Oriental Despotism

A COMPARATIVE STUDY OF TOTAL POWER

Oriental Despotism

A COMPARATIVE STUDY OF TOTAL POWER

by Karl A. Wittfogel

New Haven: YALE UNIVERSITY PRESS, 1957

NOTE

For permission to quote from the following works the author is very
grateful: H. Idris Bell, *Egypt from Alexander the Great to the Arab
Conquest*, Oxford, Oxford University Press, 1948; J. A. Dubois, *Hindu
Manners, Customs and Ceremonies*, tr. and ed. Henry K. Beauchamp,
Oxford, the Clarendon Press, 1943; Dwight D. Eisenhower, *Crusade
in Europe*, Garden City, Long Island, Doubleday, 1948; *Kauṭilya's
Arthásãstra*, tr. R. Shamasastry, 2d ed. Mysore, Wesleyan Mission
Press, 1923; S. N. Miller, "The Army and the Imperial House," in
Cambridge Ancient History, Cambridge, England, Cambridge Uni-
versity Press, 1939; Vincent A. Smith, *Oxford History of India*, Ox-
ford, the Clarendon Press, 1928; W. W. Tarn, *Hellenistic Civilization*,
London, Edward Arnold, 1927; Alfred M. Tozzer, *Landa's Relacion
de las Cosas de Yucatan*, Papers of the Peabody Museum of American
Archaeology and Ethnology, Cambridge, Harvard University, 1941;
John A. Wilson, "Proverbs and Precepts: Egyptian Instructions," in
Ancient Near Eastern Texts, ed. James B. Pritchard, Princeton,
Princeton University Press, 1950.

ACKNOWLEDGMENTS

A COMPARATIVE STUDY of total power, when it is based on documentary evidence for the institutional peculiarities of the East and the West, requires time, patience, and much friendly help. I am profoundly indebted to the Far Eastern and Russian Institute of the University of Washington for enabling me to engage in the diverse research that constitutes the factual basis of the present book. As co-sponsor of the Chinese History Project, New York, Columbia University provided facilities of office and library. For a number of years the Rockefeller Foundation supported the over-all project of which this study was an integral part. Grants given by the American Philosophical Society and the Wenner-Gren Foundation for Anthropological Research made possible the investigation of special aspects of Oriental despotism.

Scholars from various disciplines have encouraged my efforts. Without attempting to list them all, I mention in gratitude Pedro Armillas, Pedro Carrasco, Chang Chung-li, Nathan Glazer, Waldemar Gurian, Hsiao Kung-chuan, Marius B. Jansen, Isaac Mendelsohn, Karl Menges, Franz Michael, George P. Murdock, Angel Palerm, Julian H. Steward, Donald W. Treadgold, Hellmut Wilhelm, and C. K. Yang. I have been privileged to discuss crucial problems with two outstanding students of modern totalitarianism: Bertram D. Wolfe and Peter Meyer.

In the field of the Muslim and pre-Muslim Near East I was particularly aided in my researches by Gerard Salinger. In the realm of Chinese studies I drew upon the knowledge of Chaoying Fang, Lienche Tu Fang, Lea Kisselgoff, and Tung-tsu Chu, all of whom were, at the time of writing, on the staff of the Chinese History Project. Bertha Gruner carefully typed and checked the first draft of an analysis of Russian society and the Marxist-Leninist attitude toward Oriental despotism, intended originally as a separate publication but eventually included in significant part in the present volume. Ruth Ricard was indefatigable in preparing the manuscript, which offered many problems of form, source material, and bibliography.

An inquiry into the nature of bureaucratic totalitarianism is bound to encounter serious obstacles. Among those who helped in overcoming them, two persons must be mentioned particularly. George E. Taylor, director of the Far Eastern and Russian Institute of the University of Washington, never wavered in his understanding of my endeavors and in his support for what seemed at times beyond hope of completion. My wife and closest collaborator, Esther S. Goldfrank, shared every step in the struggle for the clarification of basic scientific truths and human values.

It was my belief in these values that put me behind the barbed wire of Hitler's concentration camps. My final thoughts go to those who, like myself, were passing through that inferno of total terror. Among them, some hoped for a great turning of the tables which would make them guards and masters where formerly they had been inmates and victims. They objected, not to the totalitarian means, but to the ends for which they were being used.

Others responded differently. They asked me, if ever opportunity offered, to explain to all who would listen the inhumanity of totalitarian rule in any form. Over the years and more than I can express, these men have inspired my search for a deeper understanding of the nature of total power.

KARL A. WITTFOGEL
University of Washington, Seattle

New York, July 1955

CONTENTS

INTRODUCTION

1.

When in the 16th and 17th centuries, in consequence of the commercial and industrial revolution, Europe's trade and power spread to the far corners of the earth, a number of keen-minded Western travelers and scholars made an intellectual discovery comparable to the great geographical exploits of the period. Contemplating the civilizations of the Near East, India, and China, they found significant in all of them a combination of institutional features which existed neither in classical antiquity nor in medieval and modern Europe. The classical economists eventually conceptualized this discovery by speaking of a specific "Oriental" or "Asiatic" society.

The common substance in the various Oriental societies appeared most conspicuously in the despotic strength of their political authority. Of course, tyrannical governments were not unknown in Europe: the rise of the capitalist order coincided with the rise of absolutist states. But critical observers saw that Eastern absolutism was definitely more comprehensive and more oppressive than its Western counterpart. To them "Oriental" despotism presented the harshest form of total power.

Students of government, such as Montesquieu, were primarily concerned with the distressing personal effects of Oriental despotism, students of economy with its managerial and proprietary range. The classical economists particularly were impressed by the large water works maintained for purposes of irrigation and communication. And they noted that virtually everywhere in the Orient the government was the biggest landowner.[1]

These were extraordinary insights. They were, in fact, the starting point for a systematic and comparative study of total power. But no such study was undertaken. Why? Viewed alone, the social scientists' withdrawal from the problem of Oriental despotism is puzzling. But it is readily understandable when we consider the changes that occurred in the 19th century in the general circumstances of Western life. Absolutism prevailed in Europe when Bernier described his experiences in the Near East and Mogul India and when Montesquieu wrote *The Spirit of the Laws*. But by the middle of the 19th century representative governments were established in almost all industrially advanced countries. It was then that social science turned to what seemed to be more pressing problems.

1

2.

FORTUNATE AGE. Fortunate, despite the sufferings that an expanding industrial order imposed on masses of underprivileged men and women. Appalled by their lot, John Stuart Mill claimed in 1852 that "the restraints of Communism would be freedom in comparison with the present situation of the majority of the human race." [2] But he also declared that the modern property-based system of industry, outgrowing its dismal childhood, might well satisfy man's needs without grinding him down into "a tame uniformity of thoughts, feelings, and actions." [3]

Fortunate age. Its ever-critical children could combat the fragmented despotism of privilege and power, because they did not live under a system of "general slavery." [a] Indeed they were so far removed from the image of absolutist power that they felt no urge to study its substance. Some, such as Max Weber, did examine illuminatingly, if not too systematically, certain aspects of Oriental statecraft and bureaucracy. But by and large, what Bury said at the close of the period of liberalism was true: little effort was made to determine the peculiarities of absolutism through detailed comparative study.[4]

Fortunate age. Optimistic age. It confidently expected the rising sun of civilization to dispel the last vestiges of despotism that beclouded the path of progress.

3.

BUT the high noon has failed to fulfill the promises of the dawn. Political and social earthquakes more terrifying than any that previously shook the homelands of modern science make it painfully clear that what has been won so far is neither safe nor certain. Total power, far from meekly withering away, is spreading like a virulent and aggressive disease. It is this condition that recalls man's previous experience with extreme forms of despotic rule. It is this condition that suggests a new and deepened analysis of Oriental—or as I now prefer to call it, hydraulic—society.

4.

FOR three decades I studied the institutional settings of Oriental despotism; and for a considerable part of this time I was content to designate it "Oriental society." But the more my research ad-

a. Marx (1939: 395) applied this term to Oriental despotism without realizing that more comprehensive forms of state slavery might emerge under conditions of industry.

vanced, the more I felt the need for a new nomenclature. Distinguishing as I do between a farming economy that involves small-scale irrigation (hydroagriculture) and one that involves large-scale and government-managed works of irrigation and flood control (hydraulic agriculture), I came to believe that the designations "hydraulic society" and "hydraulic civilization" express more appropriately than the traditional terms the peculiarities of the order under discussion. The new nomenclature, which stresses institutions rather than geography, facilitates comparison with "industrial society" and "feudal society." And it permits us, without circumstantial reasoning, to include in our investigation the higher agrarian civilizations of pre-Spanish America as well as certain hydraulic parallels in East Africa and the Pacific areas, especially in Hawaii. By underlining the prominent role of the government, the term "hydraulic," as I define it, draws attention to the agromanagerial and agrobureaucratic character of these civilizations.

5.

THE present inquiry goes considerably beyond the findings of the early students of Oriental society. In the following pages I endeavor to describe systematically man's hydraulic response to arid, semiarid, and particular humid environments. I also indicate how the major aspects of hydraulic society interlock in a vigorously functioning institutional going concern.

This going concern constitutes a geo-institutional nexus which resembles industrial society in that a limited core area decisively affects conditions in large interstitial and peripheral areas. In many cases these marginal areas are politically connected with hydraulic core areas; but they also exist independently. Manifestly, the organizational and acquisitive institutions of the agrodespotic state can spread without the hydraulic institutions which, to judge from the available data, account for the genesis of all historically significant zones of agrarian despotism. An understanding of the relations between the core and the margin of hydraulic society—a phenomenon barely noted by the pioneer analysts—is crucially important for an understanding of Western Rome, later Byzantium, Maya civilization, and post-Mongol (Tsarist) Russia.

In the matter of private property the early institutionalists were satisfied to indicate that the Oriental state controlled the strategic means of production, and most importantly the cultivable land. The real situation is much more complicated and, from the standpoint of societal leadership, much more disturbing. History shows that in many hydraulic societies there existed very considerable active (productive) private property; but it also shows that this development did not threaten the despotic regimes, since the property holders, as property holders, were kept disorganized and politically impotent.

Obviously, too much has been said about private property generally and too little about strong and weak property and about the conditions which promote these forms. The analysis of the varieties of private property in hydraulic society determines the limitations of nonbureaucratic (and of bureaucratic) private property under Oriental despotism. Its results contradict the belief that practically any form of avowedly benevolent state planning is preferable to the predominance of private property, a condition which modern sociological folklore deems most abhorrent.

And then there is the problem of class. Richard Jones and John Stuart Mill indicated that in Oriental society the officials enjoyed advantages of income which in the West accrued to the private owners of land and capital. Jones and Mill expressed a significant truth. But they did so only in passing and without stating clearly that under agrodespotic conditions the managerial bureaucracy was the ruling class. They therefore did not challenge the widely accepted concept of class which takes as its main criterion diversities in (active) private property.

The present inquiry analyzes the patterns of class in a society whose leaders are the holders of despotic state power and not private owners and entrepreneurs. This procedure, in addition to modifying the notion of what constitutes a ruling class, leads to a new evaluation of such phenomena as landlordism, capitalism, gentry, and guild. It explains why, in hydraulic society, there exists a *bureaucratic* landlordism, a *bureaucratic* capitalism, and a *bureaucratic* gentry. It explains why in such a society the professional organizations, although sharing certain features with the guilds of Medieval Europe, were societally quite unlike them. It also explains why in such a society supreme autocratic leadership is the rule.[5] While the law of diminishing administrative returns determines the lower limit of the bureaucratic pyramid, the cumulative tendency of unchecked power [6] determines the character of its top.

6.

THE PROPONENT of new scientific ideas unavoidably discards old ideas. Almost as unavoidably he will be criticized by those who defend the old position. Not infrequently such a controversy throws new light on the entire issue. This has certainly been the case with the theory of Oriental (or hydraulic) society.

The reader will not be surprised to learn that this theory has aroused the passionate hostility of the new total managerial bureaucracy that, in the name of Communism, today controls a large part of the world's population. The Soviet ideologists, who in 1931 declared the concept of Oriental society and a "functional" ruling bureaucracy politically impermissible, no matter what the "pure truth" might be,[7] cynically admitted that their objections were inspired by political interests and not by scientific considerations. In 1950 the leaders of Soviet Oriental studies designated as their most important accomplishment "the rout of the notorious theory of the 'Asiatic mode of production.' " [8]

The reference to the "Asiatic mode of production" is indicative of the kinds of difficulties that confront the Communist attack on the theory of Oriental society. To understand them, it must be remembered that Marx accepted many values of the Western world, whose modern private-property-based institutions he wished to see destroyed. In contrast to the Soviet conception of partisanship in art and science, Marx rejected as "shabby" and "a sin against science" any method that subordinated scientific objectivity to an outside interest, that of the workers included.[9] And following Richard Jones and John Stuart Mill, he began, in the early 1850's, to use the concept of a specific Asiatic or Oriental society. Stressing particularly the Asiatic system of economy, which he designated as the "Asiatic mode of production," Marx upheld the "Asiatic" concept until his death, that is, for the greater part of his adult life. Engels, despite some temporary inconsistencies, also upheld to the end Marx' version of the Asiatic concept. Neither Marx nor Engels clearly defined the phenomenon of a marginal Oriental society; but from 1853 on, they both emphasized the "semi-Asiatic" quality of Tsarist society and the Orientally despotic character of its government.

Lenin spoke approvingly of Marx' concept of a specific Asiatic mode of production, first in 1894 and last in 1914. Following Marx and Engels, he recognized the significance of "Asiatic" institutions for Tsarist Russia, whose society he viewed as "semi-Asiatic" and whose government he considered to be despotic.[10]

7.

I WAS UNAWARE of the political implications of a comparative study of total power when in the winter of 1922–23 and under the influence of Max Weber I began to investigate the peculiarities of hydraulic society and statecraft. I was unaware of it when, in 1924 and now with reference to Marx as well as Weber, I pointed to "Asiatic" society [11] as dominated by a bureaucratically despotic

state.[12] I was unaware of having drawn conclusions from Marx' version of the Asiatic concept, which Marx himself had avoided, when in
1926 and employing Marx' own socio-economic criteria, I wrote that
Chinese developments in the second half of the first millennium B.C.
made "the administrative officialdom—headed by the absolutist emperor—the ruling class" [13] and that this ruling class, in China as in
Egypt and India, was a "mighty hydraulic [*Wasserbau*] bureauc-
racy." [14] I elaborated this thesis in 1926,[15] 1927,[16] 1929,[17] and 1931,[18]
impressed by Marx' insistence on an unbiased pursuit of truth.[b] In
1932, a Soviet critic of my *Wirtschaft und Gesellschaft Chinas* denounced my belief in the objectivity of science.[19] It was at this time
that the Soviet publishers ceased to print my analyses of Asiatic
society in general and of Chinese society in particular.[c]

In the 1930's I gradually abandoned the hope that in the USSR
the nationalization of all major means of production might initiate
popular control over the government and the rise of a classless
society. Deepened understanding of the character of Soviet society
paved the way to further insights into the structure and ideology of
bureaucratic despotism. Re-examination of the Marxist-Leninist
view of Oriental society made it clear that Marx, far from originating
the "Asiatic" concept, had found it ready-made in the writings of the
classical economists. I further realized that although Marx accepted
the classical view in many important essentials, he failed to draw a
conclusion, which from the standpoint of his own theory seemed
inescapable—namely, that under the conditions of the Asiatic mode
of production the agromanagerial bureaucracy constituted the ruling
class.

Lenin's ambivalence toward the "Asiatic system" is perhaps even
more revealing. In 1906–07 Lenin admitted that the next Russian
revolution, instead of initiating a socialist society, might lead to an

b. I cited Marx' statements on this point in 1927 (Wittfogel, 1927: 296) and again in
1929 (*ibid.*, 1929a: 581 and n. 60; see also 585).

c. My article, "Geopolitik, geographischer Materialismus und Marxismus," which
argued the importance of the natural factor for societal growth in general and for
Asiatic society in particular (see Wittfogel, 1929: 725–8) was published in *Unter dem
Banner des Marxismus* without editorial comment, whereas in the Russian version of
the same journal (*Pod znamenem marxizma*, 1929, Nos. 2/3, 6, 7/8) the editor indicated
his disagreement with some of the author's views. In 1930, the journal refused to
publish the continuation of my article, which carried farther the analysis of the natural
foundations of Asiatic society (see Wittfogel, 1932: 593 ff., 597–608). For corrections of
certain of my early views on the man-nature relationship see below, Chap. 1; cf. Chap.
9). My book *Wirtschaft und Gesellschaft Chinas* was translated into Russian, and the
typewritten translation was circulated among a number of Soviet experts, who were
asked to write a critical introduction. To my knowledge, such an introduction was
never written. The translation was never published.

"Asiatic restoration." But when World War I opened up new possibilities for a revolutionary seizure of power, he completely dropped
the Asiatic concept, which, with oscillations, he had upheld for
twenty years. By discussing Marx' views of the state without re-
producing Marx' ideas of the Asiatic state and the Oriental despotism
of Tsarist Russia, Lenin wrote what probably is the most dishonest
book of his political career: *State and Revolution.* The gradual
rejection of the Asiatic concept in the USSR, which in 1938 was
climaxed by Stalin's re-editing of Marx' outstanding reference to the
Asiatic mode of production, logically followed Lenin's abandonment
of the Asiatic concept on the eve of the Bolshevik revolution.

8.

THE CAMPAIGN against the Asiatic concept shows the master minds
of the Communist camp unable to bolster their rejection with rational arguments. This in turn explains the oblique and primarily
negative methods with which the friends of Communist totalitarianism in the non-Communist world oppose the outlawed concept. To
the uninitiated these methods, which use distortion and de-emphasis
rather than open discussion, are confusing. To the initiated they
disclose once more the scientific weakness of the most powerful attack
against the theory of Oriental (hydraulic) society.

9.

THE PICTURE of hydraulic society given in this inquiry implies
definite concepts of societal type and development. No doubt there
is structure and cohesion in man's personal history. All individuals
base their behavior on the conviction that the regularities of yesterday are necessarily linked to the regularities of today and tomorrow.
And there is structure and cohesion in the history of mankind. Individuals and groups of individuals like to speak of institutional
units which they see operating in the present and which they expect
to operate, or to change recognizably, in the future. Agnostic withdrawal from the problem of development therefore ceases to be
plausible as soon as it is clearly defined.

However, the absurdity of developmental agnosticism provides no
excuse for a scheme of historical change that insists on a unilinear,
irresistible, and necessarily progressive development of society. Marx'
and Engels' acceptance of Asiatic society as a separate and stationary
conformation shows the doctrinal insincerity of those who, in the
name of Marx, peddle the unilinear construct. And the comparative
study of societal conformations demonstrates the empirical un-

tenability of their position. Such a study brings to light a complex sociohistorical pattern, which includes stagnation as well as development and diversive change and regression as well as progress. By revealing the opportunities, and the pitfalls, of open historical situations, this concept assigns to man a profound moral responsibility, for which the unilinear scheme, with its ultimate fatalism, has no place.

10.

CONGRUENT with the arguments given above, I have started my inquiry with the societal order of which agromanagerial despotism is a part; and I have stressed the peculiarity of this order by calling it "hydraulic society." But I have no hesitancy in employing the traditional designations "Oriental society" and "Asiatic society" as synonyms for "hydraulic society" and "agromanagerial society"; and while using the terms "hydraulic," "agrobureaucratic," and "Oriental despotism" interchangeably, I have given preference to the older formulation, "Oriental despotism" in my title, partly to emphasize the historical depth of my central concept and partly because the majority of all great hydraulic civilizations existed in what is customarily called the Orient. Originally I had planned to publish this study under the title *Oriental Society*.

The preservation of the old nomenclature stands us in good stead when we examine recent developments. For while there are some traces of hydraulic society left in certain regions of Latin America, the heritage of the old order is still very conspicuous in many countries of the Orient proper. The problem of hydraulic society in transition is therefore primarily the problem of this area.

Under what influences and in what ways are the people of the East throwing off the conditions of hydraulic society which they maintained for millennia? The significance of this question becomes fully apparent only when we understand that Oriental despotism atomized those nonbureaucratic groups and strata which, in feudal Europe and Japan, spearheaded the rise of a commercial and industrial society. Nowhere, it seems, did hydraulic society, without outside aid, make a similar advance. It was for this reason that Marx called Asiatic society stationary and expected British rule in India to accomplish "the only *social* revolution ever heard of in Asia" by establishing there a property-based non-Asiatic society.[20]

Subsequent events indicate that Marx seriously overrated the transformative strength of capitalist economy. To be sure, Western rule in India and other Oriental countries provided new possibilities for a nontotalitarian development; but at the end of the era of Western colonialism and despite the introduction of parliamentary governments of various kinds, the political leaders of the Orient are still greatly attracted by a bureaucratic-managerial policy which keeps the state supremely strong and the nonbureaucratic and private sector of society supremely weak.

11.

IN THIS CONTEXT, certain aspects of Russia's recent development deserve the most careful scrutiny. The marginally Oriental civilization of Tsarist Russia was greatly influenced by the West, though Russia did not become a Western colony or semi-colony. Russia's Westernization radically changed the country's political and economic climate, and in the spring of 1917 its antitotalitarian forces had a genuine opportunity to accomplish the anti-Asiatic social revolution which Marx, in 1853, had envisaged for India. But in the fall of 1917 these antitotalitarian forces were defeated by the Bolshevik champions of a new totalitarian order. They were defeated because they failed to utilize the democratic potential in a historical situation that was temporarily open. From the standpoint of individual freedom and social justice, 1917 is probably the most fateful year in modern history.

The intellectual and political leaders of non-Communist Asia, who profess to believe in democracy and who in their majority speak deferentially of Marx, will fulfill their historical responsibility only if they face the despotic heritage of the Oriental world not less but more clearly than did Marx. In the light of the Russian experience of 1917 they should be willing to consider the issue of an "Asiatic restoration" not only in relation to Russia but also to present-day Asia.

12.

THE MASTERS of the modern totalitarian superstate build big and integrated institutions, which, they say, we cannot emulate. And they display big and integrated ideas, which, they say, we cannot match. They are right in one respect. We do not maintain totalitarian systems of integrated power and ideology. Favorable constellations of historical events have permitted us to avoid these monstrous developments that paralyze the search for scientific truth and social improvement. But our opponents are wrong when they hold us incapable of voluntary association because we reject the disciplines of general (state) slavery. They are wrong when they hold us incapable of producing big and structured ideas because we reject state-imposed dogma.

Political freedom is not identical with the absence of organized action, though our enemies would be happy if this were so. And intellectual freedom is not identical with the absence of integrated thought. It is only under the conditions of free discussion that comprehensive sets of ideas can be genuinely tested.

In the recent past, scholars often gave themselves to the study of details because they took the broad principles of life and thought for granted. Seeing these principles threatened, they today begin to recall that the trail blazers of modern thought viewed nature and society as integrated orders whose architecture they explored. The Newtons, Montesquieus, Adam Smiths, and Darwins provided new interpretations of the world that were as spontaneous as they were coherent, and as bold as they were competent.

You cannot fight something with nothing. In a crisis situation, any theoretical vacuum, like any power vacuum, invites disaster. There is no excuse for letting the enemy have things his way when our side possesses infinite reserves of superior strength. There is no excuse for letting the totalitarian strategists parade their contrived doctrines on ground that is legitimately ours. There is no excuse for letting them win the battle of ideas by default.

Scientific inquiry has its inner laws. But it earns the privilege of freedom only when, rooted in the heritage of the past, it alertly faces the threats of a conflict-torn present and boldly exhausts the possibilities of an open future.

CHAPTER 1

C̄he natural setting of hydraulic society

A. CHANGING MAN IN CHANGING NATURE

CONTRARY to the popular belief that nature always remains the same—a belief that has led to static theories of environmentalism and to their equally static rejections—nature changes profoundly whenever man, in response to simple or complex historical causes, profoundly changes his technical equipment, his social organization, and his world outlook. Man never stops affecting his natural environment. He constantly *transforms* it; and he *actualizes* [a] new forces whenever his efforts carry him to a new level of operation. Whether a new level can be attained at all, or once attained, where it will lead, depends first on the institutional order [b] and second on the ultimate target of man's activity: the physical, chemical, and biological world accessible to him. Institutional conditions being equal, it is the difference in the natural setting that suggests and permits—or precludes—the development of new forms of technology, subsistence, and social control.

A waterfall interested primitive man little except as a landmark or an object of veneration. When sedentary man developed industry on a sophisticated mechanical level, he actualized the motive energy of water; and many new enterprises (mills) arose on the banks of rushing streams. The discovery of the technical potential inherent in coal made man geology conscious as never before, and the water mill became a romantic survival in the revolutionized industrial landscape dominated by the steam engine.

a. For the terms "transformation" and "actualization," as used here, see Wittfogel, 1932: 482.

b. This formulation differs from my earlier concept of the relation between man and nature (Wittfogel, 1932: 483 ff., 712 ff.) in its emphasis on the primary importance of institutional (and cultural) factors. From this premise follows the recognition of man's freedom to make a genuine choice in historically open situations, a point developed in the later part of the present chapter. Except for these corrections—which are essential also for my criticism of certain ideas of Marx that I had previously accepted—I am upholding the substance of my earlier views (see Wittfogel, 1931: 21 ff.; *ibid.*, 1932: 486 ff.).

11

In recent years man has uncovered the productive energies of electricity. Again he is turning his attention to falling water. But even when the engineer of the 20th century erects his power plant on the very spot that previously supported a textile mill, he actualizes new forces in the old setting. Nature acquires a new function; and gradually it also assumes a new appearance.

B. THE HISTORICAL PLACE OF HYDRAULIC SOCIETY

WHAT is true for the industrial scene is equally true for the agricultural landscape. The hydraulic potential of the earth's water-deficient regions is actualized only under specific historical circumstances. Primitive man has known water-deficient regions since time immemorial; but while he depended on gathering, hunting, and fishing, he had little need for planned water control. Only after he learned to utilize the reproductive processes of plant life did he begin to appreciate the agricultural possibilities of dry areas, which contained sources of water supply other than on-the-spot rainfall. Only then did he begin to manipulate the newly discovered qualities of the old setting through small-scale irrigation farming (hydroagriculture) and/or large-scale and government-directed farming (hydraulic agriculture). Only then did the opportunity arise for despotic patterns of government and society.

The opportunity, not the necessity. Large enterprises of water control will create no hydraulic order, if they are part of a wider nonhydraulic nexus. The water works of the Po Plain, of Venice, and of the Netherlands modified regional conditions; but neither Northern Italy nor Holland developed a hydraulic system of government and property. Even the Mormons, who established a flourishing hydraulic agriculture in the heart of arid North America, never succeeded in completely eliminating the political and cultural influence of their wider industrial environment. The history of the Latter-Day Saints illustrates both the organizational potential of large-scale irrigation and the limitations imposed on the development of hydraulic institutions by a dominant Western society.

Thus, too little or too much water does not necessarily lead to governmental water control; nor does governmental water control necessarily imply despotic methods of statecraft. It is only above the level of an extractive subsistence economy, beyond the influence of strong centers of rainfall agriculture, and below the level of a property-based industrial civilization that man, reacting specifically to the water-deficient landscape, moves toward a specific hydraulic order of life.

C. THE NATURAL SETTING

1. HISTORICAL CONDITIONS BEING EQUAL, A MAJOR NATURAL DIFFERENCE THE POSSIBLE CAUSE OF DECISIVE INSTITUTIONAL DIFFERENCES

MANY factors differentiated agrarian life prior to the industrial age, but none equaled in institutional significance the stimulating contradictions offered by arid areas possessing accessible sources of water supply other than on-the-spot rainfall. Under the just-defined conditions of preindustrial agriculture, this natural configuration decisively affected man's behavior as a provider of food and organizer of human relations. If he wanted to cultivate dry but potentially fertile lands permanently and rewardingly, he had to secure a reliable flow of moisture. Of all tasks imposed by the natural environment, it was the task imposed by a precarious water situation that stimulated man to develop hydraulic methods of social control.

2. SEVERAL NATURAL FACTORS ESSENTIAL TO FARMING

WATER is not the only natural factor essential for successful crop raising. Anyone wishing to farm must have at his disposal useful plants, an arable soil, adequate humidity, appropriate temperature (sufficient sun and a proper growing season), and a suitable lay of the land (relief, surface).[a]

All these elements are equally essential. The lack of any one of them destroys the agronomic value of all the others. Cultivation remains impossible unless human action can compensate for the total deficiency of any essential factor.

3. SOME ESSENTIAL FACTORS DEFY COMPENSATING ACTION; OTHERS RESPOND MORE READILY

THE effectiveness of man's compensating action depends on the ease with which a lacking natural factor can be replaced. Some factors must be considered constants because, under existing technological conditions, they are for all practical purposes beyond man's control. Others are more pliable. Man may manipulate or, if necessary, change them.

Temperature and surface are the outstanding constant elements of the agricultural landscape. This was true for the premachine age; and it is still essentially true today. Pre-industrial attempts to change

a. For similar attempts at defining the natural factors basic to agriculture see CM: 125; SM: 753; Widtsoe, 1928: 19 ff.; Buck, 1937: 101.

the temperature of farming areas have, for obvious reasons, met with no success; and even such achievements as central heating and air conditioning have wrought no major change. Still less has man succeeded in altering the cosmic circumstances which ultimately determine the temperature of the earth.

The lay of the land has equally defied human effort. Man has made many minor adjustments such as leveling or terracing—most frequently, it would seem, in connection with operations of hydro-agriculture. But before modern power machines and high explosives were invented, the globe's relief remained fundamentally unaltered. Even machine-promoted agriculture, like the technically less advanced forms of farming, prospers on the even surfaces of lowlands and high plateaus or on gently graded slopes and hills, and not in rugged mountainous terrain.

Vegetation and soil do not resist human action to any comparable degree. The farmer professionally manipulates plants and soils. He may transfer useful plants to regions lacking them, and he frequently does so. However, such action is sporadic and temporary; it ceases when the limited objective is achieved. In a given agricultural area the operations of crop breeding are repeated again and again; but the plants cover the ground discontinuously, and although under certain circumstances farm labor may be coordinated in work teams, there is nothing in the nature of the individual plants or plant aggregates which necessitates large-scale cooperation as a prerequisite for successful cultivation. Before the machine age the greater part of all agriculture proceeded most effectively when individual husbandmen or small groups of husbandmen attended to the crops.

The second variable factor, soil, follows a similar pattern, with special limitations dictated by the relative heaviness of pulverized mineral substance. While seeds or plants have frequently been transferred to deficient areas, soil has rarely been moved to barren regions. No doubt, poor or useless fields have been improved by bringing better soil from a distance. But such action is of little consequence for the character of any major farming area.[1] Man's efforts seek primarily to adjust the existing soil to the needs of the crops by hoeing, digging, or plowing, and on occasion by improving its chemical composition through the application of fertilizers.

Thus soil is susceptible to manipulation, but to a type of manipulation that requires work groups no larger than are necessary for the cultivation of the plants. Even when, under primitive conditions, the clearing of the ground and the gathering of the harvest are under taken by large teams, the actual task of tilling the fields is usually left to one or a few individuals.

4. THE SPECIFIC QUALITIES OF WATER

COMPARED with all other essential natural prerequisites of agriculture, water is *specific*. Temperature and surface, because of their respective cosmic and geological dimensions, have completely precluded or strikingly limited human action throughout the preindustrial era and afterward. In contrast, water is neither too remote nor too massive to permit manipulation by man. In this regard it resembles two other variables, vegetation and soil. But it differs greatly from both in its susceptibility to movement and in the techniques required to handle it.

Water is heavier than most plants. It can nevertheless be much more conveniently managed. Unhampered by the cohesiveness of solid matter and following the law of gravity, water flows automatically to the lowest accessible point in its environment. Within a given agricultural landscape, water is the natural variable *par excellence*.

And this is not all. Flowing automatically, water appears unevenly in the landscape, gathering either below the surface as ground water, or above the surface in separate cavities (holes, ponds, lakes), or continuous beds (streams, rivers). Such formations are of minor significance in an agricultural area enjoying ample precipitation, but they become immensely important in the water-deficient landscape. The human operator who has to handle water deals with a substance that is not only more mobile than other agronomic variables, but also more bulky.

This last quality presents special difficulties whenever man tries to utilize large agglomerations of moisture; and this he is prone to do whenever natural and technological conditions permit. No operational necessity compels him to manipulate either soil or plants in cooperation with many others. But the bulkiness of all except the smallest sources of water supply creates a technical task which is solved either by mass labor or not at all.

D. MUST THE HYDRAULIC POTENTIAL BE ACTUALIZED?

1. AN OPEN HISTORICAL SITUATION—BUT RECOGNIZABLE PATTERNS OF RESPONSE

THE stimulating contradiction inherent in a potentially hydraulic landscape is manifest. Such a landscape has an insufficient rainfall or none at all; but it possesses other accessible sources of water supply. If man decides to utilize them, he may transform dry lands into fertile fields and gardens. He may, but will he? What makes him engage in a venture which involves great effort and which is fraught with highly problematic institutional consequences?

Historical evidence reveals that numerous groups of persons have made this decision. Yet it also reveals that many others have failed to do so. Over millennia, tribal gatherers, hunters, fishermen, and pastoralists inhabited potentially hydraulic regions, often in close proximity to irrigation farmers, but few abandoned their traditional occupations for a hydroagricultural way of life.

Manifestly, no irresistible necessity compelled man to utilize the new natural opportunities. The situation was open, and the hydro-agricultural course was only one of several possible choices. Nevertheless, man took this course so frequently and in so many separate areas that we may assume regularity in evaluation as well as in procedure.

Man pursues recognized advantage. Whenever internal or external causes suggest a change in technology, material production, or social relations, he compares the merits of the existing situation with the advantages—and disadvantages—that may accrue from the contemplated change. Special effort is required to attain the new objective; and this effort may involve not only increased work and a shift from pleasant to unpleasant operations, but also social and cultural adjustments, including a more or less serious loss of personal and political independence.

When the sum total of the accruing benefits clearly and convincingly exceeds the required sacrifices, man is willing to make the change; but problematic advantage usually leaves him cool. Here, as elsewhere, the human budget is compounded of material and non-material items; any attempt to formulate it exclusively in terms of smaller or larger quantities of things (goods) will prove unsatisfactory. To be sure, the material factor weighs heavily, but its relative importance can be reasonably defined only when full recognition is given to such other values as personal safety, absence of oppression, and time-honored patterns of thought and action.

Culture historians have made much of the fact that during the "recent" epoch of geozoology [1] clusters of persons adopted agriculture, either as a supplementary occupation or, and increasingly, as their main subsistence economy. No doubt this transition profoundly affected the fate of mankind; but any reference to the law of recognized advantage must take into account the many primitive groups that did not turn to crop-raising either during the days of incipient agriculture or after the rise of powerful and stratified agrarian civilizations.

The agrarian alternative had a limited—and very diverse—appeal to nonfarming groups when cultivation was primitive and leadership not overly demanding. After the emergence of stratified agricultural societies, choice became even more serious. The authority wielded by the governments and wealthy landowners of nearby agrarian states acted as a deterrent, for under these conditions a shift might involve submission to distasteful methods of political and proprietary control. Often women, children, and war captives tilled some few fields close to a camp site; but the dominant members of the tribe, the adult males, stubbornly refused to abandon their hunting, fishing, or herding activities. The many primitive peoples who endured lean years and even long periods of famine without making the crucial changeover to agriculture demonstrate the immense attraction of nonmaterial values, when increased material security can be attained only at the price of political, economic, and cultural submission.

2. THE RECOGNIZED ADVANTAGES OF IRRIGATION AGRICULTURE

THE transition to irrigation farming poses the problem of choice in a still more complex form. The primary choice—whether or not to start hydroagriculture where it had not been known previously— was generally, though perhaps not exclusively, made by groups familiar with the techniques of primitive rainfall farming.

The secondary (derivative) choice—whether or not to emulate an established irrigation economy—confronts the traditional rainfall farmer as well as the nonagricultural tribesman. But the nonagriculturist is much less prepared technically and culturally to make this shift; and in both cases decision becomes more precarious when acceptance of a materially attractive irrigation economy involves reduction to an abjectly low social and political status.

It is obviously for this reason that a number of communities practicing rainfall farming in Southwest China, India, and Meso-America as well as many tribal hunters, fishermen, and herders on the fringe of the hydroagricultural world failed to make the change. The fate of those who rejected the ambivalent opportunity varied greatly; but whatever their subsequent fortunes, history offered most of them a genuine choice, and man proceeded not as the passive instrument of an irresistible and unilinear developmental force but as a discriminating being, actively participating in shaping his future.

a. If . . . , then . . .

IRRIGATION farming always requires more physical effort than rainfall farming performed under comparable conditions. But it requires radical social and political adjustments only in a special geohistorical setting. Strictly local tasks of digging, damming, and water distribution can be performed by a single husbandman, a single family, or a small group of neighbors, and in this case no far-reaching organizational steps are necessary. Hydroagriculture, farming based on small-scale irrigation, increases the food supply, but it does not involve the patterns of organization and social control that characterize hydraulic agriculture and Oriental despotism.

These patterns come into being when an experimenting community of farmers or protofarmers finds large sources of moisture in a dry but potentially fertile area. If irrigation farming depends on the effective handling of a major supply of water, the distinctive quality of water—its tendency to gather in bulk—becomes institutionally decisive. A large quantity of water can be channeled and kept within bounds only by the use of mass labor; and this mass labor must be coordinated, disciplined, and led. Thus a number of farmers eager to conquer arid lowlands and plains are forced to invoke the organizational devices which—on the basis of premachine technology—offer the one chance of success: they must work in cooperation with their fellows and subordinate themselves to a directing authority.

Again history followed no unilinear course dictated by unavoidable necessity. There were recognized alternatives; and those who were faced with them were able to make a genuine choice. But whatever their decisions, they were made within a framework that offered only a limited number of workable possibilities.

Thus the changeover to hydraulic agriculture, or its rejection, was not without order or direction. The various decisions displayed regularities in conditioning and motivation. But the relative equality of the original choices did not imply a relative equality in the final results. The majority of all hunters, fishermen, and rainfall farmers who preserved their traditional way of life were reduced to insignificance, if they were not completely annihilated. Some groups, practicing a mixed economy with little or no hydroagriculture, were strong enough to impose their will on adjacent hydraulic civilizations.

The herders came into their own at a relatively late time and in a special geohistorical setting. Often they maintained themselves against all manner of agriculturists, and in a number of instances they engaged in sweeping offensives, accomplishing conquests that profoundly modified the political and social structure of the subdued agrarian civilizations.

The representatives of rainfall farming made history in certain areas of the West, which was uniquely suited to this type of economy.

But the hydraulic agriculturists outgrew and outfought the majority of all neighboring peoples wherever local conditions and international circumstances one-sidedly favored an agromanagerial economy and statecraft.

The pioneers of hydraulic agriculture, like the pioneers of rainfall farming, were unaware of the ultimate consequences of their choice. Pursuing recognized advantage, they initiated an institutional development which led far beyond the starting point. Their heirs and successors built colossal political and social structures; but they did so at the cost of many of those freedoms which the conservative dissenters endeavored and, in part, were able to preserve.

b. Arid, Semi-arid, and Humid Areas: Hypothetical Patterns of Interaction and Growth

IN THEIR PURSUIT of recognized advantage, rainfall farmers experimented with hydroagriculture not only in desert-like areas of full aridity and steppe-like areas of semi-aridity, but also in humid areas suitable to the cultivation of useful aquatic plants, above all rice.

The first two types of landscapes, taken together, cover almost three-fifths [2]—and all three possibly something like two-thirds—of the globe's surface. Within this area each of the three types of potentially hydraulic landscapes may have played a specific role, particularly in the formative period of a hydraulic economy. In a major sector comprising all three types, the semi-arid regions are highly suitable to small and gradually growing enterprises of water control. The arid regions provide an ultimate testing ground for the new techniques. And the semi-arid and humid regions profit further from the technical and organizational experience gained in man's victory over the desert.

This may well have been the sequence in the spread of hydraulic agriculture in such widely separated areas as ancient Mesopotamia, India, and the western zone of South America. A different order of development is probable for landscapes that are homogeneously arid, and still another for those that are predominantly semi-arid.

In each case, the presence or absence of adjacent humid regions complicated the pattern of growth. In Egypt, gatherers, hunters, and fishermen seem to have practiced agriculture as a subsidiary occupation on the naturally flooded banks of the Nile long before farming became the primary pursuit. In Meso-America [a] and in

a. Some twenty years ago I considered Aztec Mexico, like pre-Tokugawa Japan, a feudal society with small-scale irrigation (Wittfogel, 1932: 587 ff.). On the basis of a

China diffusion (from South America and Inner or South Asia respectively) cannot be excluded. But such external stimulation need not have occurred; if it did, it was effective only because the rainfall farmers in the "stimulated" areas were ready to recognize the advantages of the new technique.

In ancient China the semi-arid North and the rice-growing South established noteworthy forms of interaction. The ancient Yangtze states developed early and perhaps under the influence of the rice culture of Southeast Asia; but it was the semi-arid North which,

---

growing familiarity with the early sources I came to recognize the hydraulic character of the core areas of pre-Spanish Mexico; and the recent work of Mexican archaeologists and historians fortifies me in my conclusion (see Armillas, 1948: 109; *ibid.*, 1951: 24 ff.; Palerm, 1952: 184 ff.). I quote particularly from a study by Palerm which provides a wealth of historical data on irrigation in both pre-Spanish and early Spanish Meso-America:

> 4. The majority of the irrigation systems seem to have been only of local importance and did not require large hydraulic undertakings. Nevertheless, important works were undertaken in the Valley of Mexico, and irrigation appears in concentrated form in the headwaters of the rivers Tula, Lerma and Atlixco, and in the contiguous area of Colima-Jalisco.
>
> 5. The largest concentrations and most important works of irrigation coincide, generally, with the greatest density of population, with the distribution of the most important urban centers, and with the nuclei of political power and military expansion [Palerm, 1954: 71].

How far back can we trace hydraulic activities in Meso-America? Armillas believes that the great cultural advance in the Hohokam civilization of Arizona (A.D. 500–900) was probably due to the construction of irrigation canals, a fact which is archaeologically established. And since the remains point to relations between Hohokam and Meso-America, he believes that "the same factor may underlie the cultural development in certain areas of western Meso-America during this period" (Armillas, 1948: 107). The Hohokam data tie in with the "classical" period of Meso-American history, which, in the Mexican lake area, probably began in the early centuries of the first millennium A.D. Armillas' assumption is reinforced by a recent pollen analysis, which suggests that aridity increased during the late "archaic" period (Sears, 1951: 59 ff.). Palerm has stated that this climatic change may have caused "the emergence or extension of irrigation" in Meso-America (1955: 35). Such a hypothesis, and it seems an eminently plausible one, would go far to explain the beginnings of a "classical" period of concentrated populations and monumental building, not only in the highlands but also in the marginal hydraulic Maya civilization.

If a vigorous hydraulic development occurred in Meso-America at the end of the first millennium B.C. or shortly thereafter, subsequent oscillations in hydraulic operation present no basic theoretical difficulties. Recent investigations by Palerm and Wolf indicate a rather late date for the comprehensive waterworks undertaken by the territorial state of Texcoco, which, when the Spaniards arrived, was second only to Mexico. The relative lateness of this development does not necessarily indicate that originally Texcoco was outside the hydraulic pale. More likely, the Texcocan government moved gradually from marginal to more central hydraulic conditions. (For the problem of changing hydraulic density, see below, Chap. 6.)

over a long period of time, constituted the dominant center of power and cultural advance in Eastern Asia. In India the arid, semi-arid, and humid regions of the North became historically prominent before the excessively humid area of Bengal.

These developmental sequences are presented as hypotheses. Their validity, or lack of validity, is of no consequence to our analysis of societal structure. They are worth noting, in the main, because on the basis of our present archaeological and prehistorical knowledge they suggest a highly dynamic interplay between the various types of landscapes which combine to form the larger areas of hydraulic civilization.

CHAPTER 2

$\mathcal{H}$ydraulic economy—a managerial and genuinely political economy

THE CHARACTERISTICS of hydraulic economy are many, but three are paramount. Hydraulic agriculture involves a specific type of division of labor. It intensifies cultivation. And it necessitates cooperation on a large scale. The third characteristic has been described by a number of students of Oriental farming. The second has been frequently noted, but rarely analyzed. The first has been given practically no attention. This neglect is particularly unfortunate, since the hydraulic patterns of organization and operation have decisively affected the managerial role of the hydraulic state.

Economists generally consider the division of labor and cooperation key prerequisites of modern industry, but they find them almost completely lacking in farming.[a] Their claim reflects the conditions of Western rainfall agriculture. For this type of agriculture it is indeed by and large correct.

However, the economists do not as a rule so limit themselves. Speaking of agriculture without any geographical or institutional qualification, they give the impression that their thesis, being universally valid, applies to hydraulic as well as to hydroagriculture and rainfall farming. Comparative examination of the facts quickly discloses the fallacy of this contention.

---

a. For early formulations of this view see Smith, 1937: 6; Mill, 1909: 131, 144; Marx, DK, I: 300, 322 ff. Modern economists have perpetuated and even sharpened them. Writes Seligman (1914: 350): "In the immense domain of agricultural production the possibility of combination is almost entirely eliminated." And Marshall (1946: 290): "In agriculture there is not much division of labour, and there is no production on a very large scale."

A. DIVISION OF LABOR IN
HYDRAULIC AGRICULTURE

1. Preparatory and Protective Operations
Separated from Farming Proper

WHAT is true for modern industry—that production proper depends on a variety of preparatory and protective operations [b]—has been true for hydraulic agriculture since its beginnings. The peculiarity of the preparatory and protective hydraulic operations is an essential aspect of the peculiarity of hydraulic agriculture.

a. Large-scale Preparatory Operations (Purpose: Irrigation)

THE combined agricultural activities of an irrigation farmer are comparable to the combined agricultural activities of a rainfall farmer. But the operations of the former include types of labor (on-the-spot ditching, damming, and watering) that are absent in the operations of the latter. The magnitude of this special type of labor can be judged from the fact that in a Chinese village a peasant may spend from 20 to over 50 per cent of his work time irrigating, and that in many Indian villages irrigation is the most time-consuming single item in the farmer's budget.[1]

Hydroagriculture (small-scale irrigation farming) involves a high intensity of cultivation on irrigated fields—and often also on non-irrigated fields.[2] But it does not involve a division of labor on a communal, territorial, or national level. Such a work pattern occurs only when large quantities of water have to be manipulated. Wherever, in pre-industrial civilizations, man gathered, stored, and conducted water on a large scale, we find the conspicuous division between preparatory (feeding) and ultimate labor characteristic of all hydraulic agriculture.

b. Large-scale Protective Operations (Purpose: Flood Control)

BUT the fight against the disastrous consequences of too little water may involve a fight against the disastrous consequences of too much water. The potentially most rewarding areas of hydraulic farming

b. For the concept of "previous or preparatory labor" see Mill 1909: 29, 31. The general principle was already indicated by Smith (1937), who, when discussing the division of operations in industry, pointed to the "growers of the flax and the wool" and the miners as providers of raw material (5 ff., 11), to the spinners and weavers as engaged in special processing operations (6), and to the makers of tools as combining elements of both procedures (11). Mill (1909: 36 ff.) also includes, in the category of previous labor, activities aimed at protecting industrial production proper.

are arid and semi-arid plains and humid regions suitable for aquatic crops, such as rice, that are sufficiently low-lying to permit watering from nearby rivers. These rivers usually have their sources in remote mountains, and they rise substantially as the summer sun melts part of the snow accumulated there.

Upstream developments of this kind cause annual inundations in Egypt, Mesopotamia, Turkestan, India, China, and in the Andean and Mexican zones of America. In semi-arid areas on-the-spot rains create additional dangers when they are overconcentrated (convectional) or irregular. This condition prevails in North China, northern Mesopotamia (Assyria), and the Mexican lake region. Thus a hydraulic community that resorts to preparatory labor to safeguard the productive use of water may also have to resort to protective labor to safeguard its crops from periodic and excessive inundations.

When, in protohistorical times, the Chinese began to cultivate the great plains of North China, they quickly recognized that the centers of greatest potential fertility were also the centers of greatest potential destruction. To quote John Lossing Buck: "Geologically speaking, man has settled these plains thousands of years before they were ready for occupation. . . ." [3] The Chinese built huge embankments which, although unable to remove entirely the risk inhering in the ambivalent situation, matched and even surpassed in magnitude the area's preparatory (feeding) works. [4]

In India enormous problems of flood control are posed by the Indus River [5] and, in a particularly one-sided way, by the Ganges and Brahmaputra Rivers, which in Bengal create optimal conditions for the cultivation of rice and maximal dangers from floods. By 1900 Bengal boasted ninety-seven miles of larger irrigation canals and 1,298 miles of embankments. [6]

In ancient Mesopotamia even watchful rulers could not completely prevent the inundations from damaging the densely settled plains. [7] In Turkestan excessive floods periodically threatened the Zarafshan River Valley. [8] In Upper Egypt the Nile, in very high flood, rises one meter above the level of the settled countryside, in Middle Egypt two meters, and in the Delta area up to three and a half meters. [9] The inhabitants of the lake area of Mexico could benefit from its fertility only if they accepted the periodic overflow of its short, irregular, narrow streams, [10] which they sought to control through a variety of protective works. Thus in virtually all major hydraulic civilizations, preparatory (feeding) works for the purpose of irrigation are supplemented by and interlocked with protective works for the purpose of flood control.

2. COOPERATION

A STUDY of the hydraulic patterns of China (especially North China), India, Turkestan, Mesopotamia (especially Assyria), Egypt, or Meso-America (especially the Mexican lake region) must therefore consider both forms of agrohydraulic activities. Only by proceeding in such a way can we hope to determine realistically the dimension and character of their organizational key device: cooperation.

a. Dimension

WHEN a hydraulic society covers only a single locality, all adult males may be assigned to one or a few communal work teams. Varying needs and circumstances modify the size of the mobilized labor force. In hydraulic countries having several independent sources of water supply, the task of controlling the moisture is performed by a number of separated work teams.

Among the Suk of Northeastern Africa, "every male must assist in making the ditches." [11] In almost all Pueblos "irrigation or cleaning a spring is work for all." [12] Among the Chagga, the maintenance of a relatively elaborate irrigation system is assured by "the participation of the entire people." [13] In Bali the peasants are obliged to render labor service for the hydraulic regional unit, the *subak,* to which they belong. [14] The masters of the Sumerian temple economy expected every adult male within their jurisdiction "to participate in the digging and cleaning of the canals." [15] Most inscriptions of Pharaonic Egypt take this work pattern for granted. Only occasionally does a text specify the character of the universally demanded activities, among which lifting and digging are outstanding. [16]

In imperial China every commoner family was expected on demand to provide labor for hydraulic and other public services. The political and legal writings of India indicate a similar claim on corviable labor. [17] The laws of Inca Peru obliged all able-bodied men to render *corvée* service. [18] In ancient Mexico both commoner and upper-class adolescents were instructed in the techniques of digging and damming. [19] At times the masters of this hydraulic area levied the manpower of several territorial states for their gigantic hydraulic enterprises. [20]

In 19th-century Egypt "the whole corviable population" worked in four huge shifts on Mehmed Ali's hydraulic installations. Each group labored on the canals for forty-five days until, after 180 days, the job was completed. [21] From 1881 on, at a time of decay and disintegration, "the *whole* of the corvée fell on the poorest classes," [22] the smaller number being compensated for by an increase in the labor-time to ninety days. In some regions the conscripts were kept busy "for 180 days." [23]

b. Integration

ORDERLY cooperation involves planned integration. Such integration is especially necessary when the objectives are elaborate and the cooperating teams large.

Above the tribal level, hydraulic activities are usually comprehensive. Most writers who mention the cooperative aspect of hydraulic agriculture think in the main of digging, dredging, and damming; and the organizational tasks involved in these labors is certainly considerable. But the planners of a major hydraulic enterprise are confronted with problems of a much more complex kind. How many persons are needed? And where can such persons be found? On the basis of previously made registers, the planners must determine the quota and criteria of selection. Notification follows selection, and mobilization notification. The assembled groups frequently proceed in quasimilitary columns. Having reached their destination, the buck privates of the hydraulic army must be distributed in proper numbers and according to whatever division of operations (spading, carrying of mud, etc.) is customary. If raw materials such as straw, fagots, lumber, or stone have to be procured, auxiliary operations are organized; and if the work teams—*in toto* or in part—must be provided with food and drink, still other ways of appropriation, transport, and distribution have to be developed. Even in its simplest form, agrohydraulic operations necessitate substantial integrative action. In their more elaborate variations, they involve extensive and complex organizational planning.

c. Leadership

ALL TEAMWORK requires team leaders; and the work of large integrated teams requires on-the-spot leaders and disciplinarians as well as over-all organizers and planners. The great enterprises of hydraulic agriculture involve both types of direction. The foreman usually performs no menial work at all; and except for a few engineering specialists the sergeants and officers of the labor force are essentially organizers.

To be sure, the physical element—including threats of punishment and actual coercion—is never absent. But here, if anywhere, recorded experience and calculated foresight are crucial. It is the circumspection, resourcefulness, and integrative skill of the supreme leader and his aides which play the decisive role in initiating, accomplishing, and perpetuating the major works of hydraulic economy.

d. Hydraulic Leadership—Political Leadership

THE effective management of these works involves an organizational web which covers either the whole, or at least the dynamic core, of the country's population. In consequence, those who control this network are uniquely prepared to wield supreme political power.

From the standpoint of the historical effect, it makes no difference whether the heads of a hydraulic government were originally peace chiefs, war leaders, priests, priest-chiefs, or hydraulic officials *sans phrase*. Among the Chagga, the hydraulic corvée is called into action by the same horn that traditionally rallied the tribesmen for war.[24] Among the Pueblo Indians the war chiefs (or priests), although subordinated to the *cacique* (the supreme chief), direct and supervise the communal activities.[25] The early hydraulic city states of Mesopotamia seem to have been for the most part ruled by priest-kings. In China the legendary trail blazer of governmental water control, the Great Yü, is said to have risen from the rank of a supreme hydraulic functionary to that of king, becoming, according to protohistorical records, the founder of the first hereditary dynasty, Hsia.

No matter whether traditionally nonhydraulic leaders initiated or seized the incipient hydraulic "apparatus," or whether the masters of this apparatus became the motive force behind all important public functions,[c] there can be no doubt that in all these cases the resulting regime was decisively shaped by the leadership and social control required by hydraulic agriculture.

B. HEAVY WATER WORKS AND HEAVY INDUSTRY

WITH regard to operational form, hydraulic agriculture exhibits important similarities to heavy industry. Both types of economic activities are preparatory to the ultimate processes of production. Both

c. Rüstow, who in general accepts Kern's view concerning the correlation between large-scale and government-directed water control and the centralized and despotic character of the state in ancient Egypt and Mesopotamia, assumes that in these areas nomadic conquerors developed the hydraulic works *after* establishing conquest empires (Rüstow, OG, I: 306).

Patterns of leadership and discipline traditional to conquering groups could be, and probably were, invoked in establishing certain hydraulic governments; but Pueblo, Chagga, and Hawaiian society show that such formative patterns could also be endogenous. In any case, the ethnographic and historical facts point to a multiple rather than a single origin for hydraulic societies.

provide the workers with essential material for these ultimate processes. And both tend to be comprehensive, "heavy." For these reasons the large enterprises of hydraulic agriculture may be designated as "heavy water works."

But the dissimilarities are as illuminating as the similarities. The heavy water works of hydraulic agriculture and the heavy industry of modern economy are distinguished by a number of basic differences, which, properly defined, may aid us in more clearly recognizing the peculiarities of hydraulic society.

Heavy water works feed the ultimate agrarian producer one crucial auxiliary material: water; heavy industry provides auxiliary and raw materials of various kinds, including tools for finishing and heavy industry. Heavy water works fulfill important protective functions for the country at large; the protective installations (buildings, etc.) of industry do not. Heavy water works cover at their inception a relatively large area; and with the development of the hydraulic order they are usually spread still further. The operations of heavy industry are spatially much more restricted. At first, and for a number of preliminary processes, they may depend on small and dispersed shops; with the growth of the industrial order they tend to merge into one, or a few, major establishments.

The character of the labor force varies with these spatial and operational differences. Heavy water works are best served by a widely distributed personnel, whereas heavy industry requires the workers to reside near the locally restricted "big" enterprises which employ them. The hydraulic demand is satisfied by adult peasant males, who continue to reside in their respective villages; whereas the industrial demand is satisfied by a geographically concentrated labor force.

The bulk of the hydraulic workers are expected to remain peasants, and in most cases they are mobilized for a relatively short period only—at best for a few days, at worst for any time that will not destroy their agricultural usefulness. Thus division of agrohydraulic labor is not accompanied by a corresponding division of laborers.

The contrast to the labor policy of heavy industry is manifest. Different from heavy water works, which may be created and maintained during a fraction of the year, heavy industry operates most effectively when it operates continuously. The industrial employers prefer to occupy their personnel throughout the year; and with the growth of the industrial system full-time labor became the rule. Thus division of industrial labor moves toward a more or less complete division of laborers.

The two sectors are also differently administered. In the main, modern heavy industry is directed by private owners or managers. The heavy water works of hydraulic agriculture are directed essentially by the government. The government also engages in certain other large enterprises, which, in varying combinations, supplement the agrohydraulic economy proper.

C. CALENDAR MAKING AND ASTRONOMY—IMPORTANT FUNCTIONS OF THE HYDRAULIC REGIME

AMONG the intellectual functions fulfilled by the leaders of agrohydraulic activities, some are only indirectly connected with the organization of men and material; but the relation is highly significant nevertheless. Time keeping and calendar making are essential for the success of all hydraulic economies; and under special conditions special operations of measuring and calculating may be urgently needed.[1] The way in which these tasks are executed affect both the political and the cultural development of hydraulic society.

To be sure, man is deeply concerned about the swing of the seasons under all forms of extractive economy and throughout the agrarian world. But in most cases he is content to determine in a general way when spring or summer begin, when cold will set in, when rain or snow will fall. In hydraulic civilizations such general knowledge is insufficient. In areas of full aridity it is crucial to be prepared for the rise of the rivers whose overflow, properly handled, brings fertility and life and whose unchecked waters leave death and devastation in their wake. The dikes have to be repaired in the proper season so that they will hold in times of inundation; and the canals have to be cleaned so that the moisture will be satisfactorily distributed. In semi-arid areas receiving a limited or uneven rainfall an accurate calendar is similarly important. Only when the embankments, canals, and reservoirs are ready and in good condition can the scanty precipitation be fully utilized.

The need for reallocating the periodically flooded fields and determining the dimension and bulk of hydraulic and other structures provide continual stimulation for developments in geometry and arithmetic. Herodotus ascribes the beginnings of geometry in Egypt to the need for annually remeasuring the inundated land.[2]

No matter whether the earliest scientific steps in this direction were made in the Nile Valley or in Mesopotamia, the basic correlation is eminently plausible. Obviously the pioneers and masters of hydraulic civilization were singularly well equipped to lay the foundations for two major and interrelated sciences: astronomy and mathematics.

As a rule, the operations of time keeping and scientific measuring and counting were performed by official dignitaries or by priestly (or secular) specialists attached to the hydraulic regime. Wrapped in a cloak of magic and astrology and hedged with profound secrecy, these mathematical and astronomical operations became the means both for improving hydraulic production and bulwarking the superior power of the hydraulic leaders.

D. FURTHER CONSTRUCTION ACTIVITIES CUSTOMARY IN HYDRAULIC SOCIETIES

THE masters of the hydraulic state did not confine their activities to matters immediately connected with agriculture. The methods of cooperation which were so effective in the sphere of crop-raising were easily applied to a variety of other large tasks.

Certain types of works are likely to precede others. Generally speaking, the irrigation canal is older than the navigation canal; and hydraulic digging and damming occurred prior to the building of highways. But often derivative steps were taken before the original activities had progressed far, and different regional conditions favored different evolutionary sequences. Thus the divergencies of interaction and growth are great. They include many constructional activities above and beyond the sphere of hydraulic agriculture.[a]

1. NONAGRARIAN HYDRAULIC WORKS

a. Aqueducts and Reservoirs Providing Drinking Water

A COMMONWEALTH able to transfer water for purposes of irrigation readily applies its hydraulic know-how to the providing of drinking water. The need for such action was slight in the greater part of Medieval Europe, where the annual precipitation furnished sufficient ground water for the wells on which most towns depended for their water supply.[1]

Even in the hydraulic world, drinking water is not necessarily an issue. Wherever rivers, streams, or springs carry enough moisture

---

a. Anyone interested in studying the technical and organizational details of a major hydraulic order may consult Willcocks' admirable description of irrigation and flood control in 19th-century Egypt (Willcocks, 1889: *passim*). A comprehensive survey of the hydraulic conditions in India at the close of the 19th century has been made by the Indian Irrigation Commission (RRCAI). In my study of Chinese economics and society I have systematically analyzed the ecological foundations and the various aspects of China's traditional hydraulic order (Wittfogel, 1931: 61–93, 188–300, and 410–56). Today we also have an archaeological account of the growth of hydraulic and other constructions over time and for a limited, but evidently, representative area: the Virú Valley in Peru (see Willey, 1953: 344–89).

to satisfy the drinking needs of the population throughout the year, no major problem arises. The inhabitants of the Nile and Ganges Valleys and of many similar areas did not have to construct elaborate aqueducts for this purpose.

The irregular flow of rivers or streams or the relatively easy access to fresh and clear mountain water has stimulated in many hydraulic landscapes the construction of comprehensive installations for the storage and distribution of drinking water. In America great aqueducts were built by the hydraulic civilizations of the Andean zone and Meso-America.[2] The many reservoirs (tanks) of Southern India frequently serve several uses; but near the large residential centers the providing of drinking water is usually paramount. In certain areas of the Near East, such as Syria and Assyria, brilliantly designed aqueducts have satisfied the water needs of many famous cities, Tyre,[3] Antioch,[4] and Nineveh [5] among them. In the Western world of rainfall agriculture, aqueducts were built primarily by such Mediterranean peoples as the Greeks and the Romans, who since the dawn of history maintained contact with—and learned from— the technically advanced countries of Western Asia and North Africa. No doubt the Greeks and Romans would have been able to solve their drinking-water problem without inspiration from the outside; but the form of their answer strongly suggests the influence of Oriental engineering.[6]

b. Navigation Canals

AMONG the great agrarian conformations of history, only hydraulic society has constructed navigation canals of any major size. The seafaring Greeks, making the Mediterranean their highway, avoided an issue which the ancient city states were poorly equipped to handle. The not-too-numerous Roman canals were apparently all dug at a time when the growing Orientalization of the governmental apparatus stimulated, among other things, a growing interest in all kinds of public works.[7]

The rainfall farmers of Medieval Europe, like their counterparts elsewhere, shunned rather than sought the marshy river lowlands. And their feudal masters paid little attention to the condition of the watercourses, for which they had no use. Still less did they feel obliged to construct additional and artificial rivers—canals. Few if any important canals were built during the Middle Ages,[8] and medieval trade and transport were seriously handicapped by the state of the navigable rivers.[9]

It was in connection with the rise of a governmentally encouraged commercial and industrial capitalism that the West began to build canals on a conspicuous scale. The "pioneer of the canals of modern Europe," the French Canal du Midi, was completed only in the second half of the 17th century, in 1681,[10] that is, little more than a century before the end of the absolutist regime. And in the classical country of inland navigation, England,[11] "little . . . was done in making canals . . . until the middle of the eighteenth century" [12]— that is, until a time well after the close of England's absolutist period and immediately prior to the beginning of the machine age.

As stated above, the members of a hydraulic commonwealth felt quite differently about the management of natural and artificial watercourses. They approached the fertility-bearing rivers as closely as possible, and in doing so they had to find ways of draining the lowland marshes and strengthening and reshaping the river banks. Naturally the question of inland navigation did not arise everywhere. Existing rivers and streams might be suitable for irrigation, but not for shipping (Pueblos, Chagga, Highland Peru); or the ocean might prove an ideal means of transportation (Hawaii, Coastal Peru). In certain localities inland navigation was satisfactorily served by man-managed rivers (Egypt, India) and lakes (Mexico) plus whatever irrigation canals were large enough to accommodate boats (Meso-potamia).

But when supplementary watercourses were not only possible but desirable, the organizers of agrohydraulic works had little difficulty in utilizing their cooperative "apparatus" to make them available. The new canals might be only minor additions to the existing watercourses. The ancient Egyptians constructed canals in order to circumnavigate impassable cataracts, and they temporarily connected the Nile and the Red Sea; [13] but these enterprises had little effect on the over-all pattern of the country's hydraulic economy. In other instances, navigation canals assumed great importance. They satisfied the needs of the masters of the hydraulic state: the transfer of parts of the agrarian surplus to the administrative centers and the transport of messengers and troops.

In Thailand (Siam) the different hydraulic tasks overlapped. In addition to the various types of productive and protective hydraulic installations, the government constructed in the centers of rice production and state power a number of canals, which essentially served as "waterways," that is, as a means for transporting the rice surplus to the capital.[14]

The corresponding development in China is particularly well documented. In the large plains of North China the beginnings of navigation canals go back to the days of the territorial states—that is, to the period prior to 221 B.C., when the various regional governments were still administered by officials who were given office lands in payment for their services. The difference between the state-centered system of land grants as it prevailed in early China and the knighthood feudalism of Medieval Europe is spectacularly demonstrated by the almost complete absence of public works in feudal Europe and the enormous development of such works—hydraulic and otherwise—in the territorial states of China.[b]

The geographical and administrative unification of China which vastly increased the political need for navigation canals also increased the state's organizational power to build them. The first centuries of the empire saw a great advance not only in the construction of irrigation canals,[15] reservoirs, and protective river dikes but also in the digging of long canals for administrative and fiscal purposes.[16]

When, after several centuries of political fragmentation, the Sui rulers at the end of the 6th century again unified "all-under-heaven," they bulwarked the new political structure by creating out of earlier and substantial beginnings the gigantic Imperial Canal, significantly known in China as Yün Ho, "the Transport Canal." This canal extends today for about 800 miles, its length equaling the distance from the American-Canadian Great Lakes to the Gulf of Mexico or

b. Previously I viewed Chou China as a feudal society exhibiting Oriental features, which appeared early and became increasingly conspicuous until, at the close of the period, they prevailed completely (Wittfogel, 1931: 278 ff.; *ibid.*, 1935: 40 ff.). The idea of a society that crosses the institutional divide is entirely compatible with the findings of the present inquiry (see below, Chap. 6); and by interpreting Chou society in this way, I would not have had to change a long-held position. But intensified comparative studies compel me to change. The arid and semi-arid settings of North China (17 inches annual rainfall in the old Chou domain and 24 inches in the domain of the pre-Chou dynasty, Shang) suggest hydraulic agriculture for the ancient core areas. The lay of the land, the summer floods, and the periodic silting-up of the rivers necessitated comprehensive measures of flood control especially in the heartland of Shang power. A realistic interpretation of legends and protohistorical sources (cf. Wittfogel and Goldfrank, 1943: *passim*) points to the rise of a hydraulic way of life long before the Shang dynasty, whose artifacts (bronzes) and inscriptions reflect a highly developed agrarian civilization with refined techniques of record keeping, calculations, and astronomy. The recognizable institutions of early Chou are those of a hydraulic society, which gradually intensified its managerial and bureaucratic "density" (for this concept see below, Chap. 6). The Chou sovereigns behaved toward the territorial rulers not as the first among equals but as supreme masters responsible only to Heaven. It was not their fault that their despotic claims, which possibly imitated Shang precedents, were realized imperfectly and with decreasing effect. In contrast, the rulers of the territorial states were strong enough to proceed absolutistically within their respective realms. The lands that they assigned were given not in a contractual way and to independently organized (corporated) knights and barons, but to office holders and persons permitted to enjoy sinecures. They were not fiefs but office lands (see below, Chaps. 6–8).

—in European terms—the distance from Berlin to Bordeaux or from Hamburg to Rome. For labor on part of this gigantic water work the Sui government mobilized in the regions north of the Yellow River alone "more than a million of men and women," [17] that is, almost one-half of the total population which England is said to have had from the 14th to the 16th century.[18]

The gigantic effort involved in banking the rivers and building the canals of China is indicated by the American agronomist, F. H. King, who conservatively estimates the combined lengths of the man-managed watercourses of China, Korea, and Japan at some 200,000 miles. "Forty canals across the United States from east to west and sixty from north to south would not equal in number of miles those in these three countries today. Indeed, it is probable that this estimate is not too large for China alone." [19]

2. LARGE NONHYDRAULIC CONSTRUCTIONS

a. Huge Defense Structures

THE need for comprehensive works of defense arises almost as soon as hydraulic agriculture is practiced. Contrary to the rainfall farmer, who may shift his fields with relative ease, the irrigation farmer finds himself depending on an unmovable, if highly rewarding, source of fertility. In the early days of hydraulic cultivation reliance on a fixed system of water supply must in many cases have driven the agrarian community to build strong defenses around its homes and fields.

For this purpose hydraulic agriculture proved suggestive in two ways: it taught man how to handle all kinds of building materials, earth, stone, timber, etc., and it trained him to manipulate these materials in an organized way. The builders of canals and dams easily became the builders of trenches, towers, palisades, and extended defense walls.

In this, as in all corresponding cases, the character and magnitude of the operations were determined by internal and external circumstances. Surrounded by aggressive neighbors, the Pueblo Indians ingeniously utilized whatever building material was at hand to protect their settlements, which rarely comprised more than a few hundred inhabitants.[c] The fortress-like quality of their villages is manifest to the present-day anthropologist; it struck the Spanish

c. Castañeda, 1896: 512. Bandelier upholds Castañeda's figures against divergent statements made in other early Spanish sources (Bandelier, FR, I: 120 ff. and nn.; cf. ibid., DH: 312, 46 ff., 171–3).

conquistadores, who were forced at times to besiege a single settlement for days and weeks before they could take it.[d] Rigid cooperation assured security of residence, just as it assured success in farming. An early observer stresses this aspect of Pueblo life: "They all work together to build the villages." [e]

d. Castañeda, who was the official chronicler of the first Spanish expedition, notes (1896: 494) that the defense towers of a large Zuni settlement were equipped with "embrassures and loopholes . . . for defending the roofs of the different stories." He adds, "The roofs have to be reached first, and these upper houses are the means of defending them." The experiences of the second expedition confirmed and supplemented the initial observations. Gallegos concludes his remarks concerning Pueblo building by referring to the movable wooden ladders "by means of which they climb to their quarters." At night "they lift them up since they wage war with one another" (Gallegos, 1927: 265). Obregon also stresses the military value of the ladders; in addition, he explains how the edifices themselves served to protect the community: "These houses have walls and loopholes from which they defend themselves and attack their enemies in their battles" (Obregon, 1928: 293).

One of Coronado's lieutenants, approaching certain Tigua settlements, "found the villages closed by palisades." The Pueblos, whose inhabitants had been subjected to various forms of extortion and insult "were all ready for fighting. Nothing could be done, because they would not come down onto the plain and the villages are so strong that the Spaniards could not dislodge them." Attacking a hostile village, the Spanish soldiers reached the upper story by surprise tactics. They remained in this dangerous position for a whole day, unable to prevail until the Mexican Indians, who accompanied them, approached the Pueblo from below, digging their way in and smoking out the defenders (Castañeda, 1896: 496). For a discussion of Castañeda's report see Bandelier, DH: 38 ff.)

Besieging a large Tigua settlement, Coronado's men had an opportunity to test thoroughly the defense potential of a Pueblo which was not taken by surprise: "As the enemy had had several days to provide themselves with stores, they threw down such quantities of rocks upon our men that many of them were laid down, and they wounded nearly a hundred with arrows." The siege lasted for seven weeks. During this time, the Spaniards made several assaults; but they were unable to take the Pueblo. The villagers eventually abandoned their fortress-like bulwark, not because the aggressors had penetrated their defenses, but because of lack of water (Castañeda, 1896: 498 ff.; cf. RDS: 576). Bandelier supplements Castañeda's report of this significant event by an account given by Mota Padilla, an 18th-century author, who claims to have had access to the original writings of still another member of Coronado's staff (Bandelier, DH: 323). Mota Padilla's version contains a number of details which reveal the techniques of attack as well as the strength and ingenuity of the defense. Some of the Spaniards "reached the top of the wall, but there they found that the natives had removed the roofs of many (upper) rooms, so that there was no communication between them, and as there were little towers at short distances from each other, from which missiles were showered upon the assailants on the top, the Spaniards had more than sixty of their number hurt, three of whom died of their wounds" (*ibid.,* 48).

e. Castañeda (1896: 520) qualifies this general statement by saying that the women were "engaged in making the [adobe] mixture and the walls, while the men bring the wood and put it in place." Modern reports assign the above duties to the men and credit them in addition with erecting the walls, the construction labors of the women being confined to plastering (White, 1932: 33; cf. Parsons, 1932: 212). The

The Chagga were equally effective in the transfer of their hydraulic work patterns to military constructions. Their great chieftain, Horombo (*fl.* 1830), used "thousands of people" to build great fortifications, which in part still stand today.[20] "The walls of these fortifications are some six feet high, and in length 305 yards on the south side, 443 yards on the north, 277 yards on the east side, and 137 yards on the west side." [21] Tunnels, extended trenches, and dug-outs added to the defense of the walled settlements, which appeared early in the history of the Chagga.[22] "Deep dugouts excavated under the huts and often leading into underground passages with outlets at some distance, were used for refuge. Almost every country was secured with great war trenches, which are everywhere to be seen at the present day and are often still of great depth." [23]

These instances show what even primitive hydraulic societies could achieve in the field of defense construction, when they strained their cooperative resources to the full. Higher hydraulic societies employed and varied the basic principle in accordance with technical and institutional circumstances.

In pre-Columbian Mexico the absence of suitable labor animals placed a limitation on transport, and while this restricted siege craft, it did not preclude the struggle for or the defense of the cities. In emergencies many government-built hydraulic works in the main lake area fulfilled military functions, just as the monster palaces and temples served as bastions against an invading enemy.[24] Recent research draws attention to various types of Mexican forts and defense walls.[25] Because of their size and importance, they may safely be adjudged as state-directed enterprises. The colossal fortresses and walls of pre-Inca Peru, which astonished early and recent observers,[26] are known to have been built at the order of the government and by "incredibly" large teams of corvée laborers.[27]

Many texts and pictorial representations have portrayed the walls, gates, and towers of ancient Egypt, Sumer, Babylonia, Assyria, and Syria. The *Arthashāstra* indicates the systematic manner in which the rulers of the first great Indian empire treated problems of fortification and defense.[28] At the dawn of Chinese history new capitals were created at the ruler's command, and during the last centuries of the Chou period the territorial states used their corviable manpower to wall entire frontier regions, not only against the tribal barbarians but also against each other. In the 3d century B.C. the unifier of

---

divergence between the early and recent descriptions may reflect an actual institutional change or merely a difference in the accuracy of observation. While interesting to the anthropologist, this discrepancy does not affect our basic conclusions regarding the communal character of large-scale building in the American Pueblos.

China, Ch'in Shih Huang-ti, linked together and elaborated older territorial structures to form the longest unbroken defense installation ever made by man.[29] The periodic reconstruction of the Chinese Great Wall expresses the continued effectiveness of hydraulic economy and government-directed mass labor.

b. Roads

THE existence of government-made highways is suggested for the Babylonian period;[30] it is documented for Assyria.[31] And the relationship between these early constructions and the roads of Persia, the Hellenistic states, and Rome seems "beyond doubt."[f] The great Persian "royal road" deeply impressed the contemporary Greeks;[32] it served as a model for the Hellenistic rulers,[33] whose efforts in turn inspired the official road builders of the Roman empire.[34] According to Mez, the Arabs inherited "the type of 'governmental road,' like its name, from the Persian 'Royal Road.' "[35] Beyond this, however, they showed little interest in maintaining good roads, probably because they continued to rely in the main on camel caravans for purposes of transport. The later Muslim regimes of the Near East used highways, but they never restored them to the state of technical perfection which characterized the pre-Arab period.[36]

Roads were a serious concern of India's vigorous Maurya kings.[37] A "royal road" of 10,000 *stadia,* which is said to have led from the capital to the northwestern border, had a system of marking distances which, in a modified form, was again employed by the Mogul emperors.[38] In Southern India, where Hindu civilization was perpetuated for centuries after the north had been conquered, government-made roads are mentioned in the inscriptions; and "some of them are called king's highways."[39] The Muslim rulers of India continued the Indian rather than the West Asian pattern in their effort to maintain a network of state roads.[40] Sher Shāh (d. 1545) built four great roads, one of which ran from Bengal to Agra, Delhi, and Lahore.[41] Akbar is said to have been inspired by Sher Shāh when he built a new "king's highway," called the Long Walk, which for four hundred miles was "shaded by great trees on both sides."[42]

In China, a gigantic network of highways was constructed immediately after the establishment of the empire in 221 B.C. But in this case, as in the cases of the irrigation and navigation canals or

---

f. Meissner, BA, I: 341. The term "royal road" was used in an Assyrian inscription (Olmstead, 1923: 334). The operational pattern of the Roman state post, the *cursus publicus,* can be traced back through the Hellenistic period to Persia and perhaps even to Babylonia (Wilcken, 1912: 372 and n. 2).

the long defense walls, the imperial engineers systematized and elaborated only what their territorial predecessors had initiated. Long before the 3d century B.C. an efficient territorial state was expected to have well kept overland highways, supervised by central and local officials, lined with trees, and provided with stations and guest houses.[43] Under the empire, great state roads connected all the important centers of the northern core area with the capital. According to the official *History of the Han Dynasty,* the First Emperor

> built the Imperial Road throughout the empire. To the east it stretched to Yen and Ch'i and to the south it reached Wu and Ch'u. The banks and the shore of the Chiang [the Yangtze River] and the lakes and the littoral along the sea coast were all made accessible. The highway was fifty paces wide. A space three *chang* [approximately twenty-two feet] wide in the center was set apart by trees. The two sides were firmly built, and metal bars were used to reinforce them. Green pine trees were planted along it. He constructed the Imperial Highway with such a degree of elegance that later generations were even unable to find a crooked path upon which to place their feet.[44]

In the subsequent dynasties the building and maintenance of the great trunk roads and their many regional branches remained a standard task of China's central and local administration.

The rugged terrain of Meso-America and the absence of fully coordinated empires seems to have discouraged the construction of highways during the pre-Columbian period, at least on the high plateau. But the Andean area was the scene of extraordinary road building. The Spanish conquerors described in detail the fine highways which crossed both the coastal plain and the highlands and which formed connecting links between them.[45] Commenting on the Andean roads, Hernando Pizarro writes he never saw their like in similar terrain "within the entire Christian world." [46] In fact the only parallel he could think of was the system of highways built by the Romans. The similarity is telling. As we shall discuss below, the extensive Roman roads were the fruits of a fateful transformation that made the Roman Empire a Hellenistically (Orientally) despotic state.

The efforts required to build all these great highways have attracted much less attention than the finished products. But what evidence we have indicates that like most other major government enterprises, they were mainly executed through the cooperative effort of state-levied corvée laborers. Under the Inca empire supervisory officials marked off the land and informed the local inhabitants "that they should make these roads." And this was done with little cost to the government. The commandeered men "come with their food and tools to make them." [g]

The highways of imperial China required an enormous labor force for their construction and a very sizable one for their maintenance. A Han inscription notes that the construction of a certain highway in the years A.D. 63–66 occupied 766,800 men. Of this great number only 2,690 were convicts.[47]

c. Palaces, Capital Cities, and Tombs

A GOVERNMENTAL apparatus capable of executing all these hydraulic and nonhydraulic works could easily be used in building palaces and pleasure grounds for the ruler and his court, palace-like government edifices for his aides, and monuments and tombs for the distinguished dead. It could be used wherever the equalitarian conditions of a primitive tribal society yielded to tribal or no-longer tribal forms of autocracy.

The head chief of a Pueblo community had his fields worked for him by the villagers. But apparently his dwelling did not differ from the houses of other tribesmen, except perhaps that it was better and more securely located. The Chagga chieftains had veritable palaces erected for their personal use; and the corvée labor involved in their construction was substantial.[48]

The colossal palaces of the rulers of ancient Peru were erected by the integrated manpower of many laborers. In pre-Columbian Mexico, Nezahualcoyotzin, the king of Tezcuco, the second largest country in the Aztec Federation, is said to have employed more than 200,000 workers each day for the building of his magnificent palace and park.[49]

Unlimited control over the labor power of their subjects enabled the rulers of Sumer, Babylon, and Egypt to build their spectacular palaces, gardens, and tombs. The same work pattern prevailed in the many smaller states that shaped their government on the Mesopotamian or Egyptian model. According to the biblical records, King Solomon built his beautiful temple with labor teams that, like those of Babylonia, were kept at work for four months of the year.[50]

g. Cieza, 1943: 95. The regional organization and the repair work on the roads had already been noted by a member of the conquering army (Estete, 1938: 246). The lack of payment for services rendered in the road corvée is also recorded by Blas Valeras, who states that similar conditions prevailed with regard to work on the bridges and irrigation canals (Garcilaso, 1945, I: 258).

The great edifices of Mogul India have been frequently described. Less known but equally worthy of mention are the constructions of the earlier periods. The third ruler of the Tughluq, Fīrūs Shāh (ca. 1308–88), dug several important irrigation canals, the famous "Old Jumna Canal" among them. He built forts, palaces, and palace-cities, mosques, and tombs. The palace-fort of Koṭla Fīrūs Shāh, which rose in his new capital of Fīrūsābād (Delhi), faithfully preserved the grand style of pre-Islamic Indian and Eastern architecture.[51]

The Chinese variant of the general agromanagerial building trend is revealed in many elaborate works. The First Emperor of China, Ch'in Shih Huang-ti, began to build great hydraulic works in the early days of his power; and in the course of his reign he completed colossal works of the nonhydraulic public and semiprivate types. Having destroyed all his territorial rivals, he constructed the previously mentioned network of highways which gave his officials, messengers, and troops easy access to all regions of his far-flung empire. Later he defended himself against the northern pastoralists by consolidating the Great Wall. Palaces for his personal use had been built in the early days of his reign; but it was only in 213 B.C. that work was begun on his superpalace. This monster project, together with the construction of his enormous tomb,[52] is said to have occupied work teams numbering over 700,000 persons.[53]

Eight hundred years later the second monarch of a reunified China, Emperor Yang (604–17) of the Sui Dynasty, mobilized a still larger labor force for the execution of similar monster enterprises. In addition to the more than one million persons—men and women —levied for the making of the Grand Canal,[54] he dispatched huge corvée teams to extend the imperial roads [55] and to work on the Great Wall. According to the *History of the Sui Dynasty,* over a million persons toiled at the Great Wall.[h] According to the same official source, the construction of the new eastern capital, which included a gigantic new imperial palace, involved no less than two million people "every month." [56]

d. Temples

THE position, fate, and prestige of the secular masters of hydraulic society were closely interlinked with that of their divine protectors. Without exception, the political rulers were eager to confirm and bulwark their own legitimacy and majesty by underlining the greatness of their supernatural supporters. Whether the government was

h. Over a million in 607; an additional 200,000 persons were employed in 608 (*Sui Shu* 3. 10b, 12a).

headed by secular monarchs or priest-kings, the commanding center made every effort to provide the supreme gods and their earthly functionaries with adequate surroundings for worship and residence.

Government-directed work teams, which erected gigantic palaces, were equally fitted to erect gigantic temples. Ancient inscriptions note the many temples built by the Mesopotamian rulers.[57] Usually the sovereign speaks as if these achievements resulted solely from his personal efforts. But occasional remarks indicate the presence of "the people" who toiled "according to the established plan." [i] Similarly, most Pharaonic texts refer to the final achievement [j] or to the greatness of the directing sovereign; [58] but again a number of texts refer to the government-led labor forces, "the people." [k]

In the agromanagerial cultures of pre-Columbian America, buildings for religious purposes were particularly conspicuous. Native tradition as well as the early Spanish accounts emphasize the tremendous labor required to construct and maintain the sacred houses and pyramids. The Mexicans coordinated their communal energies to erect the first temple for the newly established island city, the later Aztec capital; [59] and their increasingly powerful descendants mobilized the manpower of many subjugated countries for the construction of increasingly huge temples.[m] The city-like palace of the famous King of Tezcuco, Nezahualcoyotzin, contained no less than forty temples.[60] The great number of laborers engaged in building this palace- and temple-city has already been cited. Like the monster work teams of Mexico, those of Tezcuco could draw upon the entire corviable population.[n] In another country of the main lake region, Cuauhtitlan, the construction of large-scale hydraulic works [61] was followed by the building of a great temple. It took thirteen years to complete the second task.[62]

In the Andean zone, as in most other areas of the hydraulic world, the attachment of the priesthood to the government is beyond doubt. The Incas made heavy levies on their empire's material wealth in

i. Price, 1927: 24; cf. Thureau-Dangin, 1907: 111, and Barton, 1929: 225. Schneider (1920: 46) and Deimel (1931: 101 ff.) deplore the scarcity of concrete data concerning the Sumerian construction industry.

j. Thus in one of the oldest inscriptions of Egypt extant, the Palermo Stone (Breasted, 1927, I: 64).

k. "I have commanded those who work, to do according as thou shalt exact" (Breasted, 1927, I: 245). The "people" bring the stone for the Amon Temple; and the "people" also do the building. Among the workmen are several types of artisans (ibid., II: 294, 293).

m. Tezozomoc, 1944: 79 (the Temple of Huitzilopochtli) and 157 (the great Cu edifice of the same god).

n. Ixtlilxochitl, OH, II: 173 ff. The Annals of Cuauhtitlan also refer to this construction (Chimalpópoca, 1945: 52), without, however, discussing the labor aspect.

order to beautify their temples and pyramids.[63] They called up whatever manpower was needed to collect the raw material, transport it, and do the actual work of construction.[64]

E. THE MASTERS OF HYDRAULIC SOCIETY— GREAT BUILDERS

EVIDENTLY the masters of hydraulic society, whether they ruled in the Near East, India, China, or pre-Conquest America, were great builders. The formula is usually invoked for both the aesthetic and the technical aspect of the matter; and these two aspects are indeed closely interrelated. We shall briefly discuss both of them with regard to the following types of hydraulic and nonhydraulic construction works:

I. Hydraulic works
A. Productive installations
(Canals, aqueducts, reservoirs, sluices, and dikes for the purpose of irrigation)
B. Protective installations
(Drainage canals and dikes for flood control)
C. Aqueducts providing drinking water
D. Navigation canals

II. Nonhydraulic works
A. Works of defense and communication
1. Walls and other structures of defense
2. Highways
B. Edifices serving the public and personal needs of the secular and religious masters of hydraulic society
1. Palaces and capital cities
2. Tombs
3. Temples

1. THE AESTHETIC ASPECT

a. Uneven Conspicuousness

THE majority of persons who have commented on the great builders of Asia and ancient America are far more articulate on the nonhydraulic than on the hydraulic achievements. Within the hydraulic sphere more attention is again given to the aqueducts for drinking water and the navigation canals than to the productive and protective installations of hydraulic agriculture. In fact, these last are frequently overlooked altogether. Among the nonhydraulic works, the "big houses" of power and worship and the tombs of the great are much more carefully investigated than are the large installations of communication and defense.

This uneven treatment of the monster constructions of hydraulic society is no accident. For functional, aesthetic, and social reasons the hydraulic works are usually less impressive than the nonhydraulic constructions. And similar reasons encourage uneven treatment also within each of the two main categories.

Functionally speaking, irrigation canals and protective embankments are widely and monotonously spread over the landscape, whereas the palaces, tombs, and temples are spatially concentrated. Aesthetically speaking, most of the hydraulic works are undertaken primarily for utilitarian purposes, whereas the residences of the rulers and priests, the houses of worship, and the tombs of the great are meant to be beautiful. Socially speaking, those who organize the distribution of manpower and material are the same persons who particularly and directly enjoy the benefits of many nonhydraulic structures. In consequence they are eager to invest a maximum of aesthetic effort in these structures (palaces, temples, and capital cities) and a minimum of such effort in all other works.

Of course, the contrast is not absolute. Some irrigation works, dikes, aqueducts, navigation canals, highways, and defense walls do achieve considerable functional beauty. And closeness to the centers of power may lead the officials in charge to construct embankments, aqueducts, highways, bridges, walls, gates, and towers with as much care for aesthetic detail as material and labor permit.

But these secondary tendencies do not alter the two basic facts that the majority of all hydraulic and nonhydraulic public works are aesthetically less conspicuous than the royal and official palaces, temples, and tombs, and that the most important of all hydraulic works—the canals and dikes—from the standpoint of art and artistry are the least spectacular of all.

b. The Monumental Style

SUCH discrepancies notwithstanding, the palaces, government buildings, temples, and tombs share one feature with the "public" works proper: they, too, tend to be large. The architectural style of hydraulic society is monumental.

This style is apparent in the fortress-like settlements of the Pueblo Indians. It is conspicuous in the palaces, temple cities, and fortresses of ancient Middle and South America. It characterizes the tombs, palace-cities, temples, and royal monuments of Pharaonic Egypt and ancient Mesopotamia. No one who has ever observed the city gates and walls of a Chinese capital, such as Peking, or who has walked through the immense palace gates and squares of the Forbidden City to enter its equally immense court buildings, ancestral temples, and private residences can fail to be awed by their monumental design.

Pyramids and dome-shaped tombs manifest most consistently the monumental style of hydraulic building. They achieve their aesthetic effect with a minimum of ideas and a maximum of material. The pyramid is little more than a huge pile of symmetrically arranged stones.

The property-based and increasingly individualistic society of ancient Greece loosened up the massive architecture, which had emerged in the quasihydraulic Mycenaean period.[1] During the later part of the first millennium B.C., when Alexander and his successors ruled the entire Near East, the architectural concepts of Hellas transformed and refined the hydraulic style without, however, destroying its monumental quality.

In Islamic architecture the two styles blended to create a third. The products of this development were as spectacular in the westernmost outpost of Islamic culture—Moorish Spain—as they were in the great eastern centers: Cairo, Baghdad, Bukhara, Samarkand, and Istanbul. The Taj Mahal of Agra and kindred buildings show the same forces at work in India, a subcontinent which, before the Islamic invasion, had evolved a rich monumental architecture of its own.

c. The Institutional Meaning

IT hardly needs to be said that other agrarian civilizations also combined architectural beauty with magnitude. But the hydraulic rulers differed from the secular and priestly lords of the ancient and medieval West, first because their constructional operations penetrated more spheres of life, and second because control over the entire country's labor power and material enabled them to attain much more monumental results.

The scattered operations of rainfall farming did not involve the establishment of national patterns of cooperation, as did hydraulic agriculture. The many manorial centers of Europe's knighthood society gave rise to as many fortified residences (castles); and their size was limited by the number of the attached serfs. The king, being little more than the most important feudal lord, had to build his castles with whatever labor force his personal domain provided.

The concentration of revenue in the regional or territorial centers of ecclesiastical authority permitted the creation of the largest individual medieval edifices: churches, abbeys, and cathedrals. It may be noted that these buildings were erected by an institution which, in contrast to all other prominent Western bodies, combined feudal with quasihydraulic patterns of organization and acquisition.

With regard to social control and natural resources, however, the master builders of the hydraulic state had no equal in the nonhydraulic world. The modest Tower of London and the dispersed castles of Medieval Europe express the balanced baronial society of the Magna Carta as clearly as the huge administrative cities and colossal palaces, temples, and tombs of Asia, Egypt, and ancient America express the organizational coordination and the mobilization potential of hydraulic economy and statecraft.[a]

F. THE BULK OF ALL LARGE NONCONSTRUCTIONAL INDUSTRIAL ENTERPRISES MANAGED ALSO BY THE HYDRAULIC GOVERNMENT

1. A COMPARATIVE VIEW

A GOVERNMENT capable of handling all major hydraulic and nonhydraulic construction may, if it desires, play a leading role also in the nonconstructional branches of industry. There are "feeding" industries, such as mining, quarrying, salt gathering, etc.; and there are finishing industries, such as the manufacture of weapons, textiles, chariots, furniture, etc. Insofar as the activities in these two spheres proceeded on a large scale, they were for the most part either directly managed or monopolistically controlled by the hydraulic governments. Under the conditions of Pharaonic Egypt and Inca Peru, direct management prevailed. Under more differentiated social conditions, the government tended to leave part of mining, salt gathering, etc. to heavily taxed and carefully supervised entrepreneurs, while it continued to manage directly most of the large manufacturing workshops.

By combining these facts with what we know of the hydraulic and nonhydraulic constructional operations of the state, we may in the following table indicate the managerial position of the hydraulic state both in agriculture and industry. For purposes of comparison, we include corresponding data from two other agrarian societies and from mercantilist Europe.

a. For another peculiarity of hydraulic architecture, the "introvert" character of most of the residential buildings, with the exception of those of the ruler, see below, p. 86, n. *b.*

TABLE 1. *Government Management in the Spheres of Agriculture and Industry*

| INSTITUTIONAL CONFORMATIONS | AGRICULTURE | | INDUSTRY | | Manufacturing | |
	Heavy Waterworks	Farming	Mining, etc.	Construction Industry	Large Shops	Small Shops
Hydraulic society	**+**	—	(+) [1]	**+** [2]	+	—
Coastal city states of classical Greece	—	—	—	—	—	—
Medieval Europe	—	(+) [3]	—	(+) [3]	(+) [3]	—
Mercantilist Europe	—	—	(—)	—	—	—

Key

+ Predominant

+ Outstandingly significant

— Irrelevant or absent

( ) Trend limited or modified by factors indicated in the text

1. Simpler conditions.
2. On a national scale.
3. On a manorial scale.

In ancient Greece, mining was mainly in the hands of licensed businessmen. As long as the concessionaire delivered a fixed part of his output to the state, he enjoyed "very extensive" rights; he "was said to 'buy' the mine, he organized the working as he pleased, the ore was his, and he could cede his concession to a third party." [1] In Medieval Europe mining was also essentially left to private entrepreneurs, who, having obtained a concession from the royal or territorial authorities, proceeded independently and mostly through craft cooperatives.[2] The mercantilist governments of Europe operated some mines directly; but the majority was managed by strictly supervised private owners.[3]

All these arrangements differ profoundly from the system of government mining prevailing in Pharaonic Egypt and Inca Peru. Mercantilist usage resembles in form, but not in institutional substance, the policy pursued in certain of the more differentiated hydraulic societies, where government operation of some mines was combined with private, but government-licensed, handling of others.[4]

Except for mining, Oriental and Occidental absolutism are less similar in the industrial sphere than has been claimed, whereas a resemblance of sorts does exist between hydraulic society and feudal Europe. In hydraulic society, the majority of the not-too-many larger industrial workshops was government managed. In the mercantilist Occident they were, under varying forms of state supervision, predominantly owned and run by private entrepreneurs. In the coastal city-states of classical Greece the government was neither equipped nor inclined to engage in industrial activities. The rulers of Medieval Europe, faced with a different situation, proceeded differently. In their manorial workshops they employed a number of serf-artisans, who were kept busy satisfying the needs of their masters. The feudal lords also summoned serf labor for the construction of "big houses" —castles. The similarity between this manorial system of cooperative work and the hydraulic pattern is evident. But again the functional similarity is limited by the differences in the societal setting. The medieval kings and barons could dispose only over the labor force of their own domains and estates, while the hydraulic rulers could draw on the unskilled and skilled labor of large territories, and ultimately on that of the whole country.

The decisive difference, however, between hydraulic society and the three civilizations with which we compare it lies, insofar as industry is concerned, in the sphere of construction. It is this sphere which more than any other sector of industry demonstrates the or ganizational power of hydraulic society. And it is this sphere which achieved results never attained by any other agrarian or mercantilist society.

The full institutional significance of this fact becomes apparent as soon as we connect it with the corresponding agrarian development. Government-managed heavy water works place the large-scale feeding apparatus of agriculture in the hands of the state. Government-managed construction works make the state the undisputed master of the most comprehensive sector of large-scale industry. In the two main spheres of production the state occupied an unrivaled position of operational leadership and organizational control.

2. THE POWER OF THE HYDRAULIC STATE OVER LABOR
GREATER THAN THAT OF CAPITALIST ENTERPRISES

IN both spheres the hydraulic state levied and controlled the needed labor forces by coercive methods that were invocable by a feudal lord only within a restricted area, and that were altogether different from the methods customary under capitalist conditions. The hydraulic rulers were sufficiently strong to do on a national scale what a feudal sovereign or lord could accomplish only within the borders of his domain. They compelled able-bodied commoners to work for them through the agency of the corvée.

Corvée labor is forced labor. But unlike slave labor, which is demanded permanently, corvée labor is conscripted on a temporary, although recurring, basis. After the corvée service is completed, the worker is expected to go home and continue with his own business.

Thus the corvée laborer is freer than the slave. But he is less free than a wage laborer. He does not enjoy the bargaining advantages of the labor market, and this is the case even if the state gives him food (in the ancient Near East often "bread and beer") or some cash. In areas with a highly developed money economy the hydraulic government may levy a corvée tax and hire rather than conscript the needed labor. This was done largely in China at the close of the Ming dynasty and during the greater part of Ch'ing rule.

But there as elsewhere the government arbitrarily fixed the wage. And it always kept the workers under quasimilitary discipline.[5] Except in times of open political crisis, the hydraulic state could always muster the labor forces it required; and this whether the workers were levied or hired. It has been said that the Mogul ruler Akbar, "by his *firmān* (order) could collect any number of men he liked. There was no limit to his massing of labourers, save the number of people in his Empire." [6] *Mutatis mutandis,* this statement is valid for all hydraulic civilizations.

G. A GENUINE AND SPECIFIC TYPE OF MANAGERIAL REGIME

THUS the hydraulic state fulfilled a variety of important managerial functions.[a] In most instances it maintained crucial hydraulic works, appearing in the agrarian sphere as the sole operator of large preparatory and protective enterprises. And usually it also controlled the major nonhydraulic industrial enterprises, especially large constructions. This was the case even in certain "marginal" areas,[1] where the hydraulic works were insignificant.

The hydraulic state differs from the modern total managerial states in that it is based on agriculture and operates only part of the country's economy. It differs from the laissez-faire states of a private-property-based industrial society in that, in its core form, it fulfills crucial economic functions by means of commandeered (forced) labor.

a. Social science is indebted to James Burnham for pointing to the power potential inherent in managerial control. The present inquiry stresses the importance of the general (political) organizer as compared not only to the technical specialist (see Veblen, 1945: 441 ff.), but also to the economic manager. This, however, does not diminish the author's appreciation of the contribution made by Burnham through his concept of managerial leadership.

CHAPTER 3

$\mathcal{A}$ state stronger than society

A. NONGOVERNMENTAL FORCES COMPETING WITH THE STATE FOR SOCIETAL LEADERSHIP

THE hydraulic state is a genuinely managerial state. This fact has far-reaching societal implications. As manager of hydraulic and other mammoth constructions, the hydraulic state prevents the nongovernmental forces of society from crystallizing into independent bodies strong enough to counterbalance and control the political machine.

The relations between the governmental and nongovernmental forces of society are as manifold as the patterns of society itself. All governments are concerned with the protection of the commonwealth against external enemies (through the organization of military action) and with the maintenance of internal order (through jurisdiction and policing methods of one kind or another). The extent to which a government executes these and other tasks depends on the way in which the societal order encourages, or restricts, governmental activities on the one hand and the development of rival nongovernmental forces on the other.

The nongovernmental forces aiming at social and political leadership include kin groups (particularly under primitive conditions); representatives of autonomous religious organizations (customary in certain primitive civilizations but, as the history of the Christian Church shows, by no means confined to them); independent or semi-independent leaders of military groups (such as tribal bands, armies of feudal lords); and owners of various forms of property (such as money, land, industrial equipment, and capacity to work).

In some cases the rise of hydraulic despotism was probably contested by the heads of powerful clans or by religious groups eager to preserve their traditional autonomy. In others, semi-independent military leaders may have tried to prevent the masters of the hydraulic apparatus from attaining total control. But the rival forces lacked the proprietary and organizational strength that in Greek and Roman antiquity, as well as in Medieval Europe, bulwarked the nongovernmental forces of society. In hydraulic civilizations the men of the government prevented the organizational consolidation of all non-governmental groups. Their state became "stronger than society." [1] Any organization that gives its representatives unchecked power over its subjects may be considered an "apparatus." In contrast to the controlled state of multicentered societies, the state of the single-centered hydraulic society was a veritable apparatus state.

B. THE ORGANIZATIONAL POWER OF THE HYDRAULIC STATE

1. THE GREAT BUILDERS OF HYDRAULIC SOCIETY— GREAT ORGANIZERS

SUPERIOR organizational power may have different roots. In a hydraulic setting the need for comprehensive organization is inherent in the comprehensive constructions necessitated or suggested by the peculiarities of the agrarian order.

These constructions pose numerous technical problems and they always require large-scale organization. To say that the masters of hydraulic society are great builders is only another way of saying they are great organizers.

2. FUNDAMENTALS OF EFFECTIVE ORGANIZATION: COUNTING AND RECORD KEEPING

AN organizer combines disparate elements into an integrated whole. He may do this *ex tempore* if his aim is simple or passing. He must make more elaborate preparations if he is confronted with a permanent and difficult task. Dealing with human beings—their labor power, their military potential, and their capacity to pay taxes—he must know their number and condition. To this end he must count the people. And whenever he expects to draw from them frequently and regularly, he must preserve the results of his count either by memorizing them or, above the most primitive level, by utilizing preliterary or literary symbols.

It is no accident that among all sedentary peoples the pioneers of hydraulic agriculture and statecraft were the first to develop rational systems of counting and writing. It is no accident either that the records of hydraulic society covered not only the limited areas of single cities or city states, of royal domains or feudal manors, but the towns and villages of entire nations and empires. The masters of hydraulic society were great builders because they were great organizers; and they were great organizers because they were great record keepers.

The colored and knotted strings (*quipus*) by which the Incas preserved the results of their frequent countings [1] show that the lack of a script constitutes no insurmountable barrier to numbering and registering the population. In pre-Conquest Mexico the various forms of land and the obligations attached were carefully depicted in codices; and the procedures of local administrators were apparently based on these all-important documents.[2]

In China an elaborate system of writing and counting existed as early as the Yin (Shang) dynasty, that is, in the second millennium B.C. Under the subsequent Chou dynasty census lists were used for determining potential fighters and laborers and for estimating revenue and expenditures. Specific evidence testifies to a detailed system of counting and registering in the ruling state of Chou,[3] and we know that at the close of the Chou period the people were registered in the great northwestern country of Ch'in,[4] and also in Ch'i. In Ch'i the census is said to have been taken every year in the autumn.[5] It was in this season that people were also counted under the first long-lived imperial dynasty, Han.[6] Preserved bamboo records indicate that the Han registers follow a regular pattern.[7] The two sets of Han census figures contained in the official history of the period [8] are the most comprehensive population data to come down to us from any major contemporary civilization, including the Roman Empire.

The later history of the Chinese census presents many problems which are far from solved. The methods and the accuracy of procedures changed greatly with time, but the government's role in the handling of these matters cannot be doubted. In one way or another, the imperial bureaucracy succeeded in keeping track of its human and material resources.

The same holds true for India. The *Arthashāstra* [9] and the Islamic sources [10] reveal the interest which both native and foreign rulers took in counting their subjects and estimating their revenues. And this interest was by no means academic. Megasthenes found various groups of officials in the Maurya empire charged with such tasks as measuring the fields and counting the people.[11] Numerous inscriptions throw light on surveys made during the last period of Hindu India.[12]

After China, we are probably best informed on the Near Eastern development of governmental counting and registering. The oldest deciphered inscriptions dealing with the economy of a Mesopotamian temple city contain many numerical data on land, people, agriculture, and public services.[13] In Pharaonic Egypt the people were counted regularly from the time of the Old Kingdom.[14] Documentary evidence for the connection between the census and fiscal and per-

sonal obligations exist only for the Middle and New Kingdoms, but
the absence of still earlier data on this point is certainly accidental.[15]
On the eve of the Hellenistic period persons and property seem to
have been listed annually; [16] and the Ptolemies probably perpetuated
the ancient system. The papyri suggest that there were two cadasters
used for mutual checking, one in the individual villages and one in
the metropolis.[17]

Under the succeeding regimes the methods of counting people and
property, particularly land, underwent many modifications; but as
in India and China the underlying principle continued to receive
recognition. The Romans inherited the Hellenistic pattern [18] and the
Arabs based their system on that of Eastern Rome.[19] The Mamluks
upheld the time-honored system of record keeping,[20] as did the Ottoman Turks, who during the heyday of their power insisted that
"every thirty years a census must be taken, the dead and the ill must
be separated off, and those not on the rolls must be newly recorded." [21]

3. Organizational and Hydraulic Management

A GLANCE at the metropolitan and local centers of hydraulic record
keeping recalls the original meaning of the term "bureau-cracy":
"rule through bureaus." The power of the agromanagerial regime
was indeed closely interlinked with the "bureaucratic" control which
the government exerted over its subjects.

a. The Organizational Task Inherent in Large Constructions, Hydraulic and Otherwise

As stated above, enormous organizational tasks are inherent in the
large constructions which the agrarian apparatus state accomplishes
and which, particularly in their hydraulic form, play a decisive role
in crystallizing the over-all conformation. Having, in the preceding
chapter, dealt at some length with the constructional developments of
hydraulic society, we shall confine ourselves here to re-emphasizing
once more the cardinal importance of organization in this field.

b. Hydraulic Management

THE outstanding forms of hydraulic management (as juxtaposed to
construction) are the distribution of irrigation water and flood
watching. In general, these two operations require much less manpower than does the work of construction and repair, but those engaged in the former must cooperate very precisely.

Megasthenes describes the care with which officials of the Maurya empire opened and closed the canals and conduits to regulate the distribution of the irrigation water.[a] The highly systematized handbook of Chinese statecraft, the *Chou Li,* speaks of special officials who conducted the irrigation water from the reservoirs and larger canals to the smaller canals and ditches.[22] Herodotus, in a frequently quoted passage, tells how in Achaemenian Persia the sovereign himself supervised the major hydraulic operations: "The king orders the floodgates to be opened toward the country whose need is greatest, and lets the soil drink until it has had enough; after which the gates on this side are shut, and others are unclosed for the nation which, of the remainder, needs it most." [23]

Megasthenes and Herodotus make it very clear that the government was the distributing agent of the irrigation water; but they do not furnish organizational details. Such data are buried in administrative manuals and regulations which, because of their predominantly technical nature, have received little scholarly attention. Among the exceptions are some accounts of 10th- and 16th- (or 17th-) century Persia and several irrigation codes discovered in Bali.

The documents dealing with Persian conditions show the care with which the available water was assigned. They indicate also the clocklike cooperation between the "water master" (*mīrāb*), his subordinate officials and aides, and the village heads.[b] The Bali data familiarize us with the workings of a well-integrated hydraulic order. Here the ruler and the minister of revenues (*sedahan agong*) make the key decisions as to when and how to flood the various local hydraulic units, the *subak.*[24] The official head of a cluster of such units supervises the supply for each *subak;* [25] and the chief of the local unit, the *klian subak,* coordinates the individual peasants, who swear a solemn oath to submit to regulations while the rice fields, *sawah,* are being flooded.[26] "Thus the orderly distribution of the water among the various *sawah*-holders is accomplished with extreme care, and also with well-based reasons. The *sawah*-holder cannot at any time dispose over his share of the water supply where the water is scarce. The

a. Strabo 15. 1. 50. Smith, 1914: 132. Buddha himself is said to have settled a conflict between two city states over their rights to use the waters of a nearby river (*Jātakam,* V: 219).

b. Lambton, 1948: 589 ff. *Ibid.,* 1938: 665 ff. The organization of the irrigation system in East Persia at the time of the Abbassid caliphate is described in Arab sources. The head of the water office in Merv had at his disposal ten thousand hands, and his power surpassed that of the district police chief. The storage dam below the city was operated by four hundred guards; and the technique of measuring and distributing the water was minutely regulated (Mez, 1922: 423 ff.). For the institution of the water master in ancient and modern South Arabia see Grohmann, 1933: 31.

various *sawah*-holders, even if they belong to the same *subak,* must share the available water and must have their *sawah* flooded in sequence." [27]

The organizational operations involved in the distribution of the irrigation water are remarkable for their subtlety and for their centralization of leadership. Conflicts are frequent between cultivator and cultivator and between *subak* and *subak.* "If each *sawah*-holder could do as he pleases, there would soon arise the greatest disorder and the lower *subak* would probably never get their water." All these problems are successfully resolved because essentially "the distribution of the water as well as the water law lies in the hands of a single person." [28]

The control of flood water necessitates greater organizational effort only under special circumstances. An operational problem arises primarily where the seasonal overflow of an extended source of water threatens the irrigation system and the safety of those depending on it. In Bali the upper courses of the river have to be watched; and especially assigned men fulfill this function as a regular part of their hydraulic corvée.[29] In imperial China, even in times of decay, the government placed thousands of persons along their extended embankments in the battle against potential floods.[30] Between 1883 and 1888 the Egyptian government levied about one hundred thousand corviable persons annually to watch and fight the flood.[31]

4. The Organization of Quick Locomotion and Intelligence

UNDER hydraulic conditions of agriculture, certain large operations of construction and management must be organized. Other organizational activities are not imperative, but they are made possible by a political economy which compels the government to maintain centers of direction and coordination in all major regions of production. Being able to establish its authority not only over a limited "royal domain" and a number of royal towns—as does the typical feudal state—the hydraulic regime places its administrators and officers in all major settlements, which virtually everywhere assume the character of government-controlled administrative and garrison towns.

Effective governmental control involves first the political and fiscal superiority of the directing agency and second the means for conveying commands and commanders to the subcenters of control. The desire to exert power through the control of communications characterizes all political hierarchies; but circumstances determine the extent to which this desire will be satisfied. The overlord of a feudal society valued fast communications as much as any Oriental despot; but the spotty distribution of his administrative centers and the politically conditioned lack of good roads prevented his messages from traveling as quickly or as safely as did the messages of the hydraulic sovereign.

The development of long highways and navigation canals is only another manifestation of the extraordinary construction potential of hydraulic society. Similarly the development of effective systems of communication is only another manifestation of its extraordinary organizational potential. Almost all hydraulic states bulwarked their power by elaborate systems of "postal" communication and intelligence.

The terms "post" or "postal service" express the fact that persons are "posted" at intervals along the road; the formula "relay system" points to the regulated interaction between the persons so posted. The terms will be used interchangeably and with the understanding that, within our context, they refer to an organization maintained by the state for the purposes of the state. On occasion the post handled rare and perishable goods (fruit and fish for the court, etc.). But its primary aim was the movement of persons of privilege (envoys, officials, foreign diplomats), messengers, and messages—these latter including intelligence of the most confidential, important, and delicate nature.

In the decentralized society of Medieval Europe individuals or groups of individuals (merchants, butchers, towns) established overland communications long before the government undertook the organization of a systematic postal service.[32] In the hydraulic world, private communications were not lacking,[33] but they never competed with the far-flung and effective relay system of the state. By running the post as a political institution, the representatives of Oriental government maintained a monopoly over fast locomotion, which—interlocked with an elaborate system of intelligence—became a formidable weapon of social control.

The hydraulic countries of ancient America present the relay system in a simple but highly effective form. In the absence of suitable transport animals, messages were carried by runners, who in the Mexican area proceeded along more or less informal routes and in the Andean area, along excellent state highways. The Mexican relay stations are said to have been set something like two leagues (*ca.* 6 miles) apart;[34] and, according to Torquemada, the speed with which messages could be delivered exceeded one hundred leagues (300 miles) per day.[35] The stations along the Inca road were closer to each other, at times no more than three-quarters of a mile separating them. The runners could move at a speed of one hundred and fifty miles per day. According to Cobo, one message was carried from the coastal town of Lima to Cuzco, the capital of the *altiplano,* over approximately four hundred miles of difficult and often steep terrain, in something like three days. A hundred years after the conquest it took the Spanish horse-mail twelve to thirteen days to cover the same ground.*c* While on service, the runners had to be fed; and this was the responsibility of the settlements through which the relay routes passed.[36] As a matter of fact, in all parts of the hydraulic world those who lived along the post roads were generally compelled to provision the stations, furnish auxiliary labor, and supply the draft and transport animals, carriages, sedan chairs or boats demanded by the relay officials.

The Incas are said to have been extremely well informed about the remotest regions of their empire.[37] The far-flung organization of the postal system of Achaemenian Persia greatly impressed Herodotus.[38] Private letters might also be carried, but for security reasons they were read by the postal officials.[39] Xenophon stressed the intelligence angle. Through the royal post the Achaemenian kings were able "to learn with great celerity the state of affairs at any distance." [40]

The technical peculiarities of the Roman state post have been frequently described. The layout of its larger and smaller stations (*mansiones* and *mutationes*) and the organizational pattern of the institution are indeed remarkable.[41] But it is important to remember that from the very beginning the *cursus publicus* was primarily aimed at providing the imperial center with information.[42] By establishing the post, Augustus laid the foundations for a comprehensive intelligence system. Special officials, first called *frumentarii* and from Diocletian on *agentes in rebus,* operated in conjunction with the technical staff. Their activities enormously strengthened the hold of the autocracy over its subjects.[43]

At the beginning of the Byzantine period the postal system is said to have been excellent.[44] According to Procopius, it enabled the couriers to cover in one day a distance otherwise requiring ten days.[45] The Sassanid rulers of Persia followed the Achaemenian tradition both in maintaining an effective postal service and in using it essentially for the purposes of the state.[46]

It is generally claimed that the caliphs shaped their postal system after the Persian model.[47] This seems to be true with one important qualification. The Arabs, who carried with them the tradition of the steppe and the desert, moved on horseback or by means of camel

c. Cobo, HNM, III: 269; Rowe, 1946: 231 ff. According to Cieza (1945: 137), a message was carried this distance in eight days.

caravans. Consequently they paid little attention [48] to the well-kept highways, which had been the glory of the Near Eastern postal service until the days of the Sassanids. Otherwise they were indeed eager to keep the state post in good condition. In the 9th century the caliphate is said to have maintained over 900 relay stations.[49]

Under the caliphs the postmaster-general was often at the same time the head of the intelligence service.[50] An appointment decree of the year A.H. 315 (A.D. 927–28) states clearly that the caliph expected the head of the postal service to observe in detail the state of farming, the condition of the population, the behavior of the official judges, the mint, and other relevant matters. The secret reports were to deal separately with the various classes of functionaries, judges, police officials, persons in charge of the taxes, etc.[51] The directives imply elaborate methods of gathering and tabulating information.

The Fatimids perpetuated the postal tradition of their Arab predecessors; [52] and the Mamluks were at least as eager to maintain the state post, which during the period of their prosperity connected the Egyptian metropolis with the various regions of Syria.[53] Qalqashandi notes the connection between the regular postal system and the organization of intelligence and espionage. Government offices dealing with these matters were under the same ministry, the *Diwan* of Correspondence.[54] The dispatch-bearers of the Ottoman government carried the regime's political and administrative correspondence "through the length and breadth of the Ottoman Empire." [55]

Megasthenes mentions the activities of intelligence officials in Maurya India; [56] and the *Arthashāstra* and the *Book of Manu* discuss in some detail the methods to be employed by spies.[57] The relation between the government-maintained courier system and secret intelligence becomes clearly apparent in texts dealing with the Gupta period (3d–8th century A.D.); [58] and it can also be documented for the Muslim period.[59] In Mogul times local intelligence was bureaucratically organized under an official designated as *kotwāl*.[60] It seems legitimate to assume that the national intelligence service was interlinked with the road system, whose public inns (*sarāis*) and other conveniences were organized "in accordance with the practice of the best Hindu kings in ancient times." [61]

In China the relay system developed together with state roads and man-made waterways. Perpetuating and elaborating earlier patterns,[62] the masters of the empire established a postal service which, with numerous disruptions and modifications, lasted for more than two thousand years. The imperial post provided the government with quick and confidential information on all parts of the country. During the Han period, rebellious barbarians not infrequently burned the postal stations.[63] A high dignitary, titled King of Yen, who conspired to become emperor, set up a relay system of his own for the speedy transmission of messages.[64] A former official, wanted by the government, stated in a plaintive memorandum that the government began its search for him by dispatching "messages by the post service and the post-horse system to make a proclamation near and far." His pursuers "examined every footprint of man" and "followed every rut of the carriage." Eventually the net that was "spread all over the empire" closed in upon the fugitive; he was caught and delivered to his death.[65]

The relay system of the T'ang government (618–907) operated through more than 1,500 stations, of which nearly 1,300 served overland communications, 260 functioned as "water posts," and 86 as both.[66] The Liao post was also exclusively reserved for the use of the state; its support remained the burden of the people. "Every county was supposed to have its own relay stations for which the local population had to provide the necessary horses and oxen." [67]

Viewed against such historical precedents, Marco Polo's report of the postal system of Mongol China does not seem unreasonable, particularly if we remember that the Great Khan's empire included many a "roadless tract." [68] The Mongol rulers of China kept an unusually large number of horses. But it is noteworthy that in addition to maintaining many major "horse post houses," even these mounted conquerors had many smaller stations for the use of foot runners. Through the runners, whose number was "immense," the Mongol Empire received "despatches with news from places ten days' journey off in one day and night." [69]

The use of foot runners—as a supplement to the horse- and boat-post—continued until the last imperial dynasty, Ch'ing (1616–1912). In 1825 the postal service operated an elaborate network of trunk and branch roads with more than 2,000 express stations and almost 15,000 stations for foot messengers. For the former the administration budgeted 30,526 horses and 71,279 service men and for the latter, 47,435 foot messengers. These figures cover only the technical personnel. Official information and secret intelligence were handled by regional and local officials, whose vigilance was sharpened by threats of severe punishment.

The organizational effort involved in maintaining this gigantic network is obvious. The extraordinary opportunities for speedy and confidential information are no less striking. The metropolitan province, Chihli, alone had 185 express stations and 923 foot dispatch posts. Corresponding figures for Shantung are 139 and 1,062; for Shansi, 127 and 988; for Shensi, 148 and 534; for Szechwan, 66 and

1,409; for Yunnan, 76 and 425. During the 17th and 18th centuries the Ch'ing government allocated as much as 10 per cent of its total expenditures for the maintenance of its postal system.[70]

5. The Organizational Pattern of Warfare in Hydraulic Society

ORGANIZED control over the bulk of the population in times of peace gives the government extraordinary opportunities for coordinated mass action also in times of war. This becomes manifest as soon as we contemplate such crucial aspects of defense as the monopolization and coordination of military operations, organization of supplies, military theory, and potential size of the armed forces. A comparative view of these and related features reveals the institutional peculiarities of hydraulic society in this field as in others.

a. Monopolization and Coordination

THE sovereign of a feudal country did not possess a monopoly of military action. As a rule, he could mobilize his vassals for a limited period only, at first perhaps for three months and later for forty days, the holders of small fiefs often serving only for twenty or ten days, or even less.[71] This temporary levy tended to affect only part of the vassals' military strength, perhaps a third or a fourth, or a still smaller fraction.[72] And frequently even this fraction was not obliged to follow the sovereign, if he campaigned abroad.[73]

The national sovereign had full control only over his own troops, which in accordance with the decentralized character of society constituted only a part—and often a not very large part—of the temporarily assembled national armies. In England the Norman Conquest accelerated the growth of governmental power; but even here the royal core was slow in prevailing. In 1300 during the Carlaverock campaign, the king accomplished what Tout considers a maximal mobilization of "horse guards of the crown." At this time the "household" element was "roughly about a quarter of the whole number of men-at-arms"; at best it was "nearer a third than a quarter." [74] In 1467 the German emperor tried to gather an army of 5,217 horsemen and 13,285 foot soldiers for fighting against the Turks. Out of the aimed-at total, the emperor's own contingent was expected to comprise 300 horsemen and 700 foot soldiers, while six electors were expected to contribute 320 and 740 respectively; forty-seven archbishops and bishops 721 and 1,813; twenty-one princes 735 and 1,730; various counts and seigneurs 679 and 1,383; and seventy-nine towns 1,059 and 2,926.[75]

In all these respects the armies of the hydraulic state proceeded on an entirely different level. The soldiers were not protected by democratic checks or feudal contracts. No matter whether they held office land or not, they came when they were summoned; they marched where they were told; they fought as long as their ruler wanted them to fight; and there was no question as to who gave the orders or who obeyed.

The constant rotation of the many armed contingents that in accordance with the feudal contract served only for a short period constituted a major reason for the restlessness that characterized virtually all compound feudal armies. Another reason was the lack of a definite authority. Where the sovereign was little more than the first among equals, and where the many lords proudly insisted on the privileges of their position, argument easily replaced obedience. Consequently military action was marked as much by the lack of discipline as by individual valor.[76]

b. Training and Morale

THE army of a hydraulic state might include among those it drafted many persons of poor training and little fighting spirit. With regard to skill these men might compare unfavorably with a feudal host, whose members were carefully trained, and with regard to morale they might be inferior to the warriors of both ancient Greece and feudal Europe. But in planned coordination they approached the ancient Greeks; and they far surpassed the European chevaliers.

TABLE 2. *Types of Societies and Types of Fighters*

	ARMIES OF			
QUALIFICATIONS	*Hydraulic Society*		*Classical Greece*	*Feudal Europe*
	Professional troops	*Drafted men: "militia"*		
Training	+	—	+	+
Spirit	+	—	+	+
Coordination	+	+	+	—

Key
+ Feature developed
— Feature weak or absent

The Greeks, who recognized the high quality of the Oriental elite warriors,[d] commented contemptuously on the poorly trained mass of auxiliary soldiers,[77] who obviously were draftees. Most of them did indeed lack the spirited integration which was the pride of the

d. See Herodotus' account of the conversation between the exiled Spartan king, Demaratus, and Xerxes (Herodotus 7. 103 f.).

Greek citizen armies.[78] But opposed to the disorderly hosts of Medieval Europe the well-coordinated troops of the Eastern monarchies made formidable enemies. About A.D. 900 the author of the *Tactica,* Emperor Leo VI,[e] advised his generals to "take advantage of their [the Franks' and Lombards'] indiscipline and disorder." "They have neither organisation nor drill" and therefore, "whether fighting on foot or on horseback, they charge in dense, unwieldy masses, which cannot manoeuvre." [79] In the organization of the Western armies "there is nothing to compare to our own orderly division into batallions and brigades." Their camping is poor, so they can be easily attacked during the night. "They take no care about their commissariat." Under privation, their ranks tend to disintegrate "for they are destitute of all respect for their commanders,—one noble thinks himself as good as another,—and they will deliberately disobey orders when they grow discontented." [80]

This picture of "a Western army of the ninth or tenth century, the exact period of the development of feudal cavalry," [81] remains valid, with certain modifications, for the entire age of European feudalism. Oman describes the hosts of the Crusades as "a mixed multitude, with little or no organisation." [82] "Their want of discipline was as well marked as their proneness to plunder; deliberate disobedience on the part of officers was as common as carelessness and recklessness on the part of the rank and file. This was always the case in feudal armies." [83]

The modern Egyptian historian, Atiya, ascribes the victory of the Turks in the last major crusade to the Christians' lack of "unity of arms and companies" and of "common tactics." Conversely, the "Turkish army was . . . a perfect example of the most stringent discipline, of a rigorous and even fanatic unity of purpose, of the concentration of supreme tactical power in the sole person of the Sultan." [84]

c. Organization of Supplies

THE masters of hydraulic society applied the same organizational devices in the military sphere that they employed with such success in construction and communication. In many cases, the recruits for war could be as comprehensively mobilized as the recruits for toil. The assembled armies moved in orderly fashion, and camping

e. For reasons indicated in the Introduction, above, our presentation includes references to Byzantium after the Arab conquests, to the Liao empire, to Maya society, and to other marginal hydraulic civilizations. The marginal areas of the hydraulic world are more fully discussed in Chap. 6, below.

and scouting were often highly developed. Whenever feasible, the armies lived off the land; but numerous means were invoked to cope with possible shortages.

The Incas had a "superb supply system." [85] The Persian king, Xerxes, in preparation for his invasion of Greece "laid up stores of provisions in many places. . . . He inquired carefully about all the sites, and had the stores laid up in such as were most convenient, causing them to be brought across from various parts of Asia and in various ways, some in transports and others in merchantmen." [86] The Byzantine generals were definitely concerned with the "commissariat" of their troops.[87] The Arabs and Turks, at the peak of their power, paid considerable attention to the supply problem, which was handled by methods suited to their special form of warfare.[88] The history of Chinese warfare is filled with references to precisely this matter.[89]

d. Planned Warfare and Military Theory

FEUDAL warfare, being unfavorable to the development of tactics and strategy in the proper sense of these terms,[90] also failed to develop military theory. Medieval chronicles contain innumerable references to battles, and the epics of knighthood never tire of describing military adventures. But they are concerned essentially with the prowess of individual fighters. Tactical considerations remain as irrelevant in literature as in reality.

In the hydraulic world the organization of warfare was elaborately discussed. Military experts liked to evaluate their experiences in treatises on tactics and strategy.[f] The Arthashāstra shows Maurya India well aware of the problems of aggression and defense.[91] The comprehensive Byzantine literature on warfare indicates the many problems posed by the empire's defense strategy.[92]

The organizational trends of Islamic warfare are significantly foreshadowed in a passage of the Koran which assures the love of Allah to those who fight for him "in ranks as though they were a compact building." [93] Later many Muslim writers discussed military questions.[94]

Yet probably no great hydraulic civilization produced a more extensive military literature than China. Contrary to the prevailing notion, Chinese statesmen paid much attention to military problems; they already did so during the period of the territorial states, which in this respect as in so many others followed hydraulic rather

f. The military writings of ancient Greece reflect a similar, though differently rooted, interest in organized warfare.

than feudal patterns. The author of *The Art of War*, Sun Tzŭ,[95] however brilliant, was not the sole great military theoretician in this period—Sun Ping and Wu Ch'i rate as high,[96] and many of the ideas Sun Tzŭ put forth are acknowledged to have been based on earlier writings.[97]

Almost every major territorial state had its own school of military thought.[98] But no matter how early the various concepts were first formulated, it was in the period of the territorial states that they assumed their classical shape. For very pragmatic reasons the empire maintained a lively interest in the problems of warfare. To mention but one piece of evidence, all major official histories from the T'ang dynasty (618–907) on included special, and often large, sections on military affairs.

e. Numbers

THE masters of the hydraulic state, who monopolized coordinated military action, could—if they so wished—raise large armies. Their mobilization potential was entirely different from, and greatly superior to, that of feudal Europe.

In Medieval England the Normans inherited a military order which, in addition to a feudal elite, contained elements of an older tribal levy. The conquerors succeeded in preserving and developing these rudiments of a national army; but even in England the feudal state could draw on only a part of the population.

The armies of hydraulic civilizations were not so limited. Their numerical strength varied with such factors as military techniques (infantry warfare, chariots, and light or heavy cavalry), economic conditions (a natural or a money economy), and national composition (indigenous rule or submission under a conquering people). But potentially it was large.

Where all soldiers fight on foot—either because suitable animals are lacking or because charioteering or riding are unknown skills—numbers tend to be important, even when different parts of the army are differently armed and trained. In ancient Mexico,[99] as well as in Inca Peru,[100] the government levied large infantry armies. Where charioteering or riding are practiced, foot soldiers may count for less and their number may decrease substantially. The rise of a money economy favors the recruiting of mercenaries, who may constitute the only major standing (cadre) army or who may serve along with a "noble" elite.

And then there is conquest. Often, and especially at the beginning of a conquest dynasty, the alien ruler will depend on his own nationals to keep his power secure; and he will give little special training to his newly acquired subjects.[101]

But no matter how the armies of agrarian despotism are conditioned, the advantages of size rarely disappear altogether. The best armies of the advanced type are usually composite bodies.[102]

As noted above, the feudal armies of Medieval Europe were small units of mounted elite fighters. An army dispatched by Charles the Bald numbered less than five thousand warriors; and on several later occasions the records speak only of a couple of hundred horsemen.[103] The international armies of the crusades were usually composed of a few thousand to no more than ten thousand men.[g] The Arabs had brilliant cadre armies of mounted fighters, which were supplemented by sizable units of auxiliary troops.[104] The standing armies of the first Umayyad caliphs are said to have numbered about sixty thousand men; and the last ruler of this dynasty is credited by Ibn al-Athīr with a host of 120,000 soldiers.[105] Harun al-Rashīd once undertook a summer campaign with 135,000 regular soldiers and an unspecified number of volunteers.[106]

Similarly illuminating is a comparison of the armies of feudal Europe with those of the "Western Caliphate" of Cordoba. According to Islamic sources, Moorish Spain in the 10th century dispatched twenty thousand horsemen on a northern campaign. Lot doubts this figure because, in the contemporary European context, it seems unbelievably large. Says he: "The whole of Europe was unable to levy at this epoch such a number." [107] His comment is as correct as it is inconclusive. The distinguished historian himself notes the enormous revenues collected by the Cordoban caliphate: "What a contrast to the Carolingian Empire or the Ottoman Empire, states without finance! Only the emperor of Eastern Rome, the Byzantine *basileus,* had perhaps equivalent resources." [108] In another part of his study he credits the early Byzantine Empire with two armies of eighteen thousand men each, plus an unknown number of occupation troops in Africa and Italy [109]—that is, with a force of more, perhaps considerably more, than 40,000 men. In view of these facts there is no reason to doubt that Moorish Spain, a hydraulic country with a very dense population and a revenue far in excess of any of its European contemporaries, could put into the field a host half

g. Lot, 1946, I: 130, 175, 201. Even at the close of the Crusades, the international European army that fought in 1396 at Nicopolis against the invading Turks had no national contingent comprising more than ten thousand warriors, except that of the immediately threatened Hungarians. The Hungarians are said to have levied some 60,000 men (Atiya, 1934: 67), which would indeed have been something like a *levée en masse.*

as large as the army of the Byzantine Empire, whose revenues, according to Lot's own statement, it easily matched.

At the time of Achaemenian Persia, foot soldiers still constituted the bulk of all fighting men. Herodotus estimates that the Persian Great King mobilized against the Greeks about two million men,[110] including his elite fighters, the ten thousand "Immortals."[111] Delbrück is certainly justified in doubting that any such large force was actually sent to Europe, but his argument becomes problematic to the extreme when he suggests that the invasion army numbered only some five or six thousand armed men.[112] Nor is there any reason to reject the possibility that, within its confines, the Persian empire was able to raise armies of several hundred thousand men. Munro suggests that Herodotus misinterpreted an official Persian source when he estimated Persia's total armed strength at 1,800,000 men. Munro himself assumes that Xerxes could muster 360,000 men and that the expeditionary force against Greece might have numbered 180,000.[h]

The size of India's earlier armies, which appears "incredible at first sight,"[113] becomes plausible through comparison with the figures we have for the later phase of Muslim India. According to Greek sources, on the eve of the Maurya empire King Mahapādma Nanda is said to have had 80,000 horsemen, 200,000 foot soldiers, 8,000 chariots, and 6,000 fighting elephants;[114] and the figures given for Chandragupta's host are, with the exception of the cavalry, much larger, totaling "690,000 in all, excluding followers and attendants."[115] Data for later periods claim armies of 100,000 foot soldiers in the Āndhra kingdom and hundreds of thousands to several million soldiers under the last Southern Hindu kings[116] and the great Muslim rulers.[117]

In ancient China elite units of charioteers fought alongside large detachments of foot soldiers. During the later part of the Chou dynasty cavalry began to supplement the chariots, but apparently the new composite armies were more rather than less numerous. On the eve of the imperial period the leading territorial states are said to have mobilized three and a half million foot soldiers, plus an undefined number of charioteers and over thirty thousand horsemen.[118]

The Liao empire had, in the *ordus,* a cadre cavalry of about fifty

h. See Munro, 1939: 271–3. Eduard Meyer (GA, IV, Pt. 1: 5) states that Herodotus' description of Xerxes' army, like the list of Darius' tributes and other specific pieces of information, was based on authentic Persian sources. Munro (*ibid.,* 271) feels certain that Herodotus' list of Xerxes' army was substantially the reproduction of "an official document."

to sixty thousand fighters; and its records boast a militia of a million men.[119] Under the Sung dynasty (960–1269) the Chinese government is said to have trained—poorly, but nevertheless trained—a standing army of more than one million soldiers.[120] The Banners of the Manchu dynasty were a standing army that at least during the first phase constituted a highly qualified cavalry elite. At the end of the 19th century these armies, which included Manchu, Mongol, and Chinese Bannermen, totaled 120,000 soldiers. In addition, the government also had an essentially Chinese "Green" Army, which numbered some five to six hundred thousand men.[121]

f. Percentages

WHILE noting this, we have to remember that the hydraulic civilizations that maintained large armies generally also had large populations. Yet different external and internal conditions made for a wide range in the percentages of the total population included in the fighting forces.

The army of late Ch'ing probably constituted less than 0.2 per cent of the total population. In the Han empire every able-bodied peasant was obliged to render both labor and defense service. Theoretically this affected 40 per cent of the rural population [122] or something like 32 per cent of the entire population. The cadre army of the Liao dynasty amounted to about one per cent of the population. The peasant militia comprised, on paper, about 20 per cent. Herodotus' data, as interpreted by Munro, suggest that in Achaemenian Persia out of a population of less than twenty millions [123] about 1.8 per cent could be mobilized. Assuming that the population of late Chou China was as large as that of the Han empire at its best, namely about sixty millions (which probably it was not), the average mobilization potential of the great absolutist territorial states would have been almost 6 per cent.

Of course, there is no evidence that in any of these cases an attempt was made to realize the full mobilization potential. The Sung government, which in the 11th century levied a million soldiers from almost twenty million families, that is, from almost one hundred million people, was actually drafting slightly more than one per cent of its population.

Comparison with ancient Greece and feudal Europe is instructive. In an emergency all able-bodied free men of a Greek city state could be mobilized. During the 5th century B.C., Athens may temporarily have had under arms over 12 per cent of the total population, and something like 20 per cent of all free persons.[124]

The army that the German emperor raised in 1467 may have represented 0.15 per cent of the total population of twelve millions, and
Charles the Bald's above-mentioned army about 0.05 per cent of
what is estimated to have been the population of France.[125] Thus
the extremely low percentage for the late Ch'ing period still is
higher than the German figure for 1467, and it is almost four times
higher than the figure for 9th-century France. The difference between the feudal ratio and our other hydraulic percentages is
enormous.

To be sure, in Medieval Europe the feudal lords, monasteries, and
burgher towns had many more soldiers; but these soldiers, being
in excess of the agreed-upon service quota, were not obliged to
fight in the armies of their supreme overlord. The feudal government was too weak to mobilize more than a fraction of the nation's
able-bodied men; the agrodespotic regimes, like the ancient city
states, were not so handicapped. Technical and political considerations might induce them to employ only a small percentage of
their subjects for military purposes. But compared to feudal conditions, even relatively small armies of hydraulic states tended to be
quantitatively impressive; and the mass armies of agromanagerial
regimes completely exceeded both in absolute and relative terms
the armies of comparable feudal governments.

C. THE ACQUISITIVE POWER OF
THE HYDRAULIC STATE

1. Organizational and Bureaucratic Prerequisites

THE men who direct the constructional and organizational enterprises of hydraulic society can do so only on the basis of an appropriately regulated income. Special modes of acquisition emerge
therefore, together with special modes of construction and organization.

The acquisition of a steady and ample governmental revenue involves a variety of organizational and bureaucratic operations as
soon as the hydraulic commonwealth outgrows local dimensions;
and the need for such devices becomes particularly great when the
administrative and managerial functions are fulfilled by numerous
full-time officials. Gradually the masters of the hydraulic state
become as much concerned with acquisitive operations as with their
hydraulic, communicational, and defense tasks. As will be shown
below, under certain conditions taxation and related methods of
proprietary control may flourish together with an integrated army
and a state post without any relevant hydraulic enterprises.

2. LABOR ON THE PUBLIC FIELDS AND/OR THE
LAND TAX

THE incipient hydraulic community may make no special arrangements for the support of its leadership. However, the consolidation
of hydraulic conditions is generally accompanied by a tendency to
free the chief from agricultural work in order that he may devote
himself completely to his communal secular or religious functions.
To this end the tribesmen cooperate on the chief's land, as they do
on the irrigation ditches, defense works, and other communal enterprises.

The Suk, who give only a fraction of their economic effort to
hydraulic agriculture, have no public land; but in the Pueblos the
commoners are rallied for work on the *cacique*'s fields.[1] This is done
largely by persuasion; but coercion is not shunned when the
situation requires it.[a] In the larger communities of the Chagga
the ruler wields more power and disposes over much land. The
communal work involved in its cultivation is by no means light,
but the tribesmen receive little or no compensation for doing it—
at most some meat and a few swallows of beer at the conclusion of
their tasks. Thus the Chagga commoner who tells his white friend,
"For you we are working, not as in the corvée, but as on our own
fields," [2] manifestly performs his agricultural corvée duty without
enthusiasm.

The masters of a developed hydraulic state depend for their
maintenance on the population's surplus labor or surplus produce,
on the cash equivalent of such produce, or on a combination of all,
or some, of these sources. Work on government (and temple) fields
was regular practice in Inca Peru, Aztec Mexico,[b] and throughout
the greater part of Chou China. The extensive temple lands of the
Sumerian temple cities were cultivated in the main by soldier-
peasants, who constituted the bulk of the temple personnel; but
the communal farmers apparently delivered only a fixed part of their
crop to the storehouses, and this they did personally and directly.[3]

a. Aitken (1930: 385) juxtaposes "the gay working parties of the Hopi" to the
"compulsory work for the priest-chief and on the communal irrigation ditches" in the
Rio Grande Pueblos. Significantly, the work on the chief's field was directed by the
war chief, the chief disciplinary agent in the Pueblos (see White, 1932: 42, 45; *ibid.*,
1942: 97 ff. and 98, n. 10; also Parsons, 1939, II: 884, 889), and this was the case not
only in the hydraulically more compact eastern Pueblos but in the western Pueblos
as well.

b. Maya commoners, like the members of the Mexican *calpulli*, cultivated special
land for the "lords," the representatives of the local and central government (see
Landa, 1938: 104).

The Sumerian arrangement contrasts sharply with the coordinated work teams of the Inca villages [4] and the "thousands of pairs" that, according to an old Chinese ode, jointly tilled the public fields in early Chou times.[5] In Pharaonic Egypt the bulk of all arable land seems to have been assigned to individual peasants, who, after the harvest had been gathered, delivered part of their crop to the appropriate officials.[6]

State farms ("domains"),[c] on which special groups of serving men were employed, occurred in a number of hydraulic civilizations; but except for pre-Conquest America and Chou China, the majority of all hydraulic states [d] seem to have preferred the land tax to corvée labor on large government fields. Why?

There is no consistent correlation between the predominance of a natural economy and the predominance of the public land system. International trade and money-like means of exchange were more developed in Aztec Mexico than in the Old and Middle Kingdoms of Egypt. Possibly the absence—or presence—of agricultural labor animals exerted a more basic influence. Peasants who, without benefit of such animals, tilled the land with a digging stick (as they did in ancient Peru and Meso-America) or with a hoe (as they did in the greater part of Chou China), may be effectively coordinated in semimilitary teams, even when they work irrigated fields, whereas plowing teams function more effectively when permitted to operate as separate units on separate fields.

Significantly, plowing with oxen spread in China during the final phase of the Chou dynasty [7] that witnessed the gradual abolition of the public field system. The peasants of Lagash, who for the most part seem to have worked the temple land individually, were entirely familiar with the use of agricultural labor animals. So were the peasants of Pharaonic Egypt and of Hindu and Muslim India. Thus most of the hydraulic states, in which work animals were used in cultivation, were maintained by the production of individual farmers and not by the joint effort of an agricultural corvée.

c. State farms, *sita,* flourished in India during the later part of the first millennium B.C. (*Arthaçāstra,* 1926: 177 ff.). These farms, however, must be distinguished from the Mogul *khālsa,* which is often referred to as the rajah's "domain." Unfortunately, the term "domain" has been applied both to large sectors of public land ("the king's land") and to limited farmlike estates. The Mogul *khālsa* certainly falls within the first category. According to Baden-Powell (1896: 198), the Mogul rulers used the term *khālsa* to designate "the whole of the lands paying revenue direct to the Treasury."

d. Traces of public fields are reported for certain regions of India. Whether they reflect primitive tribal institutions, possibly of Dravidian or pre-Dravidian origin, is an open question (see Baden-Powell, 1896: 179, 180; *ibid.,* 1892, I: 576 ff.; Hewitt, 1887: 622 ff.).

The following table indicates different forms in which a number of representative hydraulic governments obtained their rural revenues.

TABLE 3. *Rural Revenue of Hydraulic Governments*

REPRESENTATIVES	SOURCE OF REVENUE		
	"Public" Land	Taxes	
		Essentially in Kind	Partly in Kind, Partly in Cash
Tribal societies:			
Suk	—		
Pueblos	+		
Chagga	+		
Hawaii	(+)[1]	+	
Ancient America:			
Inca Peru	+		
Mexico	+	(+)[1]	
The Near East:			
Sumerian temple cities (Lagash)	+[2]		
Babylonia		+	
Pharaonic Egypt		+	
Hellenistic and Roman period			+
Early Byzantium			+
The Arab caliphates			+
Ottoman Turkey			+
India	traces	+	
China:			
Early Chou	+		
Late Chou	Documented Transition		
The Imperial period (roughly)			+

Key	
+ Feature developed	*1.* Some.
— Feature undeveloped or absent	*2.* Individual responsibility.

3. UNIVERSALITY AND WEIGHT OF THE HYDRAULIC TAX CLAIM

THE fact that work on the public fields was usually shared by all corviable adult males indicates the power of the hydraulic leadership to make everyone contribute to its support. The establishment of a money economy goes hand in hand with greater differentiations in property, class structure, and national revenue. But the hydraulic state, as the master of a huge organizational apparatus, continues to impose it fiscal demands on the mass of all commoners. Comparison shows that in this respect it was much stronger than the governments of other agrarian societies.

In classical Athens "the dignity of the citizen could not submit to personal taxes." [8] When the famous city "already held the hegemony in Greece, she had neither regular taxes nor a treasury"; [9] and her national support came essentially from customs and oversea revenues. In republican Rome the free citizens were equally eager to keep public expenses low. The only major direct tax, the *tributum*, amounted to 0.1–0.3 per cent of the taxed person's property.[e] In both cases the nongovernmental forces of society kept the administrative apparatus small in both personnel and budget, distinguished office holders receiving only an insignificant salary or none.

The rulers of Medieval Europe supported themselves essentially from their personal domains, which comprised only a fraction of the nation's territory. The occasional or regular fees which they collected in their wider territory were so limited that they demonstrate the weakness rather than the strength of the sovereign's fiscal power. The Norman conquerors pioneered in establishing a stronger state; but for reasons discussed below even they were able to impose taxes on all their subjects only intermittently.[10] After a century of struggle a mighty knighthood restricted the king's right to levy taxes without the consent of the "common council" to the three "aids," as was the custom in almost every feudal country on the continent.

It is with these agrarian societies, and not with the proto-industrial and industrial West, that the great societies of the East must be compared. The masters of hydraulic agriculture spread their tax-collecting offices as widely as their registering and mobilizing agencies. All adult males were expected to toil, fight, and pay whenever the state willed it. This was the rule. Exemptions had to be especially granted, and even when granted, they were often canceled either after a prescribed period or when the grantor's reign ended.

Rural revenue was calculated in varying ways. Sometimes adult males, sometimes family "heads," and sometimes land units formed the basis for assessment. In Babylonia the land tax was collected even from soldiers who held service fields.[11] The government might demand as a general land tax 20 per cent of the annual crop. The same official rate is suggested also for the New Kingdom of Pharaonic Egypt.[12] In India during the later part of the first millennium B.C. it was one-twelfth, one-sixth, or one-fourth of the crop. The *Arthashāstra* permits the king, in an emergency, to take up to one-third (instead of one-fourth) of the crop of the cultivator of good irrigated land.[13] Many different rate-scales are recorded for late Chou and imperial China. Originally the Islamic regulations made

e. Originally taxable property was confined to land, slaves, and animals; later it included property of all kinds (Schiller, 1893: 196; cf. Homo, 1927: 237).

distinctions mainly in accordance with creed; but gradually conditions became much more involved; and, of course, they differed widely in time and space. The many arguments about heavy taxation show that, under Islamic rule, the land tax was as burdensome, and tended to become as universal, as in other parts of the hydraulic world.

A government that keeps to the official rates is considered just; but most governments preferred material to moral satisfaction. Many a sovereign went beyond the letter of the law. The clay tablets of Babylonia indicate that the state, which theoretically was content with about 10 per cent, occasionally raised the tax "to 1/5, 1/4, 1/3, and even one half" of the crop.[14]

Nor is this all. The payments, which appear in official lists, are in most cases below, and often far below, the payments which the tax gatherers actually extracted. Even in the most rational of all hydraulic states the higher echelons of the bureaucracy found it difficult to exert full control over their subordinates. Often the very effort to compel complete delivery was lacking.

The distribution of the total tax income among the various strata and categories of the officialdom varied greatly. The divergencies are highly significant for the distribution of power within the bureaucracy; but they are irrelevant from the point of view of the state as a whole. The fiscal power of the hydraulic apparatus state must be measured by the total tax that the bureaucracy in its entirety is able to extract from the nongovernmental population in its entirety. Contrasted with the almost complete absence of universal and direct taxation in the city states of ancient Greece and in Rome, and compared with the pathetically feeble fiscal policy of feudal Europe, the scope and strength of the hydraulic system of taxation is striking.

4. CONFISCATION

THE hydraulic state, which asserts its fiscal power so effectively in the countryside, pursues a similar policy also toward artisans, merchants, and other owners of mobile property not protected by special prerogatives. The fact is so obvious that in the present context we shall refrain from discussing the methods invoked for taxing handicraft and commerce. However, another acquisitive feature of hydraulic statecraft does deserve comment: the seizure of conspicuous property by outright confiscation.

An association of free men may ask of itself whatever sacrifices it holds necessary for the common weal; and occasionally it may employ the weapon of confiscation against criminals or excessively powerful men.*' But arbitrary confiscation as a general policy is characteristic of a genuinely absolutist regime. Having established unrestricted fiscal claims, such a regime can modify them at will. In addition, it can encroach on private property even after all regular and irregular taxes have been paid.

Under simpler conditions of power and class, there is little or no large independent business property; and whatever confiscation occurs essentially hits members of the ruling group. Under more differentiated conditions, business wealth becomes a favorite target, but attacks on the property of officials do not cease.

Large landed property is by no means immune to confiscation. But it is more readily accessible to taxation than are precious metals, jewels, or money, which can be hidden with relative ease and which are indeed carefully hidden by all except the most powerful members of the apparatus government. The confiscatory measures of the hydraulic state therefore hit with particular harshness the owners of mobile—and concealed—property.

The declared reasons for confiscating the property of officials and other members of the ruling class are almost invariably political or administrative. The political reasons include diplomatic blunders, conspiracy, and treason; the administrative, mismanagement and fiscal irregularities. Serious crimes frequently lead to the wrongdoer's complete political and economic ruin; lesser ones to temporary or permanent demotion and total or partial confiscation. Businessmen are primarily prosecuted for tax evasion, but they too may become involved in a political intrigue. In the first instance they may be partially expropriated; in the second, they may pay with their entire fortune and with their life.

Within the ruling class, conspiracies to replace the ruler or an important dignitary occur periodically, and particularly during times of insecurity and crisis. Wanton persecutions are equally frequent. A power center which is both accuser and judge may declare any activity criminal, whatever the facts. Manufactured evidence appears with great regularity; and legally disguised political purges are undertaken whenever the masters of the state apparatus deem them expedient.

The danger of being persecuted is augmented by the fact that under conditions of autocratic power the majority of all officials and the bulk of all wealthy businessmen tend to commit acts that,

f. For confiscation in ancient Greece, see Busolt, GS, II: 1109 ff. The confiscations during the last phase of republican Rome reflect the rise of uncontrolled Orientally despotic power (see below, Chap. 6).

legally speaking, are crimes, or may be so interpreted. At the court and/or in the administration there are always individuals or groups that try to promote their own interests by winning the favor of the ruler or other persons of high rank. The sovereign and his close relatives or friends, the chancellor (vizier) or other prominent members of the bureaucracy are all potential targets of political intrigues. And in an atmosphere of absolutist power, secrecy and quasiconspiratorial methods appear perfectly normal. This being the case, the dominant center has little difficulty in pinning the label of conspiracy on whomever it wishes to destroy.

To be sure, many persons who engage in such intrigues are never brought to book; and many others escape with minor bruises. In periods of prosperity and calm this is by no means rare. But politically phrased accusations are an essential feature of the absolutist order; and any unusual tension may spell the doom of many individuals or groups.

In the administrative sphere the borderline is similarly fluid, and the possibilities of disaster are similarly great. Many officials have to make decisions regarding goods or money; and in the absence of rational methods of procedure and supervision, deviations from prescribed standards are as usual as the attempts to increase personal income are alluring. The classic of Hindu statecraft describes the almost unlimited opportunities for embezzlement offered by such conditions. In what amounts to a veritable catalogue, the *Arthashās-tra* mentions some forty ways in which government funds may be diverted.[15] The author of the *Arthashāstra* doubts whether any person can resist so many tempting opportunities. "Just as it is impossible not to taste the honey or the poison that finds itself at the tip of the tongue, so it is impossible for a government servant not to eat up, at least, a bit of the king's revenue." [16]

The wealthy businessman is equally vulnerable. Taxation being the prerogative of a government whose declared demands are heavy and whose agents tend to go beyond the official demands, the private men of property seek to protect themselves as best they can. They hide their treasure in the ground. They entrust it to friends. They send it abroad.[g] In brief, they are driven to commit acts which make most of them potential fiscal criminals.

In many instances their efforts are successful, particularly when they are buttressed by well-placed bribes. But a technical error or a

g. In classical India "capital wealth was hoarded, either in the house—in large mansions over the entrance passage . . . under the ground, in brazen jars under the river bank, or deposited with a friend" (C. A. F. Rhys-Davids, 1922: 219).

change in the bureaucratic personnel may shatter the uneasy balance; and warranted accusations combined with trumped-up charges will initiate actions that may ruin the accused businessman economically, and perhaps also physically.

In Pharaonic Egypt officials were the essential targets of confiscatory actions. Members of the bureaucracy who were found guilty of a major crime were severely punished. A demotion usually involved the loss of revenue and property, including whatever fields the culprit possessed either in the form of office land or as a sinecure.[17] At the beginning of a new dynasty the new ruler resorted to such measures to consolidate his position.[18]

Disobedience to the Pharaoh, even when conspiracy was not involved, might be severely punished. A decree of the Fifth Dynasty threatened "any official or royal intimate or agricultural officer," who disregarded a certain royal order, with the confiscation of his "house, fields, people, and everything in his possession." The culprit himself was to be reduced to the status of a corvée laborer.[19]

The history of Chinese bureaucracy abounds with incidents of demotion and confiscation. When the Ch'ing emperor, Kao-tsung (reign-title Ch'ien-lung) died, his all-powerful minister, Ho Shên, was immediately arrested and "although out of respect to the memory of his master he was permitted to take his own life, his huge accumulation of silver, gold, precious stones, and other forms of wealth, was confiscated." [20]

The expropriation of officials for administrative and fiscal offenses demonstrates the vulnerability of almost all officials. Again the *Arthashāstra* neatly formulates the crux of the matter. Since every official who deals with the king's revenue is inevitably tempted to embezzle, the government must use skilled spies [21] and informers [22] to aid in the recovery of the state's property. Crude criteria determine whether an official is guilty or not. Whoever causes a reduction of the revenue "eats the king's wealth." [23] Whoever is seen enjoying the king's possessions is guilty.[24] Whoever lives in a miserly way while accumulating and hoarding wealth is guilty.[25] The king may "squeeze them after they have drunk themselves fat, he may transfer them from one job to another so that they do not devour his property or that they may vomit up what they devoured." [26]

Of course, in all these matters discrimination is of the essence. The king should treat petty crimes indulgently.[27] And he should also be lenient when circumstances permit. Do not prosecute even for a serious crime, if the offender "has the support of a strong party"; but "he who has no such support shall be caught hold of" and, the commentary adds, "be deprived of his property."[28] These bald maxims do not even bother with an appearance of justice.

Confiscation may be partial or total; and it may be invoked during the victim's lifetime or after his death. Post-mortem expropriation is frequently made easy by the fact that the deceased's family is no longer influential. In 934 the Abbassid caliph seized the entire property of his deceased vizier, al-Muhallabī, squeezing money even from his servants, grooms, and sailors.[29] After the death of the mighty North Persian vizier, the aṣ-Ṣāḥib, "his house was surrounded at once; the ruler searched it, found a bag with receipts for over 150,000 dinars, which had been deposited out of town. They were cashed without delay, and everything contained in the house and treasure room was brought into the palace."[30] After the death of the great general, Bejkem, in 941, the caliph "sent immediately to the house, dug everywhere, and gathered two millions of gold and silver. Eventually he ordered the earth in the house to be washed, and this yielded a further 35,000 dirhem," but it is doubtful whether he found the chests of money that Bejkem had buried in the desert.[31]

Persons suspected of having defrauded the government suffered all manner of mistreatment. The caliph al-Qādir (991–1031) had his predecessor's mother severely tortured. After her resistance was broken, she handed over her ready cash as well as the proceeds from the sale of her land.[32]

The confiscation of business fortunes follows a similar pattern. As stated above, any prosecution could be justified politically; and the international connections of the big merchants made political accusation easy. But in the majority of cases the offense was openly declared to be fiscal in nature. Frequently the line between a special tax (for a military campaign or other emergencies) and partial confiscation is hard to draw; but whatever the pretext, the consequences for the victim could be grim. The *Arthashāstra* encourages the king to enlarge his treasure by demanding money from rich persons according to the amount of their property.[33] He may squeeze such persons "vigorously, giving them no chance to slip away. For they may bring forth what others hold (for them), and sell it."[34]

In the case of political accusation, spies and agents could be depended upon to supply the required evidence. A middle-class "traitor" might be framed in several ways. An agent could commit a murder on a businessman's doorstep. The owner could then be arrested and his goods and money appropriated.[35] Or an agent could smuggle counterfeit money, tools for counterfeiting, or poison into the house of the potential victim, or plant a sign of allegiance to some other king on his property, or produce a "letter" from an enemy of the state.[36] Theoretically these measures were only to be invoked when the victim was known to be wicked; [37] but along with other devices they are recommended in a chapter discussing ways for replenishing the treasury. History shows how ready the average despot was to use them for precisely this purpose. "Just as fruits are gathered from a garden as often as they become ripe, so revenue shall be collected as often as it becomes ripe. Collection of revenue or of fruits, when unripe, shall never be carried on, lest their source may be injured, causing immense trouble." [38]

In the Islamic world the death of a wealthy man provided the government with untold opportunities for decimating or liquidating his possessions. "Woe to him," wails an Arab text of the 9th century, "whose father died rich! For a long time he was kept a prisoner in the house of misfortune, and he [the unjust official] said [to the son]: 'Who knows that you are his son?' And if he said: 'My neighbor and whoever knows me,' then they tore his mustache until he grew weak. And they beat and kicked him generously. And he stayed in closest captivity until he threw the purse before them." [39] During certain periods of the Abassid caliphate, "the death of a rich private person was a catastrophe for his whole circle, his bankers and friends went into hiding, objection was raised against the government's inspecting the testament . . . and eventually the family bought itself off with a major payment." [40]

To be sure, violence and plunder are not the monopoly of any society. But the hydraulic mode of confiscation differs in quality and dimension from the acts of arbitrary violence committed in other higher agrarian civilizations. In classical Greece it was not an overwhelmingly strong government but the community of propertied and (later also) propertyless citizens who checked a potentially over-powerful leader by sending him into exile and seizing his wealth. In Medieval Europe the rulers had only a small staff of officials, so small a staff indeed that intrabureaucratic struggles of the Oriental kind had little chance to develop. The conflicts between the feudal centers of power were many and often violent; but the rival forces fought it out more often on the battlefield than *in camera*. And those who wished to destroy their enemies by tricks preferred the ambush to the legal frame-up. The opportunities for using the first device were as numerous as those for using the second were rare.

As to the fate of businessmen, men of property in classical Greece were not plagued by heavy direct taxes; and their medieval counterparts were extremely well protected against the fiscal claims of territorial or national overlords. Like the former, the burghers of the semi-independent guild cities were in no permanent danger of being arrested, questioned, tortured, or expropriated by the officials of a centralized autocracy. True, medieval trade caravans were held up and robbed as they moved from town to town. But within the confines of their walled cities the artisans and merchants enjoyed reasonable safety of person and possession.

The rulers of European absolutism schemed as ruthlessly and killed as mercilessly as did their Eastern confrères. However, their power to persecute and appropriate was limited by the landed nobles, the Church, and the cities, whose autonomy the autocratic overlords could restrict, but not destroy. In addition to this, the representatives of the new central governments saw definite advantages in developing the newly rising capitalistic forms of mobile property. Emerging from an agrarian order, which they had never controlled or exploited in the hydraulic way, the Western autocrats readily protected the incipient commercial and industrial capitalists, whose increasing prosperity increasingly benefited their protectors.

In contrast, the masters of hydraulic society spun their fiscal web firmly over their country's agrarian economy. And they were under no pressure to favor the urban capitalists as did the postfeudal Western rulers. At best, they treated what capitalist enterprise there was like a useful garden. At worst, they clipped and stripped the bushes of capital-based business to the stalk.

D. HYDRAULIC PROPERTY—WEAK PROPERTY

1. Four Ways of Weakening Private Property

In a number of stratified civilizations the representatives of private property and enterprise were sufficiently strong to check the power of the state. Under hydraulic conditions the state restricted the development of private property through fiscal, judicial, legal, and political measures.

In the preceding pages we have discussed the pertinent fiscal and judicial methods (taxes, frame-ups, and confiscations). Before turning to the political aspect of the matter we must first deal with a legal institution which, perhaps more than any other, has caused the periodic fragmentation of private property: the hydraulic (Oriental) laws of inheritance.

2. HYDRAULIC LAWS OF INHERITANCE: THE PRINCIPLE

THROUGHOUT the hydraulic world the bulk of a deceased person's property is transferred not in accordance with his will but in accordance with customary or written laws. These laws prescribe an equal, or approximately equal, division of property among the heirs, most frequently the sons and other close male relatives. Among the sons, the eldest often has special duties to fulfill. He must care for his mother and his younger siblings; and he may be primarily responsible for the religious obligations of the family. The laws take all this into account. But their modification does not upset the basic effect: the parceling out of a deceased person's estate among his heirs.

3. THE APPLICATION

IN Pharaonic Egypt the eldest son, who had important ceremonial tasks, received a larger share of his father's estate. But the remaining children also could claim a legally prescribed share of the total.[1]

The principle of more or less even division is clearly stated in the Babylonian code. A present made by a father during his lifetime to the first-born is not included in the final settlement, but "otherwise they [the sons] shall share equally in the goods of the paternal estate."[2] Assyrian law is more complicated. Again the eldest son has an advantage, but all other brothers are entitled to their share.[3]

In India the eldest son's originally privileged position was gradually reduced, until the difference between him and other heirs virtually disappeared.[4] In the Islamic world inheritance was complicated by a number of factors, among them the freedom to will up to one-third of an estate.[a] But the system of "Koranic heirs" is definitely fragmenting: it strictly prescribes division among several persons.[5] The last imperial code of China reasserts what seems to have been regular practice during the whole period of "developed" private property. A family's possessions must be divided equally among all sons. Failure to comply was punishable by up to one hundred blows with a heavy stick.[6]

In Inca Peru the bulk of all land was regulated by the state and its local agencies. Some grants made to relatives of the ruler or meritorious military or civil officials might be transferred hereditarily; but the usufruct from the inherited land was subject to equal

a. The Koran prescribes a highly intricate division of heritable property (Koran 4. 7–14).

division.[7] In Aztec Mexico the bulk of all land was occupied by village communities and thus barred from full transfer at the will of the possessor. Some land, privately held by members of the ruling group, was after the holder's death divided among his heirs.[8]

4. THE EFFECT

a. On Regulated Villages

A LAW of inheritance which prescribes a periodic division of private property affects different groups in hydraulic society differently. Peasants who live in regulated village communities may divide the movable property of a deceased family head, but not his fields. These must be kept intact or, from time to time, reassigned according to the recognized prerogatives or needs of the members of the community.

b. On Holders of Small Private Property

ENTIRELY new problems arise when the peasants own their land privately and freely. Scarcity of food may reduce the number of potential heirs, and this is an important demographic factor in all hydraulic societies. However, the will to live often outwits want; and despite periodic or perpetual shortages, the population tends to increase. This inevitably means smaller farms, more toil, more hardship, and, frequently, flight, banditry, and rebellion.

Demographic pressures are certainly not lacking in regulated villages. But they are particularly serious where private landed property is the rule. For in such areas the impoverishment of the economically weaker elements is not counterbalanced, or retarded, by the corporate economy of the village, which prevents both individual economic advance and collapse.

c. On Holders of Large Private Property

AMONG the wealthy property owners another factor of hydraulic demography becomes important: polygamy. In hydraulic civilizations rich persons usually have several wives; and the greater their fortune, the larger their harem is apt to be. The possibility of having several sons increases proportionately. But several sons mean several heirs; and several heirs mean a quicker reduction of the original property through equal inheritance.

Commenting on the dynamics of Chinese traditional society, two modern social scientists, Fei and Chang, find it "all too true" that in this society "land breeds no land." Why? "The basic truth is that enrichment through exploitation of land, using the traditional technology, is not a practical method of accumulating wealth." Landed wealth tends to shrink rather than to grow; and this essentially because of the law of inheritance; "so long as the customary principle of equal inheritance among siblings exists, time is a strong disintegrative force in landholding." [9]

The Islamic law of inheritance has a similarly disintegrative effect. Wherever it prevails, it "must in the long run lead to the inevitable parceling out even of the largest property. . . ." [10] The land grants in the Inca empire apparently fared no better. After a few generations the revenue received by individual heirs might shrink to insignificance. [11]

5. PERTINENT WESTERN DEVELOPMENTS

a. The Democratic City States of Ancient Greece

THE fragmentation of landed property through more or less equal inheritance is certainly a significant institution. But are we justified in considering it characteristic primarily for hydraulic civilizations? "The rule of dividing up an estate on succession" also operated in the city states of classical Greece. Consistently applied, it "split up the land without ceasing." [12] In the 4th century "apart from one exceptional case, the largest property which Attica could show . . . measured 300 *plethra* or 64 acres." Glotz adds: "This state of things was common to the democratic cities." [13]

b. The United States after the War of Independence

AND then there is the fight against entail and primogeniture in the early days of the United States. During and immediately after the American Revolution the spokesmen of the young republic vigorously attacked the perpetuities, which were correctly described as remnants of Europe's feudal tradition. Once the law of entail was abolished, the colossal aristocratic landholdings quickly dissolved. "By about the year 1830 most of the great estates of America had vanished." [14]

c. A Spectacular Contrast: the Strength of Landed Property in Late Feudal and Postfeudal Europe

SIMILAR attempts at breaking the power of large landed property were made in Europe after the close of the feudal period. The governments of the new territorial and national states attacked entail and primogeniture through a variety of measures, statutory enactments prevailing on the continent and judicial reforms in England.[15] Resourceful protagonists of absolutism lent the struggle impetus and color. But in the leading countries of Western and Central Europe the governments were unable for a long time to abolish the perpetuation of big property. In France this institution persisted intact until the Revolution, and in a modified form until 1849. In England and Germany it was discarded only in the 20th century.[16]

6. DIFFERENT SOCIAL FORCES OPPOSED TO PROPRIETARY PERPETUITIES

a. Small and Mobile Property

MANIFESTLY, the perpetuation of large landed property may be opposed by different social forces. The Greek legislators, who, according to Aristotle,[17] recognized the influence of the equalization of property on political society, very possibly did not identify themselves with one particular social group or class. But their efforts benefited smaller rural property [18] as well as the new forms of mobile (urban) property and enterprise. It stands to reason that the groups which profited from a weakening of big landed property accomplished this result through methods that became increasingly effective as the city states became increasingly democratized.

In the young United States Jefferson fought for the abolishment of entail and primogeniture as a necessary step toward the elimination of "feudal and unnatural distinctions." [19] And he based his policy on a philosophy which distrusted commerce and industry as much as it trusted the independent landowning farmers. Middle and small rural property may not have been directly represented among those who wrote the Constitution; [20] but its influence was nevertheless great. The Revolution, which "was started by protesting merchants and rioting mechanics," was actually "carried to its bitter end by the bayonets of fighting farmers." [21]

And not only this. A few decades after the Revolution the agricultural frontier prevailed so effectively over the commercial and banking interests of the coastal towns that it "brought about the declaration of hostilities against England in 1812." [22] It therefore seems legitimate to claim that it was a combination of independent rural (farming) and mobile urban property that brought about the downfall of the feudal system of entail and primogeniture in the United States.

b. The States of Feudal and Postfeudal Europe

THE consolidation of feudal and postfeudal landed property in Europe was challenged by a very different force. At the height of the conflict the attack was conducted by the representatives of the absolutist state; and the external resemblance to the Oriental version of the struggle makes it all the more necessary to understand the exact nature of what happened in the West.

Why were the feudal lords of Europe able to buttress their landed property to such an extraordinary degree? Because, as indicated above, in the fragmented society of Medieval Europe the national and territorial rulers lacked the means to prevent it. Of course, the sovereign, the most powerful master of land and men, did exercise a certain public authority.[23] He claimed certain military services from his seigneurs, vassals, or lords; he had certain supreme judicial functions; he was expected to handle the foreign relations of his country; and his authority was strengthened by the fact that the bulk of his vassals held their fiefs only as long as they fulfilled the obligations mentioned in the investiture. Thus the lords were originally possessors rather than owners of their lands; and they remained so, at least theoretically, even after tenure became hereditary.

This state of affairs has been frequently described. With certain differences—which became especially important in such countries as post-Conquest England—it prevailed in the greater part of Western and Central Europe during the formative period of feudalism. However, the conventional picture stresses much more strongly the relation between the feudal lord and his ruler than the relation between the various lords. From the point of view of proprietary development, the second is pivotal.

No matter whether the baron held his fief temporarily or hereditarily, his life was centered in his own castle and not at the royal court; it was his detached position that determined his personal and social contacts. The king might claim the military services of his vassal for some few weeks; but beyond this contractually limited period —which might be extended if proper payments were offered [24]—he was unable to control his movements. The baron or knight was free to use his soldiers for private feuds. He was free to engage in the chase, in tournaments, and in expeditions of various kinds. And most important, he was free to meet with lordly neighbors who, like himself, were eager to promote their joint interests.

The atomized character of the political order stimulated the association of the local and regional vassals, who singly were no match for the sovereign but who together might successfully oppose him. In the race between the growth of lordly (and burgher) power on the one hand and royal power on the other, the rising central governments found themselves confronted not by the scattered feudal and urban forces of the early days but by organized estates capable of defending their economic as well as their social rights.

In England as early as the 11th century the king's tenants-in-chief were known as *barones;* originally the term connoted a group rather than an individual: "that word is not found in the singular." [25] But it was only when the government tried to check their independence that the barons felt the need for united action. The final section of the Magna Carta has been correctly called "the first royal recognition of the baronial right collectively to coerce the king by force." [26] Shortly afterward, *"totius Angliae nobilitas . . .* took an oath each to the other that they would give the king no answer except a *communis responsio."* [27] It was in the very century in which the English lords incorporated themselves as an estate that they laid the foundations for the perpetuation of their lands by entail and primogeniture.[28]

On the continent the timetable and many other details differed. But the over-all trend was the same. Applying to their fiefs the principle of indivisibility—which, with the abandonment of the feudal form of military service, had lost its original meaning—the noble landholders consolidated their property in Spain, Italy, France, and Germany.[29]

It is worth noting that the nobles, who kept the late feudal and postfeudal societies balanced, owed their proprietary success partly to the attitude of the absolutist bureaucracy. Among the aristocratic members of this bureaucracy not a few felt a deep affinity for the landed gentry, to which they were linked by many ties. Torn by conflicting proprietary and bureaucratic interests, the representatives of Western absolutism did not press to the extreme their organized resistance against the privileged big landowners. In consequence, there emerged out of the womb of feudal society one of the strongest forms of private property known to mankind.

c. Hydraulic Absolutism Succeeded Where the States of Occidental Feudalism and Absolutism Failed

In late feudal and postfeudal Europe the state recognized a system of inheritance for the landed nobles which favored one son at the expense of all others. And in the modern Western world the state by and large permitted the individual to dispose over his property at will. The hydraulic state gave no equivalent freedom of decision either to holders of mobile property or to the landowners. Its laws of inheritance insisted upon a more or less equal division of the deceased's estate, and thereby upon a periodic fragmentation of property.

Among primitive peoples living on an extractive economy or on crude agriculture, the pattern of inheritance apparently varied greatly; [30] thus it is unlikely that the predecessors of hydraulic society in their majority maintained a one-heir system of inheritance which the hydraulic development had to destroy. In some cases, the germs of a single-heir system may have had to be eradicated. Where no such germs existed, the hydraulic rulers made sure that efforts to undermine the traditional distributive pattern could get nowhere. They achieved their aim by a multiplicity of methods, among which the standardization of the fragmenting law of inheritance was only the most prominent one.

In the later feudal and postfeudal societies of the West the landed nobles were able to create the one-sided system of inheritance called entail and primogeniture primarily because they were armed and because they were nationally and politically organized. In hydraulic society the representatives of private property lacked the strength to establish similarly consolidated and strong forms of property, first because the governmental monopoly of armed action prevented the property holders from maintaining independent military forces, and second because the governmental network of organization (corvée, state post and intelligence, integrated army, and universal taxation) prevented the property holders from protecting their interests by means of an effective national organization.

In this setting the struggle for or against the divisibility of property did not become a clear-cut political issue as it did in ancient Greece, absolutist Europe, or the United States. And in contrast to the areas of open conflict the hydraulic world did not favor political arguments which justified—or challenged—the fragmenting law of inheritance.

7. The Organizational Impotence of Hydraulic Property Holders

As an armed and ubiquitously organized force, the hydraulic regime prevailed in the strategic seats of mobile property, the cities, as well as in the main sphere of immobile property, the countryside. Its cities were administrative and military footholds of the government; and the artisans and merchants had no opportunity to become serious political rivals. Their professional associations need not have been directly attached to the state, but they certainly failed to create strong and independent centers of corporate burgher power such as arose in many parts of Medieval Europe.

The countryside fared no better. The owners of land were either wealthy businessmen and as limited in the scope of their organization as were the representatives of mobile property, or—and more often—they were officials or priests, and a part of—or in association with—the nationally organized bureaucracy. This bureaucracy might permit its property-holding members or associates to establish local organizations, such as the Chinese "sash-bearers" (inadequately translated as "gentry") and as the priests of various temples or creeds. But it discouraged any attempt to coordinate landed property on a national scale and in the form of independent corporations or estates.

The holders of family endowments (*waqfs*) in the Islamic Near East kept their land undivided, because these lands were destined ultimately to serve religious and charitable purposes. But while the family *waqf* temporarily benefited the grantee and his descendants, it represented neither a secure nor a free and strong form of property. Although less frequently singled out for confiscation, the family *waqfs*, like the other *waqfs*, might be seized if the state wished it. They were taxed; and their beneficiaries never consolidated their power through a nationwide political organization.

The family *waqf* resembles in its announced purpose, though frequently not in its immediate functions, the lands held by temples and priests. But contrary to the religious functionaries, the holders of these endowments are conspicuous not for any active participation in public life but for their rentier-like position. Temple land, like secular office land, was undivided; but it is indicative of the relation between the hydraulic state and the dominant religions that the landholding priests or temples did not engage in any effective struggle to limit the absolutist state by constitutional checks.

Nor did the landowning members of the bureaucracy—those in office as well as the nonofficiating "gentry"—organize themselves into a national body capable of upholding their proprietary rights against the acquisitive and legal pressures of the state apparatus. They were content to use their land as a means for comfortable living, leaving it to those in office to organize and operate a nationally integrated system of political power. The Chinese general who demonstrated his political harmlessness by pretending to be exclusively interested in acquiring land [31] strikingly illustrates the political impotence of Oriental property, even when it is held by men of the apparatus itself. [b]

b. These conditions favored what may be called the introvert character of most residential architecture in agrobureaucratic society, as juxtaposed to the extrovert architecture of the corresponding type of buildings in the West. The tendency to hide luxurious courtyards and dwellings behind a noncommittal facade was not

E. THE HYDRAULIC REGIME ATTACHES TO ITSELF THE COUNTRY'S DOMINANT RELIGION

SIMILAR causes led to similar results also in the field of religion. The hydraulic state, which permitted neither relevant independent military nor proprietary leadership, did not favor the rise of independent religious power either. Nowhere in hydraulic society did the dominant religion place itself outside the authority of the state as a nationally (or internationally) integrated autonomous church.

1. SOLE, DOMINANT, AND SECONDARY RELIGIONS

A DOMINANT religion may have no conspicuous competitors. This is often the case in simpler cultures, where the only relevant representatives of heterodox ideas and practices are sorcerers and witches. Here the very problem of choice is lacking; and the hydraulic leaders readily identify themselves with the dominant religion.

Secondary religions usually originate and spread under relatively differentiated institutional conditions. Wherever such beliefs are given a chance to persist (non-Hindu creeds in India; Taoism and Buddhism in Confucian China; Christianity and Judaism under Islam), the rulers tend with time to identify themselves with the dominant doctrine. It need scarcely be asserted that in the present context the word "dominant" merely refers to the social and political aspects of the matter. It implies no religious value judgment. Whether the societally dominant religion is also superior in terms of its religious tenets is an entirely different (and legitimate) question, but one which does not come within the scope of the present study.

2. RELIGIOUS AUTHORITY ATTACHED TO THE HYDRAULIC STATE

a. The Hydraulic Regime—Occasionally (quasi-) Hierocratic

IN seeking to determine the relation between hydraulic power and the dominant religion, we must first discard a widespread misconception. In the hydraulic world, as in other agrarian societies, religion plays an enormous role; and the representatives of religion tend to be numerous. However, the importance of an institution does not necessarily imply its autonomy. As explained above, the government-supported armies of hydraulic civilizations are usually large, but the same factors which make them large keep them dependent.

confined to wealthy commoners. It also dominated the men of the apparatus—but, of course, not their supreme master.

Of course, the patterns of religion cannot be equated with the patterns of defense. But in both cases size results essentially from closeness to a governmental machine, which is capable of mobilizing huge resources of income.

The majority of all hydraulic civilizations are characterized by large and influential priesthoods. Yet it would be wrong to designate them as hierocratic, "ruled by priests." Many attempts have been made to determine the meaning of the word "priest"; and outstanding comparative sociologists, such as Max Weber,[1] have provided us with a wide choice of definitions for a phenomenon whose institutional borders are not easily established.

Obviously the priest has to be qualified to carry out his religious tasks, which generally include the offering of sacrifices as well as prayers. A qualified priest may give only a fraction of his time to his religious duties, the greater part of it being spent to insure his livelihood, or he may serve professionally, that is, full time.

If we define priestly rule as government rule by professional priests, then few if any of the major hydraulic states can be so characterized. In a number of cases the officialdom included many persons who were trained as priests and who, before assuming a government position, acted as priests. It is important to note such a background, because it illuminates the role of the temples in the ruling complex. But it is equally important to note that when persons with a priestly background become prominent in the government, they do not, as a rule, continue to spend most of their time fulfilling religious duties. Thus their regimes are not hierocratic in the narrow sense of the term, but quasihierocratic. The few hydraulic governments headed by qualified priests are almost all of them of this latter type.

The hydraulic tribes of the Pueblo Indians are ruled by chiefs who play a leading part in many religious ceremonies. However, except for one or a few among them—often only the *cacique*—these priest-chiefs spend the bulk of their time in farming. The Pueblo government is therefore represented by a hierarchy of men who, though qualified to hold ceremonial offices, are not in their great majority full-time priests.

The city states of ancient Sumer are said to have been usually ruled by the head priests of the leading city temples,[2] and the prominent courtiers and government officials, who had an important role in the administration of the temple estates,[3] were quite possibly also qualified priests.[a] But did these men, who were theologically

a. In the history of Sumer, professional priests appear early (Deimel, 1924: 6 ff.; Falkenstein, 1936: 58; Meissner, BA, II: 52). The ancient inscriptions mention priests

trained, still have time to fulfill the many religious functions of a professional priest? Deimel assumes that the priest-kings officiated in the temples only on particularly solemn occasions.[4] Their subordinates were kept equally busy by their secular duties—and equally restricted in their religious activities.

The ruler's top-ranking aides, and also no doubt many of his lower officials, entered the political arena because they were members of the country's most powerful economic and military sub-units, the temples. The governments of the Sumerian temple cities were therefore quasihierocratic. But even in Sumer the power of the temples seems to have decreased. The reform of the priest-king, Urukagina, of Lagash indicates that as early as the third millennium B.C. leading priestly families tried to secularize the temple land;[5] and soon after Urukagina, the great kings of Akkad and Ur succeeded in transferring some temple lands to the royal domains.[6] During the subsequent Babylonian period the temples ceased to be the outstanding economic sector of the society, and the bulk of the high officials were no longer necessarily connected with the priesthood.

The Babylonian pattern is much more frequent than the Sumerian. As a rule, the hydraulic governments were administered by professional officials who, though perhaps educated by priests, were not trained to be priests. The majority of all qualified and professional priests remained occupied with their religious tasks, and the employment of individual priests in the service of the state did not make the government a hierocracy.

Among the few attempts at priestly rule in a hydraulic country [b] the Twenty-first Dynasty of Pharaonic Egypt seems particularly worthy of note. But the usurper-founder of this dynasty, Herihor, who started out as a priest, held a secular government position before the Pharaoh made him high priest; and he was given this position not to strengthen but to weaken the power of the leading priesthood, that of Amon.[c] Like the priest-kings of Sumer, the rulers of Pharaonic Egypt—Herihor included—obviously spent the greater part of their time in carrying out their governmental tasks. From the standpoint of ancient Egyptian history, it is significant that out

---

as well as representatives of secular occupations (Schneider, 1920: 107 ff.; Deimel, 1924: 5 ff.; Falkenstein, 1936: 58 ff.; Deimel, 1932: 444 ff.).

b. Tibet is discussed as a marginal hydraulic society in Chap. 6, below.

c. Kees, 1938: 10 ff., 14, 16; cf. Wilson, 1951: 288 ff. Even E. Meyer (GA, II, Pt. 2: 10 ff.), who strongly, and probably unduly, stresses the priestly background of Herihor's rise to power, feels that the Twenty-first Dynasty did not succeed in establishing "a real theocracy."

of the twenty-six dynasties of the Pharaonic period at best only one can be classed as quasihierocratic.

b. The Hydraulic Regime—Frequently Theocratic

THE constructional, organizational, and acquisitive activities of hydraulic society tend to concentrate all authority in a directing center: the central government and ultimately the head of this government, the ruler. From the dawn of hydraulic civilization it was upon this center that the magic powers of the commonwealth tended to converge. The bulk of all religious ceremonies may be performed by a specialized priesthood, which frequently enjoys considerable freedom. But in many hydraulic societies the supreme representative of secular authority is also the embodiment of supreme religious authority.

Appearing as either a god or a descendant of a god, or as high priest, such a person is indeed a theocratic (divine) or quasitheocratic (pontifical) ruler. Obviously, the theocratic regime need be neither hierocratic nor quasihierocratic. Even if the divine or pontifical sovereign was trained as a priest, the majority of his officials would not necessarily have to be so qualified.

The chieftains of the Pueblo Indians and the Chagga, who are the high priests of their respective communities, occupy a theocratic position; and the divine quality of the Hawaiian kings is beyond doubt. However, under primitive agrarian conditions religious and secular authority are often closely combined, whether cultivation is carried out by means of irrigation or not.

In contrast to the wide distribution of theocratic institutions among primitive agrarian peoples, theocracy developed unevenly in the higher agrarian civilizations. Theocratic or quasitheocratic trends prevailed in many state-centered hydraulic societies, whereas they came to nothing in ancient Greece and Medieval Europe.

In Homeric Greece the king was of divine origin,[7] and his pre-eminence in religious matters was so strong that he has been called the "chief priest." [8] Subsequent democratic developments did not destroy the relation between state and religion; but they placed the control of both types of activities in the hands of the citizens. Strictly supervised by the citizen community, the state religion of ancient Greece developed neither a clerical hierarchy [9] nor a closed priestly order.[10] As a rule, those destined to officiate as priests were chosen by either lot or election.[11] Hence they lacked the training which plays so great a role in professional and self-perpetuating priesthoods. The finances of the temples were strictly controlled by political authorities, who in their majority were similarly chosen. More-over, governmental leaders were not considered divine, nor did they act as high priests or heads of any coordinated religious order. The designation "theocracy," which may be applied to the primitive con-ditions of early Greece, therefore hardly fits the "serving" citizen state of the democratic period.

In the great agrarian civilizations of Medieval Europe, nontheo-cratic development went still further. Attempts by Pepin and Char-lemagne to establish theocratic authority [12] were unable to reverse the trend toward feudal decentralization. Among the many secondary centers of proprietary, military, and political power, which restricted the authority of the national and territorial rulers, the Church proved eminently effective, since a unified doctrine and an increasingly unified leadership endowed its quasifeudal local units with quasi-Oriental organizational strength. After a prolonged period of intense conflict, the Church gained full autonomy. In the 11th century the French crown "had given way to the Holy See," [13] and the German Emperor Henry IV humiliated himself before Pope Gregory VII. For some time the struggle between secular and eccle-siastical power continued inconclusively, until Innocent III (1198–1216) raised papal authority to such a peak that he could try, al-though without success, to subordinate the state to the leadership of the Church.

Among the many manifestations of autonomous ecclesiastical be-havior the English instance is particularly instructive. In 1215 the English bishops together with the feudal lords forced King John to recognize, in the Magna Carta, the legitimacy of a balanced con-stitutional government. The Carta was " 'primarily' a concession made 'to God' in favour of the Anglican Church. . . . By the first article the king granted 'the English Church should be free, enjoy its full rights and its liberties inviolate' and, in particular 'that liberty which is considered the greatest and the most necessary for the English Church, freedom of elections.' Article 42 concerning freedom to leave the kingdom involved for the clergy the extremely important right to go to Rome without the king's permission." [14]

The Church under the Carta was not just one of several groups of effectively organized feudal landowners. In its national as well as in its international organization it was different from, and in a way superior to, the corporations of the secular nobility. Further-more, it struggled for autonomy as a religious body with specific religious objectives and claims. But however crucial these peculi-arities were, the Church could not have checked the power of the political regime if it had not, at the same time, strengthened the proprietary and organizational forces of the secular nobility. As the religious sector of these forces, the Church in the agrarian society of Medieval Europe became an essentially independent entity.[15] In achieving this goal, it fatefully supported the growth of the balanced late feudal order, which eventually gave birth to modern Western society.

Thus whether originally they were theocratically ruled or not, the higher agrarian civilizations of the West did not evolve massive theocratic power structures. The city states of classical Greece presented a nontheocratic combination of government and religion; and in Medieval Europe the secular and religious authorities, far from establishing an integrated system of Caesaro-Papism, crystallized into two spectacularly separate bodies.

Hydraulic civilization moved in a radically different direction. Where tribal hydraulic governments were theocratically shaped, the original pattern usually persisted even under more complex institutional conditions. And where theocracy was lacking in prehydraulic times, it frequently emerged as part of the hydraulic development.

A society which provided unique opportunities for the growth of the governmental machine left no room for the growth of a politically and economically independent dominant religion. The agro-managerial sovereign cemented his secular position by attaching to himself in one form or another the symbols of supreme religious authority. In some instances his position is not conclusively theocratic, but this is more the exception than the rule. In the majority of all cases hydraulic regimes seem to have been either theocratic or quasitheocratic.

The institutional diversity of the hydraulic world precludes a rigid correlation. But it seems that divine sovereigns appear primarily under less differentiated societal conditions. On a neolithic level of technology the Incas ruled theocratically over a simple hydraulic society. The supreme ("Unique," *Sapa*) Inca was a descendant of the Sun, and thus divine;[16] and in varying degrees his relatives shared this status.[17] The Sapa Inca performed the most solemn sacrifices,[18] ranking ceremonially above the professional high priests, who were usually chosen from among his uncles or brothers.[19] His officials managed the distribution and cultivation of the temple land,[20] and they administered the storehouses of the temples as well as those of the secular government.[21] Thus the government, headed by a divine ruler, controlled both the country's secular affairs and the priesthood of its dominant religion.

The theocratic development of the Near East is evidenced by many literary and pictorial records. Arising without any conspicuous

institutional attachment to—though not without cultural connections with—Mesopotamia,[d] the state of ancient Egypt demonstrates
the power potential of a highly concentrated and relatively simple
hydraulic order. The Pharaoh is a god or the son of a god,[22] a great
and good god.[23] He is the god, Horus,[24] a scion of the Sun god, Re.[25]
He derives "bodily" from his divine parent.[26] Being thus distinguished, he is the given middleman between the gods and mankind.
Lack of time prevents him from personally attending to most of his
religious duties; [27] but he is a high priest,[28] and the priest of all
gods.[29] About the exaltedness of his position there can be no doubt.

Originally the temple services were performed in considerable
part by royal officials,[30] and the temple administration was managed
by the king's men.[31] But even after the crystallization of a substantial professional priesthood, the state continued to have jurisdiction over the temple revenues; and the Pharaohs appointed the
individual priests.[32] This system of control prevailed throughout
the Old and Middle Kingdoms, and even at the beginning of the
New Kingdom. It disintegrated during the period of crisis and unrest, which at the end of the Twentieth Dynasty [e] enabled a high
priest to ascend the throne.[33] From the Twenty-second to the
Twenty-fifth Dynasty, Egypt was ruled by Libyan and Nubian conquerors, but the Pharaohs' divine position persisted despite all
political changes down to the Twenty-sixth and last dynasty.[34]

In ancient Mesopotamia society was from the dawn of written
history more differentiated than in early Egypt. This may be the
reason—or one of the reasons—why the divinity of the Sumerian
kings is formulated in a relatively complicated way. In contrast to
the Pharaoh who was "begotten by the god—corporealized in the
king—and the queen," [35] the Sumerian king is in his mother's womb
"endowed with divine qualities, first of all strength and wisdom." [36]
After his birth he is nurtured by the gods; and enthronement and
coronation confirm his divinization.[37] If, as Labat suggests, the
deities recognize the king as divine only after his birth, he is not
the divine offspring of divine parents, but rather their adopted
son.[38]

The controversy concerning the exact nature of the king's divinity
in ancient Mesopotamia [39] indicates the complexity of the early
Mesopotamian pattern, but it cannot hide the fact that the Sumerian
king, in one way or another, represented supreme divine authority

----

d. Contact between the two civilizations probably began long before the dawn
of written history (cf. Kees, 1933: 7 ff.).

e. For the establishment of an independent temple economy during the Twentieth
Dynasty see Breasted, 1927, IV: 242 ff.; cf. Rostovtzeff, 1941, I: 281 ff.

on earth.[40] He held the position of high priest.[41] In principle he was "the only sustainer of the high priest's office." [42] His administrative control over the temples was easily maintained, since in the Sumerian city states all major temples were headed by the priest-king, his wife, or some other member of his family.[43]

From the end of the Sumerian period on, the relations between the governments of Mesopotamia and the temples grew less close, but the temples were unable to free themselves from the control of the secular ruler. The king continued to occupy a quasidivine position, similar to that held by his Sumerian predecessors. As of old, he had the right to perform the highest religious functions. In Assyria he did so personally,[44] whereas in Babylonia these tasks were usually delegated to a representative.[45] Usually, not always. In the great "creation" rites at the New Year he played so important a religious role [46] that "during these ceremonies the sovereign was for his people really the very incarnation of the gods." [47]

In Assyria the government maintained strict administrative and judicial control over the dominant religion; [48] in Babylonia control was much less rigid. But here, too, the kings successfully upheld their right to appoint the high-ranking priests,[49] and having been appointed by the sovereign, "the priest had to swear an oath [of allegiance] like all other officials." [50]

The Achaemenian kings, who through conquest made themselves masters of the entire Near East, are said to have lacked divinity. Did they retain in their Persian homeland certain of their earlier non-theocratic concepts? Or were they worshiped as divine beings by their Persian subjects, because they were imbued with a divine substance? [51] Whatever the answer to these questions may be, the victorious Cyrus adopted in Babylonia "all the elements of Chaldean monarchy," [52] including royal divinity; and his successors acted similarly in Egypt. Like all earlier Egyptian rulers known to us, Darius was called divine: "Horus" and the "good god." [53]

The Hellenistic sovereigns of the Ptolemaic and Seleucid empires quickly learned to combine religious and secular authority.[54] Significantly the worship of the king was less fully developed at the institutional fringe of the hydraulic world, in Anatolia. But here, too, the Hellenistic rulers definitely, if cautiously, sought theocratic status.[55]

The Romans adopted many of the institutions of their new Oriental possessions. Acceptance of the emperor's divinity was gradual; but the beginnings of emperor worship go back to the early days of the empire. The cult, which had already been proposed by Caesar,[56] was officially established by the first emperor, Augustus.[57]

In Early Byzantium, Christianity adjusted itself to an autocratic regime that felt "completely competent to legislate in all religious as in all secular affairs"; [58] but it proved incompatible with the concept of a divine ruler. Despite significant efforts to assert the quasi-divine quality of the emperor,[59] the Byzantine government was, according to our criteria, at best marginally theocratic.

Islam objects to the divinization of the ruler for reasons of its own: Mohammad was Allah's prophet, not his son; and the caliph, who inherited the prophet's authority, had no divine status. Although he was in charge of important religious matters,[60] he cannot well be called a high priest either. Measuring the position of the caliph by our criteria, we therefore, and in conformity with expert opinion, consider it neither theocratic nor hierocratic.[f]

In China the ruler emerges in the light of history as the supreme authority both in secular and religious matters. Whether the traditional designation, "Son of Heaven," reflects an earlier belief in the sovereign's divinity, we do not know. The overlords of the Chou empire and of the subsequent imperial dynasties, who all used this appellation, were considered humans, yet they occupied a quasi-theocratic position. Entrusted with the Mandate of Heaven, they controlled the magic relations with the forces of nature by elaborate sacrifices. In the great religious ceremonies the ruler and his central and local officials assumed the leading roles, leaving only secondary functions to the professional sacerdotalists and their aides. The emperor was the chief performer in the most sacred of all ceremonies, the sacrifice to Heaven; [61] and he was the chief performer also in the sacrifices to Earth, for the prospering of the crop,[62] for the early summer rains,[63] and for the national deities of Soil and Millet.[64] Some of these rites were confined to the national capital. Others were also enacted in the many regional and local subcenters of state power by distinguished provincial, district, or community officials: the great rain sacrifice,[65] the ceremonial plowing,[66] the sacrifices to Confucius [67] and to the patron of agriculture,[68] etc.[g]

To sum up: in the Chinese state religion, the ruler and a hierarchy of high officials fulfilled crucial priestly functions, although in their

f. See Arnold, 1924: 189 ff., 198 n.; *ibid.*, 1941: 294. All this is true essentially for the Sunnite sector of the Islamic world. In the Shi'ite sector the theocratic tendencies occasionally became very strong. For instance, Shah Ismā'īl of the Safawid Dynasty apparently "considered himself as God incarnate" (Minorsky, 1943: 12 n.).

g. Thus in the political order of traditional China religious ideas and practices played a significant role, and certain of the latter were as comprehensive as they were awe-inspiring. The outstanding European expert on Chinese religion, De Groot, calls the great sacrifice to Heaven "perhaps the most impressive ceremony ever performed on earth by man" (De Groot, 1918: 180).

vast majority these officials and the emperor himself were primarily occupied with secular matters. The government of traditional China therefore presents a consistent—and unusual—variant of theocracy.

c. Agrarian Despotism Always Keeps the Dominant Religion Integrated in Its Power System

THUS within the hydraulic world some countries were ruled quasi-hierocratically by qualified priests who, however, no longer engaged professionally in their vocation; and many were ruled theocratically, or quasitheocratically, by divine or pontifical sovereigns. Of the remainder some were borderline cases; and others were probably neither hierocratic nor theocratic. But even among the latter the dominant religion was unable to establish itself as an independent church vis-à-vis the government. In one form or another, it became integrated in the power system of the hydraulic regime.

In certain regions of pre-Conquest Mexico the political ruler was originally also the supreme priest,[69] and in Michoacán this pattern persisted until the arrival of the Spaniards.[70] In the territorial states on the Lake of Mexico the two functions were manifestly separated long before the conquest, but the king continued to fulfill certain religious tasks, and the temples and their personnel were under his authority. On occasion the sovereign, alone or together with his top-ranking aides, might don priestly attire;[71] and he personally performed certain sacrifices.[72] Furthermore, and perhaps most important, the king and his top-ranking aides appointed the Great Priests;[73] and temple land was apparently administered together with government land.[74]

Should we for this reason call pre-Conquest Mexico quasitheocratic? Perhaps. The Mexican constellation defies simple classification, but this much is certain: The priests of the various temples who assembled for ceremonial purposes had no independent nationwide organization of their own. Cooperating closely with the secular leaders, whose offspring they educated and in whose armies they served,[75] they were no counterweight to, but an integral part of, the despotic regime.

The borderline cases of early Achaemenian Persia and of Byzantine and Islamic society have already been touched upon. But even when in these cases the government was only peripherally theocratic, the dominant religion was everywhere firmly enmeshed in the secular system of authority. The Achaemenian king, who in secular matters ruled absolutely, in theory also had the final say in religious matters. And not only in theory. The case of Artaxerxes II shows that the Achaemenian king could change the religious cult in significant ways.[76] The dominant priests, the *magi,* constituted a privileged group,[77] but they did not establish a national and autonomous Church.

Early Byzantium is among the very few hydraulic civilizations that permitted the dominant religion to function as a Church. But while this Church was well organized, it did not evolve into an independent entity, as did the Roman branch after the collapse of the Western half of the empire. During the early period of Byzantine history—that is, from the 4th to the 7th century—the "saintly," [78] if not divine, emperor followed Roman tradition which held that the religion of his subjects was part of the *jus publicum;* he consequently exerted "an almost unlimited control over the life of the Church." [79]

Under Islam, political and religious leadership was originally one, and traces of this arrangement survived throughout the history of the creed. The position of the Islamic sovereign (the caliphs and sultans) underwent many transformations, but it never lost its religious quality.[80] Originally the caliphs directed the great communal prayer. Within their jurisdictions, the provincial governors led the ritual prayer, particularly on Fridays, and they also delivered the sermon, the *khutba.* The caliphs appointed the official interpreter of the Sacred Law, the *mufti.*[81] The centers of Muslim worship, the mosques, were essentially administered by persons directly dependent upon the sovereign, such as the *kadis;* and the religious endowments, the *waqfs,* which provided the main support for the mosques, were often, though not always, administered by the government. Throughout the history of Islam the ruler remained the top-ranking authority for the affairs of the mosque. "He interfered in the administration and shaped it according to his will," and he "could also interfere in the inner affairs of the mosques, perhaps through his regular agencies." [82] All this did not make the caliphate a theocracy, but it indicates a governmental authority strong enough to prevent the establishment of an Islamic Church that was independent of the state.

In India the relation between secular and religious authority underwent considerable transformation, but certain basic features persisted throughout and even after the close of the Hindu period. Available evidence suggests that in the early days of Hindu history the government depended less on priestly participation than it has since the later part of the first millennium B.C.[83] But whatever changes have occurred in this respect, secular and religious authority remained closely integrated.

Were the Brahmins disinclined, or unable, to create an autonomous position similar to that of the Church in feudal Europe? Did they live by gifts and government grants because they wanted to or because they had no choice? Everything we know about the attitudes of the Brahmins shows that they, like other priestly groups, preferred a strong and secure position over one that was weak and insecure. However, the Hindu sovereigns willed it otherwise. Like their hydraulic fellow monarchs, they favored regulated and weak forms of property for their subjects. They paid their secular aides in money, consumable goods, and the usufruct of land ("villages"); and they remunerated the representatives of the dominant religion in exactly the same way. In India this was still the policy at the end of the Hindu period, when an increase in private landownership failed to consolidate proprietary power in any way comparable to that of late feudal or postfeudal Europe.

To say this does not mean to deny the extraordinary role of Brahminism—and of the Brahmins—in the governments of Hindu and Muslim India. All four castes are said to have been made from parts of Brahma's body, and the Brahmin caste from a particularly noble part, the mouth.[84] But the great Law Book ascribed to Manu especially stresses the divinity of the king.[85] It thus credits his rule with a definitely theocratic quality.

Hindu government also had significant quasihierocratic features. From Vedic times the king had had a priest attached to his person, the *purohita;* [86] and this dignitary soon became his advisor in all matters of importance.[87] The Law Books, which were written by Brahmins and accepted by the government as guides for action, require the king to have a *purohita* [88] "(who shall be) foremost in all (transactions). Let him act according to his instructions." [89]

A priest advised the king; and a priest aided him in administering the priest-formulated laws. The Book of Manu insists that "a learned Brâhmaṇa must carefully study them, and he must duly instruct his pupils in them, but nobody else (shall do it)." [90] In doubtful cases well-instructed Brahmins were to decide what was right,[91] and in the courts the priests, either with the king and his aides or alone, were to act as judges.[92]

Well educated and politically influential, the priests had unique opportunities for handling administrative tasks. The *purohita* might become the king's top-ranking minister.[93] In a similar way, priests might be entrusted with all manner of fiscal tasks. This was so during the classical days of Hindu culture,[94] and it continued to be a major trend until the end of the Muslim period. Du Bois states that "Brahmins become necessary even to the Mussulman princes themselves, who cannot govern without their assistance. The Mohamedan rulers generally make a Brahmin their secretary of state, through whose hands all the state correspondence must pass. Brahmins also frequently fill the positions of secretaries and writers to the governors of provinces and districts." [95]

The English did little to change this age-old pattern. The Brahmins

> occupy the highest and most lucrative posts in the different administrative boards and Government offices, as well as in the judicial courts of the various districts. In fact there is no branch of public administration in which they have not made themselves indispensable. Thus it is nearly always Brahmins who hold the posts of sub-collectors of revenue, writers, copyists, translators, treasurers, book-keepers, etc. It is especially difficult to do without their assistance in all matters connected with accounts, as they have a remarkable talent for arithmetic. I have seen some men in the course of a few minutes work out, to the last fraction, long and complicated calculations, which would have taken the best accountants in Europe hours to get through.[96]

During the Hindu period and after, many trained and qualified priests indeed fulfilled important government functions. But except for the *purohita* and perhaps certain others who temporarily acted as judges, the priests became full-time officials. As in other hydraulic civilizations, they preserved their religious quality, but they ceased to be professional priests. In all probability, they did not constitute the majority of all officials, for there already existed a numerous "ruling" caste,[97] the Kshatriya, who were specialists in administrative and, particularly, military matters.

d. The Changing Position of the Dominant Priesthood in Hydraulic Society

THESE observations protect us against assuming that, during an early phase, hydraulic civilization was ruled by priests and that, later on, it was dominated by a secular group, preferably warriors.

To repeat: hierocracy, the rule of priests who remained officiating priests while they governed, was rare; and rule by trained priests was far from being a general feature of early hydraulic civilizations. Theocracy characterized many hydraulic civilizations, both late and early; but it did not necessarily involve priest rule.

True, in the early days of Mesopotamia and of many (most?)

hydraulic areas of the Western hemisphere, the temples apparently played a dominant role in the choice of sovereigns and officials; but in several major hydraulic centers of the Old World this was not the case. In China no conspicuous body of professional priests represented the dominant religion. In Pharaonic Egypt a professional priesthood was not lacking; but in the Old Kingdom many important religious functions were fulfilled by the ruler and certain ranking officials. In the early days of Aryan India the government was run by secular "warriors" (Kshatriyas). Only later and gradually did the priests, directly or indirectly, participate in the government.

Nor can it be said that later and larger hydraulic societies were generally ruled by military men. As will be explained more fully in subsequent chapters, military officials and "the army" might indeed prevail over the civil bureaucracy. But this development was by no means confined to later and more complex hydraulic societies. Moreover, for obvious reasons, it was the exception rather than the rule, since in an agromanagerial state the political organizer (the "pen") tends to be more powerful than the military leader (the "sword").

F. THREE FUNCTIONAL ASPECTS, BUT A SINGLE SYSTEM OF TOTAL POWER

BUT whatever the deficiencies of this assumption of a development from priest rule to warrior rule, it has the merit of drawing attention to the multiple functions of the hydraulic regime. Different from the society of feudal Europe, in which the majority of all military leaders (the feudal barons) were but loosely and conditionally linked to their sovereigns, and in which the dominant religion was independent of the secular government, the army of hydraulic society was an integral part of the agromanagerial bureaucracy, and the dominant religion was closely attached to the state. It was this formidable concentration of vital functions which gave the hydraulic government its genuinely despotic (total) power.

CHAPTER 4

Despotic power—total and not benevolent

THE despotic character of hydraulic government is not seriously contested. The term "Oriental despotism," which is generally used for the Old World variants of this phenomenon, connotes an extremely harsh form of absolutist power.

But those who admit the ruthlessness of Oriental despotism often insist that regimes of this type were limited by institutional and moral checks which made them bearable and at times even benevolent. How bearable and how benevolent was hydraulic despotism? Obviously this question can be answered only by a comparative and reasoned examination of the pertinent facts.

A. TOTAL POWER

1. ABSENCE OF EFFECTIVE CONSTITUTIONAL CHECKS

THE existence of constitutional regulations does not necessarily involve the existence of a constitutionally restricted government. All governments that persist over time—and many others as well—have a certain pattern (constitution). This pattern may be expressed in written form. Under advanced cultural conditions, this is usually done, and at times in an orderly collection, a code.

The development of a written constitution is by no means identical with the development of a "constitutionally" restricted government. Just as a law may be imposed by the government (*lex data*) or agreed upon both by governmental authority and independent nongovernmental forces (*lex rogata*), so a constitution may also be imposed or agreed upon. The term *constitutiones* originally referred to edicts, rescripts, and mandates that were one-sidedly and autocratically issued by the Roman emperors.

Even a highly systematized law code does not bind the autocratic lawgivers by restrictions other than those inherent in all self-imposed norms. The ruler who exercises complete administrative, managerial, judicial, military, and fiscal authority may use his power to make whatever laws he and his aides deem fit. Expediency and inertia favor the perpetuation of most of these laws, but the absolutist regime is free to alter its norms at any time; and the history of hydraulic civilizations testifies to the periodic promulgation of new laws and new codes. The "Collected Regulations" (*hui yao*) of imperial China,[1] the Law Books (*dharma shāstra*) of India,[2] and the administrative and judicial writings of the Byzantine and Islamic East are all cases in point.

Having been imposed one-sidedly, constitutional regulations are also changed one-sidedly. In China "all legislative, executive and judicial powers belonged to him [the emperor]."[3] In Hindu India "constitutionally the king was in a position to accept or repudiate the laws accepted by his predecessor."[4] In Byzantium "there was no organ in the state that had a right to control him [the emperor]." Or, more specifically: "For his legislative and administrative acts, the monarch was responsible to none, except to Heaven."[5]

In Islamic society the caliph, like all other believers, was expected to submit to the Sacred Law,[6] and generally he was quite ready to uphold it as part of the dominant religious order. But he asserted his power whenever he thought it desirable by establishing (administrative) secular courts and by directing them through special decrees (*qānūn* or *siyāsa*).[7] And the religious judges, the *kadis*, were eager to support a government that appointed and deposed them at will.[a] Thus the theoretical absence of a legislature modified the appearance but not the substance of Islamic absolutism. "The Caliphate . . . was a despotism which placed unrestricted power in the hands of the ruler."[8]

In these and other comparable instances the regime represents a definite structural and operational pattern, a "constitution." But this pattern is not agreed upon. It is given from above, and the rulers of hydraulic society create, maintain, and modify it, not as the controlled agents of society but as its masters.

2. ABSENCE OF EFFECTIVE SOCIETAL CHECKS

a. No Independent Centers of Authority Capable of Checking the Power of the Hydraulic Regime

OF COURSE, the absence of formal constitutional checks does not necessarily imply the absence of societal forces whose interests and

---

a. Schacht, 1941: 677. The Sacred Law, the Islamic law proper, was in time confined essentially to personal matters, such as marriage, family, and inheritance, while secular law dealt primarily with criminal cases, taxation, and land problems. This was so not only under the Arab caliphs, but also under the Turkish sultans.

intentions the government must respect. In most countries of post-feudal Europe the absolutist regimes were restricted not so much by official constitutions as by the actual strength of the landed nobility, the Church, and the towns. In absolutist Europe all these nongovernmental forces were politically organized and articulate. They thus differed profoundly from the representatives of landed property, religion, or urban professions in hydraulic society.

Some of these groups were poorly developed in the Orient, and none of them congealed into political bodies capable of restricting the hydraulic regime. The Indian scholar, K. V. Rangaswami, correctly describes the situation when, in his discussion of Hindu absolutism, he defines genuine absolutism as "a form of government in which all the powers *must* be vested in the hands of the Ruler, there being *no other concurrent and independent authority,* habitually obeyed by the people as much as he is obeyed, and which lawfully resist him or call him to account." [9]

b. The So-called Right of Rebellion

THE lack of lawful means for resisting the government is indeed a significant feature of despotism. When such means are not available, discontented and desperate men have time and again taken up arms against their government, and under extreme conditions they have succeeded in overthrowing it altogether. Subsequently the new rulers justified their procedure by juxtaposing the worthiness of their cause to the unworthiness of the former regime; and the historians and philosophers have in the same manner explained periodic dynastic changes. It is from events and ideas of this kind that the so-called right of rebellion has been derived.

The term "right of rebellion" is unfortunate in that it confuses a legal and a moral issue. The official discussions on the rise and fall of dynastic power were presented as warnings against rebellious action rather than as guides for it; and they were certainly not incorporated into any official constitutional regulations or laws. The right of rebellion could be exercised only when the existing laws were violated and at the risk of total destruction for whoever asserted it.

Traces of the so-called right of rebellion can be found in virtually all hydraulic societies. Pueblo folklore proudly relates successful action against unworthy *caciques,*[10] and revolutions in Bali have been so justified.[11] Hindu and Muslim rulers have been similarly warned—and similarly challenged.[12] The fact that in China the right of rebellion was formulated in the Confucian classics did as little to check total power [13] as does the presence in the USSR of Marx' and Lenin's writings, which postulate revolutionary action against oppression.

c. Election of the Despot—No Remedy

NOR does the regime become less despotic because the ruler attains his position through election rather than through inheritance. The transfer of title and authority to a close relative of the deceased sovereign, preferably to the oldest son, favors political stability, while election favors gifted leadership. The first principle prevails among the indigenous rulers of hydraulic societies, the second among pastoral or other peoples who, as conquerors of such societies, frequently perpetuated their original patterns of succession.[14]

The Byzantine custom of determining the emperor through election goes back to republican Rome. It suited the conditions of the early empire, which, being largely controlled by military officials, chose its sovereigns more often through "the army" [15] than through the top-ranking body of civil officials. When, from Diocletian on, the Senate took a more prominent part in the election of the emperor, the political center of gravity shifted from the military to the civil branch of the officialdom.[b] Election was not the best method by which to establish a new emperor, but wrapped in the cloak of tradition and legitimacy it proved definitely compatible with the requirements of bureaucratic absolutism.[c] And the frequent changes in the person of the supreme leader deprived neither his position nor the bureaucratic hierarchy, which he headed, of its despotic character.

In ancient Mexico and in most Chinese dynasties of conquest the new ruler was elected from members of the ruling kin group. The procedure combined the principle of inheritance with the principle of limited choice; and, as in the case of Byzantium, those who made the choice were top-ranking members of the political hierarchy. This arrangement increased the political opportunities among the masters of the apparatus, but it did not increase the authority of the nongovernmental forces of society.

Two nonhydraulic parallels may aid in dispelling the misconception that despotic power is democratized by an elective system of succession. The regime of Chingis Khan, which was perpetuated

b. The Byzantine Senate was nothing but "the rallying-point of the administrative aristocracy" (Diehl, 1936: 729).

c. Dynastic forms of government crystallized only after the Byzantine state had lost its hydraulic provinces.

through limited election, remains one of the most terrifying examples of total power. And the transfer of leadership from one member of the Bolshevik Politburo to another makes the Soviet government temporarily less stable but certainly not more democratic.

Mommsen called the state of Eastern Rome "an autocracy tempered by a revolution which is legally recognized as permanent." [16] Bury translates Mommsen's unwieldy formulation as "an autocracy tempered by the legal right of revolution." [17] Both phrasings are problematic because they imply that the subjects were legally entitled to replace one emperor by another. Actually no such right existed. Diehl recognizes this by speaking of "an autocracy tempered by revolution and assassination"; [18] and Bury admits that "there was no formal process of deposing a sovran." But he adds, "the members of the community had the means of dethroning him, if the government failed to give satisfaction, by proclaiming a new emperor." [19]

This was indeed the pattern established by the military officials of Eastern Rome; and congruent with it, usurpation was considered legitimate if and when it was successful. That is, rebellion becomes legal—*post festum*. Says Bury: "If he [the pretender] had not a sufficient following to render the proclamation effective and was suppressed, *he was treated as a rebel*." [20]

Thus, in Byzantium as in other states of the hydraulic world, anyone might try to usurp power; and the elective nature of sovereignty combined with the temporary dominance of military leadership inspired frequent attempts of this kind. But no law protected such actions while they were being undertaken. In Byzantium persons attacking the existing government were punished with barbarous brutality.[21] In China persons caught while trying to exercise the right of rebellion were executed. Under the last three dynasties they were cut to pieces.[22]

If armed conflict, rebellion, and the assassination of weak rulers do not make Oriental despotism more democratic, do they not at least give the populace some relief from oppression? The argument has less validity than may appear at first glance. Such diversions rarely reduce in any decisive way the traditional administrative and judicial pressures; and the inclination to assert supreme leadership through open violence is more than likely to intensify the tendency to brutality among those in power. Furthermore, the devastations of any major civil war generally lay increased economic burdens on the commoners. The frequent occurrence of violence within the ruling circles, far from tempering despotism, tends to make it more oppressive.

d. Intragovernmental Influences: Absolutism and Autocracy

BUT are there perhaps forces inside the government that mitigate the ruthlessness of agromanagerial despotism? This question focuses attention on the relation between absolutism and autocracy. Absolutism and autocracy are not identical, but they interlock closely. A government is absolutist when its rule is not effectively checked by nongovernmental forces. The ruler of an absolutist regime is an autocrat when his decisions are not effectively checked by intragovernmental forces.

The absolutist regimes of hydraulic society are usually [d] headed by a single individual in whose person is concentrated all the power over major decisions. Why is this so? Do the great water works, which characterize the core areas of the hydraulic world and which indeed require centralized direction, necessitate autocratic leadership? After all, controlled (democratic or aristocratic) governments also initiate and maintain huge public enterprises. They muster large and disciplined armies and/or fleets; and they operate thus, for substantial periods of time, without developing autocratic patterns of rulership.

Manifestly, the rise of autocratic power depends on more than the existence of large state enterprises. In all hydraulic societies proper such enterprises play a considerable role; and there, as well as in the institutional margin, we always find disciplined armies and almost always, also, comprehensive organizations of communication and intelligence. But there is no technical reason why these various enterprises could not be headed by several leading officials. This is indeed the case in controlled governments, whose department chiefs are carefully separated from, and balanced against, one another.

However, despotic states lack appropriate mechanics of outside control and internal balance. And under such conditions there develops what may be called a *cumulative tendency of unchecked power*. This tendency could be countered if all major subsections of authority were more or less equally powerful. It could be countered if the chiefs of the public works, of the army, of the intelligence service, and of the revenue system were more or less equally strong in terms of organizational, communicational, and coercive power. In such a case, the absolutist regime might be headed by a balanced oligarchy, a "politburo," whose members would actually, and more or less equally, participate in the exercise of supreme authority. However, the organizational, communicational, and coercive power of the major sectors of any government is rarely, if ever, so balanced; and under absolutist conditions the holder of the strongest position, ben-

d. For a few temporary exceptions, like early India, see below, Chap. 8.

efiting from the cumulative tendency of unchecked power, tends to expand his authority through alliances, maneuvers, and ruthless schemes until, having conquered all other centers of supreme decision, he alone prevails.

The point at which the growth of government functions precludes effective outside control differs in different institutional configurations. But it may safely be said that whenever this critical point is passed, the cumulative strength of superior power tends to result in a single autocratic center of organization and decision making.

The crucial importance of this center is not negated by the fact that the supreme power-holder may delegate the handling of his affairs to a top-ranking assistant, a vizier, chancellor, or prime minister. Nor is it negated by the fact that he and/or his aide may lean heavily for advice and speedy action on selected groups of strategically placed and carefully tested officials. The governmental apparatus as a whole does not cease to be absolutist because the actual center of decision making temporarily, and often in a veiled manner, shifts to persons or groups below the ruler.

The sovereign of an agrobureaucratic state may be completely under the influence of his courtiers or administrators; but such influence differs qualitatively from the institutional checks of balanced power. In the long run the head of a controlled government must adjust to the effective nongovernmental forces of society, while the head of an absolutist regime is not similarly restricted. Simple self-interest urges any intelligent despot to listen to experienced persons. Councillors have existed in most agromanagerial civilizations, and not infrequently councils were a standard feature of government. But the ruler was under no compulsion to accept their suggestions.[23]

Whether the sovereign was his own chief executive, whether he delegated many of his functions to a vizier, or whether he or his vizier largely followed the advice of official and nonofficial advisors depended, in addition to custom and circumstance, on the personalities of the ruler and his aides. But despite significant bureaucratic attempts to subordinate the absolutist sovereign to the control of his officialdom, the ruler could always *rule,* if he was determined to do so. The great monarchs of the Oriental world were almost without exception "self-rulers"—autocrats.

3. LAWS OF NATURE AND PATTERNS OF CULTURE—NO EFFECTIVE CHECKS EITHER

SERIOUS observers do not generally contest these facts. However, not a few among them seek to minimize their significance by reference to mores and beliefs, which are assumed to restrict even the most tyrannical regime.

Mores and beliefs do indeed play a role; and so, for that matter, do the laws of nature. However, the potential victims of despotic power seem to find little consolation in either fact. They know that their masters' behavior, like their own, is affected by the laws of nature and by more or less firmly established cultural circumstances. But they know also that, nevertheless and in the last analysis, their fate will be determined by the will of those who wield total power.

The mechanics of administration and coercion depend on man's insight into the laws of nature and his ability to use them. A despotic regime will proceed in one way in the neolithic period, in another in the iron age, and in still another in our own time. But in each case the ruling group asserts its total superiority under the then actual natural conditions and by means of the then available technology. The victim of a crude form of despotism does not consider his persecutors less powerful because, under more advanced technical conditions, they may catch and destroy him by different methods or with greater speed.

Nor does he doubt their absolute superiority because they act in conformity with prevailing cultural patterns. Such patterns always shape the manner in which the ruler (and his subjects) act; and occasionally they mitigate or prolong governmental procedures at particular stages. But they do not prevent the government from ultimately achieving its goal. The fact that in many countries persons under sentence of death are normally not executed in certain seasons or on certain days [24] does not mean that they escape their doom. And the fact that a dominant religion praises acts of mercy does not mean that it refrains from invoking measures of extreme harshness.

The potential victim of despotic persecution knows full well that the natural and cultural settings, whatever temporary respites they may provide, do not prevent his final destruction. The despotic ruler's power over his subjects is no less total because it is limited by factors that mold human life in every type of society.

B. THE BEGGARS' DEMOCRACY

THE power of hydraulic despotism is unchecked ("total"), but it does not operate everywhere. The life of most individuals is far from being completely controlled by the state; and there are many villages and other corporate units that are not totally controlled either.

What keeps despotic power from asserting its authority in all spheres of life? Modifying a key formula of classical economics, we may say that the representatives of the hydraulic regime act (or refrain from acting) in response to the *law of diminishing administrative returns*.

1. THE MANAGERIAL VARIANT OF THE LAW OF CHANGING ADMINISTRATIVE RETURNS

THE *law of diminishing administrative returns* is one aspect of what may be called the *law of changing administrative returns*.[1] Varying efforts produce varying results not only in a property-based business economy [a] but also in governmental enterprise. This fact affects decisively both the political economy and the range of state control in hydraulic society.

a. Hydraulic Agriculture: the Law of Increasing Administrative Returns

IN a landscape characterized by full aridity permanent agriculture becomes possible only if and when coordinated human action transfers a plentiful and accessible water supply from its original location to a potentially fertile soil. When this is done, government-led hydraulic enterprise is identical with the creation of agricultural life. This first and crucial moment may therefore be designated as the "administrative creation point."

Having access to sufficient arable land and irrigation water, the hydraulic pioneer society tends to establish statelike forms of public control. Now economic budgeting becomes one-sided and planning bold. New projects are undertaken on an increasingly large scale, and if necessary without concessions to the commoners. The men whom the government mobilized for corvée service may see no reason for a further expansion of the hydraulic system; but the directing group, confident of further advantage, goes ahead nevertheless. Intelligently carried out, the new enterprises may involve a relatively small additional expense, but they may yield a conspicuously swelling return. Such an encouraging discrepancy obviously provides a great stimulus for further governmental action.

b. The Law of Balanced Administrative Returns

THE expansion of government-directed hydraulic enterprise usually slows down when administrative costs approach administrative

---

a. Significantly, the law of diminishing returns has so far been studied primarily in connection with private economy (see Clark, 1937: 145 ff.).

benefits. The upward movement has then reached "Saturation Point 'A' (Ascent)." Beyond this point further expansion may yield additional rewards more or less in proportion to additional administrative effort; but when the major potentials of water supply, soil, and location are exhausted, the curve reaches "Saturation point 'D' (Descent)." The zone between Points "A" and "D" is characterized by what may be called the *law of balanced administrative returns.*

c. The Law of Diminishing Administrative Returns

WHETHER Saturation Points "A" and "D" are close together or far apart, or whether they coincide, any move beyond this zone of balanced returns carries man's action into an area of discouraging discrepancy. Here similar, and even increased, administrative endeavors cost more than they yield. It is under these conditions that we observe the workings of the *law of diminishing administrative returns.* The downward movement is completed when additional outlay yields no additional reward whatsoever. We have then reached the absolute administrative frustration point.

d. Ideal Curve and Reality of Changing Returns

THIS ideal curve does not describe the development of any specific government-directed system of water works in any specific hydraulic society. It indicates in a schematic way the critical points through which any hydraulic enterprise passes, if it moves steadily through all zones of growing and shrinking returns.

Rarely, if ever, do the actual and the ideal curves coincide. Geology, meteorology, potamology, and historical circumstance make for countless variations. Progress toward saturation and beyond may be interrupted by longer or shorter countermovements. But every section of the curve reflects a genuine trend; and the entire curve combines these trends to indicate all possible major phases of creation and frustration in hydraulic enterprise.

e. Nonhydraulic Spheres of Political Economy

IN the sphere of agricultural production itself, coordinated and government-directed action yields increasing administrative returns only under primitive and special conditions. It is only in technologically crude hydraulic societies that mass labor on "public" fields prevails. And even in these societies the government does not try to assume managerial direction over the fields which have been set aside for the support of the individual farmer. In a technically more advanced setting, the administrative creation point and the administrative frustration point tend to coincide. For there the hydraulic regime prefers to refrain altogether from agricultural production, which from the standpoint of administrative returns is more reasonably handled by many small individual farming units.

Of course, political needs take precedence over economic considerations. The great agromanagerial enterprises of communication and defense are cases in point, as are certain government-run workshops (arsenals, shipyards). However, the hydraulic regime's reluctance to assume direct control over the finishing industries derives from the realization that in this field state management would involve deficits rather than gains. In hydraulic as well as in other agrarian societies the government is therefore satisfied to leave the bulk of all handicraft to small individual producers.

2. THE POWER VARIANT OF THE LAW OF CHANGING ADMINISTRATIVE RETURNS

a. Imperative and Worth-while Efforts

IT is easy to recognize the workings of the law of changing administrative returns also in the sphere of political power. The efforts of the hydraulic regime to maintain uncontested military and police control over the population prove increasingly rewarding until all independent centers of coercion are destroyed. The expenses incurred in supporting speedy communications and intelligence follow a similar pattern; and the expansion of fiscal and judicial action appears reasonable as long as it satisfies the rulers' desire for uncontested political and social hegemony.

Some of these operations are imperative, others at least worth while. But carried beyond Saturation Point "D", they all become problematic. The discouraging discrepancy between continued endeavor and decreasing political rewards makes the government reluctant to use its apparatus much below this point.

b. The Forbidding Cost of Total Social Control in a Semimanagerial Society

THE developed industrial apparatus state of the USSR has crushed all independent nationwide organizations (military, political, proprietary, religious); and its total managerial economy permits the establishment of innumerable bureaucratic bases for controlling all secondary (local) professional groupings and even the thought and behavior of individuals. The hydraulic apparatus state does not have equal facilities. It is strong enough to prevent the growth of effective primary organizations; and in doing so, it brings about that one-sided concentration of power which distinguishes it from the ancient and medieval agrarian societies of the West. But being only semimanagerial, it lacks the ubiquitous bases which enable the men of the apparatus to extend their total control over secondary organizations and individual subjects. In the USSR such total control was initiated through the nationalization of agriculture (the "collectivization" of the villages); and it was accomplished through the pulverization of all nongovernmental human relations. Hydraulic society never made the first step, and it therefore never laid the foundations for the second.

To be sure, the notion of a ubiquitous control also attracted the master minds of hydraulic despotism. Garcilaso de la Vega, a scion of native royalty, claimed that under Inca rule special officials went from house to house to make sure that everybody was kept busy. Idlers were punished by blows on the arms and legs "and other penalties prescribed by the law." [2] The great Chinese "Utopia" of bureaucratic government, the *Chou Li,* lists several officials who, in a well-managed state, should regulate the people's life in village and town.

There is no reason to doubt that the Incas wanted their subjects to work as much as possible; but any effective inspection of the commoners' domestic life would have required an army of officials, which would have eaten up a great part of the public revenue without providing a compensatory increase in income. It is therefore hard to believe that the "laws" mentioned by Garcilaso went far beyond a general—and therefore not too costly—supervision. The same may be said for the classic book of Chinese bureaucracy. All educated Chinese officials studied the *Chou Li;* but once in office, they soon learned to distinguish between the sweet dream of total social control and the sober administrative reality. Except for some short-lived attempts at extreme interference, they were content to maintain firm control over the strategically important spheres of their society.

c. Total Social Control Not Necessary for the Perpetuation of Agromanagerial Despotism

To say that the law of diminishing administrative returns discourages the hydraulic state from attempting to control individuals and secondary organizations totally is only another way of saying that the government feels no fundamental need to do so. If it were otherwise—that is, if total control were imperative for the perpetuation of the despotic regime—the rulers might have to spend all their income to be safe. Obviously, such a power system would be unworkable.

Historical experience shows that during long periods of "peace and order" the hydraulic rulers can maintain themselves without resorting to excessively costly measures. It also shows that under "normal" conditions they need not make severe material sacrifices. Except in times of unrest, they are adequately protected by their wide-flung network of intelligence and coercion, which successfully blocks the rise of independent nationwide primary organizations and prevents discontented individuals or secondary organizations from gaining prominence.

The political crises that develop periodically may be caused in part by the dissatisfaction of such individuals and organizations.[3] But serious unrest, whatever its origin, soon assumes a military form, and it is combated by outright military measures. Responding to the law of diminishing administrative returns, the masters of the agrarian apparatus state run the risk of occasional uprisings and do what their modern industrial successors do not have to do: they grant a certain amount of freedom to most individuals and to certain secondary organizations.

3. SECTORS OF INDIVIDUAL FREEDOM IN HYDRAULIC SOCIETY

a. Limitations of Managerial Control

THE duration of the state corvée determines the period during which a member of hydraulic society is deprived of his freedom of action. The corvée may have many objectives, but it must allow the mass of the laborers—the peasants—sufficient time to attend to their own economic affairs. Of course, even in the villages the peasants may have to submit to a policy of economic planning, but at most this policy involves only a few major tasks, such as plowing, sowing, harvesting, and perhaps the choice of the main crop. Often it does not go this far; and at times it may be altogether absent.

Under conditions of advanced technology the corvée also tends to change and shrink. Work on the public fields may be replaced by a tax; and larger or smaller segments of the nonagricultural corvée may be similarly commuted.

But whatever the character of the rural communities and whatever the duration of the public labor service may be, there are definite and at times considerable periods in the peasant's life during which he proceeds at his own discretion. This is still more true for the nonagrarian commoners. Artisans and traders who, in a differentiated societal setting, pursue their occupations professionally and privately [4] may become more valuable as taxpayers than as corvée laborers. Their freedom of movement will increase correspondingly.

Marx speaks of the "general slavery" of the Orient. According to him, this type of slavery, which is inherent in man's attachment to the hydraulic commonwealth and state,[5] differs essentially from Western slavery and serfdom.[b] The merit of Marx' formula lies in the problem it raises rather than in the answer it gives. A person commandeered to toil for an "Asiatic" state is a slave of the state as long as he is so occupied. He is perfectly aware of the lack of freedom, which this condition involves, and he is equally aware of the pleasure of working for himself. Compared with the total state slavery of the total managerial industrial society, the partial state slavery of the partial managerial hydraulic society makes indeed considerable concessions to human freedom.

b. Limitations of Thought Control

A COMPARABLE tendency to make concessions arises also in the sphere of thought control. To appreciate fully what this means, we must understand the enormous stress that the masters of the hydraulic state place on the society's dominant ideas. The close coordination of secular and religious authority makes it easy to apply this stress to both the higher and the lower strata of society. The sons of the dominant elite are generally educated by representatives of the dominant creed; and the whole population is in continued and government-promoted contact with the state-attached temples and their priesthoods.

Education usually is a long process, and its influence is profound. In India the young Brahmin who prepared himself for priestly office had to study one, two, or all three Vedas, applying himself to each one of them for twelve long years. And the members of the "protecting" Kshatriya caste, and even those of the next lower caste, the Vaisya, were also advised to study the Sacred Books.[6] In China "learning"—the study of the canonical (classical) writings—was already considered a basic prerequisite for administrative office in Confucius' time.[7] Increasing systematization led to the holding of

b. Marx assumed that from the European point of view, in this general Asiatic slavery, the laborer seems to be a natural condition of production for a third person or a community, as under [private-property-based] slavery and serfdom, but that actually "this is not the case" (Marx, 1939: 395).

elaborate and graded examinations, which fostered perpetual ideological alertness in all energetic and ambitious young, and in many
middle-aged and even elderly, members of the ruling class.

But the same societal forces that led to the systematic perpetuation of the dominant ideas also encouraged a variety of secondary
religions. Many simple hydraulic civilizations tolerated independent diviners and sorcerers,[8] whose artisan-like small-scale activities
modestly supplemented the coordinated operations of the leading
tribal or national creed. Under more complex conditions, ideological divergence tended to increase. Often the subject of a hydraulic
state might adhere to a secondary religion without endangering his
life. Non-Brahministic creeds, such as Jainism or Buddhism, are
documented for India from the first millennium B.C. Buddhism persisted in traditional China, despite temporary persecutions, for almost two thousand years. And the Islamic Near East, India, and
Central Asia were similarly indulgent.

In the ideological as in the managerial sphere, the policies of the
agrarian apparatus state contrast strikingly with policies of the
modern industrial apparatus states, which, while feigning respect
for traditional ("national") culture and religion, spread the Marxist-
Leninist doctrine with the avowed aim of eventually annihilating
all other ideologies. Again, the difference between their policies is
not due to any innate tolerance on the part of the agrobureaucratic
rulers, whose insistence on the unique position of the dominant
religion is always uncompromising and frequently ruthless. But the
law of diminishing administrative returns places an exorbitant price
on the attempt to maintain total ideological control in a differentiated semimanagerial society. And here, as in the operational
sector, experience shows that the absolutist regime can perpetuate
itself without making so costly an effort.

4. Groups Enjoying Varying Degrees of Autonomy

EXPERIENCE shows still more. It assures the hydraulic rulers that
they may—for the same reasons—permit some autonomy not only
to their individual subjects but to certain secondary groups as well.
In referring to heterodox creeds, we are aware that their adherents
are usually permitted to establish congregations, which support
either individual priests or larger or smaller priesthoods. Since the
early days of written history, the artisans and traders of hydraulic
civilizations have formed professional organizations (guilds). More
ancient still are the village communities, which have probably existed
as long as hydraulic civilization itself. Kin groups are institutionally

older than agriculture; and like the village community, they are present everywhere in the hydraulic world.

These types of associations differ greatly in distribution, composition, quality, and purpose. But they have one thing in common. All of them are tolerated by the despotic regime. Many supervisory measures notwithstanding, they are not subjected to total control.

a. Less Independence than Frequently Assumed

ROMANTIC observers have taken the absence of such control as evidence for the existence of genuine democratic institutions in the lower echelons of hydraulic society. In this form, the claim cannot be accepted. Throughout the hydraulic world, government authority and family authority are interlinked; and measures of political control affect the majority of all villages, guilds, and secondary religious organizations.

Parallels can be found in other agrarian societies for most of these restrictive trends. (The free guilds of feudal Europe are as exceptional as they are significant.) This, however, is not the issue here. What we are concerned with is whether, in contrast to corresponding developments in other despotic states—and also in contrast to restrictive developments in other agrarian civilizations—the secondary organizations of hydraulic society were genuinely autonomous. The answer to the question is "No."

i. THE FAMILY

THE family of traditional China has often been said to be the institution that gave Chinese society its peculiar character and strength. This thesis is correct insofar as it stresses the family as a basic component of society; but it is misleading insofar as it implies that the family determined the quality and power of the institutional setting of which it was a part.

The authority of the Chinese *pater familias* was much stronger than intrafamilial leadership required; [c] and he owed his extraordinary power essentially to the backing of the despotic state. Disobedience to his orders was punished by the government.[9] On the other hand, the local officials could have him beaten and imprisoned, if he was unable to keep the members of his family from violating the law.[10] Acting as a liturgical (semi-official) policeman of his kin group, he can scarcely be considered the autonomous leader of an autonomous unit.

c. For the nongovernmental roots of paternal authority in the Chinese family see Wittfogel, 1935: 49; *ibid.*, 1936: 506 ff.

The Babylonian father, who could place his wife, son, or daughter in the service of a third person for several years,[11] also owed his power to the government which backed him up in his decision. Whether he was legally responsible for the behavior of the family members is not clear.

The *patria potestas* of ancient Egypt has been compared with that of Rome. The strongly militarized society of republican Rome did indeed encourage the development of highly authoritarian family relations; but the Egyptian father seems to have had still greater power than his Roman counterpart.[d]

In the Islamic world, respect for the parents is prescribed by the Sacred Law; [12] and the degree to which paternal authority operated, particularly in the villages, may be judged from the fact that in such countries as Syria the father customarily was the master over his family until his death.[13]

The Law Books of India give the father an almost kinglike power over members of his kin group.[14] Despite several restrictions,[15] his authority over his wife and children seems to have been extremely great.[e]

Evidently the father's power varied notably in different hydraulic civilizations. But almost everywhere the government was inclined to raise it above the level suggested by his leadership functions in the family.

ii. THE VILLAGE

GENERALLY the villages of hydraulic civilizations are under the jurisdiction of headmen who are either government-appointed or elected by their fellow villagers. Appointment seems to be frequent in the regulated rural communities of compactly hydraulic civilizations, whereas free choice is more apt to be permitted in less compactly hydraulic societies. In Inca Peru the local officials down to the lowest functionary—the head of ten families—was appointed.[16] In pre-Conquest Mexico, too, the village land was communally regulated. But its agrarian economy was much less bureaucratized

---

d. Dr. Taubenschlag's assertion that the Egyptian father's right to sell his child has a Roman precedent is documented only for "the fourth century" (Taubenschlag, 1944: 103 ff.).

e. Jolly, 1896: 78. At the beginning of the 19th century, Dubois (1943: 307 ff.) found the authority of the Brahmins enormous, whereas paternal authority was weak. The author lived in India from 1792 to 1823. Assuming that he observed the phenomenon correctly, we are at a loss to explain it. Was it, at least in part, due to the turmoil of the time?

than that of the Inca empire. The heads of the Mexican local administrative units, the *calpulli*, were elected.[17]

However, this correlation does not prevail generally, perhaps because appointment is only one among several ways of controlling a
local functionary. Almost everywhere the hydraulic government
holds the headman responsible for the obligations of his co-villagers.
It thus places him in a position of state dependency. Where land is
communally held and where taxes are communally paid, the village
headman is likely to wield considerable power. Assisted by a scribe
and one or several policemen, he may become something of a local
despot.

The inscriptions of the early Near East show the regional officials
actively concerned with plowing and the collection of the revenue; [18] but we are unable to get a clear picture of how the village
functionaries fitted into the administrative nexus.[19] As in other
spheres of life, the Persians and their Hellenistic and Roman successors may well have perpetuated an earlier village pattern. In
Ptolemaic and Roman Egypt the leading village official, the scribe,
assisted by the elders, executed his government-imposed tasks.[20]
These men, no matter whether they were appointed [21] or elected
like the elders,[22] were all "directly dependent on the central government . . . they all especially obeyed the *strategos* of the district." [23]

The data for Roman Syria seem to suggest considerable popular
participation in village affairs,[24] whereas the Egyptian village officials
probably acted in a very authoritarian manner. But this divergence
must not make us overlook the basic similarities that existed throughout the ancient Near East in village organization and government
dependency.[25] In Hellenistic times,[26] as previously, the "royal"
villagers were attached to the land they cultivated.[27] It therefore
seems safe to conclude that in the pre-Roman as well as in the Roman
period the peasants of Syria and Asia Minor did not administer their
villages autonomously.

In Arab Egypt, as in Byzantine Egypt,[28] the village administration
was in the hands of a headman and the elders. Under the Arabs
the headman, who possibly was nominated by the peasants and confirmed by the government,[29] seems to have apportioned and collected
the tax.[30] He designated the corvée laborers and exercised police and
judicial functions.[31]

In the Arab provinces of the Turkish Near East the village headman (*sheikh*) assisted the official and semi-official representatives of
the government in allocating the tax.[32] He "policed the *fellāhs* who
cultivated the lands under his charge, and the principal *seyh* acted
as magistrate and arbitrator, with authority not only over the culti-

vators but over all the inhabitants." [33] Controlling "his" peasants in an arbitrary way and being in turn controlled with equal severity by the state bureaucracy,[34] he certainly was not the representative of a free rural village community.

In India the village headman may have been elected originally; [35] but from the time of the later Law Books on—that is, from the end of the first millennium B.C.—his appointment is documented.[36] As the king's representative in the villages, who "collected taxes for him" [37] and who also fulfilled policing and judicial functions,[38] the headman held a position of authority not dissimilar to that enjoyed by his Near Eastern counterpart. Muslim rule did not fundamentally change this administratively convenient arrangement, which in fact persisted in the majority of all Indian villages up to modern times.[39]

In China the regulated village yielded to a property-based pattern more than two thousand years ago. The duties of the village officials shrank correspondingly, but they did not disappear altogether. At the close of the imperial period most sizable villages had at least two functionaries, a headman, *chuang chang,* and a local constable, *ti fang* or *ti pao.*[40] The headman, who was usually chosen by the villagers, executed the directing, and the constable, who usually was government appointed,[f] the coercive, functions of the village government. They cooperated in their official tasks: the collection of taxes and materials for public constructions, the organizing and directing of corvée services ("government transportation . . . work on riverbanks, patrols for the Imperial roads" etc.),[41] and the making of intelligence reports.[42]

All these activities linked the headman to the central government, although he was not part of its bureaucracy.[g] The villagers found it hard to bring a complaint against him, even if their case was good, for he monopolized communication with the district magistracy.[43] The constable was controlled by the county officials. They could

f. According to Smith (1899: 227), the candidates for this position were "not formally chosen, nor formally deposed." Instead they used to "drop into their places" as the result of what Smith calls "a kind of natural selection."

It would probably be better to speak of an informal election based on an understanding between all family heads of some standing. Dr. K. C. Hsiao, who has almost completed his comprehensive study, *Rural China, Imperial Control in the Nineteenth Century,* ascribes "a certain amount of informal local influence on village leadership," especially that of "wealthy or gentry families." But he finds it impossible to give quantitative data about "the proportion of government-appointed village headmen (pao-chang, chia-chang, etc.; and later, chuang-chang, ti-pao, ti-fang, etc.)." He adds: "The official scheme called for universal institution of such headmen, wherever rural communities existed" (letter of January 15, 1954).

g. Usually the village paid him a salary (Werner, 1910: 106 ff.). In addition there were the usual material advantages inherent in the handling of public money.

have him "beaten to a jelly" for neglecting his duty as a local intelligence agent.[44]

The villages of imperial China were less strictly controlled than those of pre-Conquest Peru, India, and most Near Eastern civilizations, but even they did not govern themselves. Their main functionaries, who were either appointed or confirmed by the government, were inescapably tied to an operational system that served the interests of the government rather than the interests of the villagers.

iii. THE GUILDS

THE professional corporations of the artisans and traders in hydraulic civilizations were similarly conditioned. Again the appointment of the leading official is significant; but again it is only one of several ways in which the despotic state assures its unchecked superiority and the weakness of the tolerated organization.

Hellenistic Egypt seems to have followed ancient usage in having persons "working for the State in industry, transport, mining, building, hunting, etc." gathered into professional groups that were *"organized and closely supervised* by the economic and financial administration of the king." [45]

In the later part of the Roman empire and in Byzantium, the government "strictly regulated" the activities of the guilds.[h] Until the third century the members elected their own headmen; but from that time on the government made the final decision on guild-nominated headmen, who, after installation, were supervised and disciplined by the state.[46]

In Ottoman Turkey officials inspected the markets [47] and controlled the prices, weights, and measurements,[i] thus fulfilling functions which in the burgher-controlled towns of Medieval Europe were usually the responsibility of the urban authorities.[48] Furthermore, the state, which in most countries of feudal Europe collected few if any regular taxes from the urban centers of strongly developed guild power, was able in Turkey to tax the guilds and, as elsewhere in the Orient, to employ as its fiscal agents the headmen of these corporations, who "distributed the tax-quotas of their members" and who were "personally responsible for their payment." [49]

In Hindu India, the *setthi,* the head of the merchant guild, was a semi-official closely attached to the ruler's fiscal administration.[50]

h. Stöckle, 1911: 11. For reference to guild heads as tax collectors in Byzantine and Arab Egypt, see Grohmann, PAP: 279 and n. 8. For conditions at the beginning of Arab rule, see *ibid.:* 131, n. 3, and Crum, 1925: 103–11.

i. Specifically this was done by agents of the *kadi* (Gibb and Bowen, 1950: 287).

The merchants represented considerable wealth, and their corporations seem to have been more highly respected than those of the artisans.[51] But this did not make the merchant guild a significant political entity.

It has been said that the Indian guilds came into prominence in early Buddhist days.[52] In agreeing with this observation, however, we must be careful not to exaggerate its political significance. According to Fick, "the corporations of the manufacturers fall—partly at any rate—undoubtedly under the category of the despised castes"; [53] and Dr. Rhys-Davids insists that there is "no instance as yet produced from early Buddhist documents pointing to any corporate organisation of the nature of a gild or Hansa league." [54] A legend of the 3d or 4th century, which is supposed to show that the town of Thana [j] was "ruled by a strong merchant guild" actually describes the unsuccessful attempt of a group of merchants to combat a competitor by cornering the market.[k]

In China the existence of guilds is reliably documented only since the second half of the first millennium A.D. Under the T'ang and Sung dynasties the guild heads could be held responsible for the improper professional behavior of their members, such as violations of the currency regulations,[55] theft, and other misdeeds. And in many cases membership was compulsory.[56] The guilds as a unit also had to render special services to the state.[57] In recent centuries the government seems to have left the less significant craft and trade guilds largely to their own devices; [m] but the corporations of such important groups as the salt merchants [n] and a number of Cantonese firms dealing in foreign trade [o] were strictly supervised.

iv. SECONDARY RELIGIONS

OUR information on secondary religions is particularly plentiful for Islamic society and traditional China. Muslim rulers tolerated Christianity, Judaism, and Zoroastrianism.[p] But followers of these creeds had to accept an inferior status both politically and socially, and

j. Poona, south of modern Bombay.

k. Hopkins, 1902: 175. Hopkins' erroneous thesis is taken up by Max Weber in an argument stressing the temporary political prominence of the Hindu guilds (Weber, RS, II: 86 ff.). See below, p. 266.

m. Wittfogel, 1931: 580 ff., 714 ff. My 1931 analysis overlooked the state-controlled guilds of important trades, such as the salt business.

n. The guild heads collect the tax from the "small merchants" (Ch'ing Shih Kao 129. 1b).

o. The headmen were appointed by the government (Yüeh Hai Küan Chih 25. 2a).

p. Macdonald, 1941: 96; Grunebaum, 1946: 117. Zoroastrians were tolerated originally (Mez, 1922: 30); later they were more harshly treated (Büchner, 1941: 381).

they were prevented from spreading their ideas. The laws forbade conversion from Christianity to Judaism or vicè versa; and penalties for apostasy from Islam were severe. Christians were not permitted to beat their wooden boards loudly,[q] or sing in their churches with raised voices, or assemble in the presence of Muslims, or display their "idolatry," "nor invite to it, nor show a cross" on their churches.[58] No wonder that the religious minorities—who during the Turkish period were set apart in organizations called *millet* [59]—vegetated rather than throve. The head of the *millet* was nominated by the *millet* [r] but appointed by the sultan; [60] once in office he was given "just enough executive power . . . to enable him to collect the taxes imposed on his community by the state." [61]

In traditional China, Buddhism was the most important secondary religion. It reached its greatest prominence in the barbarian dynasties of infiltration and conquest which ruled over the old northern centers of Chinese culture during the middle period of the first millennium A.D.[62] The harsh persecutions of 845 initiated a policy which over time reduced it to a carefully restricted secondary religion.

Specially designated officials supervised Buddhism and other problematic creeds.[63] The government limited the erection of monasteries and temples; [64] it licensed the number of priests and monks; [65] it forbade certain religious activities which in other countries went unrestricted; and it prescribed that "the Buddhist and Taoist clergy shall not hold sutra-readings in market-squares, nor go about with alms-bowls, nor explain the fruits of salvation, nor collect moneys." [66] Concluding his classical survey of what others have hailed as the elements of religious liberty, De Groot asks: "What is the good of this liberty where the State has cast its system of certification of clergy within such strict bounds, and has made the admission of male disciples extremely difficult, of females almost impossible, so that the number of those who could avail themselves of such liberty, is reduced to a miserably small percentage of the population? It makes this vaunted liberty into a farce." [67]

b. Genuine Elements of Freedom Nevertheless Present

THUS the hydraulic state restrictively affects practically all secondary groups and organizations, but it does not integrate them completely into its power system.

The traditional Chinese family, whose head enjoyed a particularly

q. These boards were used as bells (Grunebaum, 1946: 179).
r. Or its clergy?

distinguished position legally, was not forced by political and police pressure to set one family member against another, as is the case in modern apparatus states. In China and in India the government permitted the kin groups to settle their internal affairs in accordance with their own family "laws." [68] In other hydraulic civilizations the families enjoyed a less formal, but equally effective, quasi-autonomy.

Government control over the villages, although very specific, is also definitely limited. Even where village officials wield much power, the peasants who live alongside them have many opportunities to make their opinions on the day-to-day affairs of the community felt. And once the demands of the government are satisfied, the headman and his aides usually settle the affairs of their village with little, if any, interference from above.

Certain opportunities for self-government seem to have existed in the villages of Roman Syria [69] and in the Egyptian villages of the Roman and Byzantine period.[70] The village chief of Ottoman Turkey, like his counterparts in other Oriental civilizations, acted with great independence as far as the internal affairs of the rural community were concerned.[71]

The headman of an Indian village could fulfill his functions successfully only by trying "to conciliate the villagers." [72] He could not be "proud, intolerant, and haughty like the Brahmins"; instead he had to be "polite and complaisant" toward his equals and "affable and condescending" toward his inferiors.[73] Full-fledged committee organizations were probably confined to the small minority of rural settlements dominated by landholding groups, primarily Brahmins.[74] But the informal assembly (panchāyat) of village elders or all villagers is said to have been a general institution; [75] and its meetings apparently softened the authority of the headman. Since the villages, except for official demands, remained more or less in the charge of the headmen and their aides, they were indeed rural islands, enjoying partial autonomy.[76]

In the traditional Chinese village the local officials were still closer to the nonofficiating co-villagers, who, particularly when they belonged to wealthy or gentry families, might exert great influence in local affairs.[77] Criticism from an "out" group of fellow villagers might compel the headman and his supporters to resign. Under such pressure, a "band of men" who had been in power for a long time might withdraw "from their places, leaving them to those who offered the criticisms." [78]

Such behavior does not imply a formal democratic pattern; but it has a democratic flavor. Of course, there are various kinds of official requests; and there is always the constable, and often a tax collector, both government appointed and both spectacularly representing the interests of the bureaucratic apparatus. But here outside control usually ends. The government "places no practical restrictions upon the right of free assemblage by the people for the consideration of their own affairs. The people of any village can if they choose meet every day in the year. There is no government censor present, and no restriction upon liberty of debate. The people can say what they like, and the local Magistrate neither knows nor cares what is said." [79]

In many hydraulic civilizations the government was as little concerned about the internal affairs of the guilds. The Indian Law Books advised the king to recognize the statutes (laws) of the guilds.[80] And similar statutes existed elsewhere.[81] The Turkish guilds were subject to "the overriding authority of the temporal and spiritual powers, represented by governors, police officers, and *ḳâḍîs*"; [82] and their headmen were held responsible by the government for the execution of its fiscal tasks. However, otherwise and "within the limits imposed by religion, tradition, and 'usage,' . . . the corporations were relatively free and autonomous." [83] Gibb and Bowen therefore list them among "the *almost* self-governing groups." [84]

Gibb's and Bowen's formula is valid also for the secondary religions. All external restrictions notwithstanding, these religions did enjoy "some fragments of religious liberty." In traditional China the priests of the secondary religions, "seeking their own and other people's salvation, are not forbidden to preach, recite sutras, and perform ceremonies within doors." [85] And under Islam, "each non-Moslem congregation administers its own affairs under its responsible head, a rabbi, bishop, etc." [86] As long as their worship disturbed no "true believers," and as long as their organization presented no security threat, the government usually permitted the religious minorities to live, within their congregations, a more or less autonomous life.

5. Conclusion

a. Politically Irrelevant Freedoms

THESE are indeed modest freedoms! They occur in varying combinations in several spheres of life. And by now we should be able to understand why they do occur, and why they are so limited.

Hydraulic society is certainly not immune to rebellious movements, but kin organizations even in their extended forms are no political threat to a normally functioning agrobureaucratic despotism. Nor are the villages a serious threat. The relatively far-reaching autonomy of the traditional Chinese village could, in case of an insurrection, "be extinguished in a moment, a fact of which all the people are perfectly well aware." [87] Secondary religious groups might be a danger in times of great unrest. And this is probably why the government of imperial China never relaxed its control over the tolerated creeds and was so ready to suppress certain sects.[88] The rebellious potential inherent in the guilds was perhaps never completely eliminated, but the hydraulic government was able to paralyze it without exhausting its revenues.

Grunebaum finds it "remarkable to observe how little the Muslim state was really hampered in its operation by the dead weight of these semi-foreign organizations within its structure." [89] And others have commented in the same vein on the political effect of guilds in hydraulic civilizations. The early Byzantine state had no need to liquidate the still-existing Roman guilds, "since they were not at all dangerous politically, and since they could exert no pressure whatsoever on the government and administration, as did, for instance, the German guilds of the Middle Ages." [90] Massignon, who more than most of his colleagues considers the Muslim guilds at least temporarily a political factor, is nevertheless aware that they "never attained a political influence comparable to that of the medieval European guilds." [91] Gibb and Bowen consider the powers of the medieval guilds in Europe so much broader than those of the Islamic corporations that they doubt the suitability of the very term "guild" for the latter.[92] An equation between the guilds of the Medieval West and the guilds of India [93] or of China [94] has been rejected for similar reasons.

To be sure, there existed many resemblances between the two types of corporations, resemblances created by the peculiarities and needs of the organized professions; [95] but the profoundly different societal settings in which they operated gave them profoundly different political and social qualities. The guildsmen of the later European Middle Ages frequently became the masters of their towns; and as such they might play an active part in the power struggles of their time. The guildsmen of the hydraulic world were permitted a certain autonomy, not because, politically speaking, they were so strong, but because they were so irrelevant.

b. A Beggars' Democracy

IN modern totalitarian states the inmates of concentration and forced labor camps are permitted at times to gather in groups and talk at will; and not infrequently certain among them are given minor supervisory jobs. In terms of the law of diminishing administrative returns such "freedoms" pay well. While saving personnel, they in no way threaten the power of the commandant and his guards.

The villages, guilds, and secondary religious organizations of agro-managerial society were no terror camps. But like them they enjoyed certain politically irrelevant freedoms. These freedoms—which in some instances were considerable—did not result in full autonomy. At best they established a kind of Beggars' Democracy.

C. HYDRAULIC DESPOTISM—BENEVOLENT DESPOTISM?

1. TOTAL POWER—FOR THE BENEFIT OF THE PEOPLE?

THE hydraulic state is not checked by a Beggars' Democracy. Nor is it checked by any other effective constitutional, societal, or cultural counterweights. Clearly it is despotic. But does it not at the same time benefit the people?

2. THE CLAIM AND THE REALITY

a. Operational Necessity Not to Be Confused with Benevolence

THE hydraulic state is a managerial state, and certain of its operations do indeed benefit the people. But since the rulers depend on these operations for their own maintenance and prosperity, their policies can hardly be considered benevolent. A pirate does not act benevolently when he keeps his ship afloat or feeds the slaves he plans to sell. Capable of recognizing his future as well as his present advantages, he is rational but not benevolent. His behavior may temporarily benefit the persons in his power; but this is not its primary purpose. Given a choice, he will further his own interests, and not the interests of others.

b. The Rationality Coefficient of Hydraulic Society

ON the level of total power, the representatives of hydraulic regimes proceed in a similar way. Their behavior may to some degree benefit the persons in their power, and far-sighted advisors and statesmen may stress the importance of satisfying the people; [a] but taken as a group they consider the needs of their subjects in the light of their own needs and advantages. For this purpose they must (1) keep the agrarian economy going; (2) not increase corvée labor and taxes to a

a. For India see Bhagavadgītā, *passim*, and Manu, 1886: 229, 396 ff. For China: the sayings of Confucius and still more important, those of Mencius.

point where the discouraged peasants stop producing; and (3) not permit internal and external strife to disrupt the life of the population.

The third task—the maintenance of peace and order—confronts the governments of all societies. The first and second tasks distinguish hydraulic from other agrarian civilizations. The continued existence of agrarian despotism depends on the satisfactory execution of these three functions. They constitute what may be called the regime's rationality minimum.

Conquest societies, whose rulers are steeped in nonhydraulic traditions, often proceed along or near the lowest hydraulic rationality level. And endogenous masters frequently sink to this level during periods of decay and disintegration. Strong moves toward a higher rationality coefficient occur particularly during the earlier phases of endogenous rule, but they may also occur during later periods of growth or consolidation.

The formative phase of a conquest society is largely determined by the conquerors' ability to identify themselves with their new institutional environment. The Mongols were completely alien to the traditions and mores of the hydraulic civilizations they overran. Chingis Khan's son, Ogotai, is said to have planned to convert the cultivated fields of China into pastures; and he refrained from doing so only because Yeh-lü Ch'u-tsai convincingly explained to him the superior tax potential of the agrarian order.[1] But although the Mongols maintained the hydraulic economy of their new realm, they remained indifferent to its subtler needs. Virtually everywhere they stayed close to the rationality minimum of hydraulic society.

Mohammed, who lived in arid Arabia, certainly understood the importance of irrigation for successful crop-raising, although in his official utterances he rarely refers to the problem, and then essentially to small-scale (well) irrigation.[2] His followers preserved, restored, and even created vigorous hydraulic economies in Syria, Egypt, Iraq, Northwest Africa, Spain, and briefly also in Sicily. The Manchus were familiar with irrigation agriculture before they moved southward across the Great Wall to conquer China.[3] In this respect they were not unlike the Incas, who practiced irrigation in the Andean highlands before they established their hydraulic empire.[4] When they were overrun by the Spaniards, they were probably operating close to their rationality maximum.

c. Whose Rationality Coefficient?

BUT no matter whether a hydraulic society is operated crudely or subtly, the claim of benevolence compels us to ask: *cui bono?* Evidently operational tasks may be handled in a way that satisfies the interests of the rulers at the expense of the nongovernmental forces of society. Or they may be handled in a way that satisfies the needs of the people and gives few, if any, advantages to the government. Intermediate solutions compromise between the two extremes.

As a rule, the three alternatives are seriously considered only if the actual circumstances permit genuine choice. In the managerial, the consumptive, and the judicial spheres of hydraulic life this is indeed the case. But in all these spheres we find the people's interests sacrificed to the rulers' rationality optimum.

3. THE RULERS' RATIONALITY OPTIMUM PREVAILS

a. Necessity and Choice in the Policy of the Hydraulic Regime

IN the territorial states of ancient China, as in other hydraulic civilizations, philosophers discussed the alternatives of altruistic, balanced, or crudely selfish rule before the representatives of absolutist power. Confucius pointed out that Yü, the legendary founder of the protohistorical Hsia dynasty, ate coarse foods, dressed poorly, dwelt in a modest house, and concentrated his energies on the irrigation canals. This great culture hero, whom Confucius considered flawless,[5] combined a minimum of personal demand with a maximum of public devotion.

In the later period of China's early history the kings lived very comfortably; but the best among them are said to have sought a balance between their own and their subjects' interests. The philosopher Mencius, who discussed this point, did not challenge the rulers' right to build lofty edifices, parks, and ponds by corvée labor; but he asked that the people be permitted to share these enterprises with their king.[6]

Thus the philosophers of ancient China assumed that within the framework of governmental needs there existed genuine alternatives for action. Without exception, however, the masters of the agrarian apparatus state satisfied the constructional, organizational, and acquisitive needs of their realm with a maximum stress on their own advantage and a minimum stress on the requirements of their subjects.

b. The Rulers' Managerial Optimum

IN its early phase the hydraulic regime becomes stronger and wealthier with the growth of its hydraulic economy. But at a certain point the government can obtain additional revenue by intensifying its acquisitive rather than its productive operations. It is at this point that different power constellations lead to a different managerial optimum.

The rulers' managerial optimum is maintained whenever the government collects a maximum revenue with a minimum hydraulic effort. The people's managerial optimum is maintained whenever a maximum hydraulic achievement is accomplished with minimum administrative expense. Intermediate arrangements involve the collection of a large but not maximum revenue, a good part of which is used to produce sizable but not maximum hydraulic works.

The rulers' responses to these alternatives show clearly the effect of total power on those who wield it. Beyond the zone of stimulating discrepancy, they generally push only those hydraulic enterprises that improve their own well-being; and they are most ingenious in developing new methods of fiscal exploitation. In short, they aim at the rulers', and not at the people's, managerial optimum.

c. The Rulers' Consumptive Optimum

THREE major alternatives may also be distinguished in the sphere of consumption. The rulers' consumptive optimum is maintained whenever the masters of the hydraulic state arrogate to themselves a maximum of goods, which they may consume with a maximum of conspicuousness ("splendor"). The people's consumptive optimum is maintained whenever the nongovernmental members of society receive a maximum of goods, which they may consume as conspicuously as they please. Intermediate arrangements to some degree favor the representatives of the government without, however, seriously restricting the quality or conspicuousness of popular consumption.

Again the responses to these alternatives show the effect of total power on those who wield it. The proverbial splendor of Oriental despotism as well as the proverbial misery of its subjects have their roots in a policy that is directed toward the rulers', and not the people's, consumptive optimum.

This optimum has both an economic and a legal aspect. By concentrating the national surplus in their own hands, the rulers restrict the amount of goods physically available to nongovernmental consumers. By legally forbidding the general use of prestige-giving objects, they reserve to themselves conspicuous consumption. In simpler hydraulic civilizations both aims can be achieved without much difficulty. Increasing social differentiations complicate matters, but they do not preclude a situation that, for all practical purposes, realizes the rulers' optimum.

In the Inca empire the common people ate poorly and had little opportunity to drink heavily.[7] Their rulers ate extremely well, and they imbibed to excess.[8] Moreover, the gulf between the two groups was widened by laws which reserved the use of gold, silver, precious stones, colored feathers, and vicuña wool to the rulers. The commoners were permitted some modest ornaments, but even these could be worn only on special occasions.[9]

Arrangements of this kind are most easily enforced when the great majority of the commoners are peasants living in government-controlled and more or less equalitarian villages. The emergence of many property-based enterprises involves the growth of nonbureaucratic forms of wealth, both mobile and immobile; and such a development inevitably affects the pattern of consumption.

Even under these circumstances the bulk of the rural and urban population continues to live poorly; and the small stratum of nonbureaucratic property-holders sees their fortunes constantly threatened by taxation and confiscation (and in time split up through the laws of inheritance). But wherever large property-based business became essential, private wealth could not be eradicated, and those possessing it could not be prevented from enjoying at least some part of it.

Thus the laws which reserved certain types of dress or other conspicuous goods to the ruling class became a crucial means for placing the men of the governmental machine and the priests of the dominant religion above the mass of the commoners. In traditional China the officials and their nonofficiating relatives were distinguished by their houses, furniture, clothes, and vehicles.[10] The Indian Law Books prescribe very precisely the garments, girdles, staffs, etc. to be used by Brahmins, Kshatriyas, and Vaisyas.[11] In the Near East distinct bureaucratic features of dress are documented for Pharaonic Egypt,[12] Assyria,[13] Byzantium,[14] the Arab caliphate,[15] the Mamluks,[16] and Ottoman Turkey.[17]

Within the limits of these regulations the commoners might—theoretically speaking—enjoy their wealth. But they always hid their most precious possessions, and frequently their fear of confiscatory action was so great that they avoided all ostentation. The sweeping persecution of the merchants under the Earlier Han dynasty was provoked by the blatant show which the rich businessmen had made of their wealth.[18] Under a government which makes no effort to approach the rationality maximum, potential victims of confiscation may act with extreme caution. The French physician, Bernier, who from 1655 to 1658 lived in the Near East and afterward spent almost ten years in Mogul India, was struck by the frustrating atmosphere in which the businessmen of Asia operated. Enterprise found "little encouragement to engage in commercial pursuits," because greedy tyrants possessed "both power and inclination to deprive any man of the fruits of his industry." And "when wealth is acquired, as must sometimes be the case, the possessor, so far from living with increased comfort and assuming an air of independence, studies the means by which he may appear indigent: his dress, lodging, and furniture continue to be mean, and he is careful, above all things, never to indulge in the pleasures of the table." [19]

Bernier's observations must not be pressed. Under more far-sighted rulers the wealthy merchants of Asia lived luxuriously as long as their behavior did not invite disaster. And even in the India of Aurangzeb some few government-protected persons of wealth, Bernier tells us, "are at no pains to counterfeit poverty, but partake of the comforts and luxuries of life." [20]

But such exceptions do not negate the basic trend. In hydraulic civilizations wealthy commoners were denied the proprietary security which the burghers of the later Middle Ages enjoyed; and they did not dare to engage in the conspicuous consumption which the medieval businessmen practiced, despite the many sumptuary laws to which they too had to submit. The lavish display by the representatives of the state on the one side and the predominance of genuine and feigned poverty on the other spectacularly show the effect of total power on the consumptive optimum of hydraulic society.

d. The Rulers' Judicial Optimum

SIMILARLY one-sided decisions characterize the judicial field. As explained above, no society is without standardized norms; and few advanced agrarian civilizations are without written or codified laws. Thus it is the special setting and intent that separate the laws of hydraulic despotism from those of pluralistically controlled states.

The rulers' judicial optimum is maintained whenever the representatives of government exert a maximum influence on the formulation and application of their country's laws. The people's judicial optimum is maintained whenever the nongovernmental elements of society are decisive. In democratic commonwealths the constitutionally qualified citizen may participate in the formulation of the laws. He may exercise the functions of a judge, as he did in democratic Athens, or he may, as a lay juror, cooperate with professionally trained, but elected judges. In both cases the nongovernmental forces of society, and not a despotic state, are charged with the application of the law. Intermediate variants are characterized by an increased, but not absolute, governmental power and by a proportionately decreased popular control over the legislature and judiciary.

It is obvious that the first type of judicial optimum prevails in hydraulic society. And it is equally obvious that in the judicial sphere, as in others, the masters of the hydraulic state seek a maximum of results (internal order) with a minimum of governmental effort and expense. This they accomplish not by yielding important judicial functions to quasi-independent secondary centers of power, as did the sovereigns of feudal Europe,[b] but by permitting politically irrelevant groups to handle certain of their own legal affairs, or by permitting magistrates to handle legal matters along with their other duties, or, where professional judges are the rule, by having as few full-time judges as possible.

Such conditions preclude the development of independent juries. They discourage elaborate judicial procedures. And they leave little room for the functioning of independent professional lawyers. With these limitations the judges of a hydraulic society settle legal cases —many of which arise from clashes of proprietary interests, and in countries with a highly commercialized urban life this field of action may become very important indeed.[21]

However, even at their rational best, the laws of such countries express a fundamentally unbalanced societal situation. Even if they protect one commoner against the other, they do not protect the commoners—as individuals or as a group—against the absolutist state. Shortly after Bernier had commented on this phenomenon, John Locke did likewise; and his references to Ottoman Turkey, Ceylon, and Tsarist Russia show him aware that the tyrannical variant of judicial procedure, which English autocracy failed to develop fully, flourished unhampered under Oriental despotism.

Locke insists that the presence of laws in a despotic regime proves nothing as to their justness:

> "if it be asked what security, what fence is there in such a state against the violence and oppression of this absolute ruler, the very question can scarce be borne. They are ready to tell you that it deserves death only to ask after safety. Betwixt subject and subject, they will grant, there must be measures, laws, and judges for their mutual peace and security. But as for the ruler, he ought to be absolute, and is above all such circumstances; because he has a power to do more hurt and wrong, it is right

b. The holders of office land and the tax collectors who occasionally act as judges are, either fully or partially, integrated in the bureaucratic apparatus. See below, Chap. 8.

when he does it. To ask how you may be guarded from harm or injury on that side, where the strongest hand is to do it, is presently the voice of faction and rebellion. As if when men, quitting the state of nature, entered into society, they agreed that all of them but one should be under the restraint of laws; but that he should still retain all the liberty of the state of Nature, increased with power, and made licentious by impunity. This is to think that men are so foolish that they take care to avoid what mischiefs may be done them by polecats or foxes, but are content, nay, think it safety, to be devoured by lions.[22]

4. "ABSOLUTE POWER CORRUPTS ABSOLUTELY"

THIS is a bitter indictment. Contrary to modern apologists for totalitarian laws and constitutions, Locke refuses to put any trust in the autocrat's potential benevolence: "he that thinks absolute power purifies men's blood, and corrects the baseness of human nature, need read but the history of this, or any other age, to be convinced to the contrary." [23] Lord Acton's affirmative version of Locke's thesis is well known: "Power tends to corrupt and absolute power corrupts absolutely." [24]

Acceptance of this idea need not include an acceptance of Locke's pessimistic views on "the baseness of human nature." Man acts from many motives, which under different circumstances operate with different strengths. Both self-centeredness and community-centeredness seek expression; and it depends on the cultural heritage and the over-all setting whether one or the other of them will prevail. A governmental—or proprietary—order leading to the emergence of absolute power encourages and enables the holders of this power to satisfy their own interests absolutely. It is for this reason that agrarian despotism, like industrial despotism, corrupts absolutely those who bask in the sun of total power.

5. THE RULERS' PUBLICITY OPTIMUM

THE corrupting influence is further consolidated by a one-sidedly manipulated public opinion. Public opinion may be shaped in a number of ways; and here, as elsewhere, the rulers' and the people's interests diverge sharply. This becomes clear as soon as the major alternatives are outlined.

The rulers' publicity optimum is maintained whenever the government's real or alleged achievements are given a maximum of uncritical publicity, while the people's experiences, sufferings, and views receive a minimum of notice. The people's publicity optimum combines a full presentation of the government's achievements and shortcomings. Intermediate arrangements favor the government without keeping the nongovernmental forces of society from stating their own case.

Independent popular criticism differs both in quality and intent from the many and continued criticisms made by leading members of the officialdom. Bureaucratic criticism is vital to the proper functioning of complex administration, but it is voiced either behind closed doors or in publications accessible only to a limited number of educated persons, who are usually members of the ruling group. In both cases, the people's problems are viewed essentially from the standpoint of a more or less rationally conceived government interest.[c]

Wielding total power, the masters of the hydraulic state can readily maintain the rulers' publicity optimum. Under socially un-differentiated conditions, the government's (frequently the sovereign's) voice drowns out all criticism except as it may appear in such inconsequential media as popular tales and songs. More differentiated conditions provide additional outlets in secondary religions and philosophies, in popular short stories, novels, and plays. But even these media remain significantly feeble. In contrast to the independent writers who, under Western absolutism, challenged not only the excesses but the foundations of the despotic order, the critics of hydraulic society have in almost every case complained only of the misdeeds of individual officials or of the evils of specific governmental acts.[d] Apart from mystics who teach total withdrawal from the world, these critics aim ultimately at regenerating a system of total power, whose fundamental desirability they do not doubt.

6. THE TWO-FOLD FUNCTION OF THE BENEVOLENCE MYTH

a. It Stresses the Long-range Interest of the Despotic Regime

THE advantages of the benevolence myth for the despotism which it glorifies are twofold. By presenting the ruler and his aides as

c. In the total managerial societies of today, state-directed popular criticism is used to supplement and dramatize the government's criticism of problematic elements, particularly in the middle and lower echelons of the bureaucracy. Criticism of this kind has been encouraged in many hydraulic societies. The letters to Stalin differ technically, but not institutionally, from the letters and petitions addressed in the past to Oriental despots.

d. Often government functionaries indict blundering fellow functionaries or harmful administrative procedures more sharply than do persons who are not part of the regime.

eager to achieve the people's rationality optimum, they enable the official spokesmen to educate and discipline the members of their own group. The holder of power, who operates below the rulers' rationality minimum, endangers the safety of the governmental apparatus, whereas one who operates above this level enhances the stability of the regime. He exploits his orchard as an intelligent gardener should.[26] Moreover, the ruler and his men must not weaken their position by crude managerial neglect, excessive taxation, or provocative injustice. The myth of an unselfish (benevolent) despotism dramatizes these desiderata which, consciously or unconsciously, are underwritten by all thoughtful members of the ruling class.

b. It Weakens Potential Opposition

MORE important still than the impact of the benevolence myth on the holders of power is its effect on the nongovernmental forces of society. The myth admits that individual sovereigns and officials may be unworthy, but it depicts the despotic order as fundamentally good—in fact, as the only reasonable and commendable system of government.

Thus the embittered subject, who is permanently exposed to such propaganda, cannot well strive for the creation of a new and less despotic order. He and others who feel as he does may withdraw to the mountains. They may kill some local officials. They may defeat the government's men in arms. They may even overthrow a tottering dynasty. But eventually they will only revive—and rejuvenate—the agromanagerial despotism whose incompetent representatives they eliminated. The heroes of China's famous bandit novel, the *Shui-hu Ch'uan,* could think of nothing better to do than to set up on their rebel island a miniature version of the very bureaucratic hierarchy which they were so fiercely combating.

c. The Presence of Good Sovereigns and Just Officials Fails to Upset the Prevailing Trend

IF man were exclusively self-centered, the result of all this would be very simple indeed. And very sad. But man is also community-centered. And this side of his character finds expression also in hydraulic society. To be sure, under the conditions of agrarian despotism, it is difficult to be a good sovereign or a just official. But it is not impossible. Throughout the hydraulic world serious-minded rulers attended to their managerial and judicial duties conscientiously, and honest officials strove to prevent fiscal and judicial oppression. Courageous functionaries insisted on what they considered proper policies, although by doing so they opposed the wishes of powerful superiors, and occasionally even of the sovereign himself.

But those who pursue such a course clash with the interest of the vast self-indulgent and scheming ruling group; and history shows that only a handful of unusually community-minded (ethically "possessed") persons was so disposed. Furthermore, even this pathetically small number of "good" men was not completely aware of how slanted the rulers' optimum was, which they recommended. Confucius' gentleman bureaucrat, the ideal ruler of the *Bhagavadgītā*, and the "just" statesmen of the ancient Roman or Islamic Near East all try to be fair within the framework of a society which takes the patterns of despotic power, revenue, and prestige for granted.

7. Hydraulic Despotism: Benevolent In Form, Oppressive in Content

Thus agromanagerial despots may present their regimes as benevolent; actually, however, and even under the most favorable circumstances, they strive for their own, and not for the people's, rationality optimum. They plan their hydraulic enterprises according to what benefits their might and wealth. And they write their own ticket as fiscal masters of the national surplus and as conspicuous consumers.

Stalin claims that in a modern industrial apparatus state the culture of a national minority is national in form and socialist in content.[26] Experience shows that the "socialist" (read: *apparatchik*) substance quickly wipes out all but the most insignificant national elements. A similar mechanism is at work in the agrarian apparatus state. Paraphrasing Stalin's formula and replacing myth by reality, we may truthfully say that hydraulic despotism is benevolent in form and oppressive in content.

CHAPTER 5

Total terror—total submission —total loneliness

A. AUTONOMOUS MAN UNDER TOTAL POWER

MAN is no ant. His efforts to escape from freedom [1] show him ambivalently attracted by what he ambivalently abandons. The urge to act independently is an essential attribute of *homo sapiens,* and a highly complex one. Not all of its components are socially valuable; but among them is man's most precious motivating force: the urge to obey his conscience, all external disadvantages notwithstanding.

What happens to man's desire for autonomy under the conditions of total power? One variant of total power, hydraulic despotism, tolerates no relevant political forces besides itself. In this respect it succeeds on the institutional level because it blocks the development of such forces; and it succeeds on the psychological level, because it discourages man's desire for independent political action. In the last analysis, hydraulic government is government by intimidation.

B. TERROR ESSENTIAL FOR MAINTAINING THE RULERS' RATIONALITY OPTIMUM

1. THE NEED

MAN is no ant. But neither is he a stone. A policy that upholds the rulers' publicity optimum confuses the people's mind, without however eliminating their feelings of frustration and unhappiness. Unchecked, these feelings may lead to rebellious action. To counter this dangerous trend the hydraulic regime resorts to intimidation. Terror is the inevitable consequence of the rulers' resolve to uphold their own and not the people's rationality optimum.

2. Its Official Recognition: "Punishment Is the King!"

MANY spokesmen of hydraulic despotism have emphasized the need for rule by punishment. Such a policy may be justified by the argument that guiltless people are few.[1] Confucius preferred education to punishment; yet he, too, believed that it would take a hundred years of good government "to transform the violently bad and to dispense with capital punishment." [2]

Thus with varying arguments, punishment has been viewed as an essential tool of successful statecraft. The Hindu law book of Manu establishes fear-inspiring punishment as the foundation of internal peace and order. Punishment, which—of course—must be just, makes everyone behave properly.[3] Without it caste barriers would be crossed; and all men would turn against their fellows. "Where Punishment with a black hue and red eye stalks about," [4] subjects live at peace. *The whole world is kept in order by punishment.*" [5]

By punishment the ruler protects the weak against the strong, sacrifice against animal violation, property against its (nongovernmental) enemies and social superiority against assaults from below. "If the king did not, without tiring, inflict punishment on those worthy to be punished, the stronger would roast the weaker, like fish on a spit: The crow would eat the sacrificial cake and the dog would lick the sacrificial viands, and ownership would not remain with any one, the lower ones would (usurp the place of) the higher ones." [6] Thus "punishment alone governs all created beings, punishment alone protects them, punishment watches over them while they sleep." [7] Indeed, "punishment is . . . the king." [8]

The rulers of ancient Mesopotamia claimed that they received their power from the great Enlil.[9] This terrifying god symbolizes "the power of force, of compulsion. Opposing wills are crushed and beaten into submission." [10] Although he is supposed to use his cruel might judiciously,[11] "man can never be fully at ease with Enlil but feels a lurking fear." [12] This being so, the sovereign's readiness to identify himself with Enlil or with deities descended from him is deeply significant. The Sumerian kings usually identified themselves with Enlil directly.[13] The Babylonians upheld the basic idea, but modified it. Hammurabi pictured himself as having been "called" by Enlil; and he names Enlil's son, Sin, as his divine father.[14] In both cases the Mesopotamian rulers stressed the terroristic quality of their position.

The terror inherent in Pharaonic despotism is symbolized by the poisonous Uraeus snake, which lies coiled on the ruler's forehead and threatens his enemies with destruction.[15] The king's actions are also compared with those of the fear-inspiring lion goddess, Sekhmet.[a]

Chinese statecraft learned to express its need for terrifying punishment in the rational and moral form of Confucianism. But punishment was the primary weapon of the so-called Legalists and of such Legalist-influenced Confucianists as Hsün Tsŭ. And it remained a cornerstone of official policy throughout the imperial period. What we would call the Ministry of Justice was known in traditional China as the Ministry of Punishments.

The Islamic ruler saw to it that he was both respected and feared.[16] The *Arabian Nights,* which depicts Harun al-Rashīd usually accompanied by his executioner, presents in fictional dress a historic truth. The executioner was a standard feature of the Abbassid court.

3. THE MORPHOLOGY OF VIOLENCE

To be sure, all governments deserving the name have ways of imposing their will on their subjects, and the use of violence is always among them. But different societies develop different patterns of integrating (or fragmenting) violence and of controlling (or not controlling) it.

a. Integrated versus Fragmented Patterns of Violence

In ancient Greece, free men ordinarily wore arms—according to Thucydides, "because their homes were undefended." [17] In other words, the government did not monopolize the use of force. With the growth of public safety the early custom disappeared in most city states; [18] but the citizens, who were potential warriors, were still permitted to keep the tools of violence in their homes. Pictorial evidence portraying the start of a campaign shows "mostly the woman bringing the weapons from the home to the departing man." [19]

In Medieval Europe the semi-independent feudal lords from the beginning represented important secondary centers of military action, and in the course of time many towns developed their own armed forces. These feudal and urban nuclei of political and military life were free to use violence both within their own jurisdictions and against one another. The vassal, who appeared before his sovereign

a. See Breasted, 1927, I: 327, and cf. II: 92, and IV: 166; Erman, 1923: 78 ff.; and Wilson, 1950: 11. According to one story, Sekhmet emerged as the suppressor of a conspiracy. When the supreme god Re "perceived the things which were being plotted against him by mankind," he conjured up a force to crush the evil schemers. Then "Sekhmet came into being." She quickly "prevailed over mankind," and desiring to drink human blood—or what she believed to be human blood, "she drank, and it was good in her heart" (Wilson, 1950: 11). Cf. Erman, 1923: 78 ff.

with his sword at his side, expressed strikingly the fragmented and balanced pattern of violence that characterized feudal society.

Concentration of the legitimate uses of force in the hands of the state does not occur under conditions of total power only. Modern constitutional government restricts private violence more and more. But it differs from agrarian and industrial apparatus states in that the size, quality and use of coercion (army and police) are determined by the nongovernmental forces of society. The experiences of classical Greece and the modern West show that a country may rally powerful armies without its citizens losing control over them.

b. Controlled versus Uncontrolled Violence

ARMY discipline requires unquestioning subordination; and the commander in chief of a well-coordinated army—which the feudal hosts were not—rules absolutely within the limits of his jurisdiction. However, in a democratic country he remains responsible to the citizens who control the government. General Eisenhower's comments on the Soviet method of attacking through mine fields indicate the institutional alternatives. In "a matter-of-fact statement" Marshal Zhukov explained to the American general: "When we come to a mine field our infantry attacks exactly as if it were not there. The losses we get from personnel mines we consider only equal to those we would have gotten from machine guns and artillery if the Germans had chosen to defend that particular area with strong bodies of troops instead of with mine fields." Eisenhower adds drily: "I had a vivid picture of what would happen to any American or British commander if he pursued such tactics, and I had an even more vivid picture of what the men in any one of our divisions would have to say about the matter had we attempted to make such a practice a part of our tactical doctrine." [20]

The Soviet way saves materiel and time; and it suits to perfection the rulers' tactical optimum. Obviously this optimum can be realized only when organized violence is wielded by the masters of an unchecked state. The social quality of organized violence, like that of other governmental functions, changes with the over-all setting in which it develops.

C. THE TERROR OF HYDRAULIC DESPOTISM

THE subjects of an agrarian apparatus state have little opportunity to argue the problem of uncontrolled violence. They may be permitted the possession of small and simple weapons, particularly in the villages, which have to ward off bandits. But the organized and military use of coercion is essentially concentrated in the hands of the absolutist rulers, who usually give audience only to unarmed men. In hydraulic society the monster with "a black hue and red eye" is no watch-dog tied up by the people, but a tiger that moves at will.

1. ITS PHYSICAL ASPECT

LIKE the tiger, the engineer of power must have the physical means with which to crush his victims. And the agromanagerial despot does indeed possess such means. He exercises unchecked control over the army, the police, the intelligence service; and he has at his disposal jailers, torturers, executioners, and all the tools that are necessary to catch, incapacitate, and destroy a suspect.

2. ITS PSYCHOLOGICAL ASPECT

a. Unpredictability

FURTHERMORE, he can employ these devices with maximum psychological effect. Everywhere persons wielding great governmental or proprietary power like to shroud certain of their acts in secrecy; but the procedures of a despotic government are enigmatic because of the very nature of the regime. Accountable only to themselves, the men of the apparatus tend to handle even insignificant matters with secretiveness; and they raise mystification to an art when they want to intimidate and surprise. Unpredictability is an essential weapon of absolute terror.

b. Lenin: ". . . power not limited by any laws"

LENIN defined the dictatorship of the proletariat—which he held to be the heart of the Soviet regime—as "a power not limited by any laws." [1] Like other utterances of Lenin, this formula combines an impressive half-truth with important fallacies. First, the Soviet dictatorship was never controlled by the Russian workers; and there is ample evidence that Lenin knew this. Second, no regime, however dictatorial, operates without normative regulations or laws of some kind; and this, too, was well known to Lenin. Before he made the just-quoted statement, his dictatorial government had already issued many revolutionary statutes and decrees.[2] The despot's right to interpret, change, and override previously established laws is a fundamental constitutional and legal principle of absolutist rule. Lenin's definition stresses with brutal frankness the dictator's unchecked power to use laws as he wishes. In the sphere of terror he may go so far that it becomes difficult to distinguish between lawless terror and terror by law.

c. Lawless Terror and Terror by Law

A CHIEF or ruler does not necessarily override the laws of his hydraulic community when he himself commits—or gives orders to commit—acts of terrifying brutality.

In smaller hydraulic tribes autocratic cruelty is no issue, because the chief, being close to his fellow tribesmen, is unable to exert power over and above his directing functions. This is the case among the Suk and their hydraulic neighbors and throughout the American Pueblos.

In larger hydraulic tribes the chief may seek to bolster his incipient autocracy by the employment of spectacular terror. A Chagga chief, for instance, may commit all manner of cruelties against his subjects. Ndeserno is said to have torn the hearts from his victims' bodies while they were still alive and to have had them roasted for his children.[3] A chieftain who went to such extremes was contemplated with grave apprehension, but, according to Gutmann, "such cruelties against individuals did not harm his prestige." On the contrary, the fear they inspired cemented the stability of the regime.[4]

The spectacular terror directed by the rulers of ancient Hawaii may well have served the same purpose;[5] and the so-called Cannibal Texts of the Old Kingdom suggest a similar situation in prehistoric Egypt. One of these texts, found in a pyramid, reveals a dead ruler killing, dissecting, and cooking human beings in the nether world for his gustatory pleasure;[6] and another reveals him as taking "the wives from their husbands whenever he wants to and according to his heart's desire."[a]

In more differentiated hydraulic civilizations, there is less need to bulwark the ruler's exalted position by spectacular acts of autocratic ruthlessness. Although such acts do not completely cease, they are now initiated mainly by excessively cruel (and/or insecure) sovereigns and by the heads of dynasties which operate below the rulers' rationality maximum. Gaudefroy-Demombynes describes the irrationally terroristic quality of the Abbassid caliphate as follows: "Improvised executions and the exhibition of heads are part of the regular life of the Abbassid court. Beginning with the reign of El Mançour, when a person is urgently summoned to the palace by the guards of the caliph, he feels that he has a good chance not to

a. Sethe, PT, II: 354 ff. The Chagga chiefs seem to have made a like claim on all girls and women of their realm (Widenmann, 1899: 48; cf. Gutmann, 1909: 25).

return alive. He makes his testament, says farewell to his family, and carries his shroud under his arm." [b]

In these and other instances, the ruler's terroristic behavior was above rather than against the law. On the other hand, officials who resorted to extreme brutalities often went beyond even the broadest possible interpretation of the law. At times they might be held accountable. But many "lawless" bureaucratic terrorists were criticized only after they were dead.

The excesses of autocratic and bureaucratic terror are an extreme manifestation of human behavior under total power. Institutionally, however, they are probably less important than the innumerable acts of terror that were perpetrated as a matter of routine and within the flexible frame of despotic law. It was this routine terror in managerial, fiscal, and judicial procedures that caused certain observers to designate the government of hydraulic despotism as "government by flogging."

3. "Government by Flogging"

a. Terror in Managerial Procedures

"The language of the whip" seems to have been employed regularly in the state corvées of ancient Sumer.[7] Under the Pharaohs, every government administrator could resort to corporal punishment.[8] The pictorial records of ancient Egypt show men conducting all manner of public enterprises with sticks in their hands.[9] In the later part of the 19th century, when the British began to abolish "government by flogging," the whip was still standard equipment for insuring the success of the hydraulic corvée.[10] Present-day writers who are greatly impressed by the planned economy of the Incas would do well to remember that the Inca prince, Garcilaso de la Vega, glorying in his forebears' achievements, took it for granted that the one sure way to make people industrious was to threaten them with beating.[11]

b. Terror in Fiscal Procedures

Since the days of the Pharaohs, reluctance in paying taxes was overcome by force. A famous satire of the New Kingdom tells that the Egyptian peasant who failed to deliver his quota of grain was "beaten, tied up, and thrown into the ditch."[12] Irregularities in

b. Gaudefroy-Demombynes, 1931: 384. The friend of an Abbassid caliph, who went to the court every Friday, was "gripped by an intense fear" when he was summoned on a different day. Had he been maligned? Had he been found wanting? His "anguish and fear" increased until he discovered to his immense relief that the sovereign merely wanted him to share an hour of idleness and pleasure (Sauvaget, 1946: 62).

handling state and temple property also called for corporal punishment.[13]

The Sacred Law of Islam prohibited torture; but the tax officials of the caliphs apparently found it impossible to fulfill their task without resorting to violence.[14] Under the Abbassid dynasty, torture was a concomitant of tax gathering until the year 800; and after a short interlude of about twelve years it was invoked again, and as brutally as ever. Government agents "beat the people, imprisoned them, and suspended heavy men by one arm so that they almost died."[15]

The *Arthashāstra* made it mandatory for police and court judges to see that rural taxes were duly paid, and to use force if necessary.[16] The Law Code of imperial China prescribed beating as the standard punishment for persons who failed to fulfill their fiscal obligations.[17]

c. Terror in Judicial Procedures

THE Chinese Code carried the issue of violence beyond the spheres of fiscal action. In case of continued resistance and/or inability to deliver, the defaulter might be taken before a judge; and if necessary, fiscal terror might be replaced by judicial terror. Judicial torture to extort evidence—and frequently also to punish—was employed in virtually all hydraulic civilizations.

In Pharaonic Egypt beating was a regular adjunct of judicial procedures.[18] "He was examined with the rod" was standard phrasing in the New Kingdom.[19]

Indian, Chinese, and Islamic sources describe judicial terror in considerable detail. The *Arthashāstra* states that "Those whose guilt is *believed to be true* shall be subjected to torture."[20] With the exception of the Brahmins,[c] they could be given the "six punishments," the "seven kinds of whipping," the "two kinds of suspension from above," and the "water-tube."[21] Regarding persons "who have committed grave offences," the famous book is still more specific. They could be given the

> nine kinds of blows with a cane: 12 beats on each of the thighs; 28 beats with a stick of the tree (nakta-mala); 32 beats on each palm of the hands and on each sole of the feet; two on the knuckles, the hands being joined so as to appear like a scorpion; two kinds of suspensions, face downwards (ullambane chale); burning one of the joints of a finger after the accused has been

c. They could not be tortured to extort evidence; but if found guilty of a very grave crime, they could be branded (*Arthaśāstra*, 1923: 270).

made to drink rice gruel; heating his body for a day after he has been made to drink oil; causing him to lie on coarse grass for a night in winter. These are the 18 kinds of torture. . . . Each day a fresh kind of the torture may be employed.[22]

In particularly serious cases, such as attempts to seize the king's treasury, the accused could be "subjected once or many times to one or all of the above kinds of torture." [23]

The Chinese Law Code describes a number of instruments used to extract evidence; [24] and the writings of sincere administrators elaborate on proper and improper methods of torture.[25]

Canonic prohibitions notwithstanding, the secular courts of the caliphs extorted evidence by employing "the whip, the end of a rope, the stick, and the strap on the back and belly, on the back of the head, the lower parts of the body, feet, joints, and muscles." [26]

Similar methods seem to have persisted in the Near East until recent days. In 19th-century Egypt, "justice, such as it was, was almost as much a terror to the innocent witness as to the accused person against whom testimony was borne." [27]

d. Western Correspondences Noteworthy for Their Temporary Strength and Their Limitations

MANIFESTLY, judicial torture is widespread in the hydraulic world. But is it specific? After all, torture had a definite place in Roman law. It appears prominently in late feudal and postfeudal Western legal procedures and in the Inquisition. And it survives today in the third degree.

All these phenomena must indeed be recognized for what they are. They remind us grimly that human nature is the same everywhere and that man succumbs to the corrupting influence of power whenever circumstances permit. Fortunately, the shape of Western institutions kept these inclinations from asserting themselves lastingly. But the momentum they gained at certain times and in certain places precludes the complacent assumption that what happened under hydraulic governments—and what is happening today in the totalitarian states—cannot happen here.

The indigenous free men of ancient Greece and republican Rome did not employ managerial or fiscal terror against their fellow citizens—the citizens did not render corvée service nor did they pay substantial taxes—and "as a rule" they were not subjected to judicial torture.[28] Their societal order was too balanced for this; yet it was not sufficiently balanced to prevent the use of managerial and judicial terror against certain alien and unfree elements. In Greece, the position of most slaves was "not much different from that of domestic animals." [29] Their masters were free to punish them physically; [30] and the not too numerous state slaves occupied in public works were directed by foremen, who, frequently slaves themselves, "had a name for being very hard." [31] In Greece both slaves and free aliens were the targets of judicial torture.[32] In republican Rome only slaves were so treated.[33]

The crystallization of absolutist power under the empire deprived the Roman citizens of the protection which their forefathers had enjoyed against judicial and other forms of governmental terror. Roman law in late Roman and Byzantine times extended judicial torture to the bulk of all free persons.[34]

A similar change occurred in the later part of the Middle Ages. Early Frankish (Salic) law permitted only persons of servile status to be tortured.[35] Conflicts between free men were handled by courts composed of peers. Serious legal issues were settled by ordeal or judicial combat; [36] and the burghers in medieval towns, who originally followed these procedures, soon preferred more humane and rational methods of determining guilt or innocence.[37]

The introduction of judicial torture—significantly bulwarked by references to Roman law—coincides with the rise of centralized and despotic power on a territorial and national scale.[38] Most historians point out that the procedures of the absolutist courts superseded the feudal methods of ordeal and combat.[d] Less frequently do they mention the equally important fact that the new judicial torture also replaced the significant beginnings of rational judicial procedure developed in the burgher-controlled towns.[e]

Changes in judicial procedures were certainly intensified by the Inquisition; and anyone who studies this period is struck by the elaborate and cruel tortures employed in questioning heretics. However, three points deserve attention: First, the Church, which based itself on medieval Canonic Law, did not originally recommend the use of extreme measures against heretics.[39] Second, judicial torture was probably initiated by secular agencies.[f] Third, terroristic procedures were equally harsh under those absolutist governments of Europe which, in the course of the Reformation, had dissociated

d. Cf. Petit-Dutaillis, 1949: 309; Lea, 1892: 480, 487 ff., 500 ff., 505. Lea describes in some detail what he calls the "resistance of feudalism" to the development of judicial torture (1892: 494 ff.). See also Williams, 1911: 72.

e. In the 14th century the Italian communities continued to combat the increasing use of torture (Lea, 1892: 506 ff.); and in Lübeck, Germany's foremost city of burgher independence, legal orders discouraging ordeal, judicial duel, and torture yielded but slowly to the new absolutist law (ibid.: 483).

f. Lea, 1908, I: 221; cf. Guiraud, 1929: 86. In the 12th century, long before judicial torture was institutionalized, heretics had been tortured to death (Helbing, 1926: 106 ff.).

themselves from Rome.[40] No doubt the disintegration of medieval society stimulated both heretic tendencies and the fanatic desire to eradicate them; but it was only within the framework of rising absolutist state power that this desire took the form of the Inquisition.

The limitations of Western absolutism also determined the point beyond which the representatives of despotic power could not subdue their own subjects. For a time they were able to employ judicial terror in secular and religious matters, but managerial and fiscal terror were not invoked against the bulk of the population. With the rise of modern industrial society judicial torture was eliminated in the heartlands of European absolutism, and eventually also in the terror-ridden slave economy of our southern states. Presently, public opinion is crusading against such police actions as the third degree. These methods were never legal; their illegal use is receding before the growing vigilance and strength of public-minded citizen organizations.

Pre-Mongol ("Kievan") Russia accepted many elements of Byzantine law, but not the use of corporal punishment. This device, as well as judicial torture, seems to have emerged in Russia only when an Oriental type of despotism arose during and after the Tatar period.[41] Third degree methods continued to be employed until the last decades of the Tsarist regime; [42] but torture as a means of getting evidence was discarded early in the 19th century, when the growth of property-based industrial forms of life promoted the restriction of many absolutist features of Russian law and society.[g] It was left to the masters of the Communist apparatus state to reverse the humanizing trend and to reintroduce the systematic infliction of physical pain for the purpose of extracting "confessions." [h]

4. VARYING CONFIGURATIONS OF TERROR IN THE HYDRAULIC WORLD

a. Relatively Lenient Developments

IN different areas and phases of the hydraulic world the methods of terror differed. The indigenous Babylonian government, for in-

g. Lea, 1892: 581; Williams, 1911: 79. For occasional late occurrences see Williams, *loc. cit.*, and Scott, 1943: 264. George Kennan, who at the close of the 19th century, studied the life of political prisoners and exiles in Siberia, draws attention to the arbitrary methods employed by the Tsarist police: unjust arrests and imprisonment, beating and torturing (Kennan, 1891, II: 52 ff.). These methods were certainly brutal, but the growing strength of public opinion restricted them increasingly; and a comparison of the conditions described by Kennan and those to which Soviet prisoners are subjected today reveals an abysmal retrogression in judicial procedure.

h. The Communist methods of judicial terror vary with time, space, circumstance,

stance, proceeded close to the rulers' rationality maximum; and Babylonian laws known to us mention, as means of establishing guilt or innocence, the ordeal, the oath, and witnesses, but not torture.[43] To be sure, judicial torture may well have been employed in cases involving the security of the regime (the Code does not discuss these matters); even for minor offenses against the interests of the government punishment was terrifyingly harsh; [i] and there is no reason to assume that the "language of the whip," which accompanied the Sumerian corvée, was not used by Babylonian master builders and master irrigators. But while the Babylonian state, local administrative councils notwithstanding, remained an absolutist regime, it acted as rationally in judicial and many other matters as could be expected under the conditions of an agromanagerial system of total power.

b. Average and Excessive Developments

IN most hydraulic civilizations the rulers employed fully all major forms of terror, the managerial, the fiscal, and the judicial. In doing so, they established procedural averages, which occasionally were codified. These averages usually sufficed to satisfy the needs of the regime; but not infrequently those who applied them resorted to methods of extreme brutality, which besides producing quicker results, yielded a surplus income for the officials who perpetrated them.

As shown above, not all officials went to such lengths; and for various reasons extreme malpractice might be punished. But "moderate" excesses tended to remain unchallenged. And from

---

and purpose; but despite a certain ingenuity in applying psychological devices, the main techniques can hardly be claimed as inventions. The "keeping-awake" torture, a seemingly mild but actually irresistible way of breaking the will of a person under interrogation, appeared in the Roman arsenal of planned cruelty under the name *tormentum vigiliae* (Helbing, 1926: 45). It was re-"invented" in 1532 by Hippolytus de Marsiliis (Williams, 1911: 77). The starvation torture was known as *tormentum famis* (Helbing, 1926: 45). Certain Communist methods parallel procedure used by the Inquisition. Compare the abrupt changes from bad to good treatment and from good treatment to bad, and the facing of the prisoner with confessions or alleged confessions of others (Lea, 1908, I: 415 ff.). Cruder methods of torture, beginning with simple beating—Roman forerunner: the *verbera* (Helbing, 1926: 45)—attain their goal faster than the more "cultivated" *tormentum vigiliae*. They seem to be extensively employed particularly in times of crisis, such as the Great Purge, World War II, and the period of continued stress that followed this war (see Beck and Godin, 1951: 53 ff.; Weissberg, 1951: 238 ff., 242, 246, 296; SLRUN, 1949: 56, 67, 74 ff.). Of course, many Soviet modes of torture were foreshadowed by Ivan IV and his successors.

i. Stealing government or temple property was punished with death (Hammurabi, Secs. 6, 8. See also translator Meek's note 45.

the standpoint of the commoner, the despotic apparatus remained irrationally formidable even when it employed only the standard methods of terror. It became frightening when it exhausted its terroristic potential.

D. TOTAL SUBMISSION

1. MAN'S RESPONSE TO THE THREAT OF TOTAL TERROR

a. The Postulate of Common Sense and the Virtue of Good Citizenship: Obedience

LIVING under the threat of total terror, the members of a hydraulic community must shape their behavior accordingly. If they want to survive, they must not provoke the uncontrollable monster. To the demands of total authority common sense recommends one answer: obedience. And ideology stereotypes what common sense recommends. Under a despotic regime, obedience becomes the basis of good citizenship.

Of course, life in any community requires some degree of coordination and subordination; and the need for obedience is never completely lacking. But in the great agrarian societies of the West obedience is far from being a primary virtue.

In the democratic city states of ancient Greece the good citizen was expected to display four major qualities: military courage, religious devotion, civic responsibility, and balanced judgment.[1] Prior to the democratic period, physical strength and courage were particularly valued.[2] But neither the Homeric age nor the classical period considered unquestioning obedience a virtue in a free man, except when he served in the army. Total submission was the duty—and the bitter fate—of the slave. The good citizen acted in accordance with the laws of his community; but no absolute political authority controlled him absolutely.

Nor did the loyalty which the medieval knight owed his overlord result in total submission. The feudal contract bound him to follow his sovereign only in a qualified and limited way. Among the virtues of the good knight, good horsemanship, prowess in arms, and courage ranked high.[3] Unquestioning obedience was conspicuously lacking.

In hydraulic society the relation between the ordinary members of the community and their leaders was regulated very differently. The quest for integrated subordination appears even at the tribal level. In the American Pueblos submissiveness and a yielding disposition are systematically cultivated.[4] Among the Chagga, "respect for the chief is the first command, which the parents impress upon their children." [5]

In state-centered hydraulic civilizations the supreme holders of power are not as close to the people as they are in Pueblo society, nor are they, as in certain Pueblos and among the Chagga, restrained by clan influence. The masters of an agrarian apparatus state make greater demands than the Pueblo leaders; and their means for enforcing their will far surpass the modest political devices of Chagga chieftainship.

Thorkild Jacobsen, discussing society and religion in ancient Mesopotamia, lists obedience as the prime virtue. Essentially "in Mesopotamia the 'good life' was the 'obedient life.' " [6] Unlike the warriors of Medieval Europe, who often fought in small bands and with little concern for a ranking leader, the Mesopotamians felt that "soldiers without a king are sheep without their shepherd," "peasants without a bailiff are a field without a plowman," and "workmen without a foreman are waters without a canal inspector." [7] Thus the subject was expected to carry out the orders of his foreman, his bailiff, and—of course—his king. "All these can and must claim absolute obedience." [8] Submission which cannot be avoided is conveniently rationalized: "The Mesopotamian feels convinced that authorities are always right." [9]

Similar concepts can be found in Pharaonic Egypt. A ship must have its commander, a gang its leader; [10] and whoever wants to survive—and to succeed—must fit himself into the edifice of superordination and subordination: "Bow thy back to thy superior, thy overseer from the palace [the government]. . . . Opposition to a superior is a painful thing (for) one lives as long as he is mild." [11]

The law of Hindu India prescribes subordination to both secular and priestly authority. Those who oppose the king's commands suffer "various kinds of capital punishment." [12]

The Koran exhorts believers to obey not only Allah and his prophet but also "those in authority amongst you." [13] In the absolutist states established by Mohammed's followers, this passage was invoked to emphasize the basic importance of obedience in maintaining governmental authority. [14]

Confucius envisioned an authority that would realize the ruler's rationality maximum. He therefore insisted that every official should judge the propriety of the ruler's actions; and when conflict became serious, a top-ranking minister might retire. [15] Normally, however, the ideal functionary obeyed his ruler; [16] and reverence toward a superior was a basic duty. [17] The commoner was given no choice whatsoever. Since he could not understand the issues involved, he had to be "made to follow" what superior authority and insight dictated.[18] In Confucius' good society, as in its Indian and Near Eastern variants, the good subject was the obedient subject.

2. PREPARATION FOR TOTAL OBEDIENCE: DISCIPLINARY EDUCATION

THE good subject was also the obedient son. For Confucius an education that demands absolute obedience to parent and teacher forms the ideal foundation on which to build absolute obedience to the masters of society.

No similar correlation can be established for Medieval Europe. The son of a feudal knight was mercilessly disciplined. At an early age he was compelled to ride a high horse, while tied to the saddle; and to toughen him further he was buried in horse manure.[19] Curses and blows were frequent accompaniments to growth. Feature for feature, the early education of the young feudal knight seems to have been as harsh, or harsher, than the education of the young son of an Oriental official. And the apprenticeship of the young European craftsman was no bed of roses either.[20]

But the behavior of the young burghers on festive occasions showed that the educational disciplines to which they had been exposed were not seriously inhibiting,[21] and the behavior of young knights remained equally carefree. Both groups matured under conditions that were built on contractual relations rather than on absolute authority, and they took their early frustrations as the passing experience that it actually was.

Conversely, similar—or even less harsh—disciplines may be eminently effective for assuring total submission. In ancient Mesopotamia, "the individual stood at the center of ever wider circles of authority which delimited his freedom of action. The nearest and smallest of these circles was constituted by authorities in his own family: father and mother, older brother and older sister."[22] And "obedience to the older members of one's family is merely a beginning. Beyond the family lie other circles, other authorities: the state and society." Each and every one of them "can and must claim absolute obedience."[23]

The wisdom of ancient Egypt consciously interlinks obedience at home to obedience to the official. The obedient son "will stand well in the heart of the official, his speech is guided with respect to what has been said to him."[24] In Hindu India the demand for subordination to the secular and priestly authorities is reenforced by the demand for subordination in the personal spheres of life. Obedience is particularly due "the teacher, the father, the mother, and an elder brother." [25]

Confucianism describes filial piety as a unique preparation for civic obedience: "There are few who, while acting properly toward their parents and older brothers, are inclined to oppose their superiors. And there is nobody who, while averse to opposing his superiors, is inclined to making a rebellion." [26]

3. The Great Symbol of Total Submission: Prostration

EDUCATION teaches man to obey without question, when despotic authority so demands. It also teaches him to perform gestures of reverence when the symbol rather than the submissive action is required. True, all cultures have ways of demonstrating respect; and many gestures indicate subordination.[27] But no symbol has expressed total submission as strikingly, and none has so consistently accompanied the spread of agrarian despotism, as has prostration.

Total submission is ceremonially demonstrated whenever a subject of a hydraulic state approaches his ruler or some other representative of authority. The inferior man, aware that his master's wrath may destroy him, seeks to secure his good will by humbling himself; and the holder of power is more than ready to enforce and standardize the symbols of humiliation.

The inferior person may indicate his submissiveness by placing one hand over the other, as if they were tied together.[28] He may raise his open hands as a gesture of self-disarmament.[a] Or going to extremes, he may fall forward on all fours like an animal, strike his head on the ground, and kiss the dust. Under the shadow of Oriental despotism, prostration is an outstanding form of saluting the sovereign or other persons of recognized authority. The details vary; and occasionally symbols with similar intent are used. Generally speaking, however, prostration is as characteristic for hydraulic society as it is uncharacteristic for the higher agrarian civilizations of classical antiquity and the European Middle Ages.

The absence of prostration in primitive hydraulic societies indicates the limitations of chiefly authority under tribal conditions. The Pueblo Indians hold their *cacique* in the highest esteem; but there are no evidences of the demonstrative submission that found open expression in the higher hydraulic civilizations of Aztec Mexico or Inca Peru. The Chagga tribesmen hail their chieftain;

a. Østrup, 1929: 28 ff. Cf. the modern "hands up."

and they murmur respectfully when he arrives or rises.[29] But this apparently is as far as their display of deference goes.[30]

In state-centered hydraulic civilizations prostration occurred almost everywhere. In ancient Hawaii political power was sufficiently terrifying to make the commoners crawl before their rulers.[b] In Inca Peru, even the highest dignitary approached his sovereign like a bearer of tribute, his back bent under a load.[31] In pre-Conquest Mexico supreme reverence was expressed by prostration. Taught in the "colleges," [32] it was performed before royalty, men of distinction,[33] and persons believed to be divine.[34]

In China prostration was practiced from the early days of the Chou dynasty—that is, during the pre-empire period of the territorial states; [35] and it prevailed throughout all subsequent phases of Chinese history. The experiences of the European envoys, who were asked to kowtow before the Manchu emperor, reveal both the importance of the custom and the embarrassment it caused Western visitors.

In the classical days of Hindu India great respect was shown by embracing a person's feet; and the king seems to have been approached in an attitude of prayer.[36] Prostration was performed before deities and the teacher's young wife.[c] However, in the later part of the Hindu period, the prime gesture of total submission was also performed before the sovereign.[37] Under Muslim rule both the sovereign [38] and venerable Hindus [39] were so honored.

The importance of prostration in the Near East can be amply documented. The records of Pharaonic Egypt describe the whole country as "prone upon the belly" before a representative of the king.[40] Faithful subordinates are shown crawling, and kissing (or sniffing) the monarch's scent.[41] Pictorial evidence suggests that in the New Kingdom high dignitaries employed other gestures of reverence; [42] but contemporary sources do not say that they ceased prostrating altogether. They indicate clearly that lowly persons and subject peoples continued to prostrate.[43]

In ancient Mesopotamia prostration was performed before the gods, the ruler, and other distinguished personalities,[44] and it was performed also in Achaemenian Persia.[45] It persisted in the Hel-

b. Fornander, HAF, VI: 12, 34 (religious prostration), 26 (before the king's idol); prostration before ruler: Kepelino, 1932: 12; Alexander, 1899: 26 ff.; Blackman, 1899: 23.

c. Cf. Manu, 1886: 69. In the second case, prostration obviously was performed in order to prevent bodily contact. For religious prostration, see *Jātakam*, III: 284; IV: 231; V: 274; VI: 302.

lenistic empires of the Seleucids [46] and the Ptolemies,[47] and also in Sassanid Persia.[48] It became the standard gesture of reverence in Eastern Rome on the eve of the Byzantine period.[49] Needless to say, it fitted the social climate of Byzantium to perfection.[50]

The followers of Mohammed originally prostrated only in prayer. Eventually, however, the "Orientalized" Arabs, like the Greeks before them, prostrated also in secular life.[51] In Ottoman Turkey the practice prevailed until close to the end of the Sultanate.[d]

Thus in the hydraulic world prostration was the outstanding expression of submission and reverence. Occasionally, equivalent gestures were used for the same purpose; and in a number of cases prostration spread to countries that were not ruled by Orientally despotic governments. However, the fate of the *proskynesis* in Medieval Europe shows how difficult it was to force this humiliating salutation on a politically balanced society. Some rudiments of the Byzantine ceremony survived in the ceremonial of the Western Church; yet the attempt of certain Carolingian rulers to uphold it as a secular ritual did not succeed. In Sicily under Roger II and Frederick II prostration was practiced temporarily probably under the influence of the Byzantines,[52] or the Arabs, who immediately preceded the Norman rulers.[53]

No doubt usage dulled man's sensitivity to the humiliating intent of prostration, and aesthetic accomplishment sweetened performance. But no matter how much prostration was rationalized, it remained through the ages a symbol of abject submission. Together with managerial, fiscal, and judicial terror, it spectacularly marked the range—and the total power—of agrarian despotism.

E. TOTAL LONELINESS

1. LONELINESS CREATED BY FEAR

DEMONSTRATIVE and total submission is the only prudent response to total power. Manifestly, such behavior does not gain a superior's respect; but other ways of proceeding invite disaster. Where power is polarized, as it is in hydraulic society, human relations are equally polarized. Those who have no control over their government quite reasonably fear that they will be crushed in any conflict with its masters.

And the formidable might of the state apparatus can destroy not merely objectionable nongovernmental forces—with equal thoroughness it may also overwhelm individual members of the ruling

d. Østrup, 1929: 32; Lane, 1898: 211 (kissing the feet as a sign of abject submission).

group, the ruler himself included. Many anxieties darken the path of life; but perhaps none is as devastating as the insecurity created by polarized total power.

a. The Ruler: Trust No One!

THE ruler, being most illustrious, is also most to be envied. Among those near him, there are always some who long to replace him. And since constitutional and peaceful change is out of the question, replacement usually means one thing and one thing only: physical annihilation. The wise ruler therefore trusts no one.

For obvious reasons the innermost thoughts of despots have been little publicized. But observable behavior and utterances confirm our assumption. Egyptian papyri preserve what is said to be a Pharaoh's advice to his son. The message reads: "Hold thyself apart from those subordinate to (thee), lest that should happen to whose terrors no attention has been given. Approach them not in thy loneliness. Fill not thy heart with a brother, nor know a friend. . . . (EVEN) WHEN THOU SLEEPEST, GUARD THY HEART THYSELF, because no man has adherents on the day of distress." [1]

The *Arthashāstra* specifies the dangers which surround the ruler, and it discusses the many means by which they can be averted. His residence must be made safe. Measures must be taken against poisoning.[2] All members of his entourage must be watched and controlled. The king must spy on his prime minister.[3] He must beware of his close friends,[4] of his wives,[5] of his brothers,[6] and most particularly of his heir apparent. According to an authority frequently quoted in the classic of Indian despotism, "Princes, like crabs, have a notorious tendency of eating up their begetter." [7] To prevent this from happening, the manual lists numerous ways by which a ruler can protect himself against his son.[8]

b. The Official: Eternal Suspicion

NOR does the official live securely. "Self-protection shall be the first and constant thought of a wise man; for the life of a man under the service of a king is aptly compared to life in fire; whereas fire burns a part or the whole of the body, if at all, the king has the power either to destroy or to advance the whole family." [9]

A Persian variant stresses particularly the danger that lurks behind seeming bureaucratic safety and success: "Should [the ruler] at any time pretend to you that you are completely secure with him, begin from that moment to feel insecure; if you are being fattened by someone, you may expect very quickly to be slaughtered by him." [10]

And the need for eternal suspicion is by no means confined to those occupying the top of the bureaucratic pyramid. In traditional China, as in other hydraulic civilizations, "high officials cannot but be jealous of those below them, for it is from that quarter that their rivals are to be dreaded. The lower officials, on the other hand, are not less suspicious of those above them, for it is from that quarter that their removal may be at any moment effected." [11]

c. The Commoner: the Fear of Being Trapped by Involvement

THE commoner is confronted with problems of a very different kind. He is not worried by the pitfalls inherent in autocratic or bureaucratic power, but by the threat which this power presents to all subjects. A regime that proceeds unchecked in the fields of taxation, corvée, and jurisprudence is capable of involving the commoners in endless predicaments. And caution teaches them to avoid any unnecessary contacts with their government.

Smith ascribes the mutual distrust that, according to him, prevails in traditional China to the people's fear of getting involved.[12] In the *Arabian Nights,* a corpse is shoved from door to door, because each house owner is convinced that the authorities will hold him responsible for the death of the unknown man. The frequently observed reluctance to help a drowning stranger is caused by similar reasoning: If I fail to rescue the poor devil, how shall I prove to the authorities that I did not plan his submersion?

Those who walk away when they can be of help are neither different from nor worse than other human beings. But their behavior makes it clear that voluntary participation in public matters, which is encouraged in an open society, is extremely risky under conditions of total power. The fear of getting involved with an uncontrollable and unpredictable government confines the prudent subject to the narrow realm of his personal and professional affairs. This fear separates him effectively from other members of the wider community to which he also belongs.

2. THE ALIENATION POTENTIAL OF TOTAL POWER

OF course, separation is not necessarily alienation: an artisan whose forebears left their rural community may consider himself different from the inhabitants of his home village. Or an intellectual may feel himself out of tune with his co-nationals, or in times of crisis he may completely reject a social order that apparently has no use for him. In such situations he may know loneliness. But as long as he can join with others of like mind, his alienation from society will be only partial.

And this partial alienation differs profoundly from total alienation. Only when a person believes he is deserted by all his fellows and when he is unable to see himself as an autonomous and inner-directed entity, only then can he be said to experience total alienation. Under the terror of the semimanagerial agrarian apparatus state he may know total loneliness without total alienation. Under the terror of the modern total managerial apparatus state he may suffer total alienation. Persistent isolation and brainwashing may bring him to the point where he no longer realizes he is being dehumanized.

3. Every-day Adjustments

There were many lonely people among the free men of classical Greece; [a] and there are many lonely people in the democratic countries of today. But these free individuals are lonely in the main because they are neglected and not because they are threatened by a power that, whenever it wants to, can reduce human dignity to nothingness. A neglected person can maintain associations of some kind with a few relatives or friends; and he may overcome his passive and partial alienation by widening his associations or by establishing new ways of belonging.

The person who lives under conditions of total power is not so privileged. Unable to counteract these conditions, he can take refuge only in alert resignation. Eager to avoid the worst, he must always be prepared to face it. Resignation has been an attitude of many free individuals at different times and in different segments of open and semi-open societies. But prior to the rise of the industrial apparatus state it was a predominant attitude mainly within the realm of Oriental despotism. Significantly, stoicism arose in antiquity when the balanced society of classical Greece gave way to the Hellenistic system of total power initiated by Alexander.

4. Total Loneliness in the Hour of Doom

The hour of doom realizes what every-day life foreshadows. The methods of final destruction operate in one way in a democratically balanced world and in another under the rule of total power.

The free citizen of an open society may fear severe punishment

a. The tragic and permanent alienation of the slave is too obvious to need elaboration.

at the hands of a state whose laws he has violated. But after arrest he expects to be visited and aided by his friends and legal counsel. He expects to be tried before a court that is not the tool of government. Moreover, he can insist that he is not guilty as charged; and the court will not prevent him from continuing to do so, even after it has sentenced him to death. Execution will destroy him physically, but the government that has thus shown its authority will not keep his friends from extolling his virtues or reasserting their belief in his innocence.

Socrates' end was unique in several ways, but it was typical for one aspect of enforced death in an open society. Sentenced to die for politically "corrupting" the youth of Athens, he was not made to denounce his acts publicly. Nor was he deprived of the company and admiration of his friends. His ordeal, far from alienating him from his followers—or from his ideas—cemented his union with both.[b]

In an open society governmental disapproval may leave the criti-

b. Plato's description of Socrates' death may have been colored by the affectionate reports of eyewitnesses. Yet it is accepted as substantially true, and it certainly shows that even those who were saddened by the verdict considered it legally proper. The jailer brought the cup of hemlock, and Socrates, after listening to his directions, raised the vessel to his lips and "quite readily and cheerfully . . . drank off the poison." Plato's narrator continues:

> And hitherto most of us had been able to control our sorrow; but now when we saw him drinking, and saw too that he had finished the draught, we could no longer forbear, and in spite of myself my own tears were flowing fast; so that I covered my face and wept over myself, for certainly I was not weeping over him, but at the thought of my own calamity in having lost such a companion. Nor was I the first, for Crito, when he found himself unable to restrain his tears, had got up and moved away, and I followed; and at that moment, Apollodorus, who had been weeping all the time, broke out into a loud cry which made cowards of us all.
>
> Socrates alone retained his calmness: What is this strange outcry? he said. I sent away the women mainly in order that they might not offend in this way, for I have heard that a man should die in peace. Be quiet then, and have patience. When we heard that, we were ashamed, and refrained our tears; and he walked about until, as he said, his legs began to fail, and then he lay on his back, according to the directions, and the man who gave him the poison now and then looked at his feet and legs; and after a while he pressed his foot hard, and asked him if he could feel; and he said, No; and then his leg, and so upwards and upwards, and showed us that he was cold and stiff. And he felt then himself and said: When the poison reaches the heart, that will be the end. He was beginning to grow cold about the groin, when he uncovered his face, for he had covered himself up, and said (they were his last words)—he said: Crito, I owe a cock to Asclepius; will you remember to pay the debt? The debt shall be paid, said Crito; is there anything else? There was no answer to this question; but in a minute or two a movement was heard, and the attendants uncovered him; his eyes were set, and Crito closed his eyes and mouth.
>
> Such was the end, Echecrates, of our friend, whom I may truly call the wisest, and justest, and best of all men whom I have ever known [Plato: 270 ff.].

cized citizen cold; but under conditions of total power, official displeasure may bring disaster. The Chinese official and historian, Ssŭ-ma Ch'ien, was not accused of high treason. He only dared to differ with his emperor's evaluation of a defeated general, and he was only sentenced to be castrated. Living on, he described in an extraordinary letter the abject loneliness he suffered during the time of his ordeal.

According to the law of the then ruling Han dynasty, Ssŭ-ma Ch'ien's punishment could have been remitted by the payment of a sum of money; and this could have been done, for he had wealthy and high-ranking friends. But no one dared to aid him. No one dared to show sympathy for a man who had angered the emperor. Ssŭ-ma Ch'ien writes "My friends did not come to my assistance. Those who were near and intimate with me did not say a single word in my favor." *c* So he was led into the dark room and mutilated as if he had been an animal.

The tragedy of a bureaucratic Timon of Athens has not as yet been written. But Ssŭ-ma's fate shows what can happen to a man who, shunning a basic principle of bureaucratic prudence,*d* contradicts the holder of total power. It shows that what is expected behavior in an open society approaches madness under the shadow of total terror. Ssŭ-ma Ch'ien's environment being what it was, his intervention on a friend's behalf was the glorious exception; his friend's failure to intervene on his the sad norm.

Measured by the standards of an open society, the Chinese historian suffered appallingly. Measured by the standards of his own world, he was not without luck. Although he was emasculated, he remained alive; and being of no political significance, he could continue to work on his history. He even commented critically on the treatment accorded him in a letter, which, however, was cautiously kept out of sight until he was dead.[13]

When persecution is total, the victim of hydraulic terror may be separated not only from his friends but from his good name as well. The great Persian vizier and writer Rashīd ad-Dīn was accused by envious and rival officials of having poisoned the young sultan's father. The crime which Rashīd was said to have committed did not fit his personality, and it was contrary to his most elementary interests. Rashīd ad-Dīn was the outstanding Asiatic historian of his period, "the author of Ghazan's famous code of laws (*kanun*), the greatest vizier of the Ilkhan dynasty, and one of the greatest men the East has produced." [14] The sovereign he was accused of having mur-

---

c. *Han Shu* 62. 18b. Our translation of this passage differs somewhat from that of Chavannes, who has rendered the whole letter (see Chavannes, MH, I: ccxxxii).

d. According to the *Arthaçāstra* (1926: 387) the prudent official avoids "those who have been forced out of position and favor."

dered esteemed him so highly that he is believed to have made him a gift of gold that exceeded the amount Alexander bestowed on Aristotle.[15] Indeed, Rashid ad-Din's talents were said to be "as indispensable to the State as salt was to meat." [16]

It is difficult to see why a man should kill his generous admirer. It beggars comprehension why he should willfully destroy the source of his power, security, and wealth. But no such considerations stayed the hands of Rashīd's enemies. They declared him guilty. They executed his son before his eyes. They cut his own body in two—certainly without permitting him any last comfort from friends or relatives. Thus Rashīd died, a lonely man, deprived of both worldly and spiritual honor. For at the end he was also denounced as a religious imposter.[17]

But no matter how cynically Rashīd's accusers proceeded, they did not force him to confess publicly to crimes he was alleged to have committed. On the contrary, he seems to have maintained his innocence to the end.[18] No such leniency has been shown in the great political trials of the modern total managerial states.

The difference does not arise from any lack of terroristic efficiency on the part of hydraulic despotism. Those who tortured for the hydraulic rulers could have broken anyone, and they certainly could have extorted public confessions if they had wanted to. But the masters of the hydraulic regime saw no reason to publicize their conflicts in the villages or guild quarters where semi-autonomous Beggars' Democracies vegetated in a subpolitical atmosphere. Thus there was no need to promote the spectacular and articulate self-alienation in which the totalitarian "People's" courts now specialize.

The last days of the Soviet Communist Bukharin indicate how, under modern conditions, a victim may be made to cooperate publicly in his own debasement. Lenin, in his "Testament," had written that Bukharin was "the most valuable and biggest theoretician of the party," that he "may legitimately be considered the favorite of the whole party." [19] But the favorite of today is the monster of tomorrow. Framed and sentenced to die during the Great Purge of the 1930's, Bukharin overnight lost his popularity and fame. Vyshinsky, the then State Prosecutor, voiced the opinion of the party leaders when he called Bukharin a "theoretician in quotation marks," [20] a "damnable cross of a fox and a swine," [21] to be listed among the spies and traitors who "must be shot like dirty dogs." [22] And the psychological engineers of the Soviet government handled the defendant so skillfully that he confessed publicly and at length to treasonable acts that he could never have committed.

Manifestly total loneliness, like total terror, also has its varieties.

CHAPTER 6

The core, the margin, and the submargin of hydraulic societies

A. PRELIMINARY STOCK-TAKING IN THE MIDDLE OF THE JOURNEY

1. SOME BASIC RESULTS

OUR inquiry has led to several basic conclusions. First, the institutional order, hydraulic society, cannot be explained by reference to geographical, technological, and economic factors alone. While response to the natural setting is a key feature, it plays a formative hydraulic role only under very specific cultural conditions. And it involves organizational rather than technological changes. Second, some features of hydraulic society appear also in other agrarian orders. But hydraulic society is specific in the quality and weight of two of its features (hydraulic organization and agrohydraulic despotism). And it is their effective combination that brings into being an operational whole, a "going concern" which is able to perpetuate itself over millennia. The historian of human freedom must face this fundamental empirical fact: among the world's higher preindustrial civilizations, hydraulic society, the most despotic of them, has outlasted all others.

2. THREE PROBLEMS DESERVING FURTHER INVESTIGATION

WHY does hydraulic society show such persistence? Is it because of its state-managed system of hydraulic agriculture? An upholder of the economic interpretation of history will believe this; indeed Marx himself argued so.

But it is significant that Marx and Engels viewed the Tsarist government of post-Mongol Russia as Orientally despotic,[1] although both certainly knew that Russian agriculture was not hydraulic. The difficulty from the standpoint of the economic determinist is manifest; and it is increased when we realize that, beside Tsarist Russia, certain other agrodespotic states fulfilled the vital organizational and acquisitive functions of hydraulic society without maintaining a hydraulic economy proper. The capacity of these regimes to perpetuate themselves successfully suggests a decisive developmental role for the organizational and power features of the agromanagerial order.

Obviously the issue is highly important, not only theoretically and for the past, but politically and for the present. It is for this reason that in this chapter we shall examine the peculiarities and the interrelation of the core and the margin of hydraulic society. In the chapters immediately following we shall analyze two other aspects of the matter: the power-determined character of private property and class rule in the hydraulic world.

3. PROBLEMS OF HYDRAULIC DENSITY

How hydraulic was hydraulic society? Obviously there are areas of maximum hydraulic density and others which, although they are hydraulically less dense, may still be considered hydraulic societies proper. What is the institutional pattern of the margin of hydraulic society? And at what point does this margin lose its societal identity? Is there an institutional divide beyond which features of hydraulic society occur only sporadically in a submarginal form?

Assuming that such shades of institutional density exist, are they static and permanent? Or did hydraulic civilizations shift from the margin to the submargin and vice versa? With these questions in mind we shall now discuss the core areas, the margin, and the submarginal zones of the hydraulic world.

B. HYDRAULIC CORE AREAS

THE institutional quality of a hydraulic area varies in accordance with its spatial cohesiveness and the economic and political weight of its hydraulic system. It may be modified further by the relative significance of the second major element of hydraulic operation: flood control.

1. How CONTINUOUS IS THE HYDRAULIC SYSTEM OF A GIVEN HYDRAULIC AREA?

THE spatial (and organizational) cohesiveness of a given hydraulic economy is primarily determined by the continuous or discontinuous form of its water supply. A hydraulic commonwealth is apt to create a single more or less continuous system of irrigation and flood control in a landscape that contains only one major accessible source of humidity. Such a development frequently occurs in oasis-like regions crossed by a river that gathers the bulk of its water in a more humid hilly or mountainous hinterland. The river-valley states of ancient coastal Peru maintained continuous hydraulic systems. In the Old World, Sindh and the Nile Valley civilization of Egypt are classical variants of the same pattern.

If an arid landscape includes several not too widely separated rivers, the canals leading from them may form a relatively continuous hydraulic network. However, few arid regions are so privileged. Lower Mesopotamia is more the exception than the rule.

In most cases the rivers of a potentially hydraulic landscape lie too far apart to permit interlocking through connecting canals. Consequently a hydraulic commonwealth covering a multi-river area generally maintains a discontinuous system of embankments and canals. Individuals depending on a limited and single water supply may reproduce a limited tribal or national culture for a long period of time. This happened in the Rio Grande area and, on a much more impressive scale, in Pharaonic Egypt. But the self-perpetuating hydraulic tribes played an insignificant part on the stage of human history; and even such national complexes as Egypt eventually outgrew their early political isolation. The great majority of all historically conspicuous hydraulic nations and empires include regions which depend on a continuous hydraulic unit; yet, taken as a whole, the hydraulic system of these larger political units have a definitely discontinuous form.

2. How Great Is the Economic and Political Weight of a Given Hydraulic Economy?

SINCE most of the larger hydraulic civilizations maintain discontinuous hydraulic systems, lack of cohesiveness obviously is no reliable index for establishing hydraulic density. The economic and political weights of a discontinuous hydraulic system must be established by other means.

In arid areas a discontinuous hydraulic system occurs occasionally; in semi-arid areas it is virtually the rule, at least for societies that have outgrown their most primitive beginnings. As indicated above, the semi-arid areas which have given rise to hydraulic developments are numerous and large; and within them the relation between hydraulic agriculture and nonhydraulic (small-scale irrigation and rainfall) farming varies enormously.

Three major shades of this relation can be distinguished:

1) The hydraulically cultivated land may comprise more than half of all arable land. Since hydraulic agriculture tends to produce

yields that, by and large, are as high as those produced by small-scale irrigation and definitely higher than the average yields of the rainfall farmers, a hydraulic agriculture which covers more than 50 per cent of all arable land may be said to be in a position of *absolute economic superiority*.

This condition is found most frequently in arid regions; and frequently, although not necessarily, it is found together with a continuous hydraulic system. In most Rio Grande Pueblos the bulk of all land is irrigated; and the bulk of irrigation water is drawn from communally operated irrigation ditches. In Egypt, from the dawn of history, the great majority of all fields was irrigated either by inundation or through canals.[1] In the delta a meager crop can be grown by methods of rainfall farming; [a] and throughout the country, wells can be used to water vegetables, gardens, and orchards.[2] But as in the case of the Rio Grande Pueblos, these supplementary forms of cultivation do not challenge the overwhelming economic superiority of the hydraulic economy.

2) The hydraulically cultivated land, even when it comprises less than half the country's arable acreage, may nevertheless yield more than all other arable land. In this case, hydraulic agriculture may be said to hold a position of *relative economic superiority*. On the eve of China's unification the state of Ch'in enormously strengthened its agrarian heartlands (in present Shensi) by constructing the Chêng Kuo irrigation works; and this action made Ch'in richer and more powerful than any other territorial state. In the subsequent period, the whole area of what had been Ch'in [b] comprised about one-third of the empire's area, but, according to Pan Ku, it accounted for 60 per cent of its wealth.[3] Ssŭ-ma Ch'ien considered the former Ch'in territory "ten times as rich as [the rest of] the empire." [4] Neither of these statements can be verified, and they certainly should not be pressed. Yet they illustrate what we mean by the relative economic superiority of a vigorous hydraulic system of agriculture.

3) The hydraulically cultivated land, even if it is inferior both in acreage and yield to the remaining arable land, may nevertheless be sufficient to stimulate despotic patterns of corvée labor and government. In this case the larger, nonhydraulic area essentially produces food, whereas the smaller, hydraulic area, in addition to producing

a. After mentioning the cultivation of barley in the Nile delta as one of the examples of rainfall agriculture close to the minimum limit, the *Agricultural Yearbook* of 1941 concludes: "Production year after year with these small amounts of moisture is possible only where the distribution of rainfall during the year and other climatic conditions are favorable and where the moisture falling in two or more years is stored for one crop" (CM: 322).

b. In addition to the Chêng Kuo complex, this included among other regions the classical irrigation plain of Szechwan.

food, produces power, and it produces power that is sufficiently strong and sufficiently despotic to control both sectors of the agrarian society.

This evidently happened in numerous semi-arid regions that were suitable—in key areas—for hydraulic operations. During the formative period of many great hydraulic civilizations despotic power probably arose under exactly such conditions; and the pattern has been perpetuated in historic times. Assyria and Mexico applied methods of mass control that were imperative only in relatively small hydraulic regions to large areas of small-scale irrigation and rainfall farming. Under these conditions the hydraulic economy, though predominant neither in acreage nor yield, nevertheless occupied a position of *organizational and political superiority*.

3. How Strong Is the Second Major Element of Hydraulic Operation: Flood Control?

WHERE the hydraulic system prevails economically, the relative strength of protective (as compared with productive) water works is of little concern. An elaborate hydraulic agriculture involves an elaborate bureaucratic development; and the despotic regime is thus conveniently bulwarked.

Things are different when the hydraulic system, although sufficient to establish political supremacy, involves only modest bureaucratic developments. To be sure, the maintenance of large installations for flood control always necessitates comprehensive operations of mobilization and on-the-spot direction; and it also heightens the quasimilitary authority of the managerial government in situations of absolute or relative economic hegemony. But the protective factor becomes particularly important when economic hegemony is lacking. The fight against large and disastrous floods tends to expand government-directed mass mobilization further than would productive hydraulic action alone. And the disciplinary measures involved in protective enterprises do much to cement the power of a government that derives only a limited managerial authority from its agromanagerial achievements. In the lake area of ancient Mexico the struggle against periodic and devastating floods probably re quired much larger corvée teams than did the regional irrigation works. The significance of this fact for the aggrandizement of government power can be easily imagined.

4. Compact and Loose Hydraulic Societies

OUR argument does not exhaust all morphological possibilities. But it establishes one point beyond doubt: The core areas of the hydraulic world manifest at least two major types of hydraulic density. Some are hydraulically compact, whereas others are hydraulically loose.[5] A hydraulic society may be considered "compact" when its hydraulic agriculture occupies a position of absolute or relative economic hegemony. It may be considered "loose" when its hydraulic agriculture, while lacking economic superiority, is sufficient to assure its leaders absolute organizational and political hegemony.

This primary division may be supplemented by some important secondary divisions. A hydraulic society, whose hydraulic agriculture is economically dominant and spatially continuous, is an extreme variant of the compact pattern (C 1). A hydraulic society whose hydraulic agriculture is economically dominant but discontinuous is a less extreme variant of this same pattern (C 2). Distinction between absolute (a) and relative (r) economic hegemony enables us to carry the differentiation still further (Ca 1 and Cr 1, Ca 2 and Cr 2).

A loose hydraulic society may include among its installations large units which are compact within their immediate locale or which go beyond the borders of a single region. The relatively great hydraulic weight of this pattern may be indicated by the symbol "L 1." A loose hydraulic society whose largest hydraulic units fail to achieve economic hegemony even regionally represents the lowest hydraulic density type (L 2). Another differentiating factor, the relatively strong development of *protective* hydraulic works, may be indicated whenever this seems desirable by the formula "+ prot."

A few examples indicate, on a tribal or national scale, the four main categories of hydraulic density:

> *Compact 1:* Most Rio Grande Pueblos, the small city states of ancient coastal Peru, Pharaonic Egypt.
> *Compact 2:* The city states of ancient Lower Mesopotamia, probably the state of Ch'in on the eve of the Chinese empire
> *Loose 1:* The Chagga tribes, ancient Assyria, the old Chinese state of Ch'i (L 1 + prot.), and perhaps Ch'u.
> *Loose 2:* Tribal civilizations: The Suk of East Africa, the Zuni of New Mexico. State centered civilizations: indigenous Hawaii, many territorial states of ancient Mexico (L 2 + prot.).

5. THE GREAT AGROMANAGERIAL EMPIRES—USUALLY LOOSE HYDRAULIC SOCIETIES

DOMINION of one city state over a number of other city states leads to the establishment of rudimentary empires. Conformations of this kind arose in ancient Lower Mesopotamia, on the coast of ancient Peru, in Chou China, and in Buddhist India.

In the first two cases the components were of the compact hydraulic type; and the quasi-imperial units were also hydraulically compact. Usually, however, military and political expansion resulted in the creation of larger and less homogeneous conformations. The great hydraulic empires tended to include territorial and national units of different hydraulic densities. They formed loose hydraulic societies, which frequently included compact hydraulic subareas. The Babylonian and Assyrian empires, China during the periods of unification, the great empires of India, Achaemenian Persia at the height of its expansion, the Arab caliphate, Ottoman Turkey, the Inca empire, and the federation of Aztec Mexico—all were hydraulic societies, and all, perhaps with the exception of Mexico, belonged to the category L 1.

The hydraulic glands of the great agromanagerial empires have been accorded little systematic attention. A morphological study of the hydraulic order of traditional China reveals many density patterns and significant super-regional arrangements.[c] Mez' thoughtful analysis of Abbassid power indicates the number and variety of the great hydraulic areas that for shorter or longer periods lay within the jurisdiction of the Baghdad caliphate: Egypt, South Arabia, Babylonia, Persia (northeast and south Transoxania and Afghanistan).[6] All these areas posed "great irrigation problems," [7] and the Arab sources note both the technological means and the numerous personnel required to solve them.[8]

6. Degrees of Hydraulic Density and Degrees of Bureaucratic Density

a. The Principle

THE bureaucratic density of an agromanagerial society varies with its hydraulic density. This correlation is affected by such factors as the institutional weight of large nonhydraulic constructions (the Zuni Pueblos, the territorial states of Chou China, the Roman empire) and the dimensions of communicational and/or military organizations (Assyria, the state of Ch'in, Aztec Mexico). But such factors modify rather than negate the basic hydraulic-bureaucratic relation. Pharaonic Egypt was highly bureaucratized long before it developed a comprehensive military officialdom. And while both the Incas and the Aztecs maintained strong military organizations, there

c. For a discussion of the varying territorial dimensions and character, as well as the interarea relations, in the "loose" hydraulic order of traditional China, see Wittfogel, 1931: 252–72.

can be little doubt that the former had a more comprehensive managerial bureaucracy than the latter.

On the acquisitive level correlations also vary. To be sure, an agrarian despotism, no matter what its hydraulic density pattern, insists upon its right to tax universally. Yet the way in which this right is exercised differs significantly. Although a loose hydraulic society with a strong government may be able to gather in a larger percentage of the estimated revenue than a compact hydraulic society with a weak government, other conditions being equal, the more comprehensive bureaucracy of an intensively managerial state is better equipped over time to handle the business of taxation than is the less comprehensive bureaucracy of a less intensively managerial state.

The collecting of the rural surplus was more centralized in Inca Peru than in Aztec Mexico, where local affairs were handled not by representatives of the government but by heads of the local *calpulli*. In the compact hydraulic societies of the ancient Near East the bulk of the revenue seems to have been gathered by government functionaries, although intermediaries are known to have been used in certain periods in Pharaonic Egypt.[9] Under Greek and Roman influence respectively, tax farming appeared in the Hellenistic and Roman Near East;[10] but the absolutist regimes soon asserted their power, first by modifying the system of tax farming and later by reducing it to insignificance.[11] State-appointed (liturgical) tax collectors, mostly wealthy townsmen, supplemented the fiscal bureaucracy; and big (bureaucratic) landowners fulfilled a similar function with more advantage as well as less danger to themselves.[12] Thus the hydraulically loose Roman empire discarded the independent tax farmers of ancient Greece and republican Rome without reverting to the old Egyptian and Babylonian ways of directly and bureaucratically collecting the revenue.

This step was taken by the Arab masters of the Near East, whose power was rooted in such hydraulic centers as Damascus, Cairo, and Baghdad. Under the Umayyads the bureaucratic fiscal system prevailed; and the tax farmers, whom the Abbassid government began to employ, were still closely integrated in the bureaucratic order. In Mesopotamia they were part of the officialdom.[13] In China some local tax collectors were not members of the regular officialdom;[14] but bureaucratic methods of tax collection seem to have prevailed throughout the ages.

b. Changing Bureaucratic Density of a Hydraulic Territory

THE inclusion of incipiently hydraulic or nonhydraulic territories in a loose hydraulic society is usually followed by the development of a bureaucratic network in these territories. This is what happened when the ancient centers of Chinese culture conquered certain "barbarian" regions in Central and South China.

The inclusion of a compact hydraulic territory in a hydraulically loose empire tends to have the opposite effect. The rulers, who are accustomed to operate with a less compact officialdom, may also reduce the bureaucratic apparatus of the hydraulically compact area. This is what happened when the Nile Valley became part of the Roman empire.

7. HYDRAULICALLY CONCERNED AND HYDRAULICALLY UNCONCERNED MASTERS OF HYDRAULIC SOCIETY

A SECOND FACTOR that may change the bureaucratic density of a hydraulic society is the rulers' concern (or lack of concern) for hydraulic management. As discussed previously, a hydraulic society may sink to a low rationality level if it is ruled by conquerors who take little interest in managerial agriculture or if its indigenous masters slacken their productive efforts. The conquerors' lack of hydraulic concern is usually a consequence of their nonhydraulic background. Internal decay may be due to a reduction in government revenue resulting from the excessive growth of proprietary forces or from the degeneration of a ruling group that reveled in the luxury of total power.

The spatial relation between the main areas of political power and hydraulic economy also plays a part. Rulers may establish their capital close to the major regions of agricultural wealth and surplus; or they may establish it at a considerable distance from these regions. Defense is often given as the reason for the latter decision, and at times it may indeed be the whole reason. Often, however, the rulers—particularly conqueror-rulers—preferred to set up their capitals in a nonhydraulic frontier, because they had a stronger affinity to the periphery than to the core areas of the hydraulic world.

In China the centers of political direction and hydraulic economy coincided more or less until the first millennium A.D., when the growing fertility of the Yangtze area conflicted with the defense needs of the vital northern border zone. From then on, the seat of the central government shifted back and forth; but the northern region never ceased to be hydraulic to some extent, and the northern capitals were ingeniously and hydraulically connected with the main rice areas of Central China through the Grand Canal.

In India the great northern plain, which was the main area of hydraulic agriculture, was also the logical place for the political metropolis; and the Muslim masters of India, like their Hindu predecessors, established their capitals there. But they exhibited less hydraulic concern than had the previous indigenous rulers. Although they were not lacking in managerial interest, and although they created and maintained large irrigation works, they never fully restored the grandiose hydraulic economy that appears to have flourished in the Maurya empire. The role they assigned to local "chiefs" and tax farmers reflects the relatively low bureaucratic density of Muslim India.

The later Roman emperors responded to the lure of the East. Yet they established their new capital, not in one of the great classical areas of hydraulic agriculture (Egypt, Syria, or Mesopotamia) but at the Hellespont, the classical divide between the Orient and the non-hydraulic West. And despite the fact that long acquaintance with managerial despotism stimulated them to plan and build on a large scale, they were content to administer their hydraulic possessions from afar. Immensely bold in the creation of nonhydraulic constructions (highways and frontier walls), they exhibited much less initiative in the agromanagerial sphere. While by no means lacking in hydraulic concern, they aimed at gathering as large a rural revenue as possible with as small a bureaucracy as possible. Rational rulers though they were, they did not realize the rationality maximum of the hydraulic world they controlled.

The Romans, who made Constantinople the capital of their empire, had behind them five hundred years of practical experience with the Hellenistic version of hydraulic statecraft. The Turks, who had conquered Adrianople in 1362, Constantinople in 1452, Egypt in 1517, and Mesopotamia in 1534, were not unacquainted with higher agrarian civilizations of the hydraulic type either; as a matter of fact, they had lived at the edge of the hydraulic world since the dawn of history. But perhaps because of their pastoral background they were less interested in the promotion of agriculture [15] than in military enterprises; and they preferred extending the non-hydraulic margin to intensifying the hydraulic core. True, the great irrigation works of Mesopotamia lay in ruins when the Turks came; but the history of China and India shows that hydraulic effort can restore quickly what antihydraulic action has destroyed. The Turks did not break with agromanagerial tradition in Egypt or Syria; but they furthered no significant reconstruction work in Irak. Speaking generally, they displayed no effective zest for hydraulic development.[16] As Orientally despotic organizers of war, peace, and fiscal exploitation, they were extraordinarily successful; and in some few major administrative centers they employed many officials. Being managerially unconcerned, however, they governed their far-flung empire with a relatively small professional bureaucracy.

8. PERIODS OF AGROMANAGERIAL ADJUSTMENT, DEGENERATION, AND RESTORATION

OF COURSE, the economic ethos (the *Wirtschaftsgesinnung*) of a ruling group is not unchangeable. Great differences in cultural and social assimilation notwithstanding, this is true also for pastoral invaders.

The tribal conquerors of China were usually willing to uphold the indigenous tradition in certain spheres of nonhydraulic construction and management; and many of them became at least superficially aware of the importance of irrigation agriculture. Perhaps none of the northern conquerors equaled the active hydraulic concern of the Manchus, who had practiced irrigation in their homeland prior to their conquest of China.[17] In the Near East the Umayyads, who consolidated a conquest regime established by the first followers of the Prophet, also showed extraordinary hydraulic concern.[18]

Pastoral and semipastoral conquerors who develop an interest in hydraulic matters do so, as a rule, not during the first period of their dominion but later; and often they grow managerially lazy and negligent before their rationality potential has been exhausted. Indigenous rulers, on the other hand, frequently show the greatest hydraulic concern during the earlier periods of their regime, tending to grow managerially less insistent when their power is consolidated. In either case, decay may be retarded by challenging external circumstances; or it may be accelerated by the expansion of large proprietary forces, whose representatives arrogate to themselves an increasing part of the national surplus.[d] When one segment of the despotic elite (primarily the court and clusters of officials close to it) succumbs to the corrupting influence of total power, another segment (other members of the officialdom and their relatives and friends among the bureaucratic "gentry") may seize power. As the result of this process, excessively irrational features may be eliminated in a "cathartic" and "regenerative" revolution.

d. For an attempt to explain the great agrarian and political crises in Chinese society by means of this and other social factors see Wittfogel, 1927: 322 ff., 328 ff.; *ibid.,* 1935: 53. Cf. Wittfogel and Fêng, 1949: 377. For an analysis of agrarian crises as a general feature of Oriental society see Wittfogel, 1938: 109 ff.

A development of this type does not change the traditional hydraulic and despotic order; it merely restores its vitality. The first rulers of many Egyptian, Babylonian, Chinese, Indian, Persian, Islamic, and Mexican dynasties have been praised for their vigor and efficiency. Regenerative upsurges may also occur during a later phase of a dynastic reign; and then, as during the formative period, serious attempts may be made at effective hydraulic management and rational fiscal administration. In both cases the more farsighted and less compromised elements within the ruling bureaucracy demonstrate that they can run the country in a more effective way than their self-indulgent and "corrupt" rivals.

9. The Staying Power of Deteriorated Agro-managerial Hydraulic Societies

The dominant myths of Oriental despotism ascribe regenerative achievements to almost every founder of a new dynasty; but an unbiased evaluation of the evidence leads to less flattering conclusions. Under conditions that permit no independent criticism or political pressure, the immediate benefits of total power have a much greater appeal to the masters of the absolutist apparatus than do the potential fruits of rational—albeit, selfishly rational—managerial effort. Self-indulgence is, therefore, a more typical motive for behavior than the desire to maintain the rulers' rationality optimum.

And this is true not only for most later sovereigns but also for many a dynasty's founding father. Such persons, however vigorous, are often more sensitive to the political weaknesses of the old regime than to the managerial possibilities of the new. Having won over the bulk of the military and civil officials, they readily correct the most glaring abuses in taxation, forced labor, or jurisdiction, and they make the most urgent constructional and agromanagerial improvements; but they have neither the vision nor the personnel to raise the hydraulic government to a conspicuously higher level of hydraulic and fiscal management. In the many dynastic changes that characterize the history of agromanagerial civilizations, thorough regenerative upsurges are probably more the exception than the rule.

Of course, a stoppage of all hydraulic operations would paralyze agricultural life, and this not only in areas of full aridity but in many semi-arid regions as well. Consequently, even a hydraulically unconcerned Oriental government will devote some effort to its managerial duties. It has to carry on somehow, even if it must depend largely and not too rationally on local groups. During the last phase of Byzantine rule over Egypt, influential landlords, most of whom had bureaucratic connections,[19] are said to have maintained the dikes and canals in many localities.[20] To what extent governmental hydraulic action was reduced by this arrangement is hard to decide. Even during this critical period, however, Egypt's irrigation economy was sufficiently continuous and sufficiently effective to feed the people and to furnish a huge revenue. Somehow it succeeded in perpetuating itself. When the Arabs appeared in 639, they found in the Nile Valley a population of about seven millions,[e] that is, about as many persons as had lived there under Ptolemaic rule.

C. THE MARGIN OF THE HYDRAULIC WORLD

IN arid or semi-arid landscapes sedentary agrarian civilizations can persist permanently and prosperously only on the basis of a hydraulic economy. Along the moderately humid periphery of the arid and semi-arid world agrarian life is not so conditioned. Here Oriental despotism may prevail with little or no dependence upon hydraulic activities.

1. VARYING OPERATIONAL AND BUREAUCRATIC DENSITY PATTERNS IN MARGINAL AREAS OF THE HYDRAULIC WORLD

IN the hydraulic core areas degrees of hydraulic density provide a crucial means for distinguishing degrees of institutional density. In the margins, however, this criterion loses its significance. Instead, degrees of bureaucratic density are best determined by an approach that evaluates the relative development of absolutist methods in the spheres of construction (mostly nonhydraulic), organization, and acquisition.

Comparison between the states of Middle Byzantium and post-Mongol Russia reveal significant differences. Byzantium maintained considerable hydraulic installations, in the main for providing drinking water; [a] and these have no parallel in Muscovite Russia. Nor did the Muscovite Russians engage in comprehensive nonhydraulic constructions as did the Byzantines. The founders of Eastern Rome reshaped the earlier network of roads; [1] and their highways were the foundation of the Byzantine system of communications,[2] which in a limited way continued in use even under the Turks.[3]

e. For the beginning of the Arab era see Johnson and West, 1949: 263 (6,000,000, plus children and old people); cf. Munier, 1932: 84. For Ptolemaic Egypt see Diodorus, I, sec. 31 (7,000,000); cf. Josephus, JW 2.16 (7,500,000); Wilcken, 1899, I: 489 ff.

a. Bréhier, 1950: 90 ff. For a description of some of these works see Ritter, 1858: 155, 160, 167, 202, 346, 378, 406, 496, 547. Most of the local and regional hydraulic works that existed under the Turks probably go back to the Byzantines.

The Byzantines also made enormous building efforts for purposes of defense. They protected their borders by a great chain of fortifications; and here, as in the sphere of communications, corvée labor was mobilized for the task.[4] After the victory of the Seljuq Turks at Manzikert (in 1071), the absolutist state still functioned; and the road corvée was still levied in the 12th century;[5] but the vigor of the early days was gone. The great military road, which in the preceding years had had its periods of decay and reconstruction, appears to have been properly maintained only "until the eleventh century."[6]

When the Mongols established their rule over Russia, they did not construct massive roads, nor did they erect frontier walls or chains of border fortresses. They were satisfied to establish organizational and acquisitive methods of total control. It is in these two last fields of action that Byzantium and absolutist Russia, although not identical, were similar.

The Byzantines kept account of their country's wealth in elaborate cadasters.[7] They monopolized quick communication and intelligence by means of the state post.[8] They closely controlled the major sectors of handicraft and commerce, again until the 11th century.[9] And they maintained armies whose orderly integration contrasted strikingly with the amorphous hosts of feudal Europe.[10]

All these features have parallels in Muscovite Russia. The mature Muscovite state registered the mass of its population for fiscal and military purposes;[11] it operated an elaborate "postal" (relay) system;[12] it occupied a key position in the country's trade;[13] and it despotically drafted and directed its fighting men.[b]

During the earlier periods of both absolutist regimes office land was assigned to persons serving the state. In Byzantium this system emerged on the eve of the Arab conquest in a time of turmoil and invasion and as a means of strengthening defense against the Persian attack. Rooted in earlier Roman institutions[14] and set in its classical form by Heraclius I (610–641), it continued patterns that had existed in the ancient Orient from the days of Sumer and Babylon and that prevailed also in contemporary Persia.[15] Under the system of *themes,* each Byzantine soldier received a farm which, like his service, was hereditary and indivisible.[16]

This plebeian version of an absolutist office land system lasted until the 11th century. Then, after the catastrophic defeat at Manzi-

b. For the principle see Herberstein, NR, I: 95 ff.; for its full development, Staden, 1930: 58; cf. Kluchevsky, HR, II: 48, 111, 115. As will be shown below, all these institutions existed before Ivan III (1462–1505), during whose reign the Tatar Yoke collapsed.

kert, the state placed at the center of its reorganized military (and office land) system the big landowners, who, with the development of a heavy cavalry, were more useful militarily than the *themes* peasants.[c]

Hand in hand with this transformation went the transformation of the acquisitive order. From the 7th to the 11th century the government collected the bulk of its revenue through its officials. The *themes* soldiers, who lived essentially off their service land, presented no major fiscal problem.[d] The holders of the *pronoia,* the larger land units that constituted the core of the later office land system, provided a certain number of heavily armed soldiers and collected taxes from the peasants of the *pronoia.*[17] Together with the newly established tax farmers,[18] the *pronoetes* formed a group of semi-official tax collectors, who were less directly controlled by the state than were the members of the regular fiscal bureaucracy.

The corresponding Russian development has certain distinct features. The Muscovite holders of office land, the *pomeshchiki,* insofar as they rendered military service, were from the beginning and in the main heavily armed horsemen, and because of the greater burden of their equipment they were usually assigned estates larger than a peasant farmstead. Within their *pomestye* they collected taxes from their peasants. Consequently their government, like the government of later Byzantium, gathered only a part of its revenue through professional fiscal officials.

Both regimes employed despotic methods of government in the organizational and acquisitive fields. In the constructional field such methods were used to a major degree only by Byzantium, and there essentially during the middle period (until the 11th century). The shrinking range of constructional operations in post-Manzikert Byzantium was interestingly paralleled by the shrinking range of its fiscal bureaucracy. In Muscovite Russia constructional activities were irrelevant from the start; and the fiscal system was, also from the start, characterized by a large nonbureaucratic sector.

Thus a positive correlation between operational and bureaucratic density can be formulated for the margin as well as for the core areas of hydraulic society. This correlation may be influenced by other factors, and strongly so. But experience bears out what theoretical considerations suggest: Other conditions being equal, the

c. Cf. Ostrogorsky, 1940: 262. Ostrogorsky describes the military difference between the two groups, which I correlate here with the two types of office land.

d. Ostrogorsky, 1940: 58. According to the *Tactica leonis* 20.71, they seem to have paid some minor imposts (*ibid.:* 48).

density of the despotic bureaucracy tends to increase or decrease
with the increase or decrease of its functions.

2. THE GROWTH OF PROPRIETARY FORCES

IN Byzantium and post-Mongol Russia the state controlled the bulk
of the land either fiscally or administratively, a large part of it being
assigned as office land to the soldiers of the *themes,* the *pronoetes,*
or to the *pomeshchiki.* Socially and economically, the *pronoia* holders
were more powerful than the plebian peasant warriors of the *themes;*
but they bore a closer resemblance to the Russian *pomeshchiki* than
to the feudal lords of Western Europe. Both the *pronoetes* and
pomeshchiki delivered part of their rural revenue to the state. Both
owed absolute obedience to their respective governments. And both
lacked the decisive capacity of feudal and postfeudal landlordism—
the capacity to organize independent nationwide political corporations (estates, *stände*).

However, these conditions did not prevail unaltered. They existed
in Late Byzantium up to 1204, the year in which the completely
defeated empire was replaced by the Latin Empire; and they underwent a great change in the final period of Byzantium, which ended
in 1453. In Russia they existed up to 1762, the year in which the
former *pomestye* land became the private property of its holders.

In later Byzantium and in post-Muscovite Russia private property
and enterprise gained considerable strength. In view of this fact
we may ask first, is such a development typical of agrarian despotisms and second, to what degree was the growth of proprietary
forces responsible for the societal changes that occurred in Byzantium
from 1261 to 1453 and in Russia from 1861 to 1917?

In Byzantium big landownership was an important factor even
before 1071; but its significance increased greatly when, at the end
of the 11th and at the beginning of the 12th century, the landlord-
pronoetes were given additional economic and judicial power. After
the fall of the Latin Empire, the *pronoetes,* who formerly had held
their grants for a limited time only, achieved the "hereditary and
unrestricted ownership" of their lands. And they also obtained tax
exemptions far greater than anything that had been customary.[19] The
corresponding shrinkage in the government revenue was a decisive
factor in the weakening of the Byzantine empire, which eventually
was unable to resist the Turks.

In Tsarist Russia events took a different course. Here industrialization made substantial advances in the 18th and particularly in the
19th century; and this development was closely related to the growth

of private property, first immobile (land) and ultimately also mobile (capital).

3. The Institutional Staying Power of Marginal Oriental Despotism

BUT the growth of proprietary forces did not bring about a transformation in Byzantine society like that achieved in Western Europe. Nor did it, prior to 1917, enable the Russian men of property to prevail over the men of the state apparatus. Why not? Were the beneficiaries of total power fully aware of the issue involved? And did they aim at isolating and crippling the representatives of property?

It is easy to juxtapose neatly separated camps. The real conditions, however, were much more complicated. In Byzantium, in Tsarist Russia, and in most other Orientally despotic countries the men of the apparatus were frequently also men of property. Consequently the conflict between the interests of the absolutist regime and the interests of private property and enterprise appear also—and often primarily—as a conflict between different members of the same ruling class or even as a conflict between different interests of individual members of this class. Why do such persons—as a group and over time—place their bureaucratic above their proprietary interests?

a. Bureaucratic Interests Favoring the Reproduction of the Despotic Order

THE civil or military official of an agrarian despotism is part of a bureaucratic hierarchy, which, taken in its entirety, enjoys more power, revenue, and prestige than any other group in the society. Of course, the post he holds today and the one he hopes to hold tomorrow carry with them the risk of total destruction; and he is therefore never safe. However, under the shadow of total power the man of property is never safe either; and the dangers of his position are not outweighed by satisfactions derived from active participation in the gambles and privileges of total power. Thus, not even the members of the bureaucratic class who hold no office challenge the principles of the absolutist regime, which they may rejoin tomorrow. And the officiating members of this class, confronted with the Big Conflict, aggressively uphold the privileges of bureaucratic power, revenue, and prestige which they are enjoying now.

Narrow and oversimplified interpretation has obscured the issue by formulating it only in terms of the interests of a single person, the autocratic ruler. To be sure, the despot is eager to perpetuate his absolute power, but, lacking an effective governmental apparatus, he cannot achieve this aim. The kings of Medieval Europe found absolutist power as sweet as did their Byzantine confrères. But the latter succeeded where the former failed, because the integrated Byzantine bureaucracy upheld the system of total power that favored both the sovereign and the men of the apparatus, whereas the enfeoffed vassals of the Western kings safeguarded and reproduced their privileges by keeping the king's power fragmented and checked.

To what extent can the prominence of the army in certain agro-managerial countries be taken as a sign of feudal decentralization? Military officials are as much men of the state apparatus as are their civil opposites; and if the first centuries of the Roman empire demonstrate anything, it is exactly this. For it was just when military leadership was prominent that Roman absolutism attained its maturity. The crystallization of despotic power in Muscovite Russia involved considerable bureaucratic activity; but the overwhelming majority of the new serving men wielded the sword and not the pen. The fact that in later Byzantium the heads of the military sector of the state apparatus figured prominently also as political leaders reflects the increasing pressure of foreign aggression. But it does not mean that these individuals served their government in a limited and conditional way as members of a baronial and feudal class.

b. Late Byzantium: Marasmus rather than Creative Transformation

WE must remember all this when we try to evaluate the effect of big property on the society of later Byzantium. Landed property increased during the first centuries of the Middle Empire; yet state protection of peasant holdings and periodic confiscations of large estates [20] notably retarded this development. After 1071, controls grew looser, but the state still had a rein on the country's rural economy. Contrary to corresponding developments in feudal Europe, conversion of the cadaster from a public to a private institution *"never* occurred in the East." [21] And the *pronoetes,* however they may have benefited personally, had to deliver a large part of the taxes they collected to the government.[22]

After the interlude of the Latin Empire, the state of Byzantium never regained its earlier authority. The landowners were now strong enough to withhold a much greater proportion of the national surplus than they had done previously, but they did not consolidate their ranks. Neither the great landowners nor the representatives of mobile urban wealth established nationwide corporations: estates. Private property became big; but it remained politically unorganized. Contrary to corresponding developments in the West, the growth of big private property in Byzantium did not give birth to a new society. It succeeded only in weakening and paralyzing the old one.

c. The Extraordinary Staying Power of Tsarist Bureaucracy

AFTER 1204 the Latin Empire temporarily replaced the traditional despotic regime. Could it be that the quasifeudal institutions of this empire (and of the Western enemies of Constantinople in general) influenced the bureaucratic absolutism of Byzantium so seriously that it was never able to regain its former superiority? In other words, did the rural and urban proprietors succeed in paralyzing the Byzantine government in the last centuries only because external forces broke the backbone of despotic power?

In terms of the fundamental issue the experiences of Tsarist Russia are eminently instructive. Post-Mongol Russia was invaded several times; but prior to the democratic revolution of 1917 the absolutist government was never completely broken. Russia's industrialization was strongly stimulated by Western developments. Foreign money flowed into private (capitalist) enterprises, increasing the weight of the proprietary sector. And Western methods and ideas notably affected Russian thought and performance. But all these external influences did not destroy the absolutist character of the state. The relation of the Tsarist bureaucracy to the forces of property—and eventually also to labor—continued to be determined by conditions that had long been operative in traditional Russian society. And this relation was, and remained, a relation of absolute bureaucratic superiority.

The masters of the despotic state apparatus responded to the changing historical situation with changing attitudes, but until 1917 they did not relinquish their total power. When in the early 18th century it became obvious that industrialization was vital for the country's defense, the Tsarist government was not satisfied with supervising and regulating the new industries, as the absolutist governments of Western Europe were doing. Instead, it directly managed the bulk of the heavy industry and, in addition also, part of the light industry,[e] probably employing for these purposes the

---

e. In 1743 the state had some 63,000 male "souls" ascribed to its (Ural) Mountain Works and 87,000 "souls" to its potash works (Mavor, 1925, I: 441), plus an unknown number of individuals who labored outside of these two main spheres of government production, whereas private workshops and factories occupied some 30,000 (ascribed) male "souls" (ibid.: 493). Under Elizabeth (1741–62) the sector of state-majority of all industrial workers in the form of ascribed labor.[f]

The machine age posed many new problems both in the agrarian and in the industrial spheres of life. The ruling bureaucracy solved them—clumsily, no doubt, but successfully insofar as the preservation of its hegemony was concerned. The Tsarist regime emancipated the serfs, but it maintained a tight control over the villages, which were administered in a quasi-Oriental manner. During the last decades of the 19th century the Russian government, by direct and indirect taxes, seems to have taken from the peasants almost the whole of their agricultural produce proper—almost 50 per cent of the entire peasant income.[23] And the same bureaucracy, which so effectively upheld its acquisitive interests, was perfectly willing to let the landed aristocracy lose a large part of its estates. Between 1861 and 1914 the land owned by this group shrank by over 40 per cent.[24] And Stolypin's reform program of 1908 showed the absolutist officialdom considerably more interested in creating a class of strong peasant owners than in protecting the landed prerogatives of its proprietary wing.

In the nonagrarian sector of economy the adjustments were similarly ingenious. The government encouraged private capitalist enterprise in industry and commerce and—to a lesser extent—also in communications and banking. But at the beginning of the 20th century it managed the bulk of the country's railroads; it maintained fiscal control over the comprehensive "monopoly" industries, and it occupied a key position in foreign investments. By means of state guarantees it influenced something like a third of the nonmonopolized light industry, and in 1914 no less than 90 per cent of the core of heavy industry, mining.[25]

These data indicate the strategic position that the Tsarist regime occupied in the economy of Russia at the beginning of the 20th century. In conformity with the majority of other analysts, the prominent Soviet economist, Lyashchenko, notes that the Russian banking system prior to the revolution "differed materially from the

managed industry temporarily shrank (*ibid.*: 440 ff.), but it rose again impressively during the later part of the century. The fourth census reports that for 1781–83 there were about 210,000 "souls" ascribed to the state-owned Mountain Works and 54,000 "souls" to private units (*ibid.*: 441). The somewhat less complete report of the Manufactures Collegium noted for 1780, 51,000 ascribed "souls" for the private Mountain Works and about 24,000 ascribed "souls" outside the key region of Russian industry, the "Mountains" (*ibid.*: 493).

f. Heavy industry formed the core of the state works, and until "the beginning of the nineteenth century, the iron mines and smelting works were manned exclusively by forced labor" (Mavor, 1925, I: 534).

banking system of the Western capitalist countries. . . . The state bank was the central bank of the entire Russian credit system," and the director of the credit department of the treasury "controlled the entire financial apparatus of the country." [26]

There is no need to rest the evaluation of Russia's societal order on the single criterion of financial control; but it certainly is worth noting that one bureau of the Tsarist state apparatus did control the country's entire financial system. Considering the role of the Tsarist bureaucracy in rural and urban society, it is difficult to avoid the decision that even at the beginning of the 20th century the men of the state apparatus were stronger than society.[27]

d. Ottoman Turkey

THE later development of Ottoman Turkey combines features of the Byzantine and the Russian patterns. The Turkish empire resembled Byzantium, with whose territory it was largely congruent, in that it also originally controlled classical areas of hydraulic economy; and it resembled Tsarist Russia in that it was also deeply influenced by the industrial society of modern Europe. It differed from Byzantium in that the loss of its hydraulic provinces virtually coincided with the decline of its political prominence; and it differed from Russia in that the growing economic and cultural influence of the industrial West was accompanied, and partly preceded, by a successful encroachment upon Turkey's sovereignty.

e. Diversified Final Evolutions

IN all three countries outside aggression was a crucial factor in the weakening of the despotic regime; and this indirectly confirms the staying power of the Orientally despotic order.

In the case of Byzantium, it is not entirely clear whether the final marasmus of the despotic regime was caused primarily by external or internal factors—that is, by the conquest of 1204 or by the excessive growth of landlordism. It is clear, however, that the growing proprietary forces did not dissociate themselves sharply and creatively from the decaying state. The impact of the West was sufficiently strong to paralyze the traditional despotic government, but it was not strong enough to pave the way for the growth of a new balanced and property-based (capitalist) society.

In the case of Russia, bureaucratic absolutism suffered a mortal blow from outside only in 1917. Prior to this date a marginal Oriental despotism adjusted itself successfully to the conditions of an advancing industrialization. The Tsarist government made more and more concessions to mobile and immobile property; and during the last period of its existence it even permitted a number of political organizations to operate on a national scale.[28] But these developments notwithstanding, the bureaucratic regime perpetuated itself until the beginning of the year 1917.

In the case of Turkey, foreign powers broke the backbone of Ottoman independence in a series of wars; and although Russia participated in the military defeat of Turkey, Western European influence prevailed in the ensuing transformation. It was under Western European influence that Turkey undertook important constitutional reforms. Due to the lesser significance of independent proprietary developments both in land and capital, the Turkish reforms were at first even more superficial than the reforms accomplished in the Tsarist empire, and this despite the fact that a first parliament was established in Turkey as early as 1876/7. But the weakness of the independent internal forces was to some degree compensated for by the increasing decay of the traditional state apparatus, which finally collapsed after the defeats suffered in the Second Balkan War and in World War I.

4. Marginal Agrarian Despotisms Containing Conspicuous Hydraulic Elements

AMONG marginal agrarian despotisms Muscovite Russia and Middle Byzantium, which exhibit numerous cultural similarities, share one trait that is particularly relevant to our inquiry: in neither civilization did agrohydraulic operations play a significant role. On the other hand, Liao and Maya society, which culturally had little in common, are alike in that hydraulic features were clearly apparent in both of them.

a. The Liao Empire

THE Liao empire deserves special attention for a number of reasons. It is one of the few Far Eastern societies of conquest in which "barbarian" (pastoral) conquerors—in this case, the Ch'i-tan—ruled over part of China without shifting their political center from their Inner Asiatic grazing grounds to the subdued (North) Chinese territories. Liao is the first of the four great historical Chinese dynasties of conquest, the three others being Chin (ruled by the Jurchen), Yüan (ruled by the Mongols), and Ch'ing (ruled by the Manchus). Liao institutions therefore have significant parallels in the Chin, Yüan, and

Ch'ing dynasties, and it would seem also in other dynasties of conquest and infiltration in China and elsewhere.[g]

During the two hundred years of their rule, the Ch'i-tan acquired no real understanding of the potentialities of hydraulic agriculture. Instead, and not dissimilar to other mounted "barbarians," they eyed with suspicion the irrigated fields which impeded the free sweep of their cavalry.[29] The greater part of their agrarian territories, however, had a long hydraulic tradition. Canals had been dug and rivers diked prior to the establishment of Liao power in North China and Manchuria;[30] and the Ch'i-tan conquerors seem to have been perfectly willing to preserve this hydraulic heritage. When a flood inundated thirty villages in present Hopei, "an imperial decree ordered the old canals dredged";[31] and when in 1074 excessive rains threatened the population of the Liao River basin, "the northern chancellor [ordered] large-scale mobilization of the able-bodied men along the river in order to complete the river dikes." An experienced official warned that such "large-scale works" would not be advantageous at this moment and he asked that the labor corvée be stopped. "The imperial court approved it and discontinued the work." Subsequent events indicated both the soundness of the official's warning—the river caused no calamity—and the dimension and weight of the hydraulic corvée: "Along the shores of the river for a thousand *li* there was not a person who was not highly pleased."[32]

The Liao government was equally well equipped—and considerably less reluctant—to employ its manpower for nonhydraulic constructions. Highways were maintained and repaired[33]—once with a huge corvée of two hundred thousand men;[34] chains of fortifications were erected along the frontier;[35] and two new capitals and many palaces, temples, and tombs were built north of the old seats of Chinese culture.[36] Literary descriptions and archaeological finds make it clear that the Liao labor service was as effective from the standpoint of the rulers as it was onerous from the standpoint of the people.[37]

Being great builders, the Liao rulers were also great organizers. Their offices registered the population for purposes of taxation, labor service, and military recruitment.[38] Their postal system was both elaborate and fast.[39] And their army was a well-coordinated fighting

g. This study was facilitated by the fact that the Chinese subjects of Liao, being trained in historiography, recorded the institutions of Liao society more fully than the scribes of most other conquest societies of Asia that were dominated by pastoral rulers. The reasons for this phenomenon are discussed in Wittfogel, 1949: *passim*.

machine. We have reason to believe that Chingis Khan shaped his own terrifying military organization after the Liao pattern.[40]

These constructional and organizational developments were supplemented by genuinely hydraulic methods of acquisition. True, some "entrusted" territories delivered only their wine tax to the central government; [41] but these regions comprised a mere fraction of the realm; [42] and eventually most of them came under full government control.[43] In the great majority of all administrative subdivisions the state insisted on its subjects paying taxes,[44] just as it insisted on their rendering labor and military services. Powerful families and monasteries sought to have households living on their land struck from the public registers, but evidently the state made no concessions in its claim to tax them.[45]

The final crisis of Liao power has all the earmarks of a dynastic crisis under a typical agrarian despotism. Here, as in similar circumstances, the landowners increased their acquisitive [46] but not their organizational strength. The collapse of the dynasty led to no property-based industrial order. Instead it led to the restoration and rejuvenation of the old agromanagerial society.

b. Maya Society

MAYA civilization presents ecological and cultural features that in several ways are unique. But these "unique" features overlay constructional, organizational, and acquisitive conditions remarkably similar to those of other marginal agromanagerial societies.

The ancient Maya were spread over a wide area, which comprised the greater part of present Guatemala, the western part of the Republic of Honduras, all of British Honduras, and Yucatan. Like most of Central America this area has a sharply divided rain year. From May to October precipitation is heavy, while during the remaining period there is little rain. This dichotomy encouraged elaborate hydraulic developments in territories that border the Lake of Mexico and also in several highland regions further to the south, the Maya-inhabited zones of Guatemala and Honduras among them. However, in large sections of the Maya area geological peculiarities decisively shaped and limited hydraulic enterprise. Almost the entire lowland plain of Yucatan and a great part of the hill zone between this plain and the highlands are composed of an extremely porous mineral: limestone; consequently precipitation quickly sinks below an easily accessible level.

A landscape which precludes the formation of rivers and lakes is of course entirely unsuitable for irrigation agriculture. Worse. The lack of natural storage places for drinking water, other than some well-like waterholes, presents a serious obstacle for any permanent or populous settlements. Persons desirous of establishing such settlements would therefore have to make concerted efforts not for purposes of irrigation but for the gathering and preservation of drinking water. As a result of such efforts we can expect to find hydraulic installations that play only a minor role in other agrarian societies.

When, in 1519, Cortez briefly visited Yucatan, he noted wells (*pozos*) and water reservoirs (*albercas*) in the residential compounds of the "nobles." [47] And in 1566 Landa, in the first systematic description of Maya civilization, stressed both the unique water difficulties of the area and the way in which moisture was provided "in part by industry and in part by nature." [48] It is significant that Landa, like the authors of the *Relaciones de Yucatán*,[h] places the man-made devices for providing water first.

The installations for providing drinking water were (1) artificial wells (*pozos* or *cenotes* in the primary sense of the Maya word),[49] (2) cisterns (*chultuns*), and (3) man-made large reservoirs (*aguadas*). The *Relaciones* report artificial *pozos* everywhere in the lowland; [50] and the early observers fully understood the difficulties of digging and maintaining good wells without the aid of metal tools.[51] Even after the introduction of iron implements, the maintenance and use of the man-made wells often required ingenious communal action.[52] In some cases the methods employed were intricate "past belief," [53] involving the active participation of "the population of a city." [54]

But important as the *cenotes* were, they did not as a rule provide water for large populations. Says Casares, a modern Yucatan engineer: "If we were to depend on the wells only for the supply of water, the greater part of our peninsula could not be inhabited." [55] This being so, the cisterns and *aguadas* of Yucatan become crucially significant.

Bottle-shaped subterranean constructions with circular openings, *chultuns,* have been discovered in several places. At Uxmal, Stephens noticed "so many of them, and in places where they were so little to be expected, that they made rambling out of the cleared paths dangerous, and to the last day of our visit we were constantly finding new ones." [56] These constructions seem to have provided "immense reservoirs for supplying the city with water." [57]

In part. Besides the *cenotes* and the cisterns,[i] the ancient Mayas

h. RY, I: 116, 144, 182, 206, 210, 221, 248, 266. Occasionally major emphasis is placed on the natural *pozos* (*ibid.*: 47, and perhaps 290).

i. Stephens (1848, I: 232) assumes that the *chultuns* of Uxmal had provided water for the people of the ruined city—"in part at least." Casares (1907: 227) also com-

constructed large pools or lakes, *aguadas*. Even in the hilly regions where the terrain provided natural waterholes or cavities, *sartenejos*, Casares considers the *aguadas*, whether natural or artificial, much more important. Those that were man-made differed greatly in shape and quality: "Some have a bottom made out of stones and some have not such stones, and they are of all sizes—true works of art they are—that show the ingenuity and attainments of their builders." [58]

Few students have searched for these *aguadas* as eagerly as did the pioneer explorer, Stephens. At first glance, many of them seemed natural,[59] and Stephens' informants felt sure—and recent research has proven them to be right [60]—that "hundreds are perhaps now buried in the woods, which once furnished this element of life to the teeming population of Yucatan." [61]

From the standpoint of hydraulic organization the importance of this fact can scarcely be overrated. The *cenotes* usually required the cooperative efforts of smaller communities only; and the urban cisterns were probably constructed and maintained by the work teams that "built at their own expense the houses of the lords." [62] But in the case of the *aguadas* large-scale cooperation was imperative. In the midnineteenth century a ranchero, who wanted the *aguada* near his estate cleaned, "secured the co-operation of all the ranchos and haciendas for leagues around, and at length fairly enlisting them all in the task, at one time he had at work fifteen hundred Indians, with eighty superintendents." [63] This much coordinated labor was required when a single *aguada* had to be cleaned with iron tools. Under the stone-age conditions of the ancient Maya, the cleaning, and still more the building, of a chain of *aguadas* certainly involved huge work teams.

Further studies must be made before the institutional weight of the man-made *cenotes*, cisterns, and *aguadas* can be fully determined. But even our present limited knowledge entitles us to state that the constructional operations of the Maya include a not inconsiderable hydraulic sector. *Aguadas* were in use not only in the lowlands but also in the hill zone,[64] where some of the most ancient centers of Maya civilization were located.[65] And irrigation canals, artificial lakes, and other familiar types of hydraulic works have been discovered in the highland sector of the Maya area [j] and, of course, also in the hill zone.[k]

---

ments on the limited capacity of these cisterns to satisfy the water needs of most of the ancient cities.

j. In the old Maya city of Palenque, Stephens discovered the remains of a water channel faced with large stones (Stephens, ITCA, II: 321 and 344). Blom found an elaborate drainage system "in other parts of the ruins" (Blom and La Farge, TT, I:

The nonhydraulic constructions of the ancient Maya have been frequently described. The early Spanish records stress the magnitude of the "houses" and "edifices," which the people built for their secular and priestly masters; [66] and grandiose ruins confirm the early written evidence. Massive stone highways connected a number of cities, and like the pyramids, palaces, and temples they must have required great levies of corvée labor.[67]

No compensation was given for certain types of the construction corvée; [68] and a similar policy may have prevailed also with regard to other corvée services, including agricultural labor for "the lords." [69] But whether the pay arrangements for labor services were uniform or not, there can be little doubt that the commoners worked for their masters in a disciplined manner. Prominent men, obviously officials, "who were very well obeyed," [70] acted on the ruler's behalf. And the power of the sovereign, who controlled either a single city-state or a cluster of such units, can be judged from the fact that local officials received no share of the tax they collected for delivery to the center.[m] The so-called "town councilors," who assisted the highest local official, were "in charge of certain subdivisions of the town, collecting tribute and attending to other municipal affairs." [71] According to a regional description, the officials of the town wards had "to attend to the tribute and services (communal labor?) at the proper time and to assemble the people of their wards for banquets and festivals as well as for war." [72] In addition to a variety of civil officials, who used a hieroglyphic script and who, among other things, kept land records,[73] there were military officials, some holding their posts for life, some being appointed for three-year

189). He also noticed a "fairly elaborate" irrigation system in Amatenango, Chiapas (*ibid.*, II: 396), a region which was formerly part of the Old Maya empire. Further to the east, in Guatemala, Stephens (ITCA, I: 206) encountered "a large artificial lake, made by damming up several streams." A canal in Honduras, probably prehistoric, may have "served to irrigate a large portion of the lower plain" near Lake Yojoa (Strong, Kidder, and Paul, 1938: 101).

k. The hill zone, intermediate between the mountain region and Northern Yucatan, contains troughlike depressions, whose clay bottoms hold "lakes, swampy lowlands, and streams" (Lundell, 1937: 5; Ricketson, 1937: 9; Cooke, 1931: 287), but even here the greater part of the terrain is composed of a limestone so porous that the natural precipitation quickly sinks below a readily accessible level, creating a dangerous deficiency during three or four months of every year (Ricketson, 1937: 10). Bottle-shaped *chultuns*, "excavated in the solid limestone throughout the region," may have been used for storing water, if their walls were "rendered impervious by plaster" (*ibid.:* 9 ff.). An *aguada* near Uaxactun is "doubtless the remains of an ancient reservoir, and excavation in its bottom would probably lay bare the stone flooring with which it originally had been paved" (Morley, 1938: 139).

m. The local officials were supported by the people, who worked their fields, maintained their houses, and served them personally (Tozzer, 1941: 62 ff., n. 292; Roys, 1943: 62).

terms.[74] Picked men, who did most of the fighting and who received a special compensation, seem to have constituted cadre troops, but "other men could also be called out." [75] The rulers determined (and limited) the duration of a campaign in accordance with pragmatic considerations, October to the end of January, the agricultural slack season, being considered the most suitable time for waging war.[76]

In the acquisitive sphere the power of the regime over its subjects was equally unchecked; and there is no reason to doubt that the rulers used their opportunities to the full. It has been said that "tribute" was light; [77] and the amounts requested from individual households may indeed have been modest. But it must be remembered that under Mexican and Inca dominion, subjects who cultivated the fields for the state and the temples paid no taxes. In contrast to this, the Maya commoners who worked the fields of their masters delivered in addition "maize, beans, chile, poultry, honey, cotton cloth, and game." [78] One regional report implies that such tributes were voluntary, but another dealing with the same locality notes that anyone who failed to pay would be sacrificed to the gods.[79]

5. "LOOSE 2" OR "MARGINAL 1"?

OUR survey of Byzantium and Russia and of the Liao empire and Maya civilization leads to several conclusions. The hydraulic density of the four institutional complexes differs greatly: it is very low or zero in the first two cases and relatively high in the last two. As a matter of fact, a reasonable argument can be made for classing Liao and the Maya as borderline cases of loose hydraulic societies— variants of "Loose 2," to use our symbols. For the time being we shall view them conservatively as marginal Oriental societies with substantial hydraulic elements, "Marginal 1" (M 1), as juxtaposed to "Marginal 2" (M 2), that is, Oriental societies with little or no hydraulic substance.

The closeness of M 1 to L 2 and the gap between M 1 and M 2 are as significant as the fact that all variants of the marginal type utilize the organizational and acquisitive methods of despotic statecraft. Thus, however marginal they may be hydraulically, their methods of social control place all of them definitely in the "Oriental" world.

6. FRAGMENTING PATTERNS OF INHERITANCE AND A GOVERNMENT-DEPENDENT DOMINANT RELIGION

MANY supplementary data can be adduced to strengthen our basic classification. But here we shall refer only to two particularly significant criteria: the fragmenting system of inheritance and the dependence of religious authority.

The Justinian Code—*Novella* 118—prescribes the equal division of property among the children of a deceased person. This provision, whatever its origin, fits to perfection the needs of agrarian despotism.

In Russia proprietary conditions changed as greatly as the institutional patterns of which they were a part. *Votchina* land, a pre-Mongol form of strong noble property, was not subjected to fragmentation; and this continued to be the custom until long after the noble owners of such land were compelled to serve the state. *Pomestye* land was office land. Originally it passed from father to one son; [80] but since all adult males were obliged to render civil or military service, the *pomestye* estate was finally considered a family possession to be divided among the father's several heirs.[81] When the growing importance of firearms changed the aristocratic cavalry army into a plebeian infantry army, fewer noble serving men were needed, and Peter I, who merged *pomestye* and *votchina* land, made the use of the new type of service (state) land hereditary.[82] The law of 1731 is an important milestone in the process of making *pomestye* land private. From this year on, *pomestye* land was divided among all the children and, according to the Law Book, "equally among all of them." [83]

In Western Europe the nobles emerged from a period of contractual and limited (feudal) state service with their landed property strengthened through primogeniture and entail. Contrary to this, and contrary also to the indigenous *votchina* tradition, the nobles of Tsarist Russia emerged from a period of compulsory and unlimited state service with their landed property weakened through a law of inheritance that prescribed fragmentation.

In Liao society the ruling tribal stratum—except in the matter of imperial succession—seems to have rejected primogeniture,[84] thus maintaining its pastoral *mores,* which permitted all sons to share in the family property. In its Chinese sector the regime was careful to uphold the traditional Chinese laws.[85] Many edicts praised Chinese subjects who conformed to what were considered ideal patterns of Chinese familism.[86] This being so, we have no reason to doubt that the government also upheld the fragmenting Chinese law of inheritance.

A fragmenting pattern of inheritance certainly prevailed among the Maya. Says Landa: "These Indians did not permit their daughters to inherit with their brothers, except it was through kindness or good will; and in this case they gave them some part of the accumulation, and the brothers divided the rest equally, except that to the one who had aided the most notably in increasing the property, they gave the equivalent." [87]

In Byzantium the Church, being nationally organized from the beginning, was well prepared to strive for independence. But the rulers of Eastern Rome and Early Byzantium treated religion as part of the *jus publicum;* and even after the catastrophies of the 7th century, the Byzantine government was able to combat the Church's drive for autonomy. In the 10th century the emperor still played a decisive role in the selection of the Patriarch. And by virtue of his judicial position he could also interfere in church administration.[88]

Significantly, the Church became more independent in the last phase of the Middle Empire; but even then the emperor could still force an obstructing Patriarch to abdicate.[n] It was only after the period of the Latin Empire that a completely shattered autocracy was compelled to tolerate an almost autonomous Church.[89]

In Tsarist Russia the bureaucratic regime expressed its enormous vitality by its victory over the Eastern Church, which after the fall of Byzantium shifted its center to Moscow, the "Third Rome." At the end of the Mongol period the increasingly powerful Russian state exerted an ever-increasing authority over the Church. Ivan III seized half the monasterial land in Novgorod; Ivan IV, the Terrible, required more taxes and services from Church land; [90] and in 1649 a new "department of monasteries" further tightened the state's control over the Church.[91] In 1721, Peter I abolished the Patriarchate and placed the Church under a government body, the Holy Synod.[92] And a few decades later, in 1764, the state seized most of the Church land without compensation, assigning only one-eighth of the revenue from the land to the clergy.[93] In consequence of these combined political, religious, and economic measures, "the church became more and more a part of the administrative machinery of the state." [94]

In Liao society the problem of an independent Church never arose. Government officials, headed by the emperor, shared leadership in religious ceremonies with a variety of shamans, who, like the priests of the Buddhist temples, obviously were not coordinated in any nationwide and independent organization ("church").[95]

The close relation between secular and religious authority among the Maya has already been mentioned. The ruler of a territorial state, the *halach uinic,* is believed to have fulfilled "definite religious functions"; [96] and certain priests might also be war chiefs.[97] But

---

n. A serious conflict was finally decided in favor of the Church, not because the Church was such a strong independent factor but because the high bureaucracy turned against the sovereign (Ostrogorsky, 1940: 239 ff.).

nothing indicates that the priests of the great temples were bound together in any single organization, except insofar as they participated in the work of the government. Says Scholes: "In many cases priestly and political functions had been combined in such a manner that it was difficult, if not impossible, to differentiate them." [98]

7. LOCATION, GENESIS, AND INSTITUTIONAL VULNERABILITY OF MARGINAL AGRARIAN DESPOTISMS

MIDDLE and Late Byzantium, the Liao empire, and the Maya point up some of the institutional diversities among marginal agrarian despotisms. Discussion of other pertinent civilizations would differentiate further the picture we have of this significant subtype. The Hopi Indians of Arizona, for instance, engage in extremely modest hydraulic enterprises—mainly communal spring cleaning [99]—but their building activities are impressive.

Tibet was faced with certain irrigation tasks in the river valleys of the high plateau,[100] but the hydraulic weight of these tasks was probably not great. Nevertheless, the "monk officials" [101] did operate a well-functioning labor service [102] and an elaborate and fast postal system also.[103] Holders of land grants served the government unconditionally and as regular officials; [104] and the fiscal apparatus insisted on taxing the bulk of the population.[105]

The kings of ancient Asia Minor and certain territorial rulers in early China were more outstanding as builders and organizers than as hydraulic engineers. But once the common institutional denominator is understood, it is easy to recognize that all these civilizations are variants of the marginal type of hydraulic society.

How did these marginal configurations come into being? And how open were they to change? Before trying to answer these questions, we must consider their relative location—that is, their spacial relation to the major hydraulic areas of the world.

a. Location

TAKING the major hydraulic zones of the Old and the New World as coordinates, we find marginal developments, as for instance the nonhydraulic territorial states of ancient China, interspersed between definitely hydraulic areas. Many other marginal developments (the Hopi Pueblos, the kingdoms of ancient Asia Minor, Middle Byzantium, Tibet, Liao, and the Maya) appear at the geographical periphery of a hydraulic zone.

Russia, however, does not. Russia had no close hydraulic neighbors when, in the 13th century, the Mongols began to introduce

Orientally despotic methods of government. Cases like Russia are more the exception than the rule; but they serve to demonstrate that marginal agrarian despotisms may arise at a great distance from the nearest conspicuous center of hydraulic life.

b. Genesis

THE relative location of most marginal agromanagerial states is highly suggestive of their origins. The bulk of all such regimes obviously came into being not earlier—and often demonstrably later —than the area's oldest hydraulic civilizations. In some cases, such as Byzantium, the marginal territory split off from an older (loose) hydraulic complex. In others, the marginal territory was adjacent to a hydraulic society proper; and while interrelation cannot always be documented, it seems probable that it was the second type which stimulated the first.

The constructional, organizational, and acquisitive patterns of the hydraulic center may have been transferred directly to nonhydraulic regions during periods of temporary control. Or native leaders may have adopted .the power techniques of their hydraulic neighbors, which from the standpoint of the ruling group had much to recommend them and which could be easily imposed on a society that lacked strong, well-organized, and independent proprietary, military, and ideological forces. Or experts in managerial and despotic control may have gone from their hydraulic homeland to adjacent nonhydraulic territories either in flight or on invitation to become teachers or co-leaders in their new environment.

On an institutional checkerboard familiarity with the hydraulic techniques of organization and acquisition was probably all that was needed to encourage a changeover from a loosely coordinated nonhydraulic tribe to a nonhydraulic managerial community. Thus it is easy to understand why the Hopi Indians built fortress-like villages similar to those of the more properly hydraulic Pueblos; why, like the inhabitants of other Pueblos, they integrated their work teams under communal leaders; and why they cultivated the fields of their supreme chieftain.

A combination of state-centered hydraulic and marginal agromanagerial societies may emerge from a composite tribal root. In prehistoric and protohistoric China such a development may have been stimulated by varied and prolonged culture contacts: visits, alliances, trade relations, and conquests.

The introduction of marginal agromanagerial institutions by nonagrarian tribal conquerors presents another genetic pattern. In this case, the conquerors employ and transfer organizational and acquisitive methods of hydraulic statecraft, although they themselves do not, to any relevant extent, practice agriculture, not even in its nonhydraulic form. And being nomadic, they may carry these methods far beyond the political and cultural borders of any major hydraulic area. The Mongol conquest of Russia demonstrates both points.⁰

The power of the Ch'i-tan differed from that of the Golden Horde in character as well as in origin. The bulk of the agricultural regions of the Liao empire had previously been part of the old, loosely hydraulic world of China; and the Ch'i-tan masters found it easy to perpetuate the traditionally absolutist administration with the aid of Chinese officials, who were ready to act as junior partners in a somewhat uneasy, but workable, alliance. Like the Mongols of the Golden Horde, the Ch'i-tan tribesmen in their great majority remained pastoralists; but their ruling group integrated itself closely with Orientally despotic officials, who directed huge nonhydraulic constructions and even considerable hydraulic operations.

The marginal agromanagerial societies discussed in our survey came into being in various ways; but they all seem to have derived from compact or loose hydraulic societies. In many instances, such an origin is certain, and in others it is likely. But is it the necessary and only way?

By no means. It is entirely possible that some agrodespotic societies emerged independently. But obviously we can assume such a development only when the despotic order in question fulfills the organizational and acquisitive functions of a hydraulic government and when, for geographical and historical reasons, institutional diffusion can be excluded as altogether unlikely. Having acknowledged the possibility of independent origin, I must add that the cases in which agrodespotic regimes in the terms of our inquiry certainly or probably have a hydraulic ancestry are so numerous that the cases in which independent origins can be established will not substantially change our basic contention. Virtually all historically significant agrodespotisms that

---

o. The attempt to explain the rise of Muscovite despotism as the consequence of external military pressure usually results in the view that this pressure was exerted in the main by Eastern nomadic aggressors (see Kluchevsky, HR, II: 319 ff.). The imitation of despotic power techniques by a non-"Oriental" government is of course conceivable, particularly if the nongovernmental sector of society lacks "strong, well-organized, and independent proprietary, military, and ideological forces." However, the noble owners of *votchina* land, although not organized in a corporation, were not without strength; and the actual events of the Mongol period show that the Great Princes of Moscow, who set out to subdue them, were for a considerable time directly under Tatar leadership.

fulfill no hydraulic functions seem to have been derived from hydraulic societies.

c. Institutional Vulnerability

DIRECT or indirect connection with an agrohydraulic center seems to have been necessary for the rise of virtually all marginal agrarian despotisms. But a continued connection is not imperative for their perpetuation. Apart from Late Byzantium, which was critically weakened by external forces, marginal Oriental societies have been able to reproduce their patterns of power amazingly well.

Obviously it is enormously difficult to create an effective counterweight to an apparatus government, which has succeeded in repressing, crippling, and fragmenting those proprietary, military, and ideological forces that enabled Medieval (feudal) Europe to evolve into an industrial society. Serious political crises occurred in all hydraulic societies. But the way in which the men of the apparatus overcame them demonstrates the staying power of their methods of organization and exploitation. Purposeful political activists strove to reestablish the only thoroughly tested type of government, which, at the same time, promised them total power and total privilege. And their restorative endeavors were greatly facilitated by the political and organizational ineptitude of their nongovernmental rivals. Among the big landowners, even if they were many, politically ambitious elements were much more eager to seize than to restrict total power. And the representatives of mobile (capitalist) property, even if they were many, were so unaccustomed to think in terms of property-based state power that they were satisfied to get on with their business without making the bid for political leadership that was so characteristic of the differently conditioned bourgeoisie of the West.

In this context, Middle and Late Byzantium and post-Mongol Russia pose crucial questions. Contrary to Maya civilization and the Liao empire—and of course, contrary to all hydraulic societies proper—these two great Eurasian countries fulfilled no relevant agromanagerial functions. And the nonagricultural managerial functions which the Tsarist regime performed did not involve the broad organizational penetration usual even in loosely hydraulic societies.

Did these circumstances reduce the institutional staying power of either marginal Oriental despotism? As stated before, the Byzantine case is not altogether conclusive; but even here it may be asked whether a more intensely managerial regime could have beaten off the external attacks without yielding so much to the proprietary forces within its borders. In Russia the absolutist bureaucracy re-

produced itself ingeniously, but it permitted the growth of democratic forces of property and labor that in 1917 temporarily prevailed
over the men of the apparatus.

Evidently, marginal agrarian despotisms, like hydraulic societies
proper, tend to reproduce their basic power system, and this over a
period of time. Like hydraulic societies proper they have a stationary
quality. But they seem somewhat more open to structural change,
particularly if they entirely lack hydraulic substance.

D. THE SUBMARGINAL ZONE OF
THE HYDRAULIC WORLD

1. THE PHENOMENON

THE effective coordination of absolutist methods of organization and
acquisition is the minimum requirement for the maintenance of a
genuine agrarian despotism. Outside this margin we find civilizations that, although lacking such a combination, exhibit stray features
of hydraulic statecraft. The areas in which such stray features occur
in other societal orders constitute the submarginal zone of the
hydraulic world.

2. CASES

a. Protohistorical Greece

AN institutional analyst of protohistorical Greece cannot fail to be
struck by the hydraulic quality of Minoan Crete. This civilization
certainly owed its international prominence to its maritime relations;
but while acknowledging this, we must not forget that nearness to
the sea alone explains little. The ancient Cretans, like other seafaring
peoples, established their thalassocracy on the basis of specific internal conditions.

To what extent Aegean patterns of "fetching water by artificial
means" and of using canals and ditches for the purposes of refined
agriculture [1] made Minoan society hydraulic is not clear. It is clear,
however, that the islanders accomplished miracles regarding matters
of drainage and probably also of water supply.[2] We do know that
Crete was covered with a network of excellent roads.[3] And we have
reason to believe that the supervisor of public works occupied a
high position [4] in the country's complex and centralized administration.[5] The Minoan script is still undeciphered, but the government certainly employed it widely for "bureaucratic methods of

registration and accounting which were handed down from century
to century and were perfected in the process." [6]

These and other facts support the view that "the Minoan civilization was essentially non-European." [7] And although the Minoans
had too many cultural peculiarities to be called "part of the East," [8]
they were connected through "a few clear and even close bonds with
Asia Minor, Syria and Egypt." [9] Ehrenberg concludes that "in particular the sultan-like life of the kings of Cnossus and Phaestus, their
courts, their officials, their economy, displayed features which were
similar to those of their opposite numbers in the Near East; they
were equally unlike anything Western." [10]

The proto-Greek Mycenaean civilization, which rose when Minoan
power decayed, accounts for significant quasihydraulic developments
in Argolis and Boeotia, and probably also in other parts of eastern
Greece. Between the middle and the close of the second millennium
B.C. Mycenaean engineers executed great drainage works around the
Lake of Copais in Boeotia; and they covered Argolis with an elaborate network of roads.[11] Their rulers lived in huge castle-like
edifices, and they erected monumental tombs.[12] Bengtson compares
their constructional achievements to "the great creations of the
ancient Orient, the pyramids and the *ziqqurats*." [13] True, we hear
nothing of a bureaucracy, and the use of the early script seems to
have been restricted.[14] But despite such limitations, Bengtson believes that "only a strong central power could plan and execute these
works," which, considering their magnitude, in all probability required the services of both native corvée laborers and captured
slaves.[a]

Moreover, an Oriental origin has been suggested for the worship
of the earth gods and the stars which the historical Greeks inherited
from their Mycenaean ancestors, and it was indeed in connection
with such religious observances that they practiced prostration.[15]
But when the Greeks of the classical period refused to perform before
an Oriental despot the act of submission they considered appropriate
to the gods,[16] they demonstrated that even if Mycenaean Greece was
marginally hydraulic, post-Mycenaean Greece belonged to the submarginal zone of the hydraulic world. In the classical period also
the monumental edifices of Argolis [17] had long lost their significance;
and the grandiose temple city of Athens, the Acropolis, whose beginnings go back to Mycenaean times,[18] was administered by a government that delegated even the management of its public works to
private entrepreneurs.[19]

a. Bengtson, 1950: 41. Bengtson mentions the slaves before he mentions the native
corvée laborers, but he calls the latter as numerous as the former.

b. Early Rome

PRIOR to Roman times the Etruscans, who apparently came from the marginal hydraulic zone of Asia Minor,[20] are known to have engaged in stupendous building activities. Their waterworks in the Po Plain are impressive,[21] and others undertaken in Central Italy are equally worthy of attention.[22] While under Etruscan dominion, the Romans learned how to construct "monumental works."[23] Later, but before they established their first colony on Hellenistic ground, they began to build solid overland roads.[24] But although such developments are more characteristic of a hydraulic than a relatively simple rainfall-based agrarian order, Rome at this period manifestly was an aristocratic variant of a multicentered non-Oriental society.

c. Japan

IN ancient Greece and Rome Oriental elements have often been overlooked. In Japan they have frequently been overestimated, and this for a good reason. Japan is part of the Asian continent, and Japanese civilization shares important features with China and India. Furthermore, the Japanese have developed one of the most subtle systems of irrigation farming known to man. Nevertheless, Japanese society never was hydraulic in the terms of our inquiry.

Why did Japan's rice economy not depend on large and government-directed water works? Any competent economic geographer can answer this question. The peculiarities of the country's water supply neither necessitated nor favored substantial government-directed works. Innumerable mountain ranges compartmentalized the great Far Eastern islands; and their broken relief encouraged a fragmented (hydroagricultural) rather than a coordinated (hydraulic) pattern of irrigation farming and flood control. According to the institutional historian, Asakawa, the Japanese landscape permitted "no extensive *Bewässerungskultur* as in Egypt and in parts of western Asia and China."[25] Japan's irrigation agriculture was managed by local rather than by regional or national leaders; and hydraulic trends were conspicuous only on a local scale and during the first phase of the country's documented history.

The rulers of the dominant political center effected a loose political unification at a rather early date, but they were not faced with hydraulic tasks that required the coordinated operation of large corvée teams. Nor were they conquered by the forces of an Orientally despotic state. They therefore failed to establish a comprehensive managerial and acquisitive bureaucracy capable of controlling the nongovernmental forces of society as did the men of the apparatus on the Chinese mainland.

The attempt to establish a centralized and bureaucratic despotism in Japan reached its first spectacular climax in the Taikwa Reform of 646. From the standpoint of our key criteria, its objectives can be listed as follows:

I. Construction
    A. Hydraulic. An edict of 646 demanded uniform procedures relating to dikes and canals.[26]
    B. Nonhydraulic. The basic reform edict ordered the creation of a system of roads for the imperial post.
II. Organization
    A. The population was to be counted periodically and census registers were to be kept.
    B. A government corvée replaced older local (and quasi-feudal) obligations.
    C. A state post was to be operated.
III. Acquisition
    A. The peasants were to be taxed on the basis of the land which the government assigned to them.
    B. Service in the state corvée could be commuted by the payment of a tax.[27]
    C. A number of officials, particularly local and high-ranking dignitaries, were to be supported from land holdings, which had often been previously owned by the new appointees and which were tax exempt.

Compared with the Merovingian and Carolingian attempts at absolute rule, the Japanese program of 646 was much more Oriental. This fact cannot be explained by Japanese contact with T'ang China alone. For centuries the Japanese had practiced irrigation farming [28] and their rulers had engaged in constructing works of a nonhydraulic type. Thus the effort of the masters of the Reform government to do as the Chinese emperors did was rooted in indigenous trends that were definitely, if rudimentarily, hydraulic.

But these quasi-Oriental trends were unable to shape Japanese society. The hydraulic innovations suggested in the Reform lacked the dynamism that characterized similar attempts in early hydraulic societies. The Reform favored the execution of "public works"; but while three of the six T'ang ministries (taxation, war, and justice) were taken over with little modification and two others (administrative personnel and rites) were successfully modified, the sixth (the Board of Public Works) found no counterpart in the new Japanese set-up.[29]

This omission was no accident. A canal that was dug in 656 struck the people as "mad"; and its critics compared it with a useless colossal hill that was built at the same time.[30] Moreover, the decrees that proclaimed a universal state labor service required many less days of corvée work than did T'ang regulations. And the provisions for commuting the corvée by paying a tax showed the Japanese government more interested in revenue than in labor.[31]

The assignment (and/or reassignment) of tax-free land to important officials was perhaps the Reform government's greatest concession to the feudal forces of Japanese society. Behind the new bureaucratic facade a fierce fight was being made to extend and consolidate tax-free land. And so successful were the representatives of the centrifugal forces that the official grantees eventually established themselves as hereditary landowners who, like their European counterparts, introduced a single-heir system of succession.[32]

As the system of tenure changed, universal census taking collapsed; and attempts to reestablish it led nowhere.[33] General taxation met the same fate. Many elements of Chinese culture notwithstanding, the decentralized and property-based society of the Japanese Middle Ages resembled much more closely the feudal order of the remote European world than the hydraulic patterns of nearby China. The poets of feudal Japan, like their confrères in feudal Europe, glorified the heroic deeds of individual warriors or groups of warriors. But the loosely agglomerated armies of Medieval Japan did not stimulate tactical or strategic thinking. The Japanese writers of the period quoted Chinese military authorities, such as Sun Tzŭ; but feudal Japan, like feudal Europe, failed to develop the art of war.[b] Prior to 1543, the Japanese armies "were made up of small, independent bands of soldiers who fought more as individuals than as units of a tactical formation." [c]

b. The reader will remember that the term "art of war" connotes the practice and theory of strategy and tactics. A recent survey of ancient and medieval military organization ascribes "the beginnings of an acknowledged art of war" in postfeudal Europe to Maurice of Nassau (Atkinson, 1910: 599), who played a decisive role in the latter part of the Dutch War of Independence.

c. Brown, 1948: 236 ff. A collection of early Japanese texts, Gunsho Ruijū, contains many references to Sun Tzŭ and other military theoreticians of his period. But the Japanese treatment of warfare is "a rather scattered melange quite unlike Sun Tzŭ. . . . The first integrated treatment of the subject comes in a work by Takeda Shingen (1521–1573)" (from a letter of February 16, 1954, from Dr. Marius Jansen, University of Washington, Seattle, who established this point in collaboration with his colleague, Dr. Richard N. McKinnon)

The absolutist concentration of government power, which characterized the Tokugawa period (1603–1867), again resembled more closely Western absolutist developments, both in its economic aspect (the slow rise of property-based commercial and industrial capitalism) and in its political limitations. It was during this period—actually in 1726—that "the first tolerably exact census" was taken.[34] It was then that the road system spread vigorously; [35] and it was then that the government, like certain of the prominent feudal lords, dug a number of locally important canals.[36]

But despite these and other activities—which, except for the irrigation works, find illuminating parallels in absolutist Europe—the absolutist regime of Japan was not strong enough to establish its acquisitive power over the whole empire. Out of a national revenue of twenty-eight or twenty-nine million *koku,* the representatives of supreme power, the Tokugawa shoguns and the court, arrogated to themselves only about eight million *koku,* while by far the larger part of the revenue remained in the hands of great feudal vassals.[37] Japanese absolutism sharply restricted the power of the feudal lords. But until 1867 it was unable to eliminate them.

While stressing the similarities between traditional Japanese society and the feudal and postfeudal West, we must be careful not to oversimplify the picture. The Oriental quality of many Japanese institutions and ideas is beyond doubt. On the lower and local level, Japanese irrigation agriculture required quasihydraulic coordination and subordination; and the feudal lords' insistence upon absolute obedience may, at least in part, reflect such quasihydraulic relations. Rudiments of a postal system seem to have existed prior to the Tokugawa period; [38] and the symbol of total submission, prostration, persisted until modern times.[d] The members of the ruling group, although strongly imbued with a military spirit, continued to think in terms of a somewhat adjusted Confucianism; [39] and although they invented simplified phonetic symbols, they employed with genuine pride the Chinese script, which, like Confucius' conception of the gentleman-bureaucrat, was better suited to a civil and learned officialdom than to a war-minded knighthood.

To sum up: traditional Japan was more than Western feudalism with wet feet. While the Far Eastern island society gave birth to a property-based and genuinely feudal order, its many and cherished elements of Chinese policy and thought show that, in a submarginal way, it was related to the institutional patterns of the hydraulic world.

d. During my stay in Japan in 1935 a number of university professors greeted each other in my presence—and prior to an official banquet—by prostration.

d. Pre-Mongol (Kievan) Russia

RUSSIAN society prior to the Mongol conquest (1237–40) presents another and equally illuminating aspect of the hydraulic submargin. In pre-Kievan and Kievan days the subsistence economy of the "Rus" included stock-raising; [e] but its mainstay was agriculture, rainfall agriculture.[40] Under the conditions of a primarily natural economy this agriculture favored the development of a broadly spread landed nobility, which was subordinated to the territorial princes in a loose way.[f] Below this stratum, but above the slave-like *kholopi*,[41] a class of free cultivators moved with comparative ease; [42] and the towns-people were even less restricted. Their "council," the *veche*, could take independent political action not only in the great northern republic of Novgorod [43] but also in such capital cities as Vladimer,[44] and even in Kiev.[45] Prior to the establishment of the Kievan state (*ca.* 880) [g] legal transactions could be consummated, and without interference from any princely authority, by the heads of the rural— and urban—communities, which in the most ancient Russian law code extant are called *mir*.[h] And even in the Kievan era (*ca.* 880–1169), the government, although considerably stronger than previously, was far from being absolutist—indeed as far from such a condition as the government of any feudal state in the contemporary West. Institutionally speaking, Kievan society manifestly belonged to the protofeudal and feudal world of Europe.

It belonged to this world, but in a way that requires special investigation. Like hydraulic society, feudal society, too, has an institutional margin; and Russia's tribal civilization, which arose on the eastern periphery of the feudal world, was for centuries, and particularly after 880,[46] dominated by the Varangians,[47] who were rooted in—and repeatedly supported by—a northern fringe area: Scandinavia. But although Rurik had once received a fief from the Frankish emperor,[48] he did not impose the Western European system of land tenure on the Eastern Slavs. Nor did his successors.

---

e. The oldest known version of the Russian law, *Russkaya Pravda*, mentions crimes pertaining to oxen, sheep, goats, horses, calves, and lambs (Goetz, RR, I: 15 ff.).

f. This fact has been established through the pioneer investigations of Pavlo-Silvansky. For a survey of his major conclusions see Borosdin, 1908: 577. For an independent study arriving at similar conclusions for the early Russian society see Hötzsch, 1912: 544.

g. Vernadsky (1943: 368) places Oleg's conquest of Kiev "between A.D. 878 and 880 (tentatively, 878)."

h. *Russkaya Pravda*, I, 17 = Goetz, RR, I: 8, 9. Cf. Vernadsky, 1948: 134. In the third version of the Law, the early term, *mir*, is replaced by *gorod*, city (*Russkaya Pravda*, III: 40 = Goetz, RR, I: 28, 29, cf. 272 ff.).

The native nobles and the members of the princely retinue, the *druzhina,* operated under no feudal contract.[49] Their freedom to "ride away" [50] indicates a type of independence that in Western feudalism was more the exception than the rule.[51] On the other hand, the princely rulers of the various territorial states drew their maintenance not from royal domains, as was usual in most feudal countries, but from a general tax, custom fees, and legal fines.[52]

Thus Kievan society resembled the feudal order of the West in that the rulers shared the power of making political decisions "with the popular assembly *(veche)* and the senate *(boyarskaya duma)*"; [53] and the nobles were able to establish a form of absolute landownership that the lords of Western Europe matched only at the close of the Middle Ages. As in the feudal West, the cities—at least the large ones—and the nobles paid no taxes.[54] But this extremely loose arrangement interlocked with a fiscal system that permitted the sovereign to tax the entire rural population. The principle of levying a tax on each fireplace was employed in Byzantium; [55] and the semipastoral Khazars applied it to those Eastern Slavs over whom, prior to the victory of the Varangians, they had control. The Varangians followed the fiscal procedure of the Khazars,[56] and they continued to do so with modifications during the whole Kievan period.[57] They also adopted other "Asiatic" features from the Khazars or related tribes. For a time their rulers referred to themselves as "khagans"; [i] and prior to the introduction of Christianity they apparently kept their numerous concubines in harem-like confinement.[j]

Direct Byzantine influence made itself felt relatively early. In addition to many literary and artistic elements, the Russians adopted Eastern Christianity and Byzantine law, both of which affected the political climate of Kiev. The Byzantine ("Greek") priests, who came to Russia, carried with them significant ideas of theocratic rule and subordination. Accustomed to act as part rather than as rivals of the secular government, they certainly enhanced the power of the prince.[k] The introduction of Byzantine law further strength-

i. Vernadsky (1943: 282) assumes borrowing from the Khazars. The title *khaghan* was borne by "the first Kievan princes." Apart from Vladimir, his son Yaroslav is also known to have been thus addressed by the Metropolitan Hilarion (*ibid.:* 370, and n. 302).

j. Prior to his conversion, Vladimir is said to have had about 800 concubines (Nestor, 1931: 55).

k. This fact has been stressed by a number of historians. Platonov points out that the "Christian and Byzantine conception of the prince as a ruler by divine right . . . was opposed to the pagan view that the prince was a mere leader of a *druzhina,* and could be driven out and killed" (Platonov, 1925: 40). The Soviet academician Grekov quotes fully the pertinent statement in the Nestor Chronicle: "God gives the power to

ened the Kievan sovereigns. In the second Constantinople-influenced version of the Russian law the ruler and his functionaries emerge clearly as the possessors of supreme judicial authority.[58]

But Kievan society did not accept the legal notions of the great Eastern empire *in toto*. The Byzantine code prescribed corporal punishment for horse stealing; but the revised Russian law continued to demand a fine for this act.[59] Despite its great prestige, Byzantine law did not supersede the Kievan view that a free man should not be beaten.

3. COMMENT

EVIDENTLY, the civilizations in the submargin of hydraulic society exhibit a wide institutional range; and their basic structures can be understood only if they are viewed first in their primary institutional context. However, certain secondary qualities, which link them to the hydraulic world, must not be overlooked:

1) A civilization that was once part of this world may, in a later nonhydraulic phase, still preserve certain traces of its previous condition, which, although not necessary to the new configuration, are compatible with it. Post-Mycenaean Greece probably belongs to this category.

2) The voluntary adoption of desirable "Oriental" features accounts for such phenomena as Taikwa Japan and Kievan Russia.

Another point that is valid for marginal hydraulic societies is also valid for the submargin. It would be incorrect to view as submarginally hydraulic an agrarian society which exhibits certain despotic features of organization and acquisition but which has no known link to the hydraulic world. Individual features of hydraulic statecraft, such as the levying of a general tax or the collection of a general tribute, certainly have emerged in civilizations which had little or no contact with this world. In a number of tribal societies this obviously happened; and if we did not know of the Asiatic background of the Khazars, we might also feel tempted to place their system of tribute gathering in this independent and residual category. Comparative analysis must in each instance decide whether we are dealing with submarginally hydraulic or independent trends.

---

whomever he wishes; the Supreme Being appoints whomever he desires as the caesar or prince." Each state should be headed by a caesar or prince, and state power is of divine origin—these are indeed "the familiar features of the Byzantine conception of state power." Grekov underlines the authoritarian spirit of the famous Christian chronicle: "Anyone who attacked the authority—according to the theory—opposed God." And "Yaroslav's merit lies in the restoration of a single authority in the state" (Grekov, 1947: 133 ff.).

E. SOCIETIES WHICH CROSS
THE INSTITUTIONAL DIVIDE

THE submarginal zone of the hydraulic world cannot be explained by a simple formula. Nor is it necessarily self-perpetuating. A number of historically prominent civilizations of the submargin have crossed the institutional divide and become either marginal hydraulic societies or hydraulic societies proper. Others have moved in the opposite direction.

The civilizations discussed so far have been essentially agrarian. The very concept of a hydraulic economy implies agriculture. But the history of the Ch'i-tan, the Mongols, and other tribal conquerors demonstrates that Oriental despotism is not confined to agrarian societies. Nonagricultural peoples, too, may adopt and transmit techniques of despotic government; and they may "Orientalize" nonagricultural as well as agricultural groups. The importance of this fact for the understanding of many despotic conquest societies and of the dynamics of the institutional divide is obvious.

1. NONAGRICULTURAL PEOPLES ADOPTING AND TRANSMITTING POWER DEVICES OF AGRARIAN DESPOTISM

REPRESENTATIVES of many extractive modes of subsistence—gathering, hunting, and fishing—have lived at the fringe of the hydraulic world. In this respect, the margin of Pueblo society [1] and the early phases of Aztec history are instructive. But no primitive nonagricultural group has played as important a role as the pastoralists. The New World lacked animals suitable for drawing carts and carrying men. The Old World had several species that could be so used. Their domestication greatly benefited the plant breeders; but primarily it benefited the pastoralists, who, after the invention of riding, became the military equals, and at times the masters, of large and wealthy agrarian commonwealths. [2]

a. Such Devices Not Necessary for, but Compatible with, Nomadic Pastoralism

PASTORAL nomads frequently supplement their herding economy by farming. [3] Yet the need to move their herds prevents them from giving more than casual attention to whatever crops they plant near their camping grounds. Their migratory way of life, however well regulated, excludes the construction of elaborate and permanent works of water control, which form the foundation of hydraulic agriculture.

But this mode of life does not prevent them from adopting Orientally despotic methods of organization and acquisition. To be sure, such methods do not grow out of the needs of pastoral life. Although some coordination and subordination are imperative for effective camping and trekking, and although disciplined procedure is highly advantageous for hunting and warfare,[4] these practices do not necessarily lead to the establishment of a political apparatus stronger than all nongovernmental forces of society. Technical factors (the ever-recurring need for dispersing herds and men) and social factors (the resistance of the free tribesmen to the demand for total submission) work in the opposite direction. Even subordination under a strong military leader is essentially voluntary. Limited in time and not bulwarked by irreversible organizational arrangements, it rarely, if ever, destroys the loose and fluid character of the tribal society.[5]

The chiefly leader and those close to him are eager to place themselves in a position of permanent and total power; but as a rule they attain this goal only after submission to, or conquest of, a hydraulic country. In the first case the overlords of the agrarian state may apply their own patterns of political control (registration, corvée, taxation) to the submitting herders, whose chieftain usually emerges as the absolute and permanent master of his tribe. In the second case the supreme chieftain (khan, khaghan, etc.) seizes the power devices of the agromanagerial civilizations he has conquered. Bulwarked by indigenous officials who maintain the traditional administration and by a group of tribal followers whose number grows with his successes, he reduces his noble rivals to a shadow of their former importance, if he does not annihilate them altogether.

In both cases the tribesmen may lose their cultural—and eventually also their sociopolitical—identity. This happened to many Arab groups under the Abbassid caliphate. In such a situation the problem itself ceases to exist. However, submitting tribesmen are usually not eager to relinquish their old way of life; nor are tribal conquerors as easily absorbed as legend has it.[6] With proper modifications, the tribal masters of a compound hydraulic empire may maintain their social and cultural identity; and while doing so, they may impose their newly acquired power techniques to outlying nonhydraulic countries. This happened when the Mongols conquered Kievan Russia.

The disintegration of a compound hydraulic empire may again make all or some of its tribal elements autonomous; and it is at this moment that the perpetuation of despotic power, under conditions of tribal pastoralism, is put to the test. At times the despotic regime dissolves as completely as the empire of which it was a part. But historical experience shows that the beneficiaries of absolutist government continued in a privileged position, at least to some extent and for some time. Obviously then, despotic methods of organization and acquisition, although not a necessary adjunct of nomadic pastoralism, are definitely compatible with it.

b. The Brittleness of Orientally Despotic Power at the Pastoral Fringe of the Hydraulic World

RECENT studies have provided a wealth of data concerning all these processes for the Ch'i-tan tribes, who, as Liao rulers, were the temporary masters of the northeastern fringe of China. Many monographs have clarified corresponding aspects of Mongol history; and future investigations of the tribal conquest societies of the Near East, of Persia, India, and pre-Spanish America will certainly bring to light many other varieties of this important institutional conformation.

Already our present knowledge enables us to juxtapose the pastoral and the agrarian forms of a marginal hydraulic society. Without doubt, the staying power of genuine despotism is much greater under agricultural than under tribal, pastoral, or nomadic conditions. The fluidity of a steppe economy encourages diffusion and separation and, as a corollary, the growth of independent centers of animal wealth and military power. Natural calamities or serious military reverses weaken and dissolve a pastoral despotism as quickly as the fortunes of war and conquest bring it into being. The meteoric rise and fall of many steppe empires in Inner and West Asia and in Southeast Europe illuminate the brittleness of pastoral despotism.

The "Black" Ch'i-tan tribes, who grazed their herds in Northern Mongolia a hundred years after Liao fell, revealed few traces of the coordinated political order maintained by their forebears either in the Far East or in Turkestan.[7] After the collapse of the Great Khan's empire, Mongol power shrank to a shadow of its former self, but it did not disappear altogether. In 1640 the Mongol-Oirat were still restrained by laws which, although considerably milder than Chingis Khan's *Yasa*,[8] forced the tribesmen to participate in a relatively heavy transport corvée.[9] Manifestly, postempire Mongol society was not entirely lacking in cohesiveness when attachment to the rising Manchu star gave their secular and religious masters a chance to support, in a privileged if secondary way, another ambitious attempt to establish a despotic regime, first in the margin and later in a great core area of the hydraulic world.

2. AGRICULTURAL CIVILIZATIONS CROSSING THE INSTITUTIONAL DIVIDE

THE changeover of pastoral societies from a nonhydraulic to a hydraulic order proceeds, as a rule, on a geographical as well as on an institutional level. In contrast to this, changing agrarian societies do not change their locale. They move from one order to another exclusively on the institutional level.

A second difference concerns the potential range of the changeover. Pastoral societies, which preserve their economic identity, may shift from the submarginal to the marginal zone of the hydraulic world and vice versa. Agrarian societies that were originally submarginal may become marginal hydraulic or full-fledged hydraulic societies and vice versa.

Like pastoral societies, agrarian societies change their institutional quality most frequently at the geographical periphery of agromanagerial areas; for it is here that the forces of the hydraulic and the nonhydraulic world have wrestled with each other for millennia. The societal transmutations of Greece, Rome, Spain, and Russia are all part of this gigantic interaction.

a. Greece

FROM a marginal or submarginal hydraulic position, Mycenaean Greece evolved into a civilization whose aristocratic and democratic energies prevented the state from exerting unchecked control over the nongovernmental forces of society. The Greeks of Homer, Hesiod, and Sophocles prostrated before certain of their gods; but they refused to recognize the supreme representative of state power as their master (*despotes*).

For many centuries, and despite their proximity to the hydraulic world, the Greek cities in Western Asia upheld within their limits the principles of a multicentered society. Only in the wake of Alexander's conquests did the old constitutional freedoms begin to shrink. The Hellenistic sovereigns of the Orient reduced the political independence of their own co-nationals in Asia and at home. Together with their Macedonian-Greek aides, they readily donned the robes of Orientally despotic power.

The early Roman empire and Byzantium completed what the Hellenistic dynasties had initiated. The Greeks of the Near East—

and those of the motherland—became part of a hydraulic empire, which included impressive areas of loose (Syria) and compact (Egypt) hydraulic economy. During the 7th century this empire shifted to the margin of the hydraulic world. Later the conquering Turks restored it once more to a loosely hydraulic position.

The Byzantine and Turkish Greeks were no longer the Hellenes of Hesiod, Pericles, and Aristotle. This is probably true ethically, and it is certainly true institutionally. The scions of Mycenae, who during the classical period and for the free members of their community created exemplary models of democratic citizenship, were the ancestors of the Byzantine Greeks, whose elaborate court ceremonial made "Byzantinism" a catchword for man's total, if ritualized, submission to total power.

b. Rome

i. THE RISE OF A HELLENISTIC VERSION OF ORIENTAL DESPOTISM

IN Greece the shift to hydraulic forms of state and society was initiated by Alexander's conquest. In Rome the establishment of absolute and monarchic rule by Augustus signals not the beginning but a relatively advanced stage of a process that had been under way for about two hundred years.

In the institutional history of Rome the year 211 B.C. is a fateful date. It was in this year that in the subdued Sicilian kingdom of Syracuse the Romans "encountered for the first time a subtly elaborate legal system of a primary agrarian state patterned after Egyptian and general Hellenistic models." [10] The victorious Italian republic made this system, the so-called Lex Hieronica, "the basis for the organization of its first provincial economy." [11] By so doing, it adopted a basic principle of Hellenistic statecraft, which declared the state the holder of absolute power and the owner of all land. [12]

As the successors of Hieron, the Roman conquerors made their state, the *populus Romanus,* the supreme master of Sicily's agrarian economy. And they acted similarly also in the other territories of their growing empire. In the regions of the Eastern Mediterranean this involved little change. But in the western areas of Roman expansion nonhydraulic conditions prevailed. It is therefore extremely significant that the Italian conquerors, with proper modifications, transferred the Hellenistic system "also to the West." [13]

From the Roman point of view the Hellenistic principle of general taxation was "a complete innovation." And this innovation was a success because it was supplemented by a periodic and comprehensive census. According to Hieron's plan, which the Romans adopted, "it was the duty of the city magistrates every year to take a census of all the farmers of the district . . . recording both the complete acreage . . . and the acreage of each crop actually under cultivation." [14]

These external developments did not automatically create a state stronger than society in the Roman homeland; but the metropolis underwent internal changes which devastatingly weakened the traditional aristocratic republic. On the one hand, the unending wars of conquest enriched the senatorial landlords, who employed an ever-increasing number of slaves; on the other hand, these wars exhausted the peasantry. Together with the land-hungry veterans, the impoverished peasants offered an ideal mass basis for the policies of the *populares* and of the victorious generals, who did not hesitate to confiscate and redistribute the estates of their erstwhile opponents.[15] The civil wars also increased the vulnerability of the wealthy businessmen, the *equites,* some of whom as tax farmers, *publicani,* profited greatly from the growth of the Roman realm. During the advancing crisis the *equites* enjoyed as little personal and proprietary safety as did the members of the senatorial group.

Evidently, the internal changes were so closely tied up with the country's territorial expansion that any attempt to explain the fall of the republic exclusively on the basis of either internal or external factors must prove inadequate. The generals who dominated the political scene, particularly in the 1st century B.C., rose to power because of the size and peculiarity of the territories they occupied. It was in these areas that they secured their material support; and it was in these areas that they tested the effectiveness of Hellenistic methods of government.

How much did any single individual contribute to the changes that occurred in Roman society? For the purpose of our inquiry it is sufficient to note that in Caesar's time the senate had already lost both its social homogeneity and its uncontested political hegemony and that Caesar, who like other great politician-generals of the period gave land to the veterans, challenged the senatorial representatives of large landed property as a "man of the people," a *popularis.* Here, as elsewhere, absolute power was established through the agency of men who used a popular cause to advance their political aims.

At the time of Caesar's assassination the strongest proprietary force in Rome, the senatorial group, had been so shaken that Augustus, who officially controlled a number of "imperial" provinces (among them the old hydraulic areas of Egypt and Syria) was able to control the "senatorial" provinces too.[16] From 29 B.C. on, the senators, who previously had been the decisive force behind the administration, had to get a permit from Augustus before they could leave Italy; and "if the object of their travel was a visit to Egypt, [the request] was refused on principle." [17] During the subsequent period the once dominant aristocratic landowning senators were more and more replaced by persons who became members of the senate because they were in the emperor's service. And the representatives of mobile wealth and capitalist enterprise, who, as *publicani*, had collected taxes and customs fees for the government and, as contractors, had executed certain "public works," were plundered by Pompey, weakened by Caesar, and subordinated by Augustus.[18] Eventually they lost their significance altogether.[19] Thus the Roman metropolis, which temporarily had ruled a huge Hellenistically hydraulic empire without itself being hydraulic,[a] eventually caved in under the hammer blows of forces which drew their ultimate strength from this very empire.

In this gigantic process of transformation Augustus was not only the grave digger of the old social forces, but also the pioneer in administrative and managerial change. Despite great loyalty to the cultural values of Rome, the first emperor (*princeps*) patterned his absolutist state not on early Rome or classical Greece—from which, indeed, he would have gotten little inspiration—but on the Hellenistic Orient.[b] By laying the foundations for a salaried officialdom,[20] he initiated a bureaucratic development that rapidly gained momentum in the 1st century A.D.[21]

Agromanagerial methods of acquisition and organization had already been employed in the provinces under the Republic; now they were elaborated and systematized. Confiscations became a standard feature of the empire's economic and political life. General taxation was bulwarked by the periodic registration of the population, which under Augustus became regular administrative procedure.[22] Initiating the great nonhydraulic constructions that are still associated with the name of Rome, Augustus started to build a truly agromanagerial system of roads. He established the state post, the

a. Of course, the Roman metropolis was not hermetically sealed off from its Oriental environment. The growing influence of Hellenistic statecraft was significantly accompanied by the growing influence of Eastern religion, art, technology, and customs. The advance of a Hellenistically Oriental culture and the pathetic attempts to resist it are among the most illuminating developments of the 2d and 1st centuries B.C. (see Voigt, 1893: *passim*).

b. At this time the Roman statesmen began "to look for guidance not to Athens or Sparta but to the Persian Empire and the Hellenistic monarchies which succeeded it" (Stevenson, 1934: 183).

cursus publicus, and very consistently, he combined it with an elaborate intelligence service.[23]

These steps were supplemented by such developments as the employment of former slaves, "freedmen," in the service of the state,[24] the use of eunuchs for political purposes,[25] the worship of the emperor, and the gradual decay of independent commercial and industrial enterprise. Long before the close of the 2d century A.D., when Septimius Severus through wholesale slaughter and confiscation made the despotic center the "owner of most of the good arable land throughout the empire," [26] the old society had lost its identity. It was only logical that the "Semitic emperor," who despised Italy and "spoke Latin with a Punic accent," [27] wanted to be called *dominus,* "master." *c*

Thus when Diocletian established a spectacularly Eastern court, the actual Orientalization of the empire had already been accomplished. A prominent economic historian summarizes the great transformation as follows: "In the second and third centuries . . . not only was the State (or the emperor) the largest landed proprietor, it was also the biggest owner of mines and quarries, and in course of time came to be the greatest industrialist." [28] Furthermore, "trade—wholesale and retail—became increasingly subject to governmental control" [29] and "transport was also largely nationalized." [30] In this single-centered economic setting, "the idea of the omnipotence of the State" evolved readily. It took shape essentially "under the influence of orientalizing-hellenistic and other theories of the State." The wholesale "replacement of one economic system by the other, and the substitution of a new civilization and attitude to life for the old took more than a century and a half. It was completed by the end of the third century." [31]

A comparative analysis of the Orientalization of the Roman Empire leads to certain basic conclusions:

1) The institutional meaning of this process appears clearly only if its study is based on the understanding of hydraulic society and agromanagerial (Oriental) despotism.

2) Hellenization means Orientalization. The Hellenization of Rome started almost two hundred years before the establishment of the principate.

c. "It was as if the spirit of ancient Assyria had taken possession of the palace to make the Empire subject to a bureaucracy which should be the executive of a divine authority transmitted through a dynastic succession. In such a system there would be no place for a Senate or for the principle of delegation by the State, and it was a sign that this notion of government now tended to prevail that the title *dominus* came to be generally applied to the emperor" (Miller, 1939: 35).

3) As a societal type, imperial Rome must be equated not with the proto-industrial absolutisms of the West, but with the great agro-managerial absolutisms of the East.

ii. THE FALL OF AGROMANAGERIAL DESPOTISM IN WESTERN ROME

DIFFERENT from the absolutist rulers of post-Medieval Europe, the Roman administrators of Spain, Gaul, Western Germany, and England were not restricted by nationally organized property-based corporations (estates). And although they preserved as far as possible the indigenous political leadership and culture, they operated the political apparatus in accordance with the great traditions of agro-managerial statecraft. As elsewhere, they created huge nonhydraulic constructions, primarily state roads and frontier walls. By means of their state post they monopolized quick communications. And they counted and taxed the inhabitants of the Western provinces in much the same way as they did in the East.[32]

No innate Iberian, Celtic, or Germanic urge for freedom kept the ancestors of modern Western Europe from accepting—at first under coercion but later as a matter of course—the yoke of a state which gave the nongovernmental forces of society little chance to participate in shaping their political and economic fate. Over several centuries Oriental despotism in its Hellenistic-Roman form spread into the woodlands of Germany, to the Atlantic shores of Spain and Gaul, and to the southern borders of Scotland.

These Eastern institutions did not disappear when, in the 4th century, Western Rome, for all practical purposes, became independent of the hydraulic East. The despotic state, which had tolerated no strong and organized proprietary classes—although it did tolerate large property of all kinds—continued to reproduce itself even after its managerial and bureaucratic apparatus shrank. Indeed, until the end, the government of Western Rome insisted upon its absolutist position. Its last prominent political figure, Heraclius, was a typical representative of hydraulic statecraft, a eunuch.[33]

As in Late Byzantium, the decline of Western Rome was largely due to external factors. The loss of revenue from the wealthy eastern provinces seriously weakened the Italian metropolis, which was also having great difficulty in adjusting itself to the collapse of its slave economy. The East, being agriculturally more intensive, never had relied on slave labor as had the West. And consequently the West suffered severely when the sources of cheap slave labor dried up.

The political impotence of Rome became blatantly apparent at the beginning of the 5th century: Rome lost Gaul in 406, England in 407, Spain in 415, and Africa in 429. Within the truncated metropolis, the forces of big landed property, as represented by a new senatorial group, increased in importance. However, the emerging proprietary leaders lacked the strength to set up a non-Oriental type of government. This objective was achieved only when they joined the Germanic king, Odovacar, who in 476 formally terminated the worn-out absolutism of Western Rome.[34]

c. Europe after 476

i. UNSUCCESSFUL ATTEMPTS TO RULE ABSOLUTELY

CERTAIN symbols of hydraulic statecraft, such as the vassals' obligation to kiss the sovereign's foot, persisted for a considerable time, even outlasting the Merovingian period;[35] but lacking substantial societal foundations, they eventually ceased to be invoked. And the political development, instead of following the Roman model, produced the decentralized protofeudal system of government which characterized the first period of the Middle Ages.[36]

ii. THE "UNPARALLELED" CASE OF THE DOMESDAY BOOK

IN this period, which is assumed to have lasted until the end of the 12th century,[37] there appeared in 1086 the Domesday Book, a register of the lands of England, which was ordered in 1085 by the Norman king, William the Conqueror. European historians have indicated institutional roots of the Domesday both in England[38] and Normandy.[39] But while these roots are entirely authentic, they do not adequately explain the great English-Norman land register. Not only was this type of public cadaster unknown in the area from which William and his men came ("Normandy had no Domesday and no dooms"),[40] but it was also unknown in other parts of non-Oriental Europe. According to Maitland, it represents "an exploit which has no parallel in the history of Europe."[41]

What then inspired this unparalleled achievement? Conquest, which Maitland suggests,[42] provides no plausible explanation, since Medieval Europe saw many conquests but only one Domesday Book. The Normans of Normandy are a case in point. They did not, to our knowledge, institute a Domesday, but they certainly settled in the north of France through conquest. Could it be that by 1085 the Normans had become familiar with administrative methods which were unknown to them in the 10th or even in the earlier part of the 11th century?

When in 1066 the Normans conquered England, some of their countrymen had already set themselves up as the masters of southern Italy, an area which, with interruptions, had been under Byzantine administration until this date; and some of them had established a foothold in Sicily, an area which had been ruled by Byzantium for three hundred years and after that by the Saracens, who combined Arab and Byzantine techniques of absolutist government.

We have no conclusive evidence regarding the effect of this Byzantine-Saracen experience on William and his councilors. But we know that in 1072—that is, thirteen years before William ordered the *descriptio* of England—the Normans had conquered the capital of Sicily, Palermo, and the northern half of the island. And we also know that there were considerable "comings and goings" [43] between the Italian-Sicilian Normans and their cousins in Normandy and England, particularly among the nobility and clergy. The latter happened also to be actively engaged in administrative work.[44] No wonder, then, that on the basis of his knowledge of the period Haskins, the leading English expert on English-Sicilian relations in the Middle Ages, suggests "the possibility of a connexion between Domesday Book and the fiscal registers which the south had inherited from its Byzantine and Saracen rulers." [45]

Haskins' hypothesis explains well why a typically hydraulic device of fiscal administration appeared in feudal Europe. It also explains why for hundreds of years afterward this "magnificent exploit" had no parallel in that area. Evidently, systematic and nationwide registration was as out of place in feudal society as it was customary in the realm of Oriental despotism.

d. Spain

i. ORIENTAL CONQUEST

BUT neither the failure of the Frankish attempts nor the singularity of the English Domesday implies that after 476 the institutional divide between the hydraulic and nonhydraulic parts of Europe remained fixed. The history of southern Italy and Sicily prior to the Normans reveals two major forces of Eastern expansion: the Byzantines, who tried to uphold their way of government in certain former provinces of the Roman empire, and, far more significantly, the Arabs, who, inspired by a dynamic new creed and equipped with new methods of warfare,[46] extended their power from the Near Eastern centers of hydraulic society throughout Northwest Africa, Spain, and —temporarily—Sicily.

This colossal eruption resembled the westward growth of the Roman empire in that it, too, spread Orientally despotic patterns of government. But for a variety of reasons the institutional effects of the Islamic conquest were much more far-reaching. Under Roman influence Western Europe became part of a loosely hydraulic Oriental society without, however, adopting hydraulic agriculture; and eventually it returned to a submarginally hydraulic or altogether non-hydraulic position. Under the influence of the Arabs, the swing was considerably greater. Prior to the Islamic invasion, the Iberian peninsula was the home of a protofeudal civilization, which had small-scale irrigation agriculture but probably few hydraulic enterprises.[d] In sharp contrast to the Romans, who seized Western Europe, the Arab conquerors of Spain were entirely familiar with hydraulic agriculture, and in their new habitat they eagerly employed devices that had been extremely profitable in the countries of their origin. Under Muslim rule "artificial irrigation . . . was improved and extended . . . on Oriental models," and this included government management: "its superintendence was the business of the state." [47]

Thus Moorish Spain became more than marginally Oriental. It became a genuine hydraulic society, ruled despotically by appointed officials [48] and taxed by agromanagerial methods of acquisition. The Moorish army, which soon changed from a tribal to a "mercenary" body,[49] was as definitely the tool of the state as were its counterparts in the Umayyad and Abbassid caliphates. A protoscientific system of irrigation and gardening [50] was supplemented by an extraordinary advance in the typically hydraulic sciences of astronomy and mathematics.[51] Contemporary feudal Europe could boast of no comparable development. Reconstructing the impressions of the great Arab geographer, Ibn Hauqal, who visited Spain in the 10th century, Dozy comments on the organizational power of the Muslim state, whose police, like its hydraulic agriculture, penetrated the most remote parts of the country: "The foreigner noticed with admiration the universally well cultivated fields and a hydraulic system, which was coordinated in such a profoundly scientific manner that it created fertility in the seemingly least rewarding soils. He marvelled at the perfect order that, thanks to the vigilant police, reigned even in the least accessible districts." [52]

d. Hirth, 1928: 57 ff.; Hall, 1886: 363, 365; Lévi-Provençal, 1932: 166; Laborde, 1808: 29, 107. Laborde's memoir claims complete lack of agricultural interest for the Gothic conquerors of Spain (Laborde, 1808: 107).

In the second half of the 14th century the leading town of the Hanseatic League, Lübeck, numbered 22,000 inhabitants,[53] and London about 35,000.[54] At the height of the Western caliphate the Moorish capital, Cordoba, may have harbored a million persons,[55] and Seville in 1248 more than 300,000.[56] At the close of the Muslim period Granada was probably at least as populous. The *Encyclopedia of Islam* estimates the dwellers of this beautiful last Islamic capital in Spain at "half a million." [57]

No wonder then that the absolutist state, at the peak of its prosperity, collected a stupendous revenue.[58] And no wonder either that this state, which like other hydraulic regimes freely used eunuchs,[59] was ruthless in purging dignitaries who fell from favor. When these unfortunates were liquidated, the state was quick to confiscate whatever property they possessed.[60]

ii. THE RECONQUISTA

THE *reconquista,* which in the 13th century reestablished Christian control over the greater part of Spain, transformed a great hydraulic civilization into a late feudal society. Students of Russia, who see the rise of an Orientally despotic state in Muscovy as the consequence of an armed struggle against powerful Eastern enemies, will do well to compare the Russian story with what happened in Spain—and for that matter, in Austria.

To begin with the latter country. For several centuries, Austria was threatened by one of the greatest Oriental empires known to history: Ottoman Turkey; and extended parts of Hungary were occupied by the Turks for more than one hundred and fifty years. But the main political and military base of the counterattack, Austria, remained free; and the protracted struggle against the mighty Eastern foe did not convert the Austrian state into an Oriental despotism. Like other countries of Europe, Austria advanced toward a definitely Western type of absolutism: until the middle of the 18th century the Austrian diets (*Landtage*) had a decisive voice concerning taxation and the drafting of soldiers,[61] and even after 1740 the estates played an essential role in the fiscal administration.[62] Hungary stubbornly maintained a semi-autonomous government, whose *Landtag,* consisting of an upper house (clerical and secular magnates) and a lower house (lower nobles and urban deputies), "exerted a great influence on the country's administration." [63]

In Spain, too, the base of the Reconquest was never Orientalized. The rulers of the small northern states that had withstood the Arab onslaught depended for their military strength on the support of the nobles, the clergy, and the towns; [64] and at the end of the main phase of the Reconquest these groups, far from being politically pulverized, were able, because of their privileges, to maintain a semi-autonomous existence.[65] Similar to the development in late feudal and postfeudal France, England, Germany, Italy, and Scandinavia, Spain also developed an absolutist government.[66] This government was strong enough to prevail over the nobles, the Church, and the towns; [67] but it was unable to wipe out the entailed aristocratic landholdings [68] and the semi-autonomy of the Church; and it was unable to break the pride and dignity of the Spanish people. The estates of Aragon that had declared the recognition of their privileges to be the condition of their homage to the king (*"si no, no."*) repeated this daring formula again in 1462,[69] that is, more than a hundred years after the greater part of the Peninsula had been reconquered. And although the assemblies (*cortes*), which in Castille essentially represented the free municipalities, had ceased to exist in 1665, the absolutist regime failed to instill in its subjects the submissive attitude habitual under hydraulic regimes.

To state this is not to deny the extraordinary strength of Spanish absolutism. This phenomenon may at least in part be explained by the exigencies of the Reconquest "frontier," which enhanced the growth of royal authority in Catalonia, Navarre, and Aragon.[70] However, the *Wirtschaftsgesinnung* of the Christian kings may have been even more decisive. The northern base of the Reconquest greatly favored pastoralism; and the European demand for wool—which increased with the advance of the Reconquest [71]—led the Spanish kings one-sidedly to promote sheep breeding also in the liberated areas of central Spain, and even in parts of southern Spain.[72] While the kings gave all manner of privileges to the towns and nobles, they established a tight fiscal and jurisdictional control over the sheep breeders, who, from the 13th century on, were combined in a special organization, the Mesta.[73]

In Spain, as in England, the sheep "ate" the people. But Spain differed from England in that, almost from the beginning, the princes profited enormously from the rapidly expanding pastoral economy. State revenues from this source were large.[74] Eventually the monarchs considered "the exploitation and conservation of the pastoral industry . . . the principal sustenance of these kingdoms." [75]

The huge revenues which the Crown received from its colonial empire have frequently been held responsible for the decline of the Spanish population in the 16th century.[e] However, the depopulation

e. Seville, which in 1247 had over 300,000 inhabitants, numbered in the 16th century 200,000. Cordoba, which under the caliphs may have harbored a million people, now

of the villages, which certainly was a major cause for the depopulation of the cities, cannot be satisfactorily explained thus, since the influx of gold and silver would have enabled the enriched townspeople to buy more rather than fewer rural products.

In all probability the downward trend was caused primarily by the replacement of labor-intensive irrigation farming by labor-extensive cattle breeding. This development, stimulated by the soaring export of wool,[f] led to the promulgation of the *Leyes de Toro,* which completed the "subjection of agriculture to large scale pasturage" [76] fourteen years before Cortez took Mexico and twenty-eight years before Pizarro took Cuzco. And it also accounts for the great reduction in the Indian farming population in post-Conquest Mexico, Yucatan, and Peru.[g]

In the Spanish countryside, herds and herders now made their

---

numbered 60,000 (Laborde, 1808: 9). The population of Granada decreased from perhaps 500,000 to 80,000 (see above, and Laborde, 1808: 9). These decreases resulted in part from military destruction; but in part they express the transformation of the rural order. Some sections of the countryside never recovered from the pestilence and the Reconquest (Klein, 1920: 337). Others were allowed to lie fallow during the 16th and 17th centuries (*ibid.:* 320, 342 ff.), until the formerly flourishing fields were "smitten with the curse of barrenness" (Prescott, 1838, III: 461, n. 85), because sheep breeding had been allowed "to run riot throughout the land and to annihilate almost the last vestiges of agriculture that still remained" (Klein, 1920: 343).

The known ruins of former settlements in Catalonia, Aragon, Leon, Valencia, Mancha, Castille, etc. numbered more than 1141. The region of the Guadalquivir had boasted 1200 villages under the Caliph of Cordoba. In 1800 only 200 survived. Of the fifty villages of Malaga, only sixteen were left. One section of the diocese of Salamanca had only 333 villages out of its former 748, while of 127 villages which existed near *des partidos de Banos peña del rey* only thirteen remained (Laborde, 1808: 8). The area of the kingdom of Granada that prior to 1492 had supported three million people numbered only 661,000 by 1800 (*ibid.:* 9).

f. The rise continued until the latter part of the 16th century (Klein, 1920: 37–46).

g. Ships were small and freight expensive; and nothing much was to be gained by exporting grain to Europe. Silver was the most highly prized export article; but handsome profits could also be made in sugar and cacao, dyewoods, dyestuffs, and hides (Humboldt, 1811, IV: 368 ff.). Within a few decades "oxen, horses, sheep, and pigs multiplied to a surprising degree in all parts of New Spain" (*ibid.,* III: 224). By 1570, when Acosta arrived in America, some individuals owned as many as 70,000 and even 100,000 sheep (Acosta, 1894, I: 418; Obregon, 1928: 151). Wherever the increase of cattle was not checked, the herds grew rapidly, not only in Central America but also in the Southwest of North America (Obregon, 1928: 151), in Peru (cf. Markham, 1892: 163; see also Juan and Ulloa, 1806, I: 300, 318, and *passim*), and in Yucatan (Shattuck, Redfield, and MacKay, 1933: 15). When Cortez set up a princely estate in Oaxaca, he at once "imported large numbers of merino sheep and other cattle, which found abundant pastures in the country around Tehuantepec" (Prescott, 1936: 671). Consistently, it was Cortez who in the New World organized a Mesta patterned after the Mesta of Castille (Mendoza, 1854: 225).

lonely way over vast grasslands. It was in this landscape that Don Quixote urged on his stumbling nag. And in the cities no spectacle was so popular as the bullfight. In Valladolid, in 1527, Charles V celebrated the birth of his son, Philip II, by himself entering the ring to challenge the bull.

e. The Introduction of Oriental Despotism into Russia

"THE TATARS had nothing in common with the Moors. When they conquered Russia, they gave her neither algebra nor Aristotle." Pushkin was doubtless correct in lamenting the negative cultural consequence of the Tatar [h] conquest. He might have gone even further and noted the devastating political consequences of their fabulous military success. The Tatars, who by 1240 had crushingly defeated the Eastern Slavs, controlled their new subjects so effectively that no independent Russian power undertook to liberate them.

Nor did any internal Russian force engage in a systematic and open struggle against the Horde. The isolated military victory at the Don River, which the Grand Duke of Moscow, Dmitry, won over a Tatar army in 1380, backfired sadly: the subsequent reprisals discouraged armed resistance for another hundred years.[i] Even when, in 1480, Ivan III refused allegiance to the enfeebled Tatars, he avoided battling against them. The Tatars, while still able to lead an army against the Muscovite host, were equally reluctant. Indecision on both sides resulted in "an unbelievable spectacle: two armies fleeing from each other without being pursued by anyone." To quote Karamsin further: "So ended this last invasion of the Tatars." [j]

h. The name "Tatar" originally referred to peoples living in the eastern part of Inner Asia (see Wittfogel and Fêng, 1949: 101 ff.). After the great expansion of Mongol power during the 13th century, the name began, in Eastern Europe, to denote those Mongols and Turks who together formed the core of the Golden Horde. Merging with older Turkish and Finnish groups, these "Tatars" spoke Turkish, a language which by then had become the most important ethnic and cultural trait of the westernmost sector of the Mongol world (Spuler, 1943: 11 n.). In the present discussion the terms "Tatar" and "Mongol" are used interchangeably to designate the people of the Golden Horde.

i. After 1380 the leading principality, Muscovy, "for the time being did not think of fighting the Tatars" (Kliuchevskii, Kurs, II: 20).

j. Karamsin, HER, VI: 195–6. Karamsin considers this the most plausible version of "the course of the great event." When the Khan, irritated by the Grand Duke's disobedience and the smallness of his presents, advanced toward the Don River, Ivan mobilized his troops and, after some weeks, moved them close to the Khan. But he remembered the aftermath of the victory which Dmitry Donsky had won at the same river a hundred years before. "Dmitry had triumphed over Mamai to see afterwards

So indeed ended Tatar rule over Russia. It had lasted for almost two hundred and fifty years; and the Grand Duchy of Muscovy, which rose to prominence during this period, did so not as an independent force but as the instrument of the Khan.

This fact is not disputed. Nor is it seriously denied that 16th-century Muscovy cannot be equated with Western absolutism. However, opinions differ fundamentally concerning the origin of Muscovy's despotism. Was Ivan's autocratic control over land and people due to external conditions, namely to a continually fought-over frontier? Or was it due primarily to internal and direct Oriental influence, above all to Tatar rule?

Historians who uphold the "external" interpretation lean heavily on the authority of the foremost modern Russian historian, Kliuchevsky. I fully share the esteem in which Kliuchevsky is held by scholars of the most diverse opinion; but I find his views on the emergence of Muscovite despotism less one-sided than is generally assumed.

True, Kliuchevsky has paid little attention to the Tatar Yoke,[k] and his understanding of Oriental despotism is limited.[m] But he

---

Moscow covered with smoking ashes and to pay a shameful tribute." The memory made him proceed with "prudent circumspection." He left his troops and returned to Moscow, where some of his followers accused him of having first infuriated the Khan and of now refusing to defend his country. "Finally the Grand Duke yielded to the general desire and promised to oppose the Khan." He returned to the front, and after some minor combats sent an envoy to negotiate with the Tatars. But no understanding was reached. After fifteen days Ivan ordered his army to withdraw to what he believed to be a more suitable place for combat. His soldiers, however, thought his command was inspired by fright. They lost their nerve and "fled in the greatest disorder." At this point, Karamsin's source notes, a miracle occurred: the Khan suspected the Russians of planning to ambush him; and "gripped by a panic of fear, he hastened to take his departure" (*ibid.:* 176–95).

k. Florinsky criticizes him for suggesting that when studying the political organization of northeastern Russia, one "should forget for a time . . . that Russia was conquered by the Tartars" (Florinsky, 1953, I: 78); and Vernadsky (1953: 333 ff.) notes that except for "a few general remarks on the importance of the khans' policies for the unification of Russia . . . [Kliuchevsky] paid little attention to the Mongols."

m. Kliuchevsky was not too familiar with the institutions of Oriental society and with such of its variants as traditional China. Otherwise he would not have contrasted the service-based class system of Muscovite Russia and the conditions of Oriental despotism (Kluchevsky, HR, III: 52). In another context, however, he notes the similarities in the Muscovite methods of liquidating potentially dangerous relatives and methods of Oriental despotism in like situations (*ibid.*, II: 88). And his description of state service and land tenure in post-Mongol Russia clearly indicates institutional affinities to Ottoman Turkey and Muslim India. His discussion of Peter's efforts to develop industry is a major contribution to our understanding of the Russian version of an agrobureaucratic despotism. The omnipotent state, based on enforced service and claiming ultimate control over all land, has also been viewed as a key element of

was too great a student to overlook the crucial institutional changes which, under Tatar rule and because of it, occurred in Russia's state and society. According to his own account, these changes definitely preceded the rise of the "frontier," with whose formative role he is so impressed.

Indeed, Kliuchevsky, in his "frontier" thesis, deals essentially with the post-Tatar period. He describes the changes involved in the recruiting of "a numerous military-official class" as being closely connected with "the territorial expansion of the empire," whose new frontiers had "placed the state in direct contact with such external and alien foes of Russia as the Swedes, the Lithuanians, the Poles, and Tatars. This direct contact had put the state in such a position that it had come to resemble an armed camp surrounded on three sides by enemies." [77] Manifestly, the Tatars of whom Kliuchevsky is speaking are those that confronted 16th-century Muscovy, and the frontier of which they form a part is the 16th-century frontier. Kliuchevsky says so expressly,[78] and several times he refers specifically to the years from 1492 to 1595.[79]

In view of these facts we cannot help feeling that Kliuchevsky's "frontier" thesis raises more questions than it answers. Why should a non-Oriental Russia evolve into an enforced-service despotism, because Russia was fighting such Western countries as Sweden, Lithuania, and Poland? Many European governments dealt with comparable enemies without establishing Orientally despotic patterns of control over land and people. Or why should a non-Oriental Russia become Orientally despotic when the Oriental forces she was combating were, relatively speaking, no stronger than the Turks, with whom the Austrians and Hungarians fought, or the Moors, with whom the Spanish reconquerors were engaged in a life and death struggle? Neither Hungary and Austria nor Spain became Orientally despotic because of their Oriental "frontier." We may therefore well ask: Could the Muscovite development of the 16th century have occurred because Russia, prior to this period and as the result of her long subjection to Oriental domination, had already taken decisive organizational and acquisitive steps in the direction of a despotic "service" state?

Kliuchevsky's frame of reference prevents him from giving a consistent answer to these questions. But it is amazing how far his account

---

Tsarist society by Sumner, who considers Tsarism to be rooted in the "ideas and ritual" of Byzantium and "the fact and practice of the Tatar khans." Elaborating this point, Sumner observes that it was under the influence of the Golden Horde rather than "far-away Byzantine administration" that the Muscovite government and military system originated (Sumner, 1949: 82 f.).

of 13th-, 14th-, and 15th-century Russia goes in affirming the socio-historical significance of the Tatar period.

According to Kliuchevsky, it was during this period that the towns, which had played a prominent role in Kievan Russia,[80] lost, with a few exceptions (Novgorod, Pskov), their political importance; [81] and it was in this period that the territorial princes and independent boyars, after a temporary improvement in their conditions, were sharply curbed by the grand dukes of Muscovy. Many princes became the serving men of Muscovy, whose new prince-officials by 1500 "overlaid, if they did not crush, the older stratum of Muscovite non-titled boyars." [82]

Why did this happen? In the matter of the political emasculation of the towns, Kliuchevsky shuts his eyes to the effects of Tatar rule,[n] which were pointed out earlier by Karamsin.[o] In the matter of the fate of the boyars and territorial princes, he recognizes that Tatar power enabled Muscovy to subdue them.

Kliuchevsky is aware that for more than two generations the Tatars operated the fiscal organization that they had erected in Russia: "After their conquest of Rus, the Tartars themselves first collected the tribute they imposed on Rus." [83] He is also aware that political and jurisdictional power accrued to Moscow when, in 1328, the Khan transferred this function to his Muscovite deputy: "The simple trustee-agent in charge of collecting and delivering the tribute of the Khan, the Prince of Moscow, was then made plenipotentiary leader and judge of the Russian princes." Subsequently the Khan's commission became "a powerful instrument for the political unification of the territorial states of Rus." [84]

In all these instances, Tatar influence is clear. It becomes still more impressive when we recognize the bureaucratic innovations that accompanied the political change. Kliuchevsky knows that the methods of registering land and tax payers which were used throughout

---

n. Kliuchevsky views this development as the result of the colonization of northern Russia (Kluchevsky, HR, I: 269). "Rus" did indeed expand northward, but this is only half the story. In Western Europe many towns, which were founded by princes or feudal lords, emancipated themselves. Why was it that in 13th- and 14th-century Russia princely authority grew at the expense of the towns? And why did the *veche* cease to function, even where it had previously prevailed?

o. Karamsin (HER, V: 451) ascribes the change to the increased authority with which the princes were endowed by the Tatars. Recently Vernadsky noted that "the destruction of most of the major cities of East Russia during the Mongol invasion" was followed by an equally devastating, and even more successful, political campaign against the towns and that in this campaign the Russian princes and boyars supported their Mongol masters. In the middle 14th century, the *veche* "had ceased to function normally in most East Russian cities and could be discounted as an element of government" (Vernadsky, 1953: 345).

the 16th and 17th centuries [85] had existed at the close of the 15th century and long before.[p] He knows that after the conquest of Russia the Tatars "during the first thirty-five years of the Yoke three times took a census, *chislo,* of the entire Russia people, with the exception of the clergy, by means of *chislenniki* [census takers] sent from the Horde." [86] Subsequent studies have thrown additional light on the original Tatar organization,[87] which may have served military as well as fiscal purposes.[88] Vernadsky plausibly suggests that *"it was on the basis of the Mongol patterns that the grand ducal system of taxation and army organization was developed in the late 14th to 16th centuries."* [89] His conclusion elaborates what Kliuchevsky had intimated fifty years before.

When describing the state post of 16th-century Moscow,[90] Kliuchevsky does not expressly connect it with earlier developments. But his remark, "the *Jamskoi prikaz,* the Department of Posts, which was known from the beginning of the 16th century," [91] in all likelihood points to Ivan III,[92] that is, to the close of the Tatar period. Other scholars have connected the postal system, *yam,* which the Tatars maintained in Russia,[93] with the Muscovite institution of the same name.[q]

The rise of Muscovite despotism coincides with the rise of the new type of civil and military serving men, who, as temporary holders of state land (*pomestye*), were unconditionally and unlimitedly at the disposal of their supreme lord. From the later part of the 14th century on, the grand dukes of Muscovy began to reduce the territorial princes to the position of serving men; [94] and in the 15th century they assigned office land—which was previously given only to unfree retainers [95]—to free serving men as well, mainly to warriors but also to civil ("court") officials.[96] Kliuchevsky is fully cognizant that this type of compulsory service differs from the conditions of Western Europe; [97] and it is therefore not surprising that in his discussion of the legal principles involved in the institution of the *pomestye*

p. Kluchevsky, HR, III: 228. The Tatar origin of the Muscovite system of census taking has been stressed among others by Miljukov (1898: 128) and Kulischer (1925: 404), the latter of whom, not without reason, assumes ultimate Chinese influence.

q. Brückner, 1896: 521 ff.; Milukow, 1898: 81; Kulischer, 1925: 405; Grekov, 1939: 216 ff. The Altaic term *yam,* "post," and *jamči,* "postmaster" (Spuler, 1943: 412) appeared in Russian as *jam* and *jamshchik* (Brückner, 1896: 503, 522). During the Mongol period, "the yam was a special tax for the upkeep of post-horse stations" (Vernadsky, 1953: 221). When in the early part of the 16th century Herberstein used the Muscovite state post, he had relay horses assigned to him "by the post-master, who in their language is called 'jamschnik' [sic!]." The relay stations were called *"jama"* (Herberstein, NR, I: 108). In the 16th century the Postal Chancellery was first called *jamskaja izba,* then *jamskoj prikaz* (Staden, 1930: 13, n. 4; cf. 15, 59).

he considers only two roots, both Oriental: Byzantium and the Tatar Horde. Rejecting the former, he is left with the Tatar alternative, suggested by Gradovski. According to this view, "the idea of the prince as the supreme landowner originated only during the Mongol period. As representatives of the authority of the Khan, the Russian princes enjoyed, in their territories, the same rights as the Khan himself enjoyed in all the territory under his rule. Later the Russian princes inherited these state rights from the Khan completely; and this shattered the incipient private ownership of land." [98]

It is characteristic for Kliuchevsky's ambivalence toward the Tatar issue that he fails to verbalize what, from the standpoint of his own premises, is the only logical conclusion. But he does not hesitate to stress the rapid growth of the *pomestye* institution at the close of the Tatar period. Evidently, "traces of an intensive and systematic distribution of public land in *pomestye* tenure can already be found during the second half of the 15th century." [99] The Muscovite princes established *pomestye* lands on a large scale first in newly conquered territories such as Novgorod; but in the early 16th century "a great development of *pomestye* tenure" also took place in the vicinity of Moscow.[100]

The comparative economic historian, Kovalevsky, expressly claimed a Tatar origin for the fateful institution: "It is a fact that prior to the 15th century we never hear of Russian princes paying for services except by the distribution of money and objects taken as war loot, whereas the assignment of military tenures under the name of *iktaa* was known in the entire Mohammedan world and especially among the Tatars for centuries prior to the appearance of this practice in Muscovy. These considerations led the author to state that this kind of practice was introduced to Muscovy and the other Russian principalities through the imitation of the Tatar khanates." [101] Vernadsky does not claim a direct link; but he too calls the Mongol age the "incubation period" of the *pomestye* system.[102]

In view of these facts it is hard to reject Vernadsky's conclusion that in the days of the Tatars the old free society of Kievan Russia was "persistently chipped away without at first affecting the facade," and that when Ivan III broke with the Horde, "the framework of the new structure was all but ready and the new order, that of a service-bound society, became clearly noticeable." [103]

It became clearly noticeable indeed. And a few decades after Ivan's death, the forces of despotism had gained sufficient strength to destroy ruthlessly the obsolete facade. The time lag between incubation and maturation reflects the contradictory interests of the Tatars, who wanted their Muscovite agency to be sufficiently strong to carry out the will of the Khan but not strong enough to override it. Without foreseeing the ultimate consequences of their action, they built an institutional time bomb,[r] which remained under control during their rule but which started to explode when the "Yoke" collapsed.

Byzantium's influence on Kievan Russia was great, but it was primarily cultural. Like China's influence on Japan, it did not seriously alter the conditions of power, class, and property. Ottoman Turkey's influence on 16th-century Russia stimulated a regime that was already Orientally despotic,[104] but it did not bring it into being. Tatar rule alone among the three major Oriental influences affecting Russia was decisive both in destroying the non-Oriental Kievan society and in laying the foundations for the despotic state of Muscovite and post-Muscovite Russia.

F. STRUCTURE AND CHANGE IN THE DENSITY PATTERNS OF THE ORIENTAL WORLD

THUS Greece, Rome, Spain, and Russia all crossed the institutional divide. In Greece, Rome, and Spain the pendulum swung back and forth. In Tsarist Russia the reverse movement (away from a despotic state) came close to bringing the country back into the Western orbit. The changes that occurred in each of these cases were enormous; but their character cannot be clearly understood unless the affected institutional structures are clearly defined. Our analysis has tried to do this. Approaching both structure and change from the standpoint of varying hydraulic and bureaucratic density, we can draw the following major conclusions.

1. STRUCTURE

a. Density Subtypes of Hydraulic Society

THERE are two subtypes of hydraulically compact areas: one with economically predominant and continuous hydraulic systems (Compact 1), the other with economically predominant but discontinuous hydraulic systems (Compact 2). There are two subtypes of hydraulically loose areas: one with an organizationally predominant hydraulic system, which comprises major and regionally compact hydraulic units (Loose 1), the other without major compact units (Loose 2). And there are two subtypes of the margin of hydraulic society: one containing conspicuous hydraulic elements (Margin 1), the other lacking such elements (Margin 2). A seventh subtype, the submargin, belongs to the fringe of the hydraulic world, because its

r. Vernadsky (1953: 335) appropriately speaks of "influence through delayed action."

representatives employ conspicuous elements of Orientally despotic statecraft. But since its dominant institutions are of a definitely non-hydraulic character, it must be placed on the outer fringe of this world.

b. Differing Frequencies of Occurrence

THE hydraulically densest subtypes of hydraulic society, Compact 1 and 2, are not the most frequent ones. Nor can the other subtypes be called less "advanced," if this term is meant to imply that eventually and necessarily they will become compact. Among the historically prominent hydraulic societies, and particularly among their larger representatives, the compact patterns are more the exception than the rule.

c. Decreasing Importance of Hydraulic Economy Proper

THE decreasing importance of hydraulic economy proper becomes clearly apparent when the agromanagerial world is viewed in its spatial and temporal entirety. There is little doubt that representatives of this world had a greater hydraulic density during their formative and primary phase than during their later and secondary developments.

In the formative phase, relatively small hydraulic commonwealths arose in semi-arid and arid settings. And if our genetic hypothesis is correct, we are safe in assuming that while, during this phase, a number of marginal hydraulic societies originated through diffusion, few such societies originated through the disintegration of larger, loosely hydraulic units, which were then practically nonexistent. The greatest number of marginal hydraulic societies—both absolutely and in proportion to the number of hydraulic societies proper—appeared therefore not during the formative phase, but after it.

This developmental peculiarity is accompanied by another which, although independent of it, aggravates its effects. For reasons which in the Old World are closely connected with the spread of nomadic conquest and globally with the lessening of hydraulic concern, hydraulic societies proper tend to reduce rather than increase their hydraulic intensity.

The specific density patterns of industrial and hydraulic society develop in different ways. The representatives of industrial society tend to become more industrial without of necessity becoming industrially compact. Conversely, the representatives of agromanagerial society seem to reach their highest hydraulic density coefficient during a relatively early phase of their growth. Afterward they hold their own or recede. Taken in its entirety, agromanagerial society apparently "advances" not to higher but to lower levels of hydraulic density.

2. Capacity for Societal Change

Our density analysis clarifies both structure and change. And it clarifies change—or lack of change—not only within the same societal type, but also from one societal type to another.

1) The formation of hydraulic society apparently depends on the presence of a hydraulic economy proper as an essential condition.

2) The perpetuation of hydraulic society is assured by a plurality of factors, among which hydraulic enterprise may play a minor part, and marginally no part at all.

3) The history of hydraulic society records innumerable rebellions and palace revolutions. But nowhere, to our knowledge, did internal forces succeed in transforming any single-centered agromanagerial society into a multicentered society of the Western type.

4) More specifically: neither in the Old nor in the New World did any great hydraulic civilization proper spontaneously evolve into an industrial society, as did, under nonhydraulic conditions, the countries of the post-Medieval West. In the marginal hydraulic civilization of Late Byzantium the rise of big private property led only to societal paralysis. In Russia, after severe attacks *from the outside,* the forces of private property (and their concomitant, free labor) prevailed in 1917 for a number of months over the system of despotic state power.

CHAPTER 7

Patterns of proprietary complexity in hydraulic society

NOT all hydraulic societies comprise independent proprietary forces of consequence. When such forces are present, they seem to be more of a threat to the margin than to the hydraulic heartlands, although even in these latter, strong proprietary developments intensify social differentiations and periodic political crises.

Hence, an institutional analysis of hydraulic society should deal not only with the density of its agromanagerial apparatus but also with the complexity of its proprietary development. Having explored the major patterns of hydraulic and bureaucratic density, we shall now examine the major complexity patterns of private property and enterprise which emerge under the shadow of agromanagerial despotism.

A. THE HUMAN RELATION CALLED "PROPERTY"

PROPERTY is the individual's recognized right to dispose over a particular object. Like other rights, the right called property involves more than a relation between a person and a thing. It involves a relation between the proprietor and other individuals who, through the former's prerogative, are excluded from disposing over the object in question.

The relation also involves the representatives of government, who, on the one hand, share the restrictions placed on the private non-proprietors and, on the other, are concerned with maintaining the existing property regulations. Thus in addition to being a legal and social institution, property is a political phenomenon. And property rights in different societies, even when they are similar in form, need not be similar in substance.

Strong property develops in a societal order which is so balanced that the holders of property can dispose over "their" objects with a maximum of freedom. Weak property develops in a societal order that is not so balanced.

The preceding chapters have described those peculiarities of hydraulic society which, by making the state inordinately strong, tend to make private property inordinately weak. Of course, weakness is not nonexistence. Hydraulic society has given rise to many forms of private property that, as far as external appearance goes, have their parallels in other societies. Some of these forms show a different degree of development in different hydraulic civilizations, and these distinctions are so regular—and so manifest—that we can establish several subtypes of proprietary (and societal) complexity.

B. OBJECTS OF PROPERTY RIGHTS

THE concepts of mobile and immobile property present obvious difficulties, but they have great advantages for our inquiry. Immobile property (essentially land) is the basis of private enterprise in the main branch of hydraulic economy: agriculture; and mobile property (tools, raw materials, merchandise, money) is the basis of its two most important secondary branches: industry (handicraft) and commerce. Persons, too, may become the object of a proprietary relation. Like many other institutional conformations, hydraulic society also knows slavery. But unlike mobile and immobile property, slavery under agromanagerial despotism does not establish specific patterns of independent enterprise and social position. We shall therefore discuss the peculiarities of this type of slavery in the next chapter, which deals with classes.

C. THE POTENTIAL SCOPE OF PROPRIETARY RIGHTS

A HOLDER of strong property may dispose over his property in a variety of ways.

He may put his property to whatever use he wants, as long as he does not interfere with the rights of other members of the commonwealth. He may employ it actively, either in the economic sphere (for purposes of subsistence and material gain) or in the sphere of physical coercion (for purposes of promoting his and his group's material or political interest); or he may employ it passively, consuming it for purposes of maintenance and pleasure.[a] Occasionally he may decide not to use it at all. He may make a piece of wood into a bow to serve him in a hunt or raid, or into a digging implement for farming. He may employ a piece of land for raising what crops he wishes, or for grazing or hunting, or he may let it lie fallow.

The holder of strong property whose active property produces gains

a. The distinction between productive and nonproductive property is a narrow, if important, economic variant of the wider dichotomy.

because he, either alone or with, or through, others, employs it effectively, is free to enjoy these gains fully. He owns the calf as well as the cow. He is free to alienate his property at will. And he is free to determine who shall inherit it when he dies.

D. THREE MAJOR COMPLEXITY PATTERNS IN HYDRAULIC CIVILIZATIONS

1. SIMPLE, SEMICOMPLEX, AND COMPLEX PATTERNS OF PROPERTY

THE holder of weak property may enjoy only a shadow of these prerogatives, but this does not destroy his desire to act as freely as he can. He exercises his modest rights with respect to both mobile and immobile, passive and active property. In the sphere of mobile and active property they become institutionally important when the holders of such property employ it professionally and independently in industry and commerce. Those who engage in handicraft or trade take a decisive step forward when they begin to devote themselves to these pursuits professionally, that is, full time. However, such an advance effects no major societal change, as long as the professional craftsmen and traders constitute only a new subsection within the class of government functionaries. It is only when they use their property to operate professionally *and* independently that they appear as a new class. The difference is not one of the "mode of production"—which may not change at all—but of the producers' and traders' political (and politically conditioned societal) position.

Land is tilled professionally (that is, by peasants who spend most of their time farming) as soon as agriculture becomes an essential basis of subsistence. And elements of private (independent) landownership emerge relatively early. But the landowners, who often do not till their soil themselves, are in many Oriental societies prevented from expanding the sphere of private agrarian property, since most of the land is, in one way or another, regulated by the government. It is only when free (nonregulated) land becomes the dominant form of land tenure that private landownership becomes a societal phenomenon comparable to the predominance of independent professional handicraft and trade.

Independent active property advances unevenly in its mobile and immobile sectors. These developmental differences are sufficiently clear and regular to permit distinction between at least three major patterns of proprietary complexity in hydraulic society:

1) When independent active property plays a subordinate role in both its mobile and immobile forms, we are faced with a relatively

simple pattern of property. We shall call this conformation a simple hydraulic society.

2) When independent active property develops strongly in industry and commerce but not in agriculture, we are faced with a semicomplex pattern of property. We shall call this conformation a semicomplex hydraulic society.

3) When independent active property develops strongly in industry and commerce and also in agriculture, we are faced with the most complex pattern of property to be observed in hydraulic society. We shall call this conformation a complex hydraulic society.

2. SUPPLEMENTARY REMARKS

a. "Simple I" and "Simple II"

How far can private and independent property advance in industry and commerce? And when does private ownership in land prevail over all other forms of land tenure? We shall attempt to answer both questions when we discuss the peculiarities of semicomplex and complex configurations of Oriental property.

Another question, however, must be settled first. Are there, within hydraulic society, conditions under which professional representatives of industry and commerce are altogether absent or, for all practical purposes, as good as absent? Such conditions do exist indeed. They occur essentially in hydraulic tribes, which for this and other reasons represent the most rudimentary variant of a simple Oriental society. We distinguish the tribal type of simple hydraulic society, "Simple I," from the state-centered type of simple hydraulic society, "Simple II."

TABLE 4. *Patterns of Proprietary Complexity in Hydraulic Society (Schematized)*

PATTERNS OF PROPERTY	SPHERES OF PROPRIETARY DEVELOPMENT			
	Agriculture Pursued:		Industry and Commerce Pursued:	
	Professionally	*Predominantly with Privately Owned Land*	*In the Main [1] Professionally*	*On Basis of Private Property and in the Main [1] Independently*
Simple				
I	⊕[3]	—	—	+[3]
II	+	—	⊕	—
Semicomplex	+	—	+	⊕
Complex	+	⊕	+	+

Key
+ Feature conspicuous
— Feature inconspicuous or absent

1. The meaning of the qualification is explained in the text, p. 233.
2. The circle ⊕ indicates a developmentally new feature.
3. Farmer-craftsmen and producer-traders.

b. Proprietary Complexity and Hydraulic Density

CORRELATIONS between the patterns of proprietary complexity, on the one hand, and patterns of hydraulic density, on the other, are less easily established. The rise of property-based enterprise and social classes is due to several factors, among which hydraulic density is only one, and one that in a given area tends to change its quality very slowly and usually only because of changing relations with other areas.

This, however, does not imply the absence of significant correlations between hydraulic density and proprietary complexity. Of the two major evolutionary steps that hydraulic property may take, at least the first—the transition from a simple to a semicomplex pattern —may be greatly retarded, if not altogether blocked, when the underlying agrarian order is hydraulically compact. Like the correlation between the rise of a state-centered simple hydraulic society and the advance of professional industry and commerce, this correlation will be clarified when we systematically discuss the characteristics of simple, semicomplex, and complex patterns of Oriental property.

E. NONSPECIFIC AND SPECIFIC ASPECTS IN THE PROPRIETARY CONDITIONS OF TRIBAL HYDRAULIC SOCIETIES

1. NONSPECIFIC ASPECTS

AGRICULTURAL tribes handle their property in many different ways; and this is as true for hydraulic as for nonhydraulic communities.[1] In the simpler farming communities of Melanesia, South America, and Africa "movables are privately owned, but not land." [2] Similar trends exist also among important groups of the American Northwest; [a] but in Melanesia and West Africa a more differentiated pattern has made its appearance. "As a rule, land was common property of the village, but in regard to cultivated land we find the beginnings of sib, family, or individual ownership." [3]

Up to a point conditions of land tenure are similar in hydraulic tribes. Among the smaller irrigation tribes of equatorial Africa land can be bought and sold. This is the case among the Suk [4] and the Endo.[5] Among the En-Jemusi it was originally "marked out by the chief," but now, when division after the father's death excessively reduces an allotment, an owner can augment his holdings by pur-

a. The Iroquois have a saying: "Land cannot be bought and sold, any more than water and fire can" (Lips, 1938: 516).

chase, as do the Suk; or following the earlier pattern, he may be given additional fields by his chief.[6] In the American Pueblos communal patterns of land tenure prevailed until modern times. In the Rio Grande area "unused agricultural land reverts to the town, to be reallotted by Town chief [*cacique*] or Governor." [7] Among the hydraulically marginal Hopi a "clan system of land tenure was universally in vogue"; [8] and the village chief, who was "the theoretical owner of all the village lands," [9] asserted his authority "most frequently . . . in the settlement of land disputes." [10]

Thus in both nonhydraulic and hydraulic small farming communities the forms of land tenure vary; and the tendency toward communal control is strong but not universal. Corresponding resemblances can be discovered also with respect to mobile property. Weapons as well as tools that are used in hunting and gathering are usually owned individually by hydraulic tribesmen; but the objects thus obtained are so perishable that their passing possession does not favor the development of class distinctions, whatever the methods of distribution.

Nor, under such conditions, do industry and trade lead to significant social differentiations. This is eminently clear with regard to trade. The exchange of privately owned goods is undertaken privately; but this does not require special training or full-time handling. As in the small nonhydraulic farming communities, there is trade in hydraulic tribes, but there are no professional traders.[b]

2. SPECIFIC ASPECTS

IN industry conditions are not so simple. Property-based crafts are practiced primarily to satisfy the farmers' personal needs; and those who, because they command particular skills or have access to particular materials, produce goods for exchange usually do so on a part-time basis, their major efforts still being devoted to agriculture. This is the prevailing pattern in both nonhydraulic and hydraulic tribes, and it is a pattern that is not fundamentally altered by the presence of a few professional craftsmen, such as smiths.[c]

b. Among the Pueblo Indians exchange between the various villages or with non-Pueblo peoples is maintained by individuals (Parsons, 1939, I: 35; Beaglehole, 1937: 81) or by trading parties (Parsons, 1939, I: 34 ff.). Market-like gatherings are organized, usually by women (Beaglehole, 1937: 82 ff.; Parsons, 1939, I: 36 ff.) and, it seems, spontaneously (Beaglehole, 1937: 81 ff.). For earlier conditions see Espejo, 1916: 183; Bandelier, FR, I: 101, 163; Parsons, 1939, I: 33 ff.; Hackett, 1923, II: 234, 236, 240, 242 ff.; for recent developments, see Parsons, 1939, I: 34 ff. For the Chagga see Widenmann, 1899: 69; Gutmann, 1926: 425, 431.

c. Beech, 1911: 18. The potters mentioned by Beech (p. 17) obviously give only part of their time to their craft.

Large-scale constructions are a different matter. Small farming communities of the nonhydraulic type usually lack the organizational integration for the execution of such enterprises; and some hydraulic tribes, such as the Suk and the Endo, have not applied the organizational methods they employ in hydraulic work to nonhydraulic objectives, as the American Pueblo Indians have done with amazing success. To be sure, the tools of the Pueblo builders were privately owned; but their building materials were secured under communal leadership, and the work was done by communal labor. Such arrangements do not promote a property-based private industry nor the growth of a group that derives its strength from private industrial property and enterprise. On the contrary. They clear the way for patterns of operation that retard the rise of nongovernmental proprietary forces in industry as well as in other sectors of society.

In the sphere of hydraulic works these antiproprietary forces appear regularly. A primitive peasant, using his own tools, cultivates land that may or may not be communally regulated, and the seeds for his crops may belong to him personally or to his kin group. Under nonhydraulic conditions this is the whole story. In a hydraulic setting cultivation proper follows a similar pattern; but the "preparatory" operations do not. The tools are privately owned, but the raw materials for making the hydraulic installations (earth, stone, and perhaps timber) either are communal property—that is, owned by nobody or everybody—or, if they are to be found on land held by a particular individual, family, or clan, are taken over by the community. And the end products of the community's coordinated effort, the ditches or canals, do not become the property of the individual farmers or farming families that participate in the work, but, like the water which they carry to the individual fields, they are controlled ("owned") by the community's governing agency.[d] This proprietary peculiarity can be discerned in the incipient hydraulic communities of the Hill Suk, whose "irrigation ditches are the property of the tribe, not of the individual." [11] In the irrigation villages of the En-Jemusi the irrigation ditches are also the property of the tribe; [12] and this is equally the case with the larger, communally built, irrigation installations of the Pueblo Indians.

To evaluate these facts properly we must remember that the communities discussed so far are small farming societies—that is, communities in which the basic unit of tribal activity is almost always the village. In a nonhydraulic setting the headmen of the small units do not, as a rule, have authority over any substantial communally

---

d. Small ditches that require the labor of only a few individuals or a kin group are the property of those who make them.

owned and communally managed property. Such property, however, characterizes the hydraulic village; and in most cases it is administered by ceremonial and/or operational leaders.[e]

This proprietary development has another aspect, which has already been noted but which in the present context assumes a new significance. In small nonhydraulic farming societies a headman, who exerts little functional leadership, does not have his fields tilled for him by the community. Among small hydraulic tribes the headman, even when his leadership is overtly recognized, is not always so privileged either.[f] However, among the Pueblo Indians, who in most cases combined a compact hydraulic agriculture with large nonhydraulic constructions, the chief's fields were cultivated for him, even in villages that numbered only a few hundred inhabitants.

Among larger hydraulic tribes, such as the Chagga, the existence of the chief's fields cannot be considered specific, since such land arrangements occur in large nonhydraulic communities. But in large hydraulic tribes the chief's fields tend to be extensive; and work on them (and on the chief's houses) is done not by a limited number of retainers but by all able-bodied tribesmen.[g] Another proprietary peculiarity is entirely specific: the chief's privileged claim on the tribe's irrigation water.[13]

The extraordinary concentration of land, water, agricultural and

e. For the Pueblos the directing authority of the *cacique* and the war chief is well established. The situation among the Hill Suk is less clear. Beech (1911: 15) recognized that communal discipline was invoked in hydraulic work, but he was unable to discover any directing secular leader, or for that matter any religious leaders: "medicine men" (*ibid.:* xiv, n. 1). However, an "Elder" plays a prominent role in two crucial agricultural ceremonies, one pertaining to the clearing of the land, the other to the opening of the irrigation ditches (*ibid.:* 15 ff.). Sir Charles Eliot doubts the validity of Beech's anarchistic picture (*ibid.:* xiv, n. 1); and he does so by citing military requirements. No doubt the need for military leadership exists in almost all independent communities, but Eliot's military argument would be equally valid for the small nonhydraulic farming communities, whose chiefs rarely have more than a "purely representative position" (Lips, 1938: 515). In the Pueblos tribal leadership is definitely linked to leadership in communal activities, and among them hydraulic work ranks first. Expanding Eliot's reservations, we suggest that the germs of an operational authority were present among the Hill Suk, particularly in the matter of the tribe's most important property, its hydraulic installations.

f. The chief occupies a conspicuously strong position among the En-Jemusi (Beech, 1911: 37), but there is no evidence of any public fields being tilled for him.

g. The Chagga chieftain demands corvée labor from the tribe's adult males, from the women, and from the adolescent boys. These three groups work for the chief, in agriculture: cutting the bush (men), burning (men), hoeing (women), watering the seeds (men), raking and weeding (women), irrigating (men), and harvesting (women) (Gutmann, 1926: 376); in construction work: cutting and transporting timber (men), building proper (men), carrying of heavy loads of straw for the roofs (women), bringing up material for fences, etc. (the "boys") (*ibid.:* 376, 368).

industrial labor in the hands of the chiefs does not enhance personal, family, or clan ownership.[h] It does not benefit the social position of private craftsmen, who in the larger hydraulic tribes become somewhat more numerous.[i] Nor does it favor private professional merchants.[j] Specifically, it hampers the expansion of private property in what is frequently an important secondary branch of the subsistence economy: herding.

The tribal history of many European civilizations shows how, in an agrarian economy, growing cattle wealth is a factor in establishing societal leadership. In East Africa animal wealth is similarly esteemed; and in a predominantly pastoral community, such as the Masai, this wealth, which is eagerly displayed,[14] is an essential means of determining the owners' social position.[k] Not so among the Chagga. Cattle, which under the peculiar conditions of the Chagga area were largely stall-fed,[15] increased substantially; and some tribesmen owned as many as eighty head.[16] But in Chagga society the owners of large herds did not necessarily enjoy a higher social status, although they certainly enjoyed added material advantages. The Chagga chieftain, thanks to his quasidespotic powers, easily found a pretext for ac-

h. Until recent colonial times the bulk of all Chagga land was controlled, first by the clans and subsequently, and increasingly, by the chieftain. The clans yielded to the chief some of their authority over the banana lands, which were probably the first to be cultivated and required some irrigation (Gutmann, 1926: 303; Dundas, 1924: 300 ff.). The fields of eleusine millet, which had always required intensive irrigation "are marked out and allotted by the Chief himself. So are the maize fields in the plains, and this allotment" is one of the important duties of the Chief" (ibid.: 301). For recent colonial developments in the chieftain-controlled maize sector see Gutmann, 1926: 307.

i. Among the Chagga, even more exclusively than in the Pueblos, trade is in the hands of women (Widenmann, 1899: 69; Gutmann, 1926: 425).

j. Among the Chagga the only professional craftsmen are the smith and perhaps the tanner (Widenmann, 1899: 84; Gutmann, 1909: 119; Dundas, 1924: 270 ff.). The smiths live in special localities and they may only marry women from families of smiths (Widenmann, 1899: 84; Gutmann, 1909: 119; Dundas, 1924: 271).

k. Merker, 1904: 28. Among the Pastoral Suk, who "rather look down upon them [the Agricultural (Hill) Suk] on account of their poverty" (Beech, 1911: 15), cattle wealth seems to be decisive for the establishment of communal prominence. A certain Karôle, who had the reputation of being the "richest" of the Suk (ibid.: 7, n. 1), rose as high politically as the undifferentiated conditions of his tribe permitted; he became his group's "most important advisor" (ibid.). But the overt authority of the "advisors" was extremely slight; and it is doubtful whether, among the Pastoral Suk, any of them exerted more power covertly, since no communal enterprise known to us provided an opportunity for invoking generally accepted disciplinary methods. It is probably no accident that the poorer but incipiently hydraulic Hill Suk prosecuted persons who violated the tribal laws more severely than did the wealthier plainsmen: "The punishments for crime in the hills are far stricter than in the plains" (ibid.: 27, n. 1).

cusing conspicuous cattle owners of some malfeasance or other and for confiscating some or all of their animals.[17] And the Chagga herders, instead of boasting of their growing cattle wealth, became increasingly secretive and fearful. An earlier practice of farming out cattle to poorer tribesmen for foddering [18] became a convenient device for hiding their valuable but insecure property. The animals were now handed over to their temporary keepers furtively and by night; [19] and the owners' sons, who originally had played an important role in the transfer,[20] were at times not even informed as to where the cattle were placed. Says Dundas: "So secret does he keep the whereabouts of his stock, that he will not even tell his sons where it is." [21] This trend gained strength with the growth of chiefly power, which occurred prior to the establishment of colonial rule. It was further aggravated when, under this rule, the chief started to raise a general cattle tax.[22]

In this setting private wealth does not necessarily, or even primarily, establish public prominence.[m] Among the qualities that in the earlier time favored chieftainship, wealth probably was a desirable but not a necessary factor; and the chief's property certainly grew not in proportion to what wealth he or his forefathers may have had originally but in proportion to his growing agromanagerial and military power. For his aides the ruler chose men who were prominent in their locality [23] or—and increasingly—men whose personal qualifications fitted them for the job.[24] In both cases selection involved a conspicuous improvement in the material conditions of the chosen, for the chief provided his serving men with cattle and women.[25] In fact, Merker found that only persons in government positions were rich.[26]

3. SIMPLE I . . .

MANIFESTLY, hydraulic tribes like nonhydraulic agrarian tribes develop private property. Both conformations present undifferentiated forms of property (as in handicraft and trade) and a trend to-

---

m. Gutmann (1909: 7) says that rich tribesmen may withhold irrigation water from the poor, but in a later and more detailed study he describes the equalitarian way in which all members of a given hydraulic unit are provided with water (1926: 418).

He also refers to certain "nobles" who obviously owned cattle and who helped a chieftain obtain office (ibid.: 462). But no details are given regarding this incident, which occurred at the beginning of the 19th century (ibid.: 461), that is, before the chief's leadership in communal affairs had been fully established. And the clan leaders did not owe their rank to wealth, though, once chosen, some of them probably had opportunities for improving their economic condition (ibid.: 15). A clansman became ceremonial leader because he was the oldest male in the group (ibid.: 13), and the political leader, the "speaker," achieved his position on the basis "not of his age, nor of his wealth, but of his political shrewdness" (ibid.: 14).

ward regulated forms (as in farming with respect to land). At the same time, however, significant differences may be observed. Under hydraulic circumstances, political property already emerges in small hydraulically compact communities (the chief's land in the Pueblo villages). In larger tribes political property expands one-sidedly, and it retards and cripples private property in important spheres of activity (such as herding).

The difference between this one-sided accumulation of property in the hands of the governing authorities and the pluralistic patterns of proprietary growth in nonhydraulic agrarian tribes reflects perfectly the differences in the character and weight of political authority.[n] In the German tribes observed by Caesar and Tacitus the chieftain, although recognized as the top-ranking political leader and expected to devote much of his time to his governmental duties, was unable to restrict or tax the wealth of his nobles. Nor did he demand corvée labor or taxes from his tribesmen, who would have considered such a request an insult and who, like the nobles, participated in the public discussions of the tribe's affairs.[27]

Thus in tribal hydraulic societies property is simple, but it is simple with a specific tendency toward the predominance of political, power-based, property. This tendency increases with the size of the community. It becomes decisive in simple hydraulic commonwealths that are no longer directed by a primitive (tribal) government, but by a state.

F. PATTERNS OF PROPERTY IN STATE-CENTERED SIMPLE HYDRAULIC SOCIETIES

1. Statehood versus Primitive Government

CONTROL over a distinct territory has been considered a basic aspect of statehood. This aspect is indeed essential; but it has little value in the present context, since it is not specific. (As a rule, primitive governments also claim control over their territory.) Nor does the criterion of sovereignty help much. (Primitive governments also strive to establish sovereignty; and like states, they are not always able to.)

The differences between a primitive government and a state seem inconsequential so long as we confine comparison to external relations. They become significant when we compare internal conditions.

n. As elaborated above, in most nonhydraulic communities tribal coordination is required mainly for military and ceremonial purposes, whereas the heads of hydraulic tribes, in addition to exerting military and/or religious leadership, fulfill specific, vital agromanagerial functions.

Primitive governments are operated in the main by nonprofessionals —that is, by functionaries who devote the bulk of their time not to the civil, military, or religious affairs of the community but to their own hunting, fishing, farming, or raiding. States are operated in the main by professionals—that is, by functionaries who devote the bulk of their time to "public" affairs. From the standpoint of human relations a state means government by professionals.

Certain communal functions, such as the maintenance of internal order and the organization of defense, are vital for the perpetuation of all types of society. Consequently, man's political activities are as essential as those involved in the securing of food and shelter; and the professionalizing of government is as important an aspect of social differentiation as is the professionalizing of those economic or intellectual pursuits that under more primitive conditions are handled only by persons who are primarily engaged otherwise.

It goes without saying that a statelike government with its full-time civil and military officials, its soldiery and police can invest much more time and energy in administrative and coercive activities than a primitive government. It is this power potential of the state that makes its control by responsible and effective nongovernmental forces the only guarantee against the rise of a totally powerful (and totally corrupt) apparatus state.

Many Marxists, following Marx' and Engels' interpretation of the Western state and disregarding their stress on the peculiarity of Oriental despotism, have described "the state" as an institution that *always* serves the special interests of a property-based ruling class. This interpretation, which today, in its Soviet version, is part of an extremely widespread—and extremely potent—political myth, is not true even for modern parliamentary governments, whose plutocratic potential it generalizes and whose capacity for growth and democratization it denies. Nor does it fit the states of Western absolutism and feudalism, nor indeed the democratic states of ancient Greece. And it is completely absurd when it is applied to the agrarian and industrial apparatus states that are characterized not by the strong influence of nongovernmental proprietary forces on the state, but by the abysmal lack of any such influence.

2. Steps in the Professionalizing of Government

a. Chagga Chieftainship and the State of Ancient Hawaii

THE difference between primitive government and statehood becomes unmistakably clear when we juxtapose the single full-time and

community-supported leader of a Pueblo village and the large staffs
of government functionaries in Pharaonic Egypt, imperial China, or
Ottoman Turkey. The almost complete predominance of nonprofessionals in the first case is as manifest as the almost complete predominance of professional apparatus men in the second. The
difference is less obvious, but perhaps even more informative, when
we compare the regimes of large hydraulic tribes, such as the Chagga,
with the state of a relatively crude neolithic hydraulic civilization,
such as ancient Hawaii.

The absolutist acts of a Chagga chief are impressive: he kills, [a]
spies, seizes his subjects' cattle,[b] and keeps as many girls as he wishes
in his palace.[c] In addition and more importantly, he is the commander in chief of the tribe's laboring and fighting force.[d] Nevertheless, his ability to rule the lives of his subjects is limited by the small
number of his full-time functionaries. Highest among them is "a
person who may best be described as his prime minister, and on
whom much of the executive work devolves." [1] Below this tribal
version of a vizier are certain helpers and advisors, akida,[2] who "receive the chief's orders, convey them to the people, using for this
purpose special helpers, and supervise and organize their execution.
Such orders pertain, for instance, to the making and repairing of
canals, work for the chieftain . . . payment of taxes and religious
affairs." [3] The akida, who are expected to spend a considerable part
of their time at the chief's palace,[4] apparently have one assistant each; [5]
but the professional officialdom ends here. Clan heads may advise
the chief,[6] staying at his palace for this very purpose, and most of
the on-the-spot directing remains in the hands of the clans. The
hornblower, the actual leader of the corvée, is selected by members of
his clan and only confirmed by the chieftain.[7] Obviously, he is
not a full-time salaried functionary.[8]

a. To demonstrate his loyalty a Chagga dignitary was ready to burn his sister to
death when ordered to do so by his chieftain (Gutmann, 1914: 219).

b. As punishment for an alleged crime, Chieftain Mapfuluke is said to have seized
the cattle of one of his fathers-in-law. Later, and quite unexpectedly, he returned some
part of them (Gutmann, 1914: 231).

c. Gutmann (1926: 388 ff.) estimates that, in one instance, the chieftain assembled
from among rank-and-file families more than 5 per cent of all girls. These young
females were then assigned to his wives; but the chieftain maintained his sexual rights
over all of them: "None of the girls entered marriage untouched, the chieftain used
them as he pleased."

d. The Chagga chieftain makes the supreme decisions concerning the hydraulic
corvée and other large-scale secular enterprises. He commands his tribesmen in war;
he assigns residences to all; and he fixes the dates for sowing and harvesting (Gutmann,
1909: 25).

Nor does the chieftain have at his disposal professional guards or policemen. The warriors who protect his person—and this is particularly demanded at night—are ordinary members of the tribe who return home after their shifts are done.[9]

The supreme head of the Chagga government is occasionally referred to as a "monarch" or "king." [e] However, the majority of all observers designate him as "chieftain." [10] Conversely, the ancient Hawaiian rulers are sometimes called "chiefs," but in more scholarly treatises they are designated as "kings." The preferred titles reflect the general conviction that the Chagga ruler presides over a more primitive type of government than does his Hawaiian counterpart. This conviction seems well founded. In the first case we are faced with a primitive government that has elements of incipient statehood, in the second with a crude but genuine state.

The Hawaiian kings disposed over a much more differentiated staff of top-ranking aides than did the Chagga chieftains. In addition to a chief councilor, the Hawaiian ruler had a chief war leader, a chief steward, a treasurer, and "land experts." [11] There is no evidence that clan heads acted as his advisors or that his guards served part time. Besides a "body guard," the king had at his beck and call a detachment of armed men headed by an executioner—official terrorizers who were always ready in the king's name to accuse, arrest, and kill.[12]

In the Hawaiian government the professionals were not confined to the top echelon. Below the leading officials there were primarily and most importantly the *konohiki*. In contrast to the Chagga *akida*, who spent much of their time near their chieftain, the *konohiki* seem to have resided and officiated for the most part in the regions of their jurisdiction, directing the regime's constructional, organizational, and acquisitive operations. They kept count of the population; [13] they mobilized the corvée; [14] they directed the hydraulic enterprises; [15] they supervised agriculture; [16] they gathered the tax,[17] retaining some of it for their own use and for the use of their underlings, but passing on most of it to the higher authorities, and eventually to the king.[18]

Manifestly, the *konohiki* and their aides were government-supported full-time functionaries. The organizational and acquisitive network that they spread over the countryside probably contributed more than any other political institution to making the government of ancient Hawaii a crude, agrobureaucratic hydraulic despotism.

e. Gutmann, 1909: 10 ff. Lowie (1938: 302) calls him the head of a "monarchical system."

b. Proprietary Consequences

CONTROLLING a much more fertile territory and a much larger population—the largest Hawaiian kingdom had five times the population of the largest Chagga tribe [f]—the Hawaiian rulers were in a better position to establish and maintain a permanent officialdom. And this larger officialdom in turn enabled them to control their subjects' property more completely. In Hawaii the government's jurisdiction over the land was not restricted by any clan rights, as was the case among the Chagga.[19] Nor did a clan head stand between tax-collecting officials and individual taxpayers, as in Chaggaland.[20] Indeed the Hawaiian regime functioned so well that the masters of the apparatus state were able to syphon off over half of the entire rural produce. According to one estimate, "the common laborers did not receive on an average more than one third of the avails of their industry." [g]

On a smaller scale the difference between the two types of government appear also in the sphere of circulation. The Chagga markets were policed by the chief's wives and regional officials;[21] but a market tax on agricultural products and salt was collected by a member of one particular clan.[h] In Hawaii we find no trace of such divided authority. The functionaries who sanctioned the transactions and taxed the goods were toll collectors—that is, government officials.[22]

Thus the kings of Hawaii exerted a much more formidable power

f. In the 18th century some 300,000 Hawaiians were organized in a few sovereignties, the largest of which, Hawaii proper, numbered more than 85,000 people (Lind, 1938: 60). Lind's figure harmonizes well with an estimate made by Ellis in 1826 (Ellis, 1826: 8). Ellis considered the total of 400,000 inhabitants suggested by the earliest observers "somewhat above the actual population of that time, though traces of deserted villages, and numerous enclosures formerly cultivated, but now lying waste, are everywhere to be met with." In 1826 there were between 130,000 to 150,000 people on the archipelago (Ellis, 1826: 8). Fornander, although suggesting smaller figures than Cook and King, sees "no valid reasons for assuming a greater or more rapid depopulation between 1778 and 1832, when the first regular census taken gave an approximately correct enumeration of 130,000 than between the latter year and 1878, when the census gave only 44,088, exclusive of foreigners" (Fornander, PR, II: 165). At the beginning of the 19th century Bali had a population of about 760,000 persons, with some of the island's major kingdoms accounting for more than 100,000 persons each (Lauts, 1848: 104–5). The largest Chagga tribes numbered less than 20,000, 10,000, or 5,000 persons respectively (Gutmann, 1926: 1).

g. Alexander, 1899: 28 n. Blackman (1899: 26) presents this estimate as "the opinion of careful observers."

h. Gutmann, 1926: 426 ff. The clan functionary grasps a handful of taxable goods. The trading women have the right to kick him once; but they cannot prevent him from seizing the fee, which "at a well attended market amounts to fairly sizable loads" (ibid.: 427).

over their subjects' life and property than did the Chagga chieftains. Difference in the form of reverence strikingly expresses the difference in autocratic power. As already mentioned, the Chagga tribesmen hold their ruler in great esteem, but unlike the Hawaiians they do not perform before him the classical gesture of total submission: prostration.

3. SIMPLE PATTERNS OF PROPERTY IN LAND, INDUSTRY, AND COMMERCE

IN the early phases of state-centered hydraulic societies, private property in land is not necessarily lacking; its origins go back much further than was assumed by the pioneer institutionalists of the 19th century. But the greater part of all cultivable land is regulated, and thus kept from being privately owned, even after private and independent property emerged notably in industry and commerce. For this reason, we shall discuss the problems of hydraulic land tenure later. With respect to the simple patterns of hydraulic property we need only state here that, within the framework of these patterns, the forms of land tenure are many but that regulated land always prevails (and generally by a substantial margin) over privately owned ("free") land.

Property-based and independent handicraft and commerce, however, must be examined immediately, for their occurrence makes, as we see it, a change in the patterns of property and society. This development is not uniform.

It advances unevenly in the spheres of

A. Industry, in
  1. The extractive industries (mining, quarrying, certain forms of salt production)
  2. The processing industries
     a. Constructions
     b. Others

and also in

B. Commerce, in
  1. Foreign trade
  2. Domestic trade, dealing with
     a. Easily supervised goods (such as salt, iron, tea, wine, oil, etc.)
     b. Others.

In all hydraulic societies proper and in most marginal hydraulic societies, the government engaged in comprehensive constructions. Employing a large labor force, the agrarian apparatus state enjoys what amounts to a monopoly of all large-scale construction work.

Often it also manages those extractive operations which provide the bulk of all raw materials for the large government constructions. Other extractive industries, such as mining and certain forms of salt production, may either be directly managed by the government or, and particularly under the conditions of a money economy, they may be controlled through monopolistic licensing.

Thus property-based and independent action cannot hope to prevail in the most important sector of hydraulic industry: large-scale constructions. Nor can it hope to operate freely in the large extractive enterprises. Only in the nonconstructional sector of the processing industries is there a chance for property-based free handicraft to become significant. Indeed, apart from the making of coins, only a few manufacturing pursuits, such as the production of weapons and certain luxury goods, may be directly managed by the government, while most other crafts are handled entirely by private and independent entrepreneurs.

Free private enterprise, however, does not necessarily mean large enterprise. Large-scale industries are extremely vulnerable on the fiscal level, and except for government-protected units do not prosper under the shadow of total power. The many private and independent crafts which have emerged in certain hydraulic societies are essentially confined to small shops and small-scale operations.

The development of independent private trade may be retarded under conditions of great hydraulic and bureaucratic density (compactness), but it is not blocked by the state's managerial predominance, which, with regard to the construction industries, appears in all hydraulic societies proper and also in many marginal hydraulic societies. Above the level of the producer-trader, commercial business is transacted over significant distances, either overland or oversea. This favors large-scale action, particularly since the merchandise so handled is less conspicuous and therefore less vulnerable fiscally than a fixed and conspicuous industrial plant.

When the law of diminishing administrative returns induces a state to limit its own commercial operations, independent merchants tend to appear both in foreign and domestic trade; and governmental attempts to maintain direct and indirect controls in both sectors at a particular level or to restore them to an earlier level are based for the most part on short-range considerations.[i]

i. This is why government policy in this regard in China, India, and the Near East oscillated so considerably. The student of Chinese history will recall the discussions which Han administrators conducted concerning the way in which the sale of salt and iron should be handled. The problem arose in pre-Han days, and different solutions were found at different times. The administrative history of India is not

Hydraulic society outgrows the simple patterns of property, when private and independent handicraft becomes prominent in the processing industries (excluding, of course, large-scale construction) and when big and independent merchants handle as much or more business than all government-managed and government-controlled commerce taken together.

The almost complete absence of pertinent statistical data compels us to formulate our criteria broadly. In some branches the relative proportions are evident. In others we can at least establish prevailing trends.

4. Variants of Simple Patterns of Hydraulic Property and Society

a. Hawaii

THE Hawaiian archipelago is so distant from the more southerly regions of the Polynesian world that after an early period of daring expeditions, "all intercourse with the southern groups seems to have ceased, for there is no further evidence of it in any of the ancient legends, songs, or genealogies for five hundred years." [23]

Nor were the relations between the various Hawaiian kingdoms sufficient to stimulate the development of commerce above the producer-trader level.[24] Internal circulation consisted in the main in the transfer of rural surpluses from the peasant and fishermen producers to the local and central representatives of the government. Exchange between individuals occurred either in the form of "gifts" [25] or barter; [26] and in both instances without the aid of professional middlemen. Markets and fairs provided ample opportunity for such activity. Ellis' descriptions of what was then considered the most famous fair makes no reference at all to any professional merchants. The only professional person noted by the observer was the government official who supervised and taxed the transactions between the barterers.[27] When, in the early 19th century, contact with the outside world opened up a new outlet for sandalwood, it was the king and his lieutenants and not independent private

so well documented as that of China, but what we know about Indian fiscal policy suggests similar oscillations.

The history of state and private commerce in the great hydraulic countries of the Near East is still in its infancy; and attempts, such as that made recently by Leemans, reveal the institutional importance of this phenomenon as well as the difficulties of investigating it. The Near Eastern data show again that in contrast to the great hydraulic works and the big nonhydraulic constructions, large-scale commerce can readily be handled by private and independent merchants.

Hawaiian merchants who handled the resulting international trade.[28]

The undeveloped conditions of circulation reflect the undeveloped industrial conditions, and these in turn are closely connected with the paucity of suitable raw materials. The volcanic islands of Hawaii lack metals; and this deficiency kept the islanders, as long as they were separated from technically more advanced civilizations, at a relatively crude level of neolithic life. The archipelago had useful plants (such as taro and the coconut tree) but none of the world's major cereals; and there were no animals that could be used to ease man's labors. Lava was the only important workable stone.

The technical skill which the Hawaiians developed in this natural and cultural setting was admirable.[29] However, even maximum ingenuity produced only a modest differentiation in the crafts. Specialists built canoes [30] and houses,[31] made nets, fish lines, tapa cloth,[32] and many other articles,[33] yet the economic and political position of these artisans is none too clear. A number of them may well have worked for their own account.[j] But neither Hawaiian tradition nor early non-Hawaiian observers suggest that these private artisans could compare in importance with the craftsmen who served the king and his functionaries. The government, which controlled an enormous percentage of the country's surplus, was able to support many artisans, *poe lawelawe*. The supreme *poe lawelawe* was a member of the central government.[34] He seems to have directed the industrial activities undertaken for the benefit of the government and obviously through the use of corvée labor. In addition, he was in charge of the numerous artisans who were permanently attached to the court. Says Kepelino: "At the chief's [king's] place there were many workers or *Poe-lawelawe* of every description." [35]

Thus in ancient Hawaii professional artisans appeared most significantly as persons who, supported by the government, worked under government functionaries for the ruler and his serving men. This constellation, together with the complete absence of independent professional merchants, created in ancient Hawaii a very rudimentary variant of simple patterns of hydraulic property and society.

b. Inca Peru

THE masters of the Inca empire drew upon natural resources that were richer than those of Hawaii but poorer than those of Egypt, Mesopotamia, China, or India. The agriculturists of the Andean area entered the metal age at a relatively late date; and even then they did not process iron. Nor did they domesticate animals for use in farming. To be sure, in hydraulic civilizations the absence of labor

---

j. Several trades had special patron gods (Alexander, 1899: 37, 62 ff.; Blackman, 1899: 32).

animals is of less importance to crop-raising [k] than to transportation, which is basic to the spread of military and political control, to the collection of taxes, and to the growth of trade. However, compared with the donkey, the mule, the ox, the horse, and the camel—the chief labor animals of the Old World—the llama, although useful for its wool, was a poor instrument of locomotion. The absence of navigable rivers, in addition to a rugged coastline, discouraged experiments in shipping, except on primitive rafts; and a scarcity of culturally advanced neighbors discouraged international trade much more decisively than was the case in Pharaonic Egypt.

TABLE 5. *Factors Stimulating Commerce and Regional Division of Labor in Industry*

HYDRAULIC CIVILIZATIONS	LABOR ANIMALS	NAVIGABLE RIVERS AND BOATS	CULTURALLY ADVANCED NEIGHBORS INVITING INTERNATIONAL TRADE
Inca Peru	(—)	—	—
Pharaonic Egypt (particularly the Old and Middle Kingdoms)	+	+	(—)
The various states of ancient China	(+) [1]	+	+
Sumer	+	+	+

Key
+ Present
— Absent
( ) Development limited

1. The ox was used for plowing only at the close of the Chou period.

Our analysis has revealed a number of factors that stimulate commerce and regional division of labor in industry. We indicate in Table 5 the uneven development of these factors for a number of major simple hydraulic civilizations. Although by no means the only formative features, they aid us in recognizing the uneven development of trade and industry in these civilizations.

In the Andean area transportation was further discouraged by the desert-like conditions in large segments of the coast and by the high and steep elevations in the strategically located mountain regions. For all these reasons, effective and long-distance communication proceeded essentially on land and not on water; and it depended

k. An approach which recognizes the crucial role of hydraulic operations in the development of agriculture cannot be content with Lowie's otherwise suggestive typology of subsistence economies: "hunting, farming with hoe or dibble, farming with plow and livestock, and stockbreeding without farming (pastoral nomadism)" (Lowie, 1938: 283). The Near East, India, and China shared the plow and labor animals with Europe and Japan; and the reason for the differences between the stationary hydraulic civilizations and other agrarian civilizations that were not stationary must therefore be looked for elsewhere, and most decisively, it would seem, in the presence or absence of hydraulic agriculture.

to an extraordinary degree on roads that were built and controlled by the omnipotent hydraulic state. There were a few foreign-merchants; [36] and some of the trade in salt and fish reported for the northern border zone [37] may have been handled by professionals. But such developments were so peripheral and of so little .importance that serious scholars, such as Means, have completely overlooked their occurrence. Within the empire government officials directed the transfer of enormous quantities of goods—corn, beans, cotton, timber, metal, textiles, etc.—along the coast, on the *altiplano,* and from one zone to the other; and small producer-traders exchanged products by barter at the many fairs that were held regularly throughout the country.[38] But there is no evidence that any private agency competed with the government in long-distance transportation and distribution of goods. Trade there was, and on a local level obviously plenty of it. But there were almost no independent professional traders.

The industrial sphere of Inca life was much more differentiated, but the private artisans remained inconspicuous in comparison with government-employed craftsmen. The mines were managed either by the local heads of formerly independent territories or by nonlocal members of the imperial officialdom.[m] In both cases they were controlled by professional officeholders who, in one way or another, were part of the over-all agromanagerial apparatus.

More precise information exists concerning certain aspects of the processing industries. The large construction teams were directed by prominent Inca functionaries; and the work patterns of Hawaii, Pharaonic Egypt, and early China suggest that here, too, special officials may have been in charge of the permanent government workers and those craftsmen who, for two months or "at most" three months,[n] rendered industrial labor service in the state workshops. Among the permanent craftsmen that the government occupied there were apparently many silversmiths [39] and also not a few carpenters.[40] Weavers, shoemakers, lumbermen, and makers of copper tools are mentioned as working at home after having fulfilled their corvée obligations.[41] Garcilaso's description does not make it clear whether all, or most, of these last worked exclusively at their specialities or whether some—or even most of them—were farmer-artisans. If we assume that most of them were professional craftsmen, it is even more noteworthy that the early accounts of rural and urban

m. Local mining of gold in accordance with directions from Cuzco is indicated by Polo de Ondegardo (1872: 70 ff.). Cf. Cieza, 1945: 269; Sarmiento, 1906: 100; Rowe, 1946: 246; Garcilaso, 1945, I: 253; Sancho de la Hos, 1938: 181.

n. Notable overtime was deducted from the following year's corvée labor (Garcilaso, 1945, I: 255).

life do not mention them. It was only as permanent workers for the state or as members of the industrial corvée that the artisans became a conspicuous feature of Inca society.

The "virgins," who were selected by officials from among the young and attractive females of the empire, provided the regime with a unique, but eminently useful, labor force. The "Selected Ones" were kept under strict supervision in special houses, where they spent the greater part of their time weaving, spinning,[42] and preparing beverages.[o] The sovereign included some of them in his harem; and he assigned others to prominent dignitaries. But there were always large numbers of them confined to the "houses." Apparently there were many such establishments in the Inca empire: some had two hundred inmates,[43] the one in Caxa had five hundred,[44] the one on Lake Titicaca one thousand,[45] and the one in Cuzco usually more than fifteen hundred.[46] Economically, the Inca "houses" constitute an interesting parallel to the textile shops of 17th- and 18th-century Europe. Few of these latter employed more persons, and those employed were in the main women, who often worked only part of the year.[47]

Despite a not inconsiderable technical development, Inca society developed no conspicuous, independent, private-property-based classes. The sinecure land, which the Incas assigned to certain members of the ruling group, created no full-fledged landownership; [48] and professional private enterprises were virtually absent in the spheres of transport and trade, which in other civilizations favored the rise of independent rich merchants. Professional private artisans, who certainly existed, remained an insignificant force even in the processing industries, when compared with the numerous craftsmen who permanently or temporarily practiced their skills in the government workshops and "houses." An interesting if feeble trend toward private handicraft notwithstanding, the Inca empire represents a simple pattern of hydraulic property and society.

o. CPLNC: 309. The two Spaniards who gave Sancho de la Hos (1938: 181) a first-hand report on the Lake Titicaca temple mentioned only the preparation of sacred wine by the women, if the chronicler recorded their story correctly. But whatever the accuracy of the initial report, it seems most unlikely that the thousand "selected" women of the Lake Temple made nothing but *chicha* the year round, and this in the classical region of llama-breeding and wool production. Our doubts are strengthened by *The Anonimo's* comment on the dual activities of the women at Caxa (CPLNC: 309) and by Garcilaso's description of the institution in the Inca capital. Obviously the virgins also had to prepare *chicha* and certain ceremonial foodstuffs, but their main operation (*il principal exercicio*) was spinning and weaving (Garcilaso, 1945, I: 188 ff.). There were many other houses of the same kind throughout the country. Their inmates engaged in the same economic activities. They "spun and wove and made an enormous amount of cloth for the Inca" (*ibid.*: 189).

c. Pharaonic Egypt

A UNIQUELY serviceable river provided the masters of Pharaonic Egypt with excellent facilities for internal communication; shipping was therefore well advanced at the dawn of written history. But scarcity of raw materials did not necessitate a regular foreign trade; nor was such trade stimulated by culturally advanced neighbors. The Egyptian ships and beasts of burden permitted the establishment of some external contacts, but these contacts remained intermittent— and essentially government managed—until the close of the Middle Kingdom.

During the New Kingdom, and particularly in the days of the empire, private merchants emerged. But often they were attached to the temples [49] and apparently they were no match for the state. According to Kees, during a great part of the New Kingdom the Pharaoh remained "the only big merchant." [50]

To be sure, foreign merchants did business in Egypt, but native middlemen were given even less opportunity in domestic than in foreign trade.[51] In the local markets producer-traders exchanged their goods directly, and in the main by barter.[52] A market official of the New Kingdom significantly bore the title "Scribe of Barter." [53]

Handicraft offered more room for the development of private enterprise. No matter to what extent the census data of the Old Kingdom imply the presence of independent trades during that period,[p] the cases of Hawaii and Inca Peru show that professional artisans operated in state-centered hydraulic societies that were technically less advanced than the Old Kingdom. And a number of records from the Middle and the New Kingdom definitely speak of private artisans.[54]

These Egyptian private artisans were more conspicuous than their colleagues in the Inca empire; but, like them, they probably catered essentially to the every-day needs of small consumers.[55] Did they, at least numerically, equal the many craftsmen who in the processing industries were permanently or temporarily employed by the government and the temples? Even this is not certain. But there can be little doubt that economically they were less significant.

The government engaged particularly in three kinds of industrial work: (1) extractive and preparatory operations requiring much labor, some of it skilled, but most of it unskilled; (2) big construction enterprises, requiring a combination of skilled and unskilled labor; and (3) processing industries, carried out in the main by skilled

p. Kees (1933: 164 ff.) hesitates to accept E. Meyer's interpretation of these data as proving the existence of free artisans and merchants.

craftsmen who were gathered together in larger or smaller workshops.

In all three sectors the skilled craftsmen, who included artists of great ability,[56] seem to have been largely government employees. The "chiefs of work" [57] probably had supreme jurisdiction over them. In the branch industries they operated under specially designated foremen.[58]

On the basis of carefully weighed evidence Kees concludes that "the economic life of [Pharaonic] Egypt constituted a not very appropriate soil for an estate of *independent* free artisans." [59] He finds the concept of free handicraft, except for lowly producers who satisfied lowly needs, "poorly suited for the economic picture of the Old Kingdom." [60] After the interlude of the Middle Kingdom, during which territorial courts became outstanding centers of the arts and crafts,[61] the New Kingdom increasingly forced the artisans into state-regulated workshops and subjected them to the rigid control of the state storehouses that allocated the raw materials.[62]

Documents from the New Kingdom show the state artisans eager for promotion to higher posts. Their foremen considered themselves fairly distinguished members of the bureaucratic hierarchy.[63]

To summarize: the power of the Pharaohs was so all embracing that private and independent handicraft made little headway, and independent professional commerce during the greater part of the period even less. The prevalence of state trade and the weight of government-managed industry, together with the dominance of state-regulated landed property created—and maintained—in Pharaonic Egypt a historically and institutionally significant variant of the simple pattern of hydraulic property and society.

d. Ancient China

THE most archaic Chinese inscriptions, the divination texts of the Shang dynasty, mention sets of shells, which in all probability were used as means of exchange. But they do not clearly refer to professional merchants. Neither do merchants play a conspicuous role in the inscriptions and literary texts of the Chou dynasty. Although in early China there certainly was trade, there seem to have been few, if any, professional traders.

Big merchants, who traveled overland, are reported for the first part of the later Chou period, the time of the "Spring and Autumn Annals" (721–481 B.C.). But those on whom the data are fullest cooperated so closely with their rulers that they can probably be considered to have been government attached.[64]

During the last phase of the Chou dynasty, the time of the Warring

States, independent merchants increased in importance—so much so, in fact, that in the 4th century B.C. the state of Ch'in took measures to restrict them.[65] By the time Ch'in had welded "all-under-heaven" into an empire, the great Unifier, Ch'in Shih Huang-ti, decimated the ranks of the merchants by sentencing them to guard the frontier, at first the merchants themselves and then their sons and grandsons.[66] This policy demonstrates both the economic importance and the political weakness of nongovernmental professional traders at the end of the Chou period.

The early Chinese records that have so little to say about professional traders are more articulate about craftsmen. The beautiful bronze artifacts of Shang and early Chou reveal extraordinary industrial refinement. However, and different from conditions in feudal Europe, the Chinese crafts developed not on many and separated manorial estates or in guild-controlled burgher towns but rather in big administrative centers controlled by the Son of Heaven, the territorial rulers, or their high ranking officials. Artisan-officials, the "hundred artisans," are mentioned in the oldest literary texts as well as in the early bronze inscriptions.[67] Apparently government artisans employed their skills under the supreme direction of the Minister of Works, the *ssŭ-kung*,[68] and alongside the "people," who as part of their corvée duty constituted the unskilled labor force of the government's large constructional enterprises.

Government-attached artisans may have prevailed until the time of the "Spring and Autumn Annals"; [69] and perhaps it was only during the subsequent period of the Warring States that private artisans became increasingly important.

We have no conclusive evidence that, under the Chou dynasty and under the first imperial dynasties, private merchants or artisans organized independent professional corporations (guilds).[q] The retarded development in this regard is surprising when we remember that private handicraft and particularly private trade flourished at the close of and after the Chou period. Whatever the reasons for this unevenness, we are probably safe in suggesting that a simple Oriental society prevailed in ancient China until the end of Early Chou (722 B.C.) and probably also in the first centuries of Later Chou.

q. Shops dealing with the same goods were apparently assembled in the same locality from the close of the Chou period on or from Early Han days (Kato, 1936: 79), and probably also prior to this time. But it "was not until after the Sui period that the expression '*hang*', used in the sense of a street of shops of the same trade, came into general use"; and it was only "at the close of the T'ang period, or even later, that they [the Chinese merchants] came to organise a real merchants' association" (*ibid.*: 83).

e. Sumer

THE agricultural civilizations of Lower Mesopotamia originated in a setting that was as lacking in certain industrial materials as it was encouraging to interarea exchange. The alluvial landscape, which because of its well-watered rivers offered ideal opportunities for hydraulic development, lacked stone, timber, and metals. However, these materials, which were essential to technical, military, and political growth, were available in adjacent lands, and from the standpoint of wealth, security, and power the incentives to obtain them were enormous.

The ancient Hawaiians did not get from abroad the raw materials that they lacked at home; and the Andean Indians and early Egyptians created urban civilizations mainly on the basis of their own resources. The Sumerians developed a flourishing urban life, because they succeeded in establishing and maintaining an elaborate system of international relations and exchange.

Needed raw materials can be obtained by organized force: war. But this is not always appropriate, and particularly not when the sources of supply are remote and those in control strong. In many cases the sought-for goods had to be acquired by peaceful means— that is, primarily by trade.

Long distance trade requires the services of specialists in transportation and exchange. In Lower Mesopotamia merchants appeared early. While traders played an insignificant role in almost all other simple Oriental civilizations, they were conspicuously mentioned in the Sumerian protohistorical inscriptions of Fara; [70] and in later and more detailed inscriptions they were depicted as important professionals.

The development of urban centers of administration and religion also involved a fairly advanced division of industrial labor; and the Sumerian inscriptions contain many references to artisans, who practiced their skills professionally. How developed were private property and private enterprise in early Lower Mesopotamia?

Deimel's elaborate investigations suggest that from the dawn of history on,[r] the Sumerian temple cities probably offered less opportunity for independent craftsmen than did ancient Hawaii, Peru, and Pharaonic Egypt. Like the other members of the temple com-

r. According to Deimel, the ancient Sumerians apparently depended as much on the temples, when the Fara texts were written, as they did three or four hundred years later, when Urukagina ruled Lagash. "The population then too served the temple and lived on it" (Deimel, 1924a: 42).

munity, the artisans received land,[71] and like them also, they rendered corvée service,[72] which, according to Schneider's tentative estimate, may have lasted some four months a year.[73] A number of craftsmen were employed permanently in temple workshops,[74] as were certain slaves (in the main female).[75] The majority of all artisans, however, seems to have worked for the temples through the operation of a putting-out system: temple storehouses provided them with raw materials, which they processed at home and for a wage.[76] The position of these artisans was not unlike that of many European craftsmen who during the first centuries of industrial capitalism worked in a similarly decentralized way for their commercial or industrial employers.

Were all domestic artisans of early Mesopotamia so engaged? And did any of them engage at least in some independent business? The second question is more easily answered than the first. The fact that all (or some?) of the workmen offered the temples certain tax-like "gifts" [77] is best explained by the assumption that they were able to produce something for their own account.[s]

The private activities of the Sumerian merchants were apparently much more extensive. No doubt these merchants were not independent of the city or temples either. They, too, were assigned land, but much more than the artisans—in fact, as much as a middle official or officer.[t] They could have their fields cultivated for them by tenants, wage laborers, or slaves; and their landed possessions, instead of handicapping them in their commercial activities, probably provided them with additional means for their business enterprises. As merchants, they were attached either to the supreme authority of the city state,[78] or to a temple, the second most important unit of power.[79] And obviously and in the main, they traded for the "palace" or the temples.[80]

In their transactions the great merchants, *gal damkar,* and the ordinary merchants, *damkar,* enjoyed considerable freedom; [81] and

---

s. A. Schneider assumes that the artisans who worked at home for the temples "apart from this, and perhaps already against a remuneration, also executed orders from other members of the temple community" (1920: 85).

t. According to inscriptions collected by Hussey, a *damkar* of the Bau Temple received 19 *gan* of land (Schneider, 1920: 66). One *gan* could support more than one person and two *gan* a small family (*ibid.:* 35 ff.). A top-ranking temple executive, mentioned in Hussey's material, received 43 *gan* (*ibid.:* 35). Another text gives much higher totals for the land assigned to high officials: 90 *gan* and even 138¾ *gan* (*ibid.*). Heads of military detachments or other prominent warriors received 23, 24, 26, and 18 *gan,* and a temple official *engar* 17¾ *gan* (*ibid.:* 110 ff.). Among the artisans, a carpenter was given 1 *gan,* a chariot maker 1 to 2 *gan,* a tanner 3 *gan,* and cooks and bakers from 2¼ to 6 *gan* (*ibid.*).

in addition they were permitted to trade for their own account. They might have business dealings with the ruler,[82] with the queen,[83] with members of the ruling family,[u] and with less highly situated persons.[84] Manifestly the opportunities for amassing wealth were vast.[85]

Thus in contrast to ancient Hawaii, China, and Pharaonic Egypt, Sumer saw a very early development of private enterprise in trade. And whereas the country's artisans, even when they were engaged in domestic industry, were closely tied to the temple economy, the merchants, who were neither trading officials nor governmental commercial agents but something in between, were much less so. Few simple hydraulic societies moved as conspicuously toward a property-based and independent commerce as did ancient Sumer.

5. Origins of Bureaucratic Capitalism

THE great merchants of Sumer, who had funds of their own and who traded directly with their sovereign, occupied a position very different from that of the commercial specialists of the Pharaohs. The representatives of the Pharaohs, who traded with Punt,[86] Phoenicia,[87] Mesopotamia,[88] and Cyprus,[89] handled government property for the advantage of the government. They accomplished an exchange of goods often under the guise of diplomatic "presents," but they had a keen eye for the values involved. They asked for specific items,[90] they carefully examined the objects offered them,[91] they criticized inadequate gifts,[92] and they stressed the need for reciprocity.[93] Whatever presents were given them during, or át the end of, their expeditions were given them as servants of the king and not as independent businessmen. In short, they were governmental trading officials not too different in their position from the members of a Soviet Trade Mission.

In contrast to such trading officials, the government-attached merchants used their own capital largely, or exclusively, in the service of their rulers, who—while providing them with excellent opportunities for doing business—might also set the conditions (prices, profits) under which these opportunities could be utilized. To invoke a designation that originally pleased the Chinese Communists but that now embarrasses them, these merchants were "bureaucratic capitalists." [94]

In a wider sense, the designation "bureaucratic capitalists" is applicable to several groups: (1) tax collectors, who act as fiscal agents

u. Scholtz, 1934: 59. Princes or princesses occupied a number of artisans, servants, and slaves (Deimel, 1929: 126, 128; *ibid.*, 1931: 110).

for a ruling bureaucracy; (2) officiating or nonofficiating members of such a bureaucracy, who on the strength of their political position engage in private enterprises, such as trading, money lending, and tax farming; (3) private businessmen, who as commercial agents or contractors do business for the ruling bureaucracy; and (4) private businessmen, who attach themselves to individual members of the bureaucracy to assure the success of their transactions. Bureaucratic capitalists, then, are owners of capital who act as commercial or fiscal agents for an apparatus state, no matter whether they are members of the officialdom or functionaries of the dominant religion, or persons of wealth who are neither.

The records of ancient China are not clear on the subject of trading officials, although it seems likely that in the Shang and Early Chou periods certain functionaries of the early territorial states fulfilled commercial tasks. They are more articulate on the presence of government-attached commercial agents. Indeed such persons are sufficiently conspicuous to justify our tentatively classing Chou China, up to the period of the "Spring and Autumn Annals," as a simple Oriental society.

For Inca Peru the very problem does not arise seriously. Officials of the frontier districts may have traded government-owned goods against goods produced abroad; and some transactions may well have been concluded privately. But Inca society seems to have had little need for trading officials and still less for government-attached commercial agents.

The Sumerian inscriptions contain many references to foreign trade (internal exchange was mainly confined to barter).[95] Unfortunately, however, the texts leave many questions unanswered. What kinds of commercial transactions were involved in the many government expeditions that were undertaken to acquire stone,[96] wood,[97] metal,[98] bitumen,[99] and other items? Were the majority of all merchants primarily trading officials or governmental commercial agents? No matter what the answer to these questions may be, the character of ancient Sumerian society provides scant justification for interpreting the "merchants" of the oldest inscriptions thus far deciphered as independent entrepreneurs.

6. THE HYDRAULIC SPONGE

MOST of the hydraulic civilizations that achieved considerable proprietary differentiation seem to have maintained simple patterns of property at an earlier time. In some cases, such as India, simple conditions of property and society gave way relatively quickly to semicomplex configurations. In other cases, such as Egypt and Lower Mesopotamia, they prevailed for millennia. In the Andean area they were (still or again?) dominant when the conquistadores arrived.

The variations in the persistence of simple patterns of property assume a new meaning as soon as they are correlated with variations in hydraulic density. The hydraulic centers of Peru, Egypt, and Lower Mesopotamia all gave birth to compact systems of hydraulic agriculture, whereas many of the territorial states of India and China and, for that matter, of Mexico relied on loose or marginal types of Oriental agriculture. We do not, in this context, cite Hawaii, because in that archipelago the perpetuation of extremely simple patterns of Oriental property was obviously due to an extraordinary combination of internal and external circumstances. However, in the first instances the contrast in hydraulic density patterns is too striking to be dismissed as irrelevant. In all probability the early independent hydraulic communities of the Andean zone traded beyond their borders, and this early trade may well have been handled not only by commercial officials but also by government-attached private merchants, who may to some extent have acted for their own account. But Sumerian history demonstrates that strong hydraulic regimes can keep the bulk of all traders attached to the government even in separated city states. Thus it is not impossible that in the Andean area (as in Sumer and Pharaonic Egypt, but perhaps with more marked oscillations) there prevailed, even prior to the Incas, simple conditions of power, property, and class.

In Peru these conditions may have endured as long as state-centered and hydraulic civilizations were present in the area. In Egypt they outlasted the relative isolation of the hydraulically complex Nile Valley. And in Lower Mesopotamia they persisted even after the compact hydraulic heartland had been incorporated into larger and looser hydraulic conformations. Leemans assumes a high development of private property and trade [100] when the second Sumerian empire under Ur III for a brief period reached to the Mediterranean Sea, Assyria, and Persia. However, according to the same authority, state trade prevailed again under the last Larsa ruler, Rim-Sin,[101] under the Babylonian king, Hammurabi,[102] who defeated him, and for over four centuries under the Kassites.[103]

In these compact hydraulic societies the "dense" bureaucratic apparatus obviously acted like a powerful hydraulic sponge, whose capacity to absorb vital functions of industry and trade was superior, other conditions being equal, to that of less compact hydraulic communities.

G. SEMICOMPLEX PATTERNS OF HYDRAULIC PROPERTY AND SOCIETY

BUT such compact and self-perpetuating simple hydraulic societies are not too numerous. In many hydraulic civilizations the agromanagerial apparatus state, while keeping the bulk of the cultivable land from becoming private property, did not so seriously restrict the growth of nongovernmental, property-based, and professional handicraft and commerce.

1. OCCURRENCES

a. Pre-Conquest Meso-America

THE rise of independent professional artisans and merchants in Aztec Mexico contrasts illuminatingly with conditions in Inca Peru. A complete lack of transport animals handicapped the inhabitants of Meso-America; but this deficiency was largely compensated for by a number of other ecological advantages. The terrain was far more suitable for interterritorial communication; navigable lakes, rivers, and an extended and approachable coast stimulated the circulation of goods by boat. The Sumerians enjoyed similar advantages; and we should not be surprised to learn that like them the Aztecs and their predecessors, the Toltecs, had private professional merchants and carried on an extensive international commerce.[1] These conditions also promoted a technical and regional division of industrial labor. But neither the city states nor the larger territorial units of pre-Conquest Mexico were as hydraulically compact as were their Sumerian counterparts. Thus the professional artisans and merchants of Mexico were not equally dependent upon the hydraulic state. Their plots of land were allotted by the *calpulli,* local and stratified units that possessed a limited autonomy; [2] and apparently neither group rendered extended labor services. Except for references to houses in which females were assembled,[a] we have little evidence for government workshops.[b] According to Zurita and other early sources, the artisans rendered no corvée labor but paid over part of their produce

a. According to Torquemada, houses with females, "nuns," were "widespread" (Torquemada, 1943, II: 189, 191). Diaz, who observed traditional Aztec society before it disintegrated, asserts that there were "nunneries" in a number of Central American countries. In Mexico proper he knew of only one, in the capital (Díaz, 1944, I: 349 ff.).

b. Díaz (1944, I: 346) mentions government-managed bakeries. Sahagun (1938, III: 75) speaks of persons who made shoes for the lords. Was the work in the government shops performed by serving men, who, while hereditary members of the *calpulli,* worked exclusively for the sovereign? (Monzon, 1949: 41.) Is this what Torquemada (1943, II: 488) had in mind when he said that certain work was done by artisans as tax.[3] Except for the time they spent in tilling their fields, the many Mexican craftsmen [4] seem to have deployed their special skills for their own account, preparing articles to be sold at the markets that were held in the large communities.[5]

The small traders were probably as independent as they were insignificant.[c] But the big interterritorial merchants, the *pochteca,* were close to the governmental apparatus. Permitted to rent out their plots of land [6] and to render tax instead of labor service,[7] the *pochteca* could engage in full-time commerce. They served the government as diplomats [8] and spies.[9] Occasionally they conducted military campaigns on behalf of their sovereign.[10] Tezozomoc says that the king's own brothers and uncles were *pochteca.*[11]

Manifestly, these big merchants were part of the ruling class.[12] But they were not commercial officials. Being rich, they operated with their own funds, and essentially, it would seem, for their own account. They might also collect taxes for the government,[13] and at such times, they were bureaucratic capitalists in the narrow sense of the term. However, this was no universal practice, for we know that as a rule the taxes were levied by full-time officials.

And there is still less evidence that the Mexican *pochteca* and/or their aides traded largely on order of the ruler and the temples, as did the Sumerian *damkar.* Thus, however close the *pochteca*'s associations with the "lords" may have been socially and politically, professionally they do not seem to have been part of the state apparatus. It is for this reason and because of the independence of the artisans that we view Aztec Mexico as a semicomplex hydraulic society.

The exact position of the Maya artisans is not easily determined. Clearly they were given fields, *milpa,*[14] and contrary to practice in Aztec Mexico they seem to have received allotments, not from semiautonomous heads of the *calpulli* but from regional representatives of the central government.[15] The Maya commoners who built "houses" for the "lords" may well have included artisans; but the records are not articulate on this point. They are even less articulate on government-managed workshops, which as in Mexico were probably not absent altogether. But as in Mexico, the Maya craftsmen probably produced and traded mainly for their own account.[16]

Lacking a comprehensive agromanagerial officialdom, the Maya rulers did not maintain an elaborate state trade. Some "rich" men were members of the governing class,[17] but it is doubtful whether the

---

"for the lords"? Or are we faced with residual forms of an industrial corvée, which, although still invoked, had ceased to be institutionally relevant?

c. Apparently they dealt in foods, cloth, and cacao on a modest scale and for a lowly clientele (Sahagun, 1938, III: 40, 53, 77).

big Maya merchants in their entirety were as close socially to the secular and priestly leaders as were the *pochteca*. According to Landa, men of wealth lived near the "lords" and priests, but not in the same quarter.[18] Could it be that the crystallization of a property-based and nongovernmental group of professional merchants had advanced further in the hydraulically marginal lowlands of Yucatan than in the hydraulic core of Mexico?

b. India, China, the Near East

IN India semicomplex patterns of hydraulic property and society prevailed throughout the greater part of its recorded history. In China and the Near East simple patterns of property yielded to more complex configurations and with differing results. China operated on a semicomplex level at least twice, once during the last centuries of the Chou period and again from the later part of the 5th century to the 8th century A.D. In the Near East complex patterns of property possibly prevailed only during a certain phase of Roman rule, whereas semicomplex configurations were prominent both before and after that time.

Thus varying forms of semicomplex hydraulic property and society prevailed in India almost from the dawn of written history to the 19th century, in China altogether for some five hundred years, and in the Near East for two long periods covering two thousand years or more.

c. Byzantium and Russia

IN Byzantine society there was no lack of private craftsmen and merchants. As a matter of fact, Byzantine trade was both comprehensive and flourishing during the middle and later part of the first millennium.[19] But the Byzantine artisans and merchants no longer had the freedom of action that their predecessors had enjoyed in the Greek cities of Western Asia or in Rome prior to the victory of bureaucratic absolutism. Administrative and fiscal restrictions burdened the craftsmen and traders of Byzantium until the 11th century,[20] pressing them into a peculiarly crippled variant of a semicomplex pattern of hydraulic property.

In post-Mongol Russia private property in land evolved unevenly and as far as the peasants were concerned, very late. Professional and free handicraft recovered slowly from the setbacks instituted under the Mongol yoke. Commerce offered much greater opportunities to those who controlled it, and the masters of the Muscovite apparatus state were eager to manipulate it either directly, through trading officials, or indirectly, through commercial agents. In the sphere of domestic trade government functionaries first purchased wax, honey, and other items, "taking them at smal prices what themselves list, and selling them againe at an excessive rate to their own marchants, and to marchants strangers. If they refuse to buy them, then to force them unto it." [21] The government also sold goods that it received as taxes or tributes and obviously with a similar disregard for the buyer, for such goods were "forced upon the marchants to be bought by them at the emperours price, whether they will nor no." [d]

Foreign merchants too had to submit to government regulations. Once inside the Russian realm they had to display all their commodities before the officials, who "put a value on them"; [22] and they could not trade with private individuals before the Tsar was given an opportunity to buy what he wanted.[23]

But the Muscovite state was unable to manage the bulk of all large-scale circulation as did the regimes of Pharaonic Egypt or Inca Peru. The Tsar comprehensively employed the services of a number of rich merchants, particularly the *gosti*. These bureaucratic capitalists, who collected taxes and custom fees for the government,[24] usually acted as the Tsar's commercial councilors and agents.[25]

Outside the government trade proper, commerce was carried on, among others, by the *pomeshchiki*. These holders of office land sold the surplus grain and other surplus products of their estates for their own account,[26] thus constituting a group of bureaucratic capitalists *sui generis*. The monasteries, which were linked and subordinated to the state, also engaged in commercial transactions, not infrequently on a large scale.[27]

All this did not leave much room for the operations of professional and independent trade. The *gosti* and a small number of other privileged merchants controlled a large segment of the market,[28] seeing to it that "nowhere free commerce be permitted." [29] Such at least was the opinion of the ordinary merchants, who played a decidedly inferior role and hated the *gosti* bitterly.[30]

Privileged merchants of the Muscovite period could amass great wealth, but neither this wealth nor their semi-official position protected them against the confiscatory actions of their despotic masters. Fletcher reports a case in which three brothers of unusual energy and daring built up a thriving trade that yielded them "300,000 rubbels in money, besides landes, cattels, and other commodities." Fletcher ascribes this initial success partly to the fact that the brothers lived more than a thousand miles from Moscow. For a while they

d. The government profited particularly from the quasimonopolistic sale of furs, grain, and wood (Fletcher, 1856; 57 ff.).

stood well with the authorities, who charged them with the administration of certain customs along the Siberian border. The Tsar was
"content to use their purse, till such time as they got ground in
Siberia." Finally, however, the government took away their fortune
"by pieces, sometimes 20,000 rubbels at a time, sometime more; till
in the end their sonnes that now are, are well eased of their stocke,
and have but small parte of their fathers substance: the rest being
drawen all into the emperours treasurie." [31]

Private property and property-based enterprise suffered immensely
from this ruthless policy. "The great oppression over the poore
commons," so Fletcher,

> maketh them to have no courage in following their trades: for
> that the more they have the more daunger they are in, not onely
> of their goods but of their lives also. And if they have any
> thing, they conceale it all they can, sometimes conveying it
> into monasteries, sometimes hiding it under the ground and
> in woods, as men are woont to doo where they are in feare of
> forreine invasion. . . . I have seene them sometimes when they
> have layed open their commodities for a liking . . . to look
> still behind them and towards every doore: as men in some
> feare, that looked to be set upon and surprised by some enimie.[32]

Under such conditions most of the commoners preferred immediate
satisfaction to long-range planning: "This maketh the people (though
otherwise hardened to beare any toile) to give themselves much to
idlenes and drinking: as passing for no more then from hand to
mouth." [33] It is difficult to find a more colorful and more depressing
picture of private mobile property under the conditions of a crippled
semicomplex hydraulic society.

2. How Powerful Could the Representatives of Private Mobile and Active Property Become in Semicomplex Hydraulic Societies?

How much power may the potentially wealthiest representatives of
mobile property, the big merchants, wield in semicomplex hydraulic
societies? Can they ever dominate, or run, an absolutist government?
Wealthy merchants certainly may control absolutist governments;
and this may be the case even in commonwealths that contain elements of hydraulic statecraft. Elements. As long as such governments
fail to keep private property legally and economically weak, so long
will the patterns of property and power remain hydraulically submarginal. This is always so when the interests of private property
dominate the society; and it is so even when large hydraulic enter-

prises and/or quasi-Oriental devices of political control are present. The city state of Venice built enormous protective waterworks, but Venice remained a nonhydraulic aristocratic republic, in which big commercial property gained a maximum of strength and security.

Carthaginian society in the 4th and 3d centuries B.C. included a number of Oriental institutions. The Carthaginians certainly knew irrigation agriculture.[34] Their government was strong enough to tax the Lybian peasants of their agrarian hinterland.[e] To the disgust of their Roman enemies, they invoked the symbol of total submission, prostration, not only before their gods "as is the custom with other men," but also before their fellow men.[35] But as we have seen in Japan, irrigation techniques and prostration may occur also at the submarginal fringe of the hydraulic world; and in Carthage commercial interests were manifestly paramount[f] and private property was the key means for attaining high political office.[g] On the basis of our present knowledge we may therefore say that at least at the time of Aristotle the rich merchants probably dominated Carthaginian society and that similar submarginal configurations in all likelihood emerged in a number of other places, particularly—although not necessarily—at the geographical fringe of the hydraulic world.

In independent commonwealths based on commerce, rich merchants—who may also be big landowners—can certainly achieve social and political prominence. But while recognizing this possibility, we must ask: how much power can the representatives of independent commercial property wield in semicomplex Oriental societies?

a. Miscellaneous Developments

UNDER semicomplex conditions of property, the bulk of cultivable land is not owned privately; the big merchants must therefore derive their societal strength primarily from their mobile wealth. In a number of cases their combined wealth was enormous; but even under rational despots, such as the kings of Babylonia, commercial property generally remained subject to fragmenting laws of inheritance, to comprehensive taxation, and, insofar as transportation was concerned, not infrequently also to government regulation of oxen, carts, and

e. Gsell assumes that normally the government claimed 25 per cent of the crops as tax. Polybius (1.72.2) shows that in emergencies as much as 50 per cent might be collected (Gsell, HA, II: 303).

f. Meyer (GA, III: 644) calls the Carthaginian government a "commercial autocracy."

g. Aristotle, Politics 2.11.1273a. Aristotle, who noted that in Carthage the greatest offices, such as those of kings and generals, were bought, considered this "a bad thing." "The law which allows this abuse makes wealth of more account than virtue." For an elaboration of these points see Gsell, HA, II: 235 ff.

hired men.[36] It has been said before, and because of the importance of the issue it must be said again: the holders of active mobile property might organize in guilds, and often the state compelled them to do so; but neither the merchants nor the craft guilds were integrated in independent political machines on a local or national basis.

The gentlemen traders of Aztec Mexico seem to have been content to act as a commercial appendage to the secular and religious rulers; and nothing is known regarding any attempts on their part to dominate Mexican society. The "rich" Maya, whose quarters were close to, but not identical with, those of the masters of the state, operated at the outer edge of the power system. Commoners, "apparently men of wealth or influence," sometimes "insinuated themselves into political positions considered to be above their station," but "the official hierarchy was purged from time to time of the pretenders and upstarts, who were not versed in the occult knowledge of the upper class." [37]

In the Old World, the marginal hydraulic societies of Byzantium and Russia differed greatly from Maya society, but their private traders also failed to become politically dominant. In Byzantium the merchants, however wealthy they were individually, remained politically and socially restricted until the 11th century. During the final phases of Byzantine history, the men of property who succeeded in paralyzing the absolutist apparatus were not merchants or artisans, but landlords.

In Muscovite Russia the merchants were little more than economically useful domestic animals; nor did the big merchants in China rise to political prominence when semicomplex patterns of property prevailed at the end of the Chou period and during the middle part of the first millennium A.D.

b. Hindu India

THE corresponding developments in early India are particularly instructive because the Aryan conquest was accomplished by a group that, although aware of the importance of irrigation canals,[38] emphasized cattle wealth, trade, and traders. The Vedas speak respectfully of merchants.[h] In a hymn in the *Atharva-Veda-Samhita* merchants pray to the god Indra as "the merchant par excellence." [39] The great epics that were composed very much later [40] confirm the relatively high and influential position of the Vedic merchant in what Hopkins calls "the Aryan state." [41] However, they leave no doubt that

---

h. Grassmann, RV, I: 197; II: 113; cf. Banerjee, 1925: 155. Less esteemed, although equally prosperous, was the *pani,* a businessman who sought gain "either through trade or through usury" (Banerjee, 1925: 156).

"in distinction from noble and priests," the merchants, together with the Aryan peasants, belonged to "the people." [42] Thus whatever the status of the Aryan commoners, the Vaisyas, may have been in prehistoric times, in the Vedic era they were "oppressed by the princes." It was in this era—or even later in the subsequent Buddhist period [43] —that professional associations of merchants began to appear.[44]

Of course, the rise of such bodies proves nothing about their political independence. In simple Oriental societies—and often also under more complex conditions—the professional corporations are useful tools of government. The epics voice the king's concern with the merchants, particularly in times of war and crisis; but the merchants' chief political importance may well have been derived from their possible conspiratorial value to enemy countries.[45]

There can be no doubt regarding the prospering of trade and traders during the Buddhist period; and there can be no doubt either regarding the social prominence of the government-attached chief merchants, the *setthi.* However, this does not justify the claim that the merchants, as a group, were able in the major centers of what was then Hindu India to normally and conspicuously influence —or control—the political decisions of their respective governments.

These governments were not necessarily monarchies. In the homeland of Buddhism, northeast India, there were several republics, in which the ruler discussed public affairs in full and frequent assemblies.[46] But the merchants were not included in these bodies. The meager information we have on eight of the ten republics listed by T. W. Rhys-Davids [47] shows all of them to have been dominated by members of the warrior caste, Kshatriyas.[48] Buddha considered their assemblies an ancient institution; [49] and it may well be that the patterns of Aryan society [i] persisted somewhat longer in the northeastern area, in which hydraulic action, although highly advantageous, was not so crucial as in the more arid western parts of the north Indian plains.[j] However, irrigation agriculture and hydraulic enterprises were by no means absent in the northeast; [50] and the aristocratic republics clearly moved toward a monarchical form of power [51] which was already widespread in the days of Buddha [k] and which, after a transitional period of turmoil and conquest, came to prevail throughout the heartlands of Aryan culture.[52]

i. For the original role of an aristocracy of warriors see Hopkins, 1888: 73; Keith, 1922: 98.

j. Cf. Stamp, 1938: 299 ff. Oldenburg (1915: 284) regrets that the studies of Vedic and Buddhist India have neglected the solidly Brahmin development in the west and the great susceptibility of the east to the anti-Brahmin movement of Buddhism.

k. For the despotic character of these Indian monarchies see Law, 1941: 169 ff. Cf. Fick, 1920: 105 ff.

In the restless and changing Indian society of this important period many governments availed themselves of the services of a *setthi*. Apparently a man of means,[53] the *setthi* often advised and aided the ruler in economic matters.[54] His position, though not that of an official,[55] was distinguished and hereditary,[56] vacancies being filled by the king.[57]

The term *setthi* means "best, chief." [58] Manifestly he was a "representative of the commercial community," [59] but it is most important to note that he did not operate as the constitutionally established spokesman of organized merchant power. Nor does he seem to have been regularly—or primarily—concerned with guild affairs. His title "may possibly imply headship over some class of industry or trading"; [60] and a famous *setthi* mentioned in the *Jataka* tales apparently "had some authority over his fellow-traders." [61] But this authority, even if real, was rooted in a body whose organizational effectiveness has not yet been clearly established. In Buddhist and post-Buddhist India there certainly were merchant corporations, but C. A. F. Rhys-Davids warns against over-estimating the degree to which the traders were syndicalized.[62] To repeat her conclusion: "There is . . . no instance as yet produced from early Buddhist documents pointing to any corporate organisation of the nature of a gild or Hansa league." [63]

All this does not preclude the political prominence of merchants in some Orientally submarginal cities or city states of classical India; but it stresses the need for a most careful examination of the sources adduced to prove such prominence.

Hopkins, the well-known Sanscritist, cites a Nepalese legend of the 3d or 4th century A.D. as offering particularly valuable data on the political power of a merchant guild.[m] In his opinion this legend "records that Thana was ruled by a strong merchant guild." [64] Turning to the *Bombay Gazetteer* which Hopkins consulted,[65] we find that it makes a significantly more limited claim: "A strong merchant guild ruled *the trade of the city*." [66] The city in question is Sopara, one of several settlements located on the coast of Thana,[67] south of modern Bombay. Turning to the legend itself, we find that the merchants in question, far from controlling the government of the city, did not even control its trade. A single powerful outsider prevailed over the "500" merchants who were trying to corner the market, and he did so after both parties were summoned to appear before the king, who manifestly was the undisputed ruler of the city and the merchants.[68]

The Indian development is instructive in several respects. The

---

m. "Later literature down to our own time contains frequent reference to such bodies, but no thorough treatment of them is to be found" (Hopkins, 1902: 175).

Kshatriya republics show that hydraulic regimes need not be monarchic; but their final phases also underline the tendency toward a concentration of power that inheres in such regimes. The fate of the merchants is equally worth noting. During the formative days of the Aryan conquest society, traders enjoyed considerable social prestige. But subsequently their position deteriorated, and this happened despite the fact that they were tightly organized.

c. Ancient Mesopotamia

WERE the merchants more successful in the great Western Asiatic cradle of Oriental trade, ancient Lower Mesopotamia? Sumerian legends speak of elders and assembly-like gatherings, which the legendary king, Gilgamesh, consulted before making decisions.[69] What do these tales mean? Boas has convincingly argued that myths contain fictitious as well as realistic features and that realistic elements may be exaggerated or transformed into their opposites.[70] There may very well have been proto-Sumerian assemblies similar to the warrior assemblies of the Aryan conquest republics in northeast India. Kramer assumes the existence of a military aristocracy during the formative period of prehistoric Sumer.[71] But whatever the institutional quality of these legendary assemblies may have been, no such gatherings dominated the Sumerian city states when they emerged in the light of recorded history. To quote Jacobsen: "The political development in early historical times seems to lie under the spell of one controlling idea: concentration of political power in as few hands as possible." [72] In each of the early Mesopotamian city states "one individual, the ruler, united in his hands the chief political powers: legislative, judiciary, and executive." [73] In each of them the king handled the despotic state apparatus through the agency of an effective secular and priestly bureaucracy, "the court and temple administrators and intellectuals," as Kramer calls the new core of the "ruling caste." [74]

Significantly there are few, if any, traces of assemblies in the simple hydraulic society of historical Sumer. With regard to Babylonia the situation is otherwise. Babylonian inscriptions refer to assemblies, to elders, and—in the same context—to merchants. Could it be that the growth of Babylonian trade also increased the power of its representatives, the big merchants?

The possible extent, and the limitations, of merchant power are indicated by the Assyrian merchant colonies, which flourished in Cappadocia during the earlier part of the second millennium B.C. These Assyrian settlements were established in an area which, al though lacking political unity,[75] comprised a number of territorial governments.

The Assyrian traders who settled far to the north of their homelands did not dwell inside the Cappadocian towns. The walled sections were reserved for the native population and for the palaces of the ruler.[76] Moreover, the local authorities [77] inspected the trader's commodities in the palace and also, it seems, had a first claim on any goods they wanted to sell.[78] The presence of such local authorities did not mean that the colonies were independent of the Assyrian metropolis. In the end it was Assur that decided legal cases and that had the power to impose taxes: [79] "The authorities of Assur and ultimately the king were therefore the superiors of the Assyrian authorities in the commercial centers." [80]

Within this over-all frame the colonies dealt with their judicial matters in "a general assembly of all colonists," [81] the *karum;* and this body also settled other communal problems.[82] Evidently the members of these Assyrian trade colonies enjoyed a greater autonomy than did the merchants of Assyria or Sumer, or—after the close of the Sumerian period—Babylonia; but they did not dominate the Cappadocian towns, nor were they politically independent in their own quarters.

Babylonian absolutism, like that of Sumer, was rooted in a compact agromanagerial economy; and private property probably played a secondary role in agriculture as well as in commerce.[n] In any case, no serious institutional analyst claims that the assemblies, and through them the merchants, controlled the Babylonian government. The king and his men dominated the administration, the army, and the fiscal system. The king was also the lawgiver. Furthermore, he and his functionaries were strategically situated in the judiciary. At the king's service "judges of the king" ruled according to the "legal practice of the king." [83] But the royal judges, who frequently combined administrative, military, and legal activities,[84] re-

n. Probably. The reasons for the second part of our assumption have been given above; the reasons for the first will be given below when we discuss the extent of private landownership. Dr. Isaac Mendelsohn, in a personal communication and on the basis of an independent examination of the inscriptions, believes that in both spheres of Babylonian economy private property was more extended than the combined property of the state and the temples. No doubt the facts of the matter have to be decided by the period specialists; and our tentative classification of Babylonian society is therefore open to whatever adjustments future research may postulate. But assuming for the sake of the argument that the private property sector exceeded the public sector, there is still no need to change our evaluation of the subordinate political position of the Babylonian merchants. In the same personal communication, Dr. Mendelsohn rejects an interpretation of Babylonian society as democratic.

lied for the settlement of local issues heavily on local assemblies. These bodies dealt primarily with legal matters.[85] Operating under the king's control, they constituted "a kind of civil jury." [o]

The members of these assemblies were "elders," "notables," "merchants" (under a head merchant), and "men of the gate." [86] According to Cuq, these designations refer to separate groups that acted either alone or in combination.[87] Whether Cuq's interpretation is correct or not and whatever the terms "elders," "notables," or "men of the gate" may mean, for our present purpose it is sufficient to know that the assemblies were essentially judicial bodies and that among their members there were merchants headed by an *akil tamgari*.

In early Babylonia the *akil tamgari* seems to have been the director of the Department of Commerce or the Department of Finance, and as such the chief of the fiscal bureaucracy.[88] He headed the ordinary merchants, who undertook commercial expeditions, "at times exclusively in the interest of the crown." [p] He thus was a prominent official through whom the absolutist regime exerted control over the country's traders.

Occasionally an assembly dealt with issues that concerned a whole town; and its merchant members would therefore be participating in matters of considerable local importance. However, since the assembly was presided over by a royal governor or town prefect and since it acted essentially as a civil jury, it certainly did not control the town government; and the merchants, who were under the authority of the *akil tamgari*, were not free to control even their own professional spheres, the country's trade.

d. Conclusions

THE lessons of all this are obvious. Powerful groups of rich merchants may control the government of their commonwealth; and this may happen even in communities that fulfill substantial hydraulic functions. But as far as we know, such developments did not result in anything that can be called the rule of hydraulic merchants. The great merchants of Venice operated in a societal setting in which hy-

---

o. Cuq, 1929: 361. Occasionally they also handled political crimes, but the case cited by Jacobsen involves no deeds, but words only: "seditious utterances" (Jacobsen, 1943: 164).

p. Krückmann, 1932: 446. Was the head merchant of the king, *rab tamgar sa šarri*, who is mentioned in the Neo-Babylonian inscriptions, the successor of the *akil tamgari?* His activities were obscure. Ebeling (1932: 454) places him among the "high officials," adding that he "probably conducted commercial and monetary transactions for the king."

draulic institutions were submarginal. And Carthage, although certainly more hydraulic than Venice, may well have belonged, either from the start or eventually, to the submarginal zone of the hydraulic world.

Carthage-like or Venice-like commercial commonwealths flourished in considerable numbers at the geographical fringe of hydraulic society; and there is no reason why such commonwealths should not have constituted independent heterogeneous enclaves also within certain zones of the hydraulic world. We therefore do not reject Max Weber's assumption that independent commercial communities may have flourished in Buddhist India.[89] But the evidence adduced is not conclusive; and in a number of cases reexamination reveals that the position of the merchants is far from being politically dominant.

Further inquiries into the political role of merchants in institutionally peripheral regions will certainly deepen our insight into the diversities that exist within the margin and the submargin of the hydraulic world. They may also shed more light on the limitations of mobile private property even in those hydraulic societies in which private-property-based commerce became more important than government-managed and government-attached trade.

H. COMPLEX PATTERNS OF PROPERTY IN HYDRAULIC SOCIETY

1. HYDRAULIC LANDLORDISM, PAST AND PRESENT

THE limitations of immobile property in hydraulic society are equally significant—and equally misunderstood. The institutional pioneers who viewed the despotic state as the only major landowner tended to neglect the problem of private landownership altogether. Modern observers, who have noted the paralyzing influence of absentee landlordism in the Orient, are inclined to treat as a basic feature of hydraulic society what in many cases is only a feature of hydraulic society in transition. And they are quick to interpret in terms of past (feudal) or present (capitalist) Western institutions what is actually a specific Oriental development.[a]

a. To mention just one key issue: the establishment of private peasant land by means of a thoroughgoing land reform has one meaning when it is undertaken by the separate forces of a relatively decentralized postfeudal or industrial society and quite another when it is undertaken by the government-controlled forces of a disintegrating hydraulic order or, for that matter, by a totalitarian state of the Soviet type. Major changes in the system of land tenure that occurred in modern Japan, in Russia under the Tsars or under the Bolsheviks, in Nehru's India, or in Communist

More will be said on this subject in our concluding chapter. In the present context we are concerned essentially with the roots of the modern development: the extent and peculiarities of private landownership prior to the dissolution of hydraulic society.

2. GOVERNMENT-CONTROLLED AND PRIVATE LAND IN HYDRAULIC SOCIETY

THE extent and the peculiarities of private land in hydraulic society can be properly viewed only when we remember the extent and the peculiarities of hydraulic state power. In the majority of all hydraulic societies the despotic regime kept private land in a quantitatively subordinate position. In all hydraulic societies the despotic regime limited the freedom of the private land it permitted to exist.

a. Types of Government-controlled Land

IN order to establish the extent of private land we have to clarify the extent of government-controlled land. This last comprises three main types: (1) government-managed land, (2) government-regulated land, and (3) government-assigned land.

All land that is kept by government measures from being alienated either to or by private landowners is regulated land in the broad sense of the term, and in this sense all government land is regulated land. In a narrow sense, the term "regulated land" will be applied essentially to that part of government-controlled land that is managed not by the government but by possessors, who work for, or pay tax or rent to, the government. The term "government-managed land" will be applied to land that is farmed under the direction of government functionaries and for the immediate and exclusive benefit of the government. The term "assigned land" will be applied to land that is temporarily, or indefinitely, assigned to officials (office land), to representatives of the dominant religion (sacred or temple land), or to some distinguished persons who do not, in return, fulfill any special secular or religious functions (sinecure land).

i. GOVERNMENT-MANAGED LAND

GOVERNMENT-MANAGED "public" land was never more than a minor part of all regulated land, since the peasants who cultivated the "public" fields also needed land for their own support. Above a certain agronomical level and except in some strategically important

---

China are frequently treated as if they were more or less identical, though in their societal substance and effect they are entirely different phenomena.

regions, the hydraulic state preferred the payment of a land tax from the individually cultivated fields to products from public fields.

Imperial China, although favoring private ownership of land, maintained farm colonies for the support of the army, primarily in border areas, but at times also in critical inland areas: at places that were being "pacified" and along vital lines of communication. The tilling in these colonies was done either by soldiers (in which case they were generally called "garrison fields," *t'un-t'ien*) or by civilians (in which case they were frequently called "camp fields," *yin-t'ien*). The two types of fields together occasionally comprised as much as one-tenth of all cultivable land, but in most dynasties the fraction was much smaller.

Apart from military colonies, there were government domains for the growing of special crops, and parks and gardens for the rulers' pleasure. These secluded retreats were often built with corvée labor, but usually they were cared for by professional cultivators, palace laborers, and slaves [b]—that is, they were government-managed. But while remarkable in this respect, they were spatially insignificant. They were tiny islands in a sea of peasant farms, whose occupiers or owners supported the government not by their labor or public fields but by their tax payments.

ii. GOVERNMENT-REGULATED LAND

THE most important type of all government-controlled land is perhaps the least clearly defined: peasant land which is neither managed by government officials nor assigned to groups of grantees, nor owned by the cultivators. This type of land cannot be simply equated with the land of village communities, since not all peasants who possess regulated land live in integrated village communities—that is, in communities that distribute and redistribute the land. Nor are all village communities under the control of the government.

Regulated peasant land, in terms of the present inquiry, is land that a holder cannot alienate freely. Often, and particularly when the land is periodically redistributed, a holder may be allowed to lease it to other villagers,[c] but he cannot sell it.[d] In other cases he

b. Royal or imperial gardens and parks have been described by many authors. For the Mexican lake area see Ixtlilxochitl, OH, II: 209 ff.; for Pharaonic Egypt, Erman and Ranke, 1923: 206 ff.; for ancient Mesopotamia, Meissner, BA, I: 201, 292; Contenau, 1950: 53 ff.; for the Islamic Near East, Mez, 1922: 362 ff.; for Muslim Spain, Lévi-Provençal, 1932: 223; for India, *Jātakam: passim* and Smith, 1926: 402 ff.; for Chou China, Legge, CC, II: 127 ff.

c. This was customary among the *calpulli* members of Aztec Mexico. See Zurita, 1941: 88; Monzon, 1949: 39.

d. For an elaborate description of the regulated village community in Tsarist Russia, the *obshchina* or *mir*, see Haxthausen, SR, I: 129 and *passim*.

may sell it but only to other villagers—that is, to fellow peasants. In Byzantium earlier directives were restored and reenforced in 922 by a law which permitted the peasants to sell land to the following groups and in this order: (1) co-possessing relatives, (2) other co-possessors, (3) persons whose land was adjacent to the land to be sold, (4) neighbors who shared the seller's fiscal responsibility, and (5) other neighbors.[1] These regulations made it impossible for a landlord to purchase peasant land except in villages where he was already an owner.[2] As long as they worked, they protected the bulk of the peasant land from falling prey to the expanding forces of land-lordism.

Similar principles were employed in Hindu [e] and Muslim India. Bulwarked by the law-enforcing powers of the state, the Indian village community "protected small farming against the invasion of capitalistic interests," and it did so "by maintaining [for the villagers] the rights of entail, pre-emption, and pre-occupation."[3]

The cases of Byzantium and India, which could be supplemented by data from other civilizations, demonstrate the negative effects of regulated land on the growth of private landownership. Wherever the Orientally despotic state insisted on keeping the bulk of all land regulated, private ownership of land was kept in a secondary and not infrequently in an irrelevant position.

iii. GOVERNMENT-ASSIGNED LAND

THE despotic regime that is able to regulate all or a large part of the land is also able to assign portions of it to any individual or group of individuals. Such land assignments may differ in purpose and duration, but usually the two aspects interlock. Persons who serve the government may hold their office land for life or even hereditarily. Others may hold their offices only for a short term; in such cases tenure over their office land is equally brief. Serving men who fulfill military functions are particularly apt both to obtain and to lose their office land suddenly.

Land grants made to those who serve the gods are more stable. Enduring religious organizations, such as temples and mosques, are almost always permitted to retain their grants indefinitely.

Sinecure land is given for a variety of reasons to a variety of persons. The grantees may be so distinguished because of their meritori-

e. See Appadorai, 1936, I: 133 ff. The alienability of land has been seen as a sign of ownership, whereas it may merely be indicative of a flexible form of possession. Jolly's (1896: 94) interpretation makes allowance both for the (externally) regulated and the (internally) fluid conditions of village land. He assumes "that generally the villages were shut off from the outer world, but that within the individual villages there existed private property of land."

ous acts or merely because they are the ruler's relatives, friends, or favorites.*f* In all instances the land is assigned unconditionally. The grantees do not render service for the revenues which the sinecure land yields. This is also true for the holders of pension land. But whoever the beneficiary may be, the government remains the master of the assigned land.

Sacred (temple) land is usually supervised and/or managed by secular government officials. This has been established for Pharaonic Egypt,[4] for Ptolemaic Egypt,[5] for Babylonia,[6] and of course, for pre-Conquest Peru and Mexico. In the Islamic world, direct or indirect state control over the various types of religious property persisted, with many modifications in detail, until recent times.[7]

Control over office land is guaranteed by the government's operational control over the landholders. A normally functioning despotic regime determines the fate of its serving men and the lands allotted to them. When, at the close of the Chou period, the chancellor of the state of Ch'in made merit rather than inheritance the essential basis for office,*g* he met with no conspicuous resistance; and throughout late Chou China the decrease of areas administered by holders of office land [8] were accepted with equal meekness. No organized group of "barons" rose against the imperial unifier of China when he finally and decisively discarded the office land system in its entirety. Nor did Akbar's decision to substitute in large part salaries for office land [9] meet with any greater challenge. Akbar went far, but not so far as the Turkish Sultan Suleiman, who spectacularly demonstrated that a well-functioning despotism could abolish office land as easily as it could create it.[10]

Sinecure land might be given without any limitation as to time. In this case possession might come to an end when the ruling dynasty fell. In Pharaonic Egypt this seems to have been the rule; [11] and it is not unlikely that the land grants in ancient Peru would have suffered the same fate if the Inca regime had been replaced by other native rulers. Often sinecure land was intended to support the recipient as long as he lived, but the grantor's death might terminate the assignment earlier. The land grants of ancient Hawaii were apparently so conditioned.[12]

f. Cf. *Jātakam*, I: 56 (grant given to the king's barber); II: 193 (to a Brahmin), 270 (to a princess), 457 ff. (to a princess); IV: 116 (to a Brahmin), 309 (reward for finding a precious antelope), 415 (to a princess), 480 (reward for singing a special verse); V: 21 (reward for useful advice), 35 (to ascetics), 45 (to a hunter), 374 (to a hunter); VI: 135 (to a barber), 355 (to the king's brother or son), 422 (to a *setthi*), 438 (to good advisors), 447 (to an advisor). Cf. *ibid.*, I: 362 ff., 424, 462.

g. Shih Chi 68.4a; Duyvendak, 1928: 15, 61. The "nobles" whom he restricted more

b. Private Land

i. DEFINITIONS

LAND that is government-managed, government-regulated, or government-assigned is obviously not the property of private landowners; and it cannot be so viewed, even when possession is prolonged. Permanency of possession is not enough (hereditary tenants also enjoy this privilege); nor is the right to alienate enough (holders of regulated land are sometimes permitted to alienate it within their social group). Only when the proprietor has the right both to hold his land indefinitely and to alienate it to persons outside his social group do we encounter what, in conformance with established usage, can be called full private landownership.

ii. ORIGINS

THE commoners and nobles of early Greece, Germany, Gaul, and England owned their land not because of the decision of an autocratic ruler but because of differentiations within a tribal society, which produced multiple patterns of private property and political leadership. In hydraulic society it was essentially the ruler and his functionaries who established private landholding by transferring to individual owners what was previously government-controlled land.

Individuals usually became landowners through gifts or sale. Entire groups were made landowners by government decree. After a piece of land had been recognized as private property, it could, within government-set social limits, be transferred from one private owner to another. Large-scale conversions of regulated land into private land are relatively rare in the history of Oriental society. They seem to have occurred only where private-property-based handicraft and trade were well developed.

c. Types of Landownership

i. PEASANT LANDOWNERSHIP

WHO then are the potential owners of land in hydraulic society? In Oriental as in other agrarian societies the key figure in the basic subsistence economy is the peasant. We can therefore expect him to play an important role in the expanding sector of private landownership; and indeed in China the establishment of free private land involved the emergence of a large class of peasant owners.

and more (*ibid.:* 27; *Shih Chi* 68.8b) are said to have hated him (Duyvendak, 1928: 23; *Shih Chi* 68.6b), but his measures led to no organized "baronial" rebellion.

ii. BUREAUCRATIC LANDLORDISM

BUT the Chinese development is the exception rather than the rule. In the majority of all cases it is not the peasant owner but the non-peasant owner who first and prominently appears in the private land sector. Evidently the more complex a hydraulic society becomes, the greater the number of social groups that seek to be landed proprietors. But one group among them is outstanding: the civil and military functionaries of the government and their relatives, the bureaucratic gentry.

Under simple conditions of property few others are rich enough to buy land. And even where there are wealthy merchants or traders, the bulk of the surplus, and consequently the bulk of the purchasing power, remains in the hands of the governing class. Furthermore, it is to members of the governing class that the ruler is most likely to make gifts of land.

Bureaucratic landlordism therefore tends to appear in all types of hydraulic society, whatever their complexity. It prevails completely in those simple hydraulic societies in which private land is at all relevant. It is a significant feature in many semicomplex hydraulic societies. And it is crucial in complex hydraulic societies where privately owned land outweighs state-controlled land.

Data on landed property in Pharaonic Egypt are vague even for the New Kingdom.[13] A few statements that are specific speak essentially of princes, viziers, and other members of the governing class as owners of private land.[14]

In Aztec Mexico private lands were held by the rulers, their officials, and some merchants.[15] In Hindu India the Brahmins did not, as was the case with priesthoods in many other hydraulic societies, live on large and permanently granted temple lands. Consequently, in Hindu India land grants to individual Brahmins fulfilled a special function, and it is not surprising to find that they were numerous. Many of them carried only the right of possession, but a number of Brahmins seem to have owned land at least in the last phase of Hindu rule.[16] In Byzantine Egypt the "powerful ones" who had large estates were most frequently officials;[17] and this pattern is repeated in Islamic times. Among the persons who, during the Mamluk period, acquired private land, actual or former holders of office land were prominent.[18] In Ottoman Turkey some office lands became the private property of former holders.[19]

In Middle Byzantium functionaries were for a time forbidden without special imperial permission to purchase land while they held office. The restriction retarded the growth of bureaucratic landownership but did not prevent it.[20] In Tsarist Russia the edict of 1762 converted the *pomeshchiki*, who had been possessors of office land, into landowners. In later imperial China government functionaries were forbidden to purchase land in the district in which they officiated.[21] Nothing was said regarding the purchase of land outside this area; and the evidence at hand suggests that among the owners of land officiating and nonofficiating members of the government class were outstanding.

iii. OTHER SOCIAL GROUPS

To be sure, members of other social groups also owned land, if they had the necessary means and if they were permitted to. In semi-complex and complex hydraulic societies rich merchants particularly were likely to acquire land; and information on Aztec Mexico,[22] India,[23] and China shows clearly that they did so. Moreover, the measures invoked by the Han dynasty reveal both how well entrenched this type of landlordism might become and how ruthlessly a ruling bureaucracy might combat it.[24] Of course, even persons of modest wealth might buy land. In traditional China persons from all walks of life owned small pieces of land.[25]

iv. ABSENTEE LANDLORDISM (THE GENERAL TREND)

OCCASIONALLY a nonpeasant owner of land, who for some reason or other was deprived of his occupation, might assure his support by personally turning to farming.[h] Generally, however, nonpeasant landowners left the tasks of cultivation to tenants. In many cases they were absentee landlords.

In Medieval and post-Medieval Europe tenancy and absentee landlordism were also widespread. However, many landlords personally managed their large estates (*Güter*) or employed stewards for this purpose.

The small incidence of large-scale farming in hydraulic society is due primarily to the high crop yield obtained by labor-intensive methods, which are in part required and in part stimulated by irrigation agriculture.[26] These methods provide extraordinary advantages for small-scale peasant farming on a family basis. The advantages are so striking that the dominant hydraulic "economic ethos" (*Wirtschaftsgesinnung*) discouraged large-scale and "manorial" methods, even when they might have been profitably applied.

The significance of this attitude for hydraulic society in transition

---

h. For Brahmins who tilled their land either with or without the aid of farmhands, see *Jātakam*, II: 191 ff.; III: 179, 316; IV: 195, 334 ff.; V: 70.

is obvious. The consolidation of landlordism in postfeudal Europe encouraged many owners of large farms to cultivate their land scientifically. The recent growth of landlordism in many hydraulic countries intensified the acquisitive zeal of the absentee landlords without increasing the rationality of tenant farming.

V. ABSENTEE LANDLORDISM (TRADITIONAL RUSSIA)

AN interesting variant of absentee landlordism appeared in Tsarist Russia. The *pomeshchiki* of Muscovite and post-Muscovite Russia were kept so busy rendering military or civil services that they could not pay much attention to farming, as did the landed nobles of England or Germany. In consequence, large-scale and scientific farming was extremely limited among landholding aristocrats in Russia prior to 1762, and despite some expansion it remained the exception long after this date.

Baron Haxthausen, who made his famous study of rural Russia in the 1840's, was struck by the difference between landlords in Russia and in the rest of Europe. Although unaware of the peculiarities of Oriental despotism, he clearly recognized that Russia's landowning aristocracy lacked a feudal tradition:

> The Russian, the Great-Russian nobility, is not a landed nobility [*Landadel*] now, nor in all probability was it ever one; it had no castles, it did not pass through a period of knighthood and [private] feuding. It always was a serving nobility, it always lived at the Courts of the Great Princes and the smaller princes and in the cities, rendering military, Court, or civil services. Those among them, who lived in the countryside, peacefully pursued agriculture; but in actuality they were either insignificant or unfit. Even today the majority of the Great-Russian nobles have no rural residences, no [manorial] economies as we see them in the rest of Europe. All the land that belongs to the noble—cultivated land, meadows, forests—are left to the peasant village community that works it and pays the lord for it. Even if the lord owns, and lives in, a country house, he still does not have a [manorial] economy, but rather lives like a *rentier*. Most nobles have country houses, but they live in town and visit the country house only for weeks or months. This is the old Russian way of life of the aristocracy! [27]

The Russian nobles' peculiar detachment from the land they owned—together with the fragmenting law of inheritance—kept them from becoming "a real landed aristocracy," as Haxthausen knew it in Central and Western Europe. "I do not think that there is, in any major country in Europe, less stability of their land than in Great Russia." [28]

It is against this background that we must view the two great agrarian changes accomplished by the Tsarist bureaucracy in the second half of the 19th and the beginning of the 20th century: the emancipation of the serfs from their former landlords (in 1861) and Stolypin's reform (in 1908). In both cases resistance was great; but in both cases the new measures were introduced by members of the same governing class that comprised the bulk of all landlords.

vi. BORDERLINE CASES OF REGULATED AND PRIVATE LAND TENURE

ABSENTEE landlordism is quickly apparent, more quickly than the exact proprietary quality of a particular piece of land. How many of the land "grants" of Pharaonic Egypt or Buddhist India were given with the intention of establishing possession? How many with the intention of establishing ownership? The records often fail to provide definite information on these points. And even when they suggest the right of ownership—how secure was this right? Segrè, in comparing the proprietary developments under Oriental absolutism and in classical Greece, concludes that "private property in a sense approaching to classical ownership could not exist as long as the king could exercise the power of withdrawing rights either to land or to liberties or change these terms at will." [29]

Brahmin property was believed to be safe from confiscation. But this did not prevent Hindu rulers from seizing Brahmin land for "treason," which the king's judiciary had no difficulty in establishing when it suited his purposes.[30] In Pharaonic Egypt private landownership, although perhaps more extensive than in Hindu India, was equally insecure. Indeed it was "basically nothing but an exceptional transfer of royal prerogatives, a transfer which as a matter of principle could be reversed at any time and which was often reversed when a new dynasty came into being." [31] In such cases it is manifestly hard to draw a sharp line between possession and ownership.

Another difficulty arises from the fact that in certain hydraulic societies the right to alienate private property in land is spread unevenly. Nonpeasant landlords may be free to buy land from other landlords, whereas the peasants who live in a regulated rural order enjoy no corresponding right of alienation. In hydraulic society such mixed patterns create a major classificatory problem only when, as in Late Byzantium and in Russia after 1762, the land held by landlords comprises a large part (perhaps more than one-half) of all cultivated land. When this is the case, we can speak of an incipient pattern of complex hydraulic property and society.

d. The Extent of Private Landownership in Various Subtypes of Hydraulic Society

THE categories of government and private land developed so far enable us to advance beyond our initial tentative position and to correlate with greater precision and fuller evidence the advance of mobile and immobile private property in various hydraulic civilizations. Germs of private landownership were present even in hydraulic societies in which private-property-based industry and commerce were of little consequence, but they did not assume major dimensions. This confirms the validity of our concept of "simple" patterns of hydraulic property and society. In hydraulic civilizations with a substantial sector of mobile property and enterprise, private landownership frequently remained a secondary feature, and occasionally an insignificant one. This confirms the validity of our concept of semicomplex patterns of hydraulic property and society. Furthermore it confirms our contention concerning the relative scarcity of the complex configuration—a configuration in which immobile private property is as prominent in agriculture as, in its peculiar way and with its peculiar limitations, mobile property is prominent in industry and trade.

On the basis of these results, we shall contemplate briefly the extent of private landownership in some of the major hydraulic civilizations. In this survey certain crucial data that were adduced in the discussion of our key criteria have to be mentioned again. But they now appear in a new context and, in a number of cases, they are supplemented by important additional information. In accordance with our previously established concepts we shall advance from simple to semicomplex and eventually to complex conditions of property and society.

i. SIMPLE HYDRAULIC SOCIETIES

Hawaii: Ancient Hawaii certainly knew private possession of land. But it is doubtful whether there existed full landownership, since the "estates" even of the most powerful territorial "chiefs," the governors, "reverted to the king" after the holder's death and since "at the accession of a new king . . . all the lands of an island" were reassigned.[32]

Inca Peru: As stated above, sinecure lands were held privately and indefinitely, but the holders of such lands lacked the right to alienate them. Thus they were not owners but permanent occupiers.

Sumer: At the close of the Sumerian period, genuine private land-ownership emerged.[33] However, the governments of the earlier temple cities seem to have exercised a strict control over the cultivable land. The records so far deciphered fail to reveal the existence even of such private landed possessions as have been documented for Inca society.

Pharaonic Egypt: In addition to government land proper and to government-assigned land (temple land and office land), there was private land which could be alienated,[34] but the king could cancel a holding at any time. Generally speaking, private landownership was more the exception than the rule.[35]

ii. SEMICOMPLEX HYDRAULIC SOCIETIES

India: Numerous inscriptions document for the last southern phase of Hindu India what was already certain for the Buddhist and post-Buddhist periods,[36] namely that "most villages" were occupied by *ryotwāri* [37]—that is, by peasants who were under the direct control of the state. This implies that private landownership can have existed only in a (not very large) minority of all villages.

Mesopotamia: At the end of the Sumerian period and in Babylonian society private landownership is clearly apparent. Did it become the dominant form of land tenure? Evidence to this effect would lead us to class this period not as semicomplex but as complex. However, available data seem at best to indicate semicomplex patterns of property. At best. If state trade equaled or exceeded private trade during a large part of the Babylonian period, we would be faced with an advanced simple or an incipient semicomplex situation.

For Late Sumer—the Third dynasty of Ur—the texts frequently mention private property in fields a well as in houses and gardens.[38] But although the temples were no longer alone in leasing land, they are still most frequently mentioned in this respect.[i] For Babylonia, Meissner finds that the best and largest tracts of lands were in the hands of the government and the temples. "What still remained of the land was private property." [39] Schawe's analysis of the tenancy conditions of the period seem to confirm Meissner's view: in Babylonia land was rented out "primarily by the state and temple domains and then also by private individuals." [40]

i. Schneider, 1920: 58. Hackman's (1937: 21 ff.) numerous references to fields unfortunately are often vague concerning their property position.

Cuq stresses the specific position of land that was made private through royal gift.[41] At the same time he mentions among the features that led to differentiations in land tenure the emergence (or reemergence?) under the Kassites of communities which he characterizes as tribal and kinship-based,[42] but which he also compares with the Russian *mir* [43]—that is, with a purely administrative type of village community. The details of the Kassite rural units are still obscure,[44] but we know that they were interlinked with the governmental apparatus through certain of their leaders and that they regulated the landed possessions of their members in ways not too different from those of the Mexican *calpulli* and the Inca *ayllus*.

During the last phase of Babylonian history the two types of government-controlled land still prevailed—if what the Persians found in Mesopotamia is indicative of the Neo-Babylonian conditions. In Persian Mesopotamia there were (1) state lands that in large part were assigned to individuals, (2) "large tracts of land" held by the temples, and (3) lands "held in fee simple by the individuals." The first two categories were obviously very extensive: "With much of the land held by the state and the temples, the number of land transactions is not so large as that of other sales." [45] Again we lack statistical data, but the above statement suggests that the process of "privatization" had gone further in mobile than in landed property.

Persia: The Persians used the government-controlled land (and outside the Greek cities this was the bulk of all cultivated land) very much as had the Babylonians and Sumerians before them. They assigned it to members of the royal house and to friends of the king (obviously as sinecure land), to officials, resettled soldiers, and persons obligated to provide contingents for the army (obviously as office land).[46] Knowing the conditions under which office land was held in other Oriental despotisms, we have no reason to doubt that this land, like the regulated peasant land, was what Rostovtzeff takes it to be: state land.

The Persian office land was not a feudal institution, nor did it inspire a feudal order among the Parthians. The big Parthian landholders were no semi-autonomous fief-holders who spent most of their time attending to their personal affairs. Instead, and very much like their Persian predecessors, they were government officials.[j]

---

j. Christensen, 1933: 307. According to Christensen, the Parthian government was "despotic" in form, at least as long as the Parthian monarchy was united (*ibid.*). Did the political order change when the monarchy disintegrated into several territorial kingdoms? This is, of course, possible but it is by no means certain. On the basis of comparable cases, it seems more likely that the smaller and later Parthian kingdoms

Hellenistic Monarchies of the Near East: Private landownership was confined essentially to the Greek cities,[47] which were few in Egypt but numerous in Western Asia. Outside these Greek enclaves, the land was controlled by the government and by government-attached temples.

The Seleucid rulers established considerable private land through grant or sale [48] "on condition that the grantee joined his land to some city and made of it city-land"; [49] and, of course, they assigned office land to soldiers and probably also to civil functionaries.[50]

The kings of Pergamum do not seem to have reduced the royal land at all. "Like the Ptolemies, they must have gifted the (revocable) user of estates on King's land to officials." [51]

In Ptolemaic Egypt "private land originally meant house, gardens, and vineyard; even the house and garden of a Royal peasant were 'private.' Greeks sometimes called it property, but it was, like every other Ptolemaic form, not property but user; apart from the Greek cities, the property or legal estate in any land in Egypt never left the king." [52]

It is in the light of this statement that we have to view the existence of certain "private" grain land. Rostovtzeff suggests that this type of land had existed in Pharaonic Egypt; [53] and what we know of the earlier period confirms his assumption. However, we must remember first the instability that in Pharaonic times characterized landed property generally, and second the loose way in which the Ptolemaic (Greek) masters of Egypt employed the term "private."

The "private" land, whose spread the Ptolemies encouraged, was "regulated emphyteutic" tenure [54]—that is, a lease of "deserted land" "for a long period (hundred years) or in perpetuity." The rights over this kind of property were "transferable by alienation or succession and enjoyed in a certain measure the same protection as ownership." [55] By developing emphyteutic tenure, the Ptolemies strengthened the trend toward landownership. But until the Roman era, this trend does not seem to have gone beyond a relatively strong form of "landed possession." [56]

The Roman Interlude: Under the Romans private property emerged on a large scale.[57] The reasons for this extraordinary development—and for its limited success—are treated below in connection with the discussion of complex patterns of property.

The Islamic Near East (the first centuries): The Arab conquerors

---

were smaller Oriental despotisms, with certain leading families hereditarily holding the top-ranking positions in government and occupying very substantial tracts of office land.

of Egypt and Syria perpetuated most of the Byzantine institutions,[58] including patterns of land tenure. For obvious reasons many former holders of estates fled,[59] and those who stayed [60] lost the right to collect the taxes for the government.[61] Alongside them, prominent Arab landholders established themselves on deserted estates and the old state domain.[62] These new holders bought and sold land, and they held their property, *qati'a*,[63] hereditarily.[64] But the *qati'a* represented an emphyteutic form of possession; [65] and it is doubtful whether holders could enlarge them by freely buying peasant land. Their Byzantine predecessors had been forbidden by law to do so; [66] and the new Arab state was certainly as eager as the officials of Eastern Rome—and probably better able—to protect the regulated villages. Apparently, the *qati'a* possessions increased in extent,[67] but they remained in the hands of a limited group of leaders. The mass of the Arab tribesmen lived in military camps; [68] and it was only after several generations that the *qati'a* were spread into the villages.[69]

We need not follow here the step-by-step rise of a new system of landed property, whose beneficiaries were both tax collectors and holders of office land.[70] This system appears clearly and consistently in Mamluk society.

Mamluk Society: At the beginning of Mamluk power virtually all the cultivable land of Egypt was divided into twenty-four units, which were either controlled directly by the sultan or assigned as office land.[71] Private land, *mulk*, was "almost absent." [k] Its later growth was accomplished "mostly" by an intricate process which required a holder of office land to surrender part of it to the treasury before he purchased it from the government, either directly or through a middleman.[72]

But while *mulk* continued to increase until the end of the period, it remained only one of a number of types of land that an official (and usually a military official) might control. In addition to his office land (*iqṭā'*) and to his *mulk*, he might possess pension land,[73] and he might also be the manager of a *waqf* which he had founded [74] and which in all likelihood would yield him and his family a steady income.

Ottoman Turkey: The Turkish sultans demonstratively established the hegemony of state land by officially abolishing the bulk of privately owned land.[m] Some "landowners proper" seem to have

---

k. Poliak, 1939: 36. Poliak assumes that private lands were, at the beginning of the Mamluk period, "numerous" in Syria.

m. Gibb and Bowen, 1950: 236, 258, n. 4; cf. Poliak, 1939: 46. This refers essentially to cultivable land and pastures. The farmhouses and the land around it were always *mulk;* and vineyard and orchards were usually so considered (Gibb and Bowen, 1950: 236).

existed from the start; [75] and local "notables" (a'yāns) acquired mulk, perhaps through conversion of office and other land.[76] But until the recent period of transition, most of the land was controlled by the government, which assigned part of it as office land or waqf and taxed the remainder through the agency of its tax farmers.[n]

The tax farmers had many prerogatives. In the non-Arab provinces they might transfer a vacant peasant farm [o] to a resident of another village, but "only after offering it to the peasants of the village to which the land in question was attached." [77] In the Arab provinces their position, by the 18th century, approached that of holders of military office land. In Egypt they were given one-tenth of all village land under the name of waṣiya. They could sell this waṣiya land, but only to another tax farmer and only when they, at the same time, transferred to the buyer a corresponding amount of their jurisdictional domain.[78] In the Arab provinces the fellahs could alienate their land "to other fellâḥs." [79] Regarding the Arab territories, Gibb and Bowen expressly state that the person responsible for collecting the taxes "might not deprive a fellâḥ of his land, except for non-payment of taxation." [80] Thus in both the non-Arab and Arab provinces the majority of all peasants were hereditary occupiers of assigned or regulated state land.[81]

The prerogatives of tax farmers and of holders of assigned lands present important problems; but all of them arise within the context of government-controlled land. Since land of this type comprised the bulk of all cultivated acreage, we feel justified in saying that the Islamic Near East, up to the 19th century, was characterized by a semicomplex pattern of Oriental property and society.

Maya Society: The Maya system of land tenure is not clear.[82] There probably was some individual landownership,[83] but most of the cultivable land seems to have been "common" (regulated) land.[84]

Pre-Conquest Mexico: Early sources agree that the bulk of all land in this area, as in Yucatan and Peru, was government controlled. The great majority of all peasants (and townspeople) lived in regulated communities (calpulli).[85] But there were also certain private lands, tierras proprias patrimoniales,[86] which were tilled by mayeques,[87] peasants attached to the soil.

According to Zurita, private land had long been in existence.[88] Did it originate through grant or sale? And how freely could those who held it dispose of it? Local officials were permitted to sell

---

n. Gibb and Bowen, 1950: 237. The authors cite a statement according to which the "Sipāhīs" used to convert the state land they held into private property "in later times" (ibid.: 188, n. 6). Unfortunately the reference specifies neither the approximate date nor the extent of the development.

o. A farm whose deceased owner was without heirs (Gibb and Bowen, 1950: 239).

calpulli lands, if they were not burdened with obligations; and as stated above, the buyers of these tracts—which were then alienable—were either members of the ruling families or "some officials or merchants." [89] However, most of the *calpulli* land was burdened with serious and lasting obligations in that its yield was destined to support either the members of the *calpulli* themselves or officials of the local or central government, garrisons, or temples.[90] In consequence, the amount of land available for sale was probably small.[91]

It is not clear to what extent the *tierras proprias patrimoniales* originated from the sale of *calpulli* land. Some, or perhaps even many, of these private holdings may well have been grants made by the rulers to distinguished individuals. In contrast to the allodial estates of feudal Europe, the *tierras proprias patrimoniales* remained under the jurisdiction of the government; [92] and in contrast to the serfs of allodial or feudal estates the Mexican *mayeques* served the government "in time of war or need." [93] This formula is comprehensive. In Aztec Mexico, as in other hydraulic societies, the government determined one-sidedly what kind of services it needed.

Not being office lands, the private holdings were not kept intact by the will of the government. And not being allodial or feudal estates, they were not entailed by the will of the owner: *"no son de mayorazgo."* [94] In fact, the private lands of ancient Mexico were as similar to the sinecure lands of other Oriental societies as they were dissimilar to the strong landed property of feudal and post-feudal Europe. In all probability they represented a smaller percentage of all cultivated land than did private lands in Babylonia or in early Islamic society. According to one estimate, the private holdings in ancient Mexico amounted to little.[95] According to another, they may have comprised somewhat more than 10 per cent of the total cultivated area.[p]

iii. COMPLEX PATTERNS OF HYDRAULIC PROPERTY AND SOCIETY

ORIENTAL societies in which there was less private land than government-controlled land are many. Private land was insignificant in the higher civilizations of South and Meso-America when they were overrun by the Spaniards. It remained a secondary feature in India, Sumer, Babylonia, Persia, the Hellenistic monarchies of the Near East, and Islamic society. In the early phases of state-centered Chinese society it appears to have been as unimportant as it was in

p. This figure was suggested in a memorandum on land tenure in pre-Conquest Mexico prepared for the present inquiry by Dr. Paul Kirchhoff.

pre-Conquest America; and when China, under the impact of Inner Asian forces, temporarily discarded the free forms of landed property that had prevailed at the end of the Chou period and throughout the imperial dynasties of Ch'in and Han, regulated patterns of land tenure prevailed again.

Thus, our survey confirms what we tentatively suggested at the start of our discussion of hydraulic land tenure. Prior to the recent period of institutional disintegration and transition, private land may have prevailed in the Near East under Roman rule; it certainly prevailed in China from the later part of the first pre-Christian millennium to the 5th century A.D. and, after an interlude of almost three centuries, again and until our time.

The Roman Near East: Did such classically hydraulic countries as Egypt, under Roman rule, actually develop complex patterns of property? The conquerors did indeed establish private landed property within the terms of Roman provincial law; [96] and in Byzantine Egypt prior to the Arab conquest large estates were certainly held by the "powerful ones," the *dynatoi*. But how widespread was land-ownership at the beginning of the Roman empire? And to what extent did it prevail during the 5th and 6th centuries?

Under Roman influence private land was created through grants,[97] through transfer of cleruchic land (military office land),[98] and through the sale and grant of other government land.[99] This was a far cry from Hellenistic conditions; but even scholars who emphasize the qualitative differences [100] are usually careful also to indicate the quantitative limitations. The greater part of the former cleruchic land was taken back by the government immediately after the conquest; [101] and out of the private estates that temporarily came into being as the result of grants or sales "the majority" soon again became imperial property.[102] Thus "the best land continued for the most part to form the royal domain and to bear the name royal land." [q] And since, in the main, it was the larger estates that were confiscated, private land seems essentially to have been held by small owners. This is particularly true for Egypt and Asia Minor. A greater incidence of large estates is suggested for Syria and Palestine.[103]

The existence of private landownership is said to have reached a

q. Bell, 1948: 73. On the basis of several decades of additional research Bell confirms what Mommsen had cautiously noted in 1885, namely that the imperial domain constituted "a considerable part of the entire area in Roman as in earlier times" (Mommsen, 1921: 573). Johnson and West (1949: 22) refer to "the retention of the great bulk of arable land as the property of the [Roman] crown"; and Johnson (1951: 92) calls "the amount of privately owned land in Roman times . . . slight."

second peak on the eve of the Arab conquest, especially in Byzantine
Egypt. What actually were the conditions of land tenure in Egypt
during this period? The peasants, who because of extreme fiscal
pressure had become increasingly reluctant to farm—not a few ran
away from their villages—became the targets of elaborate "reform"
measures. Government control in the form of compulsory permanent
tenancy (epibolē) became more and more strict.[104] Increasingly the
peasants were permanent holders of land which they were forbidden
to leave. As coloni, they were attached to the land which, from
then on and within the confines of a rigidly regulated village community, became their "private" possession.[105] The continuing fiscal
burdens caused many villages to look to "powerful" protectors,
primarily members of the governing class, and to the church.[106]
These individuals, who were designated patroni until 415,[107] did not
exert authority everywhere—many villages remained directly subordinated to the fiscus and the imperial administration.[108] Nor did
they integrate "their" peasants into a typical and large-scale manorial
economy,[109] although for lack of a better term their holdings are
usually referred to as "estates."

The edict of 415, which acknowledged the position of the estate
holders, also reaffirmed the government's claim on the fiscal and corvée
services that the landholding coloni had previously fulfilled.[110] The
holders of the new estates were delegated to collect taxes for the
government from their coloni. But although this function endowed
the new landlords with great power,[111] the state upheld its fiscal
rights without compromise: "the rate of taxation was the same for
all." [112] Thus with regard to the most crucial fiscal aspect the estate
holders were not privileged: "that their tax rate was less than others,
there is no evidence whatsoever." r

Under Justinian (to be precise: in 538) the Byzantine government

r. Johnson and West, 1949: 240. In the 2d and 3d centuries the tax collectors seem
to have been in the main municipal groups or individual businessmen who had their
fiscal duties imposed upon them as a "liturgy." The government used these liturgical
obligations to destroy the economic strength of propery-based groups (Wallace, 1938:
347 ff.); and it transferred the fiscal tasks to the bureaucratic landlords, who, being
politically better connected, succeeded where the private entrepreneurs had failed. But
these estate-holders were in no sense feudal lords, who could appropriate the bulk of
the peasant surplus they collected. From the 4th to the 6th century the Byzantine
collectors were generally allowed commissions of some 2 per cent on the collection
of wheat, 2½ per cent on barley, and 5 per cent on wine and pork (Johnson and
West, 1949: 328, cf. 290). Whether these rates were valid for Egypt we do not know
(ibid.); but we do know that the Egyptian tax collector was entitled to a fee of one-
eighth to one-twelfth of the money tax he raised (ibid.: 268, 284), that is, to a commission of 8 to 15 per cent. By manipulation he could raise his share to from 10 to
20 per cent of the money tax (ibid.: 268, 284 ff.).

expected a tax revenue from Egypt that was larger than that mentioned for the time of Augustus.[113] This fact involves a number of questions which have not as yet been solved.[114] For our purpose, however, it is enough to know that the Byzantine government was able to tax the Egyptian peasants as comprehensively and successfully as did the Romans under their powerful first emperor.

To be sure, there were in Egypt at the close of the Byzantine period large units of private landed property: estates. These estates arose under a bureaucratic government; they were held mainly by bureaucratic landlords; and they were organized in a conspicuously bureaucratic way.[s]

All this we know. We do not know, however, "whether these estates of Egypt were privately owned or were leaseholds from imperial and ecclesiastical properties, or even from small farmers." [115] We do not know either whether these estates, prior to the Arab conquest, comprised more than one-half of the cultivable land. The law forbade the estate holders to purchase peasant land at will, and according to Johnson,[116] "there is no evidence" that this legislation "was ever a dead letter." The landlord's proprietary position, even if it had the character of ownership, was legally limited. The freedom of the villagers, it need scarcely be repeated, was even more severely restricted.

The historical data known today suggest that in such Near Eastern countries as Egypt private landownership did not prevail at the beginning of the Roman period and they give little reason to assume that this type of ownership spread later in such a way as to even temporarily establish complex patterns of property and society.

China: Authentic historical records state that in the 4th century B.C. in the state of Ch'in the traditional regulated field system was abolished and that from then on, land could be bought and sold freely.[117] The records dealing with the imperial dynasties of Ch'in and Han imply that after the unification of China private landownership prevailed generally.[118] When, in the first century B.C.,

---

s. Bell finds that in contrast to feudal lordship in the West, which "was a replica in little of the kingdom to which it belonged," the estate of Byzantine Egypt "reproduced in little the bureaucratic empire of which it formed a part; its organization and its hierarchy of officials were modelled on the Imperial bureaucracy. Indeed it is sometimes impossible, in dealing with a papyrus document of this period, to be certain whether the persons whose titles are mentioned in it were Imperial officials or the servants of some great family" (Bell, 1948: 123 ff.). This overlapping of titles, far from being accidental, reflects an overlapping in positions. The proprietors of these estates were for the most part, if not exclusively, officiating or nonofficiating members of the governing class, who even in their capacity as landlords functioned as semi-officials: tax collectors and leaders of the hydraulic and nonhydraulic corvées.

merchants accumulated substantial mobile and immobile property, the government took strong fiscal measures to reduce their wealth, and an edict in 119 B.C. forbade them to own land; [119] but this edict did not interfere with land transfers between other classes, and even in the case of the merchants it seems to have been maintained only temporarily.

Unfortunately the historical sources leave important aspects of the agrarian development unexplained; and this is true both for the first period of complex property relations and for the subsequent regulated agrarian order that was instituted in the 5th century A.D. and endured until the middle of the 8th century. However, the information at hand is sufficient to illuminate at least the main trends in these periods.[120] During the last millennium, dynasties of conquest reserved lands for their tribal supporters and for some Chinese who had joined their conquering armies; but for the bulk of their Chinese subjects they upheld private landownership. It has been estimated that during the last phase of the Ch'ing (Manchu) dynasty the combined bannerland of the Manchu, Mongol, and Chinese bannermen amounted to some 4 per cent and privately owned land to almost 93 per cent.[t]

Although prior to this phase nongovernment land may at times have amounted to no more than one-half of all land,[121] and although a variety of legal clauses gave the right of preemption (primarily) to relatives,[122] it seems evident that China went further than any other major Oriental civilization in maintaining private ownership in land.

The reasons for this extraordinary development are by no means clear. But certain facts are suggestive. In China the critical changes occurred after the middle of the first millennium B.C., when several important culture elements appeared simultaneously: plowing with oxen, the use of iron, and the art of horseback riding. We hesitate to dismiss this coincidence as inconsequential. None of these elements emerged in the hydraulic areas of pre-Conquest America; and in the Near East and India they emerged separately in the course of a drawn-out development. In both areas plowing with labor animals was known from the dawn of written history, whereas the use of iron spread later, and the art of horseback riding later still. Could

---

t. Buck, 1937: 193. The estimate used by Dr. Buck puts privately owned land at 92.7 per cent, land assigned to Manchu nobles together with some "crown land" at 3.2 per cent, "state land" (land set aside for the maintenance of schools, religious purposes [state cult]) at 4.1 per cent. These data are approximate. They do not make allowance for private ancestral and temple land, which, according to the same source, amounted to less than .05 per cent.

it be that the simultaneous rise of new techniques of agricultural production and of military coercion and fast communication (and the assurance the two last gave to the maintenance of government control) encouraged the masters of Chinese society to experiment confidently with extremely free forms of landed property? Whatever the reason for the fateful step may have been, once taken it was found to be politically workable and agronomically and fiscally rewarding.

The Chinese development—which requires further investigation —is remarkable not only for its success but also for its geographical limitations. It seems to have affected certain southwestern neighbors, especially Siam. But many cultural contacts with more remote Asian countries notwithstanding, the Chinese system of private landowner-ship remained essentially confined to the area of its origin.

3. How Free Is Private Landed Property in Hydraulic Society?

THUS private landownership was present in many hydraulic civiliza-tions; but except for a brief and recent period of transition, the combined private lands were less extensive than the combined public lands. More. Even where private landownership did prevail, it in-variably was prevented from achieving the kind of freedom which is possible in a multicentered nonhydraulic society.

a. Despotically Imposed versus Democratically Established Restrictions of Private Property

To be sure, in no society does an owner absolutely dispose over his property. Even under conditions of strong property the owner of bricks, who may sell or store them or use them in building his house, may not throw them at his neighbor. The early Roman emphasis on the proprietor's sovereign position, although meaningful fiscally, is not valid societally.

Even fiscally the holder of strong property is not necessarily without burdens. In most free commonwealths some public func-tionaries have to be supported, and when this is the case, the citizens may have to draw upon their property to satisfy this need. Contribu-tions from private property for the maintenance of the government will be used only for proven essentials when the property-based forces of society can keep government in a serving position. Such contributions will increase, and be spent more freely, when an im-perfectly controlled government partially determines its own budget. They will be determined one-sidedly and with primary concern for the interests of those in power when a state stronger than society prevents the representatives of property from protecting their interests. It is under conditions of the first type that we find strong, though never absolute, property. And it is under conditions of the third type that property is weak. In hydraulic society immobile property, like mobile property, remains weak even where private landownership quantitatively outweighs public land tenure.

b. Restrictions Imposed upon the Freedom to Enjoy, to Use, to Transfer, and to Organize

ORIENTAL despotism one-sidedly restricts the landowner's freedom to enjoy the fruits of his property, to decide on its use, to will it freely (through testament), and to protect it by means of political organization.

The agrodespotic government demands payments from all landholders, either for its own use or for the use of especially privileged persons or institutions (temples, mosques, churches); and it determines the land tax one-sidedly, according to its own (the rulers') rationality standard. Tenancy may stratify the proprietary sector; and the changing strength of local and central authorities may alter the distribution of state revenues within the bureaucratic order. But neither condition affects the fundamental arrangement that compels owners and/or possessors of land generally to surrender a substantial part of their revenue to the representatives of the state.

Directly, this arrangement aims at the fruits of operational landed property. Indirectly, it also influences (and limits) the use to which a given piece of land may be put. The government bases its fiscal demands on the expectation that the peasant occupiers (or owners) will grow a crop capable of yielding a certain return. This demand forces the cultivator to grow the standard crop or an acceptable substitute. Occasionally, and particularly in regulated agrarian orders, the government may expressly prescribe that certain plants or trees (rice, corn, olives, hemp, cotton, or mulberry trees) be cultivated; and in these cases the proprietor's freedom to determine how his land should be used is nil. Frequently, however, the government is content to prescribe how much should be paid over to it. In both cases the result is a crude type of planned economy, which substantially limits the cultivator's freedom of choice and action.

Restrictions on the freedom to will property and to organize for its protection have been discussed in an earlier chapter. Hydraulic laws of inheritance fragment privately owned land. The landowner's inability to strengthen his proprietary position through independent national and politically effective organizations is as apparent in complex as in semicomplex or simple hydraulic societies.

This does not mean to say that the predominance of private landownership and the spread of landlordism in such civilizations as traditional China were societally irrelevant. They were not. But the spread of landlordism, which significantly modified the relations between the officiating and nonofficiating (gentry) segments of the ruling class, did not result in the consolidation of landed property or in independent organizations of landed proprietors. From the fiscal, legal, and political points of view private landownership was as weak at the final collapse of traditional Chinese society as it had been at its birth.

I. THE EFFECT OF PRIVATE PROPERTY ON HYDRAULIC SOCIETY

1. THE PERPETUATION OF HYDRAULIC SOCIETY DEPENDS ON THE GOVERNMENT'S MAINTENANCE OF ITS PROPERTY RELATIONS

ON the basis of these facts certain general conclusions seem justified. First of all, hydraulic society, like other institutional conformations, knows private property. Human existence over any considerable period of time is impossible without the public recognition and standardization of relations between persons and things or services. Even the convict possesses his clothes while he wears them; and many slaves possess not only their clothes but certain other articles as well. A serf possesses a great variety of things in addition to his land.

In most cases possession—and, of course, ownership—are recognized by custom. Where written laws exist, important forms of property may be recognized and regulated by special statutes.

This is true for all societies, including those ruled by despotic regimes. The most elementary considerations of rationality require that even those who make—and change—laws one-sidedly and despotically should emphasize their validity by not abrogating them unnecessarily. A ruler's rationality coefficient is the higher, the more strictly he himself observes the regulations which he has imposed upon his subjects. This also includes regulations concerned with private property.

The Oriental despot may buy and sell land.[1] He may have private artisans producing goods for him and at times he may pay them generously. And he may also buy directly from merchants. In all these cases he may—though he need not—set a low price. In Muscovite Russia this seems to have been the rule,[2] and in classical Hindu

India merchants had to accept whatever figure the king's appraiser deemed appropriate.[3] But the fact that the ruler and his officials paid for certain goods and services does not negate the despotic character of the regime. It only shows that by and large the despotic regime proceeds on the basis of the legal and proprietary regulations it has established.

What is true for Oriental despotism is no less true for the modern industrial apparatus state. Superficial observation may be satisfied with the presence of laws that deal with property. But no realistic analyst will call the Hitler government democratic because it dealt with Jewish property in accordance with the Nüremberg laws. Nor will he deny the absolutist character of the early Soviet state because it bought grain at a government-fixed price from individually producing peasants.

2. The Growing Complexity of Property and the Growing Complexity of Society

In addition to being an essential feature of hydraulic society, hydraulic property is also characterized by a variety of forms. Considerable private property and enterprise may appear in industry and commerce; and private ownership may spread, and even prevail, in agriculture. The representatives of semicomplex and complex patterns of property maintain relations to one another and with the state that differ substantially from those maintained by representatives of simple patterns of property. This fact enables us to distinguish, on the basis of different patterns of property, different subtypes of the over-all societal order.

3. Small Property Offers a Considerable Economic Incentive, but No Political Power

a. Incentives Inherent in Private Possession and Ownership

The technical advantages accruing from devices that can be employed only by large teams may equal or outweigh what is achieved by individual effort or by the labor of a few kinsmen working together. But when the technical advantages are insignificant or lacking, the incentives for individual action tend to become more effective.

Individual action need not be based on ownership. The occupier of a piece of land may only be its possessor, but in premachine days and under comparable technical conditions he is likely to outproduce a member of a team who is working for hire. Throughout the hydraulic world we therefore find the peasants tilling their land individually rather than collectively; and where labor animals increased the advantages of individual cultivation, small-scale peasant work also replaced the only relevant system of collective agriculture, the public field system. In handicraft and commerce private enterprise is generally based on private ownership. In agriculture private possession is usually sufficient to make the peasant proceed with great care. Tenancy, like peasant ownership, has created a horticulture-like intensity of farming.

To be sure, the tenant's desire to own his land is enormously strong. Even under the most frustrating fiscal conditions most peasant owners cling to their fields in the hope that the irrational tax pressure will be lightened before they are forced to abandon their property.

Property-based private handicraft created many of the beautiful objects (textiles, wood-, leather-, and metal-work) that delight the student of hydraulic civilization; and the hydraulic peasants who individually tilled their fields surpassed in skill and productivity the serfs of Medieval Europe. This was so even when these peasants were only the hereditary occupiers of regulated land; and it was even more so when they were tenants or private landowners. Indeed it is not at all unlikely that the exceptional intensity of agriculture in traditional China derived from the fact that private peasant land-ownership was more widespread there than in any other major hydraulic civilization.[a]

b. The Beggars' Property

SMALL private property, both possessed and owned, was conspicuous in hydraulic societies of the semicomplex type. It became much more so, and particularly in the agrarian sphere, in complex Oriental societies. Did it in either case become an important political force?

From the standpoint of a multicentered property-based society, the question is entirely reasonable. Small proprietors (artisans and peasants) played an ever increasing political role in classical Greece.

a. The feudal landholders of Japan did not engage in large-scale manorial farming as did their European peers; and the Japanese peasants cultivated their land individually and under conditions which resembled tenancy rather than serfdom. On the basis of a highly refined irrigation economy, they too engaged in a semihorticultural type of farming. This cannot be explained entirely by geographical proximity. The Japanese did not adopt the semimanagerial bureaucratic absolutism of China; nor did they adopt their system of private landownership from their continental neighbors. But within a feudal framework of power and social relations, the Japanese nobles gave their peasants as great a proprietary incentive as the over-all pattern of their society permitted.

Independent artisans were prominent in many guild cities of Medieval Europe; and, together with the peasants, they constituted a significant element in the democratic governments of Switzerland. In a number of the predominantly agrarian states of the United States which are not given over to giant farms and large-scale production the farmers' vote is a decisive factor. Although today the farmers account for no more than one-fifth of America's manpower, they are better organized than ever, and they continue to be a substantial political force, both regionally and nationally.

There is no need here to stress the potential political importance of labor—a group whose essential economic asset is the capacity to work. Free labor became a political force during the final democratic phase of ancient Greece, and under new conditions it emerged again in the property-based industrial society of our time. Organized both professionally and politically, the representatives of this form of individual property have in some industrial countries, such as Australia, Sweden, and England, assumed political as well as economic leadership; and in many others, including the United States, their political position has improved rapidly.

Small property and labor played no comparable role in the hydraulic world. With regard to labor the issue is simple. Personally free, hired laborers have existed in many hydraulic civilizations.[4] Unskilled workers were for the most part unorganized. Skilled workers were frequently organized in local and separate professional units. But even when they were not under strict government supervision, they constituted only a politically irrelevant form of self-government, a Beggars' Democracy.

And the peasant proprietors? Whether they possessed or owned their land, they remained the representatives of a fragmented type of property and enterprise. At best they were permitted to handle their essentially local affairs within the rural version of a Beggars' Democracy, the village community.

From the standpoint of the absolutist bureaucracy, the property of both artisans and peasants was Beggars' Property, property that was economically fragmented and politically impotent.[b]

b. Did the peasants constitute an economic and political threat during the first period of the Soviet regime? Long before 1917 Lenin stressed the danger of any private property (peasant land included) for a socialist regime (cf. Lenin, S, IX: 66–7, 213–14, and passim); and he did not change his opinion after his party established its dictatorial power with the support of the peasants who had been "given" land (ibid., XXVII: 303 ff.; XXXI: 483 ff.). He insisted that property transforms men into "wild beasts" (ibid., XXX: 418); and he called the petty bourgeois and small peasants potential breeders of capitalism and thus an inherent danger to the Soviet state (ibid., XXVII: 303 ff.; XXXI: 483). In 1918, and again in 1921, Lenin viewed these petty

4. Private Commercial Property Politically Inconsequential Even When Permitted to Become Large

UNDER certain conditions, the representatives of Oriental despotism found it economically advisable to have the bulk of all trade handled by private businessmen. When this was the case, some merchants grew fabulously rich, and a few enjoyed distinguished social positions.

We do not exclude the possibility that big merchants as a group could have participated in the running of despotic governments; but the evidence at hand fails to document this development as a significant feature in any of the major representatives of semicomplex or complex hydraulic societies. In Babylonia, in Buddhist India, in pre-Conquest Meso-America, in the Islamic Near East, and in imperial China big merchant property, even when involved in large-scale operations, remained politically inconsequential.

5. Problems of Wealth within the Governing Class

PROPERTY problems of a very different kind arise within the governing class. In simple hydraulic societies almost the entire national surplus is appropriated by the ruler and his serving men. And even when intermediary groups, such as the merchants, are permitted to derive considerable profit from their transactions, the governing class continues to monopolize the greater part of the country's wealth. The members of the court and the officials may receive their share of this wealth either as revenue from assigned (office or sinecure) lands or as salary (in kind or cash). In both cases the income is based on the government's power to control land and to tax people. And in both cases it becomes private (bureaucratic) property. Its recipients may use all of it for consumption; or they may set some part of it aside as savings or for investments. Both types of use involve the problem of bureaucratic hedonism; the second raises in addition the problem of bureaucratic landlordism and capitalism.

---

bourgeois forces as his regime's "principal enemy" (*ibid.*, XXXII: 339). On the eve of the First Five-Year Plan, Stalin repeated Lenin's formula that the small producers are "the last capitalist class" (*ibid.*, XXXII: 460). He insisted that this class "will breed capitalists in its ranks, and cannot help breeding them, constantly and continuously" (Stalin, 1942: 102). There is no evidence that either Lenin or Stalin based his views on a serious study of the political position of small peasant landholders under absolutist state power. Stalin's pseudoscientific accusations of 1928 only served to prepare the Soviet bureaucracy and the Soviet people for the total liquidation of private peasant property.

a. Bureaucratic Hedonism

BUREAUCRATIC hedonism can be defined as the enjoyment of wealth without provoking the envy of high officials or the crushing wrath of the despot.[5] Such hedonism may be complicated by opportunities for saving and investing. While the members of the governing class are generally eager to enjoy their property as long as the enjoying is good, they express this desire differently under different circumstances. But the wish to consume pleasantly and to live well prevails everywhere, even in those complex hydraulic societies in which the possibility of owning land encourages economy and thrift.[c] Often and particularly in the case of very highly placed and continually endangered officials, such as viziers, chancellors, or "prime ministers," the bureaucratic *joie de vivre* is spectacularly manifested.[6]

b. Bureaucratic Landlordism and Capitalism

EVEN the most luxury-loving functionary usually tries to save part of his income. After all, he may not be in office forever; his family will always have to eat; and his children will have to be trained for the most desirable of all goals: a government career. Thus the thoughtful official buries precious metals and jewels in the ground. Or better still he converts some of his passive private property into active property. He buys land for rental and/or he uses his funds profitably as a government contractor (especially as a tax collector), or as a money lender, or as a partner in private commercial enterprise. On the basis of his bureaucratic property he becomes a bureaucratic landlord and/or a bureaucratic capitalist.

Of course, there are others who are landlords also. Wherever land can be freely alienated, small proprietors are eager to purchase it.[7] And there may also be nonbureaucratic capitalists. But since the uniquely powerful state apparatus surpasses all other forces of hydraulic society in acquiring agricultural and nonagricultural revenue, officials figure prominently as tax farmers and, wherever land can be bought, as landowners.

In imperial China predominance of private landownership enabled the officials to invest a considerable part of their income in land. A recent analysis of officialdom and bureaucratic gentry in 19th-century China suggests that at the close of the Ch'ing dynasty present and former officials, holders of official titles, and holders of high examination degrees together may have received land rents

c. The pleasures of bureaucratic consumption in late imperial China were depicted in great detail in such novels as the *Dream of the Red Chamber*.

amounting to 165 million taels annually and about 81.5 million taels from entrepreneurial activities. At the same time all lower degree-holders together received about 55 millions from the first source and 40 millions from the second.[d] These figures indicate that by far the greater part of the rent income of the official-literati went to the upper echelon of this group, which was predominantly bureaucratic (present and former officials and quasi-officials outweighed the holders of high degrees by three to one).[e] The members of this echelon received an average of 1100 taels in rent annually. The lower degree holders received from this source only about 44 taels; and this despite the fact that over a third of all members of this group were wealthy enough to purchase their degree.[f]

The civil and military officials may have derived an annual income of 91 million taels from their government positions. This suggests for the ranking official an average bureaucratic income of about 1700 taels [g]—that is, 65 per cent more than the average income from rent.

Under Oriental as well as under Occidental despotism, landlordism and officialdom overlap. But the seemingly similar configurations differ profoundly in their institutional substance. The bureaucratic landlords of Oriental society derived their political power essentially from the absolutist government, of which they themselves

d. These and many other illuminating data have been taken from a comprehensive study of the Chinese "gentry" in the 19th century by Dr. Chang Chung-li, University of Washington, Seattle, who has generously permitted their inclusion in the present study. The officials and degree-holders are classed together, because during the later part of imperial China they constituted a status group, shên-shih (see below, Chap. 8). Their entrepreneurial income stemmed mainly from investments in native banks, pawnshops, and the salt trade (Chang, GI, Pt. II). Dr. Chang's study shows that the shên-shih—"a privileged group with managerial abilities and functions"—received "from 'government services,' 'professional services' and 'gentry services' together" an income larger than that from rent or mercantile activities (letter from Dr. Chang, March 20, 1954).

e. Prior to the Taiping Rebellion, the "officials, officers and holders of official titles" together constituted 67 per cent of the upper group; after the Taiping period, the figure rose to 75 per cent (Chang, CG, Pt. II).

f. A lower degree attained through examination opened the door to regular advancement on the ladder of higher examination degrees and government office. The purchased degree carried with it no such advantages.

g. It is assumed that out of a total of 50,000 incumbent and former civil officials (Chang, CG) about 40,000 held office (see below, Chap. 8, sec. C, n. 3); and that among the 17,000 military officers (ibid.) a similar proportion prevailed. According to Dr. Chang, the figure of 40,000 civil officials, suggested by Mrs. Lienche Tu Fang, probably includes "expectant officials who gathered around the governors and governor-generals" and who "were often given temporary assignments." Although not listed in the registers of the central government, they were responsible to, and paid by, the provincial authority (letter from Dr. Chang, March 1, 1954).

or their officiating relatives formed an active part. It was only as officials that the members of the agrobureaucratic gentry were politically organized. The noble landlords of postfeudal Europe or Japan did not necessarily hold government office. And they did not need government salaries to periodically restore their landed property, since their estates were kept intact by primogeniture and entail.

The land of the bureaucratic (Oriental) gentry might facilitate a government career for certain of its members and thus give renewed access to power; but essentially this land was revenue property. Conversely, the land of the feudal (Occidental) gentry involved the perpetuation of organized political power, independent of, and at times openly conflicting with, state power. In a way unparalleled by hydraulic property (bureaucratic and other) and in addition to being revenue land, feudal property was conspicuously and significantly power property.

6. CONCLUSIONS LEADING TO NEW QUESTIONS

a. Hydraulic Property: Revenue Property versus Power Property

WHETHER hydraulic property is large or small or whether or not it belongs to a member of the governing class, it provides material advantages. But it does not enable its holders to control state power through property-based organization and action. In all cases, it is not power property but revenue property.

b. The Importance—and Limitation—of Private Property in Determining Class Differentiations within Hydraulic Society

THIS does not mean to deny the importance of property in establishing social (class) differentiations. The emergence of property-based handicraft and commerce and the spread of private landownership involve the emergence of new social elements, groups, and classes. Thus it is not only legitimate but necessary to show in which ways patterns of social differentiation correlate with patterns of private property.

However, it is quickly apparent that in hydraulic society the problem of social differentiation involves more than the question of the presence or extent of private property. Once established, bureaucratic wealth is private property, but it is rooted in, and derives from, government property, and its intrabureaucratic distribution is based on political conditions that cannot be explained in terms of private property.

CHAPTER 8

Classes in hydraulic society

A. THE NEED FOR A NEW SOCIOLOGY OF CLASS

MODERN institutional analysis emerged in a society that was decisively shaped by conditions of property. Consequently, the pioneers in the modern sociology of class saw the major segments ("orders") [1] of society as determined essentially by major types of private property and by corresponding types of revenue. According to Adam Smith, "the whole annual produce of the land and labour of every country . . . naturally divides itself . . . into three parts; the rent of land, the wages of labour, and the profits of stock; and constitutes a revenue to three different orders of people; to those who live by rent, to those who live by wages, and to those who live by profit. These are the three great, original and constituent orders of every civilized society, from whose revenue that of every other order is ultimately derived." [2] The representatives of government are supported to an extent from "public stock and public lands"; but the greater part of their expenses is met by the three major orders which render some of their revenue to the state in the form of taxes. [3]

According to this view, the representatives of government constitute not a major order of society but a secondary and derivative one. And whenever conflicts concerning property arise, civil government becomes a weapon of the propertied classes against the economically under-privileged groups. To quote Smith again: "Civil government, so far as it is instituted for the security of property, is in reality instituted for the defence of the rich against the poor, or of those who have some property against those who have none at all." [a]

This statement, which was written in a period of unbridled

---

a. Smith, 1937: 674. Smith supplements this statement by a citation from his "Lectures": "Till there be property there can be no government, the very end of which is to secure wealth and to defend the rich from the poor." He adds a reference to Locke, *Civil Government*, sec. 94: "Government has no other end but the preservation of property."

proprietary privilege, presents a crude economic interpretation of the state. It makes no allowance for power as an independent determinant of class or for the socio-economic prominence of the state in the hydraulic civilizations with which Smith was familiar.[b] Smith's successors defined the peculiarity of Asiatic society more clearly; but they, too, treated "Asia" as a residual category in a socio-economic system which considered private property and the revenue derived from it the decisive factors in the formation of class.

Despite its obvious deficiencies, the proprietary concept of class greatly stimulated the social sciences up to the beginning of the 20th century. Without doubt, this concept is essential for the understanding of societies in which strong independent private property prevails; and it remains important also for the understanding of certain secondary aspects of power-based societies. But it is insufficient when it is unqualifiedly applied to formations of the first type. And it is altogether inadequate when it is used as the essential means for explaining formations of the second type.

The growth of big government in many modern industrial countries and the rise of totalitarian states in the USSR and Germany enable us to recognize state power as a prominent determinant of class structure, both in our time and in the past. They also enable us to recognize more clearly than before the importance of power in the establishment of the ruling class in hydraulic society.

B. CLASS STRUCTURE IN HYDRAULIC SOCIETY

1. THE KEY CRITERION: RELATION TO THE STATE APPARATUS

THE pioneers of a property-based sociology of class viewed the Asiatic state as a gigantic landowner. In most hydraulic societies the bulk of all cultivated land is indeed regulated; and although the state's proprietary right over the regulated fields is hidden behind the façade of a seemingly self-governing village community, it operates negatively when the government prevents outsiders from purchasing these fields, and positively when the government assigns or sells land (or villages) at will. However, the classical formula is definitely unsatisfactory in at least one respect: It overlooks irrigation water, which in hydraulic societies is a major agent of production.

b. Smith, 1937: 789 ff. On a number of occasions Smith tries to remove the inconsistency by limiting his scheme to "civilized" societies. But he makes no effort to establish a concept of class that adequately mirrors the specific position of the state and its representatives in either the Eastern or the Western world.

Does the despotic state "own" the great accumulations of water? This has been claimed in many but not all hydraulic civilizations. I prefer to view the state as controlling rather than owning the country's "big" water.

The same approach may also be taken with regard to land. Some hydraulic states, such as imperial China, tolerated the predominance of privately owned land over a long period of time, and in this case the state restricted the owner's proprietary position by means of heavy taxation, directives as to what crops should be grown, and a fragmenting law of inheritance. Thus the hydraulic state, which frequently owned the bulk of all cultivable land, generally kept landed property weak. Its position is again best viewed as one of control.

In hydraulic society the first major division into an order of superior and privileged persons and an order of inferior and under-privileged persons occurs simultaneously with the rise of an inordinately strong state apparatus. The masters and beneficiaries of this state, the rulers, constitute a class different from, and superior to, the mass of the commoners—those who, although personally free, do not share the privileges of power. The men of the apparatus state are a ruling class in the most unequivocal sense of the term; and the rest of the population constitutes the second major class, the ruled.[a]

Within the ruling class different individuals and groups differ greatly in their ability to make decisions and handle personnel. In the civil administration, as in the army, major directives originate at the top level. But, again, as in the army, minor decisions are made by men in the middle brackets. And decisions concerned with the final execution of orders and regulations are made by the noncoms and the buck privates of the power hierarchy. Such decisions may be insignificant from the standpoint of a superior, but they are often vitally important for the commoners whose fate they affect.

The parallel between the lower strata of the apparatus hierarchy and the small businessmen of a capitalistic society is obvious. A small capitalist has little influence on the conditions of supply, marketing, or finance, except when he combines with others of his kind; but whether he does so or not, he can usually decide where and what he wants to buy and/or produce. In fact, he makes many small decisions

---

a. Max Weber drew attention to the fact that under the conditions of supreme bureaucratic power the mass of the population are all reduced to the level of "the ruled,' who see themselves confronted by "a bureaucratically stratified ruling group" that actually, and even formally, may occupy "an altogether autocratic position" (Weber, WG: 667; cf. 669, 671).

respecting the small affairs that are his world. Similarly, middle and even lower functionaries in hydraulic society are, like the top-ranking leadership, part of the power apparatus; and with proper grading they, too, enjoy advantages that accrue essentially from the unrestricted authority of the regime.

In terms of income, lower members of the apparatus hierarchy may be compared to the employees of a capitalistic enterprise who do not share in the surplus they help to realize. A property-based sociology of class would therefore consider them commoners rather than members of the upper class. Such an approach, however, overlooks the human relations that usually and specifically characterize the operations of a bureaucratic order. These operations make the lowest representatives of the apparatus state participants in the exercise of total power. In contrast to the employees of a commercial or industrial enterprise who proceed under the give-and-take conditions of the market and thus in a formally equal way, even the most lowly men of the apparatus proceed on the basis of coercion, that is, in a formally unequal way. Their position in the power hierarchy provides some of the lowest functionaries with particular opportunities for personal enrichment; and it provides all of them with a specific sociopolitical status. As representatives of the despotic state, even the lowest functionaries arouse in the commoners a mixture of suspicion and fear. They therefore occupy a social position which places them, in terms of power, prestige, and sometimes also of revenue, outside of, and ambivalently above, the mass of the ruled.

The natives of a conquered country consider the occupying army a unit; and they do so knowing full well that the power of the rank-and-file soldier is extremely restricted. Similarly, the subjects of a hydraulic despotism view the men of the apparatus as a unit, even when it is clear that individual members vary immensely in power, wealth, and social status.

2. THE MULTIPLE CONDITIONING OF SOCIAL SUBSECTIONS

THE ruling class is differentiated from the earliest beginnings of hydraulic civilizations. The ruled class is usually undifferentiated in simple hydraulic societies. It is always differentiated in semicomplex and complex hydraulic societies.

The subsections of the two classes are differently conditioned. Within the ruling class position in the power hierarchy is the primary determinant, and wealth, although at times significant, remains secondary. Within the ruled class types and dimensions of active property are the primary determinants of social status, whereas differences in relation to the government tend, in this apolitical world, to play a minor role or no role at all.

C. THE RULERS

1. THE MEN OF THE APPARATUS

a. *The Basic Vertical Structure*

THE ruling class of hydraulic society is represented first by its active core, the men of the apparatus. In virtually all hydraulic countries these men are headed by a ruler, who has a personal entourage (his court) and who controls and directs his numerous civil and military underlings through a corps of ranking officials. This hierarchy, which includes the sovereign, the ranking officials, and the underlings, is basic to all Orientally despotic regimes. Horizontal developments, which occur under certain conditions, complicate the basic vertical structure.

i. THE RULER AND THE COURT

THE despot's arbitrary cruelties and his equally arbitrary generosities form the themes of many records. His arbitrary cruelties indicate that subject to obvious physical and cultural limitations he can make or break anyone if he wants to. His arbitrary generosities indicate that, subject to obvious economic limitations, he can spend wastefully and without being restricted by any constitutional agency. The proverbial glamour of Oriental courts is merely an economic expression of the ruler's despotic control over his subjects.

In his person the ruler combines supreme operational authority and the many magic and mythical symbols that express the terrifying (and allegedly beneficial) qualities of the power apparatus he heads. Because of immaturity, weakness, or incompetence, he may share his operational supremacy with an aide: a regent, vizier, chancellor, or "prime minister." But the exalted power of these men does not usually last long. It rarely affects the symbols of supreme authority. And it vanishes as soon as the ruler is strong enough to realize the autocratic potential inherent in his position.

The unique importance of the ruler's whims and actions give unique importance to individuals who may influence him. In addition to the vizier—and sometimes more consequential than he— the best situated to do so are the members of the ruler's personal entourage: his wives and concubines, his blood relatives and affinals, his courtiers, servants, and favorites. Under the conditions of despotic autocracy, any one of them may temporarily and irrationally wield excessive power.

ii. THE RANKING OFFICIALS

IN speaking of officials, we refer to persons who are assigned a particular type of government task. Among sedentary peoples the regular duties involved in such a task tend to be permanently and physically located in an "office" or "bureau." And usually the holder of such an office keeps a record of his dealings.

Linguistically, the word "bureaucracy" is a monstrosity.[1] But the importance of some of its connotations has made it popular, despite the disapproval of the purists. Semantically, a bureaucrat is a person who "rules through bureaus." In a wider sense, the term is also applied to any official who uses secretarial devices ("red tape") to delay action, to make himself important, or to idle on the job. When Stalin criticized "bureaucracy," he particularly stressed "bureaucracy and red tape," officials who indulge in "idle chatter about 'leadership in general,'" "incorrigible bureaucrats and chair-warmers."[2]

Certainly bureaucratic chair-warmers can be annoying and harmful; and even serving and controlled governments are plagued by them. But a bureaucracy becomes truly formidable only when its offices are the organizational centers of ruthless and total power. For this reason Stalin's effort to hide the bureaucratic Frankenstein of the Soviet regime behind the semihumorous facade of inefficient "chair-warmers" is nothing more than a clumsy attempt at totalitarian myth making.

The ranking officials include civil and military functionaries of recognized status. They do not include the bureaucratic underlings. The civil officials resemble their military colleagues in that both are in positions of command and able to make limited and intermediate decisions, that both are parts of centrally directed bodies, that both unconditionally (and usually full time) serve their ruler, and that both are government-supported either by salary or by revenue derived from state-assigned office lands.

An army is essentially an instrument of coercion, and as such not necessarily a bureaucratic institution. But the management of centrally directed armies of the Oriental type involves considerable organizational planning, which in literate civilizations is usually carried out through bureaus. Many officers are both fighters and administrators; but often the fighting officials are functionally separated from the bureaucratic officials (*Militärbeamte*). In any case officers are not feudal knights but government functionaries, and as such part of the ranking officialdom.

iii. THE UNDERLINGS

THE underlings of the bureaucratic hierarchy are either scribes or menial aides. The scribes account for the bulk of all the secretarial work done at the court, in the central government, and in the provincial and local offices. The menial aides act as gate keepers, runners, servants, jailers, and, in a semimilitary capacity, as policemen.

In all sizable agrobureaucratic despotisms the underlings are numerous. During the last period of imperial China about 40,000 ranking (civil) officials had at their disposal over 1,200,000 clerks and over 500,000 runners—that is, a total of more than 1,700,000 underlings, or something more than forty underlings to one ranking official.[3]

b. Horizontal Developments

THE bureaucratic network may spread over a large territory. But as long as the central government appoints the bulk of the ranking officials and directs the provincial bureaus, no special problems of horizontal authority arise, even when the regional functionaries, for reasons of distance or political expediency, are given a relatively free hand in the conduct of their business.

Max Weber was struck by the relatively loose way in which the central government of imperial China controlled the provincial bureaucracy;[4] and indeed, in accordance with the law of diminishing administrative returns, regional and local officials were given considerable freedom of decision in matters of detail. But as Weber himself recognized, the central government appointed and transferred these officials at will; and it determined the major lines of their action.[5]

Of course, from time to time dynastic authority declined; and when the inner crisis was serious, the high territorial officials became temporarily the semi-autonomous, or even the autonomous, masters of the areas they administered. But except for periods of disruption, the most distinguished provincial dignitaries were merely prominent members of the centrally established and centrally manipulated ranking bureaucracy.

i. SATRAPS

THE Persian empire of the Achaemenids differed from the Chinese empire both in origin and structure. The unification of China was prepared for by centuries of institutional growth; and the core areas of Chinese culture were sufficiently populous and strong to make their domination over the outlying and colonized regions relatively easy. Conversely, the Persians in a single generation extended their rule beyond the confines of their homeland to four sizable countries, each of which had a well-defined culture: Media (549), Lydia (546), Babylonia (538), and Egypt (525). They abolished the ruling houses in all four of these regions and in addition changed the political map by carving them up into a number of provinces, each governed by a satrap.[6]

The heterogeneity and size of their new acquisitions compelled the Persian conquerors to give their satraps unusual freedom in the handling of political affairs. A satrap might retain his position for a long period; and at times he might be succeeded by his son.[7] Moreover, he appointed the subsatraps [8] and probably also the local officials, who were usually natives.[9] He hired mercenary troops and his bodyguard. He commanded militia-like levies raised in his territory.[10] He administered the taxes of his province.[11] He maintained diplomatic relations with neighboring states.[12] And he might organize a military expedition against a neighbor country—usually, however, with the permission of the Great King.[13] Surrounded by his court, he ruled with kinglike splendor.[14] This quasiroyal status of the satrap was actively encouraged by the Persian sovereign,[15] who apparently considered this as good a way as any to maintain his prestige in distant regions.

Nevertheless, in several crucial respects, the Great King exerted strict control over his satraps. Definitely and conspicuously, he was the master, the satrap the serving man who owed him absolute obedience. A central system of communication and intelligence,[16] inspection by metropolitan officials,[17] and the maintenance of Persian garrisons at strategic points [18] prevented the satrap from attaining military or fiscal independence. The satrapies were taxed according to centrally devised principles and with definite obligations toward the capital. "The proceeds of this taxation were forwarded annually by the satraps to Susa, where the surplus that remained, after defraying the annual outgoings, accumulated in the king's treasury as a reserve fund." [19]

The Great King considered his satrap not a feudal vassal but a top-ranking territorial agent. "The king is the master over all his

subjects and the satrap his representative; they can arbitrarily interfere everywhere, not only where this is required by the realm's
interest, but wherever they want." [20]

Thus the Persian empire was "a bureaucratic state" (*ein Beamtenstaat*); [21] and the satrap's administrative and military freedom of
action did not destroy the basic structure of the bureaucratic hierarchy of which the satrap was a part.

ii. SUBORDINATE PRINCES, CURACAS, RĀJAS

A SATRAP might be a native of the region over which he had jurisdiction. But this was not typical. Only in Cilicia did the Great King
permit a member of the former ruling house to become the governor
of a newly established province.[22] Princes who voluntarily accepted
Persian sovereignty were generally permitted to continue ruling as
vassals. Like the satraps and subsatraps, they owed the Great King
military services and tribute; [23] but they seem to have enjoyed more
political and cultural freedom than did many other native rulers who
fell under the sway of powerful hydraulic empires.

The builders of the Inca empire permitted rulers who had sur-
rendered voluntarily to hold official position; but these *curacas*
were subordinated to Inca governors.[a] Moreover, the shrines of the
region's highest deities were transferred to Cuzco; and the main
features of Inca religion were imposed upon the new subjects.[24]
While in some ways perpetuating the appearance of native rule, the
curacas were, for all practical purposes, integral parts of the imperial
officialdom.[b]

In Muslim India a number of native "chiefs" or rulers (*rāīs, rājas*)
were also, if somewhat differently, included in the ruling order. A
rāja was permitted to preserve many secondary features of his
previous power, if he vowed unconditional political (and fiscal)
submission to his new overlord. Says Moreland: "His [the chief's]
tenure depended on his loyalty, which meant primarily the punctual
payment of tribute." [25] The *rājas* were more or less free to determine
how, in their regions, the tribute should be raised.[26] In Akbar's
time the six older provinces, which constituted the core of the empire, were almost completely administered by the central govern-

a. Usually their sons were taken as hostages to Cuzco, where they were taught the
Inca way of life (Rowe, 1946: 272).

b. They were chiefs of 10,000, 5,000, 1,000, or 500 corviable men. See Rowe, 1946:
263. The chiefs of 100 were apparently the lowest ranking officials. Like the higher
functionaries, they might ceremonially participate in communal agriculture; but essentially they supervised and directed the chiefs of ten, who as foremen worked with
the peasants (Rowe, 1946: 263, 265).

ment, whereas the outlying provinces presented a mixed picture, some being headed by centrally appointed officials, some by *rājas*.[27]

The Persian satraps, the Inca *curacas,* and the *rājas* of Muslim India constitute a series of variants on the scale of political subordination. The relations between a satrap or *curaca* and their sovereign were definitely noncontractual; in substance, as well as in form, the ruler demanded total submission. The position of certain *rājas* included elements of a contractual arrangement; but these were expressed factually more than formally. Only with regard to the most loosely attached dependencies did a despotic overlord accept, under the cloak of an alliance, a quasicontractual relationship.

The contrast to feudal patterns of subordination is manifest. Under a feudal regime the contractual relationship is essential; and it characterizes the core of the feudal order. Under a hydraulic despotism relations of total submission characterize the core of the bureaucratic system and they also prevail in its horizontal extensions. Only in the loosely dependent periphery do quasicontractual (quasifeudal) features make their appearance.

The sociology of hydraulic despotism recognizes relevant differences between an ordinary member of the centrally directed bureaucracy and a satrap (or *curaca*), and between such dignitaries and a *rāja* or a loosely dependent ally. In all cases the determining force is the agrarian apparatus state; but the degree of operational dependency creates significant subdivisions in the edifice of despotic power.

iii. GRADATIONS OF POWER IN MODERN TOTALITARIAN STATES

ANALYSTS of modern industrial apparatus states are equally concerned with differences between the officials of the totalitarian heartland and the heads of the satellite countries. In these cases too it is essential to recognize both the supreme role of the metropolis and the structural differentiations that characterize its horizontal extensions.[c] It is also essential to recognize the tendency toward

c. In 1921 Stalin characterized the horizontal gradations in the newly established USSR as follows: "The Russian experiment in applying various forms of federation, in passing from federation based on Soviet autonomy (the Kirghiz Republic, the Bashkir Republic, the Tatar Republic, the Gortsi, Daghestan) to federation based on treaty relations with independent Soviet republics (the Ukraine, Azerbaidjan), and in allowing intermediate phases (Turkestan, White Russia), has fully proved the significance and flexibility of federation as a general form of state government for the Soviet republics" (Stalin, S, V: 22). Stalin considered this allegedly voluntary association a transitional step to a future and "supreme" unity; and indeed as far as the then

intensified subjugation in periods of imperialistic growth and coordination. The quasi-independent ally of yesterday may be the
dependent ally of today and the satellite, satrap, or run-of-the-mill
official of tomorrow.

In hydraulic society this trend has its counterpart in retrogressive
developments that may ultimately replace one unified despotic
regime by several such systems. Pharaonic Egypt fell temporarily
into a number of quasi-independent territories; and post-T'ang
China was even more seriously dismembered. But in both cases the
new political units perpetuated despotic methods of statecraft, and
the term "feudal," which may with a certain poetic licence be
applied to the relation between the weakened center and its larger
sub-units, is completely inappropriate when used to designate sub-
units which are actually nothing but detached and smaller replicas
of the larger despotic model.

The control mechanism of the modern apparatus states makes
separation extremely difficult as long as the despotic metropolis itself
persists. The defection of Tito's Yugoslavia was made possible by
exceptional geomilitary circumstances.[28] Manifestly, the horizontal
extensions of the modern apparatus state are not identical with—
although they offer instructive parallels to—the territories of satraps,
rājas, or dependent allies in hydraulic society.

2. SUBCLASSES ATTACHED TO THE MEN OF THE APPARATUS

THE manipulators of the despotic state apparatus are the core, but
not the whole of the ruling class. A biosocial supplement—blood
relations and affinals—must be included, and frequently also an
operational supplement—persons who enjoy a semi-, quasi-, or pre-
official status.

a. Attachment Based on Kinship

i. THE RULING HOUSE

POLYGAMY was a recognized institution in the great majority of all
hydraulic societies;[d] and for obvious reasons the sovereign had

---

"autonomous" and "independent" republics were concerned, he and his comrades
worked successfully to bring this about: "This voluntary character of the federation
must absolutely be preserved in the future, for only such a federation can become a
transitional form to that supreme unity of the workers of all countries in a single
universal economic system, the necessity for which is becoming ever more perceptible"
(*ibid.*: 23).

d. Interesting exceptions: Christian Byzantium and Russia. The prevalence of

unique opportunities to utilize it. His many relatives (by blood or marriage) usually enjoyed a distinguished social status, and usually they also enjoyed considerable material advantage. If and to what extent the despot employed them in the government depended on a number of circumstances. But when employed, they had an excellent chance to rise to positions of prominence and power.

In the Inca empire the male descendants of the sovereigns were organized in *ayllus,* whose number increased with the advance of the dynasty. The members of these *ayllus* "formed a useful court circle of educated men trained in the imperial ideology, and interested in its perpetuation. The emperors chose their top administrators from this group when possible." [29]

In certain Chinese dynasties, such as Han, the consort family played an enormous political role; and in the conquest dynasty of Liao the members of the consort clan, Hsiao, were apparently more trusted than those of the imperial Yeh-lü clan.[30] But whether the sovereign's blood relatives or his affinals were numerous or not in the bureaucratic hierarchy, the members of these two groups were generally a distinguished component of the ruling class.

ii. THE BUREAUCRATIC GENTRY

ON a less exalted level, the families of the ranking officials are equally significant. Like the relatives of the sovereign, although not entirely for the same reasons, the members of what may be called the bureaucratic gentry did not necessarily hold office. Some were too young, some too old, some inept, some women; and some who had the qualifications could not find a government post, first, because there were usually more candidates than vacancies and second, because some of the vacancies might be filled by outsiders rather than by sons of officials.

The amount and form of family possessions are important differentiating factors. Mobile passive wealth (gold, jewels, etc.) shrinks more quickly than landed property, which, although it is fragmented through equal division among the heirs, may during the owner's lifetime remain undiminished, if the rents are large enough to support him and his family. Thus hydraulic societies with highly developed private landownership provide the bureaucratic gentry with optimal, if gradually diminishing, opportunities for living on

---

monogamy in Byzantium and Russia shows that this form of marriage, despite the restrictions it imposed on the rulers, was nevertheless compatible with the main political, economic, and social trends of Oriental despotism.

the amassed family wealth. The Chinese saying that a family may rise from rags to riches in three generations and go back to rags in the next three well describes the trend toward declining wealth that in contrast to the feudal gentry characterizes the bureaucratic gentry of hydraulic society. Equally important is the speed with which a return to government service can reestablish (or increase) family wealth. No doubt, if members of an impoverished gentry family held office for three generations, the family fortune (and landholdings) at the end of that time would certainly be large. But often one family member who served the government even for a limited time was able to restore his family's property. In a Chinese case with which I am personally familiar a three-year stint in a county magistracy did the trick.

The political significance of the bureaucratic gentry is indicated by the fact that members of this group are frequently invited to fulfill auxiliary administrative, judicial, or priestly functions. In Pharaonic Egypt remunerative positions in the temple service were often given to children of notables.[31] In the judicial assemblies of Babylonia some "notables" were officeholders, others had a gentry-like status.[32]

For Buddhist India Fick assumes the existence of a "gentry of the land" that formed a part of the *gahapatis,* the "householders."[33] In his opinion these householders were neither warriors, Kshatriyas, nor Brahmins;[34] rather they were identical with, or overlapped, a "lower-land-owning nobility."[35] Fick's interpretation of the householders is open to doubt. Dutoit considers them members of the third order, the Vaisya.[e] The texts which Fick has translated show clearly that Brahmins could be householders;[36] and this indeed was

e. *Jātakam,* II: 143, n. 1; cf. IV: 541, n. 1. At this period, castes, *jati,* already existed. But the *jati,* which later increased to several thousand, are not identical with the four major *varṇa,* the Kshatriyas, Brahmins, Vaisyas, and Sūdras. The use of the word *varṇa* ("color") as a designation for these great divisions, goes back to the period covered by the Rigveda—that is, to the days when the Aryans, the persons of "the light color," subdued the indigenous Dasyus, the persons of "the dark color" (Rapson, 1922: 54; see also Renou, 1950: 63). After this period the term *varṇa* "denotes 'a social order' independently of any actual distinction of colour" (Rapson, 1922: 54) or a "class" or "order." Smith (1928: 36), following Shama Sastri, suggests these or "some equivalent term." Cf. also Rhys-Davids, 1950: 46. The rules of castes, *jati,* which most prominently regulate diet and marriage, shaped with increasing rigidity the four orders, among which, however, only the Brahmins persisted throughout India and until modern times: "No four original castes ever existed at any time or place, and at the present moment the terms Kshatriya, Vaisya, and Sūdra have no exact meaning as a classification of existing castes. In northern India the names Vaisya and Sūdra are not used except in books of disputes about questions of caste precedence. In the south all Hindus who are not Brahmans fall under the denomination of Sūdra, while

their regular condition when, after having completed their education, they married and founded a family.[37]

Fick's classification seems valid.to this extent: a householder enjoyed no "special privileges," [38] and when he lived essentially off his lands he generally belonged to the lower nobility—that is, to a segment of the ruling class that was less distinguished than the officeholding Kshatriyas, Brahmins, or Vaisyas. But land grants were made primarily to secular serving men and to Brahmins; [39] and the nonofficiating members of these groups certainly constituted a bureaucratic or priestly gentry. This was the case whether they held land grants hereditarily or for life, or not at all.[40]

In Byzantine Egypt the relatives of prominent functionaries seem to have been eager to assume office when opportunity offered. While living on their estates, they fulfilled a variety of semi-official functions in their locality.[41]

The Inca state took elaborate measures to support meritorious dignitaries and other persons of distinction. The lands assigned to them were also intended to benefit their descendants.[42] This suggests that, as in other hydraulic civilizations, a sizable bureaucratic gentry flourished in Inca society. In pre-Conquest Mexico, too, sinecure lands were held for long periods of time, not only by relatives of the ruling house but also by the families of ranking officials.[43]

In China individuals who achieved social distinction because of their bureaucratic family background can be documented as early as the Chou period; and at least since T'ang times and with due consideration for the degree of relationship, the kinsmen of ranking officials enjoyed legally established advantages.[44] Thus they constituted a bureaucratic gentry within the terms of our definition.

In a somewhat different way, Western writers have applied the term "gentry" to the *shên-shih,* the sash bearers, a group that overlaps but is not identical with the bureaucratic gentry of the present inquiry. As far as we know, the designation *shên-shih* is found only in official documents of the last dynasties. The lists of *shên-shih* included natives of a particular region who were or had been officials, and in addition persons who had attained a degree either, and in the main, through examination or through purchase, but who, as yet, had not held office.

The examination system appears relatively late in Chinese history; and the classing of holders of examination degrees as a social group

---

the designations Kshatriya and Vaisya are practically unknown" (Smith, 1928: 35). The consolidation, social rise, and persistence of the Brahmins in Hindu and Muslim India is a crucial aspect of the long and complicated history of Indian society.

appears even later. But whatever the initial date, the bureaucratic orientation of the *shên-shih* is clear. As noted above, *shên-shih* status was determined not by relations to land but to government office.[f] The top echelons of the *shên-shih* hierarchy were composed of present or former officials and holders of high degrees who expected to be in office soon. Much larger was the number of lower *shên-shih*, who, holding lower degrees, would have a long wait. However, like the high-degree holders, who had not as yet entered government service, the members of the lower *shên-shih* engaged in all kinds of semi-official activities, such as the promotion of local public works, local defense and security measures, management of relief and welfare enterprises, and the collection of contributions and fees for the government.[g] And they were, of course, always ready to accept a government position, which, in addition to opening the way to greater political and social influence, was incomparably more rewarding materially.

f. In an analysis of the Chinese gentry published in 1946, H. T. Fei emphasized both its proprietary and bureaucratic aspects; but his formulation of the second point remains somewhat vague: "Not until one of the family members [of a landlord] enters the *scholar group and into officialdom* is their position in the gentry consolidated" (Fei, 1946: 11; italics mine). In 1948 in a book which he wrote prior to joining the Communist camp, Fei, defining the gentry, mentions their connections to government office *before* landownership: "The gentry may be returned officials or the relatives of officials or simply educated landowners" (Fei, 1953: 32). To fully appreciate Fei's statement it should be remembered that he sharply rejected any idea of a self-perpetuating landlordism in China. The law of inheritance dissolved even large holdings; and traditionally the major road to acquiring land was through government office (see Fei and Chang, 1945: 302). This implies that the bulk of China's landowners, and particularly the large and educated landowners, were bureaucratic landlords—that is, typical members of a bureaucratic gentry.

Eberhard in a recent definition of the Chinese gentry mentions their "landed property" first; he refers to the proprietary aspect again, and prominently, when he describes "the gentry class" as comprising "landowners, scholars and politicians *in one and the same class*," normally with "representatives of all three occupations *in one family*" (Eberhard, 1952: 16; cf. 14. italics in original.). Eberhard "feels not qualified to write about Egypt, Mesopotamia and India" (*ibid.*: 35, n. 2); and he does not consider Rüstow's concepts of the "Hellenistic-Oriental sultanate" and of the bureaucratic state slavery of the later Roman empire (Rüstow, OG, II: 169, 187). Lacking crucial tools for a comparative study of Oriental government and property, he remains unaware of the peculiar character (and strength) of the former and of the peculiar character (and weaknesses) of the latter.

g. Chang (GI, Pt. II). A number of these tasks, such as construction and repair of local roads, irrigation canals, and river dikes and the collection of contributions and fees for the government, belong to the intermediate type of enterprises, which in hydraulic society are sometimes handled by the bureaucracy, sometimes by private persons (cf. Wittfogel, 1931: 413 ff., 445 ff.). These private persons are mostly members of the bureaucratic ruling class, and their work assumes a semi-official character when it is backed by government authority for the collection of funds and for the mobilization of people.

The average ranking civil official may have derived about 1700 taels from his office.[h] The average member of the lower *shên-shih* probably had an annual income in the neighborhood of 200 taels from "gentry services."

For some hydraulic societies our evidence on the existence of a bureaucratic gentry is merely suggestive; for others it is conclusive. But even where documentation is scanty, the presence of privileged members of the ruling house and of a similarly, if less conspicuously, privileged bureaucratic gentry seems indicated. The ranking officials were eager to share the advantages of their positions with their relatives. And within the range of their power they certainly did so.

iii. THE RELATIVES OF CIVIL UNDERLINGS AND RANK-AND-FILE SOLDIERS

AND then there are the relatives of the civil underlings and rank-and-file soldiers. About the day-to-day life of this numerous group we know little. In the 17th century in China a bureaucratic racketeer, Li San, lived splendidly because he was able to cash in on his own and his father's and grandfather's experience as government clerks.[45] His success, although short-lived and exceptional, underlines the benefits that intelligent and ambitious relatives of civil underlings could derive from their position.

The families of professional soldiers constituted a more or less analogous group. Some of their problems are indicated in Hammurabi's Code,[46] and a comparative study of the Ptolemaic cleruchs and the peasant soldiers of the Byzantine *themes* would probably reveal similar conditions.

For the most part, the relatives of these civil and military underlings were as modestly situated economically as the bulk of the artisans and peasants. But politically and socially they shared the ambivalent prestige of their serving family members. The social position, which the father, wife, or son of a policeman enjoys in a police

h. According to Dr. Chang, at the close of the 19th century the "lower" *shên-shih* group numbered about 1,250,000 persons; and it derived about 94 million taels annually from "gentry services" (see Chang, GI, Pt. II). Dr. Chang estimates the total annual income of the lower *shên-shih* as 239 million taels (55 million from rent, 40 million from various private enterprises, 50 million from professional services—mainly teaching—and 94 million from "gentry services") and that of the upper *shên-shih* as 365.5 million taels (165 million from rent, 81 million from private enterprises, 91 million from office, 5 million from professional services, and 21 million from "gentry services") (Chang, GI, Pt. II). This suggests an income of 192 taels for the average member of the lower *shên-shih* as against an income of over 1800 taels for an average member of the upper *shên-shih*.

state, gives some indication of the place occupied by the relatives of underlings in an Orientally despotic state.

b. Attachment Based on Semi-, Quasi-, or Pre-official Status

NOT all relatives of the men of the apparatus share to the same degree the social privileges of their officiating kinsmen. Relative closeness to the bureaucratic activists and the peculiarities of the prevailing kinship system define the beneficiaries' specific position within the ruling class. But whatever the variations, this position, other conditions being equal, derives from the prominence that the apparatus state gives its functionaries.

In a different way this is true also for groups that have a semi-, quasi-, or pre-official status. Although they are not properly officials, members of such groups work for the government as economic agents or they are granted official or quasi-official status because as functionaries of the dominant religion they magically bolster the security of the regime.

i. SECULAR SEMI-OFFICIALS (COMMERCIAL AND FISCAL AGENTS)

PERSONS who spend all or most of their time serving the government as economic agents (*damkar, setthi*) are sometimes included among the officials. In this case their status need not be argued. Often, however, commercial agents are not so listed; and fiscal agents (tax farmers) are rarely if ever considered part of the bureaucratic hierarchy. But although these men are denied official rank, they are recognized as servants of the government. In this capacity they are supported and given authority, sometimes even coercive authority, and to compensate them for their services they are granted a fee or commission. In Ptolemaic Egypt tax farmers were granted a fee of 5 per cent, and later 10 per cent; [47] in Byzantium of one per cent, 2.5 per cent, or 5 per cent; [48] in Muslim India up to 10 per cent.[49] In Ottoman Egypt they had assigned to them, in addition to cash income, about 10 per cent of all cultivable village land, the so-called *waṣiya*.[50]

To be sure, commercial agents and tax farmers might succeed in gathering and keeping more than the prescribed quota. But this tendency, which was vigorously combated by strong rulers, does not distinguish the economic agents from the commercial or fiscal officials, who were equally eager to gather and keep more than they should.

The commercial and fiscal agents were private entrepreneurs in that both used private means and, in some part, privately hired employees. But in acting for the government they enjoyed the advantages of government authority, and when necessary they could mobilize government personnel to impose their will. The population respected and feared them, not as private individuals but as extensions of government power.

If these persons were officials or members of the bureaucratic gentry, who sought to increase their wealth through semi-official operations, their bureaucratic position was established *a priori*. In any event, the government-based character of their functions made them semi-officials and placed them in, although often at the periphery of, the ruling class.

ii. RELIGIOUS QUASI-OFFICIALS (FUNCTIONARIES OF THE DOMINANT RELIGION)

IN a previous chapter we examined the methods by which the agro-despotic state closely attached to itself the dominant religion and its functionaries. In China and in the earlier period of Pharaonic Egypt government officials performed many of the major tasks of the dominant cult. In other Oriental civilizations the government appointed the priests of the dominant religion and from the standpoint of administration treated them like secular officials *(Staatsbeamte)*.[51]

The religious functionaries of Islam lived for the most part on endowments *(waqfs)* that were controlled directly or indirectly by the government.[52] In this respect they were more closely attached to the state than were the Brahmins of Hindu India, who only on occasion received land grants. In both cases, however, the state enforced the sacred law of the dominant religion, which bestowed a quasi-official position of authority on the religious functionary.

To be sure, any religious functionary enjoys a special kind of awe among the believers; but his prestige may be weakened or enhanced by the over-all setting in which he operates. The priest of a secondary and underprivileged creed may have difficulty in asserting his authority even among his own followers, who are constantly exposed to the disparaging value judgments of an unfriendly environment. The priest of a dominant creed is not faced with such difficulties. On the contrary. The respect of the rulers enhances his prestige; and the more so, the stronger the government happens to be. Under hydraulic despotism the functionaries of the dominant religion, even where they are not appointed officials, enjoy on the social level a quasi-official status.

iii. PERSONS OCCUPYING A PRE-OFFICIAL STATUS (TRAINEES AND DEGREE-HOLDING CANDIDATES FOR OFFICE)

THE intricacies of ideology and script, and most hydraulic civilizations above the tribal level had a script, tended to make the training for office a drawn-out affair, and those who participated in it often constituted a special group. If they were accepted in official "colleges" or "universities," they were carefully selected and restricted in number. This was the situation in Aztec Mexico and Byzantium, under the Mamluks in Ottoman Turkey and during certain periods of Chinese history such as Han.

Where the students were educated in temples and/or by priests, their training was not specifically bureaucratic but their number was similarly restricted. Where competitive examinations were open to the public generally, as was the case under the later Chinese dynasties, the students were numerous, and the lower degree-holders many. Exposed to a long and intensive process of indoctrination, the students may well have been even more sensitive to the benefits and eminence of the bureaucratic life than the office-holders. Bureaucratic class consciousness could be further consolidated if degree-holders were permitted to carry out certain semi-official functions. The members of the Chinese *shên-shih,* who held examination degrees but had not yet attained office, are a classical example of a pre-bureaucratic group.

iv. A COMPARATIVE NOTE (PROFESSIONAL IDEOLOGISTS IN THE USSR)

IN hydraulic society the rulers rarely manipulated the sacred doctrine, even if they were its high priests. In the Soviet Union the Orthodox Church, although still tolerated, is no longer a dominant creed; and when the openly expressed Soviet designs materialize, the Church will be replaced altogether by the secular state doctrine. The standard bearers of this doctrine are the masters of the apparatus state; they—and they alone—interpret and change it. The country's top-ranking ideologists are the top-ranking members of the ruling bureaucracy; and the great bulk of all professional intellectuals are, like them, government officials.

A few outstanding artists and writers may produce their works without holding office. But they follow state directives, they execute state orders, they are paid as are high officials; and since they serve

the state well and without reservation, they enjoy similar prerogatives. For all practical purposes, they have a quasi-official status.

Thus, while in hydraulic society the quasi-official ideological
(religious) functionaries are many and relatively free insofar as
doctrine is concerned, in the USSR the quasi-official intellectuals are
few and their freedom in matters of doctrine is nil. The rulers of
the total managerial state have nationalized the ideology as well as
the ideologists.

c. Subdivided, but Still an Entity

OUR survey reveals that even under the simplest conditions the
ruling class in hydraulic society is divided into several subsections.
Under more differentiated conditions it tends to be a fairly complex
entity. How conscious of the peculiarity and superiority of their class
position are the members of the various subsections?

Class consciousness is probably a less general—and certainly a less
dynamic—factor than Marxism would have us believe. But there
can be little doubt that the masters of hydraulic society, who enjoyed extraordinary privileges of power, revenue, and status, formed
one of the most class-conscious groups in the history of mankind.

To be sure, their class-consciousness did not always express itself
in images which underlined their greatness as ranking officials. The
serving men of Ottoman Turkey were proud to be the "slaves" of
their sultan. The glory of the ruling class, as they saw it, rested upon
its autocratic ruler. The political ideologists of Hindu India stressed
the prominence of the king as the supreme protector of the dominant
religion. The glory of the ruling class, as they saw it, rested upon its
priestly advisors. The Confucian philosophers paid homage to their
absolute sovereign; but they extolled the gentleman-scholar, who,
because of his training, was likely to become a gentleman-bureaucrat.
The glory of the ruling class, as they saw it, rested upon its properly
educated officials.

Confucianism presents the sociopolitical aspect of the matter with
unusual clarity. By designating the gentleman-scholar as *chün-tzŭ*,
Confucius emphasized the political quality of his ideal man. The
chün-tzŭ was thoroughly versed in the cultural tradition of the
hereditary ("noble") officialdom, but his qualifications had an
essentially political intent. The word *chün-tzŭ* originally connoted
"a ruler," "a man engaged in the business of ruling." After being
properly trained, the *chün-tzŭ* was ready to be "used" as a government official.[53] He was ready to rule the "little men," the mass of the
population.

The dichotomy between the two groups finds expression in the Chinese terms *shih* and *min*. The *shih* are those individuals who, by their training in ethical, military, and ceremonial matters, are qualified to serve their ruler and who do so when this is possible. The *min* are "the people," who are ruled by the sovereign and the officiating members of the *shih*.[i] The values placed on civil and military qualifications have varied over time.[j] But the glorification of the *shih* endured until the end of the imperial era.

Whatever the nomenclature, the *shih-min* distinction operates in all hydraulic societies. In all of them the potential and the actual rulers are deeply aware of their superiority to, and difference from, the mass of the ruled—the commoners, the "people."

D. THE RULED

1. PROPERTY-BASED SUBSECTIONS OF COMMONERS

BELOW the rulers spreads the vast world of the commoners. Its members share a negative quality: none participates in the affairs of the state apparatus. They also share a positive quality: none are slaves.

Chinese tradition distinguishes three main groups of commoners: peasants, artisans, and merchants. The sequence reflects the order of their appearance on the historical scene; but it is doubtful whether this was in the minds of those who listed them so. More likely they were concerned with relative economic importance, agriculture being the root (*pên*) and handicraft and commerce the branches (*mo*) of their agrarian civilization.[a]

i. The *Classic of History* frequently refers to the officials as *shih* (Legge, CC, III: 275, 367, 369, 626), as also do the Odes (*ibid.*, IV: 360, 409, 429 ff., 569). More narrowly the term *shih* connotes lower ranking officials (cf. *ibid.*, I: 401). As persons of proper training, the *shih* are frequently mentioned, particularly in the Confucian writings (cf. *ibid.*, I: 168, 274, 276). The ultimate test of their education is revealed in government service (*ibid.*, I: 271 ff., 339). To be sure, the friendship of a *shih* should be sought even when he is not in office (*ibid.*, I: 297).

Frequently the *shih* are juxtaposed to the *min*. The former serve elegantly at the royal ancestral temple (*ibid.*, IV: 569) or the court, while the latter look on and admire them (*ibid.*, IV: 409 ff.). Taken together, the *shih* and the *min* constitute the whole population. In periods of unrest both groups suffer (*ibid.*, IV: 560).

j. Confucius was primarily interested in the civil qualifications of the *shih;* and this obviously modified an earlier tradition (see Legge, CC, I: *passim;* cf. Wittfogel, 1935: 49, n. 3).

a. The Chinese classification which places the *shih* before the peasants, artisans, and merchants does not recognize a class of persons whose position rests essentially on landownership.

The root and the branches correspond to two basic forms of property: immobile and mobile. In our survey of the complexity patterns of property we discussed the rise, development, and social position of the three just-mentioned groups in considerable detail; [1] and there is no need to recapitulate our conclusions here. However, to round out the inquiry, we shall at this point examine the position of the most lowly social group: the slaves. Slaves played only a very limited role in hydraulic society. Why?

2. SLAVES

SOIL, water, and plants are manipulated with great care by persons who profit personally from their labors: peasant members of village communities, owner-cultivators, and tenant farmers. But no such care can be expected from full slaves—that is, from persons, who, in addition to being personally unfree, possess neither family nor property. This is true for agrarian conditions generally, and it is especially true for areas where the agronomy is largely determined by irrigation farming.

In irrigation-based hydraulic agriculture slave labor was little employed. Occasionally when easy access to slave labor suggested its use in farming (or in handicraft), such labor remained an auxiliary force. To assure the necessary care the slaves were usually given a share in what they produced, and at times they could marry.

The costs of supervision inhibited the use of great numbers of slaves in the most typical of all public works in hydraulic society: the construction and maintenance of canals, embankments, roads, and walls. It was only in spatially restricted enterprises, such as mines and quarries, the building of palaces and temples, and the transport of bulky objects that slave labor could be easily supervised and therefore advantageously employed.[2]

This explains why state slaves are found primarily at the court, in government offices, workshops, and mines, and in special types of building activities. It explains why privately owned slaves were essentially employed domestically and by wealthy persons, who could afford the luxury of lavish consumption.[3] It explains why occasional attempts to use slaves in subtler tasks compelled their public and private masters to provide conspicuous incentives and to replace full slavery by semislavery.

A victorious war might, of course, produce a sizable slave reservoir. And while the conquerors of agricultural regions usually hastened to assign the bulk of their peasant captives to farming, the occupation in which they would best profit their new masters, some might be kept as government slaves or sold to private persons.

The Aztecs, who frequently fought their neighbors, had little use for slave labor in their communally organized *calpulli* villages. But as sacrifices at the great state ceremonials many captives served the purposes of spectacular terror, a major device for keeping the crudely coordinated Mexican empire united.

In ancient Mesopotamia warfare between the independent states was also an important source of slaves; and in Babylonia slaves were used to some extent in agriculture and handicrafts. But here, too, slave labor remained a secondary feature; and usually it was employed under conditions of semislavery: the slaves could acquire property and marry.[4] In Pharaonic Egypt slavery seems to have assumed some importance only in the New Kingdom, when major wars and conquest flooded the country with unfree foreign labor.[5]

After examining the history of ancient Mesopotamia and Egypt in their entirety, Westermann finds that in these civilizations slave labor was predominantly domestic;[6] and Meyer, in his evaluation of Near Eastern slavery, asserts that "scarcely anywhere in the Orient did slavery play a major economic role."[7] Mendelsohn's recent study on slavery in the ancient Orient confirms the earlier findings. Whatever slave labor was used in agriculture "was of no great weight. On the whole, slaves were used primarily in domestic service."[8]

Studies of other Oriental countries reach the same conclusions. There were many slaves in India, China, and the Islamic world, but in none of these large civilizations did slave labor dominate agriculture or handicraft.[b]

Some slaves and freedmen were raised to positions of prominence by Oriental despots, and others were given important supervisory tasks by private slave owners. But their careers were not representative of the conditions of their group. While the domestic slaves of hydraulic society in their majority were not chattel slaves,[9] they were personally unfree and they remained at the mercy of their masters. In the case of the female slaves it was usually taken for granted that their masters had access to them.

b. For India, see C. A. F. Rhys-Davids, 1922: 205; Fick, 1920: 306 ff. Appadorai (1936, I: 317 ff.) does not correlate his findings on the use of slaves in late Hindu South India with his analysis of agriculture and industry. But his description of these two branches of economy imply what Dr. Rhys-Davids has explicitly noted for Buddhist India. In both fields slave labor was insignificant (C. A. F. Rhys-Davids, 1922: 205). For Chinese society in general, see Wittfogel, 1931: 393 ff.; for the Han period, see Wilbur, 1943: 174 ff., 195 ff. For Abbassid society, see Mez, 1922: 152 ff.; for pre-Mongol Persia, see Spuler, 1952: 439 ff.

In a society that polarized total authority and total submission individuals who lacked every personal freedom were not to be envied.
Their position was little improved by the fact that in certain hydraulic civilizations and in wealthy families they were, at times,
numerous.

E. MODIFICATIONS OF CLASS STRUCTURE THAT OCCUR IN CONQUEST SOCIETIES

SLAVERY affects the bottom rung of Oriental society, conquest the
top. Indeed, conquest may change the traditional structure of a
conquered area so greatly that we are justified in designating the
institutional result as a conquest society.[1] The sociology of conquest
has essentially stressed the relation of conquest to the beginnings of
stratified societies (primary conquest in our terms); and this process,
although not too fully recorded, certainly deserves attention. But
conquest may further differentiate already stratified societies (secondary conquest in our terms); and this process, which is more fully
recorded and which generally involves more recent developments,
deserves particular attention.

1. CONQUEST INVOLVING THE FORMATION OF STRATIFIED SOCIETIES (PRIMARY CONQUEST)

WAR between independent political commonwealths is as old as
human life. But devices for keeping a given population permanently
subdued developed only when permanent subjection was both rewarding and feasible. Was this possibility exploited first and in all
cases by conquerors? Or did the increasing facilities of production
first lead to the emergence of a native upper group, a tribal nobility
or a professional officialdom?

Lowie, who considers "internal conditions" sufficient "to create
hereditary or approximately hereditary classes," [2] cautiously evaluates
the possible range of internal differentiation and conquest by stating
that the two factors "need not be mutually exclusive." [3]

An essentially endogenous development has been documented in
a number of cases,[4] but there seems to be no question that in other
cases conquest created a conspicuous social stratification and very
often intensified and advanced incipient endogenous differentiation. Conquest of this kind—primary conquest—apparently occurred
throughout the hydraulic world, in ancient Greece and Rome, in
Japan, and in Medieval Europe. It is a general and not a specific
factor, and therefore it cannot be held responsible for the diverse

patterns of power, property, and class, which characterized these civilizations.[a]

2. CONQUEST INVOLVING THE FURTHER DIFFERENTIATION OF STRATIFIED SOCIETIES (SECONDARY CONQUEST)

SECONDARY conquest does not always lead to the establishment of a conquest society. The bulk of all members of the conquering group may remain in their homeland; and their leaders may be satisfied to exercise remote control either by placing their own nationals directly over those they have subjugated, or by utilizing native collaborators, or by establishing strategically placed garrisons. Rule by satraps, *curacas*, or *rājas* is usually an end product of military conquest; and it involves significant horizontal gradations of power. But the resulting institutional order is not a conquest society in the sense of the present inquiry.

I speak of a conquest society only when the conquerors take up residence in the lands they have seized, when they neither liquidate nor expel the native population, and when they are sufficiently numerous to establish a cohesive and distinct alien ruling body apart from, and above, their new subjects.

a. For the history of the relation of conquest to the origin of class structure, see Rüstow, OG, I: 84 ff. The phenomenon has been systematically discussed from a sociological standpoint by Gumplowicz (1905: 190 ff., 195 ff.) and Oppenheimer (1919: 32 ff.), both of whom promoted the thesis that class differentiation is generally initiated by conquest. This thesis has been convincingly challenged by the anthropologists MacLeod (1924: *passim*) and Lowie (1927: 33 ff.). Without consideration for their arguments, Rüstow (OG, I: 66 ff., 74 ff., 95 ff.) accepts in the main the earlier conquest thesis; but he admits the possibility of social differentiations resulting from internal and peaceful development (OG, I: 88 ff., 90 ff.), and he recognizes that the conquest-created societies are diversely structured. Although he suggests that these societies be called "'medieval' or 'feudal' in the widest sense" (OG, I: 79), he notes that the term "feudal" in its "political and narrower meaning" fits essentially Medieval Europe (OG, I: 312), that in ancient Rome a big-peasant aristocracy formed the dominant class (OG, II: 166), and that in Egypt from the dawn of history a planned economy doomed the mass of the population to "state slavery" (OG, II: 187).

In view of this, it is unfortunate that Eberhard, who "accepts the theory of A. Rüstow of the power factor, which creates feudal societies by superstratification" (Eberhard, 1952: 3) and who considers Rüstow's ideas "the so far most complete theory on the origin of feudalism" (*ibid.*) fails to familiarize his readers with the structural diversity of Rüstow's feudal societies. Eberhard sees "no principal difference between Oriental and Western feudalism" (*ibid.*: 2). But we have only to confront Eberhard's feudal system "based essentially on land which the vassal held as a fief" (*ibid.*: 1) with the Oriental reality and Rüstow's concept of Egypt's "spiritual feudalism" with its ruling priesthood and planned state slavery (OG, II: 17, 31, 187) to realize the inadequacy of Eberhard's view both from the standpoint of institutional facts and from that of his alleged authority, Dr. Rüstow.

Incipient conquest societies have emerged as the result of primary conquests. Full-fledged conquest societies appeared in many parts of the world and under a variety of circumstances. Their rise was inevitably stimulated by the attractiveness of the target country and by the military strength and mobility of the conquerors. Agricultural civilizations (and particularly "wealthy" hydraulic economies) were highly desirable objectives; and until modern times powerful nomadic tribes (especially pastoralists who could ride and use the saddle and stirrup) have been optimally successful in seizing them.[5]

3. CLASS MODIFICATIONS IN HYDRAULIC CONQUEST DYNASTIES

a. The Chinese Did Not Always Absorb Their Conquerors

GREAT and culturally persistent peoples, such as the Chinese, have pointed to the speed with which their "barbarian" conquerors adopted many features of their way of life. Easy-going generalizations from this cultural fact originated the widespread legend that the Chinese "always" absorbed their conquerors. However, reality contradicts this legend. Instead of relinquishing their privileges of power, prestige, and revenue the conquerors invariably sought to maintain them by all manner of political, military, and legal devices. And where they found it desirable to do so they also preserved particular features of their own cultural tradition.

Comparative analysis shows that none of the four major conquest dynasties of China confirms the myth of absorption, not even the last. The Manchus had already adopted many Chinese customs prior to the conquest;[6] but in their case, as in the others, basic differences in political and social status were maintained to the end.[b]

b. Devices for Preserving the Conquerors' Hegemony

THE reasons for this are easily understood. The "barbarian" conquerors depended for many details of civil administration on native experts and bureaucrats. But they protected their political, social, and economic hegemony by placing their own nationals above the indigenous officialdom, by concentrating their tribal soldiers in special cadres, camps, *ordus* (hordes), or banners, by making intermarriage with the subdued population difficult or impossible, and

b. Under conditions of conquest, cultural change is closely interlinked with political change. Our Chinese findings are therefore suggestive for conquest societies in general: "full cultural amalgamation obviously occurred only when the disappearance of the social divide permitted the cultural divide to disappear also—that is, after the period of conquest had come to an end" (Wittfogel, 1949: 15).

by preserving their tribal religion even when, for purposes of prestige, the ruler and his lieutenants performed the great indigenous ceremonies.[c]

The Arab warriors, who were the military mainstay of the Umayyad dynasty, lost their social prominence when that dynasty collapsed,[d] just as in China the Ch'i-tan, Jurchen, Mongols, and Manchus lost their privileged position when their respective conquest dynasties (Liao, Chin, Yüan, and Ch'ing) came to an end.

c. Duplications of Class

THUS conquest societies tend to involve a curious duplication of social strata. As a rule, an exogenous upper class (nobility) is superimposed upon a native bureaucracy; and tribal warriors become a distinguished stratum of plebeian underlings in the political hierarchy. The newly organized banners, camps, or *ordus* replace the former cadre troops, and definitely outrank the native troops which the regime may decide to maintain.

F. MANY SOCIAL ANTAGONISMS BUT LITTLE CLASS STRUGGLE

FOR obvious reasons the representatives of the despotic state are significant in any study of class structure; and this not because the men of the apparatus form the bulk of the population—which they certainly do not—but because state power, more than any other factor, shapes the fate of both the members of the ruling class and the commoners. This becomes crystal clear when we consider the three major types of social antagonisms that arise in hydraulic society: antagonisms between the members of different subsections of commoners, antagonisms between the commoners and the state, and antagonisms between the members of the various subsections of the ruling complex.

1. SOCIAL ANTAGONISM AND CLASS STRUGGLE

SOCIAL antagonism is not identical with class struggle. A conflict may be considered social when it involves members of different social groups and when it arises essentially out of the social position of those concerned. But a social conflict which is limited to a few

c. This, for instance, happened in the case of the Manchus, whose emperors performed the traditional Chinese sacrifices, while within the privacy of the palace they continued to worship their tribal gods (Wittfogel, 1949: 14).

d. Wellhausen, 1927: 557. The Umayyads did not conquer the Near East, but they consolidated the conquests accomplished under the first caliphs.

persons cannot reasonably be called a class struggle. The term "class" connotes a group—and usually a relatively large group—of socially homogeneous individuals; and a social conflict assumes the character of a class conflict only when those who participate in it represent a recognizable and representative fraction of such a group.

Class struggle involves mass action. Such a struggle may reach a point where it challenges existing social and political conditions. Marx, who perhaps more than any other social scientist of the 19th century studied classes, stressed this aspect of the matter by saying that "every class struggle is a political struggle." [1]

2. PARALYSIS OF CLASS STRUGGLE BY TOTAL POWER

THE meaning of all this for an understanding of hydraulic society is far-reaching. An agrarian despotism which is strong enough to prevent independent political organization does not need to tolerate mass action as a means of settling social conflicts. The men of the apparatus easily control the secular and religious variants of the Beggars' Democracy. They are suspicious of all rallies of socially dissatisfied persons. And usually they hasten to break up incipient mass movements.

During the middle period of the Ch'ing dynasty, in 1746, some Fukienese tenants joined together in requesting an adjustment of their rents. Apparently this was nothing but an argument between two groups of private persons, yet the local officials quickly intervened, arrested, and punished the leaders.[2] A subsequent edict blamed the provincial officials for the fact that "stupid people assemble and violate the law." [3]

A Han discussion of state and private enterprise in the manufacture of salt and iron objected to private businesses that employed more than a thousand workers, since such an accumulation of manpower might provide opportunities for treacherous action.[4] At the close of the imperial period an edict noted emphatically that there had "always been a law of this dynasty forbidding the establishment of societies and associations of any sort whatsoever." [5] The statement is significant both for its hostility to popular associations and for its lack of concern for the existing craft and trade guilds. Obviously the government did not count these organizations among the politically relevant societies and associations.

Such attitudes precluded political mass action (class struggle) as a legitimate form of social protest. And they did so even in the ruling class. Conflicts between members of different subsections of this class were often politically colored in that they involved antagonistic claims to power-based privileges; but they rarely led to open and political mass action. The history of hydraulic society suggests that class struggle, far from being a chronic disease of all mankind, is the luxury of multicentered and open societies.

G. ANTAGONISM BETWEEN MEMBERS OF DIFFERENT SUBSECTIONS OF COMMONERS

IN simple hydraulic societies peasants constitute almost the whole of the "ruled," and they continue to be the most numerous subsection of commoners in semicomplex and complex hydraulic societies. How much opportunity is there for social antagonism between them and other commoners?

Poor (and tenant) farmers may clash with rich (landowning and well-to-do) farmers, with traders, or with money lenders. However, the possibility of such frictions is minimal in the regulated village communities that prevail in the majority of all hydraulic societies. For in these communities tenancy is either a nonexistent or a marginal issue; and the economic differences between the similarly situated peasant households are slight. Moreover, the limited economic flexibility of the average community member restricts the extent to which he may deal—and clash—with nonpeasant commoners: artisans, traders, and/or money lenders.[a]

a. W. C. Smith in his article "Lower-class Uprisings in the Mughal Empire" says nothing about social conflicts of this inter-commoner type. Several times he mentions "landlords" as involved in class struggles with peasants. But in one instance he only surmises the existence of such persons (1946: 28); in others he uses the word "landlords" as an equivalent for zamīndārs (ibid.: 27, 30). Until the 18th century the zamīndārs were essentially tributary rājas (Moreland, 1929: 279); and the "nobility" which, according to Smith, seized "approximately one-third of the country's agricultural produce" did so "in the form of what is called 'taxes' or 'revenue'" (1946: 23). That is, these "nobles" were actually government functionaries who lived on government revenue. This pattern is altogether different from the system of land tenure of feudal Europe; and it is regrettable that Smith, who was aware of this (1946a: 308), nevertheless designated the Indian conditions as "feudalism" (ibid.).

Peasants apparently participated in rebellions of various kinds, but those that can be clearly recognized as involving secular issues seem mostly to have arisen from fiscal conflicts. As may be expected in a country dominated by rulers of an alien creed, religious conflicts frequently merged with secular ones; and in many cases the former probably gave voice or increased intensity to the latter (see Smith, 1946: 27 ff.). But we have no reason to doubt that certain conflicts were genuinely—or primarily—religious. In 1672 members of a small sect clashed with the authorities, defeated the local police and several contingents of regular troops, and temporarily controlled the city of Narnāwl. Smith, who views this event as a "desperate class struggle" (ibid.: 29), fails to mention any secular issue which would justify such a classification.

And then there were struggles that essentially concerned national or territorial issues. The Pathan rebellion, which Smith designates as "perhaps the most formidable

Rural conflicts increased as private landownership increased. In Tsarist Russia large peasant uprisings flared up in the 18th century when the *pomeshchiki* became the owners of their former service land and when the peasants, encouraged by rumors of all kinds, hoped also to become the owners of the land they were tilling.[1] The reform of the *pomeshchik* land in 1762 was followed by serious peasant disturbances,[2] which reached their climax in the great rebellion led by Pugachev (1772–75).[3]

Conflicts arising out of the usurious lending of grain or money and out of oppressive tenancy are well documented for Ptolemaic and Roman Egypt, for traditional China, and, of course, for many hydraulic societies in transition.

Recent studies have often concentrated on these property-based conflicts and as a consequence have paid little attention to the extraordinary forces of bureaucratic power and property that underlie and complicate the tensions between various groups of wealthy and poor commoners. But however much such studies have misunderstood the character of hydraulic society, they provide us with valuable data on conflicts arising from property; and they relieve us of the need to repeat here what their authors have industriously, if one-sidedly, said on this subject.

The rise of private property and enterprise in handicraft and commerce created conditions that resulted in social conflicts of many kinds among urban commoners. In Medieval Europe such conflicts were fought out with great vigor. Not infrequently the social movements assumed the proportions of a mass (and class) struggle, which in some towns compelled the merchants to share political leadership with the artisans and which in others assured the hegemony of the craft guilds.[4]

The contrast with the hydraulic world is striking. Although the guilds of hydraulic society have a much longer history than their Western counterparts, they rarely, if ever, engaged in militant and political activities of comparable scope.[b]

---

people's movement" of the Mogul period was the prolonged and pathetic endeavor of proud border tribesmen to resist "the attempt to impose . . . [on them] the rule of the Mughal State" (*ibid.*: 33, 34). And in the district of Kishtwar it was obviously a semi-independent group of local rulers that combated the Moguls' infringement upon them. The protagonists of the Kishtwar rebellion, local *zamīndārs,* defended the cause of their prince, who eventually was reinstated. The fact that the "lower classes" also "fought and suffered" and that the *ryots* and inhabitants of nearby Kashmir "complained" about the harshness of the Mogul commander (*ibid.*: 27) is scarcely a reason for including this affair among the "lower-class uprisings" of the period.

b. Cf. above, Chap. 4. The Kārimī merchants of Mamluk Egypt accumulated great fortunes in the international spice trade and as bankers; and their commerce with

H. THE "PEOPLE" VERSUS THE
MEN OF THE APPARATUS

THE disproportion between the intensity of social antagonism and the frequency of class struggle becomes particularly striking when we view the relations between the two main classes of hydraulic society: the "people" and the men of the apparatus. In the normal course of events the commoners suffer periodically from the demands made on them by representatives of the despotic state. Generally those who are oppressed or exploited do not dare to resist openly; and frequently they do not even dare to resist covertly. The Oriental subject's proverbial eagerness to avoid any contact at all with the feared organs of government underlines his acceptance of defeat in a contest that he never dares to enter.

Avoidance, however, is not always possible. The commoner may not lay his complaints before a judge or magistrate; but often he must render services and usually he must pay a tax. He may bitterly resent both demands, and being unable to protect himself by constitutional means, he may feign compliance. But behind this facade he will combat the men of the apparatus with all the weapons of indirect and passive resistance at his command.

When he performs his corvée labor, he will work as slowly as the overseer's control (or the stick or whip) permits.[1] When he renders his tax, he will seek to conceal certain of his assets. And not infrequently he will hand over his quota only after being severely beaten. Writers in Pharaonic Egypt have satirized this aspect of the battle of the land tax;[2] and a 19th-century account shows the Egyptian peasant's attitude in these matters to be unchanged: "All the felláheen are proud of the stripes they receive for withholding their contributions, and are often heard to boast of the number of blows which were inflicted upon them before they would give up their money."[a]

When taxation becomes unusually burdensome, the peasant may reduce his cultivated acreage,[3] and when the heavy demands continue, he may become a fiscal fugitive,[b] abandoning his fields alto-

---

such countries as Yemen may occasionally have influenced the foreign policy of the Mamluk government, which derived great revenues from it. But their economic importance notwithstanding, the Kārimī merchants failed to attain an independent political position comparable to that of the guild merchants of feudal Europe. See Fischel, 1937: 72 ff., 76 ff., 80 ff.; cf. Becker, IS, I: 186, 214.

a. Lane, 1898: 143 ff. Lane adds: "Ammianus Marcellinus gives precisely the same character to the Egyptians of his time." Ammianus lived in the 4th century A.D.

b. The founder of the Mogul Dynasty, Bābur, was infuriated by the Indian peasants,

gether. He may wander in despair, look for work elsewhere, or turn bandit or rebel.[c]

As stated above, open conflicts between peasants and government were rare where land tenure was regulated; and even in imperial China they assumed major proportions mainly during periods of disintegration which initiated the collapse of a dynasty.

Conflicts between urban commoners (or groups of commoners) and the government occurred in a different context. They frequently centered around tax issues; but the administrative (and garrison) character of most hydraulic towns generally prevented the discontented townspeople from resorting to armed rebellion. The individual merchants or artisans defended themselves as well as they could against restrictive regulations and fiscal exploitation; and the guilds of craftsmen and traders, headed by government-appointed or government-supervised functionaries, not infrequently appealed to the authorities for the adjustment of excessive demands At times artisans ceased to work and merchants closed their shops; [d] and occasionally a crowd might start a riot.[d] Government officials who

---

who, typical fiscal refugees, hid in the woods and "trusting to their inaccessible situation, often continue in a state of revolt, refusing to pay their taxes" (see Bābur, 1921: 208).

c. Chinese historiography relates many such cases (cf. Wittfogel and Fêng, 1949: 420). An incident that occurred in the Ming dynasty is illuminating in several respects. Between 1436 and 1448 a tenant, Têng Mao-ch'i, became a person of influence among his fellow villagers, whom he is said to have gotten to "work for him." His prestige was greatly enhanced through his leadership in a movement that urged the tenants not to make the customary gift to their landlords when they paid their rent. The landlords approached the local magistrate, and it may well be that some of them were members of the court or the officialdom, since in Ming days these groups were extremely successful in appropriating peasant land. In any case, the magistrate dispatched armed forces; but Têng defeated them with a rebel army, which eventually numbered several tens of thousands. Soon his power spread over twenty counties, and he received further assistance from people who escaped from the "unbearable" oppression of a "greedy and cruel" official. Subsequent developments revealed excessive corvée labor as a major reason for their discontent. After several military successes the rebels were defeated; and Têng, together with some of his followers, was beheaded (Ming Shih 165.5a–b). An episode in the middle of the fight characterizes both the strength of the government and the limited objectives of the revolt. Negotiating with a courageous official, the rebels are reported to have asked only that their lives be spared and that they be exempted from labor service "for three years." If these conditions were granted, they would lay down their arms and again be "good people" (Ming Shih 165.5b). At the close of the dynasty the government would probably have been more ready to compromise and the rebels less eager to submit. During the last phase of the Ming period rebels appeared everywhere; and the many local conflicts were merged in the final battle for the overthrow of the dynasty.

d. For Mamluk Egypt cf. Poliak, 1934: 267 ff. The members of the Indian sect who, in 1672, started an uprising are said to have been "goldsmiths, carpenters, sweepers, tanners, and other ignoble beings" (commoners?). Some apparently engaged in agri-

were charged with maintaining the rulers' rationality minimum, were expected to heed such warnings. And indeed they often did. But they were most ready to do so where private, and not state, business was involved,[5] and any sporadic moderation on their part did not keep them from exerting their authority fully and coercively in matters of consequence—for instance, over artisans and laborers who rendered corvée labor [6] or over particular persons whose wealth they wished to syphon off.

In the great majority of all cases the artisan or merchant who aroused the greed of a ranking official or underling maneuvered prudently. Whenever he could he paid his way out of his impasse. Obviously, an accommodating lie or a well-placed bribe are not exactly weapons in a war of liberation. And the unending small conflicts between the bureaucratic hunter and his petty-bourgeois or capitalist game made it unmistakably clear that in this chase the urban commoners might survive, but they could not win.

Traditional Chinese statecraft gave more leeway to private property than did the absolutist regimes of most other hydraulic civilizations; but under its shadow capitalist enterprise was as cagey as elsewhere. An edict of the short-lived reform government of 1898 puts the blame for this fact on the officials, particularly—and somewhat hypocritically—on the underlings. When a firm is in diffi-

---

culture (Elliot and Dowson, 1877: 185, 294). Smith (1946: 29) suggests that the urban sectarians were workers or poor traders: "petty traders and workers, either propertyless proletariat or men with a very small professional 'property." His second source speaks of trade "on a small scale" or, according to another translation, "their trade is on a small capital" (*ibid.*: 29 ff.). In Muslim India, as elsewhere, propertyless persons certainly participated in urban riots; but in this case the cited data point to artisans who owned their means of production rather than to proletarian elements.

Another insurrection of the period is even farther removed from being proletarian. According to Smith (*ibid.*: 25 ff.), the town of Patna was seized in 1610 "by a proletarian mob" whose leader impersonated "the popular hero Khusraw." After the success of this coup "numbers of the lower-class aligned themselves with him. These proletarians even organized a minor army from amongst themselves, which they were foolish enough to send out against the upper-class army advancing under the irate governor." This account is greatly at variance with the facts as given in Smith's own sources. The popular hero Khusraw was the emperor's oldest son, who was kept prisoner after he had made an armed attempt to seize the throne (Jahāngīr, 1909: 56–68). Khusraw had based his rebellion primarily on the support of members of the imperial army (*ibid.*: 52, 55, 58); and temporarily his chances of success had been considerable (*ibid.*: 58). It is therefore not surprising that the impostor found adherents among "a number of foot- and horsemen." These soldiers—and no "proletarian mob"— seized Patna and its fort (*ibid.*: 174); and there is no specific evidence that the "wretched creatures," who later joined the rebellion (*ibid.*: 174), were "proletarians" either. Jahāngīr applies the term "wretch" indiscriminately to rebels, including persons of the highest political and social status (*ibid.*: 55, 65, 123).

culties, "the demands and extortions of the yamen underlings are invariably so great and exorbitant that merchants become discouraged and dare not venture further afield into trade enterprise, thereby causing trade to stand immovable." [7]

The covert conflicts between state slaves and their bureaucratic masters were numerous and, generally speaking, unnoticed. Like the domestic slaves of private owners, the unfortunate bondsmen of the government tried to ease their fate by cunning and well-camouflaged devices; and like them also they were employed essentially as single individuals or in small groups and with little opportunity to revolt *en masse*.

The slave war that started in southern Mesopotamia in 869 drew its initial strength from the unusually large number of slaves employed by unusually large private enterprises [8] in the production of salt, east of Basra. The magnitude of these enterprises made them an ideal breeding ground for mass action. The revolt, which lasted some fourteen years, owed much of its temporary success to the fact that during these years the Abbassid state was shaken by civil wars between certain generals and high territorial officials and between both and the caliphate.[9]

I. SOCIAL CONFLICTS WITHIN THE RULING CLASS

EXCEPT for the peasant uprisings that occasionally, and particularly in hydraulic societies with strongly developed private landownership, challenged the authority of the officialdom, only the social conflicts within the ruling class had a definitely political quality. The military rebellions of dissenting members of the ruling family or of ambitious generals or governors against a weak monarch usually involved conflicts between persons of different grades and positions within the power hierarchy. But they occurred only sporadically and at long intervals; and when they did, they tended to evolve quickly into military tests of strength between two or more independent territories or regions.

Much more frequent, and much more difficult to discern, are the undercover conflicts that arose between ranking officials and bureaucratic underlings, between various groups of ranking officials, between officials and the bureaucratic gentry, and between ranking officials and the despot and his personal entourage, the court. These conflicts were usually concerned with political power or influence, and while most of them affected only a few individuals, some of them involved the privileges of larger groups, subsections or strata within the bureaucratic order. But although such conflicts might touch the interests of a considerable number of persons, they lacked the organized cohesiveness which characterized the great social movements of the ancient, medieval, and modern West.

1. RANKING OFFICIALS VERSUS UNDERLINGS

BROADLY speaking, the ranking officials determine the operations of their secretarial and menial underlings. But often an administrative (or fiscal or police) problem can be solved to the advantage of either the ranking officials or their underlings. Ambivalent situations of this kind are inherent in all organizations whose functions are vertically divided. But in the hydraulic setting these situations were particularly consequential because the actions of the *apparatchiki* were not checked by effective outside forces and because those involved in the conflicts disposed over the resources of a uniquely powerful state apparatus.

The ranking officials, as well as the underlings, aimed at a maximum of control over details of procedure and personnel, partly for the sake of power and partly for the sake of increasing their share of the government revenue. Status was no major issue, although the underlings, by increasing their power, also increased their social prestige. A critical examination of the Chinese government under the Manchus suggests that the underlings for some time arrogated to themselves something like 30 per cent of the government revenue.[1] Since this estimate was made by a member of the ranking officialdom,[2] it may be too high, but it indicates the dimension of the economic problem involved in the day-to-day struggle between the gentlemen-functionaries and their plebeian aides.

In this struggle the underlings could and did draw advantage from their intimate knowledge of local affairs, their familiarity with the know-how of the office, and their physical control over the ultimate execution of all administrative work. The officials could and did draw advantage from the various methods of supervision, from control over the hiring and firing of the staff personnel, and in serious cases from the power to invoke all manner of punishment.

An official Chinese statement of 1899 reveals how in the tug-of-war between the ranking officials and the underlings certain functionaries might become dependent on strategically placed scribes: "In all matters of promotion, transfer, appointment, merit or demerit, or of taxes and legal decisions, provincial officials sought to gain favors by bribing clerks in the various Boards. And officials who were charged with the delivery of revenue, or copper, or dye materials to the central government were especially harried by their demands.

From the day they reported deliveries to the time they were given the receipts the clerks found many reasons for making extortions. The sums asked reached hundreds and thousands of taels. This was known as the 'Board of Expenses' and was collected with little effort at concealment." [3]

The runners exerted their power on a different plane and, of course, with different methods. They controlled access to government buildings; they arrested people and guarded the jails. Thus they could alleviate a prisoner's lot or make it more miserable; they could regulate the force of a flogging; they could claim resistance to arrest.[4] The power and possible material benefits inherent in these situations are manifest.

The ranking officials, who wished to maintain their control over the numerous and well-entrenched host of underlings, brought into play all the administrative and disciplinary means with which they were invested. The functionaries of Ch'ing China attempted to limit the duration of the underlings' employment. But while such control strengthened the hold of the ranking officials over the lower functionaries, the costs in skill and experience could be considerable.

Underlings who abused their power to the manifest detriment of the government were to be severely punished. This aspect of the matter has been clearly defined in the *Arthashāstra,* in the dynastic regulations of China, and in other manuals of agrodespotic statecraft. For scribes and runners who were dishonest or resorted to extortion the last Code of imperial China established penalties ranging from fines to permanent exile and execution by strangulation. The attached cases show that the higher officials did not hesitate to strike when they saw fit.[5]

In the struggle between the officials and the underlings the latter could never be completely subdued. But neither could they upset the structure of the bureaucratic apparatus, which enabled the ranking officials to emerge over time, not as total victors but as the holders of superior legal, administrative, and economic authority.

2. Bureaucratic Competition

a. Patterns of Competition Different in Different Societies

COMPETITION in the market is only one of many forms of competition. And hydraulic and feudal society differ from capitalism not because in them competition is absent, but because it is differently shaped.

In the medieval world of the West serfdom reduced competition in most villages to insignificance, whereas the feudal knights openly and violently competed with their fellows for land and glory. The guilds severely restricted competition in the crafts but not in large-scale and international trade.[6]

The regulated villages of Oriental society had little opportunity for economic rivalries. In traditional China the advance of private peasant landownership encouraged competition in economic affairs, without, to be sure, making Chinese agriculture capitalist. In all types of hydraulic society the members of the ruling class competed for power, prestige, and income; and this is true not only for the ranking officials but also, and with proper modifications, for the bureaucratic underlings.

Within the capitalist system we find competition on both the employer and employee levels. But while the expansion of this system increases the quality of goods and the number of persons involved, it reduces the number of competing and bargaining elements through the rise of corporations and labor unions. In addition, legal controls tend to restrict the methods of the competitive struggle, which generally is more violent in the early than in the later phases of capitalist economy.

The difference between the three types of competition appears also as a difference in their results. The medieval knight who makes a crucial mistake while competing with his fellows (on the battle field) may forfeit his life, but his property and honor usually remain untouched. The modern businessman who makes a crucial mistake while competing with his fellows (on the market), may lose his property, but his honor is rarely besmirched, and he certainly will not forfeit his life. The official of an agrarian despotism who makes a crucial mistake while competing with his fellows (in a bureaucratic or court intrigue) is likely to lose his honor, his property, and his life. Where power is fragmented and balanced, punishment for a crucial mistake is limited. Under conditions of total power, it is total.

b. Bureaucratic Competition in Hydraulic Society

ALL bureaucratic organizations have certain technical features in common; and some methods of intrabureaucratic competition appear universally in serving, controlled, and ruling bureaucracies. However, this makes it all the more imperative to recognize, behind the familiar trees, the peculiarity of the woods of which they form a part.[a]

a. Universals of warfare appear in the military enterprises of feudal Europe as well as in the hydraulic and modern industrial societies. But no one concerned with in-stitutional specification will, for this reason, deny the peculiarities of organization and procedure that distinguish the three patterns.

The functionaries of Occidental absolutism are closest to those of Oriental absolutism insofar as the chance for a meteoric rise or fall is concerned; but under Western absolutism there are non-bureaucratic roads to social prominence. And the government officials of an open modern society have legally established rights which guarantee that the loser in an intrabureaucratic fight need suffer nothing more than the frustration of not being promoted.

Under the conditions of total power bureaucratic life is as competitive as it is dangerous. A statistical study of the officials of the first long-lasting dynasty of imperial China, Han, shows that among those whose careers can be traced in some detail [7] about 21 per cent at one time or another were imprisoned for derelictions during their official career, and about 35 per cent died a violent death outside the battlefield. More than 12 per cent were murdered or died after torture in prison, 14 per cent were executed, and 9 per cent committed suicide.[b]

3. CIVIL VERSUS MILITARY OFFICIALS

BUREAUCRATIC competition occurs not only between members of the same office or administrative unit but also between members of different branches of the state apparatus. Among these branches, the army, for obvious reasons, poses special problems.

a. The Autocrat and the Army

THE army, as the compact machine of institutionalized coercion, plays a different role in different phases of hydraulic society. During the formative period the supreme military leader is also apt to control the new political economy, since his organizational and disciplinary position prepares him uniquely to head the emerging agromanagerial apparatus. Once established, the over-all political apparatus tends to prevail over the various branches, because the heads of the former through their control over personnel and com-

---

b. A study of 19th-century China suggests that at the close of the imperial period the career of an official was still beset with many dangers, although the character of these dangers had changed in several respects. On the basis of the Tung-hua-lu, Dr. Hellmut Wilhelm assumes that between 1821 and 1895 "almost every high official was punished at least once during his career." Extremely severe punishments (execution, banishment, enslavement, corporal punishment, or imprisonment) were imposed in about 22 per cent of all cases brought to the emperor's attention, dismissal in 42 per cent, and lighter punishments (reprimands, fines, and/or demotion) in the remaining cases. The survey, which considers both Manchu and Chinese officials, was made under Dr. Wilhelm's direction, at the University of Washington, Seattle, by Cecil Cody, Robert Crawford, Chen-i Wang, and Lincoln Wong.

munication penetrate all segments, which, no matter what their economic weight or coercive potential may be, remain compartmentalized and thus strategically inferior to the coordinating center. To elaborate upon our previously established thesis we may say: it is not the technical specialist or the hydraulic manager or the head of the police, or the commander of the army, but the master of the all-pervasive political apparatus who maintains supreme power over the compartmentalized technicians, managers, police chiefs, and generals. Only during periods of political disintegration and civil war will a vigorous general seize control of the entire country or a number of generals simultaneously in separated territories become military and political leaders: bureaucratic warlords.

The agromanagerial despot is usually very much aware of the power potential inhering in the armed forces; and he therefore takes every precaution to keep them subdued. He is the supreme master of the military, first because he makes the crucial decisions concerning its organization, its personnel, and (often also) its supply, and second because he heads the centralized apparatus of communications and intelligence.

Similar sociostrategic advantages favor the political masters of modern industrial apparatus states. They largely explain why, in the 1930's Stalin was able to liquidate the discontented heads of the Soviet army and two subsequent chiefs of the GPU, and why, in 1944, the National Socialist center prevailed over the generals who sought to overthrow Hitler.

b. Civil versus Military Officials

THE military functionaries, like their civil colleagues, are part of the over-all officialdom, and not infrequently the duties of the two groups overlap. When essential civil and military tasks are concurrently executed by the same higher officials (a governor, a satrap, etc.), conflicts between military and civil functionaries occur only on lower levels of authority. Often, however, the two spheres of action are represented by two distinct groups; and then such conflicts appear in the top echelons of the hierarchy.

Outside of periods of formation, decay, and crisis, military leaders in the hydraulic world have a chance to establish positions of prominence under several conditions: (1) in all areas—core and margin—which, being situated between strong neighbors, for international reasons require strong protection; (2) in marginal areas, because the lesser importance of the managerial bureaucracy increases the weight of the army; and (3) in conquest societies, in which the army is an essential factor not only for the establishment of the regime but for its perpetuation.

A number of the states of Buddhist India fall into the first category, Middle and Late Byzantium and post-Mongol Russia in the second, and many conquest societies of the Old and the New World in the third.

The struggle between the civil and military officialdom can be clearly observed in several hydraulic civilizations. In Pharaonic Egypt functionaries who specialized in the military arts proper ("front" officers) were during prolonged periods subordinated to military administrators—that is, to officials who kept the military records and who organized supply and equipment.[8] But in another context the front officers might successfully counterbalance members of the civil administration. The king placed some of them in important government positions, where, as socially inferior *homines novi*, they could be relied upon to uphold his interests against the ambitions of the ranking civil officials.[9]

Under the Mamluks the military officers, who were exclusively Mamluks, remained apart from, and above, the native bureaucracy. They could—and did—expropriate, imprison, and execute civil officials when they felt the latter were overstepping their authority.[10]

During the last period of the Roman republic successful generals rose to the top of the political hierarchy; and under the empire the army played a dominant, although varying, role for centuries.[11]

Ostrogorsky considers "the struggle between the competing forces of the metropolitan civil aristocracy and the provincial military aristocracy" the basic trend of Byzantine society.[12] The meaning of this statement becomes clear when we remember that the Byzantine civil aristocracy was a *Beamtenadel,* an aristocracy of officials,[13] and that both groups competed within the framework of a *Beamtenstaat,* a bureaucratic state, which was "constantly swelling and which, as the *ruling stratum,* made ever-greater demands." [14]

The intragovernmental struggles in T'ang China and in comparable periods in the history of other hydraulic civilizations were largely struggles between the civil and military branches of the ranking officialdom.

4. The Bureaucratic Activists versus the Bureaucratic Gentry

CONFLICTS between the officiating functionaries and members of the bureaucratic gentry resemble the intrabureaucratic struggles in that they, too, are frequently linked with the intrigues and machinations of competing court cliques. However, they have important peculiarities of their own. The active bureaucrats wield power; the members of the bureaucratic gentry exert influence. The officiating executives have excellent opportunities to accumulate wealth; the bureaucratic rentiers have fair opportunities to preserve, at least during their lifetime, what wealth they have. These differences in position go far to explain the conflicts that occur between members of the two groups.

If the individuals concerned are of the same rank, then, other things being equal, power will prevail over influence and the executive over the rentier. Not infrequently, however, a local official of minor rank may find himself in opposition to members of the gentry, who are able to prevail because they belong to a bureaucratically powerful family. The study of powerful families in hydraulic society [15] reveals the decisive role that power plays in this society in determining status, influence, and revenue.

A gentry-bureaucracy conflict may involve only a single member of the gentry, a person, let us say, who seeks through influence to decrease his fiscal obligations or increase his landholding. Occasionally it may involve all the members of a local gentry who are seeking to shape local politics according to their interests. Members of the gentry may stress (and actually represent) the ruler's rationality maximum; and they may dramatize their intentions by getting commoners to demonstrate against the local officials. To support their interests at the local level they may even appeal to top-ranking members of the hierarchy.

In the province of Anhui, after the T'ai-p'ing Rebellion, members of the gentry, together with other landowners, were temporarily able "to cheat the government yearly of a large proportion of income from land revenue." The local officials accepted this condition for a time because they feared that an insistence on full tax payments would cause the people, "incited by the landed gentry," to rebel against the newly arrived magistrate. Eventually, however, some undaunted members of the bureaucracy suggested the restoration of the destroyed cadaster in order to reestablish government control over the revenue.[16]

Conversely, several members of the gentry of a certain region in the province of Chekiang were dissatisfied with the district magistrate because of his "extortions." They complained to his superiors, requesting his demotion.[17]

An imperial decree of April 14, 1890, deplored "the common practice among the provincial gentry and literati of mixing themselves up in matters of public business, and sometimes even bringing pressure to bear on the authorities." The former justified their actions by stating that they promoted the public good. However, according to the official view these actions were "in reality designed for selfish purposes." [18] The publication of the edict shows that the local officials, who were temporarily at a disadvantage, eventually and through the support of the central government, prevailed over the gentry.

In periods of political decay the gentry asserts itself in various ways, but officials of a strong regime usually insist that it meet their demands. This last was the case in Early and Middle Byzantium and in 19th-century Russia, where the negotiations concerning the emancipation of the serfs revealed the relative strength of the bureaucratic and the proprietary (gentry) wings of the ruling nobility. Theoretically speaking, the (bureaucratic) landowners, or the absolutist state and its functionaries, or the peasants might have become the chief beneficiaries of the Emancipation of 1861. Actually, the government one-sidedly determined that the "Editing Commission" was to be "composed of officers of the various departments which had to do with peasant affairs, together with a number of experienced landowners." [19] Thus the terms of the Emancipation were "settled by discussion in the bureaucratic field"; [20] and both the bureaucratic landowners and the officials presented their respective arguments, which were based "not upon any ideal, but upon the recognition of the needs of the landowners or of the State." [21] The bureaucratic quality of the nobles' landed interests was expressed in the person of the man who finally headed the Commission, Count Panin. Panin owned enormous estates and twenty-one thousand serfs, but he also had a prominent role in the juridical affairs of the government. Pressured by the Tsar and his aides, Panin readily subordinated the proprietary aspirations of the nobility to its bureaucratic interests. [22]

The relations between the bureaucratic activists and the rentier-like bureaucratic gentry recall patterns of conflict occurring in the big corporations of modern industrial society. Shareholders of a company, who are not among its officers, have the right at the annual meeting to comment on, or question, company policy. But such casual and optative participation is far from effective control. Satisfied with their dividends, the majority of the shareholders are willing to leave the actual management to the executive officers. These functionaries exert supreme power over decision making and personnel; and even if originally they possessed little stock, they have incomparably greater opportunities for improving their material position than do the shareholders. [23]

In contrast to the corporation shareholders, who have the right to assemble, to rally public opinion, and to resort to legal action, the members of the hydraulic gentry, even when they owned considerable amounts of land, could not organize or gather freely. These privileges were restricted to the men in office, who, controlling the bulk of the country's surplus and monopolizing coercive power, had no difficulty in stressing the bureaucratic against the proprietary interests of the ruling class. And they did so, even when, as in the case of Count Panin, they were both officials and big landowners.

Thus the conflicts between the bureaucratic gentry and the ranking officials once more thrust into sharp relief the unique power position enjoyed in hydraulic society by the men of the state apparatus.

5. Conflicts between the Autocrat and Other Members of the Ruling Class

THE autocrat has been likened to the life-giving sun, to fierce animals, and to the merciless forces of lightning, storm, and flood. To his subjects he is indeed all these, and those among them who act in his name are eager both to execute his will and to influence it.

But the master of a tool is also its servant. The autocrat depends operationally upon the persons who implement his orders. The history of Oriental courts records endless attempts to influence the autocrat and equally endless attempts by the ruler to prevail over all personal and impersonal (bureaucratic) forces. The resulting conflicts are many. Contemplating the autocrat's antagonistic relations with his relatives on the one hand and with his ranking officials on the other, we can distinguish several types of conflict and also several major devices that the antagonists employ to further their respective aims.

a. The Autocrat versus His Relatives

i. BLOOD RELATIVES

THE ruler's relatives (who they are depends upon the prevailing patterns of kinship) are ever-ready to use their socially privileged position for political purposes. To name a successor outside the established tradition or to replace a ruler in his lifetime is a risky venture; but attempts to do so have frequently been made and not always without success.

Serious problems may arise even when the established tradition is upheld. How does an autocrat control his crown prince? How does he control his kinsmen? The Han emperors granted them much property but little power. Such a policy cannot eliminate all conflicts, but it will restrict them greatly, and to the decided advantage of the autocrat.

ii. AFFINALS

THE ruler's affinals are an equally ambivalent asset. They attain political prominence because one of their female members is his wife. They thus have a vested interest in the person of the ruler, who on his part may trust them more than his blood relatives. The Han rulers almost invariably kept their blood relatives out of office, but many members of the empress' family were given high positions in the bureaucracy. The Liao emperors were less discriminatory, but they, too, often turned to their in-laws when key political positions were to be filled.[24] Of course, such a policy has its dangers. Affinals who wield great power may reduce the ruler to a figurehead during his lifetime. Or after his death they may install a child as his successor and then reign in his stead. During a great part of the Liao dynasty the empire was ruled by empress dowagers.[25]

How does an autocrat control his affinals? The limiting of political eunuchism tends to decrease the influence of the ruler's wives, and measures designed to protect the heir apparent also have obvious advantages. The Toba ruler went to extremes: He killed his wife after she bore him an heir.[26] But such radical means were rarely invoked. More often, instead of killing the mother of his son (or sons), the ruler filled his harem with slave girls. Their relatives were usually persons of lowly status, and although some among them might rise to high station, they were much less of a threat, as a group, than noble and well-established consort families. Several Chinese emperors were the sons of former "singing girls," [27] and the majority of all caliphs [c] and Turkish sultans had former slave girls as mothers.[28]

The problems raised by the blood relatives contrast sharply with those raised by the affinals. With regard to the former the ruler could narrow the basis of hostility; with reward to the latter he could, under optimal circumstances, remove it altogether.

c. All Abbassid caliphs except three had slave mothers (Goldziher, 1889: 124; cf. Mez, 1922: 140, and Kremer, CGO, I: 393).

b. The Autocrat versus the Ranking Officials

i. ONCE MORE THE PROBLEM OF AUTOCRACY

THE despot's effort to control his relatives is only a particular expression of his over-all effort to control his serving men. Neither indicates the absence of autocratic authority. As developed above, a ruler who in his person concentrates "all the power over major decisions" [29] is by no means above and beyond the influence of those who serve him. And since the interests of the officialdom frequently suggest one decision and the ruler's interests another, there is considerable room for conflict. Needless to say, the sovereign will prevail the more completely, the more he determines the choice of his civil and military functionaries, and the more he controls their executive procedures.

The fact that the ruler in peace or war may insist on an irrational policy, even when it endangers the very existence of the state, underlines the extent to which power is concentrated in his person. The fact that his minor decisions may profoundly affect the prestige, income, and security of his officials underlines the unique political sensitiveness of the ruling class under the conditions of total power.

ii. HUMAN (SOCIAL) RELATIONS EXPRESSED
THROUGH INSTITUTIONAL ARRANGEMENTS

THE despot establishes horizontal checks by giving equal authority to two or more officials. He maintains vertical checks by a multiple system of reporting and supervising. And he demonstrates his supreme power by ruthless methods of discipline and punishment. Thus he is able to counter the strivings of his ranking officials for more influence (as advisors and memorialists), for more freedom (as executives and judges), for more wealth (as manipulators of the government revenue), and for more group advantage (as the beneficiaries of hereditary privileges).

The resulting institutional arrangements are not merely organizational and technical, as some observers believe. Rather they express human (social) relations between two crucial and antagonistic subsections of the ruling class. These relations are always slanted in favor of the despot, and this is so even where the officials enjoy hereditary privileges. It is particularly so where the ruler appoints his officials without the need to consider a self-perpetuating (noble) bureaucracy.

6. AUTOCRATIC METHODS OF CONTROLLING THE BUREAUCRATIC PERSONNEL

a. The Ruler's Control over a Hereditary Officialdom (a Bureaucratic Nobility)

MEMBERS of hereditary (noble) official families usually have a hereditary claim on an office, but not necessarily a claim on a special office or one of equal rank. If a hereditary serving man blunders seriously or is disloyal, the ruler can cancel the family privilege altogether and enslave or exterminate the culprit.[30] The ruler, who is limited with respect to the group from which he chooses his officials, nevertheless asserts his power by promoting or demoting its members at will.

b. Autocratic Means of Weakening or Destroying the Self-perpetuating Quality of the Ranking Officials

BUT "despotism itself has its varieties." [31] The despot may reduce the social homogeneity of the ranking officials by the appointment of outsiders; he may place men of lowly origin above officials of upper-class background; he may give precedence to priests, "barbarian" nobles, eunuchs, or slave officials. In the sovereign's hand such devices become the weapons for asserting his autocratic power against the will, and the unending political intrigues, of the ranking officialdom.

i. PRIESTS

THE inclusion of professional religious functionaries in the government was an important means of preventing a homogeneous officialdom. Under the Mayas, priests seem to have been regularly employed as officials.[32] In India the leading position of the "warrior-rulers," the Kshatriyas, was weakened by the appointment of Brahmins to government offices [33] and by the institution of the *purohita*. The royal house-priest, who was his sovereign's main advisor, could be expected to promote the selection of priests as officials whenever circumstances permitted. Even the Muslim rulers of India used to "make a Brahmin their secretary of state." [34] The prominence of priests among the king's councilors probably goes far in explaining why both in Hindu and Muslim India eunuchs had little opportunity to advance to the top-ranking advisory positions which they attained in other Oriental civilizations.

ii. COMMONERS (GENERAL OBSERVATIONS)

THE professional functionaries of the dominant religion were members of the ruling class; and the ruler who employed them—or for that matter his relatives by blood or marriage—counterbalanced the trend toward a self-perpetuating bureaucracy without drawing upon "the people."

In the wider sense "the people" included commoners and slaves. But it is characteristic of the peculiarities of social mobility under agromanagerial despotism that in this type of regime slaves (and eunuchs) were more systematically appointed to key political positions than were commoners.

The hereditary officials and the priests in government posts laid great stress on the educational qualifications required for the execution of their bureaucratic tasks; and their overlord had little reason to discard prerequisites which, from the standpoint of effectiveness and prestige, seemed eminently desirable. These prerequisites provided serious arguments against the indiscriminate placing of commoners into government positions.

In India the Sūdras, as a group, were not permitted to study the sacred books; [35] the Vaisyas were not so restricted. [36] But how many of them actually attained as thorough an education as a Brahmin or Kshatriya? Among the Maya, wealthy commoners were employed in government positions, but, as noted above, from time to time the official hierarchy was purged of those who were "not versed in the occult knowledge of the upper class." [37] Confucius accepted commoners as disciples, [d] but like their noble colleagues, these commoners had to be thoroughly familiar with the classics and the secular and religious ceremonial before they could be "used" in office.

iii. COMMONERS: SOCIAL EFFECTS AND LIMITATIONS OF THE CHINESE EXAMINATION SYSTEM

THE Chinese examination system has frequently been viewed as an institution which, throughout the period of imperial rule, gave the commoners access to office. Since participation in the examinations was based not on invitation from above but on the would-be candidate's spontaneous application, the Chinese bureaucracy may well seem, during this period, to have been recruited in large part from "the people."

d. One, Tzŭ-kung, is known to have been a businessman (*Shih Chi* 129.5a; cf. Legge, CC, I: 144, 242). For Tzŭ-kung's prominent position among Confucius' followers see Creel, 1949: 66 ff.

The Chinese examination system did in fact make it possible for a number of qualified commoners to enter the bureaucracy; but its social effects were much more modest than popular legend would have us believe. What actually did happen? The question is sufficiently important for an understanding of mobility in hydraulic society to justify a brief statement of the function—and the limitation—of the Chinese examination system.

First of all, the Chinese examination system provided the absolutist governments of China with candidates for office only during a limited and relatively late period. In Chou times and probably also under the Shang dynasty the bulk of all officials held positions because their forefathers had done so. During the Han dynasty (206 B.C.–A.D. 220) entry upon a government career depended essentially on appointment by the emperor or by a special official; in addition, office-holding fathers might recommend their own sons. The method of "recommending sons" (jên tzŭ) [38] favored the self-perpetuation of particular families in the bureaucracy, while appointment favored the self-perpetuation of the ranking officialdom generally. An examination of the biographical data included in the dynastic histories of the Han period gives considerable insight into the effects of these procedures, which are in fact a bureaucratic variant of the aristocratic principle of cooptation.[39] Basing ourselves on this source, we find that no more than 8 per cent of all officials of known social background were commoners, the remainder being relatives of the emperor (in the main, affinals), members of other noble families, or—and in their great majority—the relatives of officials.[40]

The period of disruption which ended in A.D. 589 modified earlier patterns of government. Although wars and conquest provided opportunities for the rise of social outsiders, a limited number of families were able to perpetuate their hold on the state apparatus. Under the infiltration and conquest dynasties [41] of North China, nobles of Inner Asian origin prevailed; and in the South indigenous "hereditary families" (shih chia) were similarly prominent. The biographies of the Southern Chin dynasty (216–419) indicate that about 9.5 per cent of all officials with known background may have been commoners.[e]

e. In 1935–36, in Peiping, I organized a study of the social background of the officials listed in the biographical sections of the official histories of several imperial dynasties. In 1938 I summarized the results of a preliminary analysis of our findings as follows: "Some 'fresh blood' may have been absorbed from the lower strata of society by means of the examination system; but on the whole the ruling officialdom reproduced itself socially more or less from its own ranks. The Chinese system of examinations had a very definite function; but, as in the case of the family, this

The much-discussed examination system was established only in the time of the re-unified empire by the short-lived Sui dynasty (581–618). It was fully developed by the subsequent T'ang dynasty—that is, it came into being something like seventeen hundred years after the beginning of the Chou dynasty and eight hundred years after the beginning of the imperial era. And even during the first half of the thirteen hundred years of its existence its influence on the social composition of the imperial bureaucracy was seriously restricted by institutionalized social discrimination, by hereditary claims to office (the *yin* privilege), and, under the conquest dynasties, by the politically prominent nobles of the "barbarian" master nationality.

The Chinese examination system was established not by democratic forces but one-sidedly by a despotic ruler. The ranking officials certainly influenced the original plan; and they implemented it, once it was established. Anyone who was eligible to participate in the examinations could take the initiative in applying; and this is a significant deviation from the earlier appointment system. However, even under the examination system the emperor and his officials ultimately decided whom they would employ, and how they would employ them. The government determined in advance how many degrees would be conferred; and even the holders of the most important degree, the *chin-shih,* originally were admitted to office only after they had also passed a sort of civil service test.[42]

The insistence upon a thorough classical education gave the members of official families—and, of course, also the relatives of the ruling house—an enormous cultural and social advantage. This advantage was enhanced by measures that, on the one hand, restricted the commoners' access to office and, on the other, provided the relatives of higher and middle officials with institutionalized claims to office.

The Sui statutes that initiated the examination system expressly excluded "artisans and merchants" from holding office. A similar policy of discrimination prevailed under the T'ang, and, with certain modifications, also under the Sung dynasty.[43] Since commerce, more than any other occupation, provided commoners with opportunities

---

function is by no means, what popular legend has thus far made us believe it was" (Wittfogel, 1938a: 11 ff.).

From 1939 on, the Chinese History Project, New York, has investigated several aspects of Chinese officialdom, including the *yin* system. It has examined in detail the selection of officials in the Liao dynasty (Wittfogel and Fêng, 1949: 450 ff.); and it greatly refined an earlier statistical analysis of the biographies of the Han dynasty. For several reasons it has not yet been possible to process the biographies of the other major dynasties as fully; but since the problem of mobility is a very important one, I have felt justified in presenting above some of the results of my original pilot inquiry together with some of our more recent findings.

for acquiring wealth and education, discrimination against merchants excluded from government exactly those commoners who were materially best equipped to prepare for the examinations.[f]

Moreover, the statutes that restricted the artisans and merchants gave added advantages to the bureaucracy. On the basis of their governmental position, higher and middle officials were granted the "protective" (yin) privilege of having one or several of their sons [g] enter the civil service without having to pass an examination.[44] This privilege, which in a new guise reestablished time-honored prerogatives, emerged in the Sui and T'ang dynasties—that is, as soon as the examinations were instituted. The yin system underwent considerable change during the Sung period, but it continued to play a significant role at this time [45] and also under the two first of the four great dynasties of conquest, Liao and Chin.[46]

The Mongols were deeply suspicious of their Chinese subjects. They therefore preferred appointment for their Chinese officials to any other method of selection. During the great part of their rule the Mongols held no examinations; and when eventually the examinations were re-instituted, the number of chin-shih degrees remained grotesquely low: "averages totaled not more than seventy (including a number of 'barbarians')." [47] They also restricted the number of yin sons and grandsons to one, as compared with ten and twenty beneficiaries under Sung rule and six under Chin rule. But they favored those who held the yin privilege by permitting them to enter the bureaucratic hierarchy in the fifth rank, a higher level than that granted in T'ang days.[h] The Ming and Ch'ing emperors reduced the yin prerogative to a shadow of its former self. They granted it only to the descendants of higher officials; and its beneficiaries could attain high positions only if they had passed the examinations.[48]

f. Under the Sung dynasty, government positions might be granted to persons who contributed grain for famine relief. This policy, which amounted to an indirect sale of office, gave some merchants a chance to enter the state service. But "it seems to have been practiced only in connection with a specific emergency" (Kracke, 1953: 76).

g. The number varied from period to period.

h. Wittfogel and Fêng, 1949: 459, 463. At the same time, "the Mongols raised the level of entry into the official hierarchy for yin claimants from the seventh to the fifth rank." Originally the yin son of a father who occupied one of the three highest ranks could begin his career in the seventh rank, and yin sons of fathers who occupied posts in the fourth or fifth rank could enter in the eighth rank, whereas the holders of the distinguished chin-shih degree might apply for positions only in the lowest or ninth rank. Yin officials might rise to the highest positions, including those of prime minister; and while in T'ang times this supreme post was, in most cases, held by men with a chin-shih degree, many yin sons seem to have attained posts in the middle or upper middle brackets (ibid.: 458).

The role of the holders of the *chin-shih* degree indicates one crucial function of the examination system. The intensive knowledge of
the Chinese classics required for the examinations saturated the students both with the social philosophy of the ruling bureaucracy and
with the great traditions of its semimanagerial and absolutist statecraft. Thus the competitive examination system was an excellent
means for thoroughly indoctrinating ambitious commoners and for
compelling the talented sons of officials and bureaucratic gentry families to submit to a most·comprehensive professional ideological training.

The examinations were open to commoners during the first six
hundred years with serious restrictions, and during the last six hundred years without such hindrances. But how many commoners did
actually rise to official position in the government of imperial China
through this method? Again the biographies, included in each of the
official dynastic histories, provide us with invaluable, if selective, information. The biographies are numerous, more numerous in fact
than any other collection of corresponding data in any other agrarian
civilization, and they deal essentially with high and middle officials,
who are listed not because of their rank, but because of their achievements.

Our preliminary effort to determine the social background of the
official biographies in some of the more important imperial dynasties
indicates that during the T'ang period (618–907) some 83 per cent of
all socially definable officials had an upper-class background: about
70 per cent were from the families of officials and 13 per cent from
the ruling house or other noble families. Almost 7 per cent were
"barbarians" (the T'ang ruling house was, at least in part, of Turkish
origin). And less than 10 per cent were commoners.

The corresponding figures for the Sung dynasty (960–1279) suggest
a minimum figure of some 85 per cent of officials with an upper-class
background: 72 per cent descended from the families of officials and
13 per cent from the ruling house. About 15 per cent were commoners.

Our survey of the biographies of the Mongol dynasty (1234–1368)
suggests that about 85 per cent of all socially definable officials had
an upper-class background: 74 per cent were descended from the families of officials and 11 per cent from the ruling house. About 15 per
cent were descended from commoners.

The indigenous rulers of the Ming dynasty were not at all eager
to restore the pre-Mongol privileges of the bureaucracy. They controlled the officials from above through political eunuchism. And they
made it easier for commoners to enter the state service by crippling

the *yin* privilege and by not discriminating against artisans and merchants, as the Sui, T'ang, and Sung governments had done. Under the Ming dynasty 77 per cent of all socially definable officials had an upper-class background: 63 per cent were descended from the families of officials, 14 per cent from the ruling house. And about 23 per cent were descended from commoners.

The Manchu rulers were no more inclined than their Ming predecessors to favor the bureaucracy's tendency toward self-perpetuation. They controlled their Chinese officials from above through tribal nobles, whose political position was bulwarked by the preservation of their hereditary prerogatives. And they facilitated the access of commoners to examinations and office, as the Ming rulers had done, through curtailing the *yin* privilege and through not discriminating against artisans and merchants. They particularly stressed purchase of degrees as a means of preventing the *shên-shih* (the officials and degree-holders) from becoming a socially homogeneous body.

An imperial edict of 1727 expressed sharp criticism of many persons who attained office through examinations. "If the official career should be left completely to those who rise through examinations, they would just firmly join together and work for their private interest against the public interest. This is of great harm to the public welfare and to the livelihood of the people. The purchase system should be appropriately expanded." [49]

According to a recent analysis of the social background of *chin-shih* candidates, the percentage of candidates whose forebears were neither officials nor degree-holders increased greatly during the 19th century.[i] And a study of the 19th-century *shên-shih* reveals that persons who joined this group not through examination but through purchase of a degree constituted about 32 per cent of the "lower gentry" during the first half of the century and about 36 per cent after 1854.[j]

The results of our analysis are confirmed for the Sung period by two lists of *chin-shih* graduates for 1148 and 1256 respectively, which, although incomplete as to social background data,[k] throw additional

i. See the unpublished study of the Ch'ing officialdom undertaken by Dr. C. K. Yang for the Modern Chinese History Project, Far Eastern and Russian Institute of the University of Washington, Seattle.

j. Chang, CG. For further data on the position of the *shên-shih* at the close of the Ch'ing dynasty see below, and Chap. 7 above.

k. For details concerning the two lists see Kracke, 1947: 107 ff. The second list has conspicuous gaps (*ibid.*: 113), and both, like the dynastic biographies, provide only selected data concerning the protagonists' official background. In his thoughtful study of this background, Kracke considered only relatives in the direct line up to, and including, the great-grandfathers (*ibid.*: 115). However, besides such individuals the list of 1256 mentions regularly the brothers of "graduates" who held degrees or offices.

light upon our problem. Assuming that during the thirty-year period from 1142 to 1171 almost forty-five hundred persons ^{m} passed the examinations, that all these persons and an equal number who "presumably entered the service by other methods" [50] achieved government positions, that at least one-half of all *chin-shih* graduates, as relatives of the emperor, acting officials, or members of the bureaucratic gentry, belonged to the ruling class,^{n} and that the average length of office tenure was something like twenty years,^{o} we find among the

---

In two cases, in which no direct forebears had held public office, five (69a) and seven (66a) brothers respectively did so. And both lists note brothers, uncles, granduncles, and great-great-grandfathers whenever they are family heads. Differing from Kracke, we view graduates with such relatives as having an official background; and in consequence we add sixteen more cases for 1148 and twenty more for 1256 to his graduates with official background. This raises the percentages of graduates with known official background from 42.1 to 45.6 per cent in the first case and from 43.7 to 49.5 per cent in the second.

m. The exact figure, according to Kracke (1947: 120), is 4428.

n. In his 1947 study, Dr. Kracke distinguishes essentially between graduates with and without an official background. Our figures, therefore, can be expected to be somewhat larger than his. All graduates of 1148 who are members of the imperial family, Chao, are listed in the Sung account as having relatives who held official position; and they are therefore included by Dr. Kracke. However, in the 1256 record only the names of the Chao graduates, who numbered twenty-seven, are listed. Dr. Kracke is consistent in not including them; but we are equally consistent in doing so. We thus find that 50.3 per cent of all graduates of 1256 belonged to the ruling class. In view of the limited character of the background data contained in both lists, our above estimate that "at least one half of all *chin-shih* graduates . . . belonged to the ruling class" is probably a conservative one. I should like to take this opportunity to thank Mr. Fang Chao-ying for calling my attention to the imperial relatives mentioned in the lists and Professor Tung-tsu Chu for his careful reexamination of the social data contained in the two Sung lists.

o. Dr. Kracke assumes that the (civil) officials "served an average of some thirty years each (the examinations were passed by men commonly ranging in age from the twenties to the fifties)" (Kracke, 1947: 120). The last mentioned fact indicates that part of the candidates were physically and mentally vigorous until their fifties; but it tells us nothing about the political conditions that determine and shorten an official career under Oriental despotism. Lacking pertinent Sung statistics, I revert to the biographical data of the Han period, which has been analyzed in detail by the Chinese History Project. Among the Han officials for whom such information is given, about 45 per cent were in office for less than ten years, and more than 18 per cent from ten to nineteen years. This suggests an average office tenure of not more than ten years. At the end of Northern Sung, in 1119, the *yin* privilege was sharply, if temporarily, reduced by granting it only to civil and military functionaries, who had held office for more than fourteen and nineteen years respectively (*Wên-hsien T'ung-k'ao* 34: 325). Obviously, these terms of tenure were not considered excessively short (or the measure would have had little restrictive value) or excessively long (or it would have been forbidding). Assuming that the average office tenure in Sung time was definitely higher than during the Han dynasty and somewhat higher than the figures mentioned for 1119, an average of twenty years seems a reasonable estimate.

thirty-three thousand civil and military officials [p] a total of 9 per cent who may have come from the rank of commoners. These figures are well below the 15 per cent suggested by our earlier analysis. To adjust them, we would have to assume that the Sung emperor appointed more than the above-suggested number of commoners without benefit of a degree.

Many details of the Chinese examination system still need clarification, but this much seems certain: if the Sui and T'ang emperors established the examination system, in part at least, in order to alter the social composition of the ranking officialdom, then it must be said that the system failed to achieve this purpose. The examinations provided the ambitious core of the ruling class with a most intensive intellectual and doctrinal training; and they added a varying amount of "fresh blood" to the ranking officialdom. But they did not destroy the trend toward sociopolitical self-perpetuation which dominated the thoughts and actions of this group.

iv. EUNUCHS: THE PRINCIPLE

A VERY different method of strengthening the ruler's autocratic grip on his officials was provided by the employment of castrated persons —political eunuchs.

Castration was probably first used on large domesticated animals. In ancient America, which knew no such animals, there is no evidence of eunuchism. In the Near East, however, references to castrated animals appear in the middle of the 2d millennium B.C., and perhaps before that time.[q] Castration of human beings as a form of punish-

---

p. Chinese tradition views both civil and military functionaries as government officials (po kuan); and throughout the imperial period civil officials were time and again given military posts and military officials civil posts. (For Sung see Kracke, 1953: 56). Accepting for the sake of the argument an average office tenure of thirty years (an improbably high estimate on the basis of our data) and considering only civil officials (according to Kracke some 11,000 persons), we find that as graduates of the examinations, commoners might constitute 20.4 per cent of the civil officialdom. An average office tenure of twenty years would reduce the figure to 13.6 per cent. Our calculation is based on Chin Yü-fu's "combined numbers of civil and military [Sung] officials" given by Kracke in the next to last note of his study (Kracke, 1947: 122, n. 31).

q. A few passages in the Pyramid Texts have been considered as possibly referring to castration; but the Berlin Dictionary and such outstanding Egyptologists as Sethe indicate the problematic character of such an interpretation (Sethe, PT, III: 213, 215, 216; Wb, IV: 43, 264; V: 410). The caution exercised by these authorities should pertain also to passage 1462c (see Mercer, 1952, II: 323; III: 712 ff.). The inscriptions that refer to tribute bullocks from Syria (Breasted, 1927, II: 191, 199, 203) originated under Pharaoh Thutmose III (15th century). Thus in the middle of the second millennium B.C. castration of animals was known in Egypt and obviously also in Western Asia, but we have no equally reliable evidence for the castration of humans.

ment was used in Assyria in the second half of the 2d millennium. But political eunuchism is clearly evidenced in the Near East and China only from the first millennium B.C. on.[r]

In all likelihood eunuchs were used as harem guards before they became political functionaries. It is not difficult to see how a ruler who as a boy had known eunuchs as his mother's personal servants would be inclined to rely on such trusted attendants when he came to power and was faced with an elaborate and alien bureaucracy. Having been castrated as adults (and then usually for a crime) or as children (and then usually after being sold off by poor parents), eunuchs, unlike the regular officials, did not come from prominent families. Socially rootless, they owed everything they had and everything they were to their ruler; and their doglike devotion to him therefore resulted as consistently from their position as did their detachment from, or their open hostility to, the regular members of the officialdom. The Achaemenian Persians, who employed political eunuchs exclusively,[51] told Greek visitors that such persons were the most reliable tools a ruler could have.[52]

Oriental despots were pleased to use eunuchs in many semipersonal and semipolitical spheres of court life and in government proper. Often the eunuchs were entrusted with confidential tasks of intelligence. Not infrequently they were responsible for their sovereign's personal safety (as heads of his bodyguard); and at times they were placed in command of important armies or navies, or in charge of the royal treasury.

Such arrangements proved highly satisfactory since, although mutilated in body and spirit,[53] a eunuch retained his intellectual powers and his ability to act. One of their number, Ts'ai Lun, is credited with having invented paper;[54] and the most eminent Chinese historian, Ssŭ-ma Ch'ien, completed his great historical work after he had been castrated. Eunuch generals and admirals seem to have been no less ingenious and daring than those who had not been emasculated. In the political arena eunuch cunning at times astounded veterans of Oriental court intrigue. It was here that they were most

---

r. Meissner (BA, I: 120) is not sure whether the *girsequm* of Hammurabi's Code (secs. 187, 192, 193) were eunuchs. The Code punishes adultery with death (Hammurabi, secs. 129, 130), whereas the Middle Assyrian Laws order castration for this and other sex crimes (Meek, 1950: 181). The tables on which these laws are recorded originated in the 12th century B.C., but the laws themselves "may go back to the 15th century" (*ibid.:* 180). Assyrian references to what seem to be political eunuchs are contained in inscriptions made under Adad-Nirari II (911–891 B.C.) and Sargon (724–705 B.C.) (Luckenbill, AR, I: 116); but as far as pictorial representations of beardless men are concerned, Meissner (BA, I: 411) warns that these need not always indicate eunuchs.

feared, because it was here that they came closest to the nerve centers of despotic power.

v. EUNUCHS: A FEW HISTORICAL FACTS

THUS institutionalized eunuchism seems to have been altogether absent in ancient America. Domestic eunuchism was known in many major areas of Old World Oriental society. Political eunuchism was weakly developed in Hindu India, where an enormously influential priesthood provided the most important group of non-Kshatriya candidates for government office. In China and the Near East it temporarily became a formidable weapon of autocracy for supervising and controlling the ranking officialdom.

In China eunuchs emerged as political advisors and heads of armies during the second half of the Chou period—that is, at a time when the ranking officials still constituted a hereditary (noble) bureaucracy.[55] The founder of the empire, Ch'in Shih Huang-ti, had at the close of his life as his most intimate companion the eunuch, Chao Kao. After the emperor's death, Chao Kao succeeded in destroying the great chancellor, Li Ssŭ, and many other prominent functionaries. And so powerful was this eunuch that after having brought about the suicide of the second emperor he, and not a high-ranking official, chose the new emperor.[56]

The first sovereigns of the long-lasting imperial dynasty, Han, soon began to use eunuchs to maintain their autocratic rule. Under Empress Dowager Lü (188–180 B.C.) the eunuch Chang Shih-ch'ing handled the edicts and commands.[57] Under Emperor Wên (180–157) two eunuchs enjoyed considerable favor.[58] Emperor Wu (141–87) left political matters to his trusted eunuchs when he withdrew to his harem,[59] and two eunuchs, Hung Kung and Shih Hsien, played a prominent role in the government of Emperor Yüan (48–33 B.C.).[60]

Under these rulers of Early Han individual eunuchs were prominent. During the Later Han period (A.D. 25–220) eunuchs were merged in a powerful group. Their influence increased notably in the second half of the first century A.D. and, in the second century they held in their hands "kingdoms and noble ranks and they had in their mouths the decrees of Heaven." [61] As tools of the emperor or of his wives or in-laws, they temporarily exerted an almost unlimited control over the bureaucracy.[62]

Similar developments also characterized the "typically" Chinese [63] dynasties, T'ang and Ming. The prominence of political eunuchs in T'ang times coincided significantly with the establishment of the examination system, and in Ming times with the restrictions of the *yin* prerogative. Under the Ming emperors [s] eunuchs were in charge of special agencies for supervising the metropolitan officials and commoners. The eunuch Liu Chin, the most famous of the "Eight [eunuch] Tigers," systematically persecuted his bureaucratic opponents, and he was equally merciless in his dealings with members of the bureaucratic gentry.[64] Although Liu was eventually executed, eunuchs remained powerful until the dynasty fell under the combined onslaught of Chinese rebels and Manchu invaders.

The Sung emperors relied less on political eunuchism than did the Han, T'ang, and Ming rulers; but at the beginning of the 12th century the eunuch T'ung Kuan was raised to the highest military rank and set over the empire's supreme defense council.

In Western Asia eunuchism flourished under the Achaemenids. It receded under the Hellenistic monarchs, but it acquired great strength as the Roman empire became increasingly Orientalized.

In strong contrast to earlier custom the emperors Claudius, Nero, Vitellius, and Titus included eunuchs in their entourage. Claudius was influenced by two, Posides and Halotus; and Nero, who "married" the eunuch Spores, placed the eunuch Pelago in charge of a terror squad.[65] Under Elagabalus and Gordian eunuchs became a permanent feature of the administration.[66] Diocletian gave them a prominent place in his new court hierarchy.[67]

Of the eighteen ranks of Byzantine officialdom eunuchs could hold eight, among them the distinguished Patrikios; and eunuch patricians were rated above ordinary patricians.[68]

Runciman calls the employment of eunuchs "Byzantium's great weapon against the feudal tendency for power to be concentrated in the hands of a hereditary nobility, which provided so much trouble for the West." [69] Since eunuchism was already fully institutionalized in Byzantium in the 4th century, it cannot have been instituted as a weapon to combat a feudal tendency, which was certainly no issue in the bureaucratic regime of Eastern Rome and which, even in the West, only became an issue several centuries later. The suggestion that the eunuchs "gave the Emperor a governing class he could trust" [70] comes closer to the heart of the matter. As elsewhere the political eunuchs of Byzantium constituted an entirely trustworthy control group within the absolutist bureaucracy. And they functioned so well that Byzantium became a "eunuch's paradise." [71] Among the eunuch generals, Narses, Solomon,[72] and Nicephorus Uranus [73] were

s. The rise of the eunuchs in Ming times began soon after the founding of the dynasty (1368). Eunuchs were entrusted with the defense of the northern border in 1403, and in 1406 the eunuch Chêng Ho commanded the large imperial fleet that visited India, Arabia, and East Africa.

outstanding, among the eunuch admirals Eustathius Cymineanus [74] and Nicetas, who commanded the Byzantine fleet in the battle for Sicily in 963.[75] After the military and political catastrophe of Manzikert, a eunuch, Nicephorus the Logothete, "managed to reform the army." [76] "No religious or secular office, however high—with the imperial dignity as the only exception—was closed to them as a matter of principle." [77] "A large proportion of the Patriarchs of Constantinople were eunuchs." [78] At times eunuchs exerted unlimited power over the sovereign. Constantius II (d. A.D. 361) was so completely dominated by the eunuch Eusebius that the historian Ammianus quipped: "To speak truly, Constantius had much influence with him." [t]

Political eunuchism flourished during and after the Abbassid caliphate in the centers of Muslim power. From the 9th century on, the caliphs placed eunuchs in important positions at the court and in the army and navy. The Abbassid general Munis, the Samanid general Fa'ig, and the Muslim admiral Thamil were eunuchs. How high, at this time, eunuchs might rise in the military hierarchy is illustrated by the fact that when the naval forces of Baghdad and Fatimid Egypt fought each other in 919, both fleets were commanded by eunuch admirals.[79]

vi. THE DESPOT'S PERSONAL AGENCY NO INCIPIENT PARTY

UNDER the conditions of advancing industrialization and intensive communications between the various segments of society and the ruling center, an all-pervasive superorganization, such as the Communist or Fascist state party,[80] provides unique means for maintaining total autocratic power.

Oriental despotism needed no such superorganization. The compartmentalized peasant or urban communities, and also the individual officials who lacked modern facilities for communication and potential conspiracy, could be satisfactorily controlled by the postal and intelligence service, by the ruler's "men," and by special segments of his officialdom, such as the eunuchs. The intelligence service took care of the country's vital administrative and military centers, the eunuchs in the main of the court and, often also, of the capital. It is interesting to note that the eunuchs never formed a very large group. In many hydraulic societies a limited number of personal agents sufficed to assure the ruler's autocratic position.

t. Ammianus Marcellinus 18.4.3: "Eusebi . . . apud quem - - si vere dici debeat— multa Constantius potuit."

vii. THE TRIBAL NOBLES OF CONQUEST DYNASTIES

IN many Oriental societies, but not in all. To mention only one exception: even in the hydraulic societies of the Old World that knew institutionalized eunuchism, political eunuchs were of no great importance in conquest societies.

We have already commented on the peculiar role played in Oriental conquest societies by the nobles and commoners of the conquering nationality. Alien commoners were ideal instruments of coercion, and alien nobles, ranking above the native bureaucracy, formed a social elite whose prominence and security depended on their loyalty to the ruler and their ability to control the native officials. Alien nobles regularly commanded the cadre armies and usually headed strategic civil offices. They were political agents who, as faithfully as any eunuch, upheld the interests of the conquering dynasty—which indeed was substantially identical with their own.

Why did the Umayyad caliphs have little use for political eunuchs? Religion has been invoked to explain this interesting phenomenon.[81] But the Abbassid development shows that theological difficulties could be easily overcome, if the ruler wanted it so. More probably, the Umayyads, as a conquest dynasty, found it quite satisfactory to base their autocratic power essentially on their Arab nationals, nobles and commoners.

The Ch'i-tan masters of the Liao empire established their domination over northeastern China without engendering an excessive antagonism between pastoral victors and sedentary subjects. Nevertheless, they prudently reserved for themselves the key positions of power, and the emperor personally handled both strategic communications and the supreme command.[82] The only high-ranking Chinese who was thoroughly trusted (because of his great achievements in the war against the Sung empire) did not shift the center of authority to the Chinese sector of the government. Instead, he was given a Ch'i-tan clan name, a symbol of his inclusion in the "barbarian" nobility of the conquerors. When the last Liao emperor, in desperation and already deprived of a great part of his realm, offered the command of the remnants of his eastern forces to a Chinese, the man of his choice declined, noting bitterly and correctly that "under the old system Chinese did not participate in the important military and state policies . . ."[83] Indeed under the old system the major military and civil decisions were made by the alien ruler and his "barbarian" nobles. No wonder then that "eunuchs . . . were marginal men in Liao society. . . . no real political influence was ever concentrated in the hands of any Liao eunuch mentioned in the historical records." [84]

In the Manchu dynasty, too, the Manchu nobles made eunuchs superfluous. The T'ai-p'ing Rebellion (1850–1863) weakened, but did not destroy, the hegemony of the tribal aristocrats, and the short-lived attempt of 1898 to modernize the government, which under a heretic Manchu emperor was undertaken by Chinese reformers, was crushed by the Empress Dowager. In her first restoration edicts she significantly appointed a number of Manchus to positions of power.[85] Thus even the Manchus who had accepted more of Chinese culture than any of the three preceding conquest dynasties relied not so much on eunuchs as on "barbarian" nobles. These nobles came as close to constituting a totalitarian "quasiparty" as any dominant segment in the ruling class of hydraulic society anywhere.[u]

viii. SLAVES

IN nonconquest societies eunuchs are a formidable weapon of auto-cratic policy. However, slaves (and ex-slaves) may serve similarly, since they too are socially rootless. And they may fulfill their purpose even more effectively, since their more normal physique makes them seem more suitable to represent the despot's authority everywhere.

Some early Roman emperors employed freed slaves (*libertini*) in important political positions; [86] but later emperors preferred eu-nuchs, who, unlike the slaves, were traditionally associated with the power of Oriental despotism.

The use of slaves as the ruler's serving men was more frequent in the Islamic Near East, where quickly changing conditions of war and political alignments strongly encouraged experiments with hired sol-diers. In contrast to the Umayyads, who maintained their conquest regime essentially by means of tribal supporters, the Abbassids re-lied increasingly on mercenaries. Eventually, and particularly for the caliph's bodyguard, they bought Turkish slaves. The Samanid and Seljuk rulers of Persia followed the Abbassid example.[87] In the Mam-luk empire an alien elite of ex-slave warriors perpetuated itself by systematically filling vacancies with slaves purchased abroad. When entering upon their official careers, these slaves were solemnly en-franchised; but they remained a socially self-contained stratum.[88] In

---

u. Political eunuchs emerged temporarily under Emperor Shih-tsu (d. 1661) (Hummel, ECCP, I: 256 ff.). But the trend was stopped abruptly and never showed strength again except under the last Empress Dowager (cf. Hummel, ECCP, I: 296; II: 724; cf. also I: 298). Even this extraordinary woman despot, however, sought to enhance her power not by intensifying eunuchism, but by restoring Manchu control over the Chinese official-dom.

Ottoman Turkey tribute boys and persons of slave or slavelike origin were trained to be cadre warriors and top-ranking administrators.

These Turkish "slave" functionaries were offered many incentives: substantial earnings, honors, opportunities for advancement, and, at times, also a chance to marry. They were no chattel slaves but highly privileged half-slaves, if they were not completely enfranchised. But even as ex-slaves, they remained closely attached to the ruler.[v] More favorably situated in many ways than the great majority of the free population, they considered it an honor to be his personal property.

But the distinctions they enjoyed did not remove the basic deficiency of their position—their essential rootlessness. True, they might at the height of their career invite certain of their relatives to share their glory and wealth, but this was more the exception than the rule. In any case—and this was to the benefit of the ruler—the fortunate relatives were almost always persons of humble status; and thus they formed no link to an ambitious and self-perpetuating (noble) bureaucratic gentry.

Their rootlessness was further aggravated when the ruler selected his slave functionaries from among the children of nonbelievers, particularly from among the children of Christians. Of course, they were given a thorough Muslim education, but their special training widened the gap between them and the upper-class believers, from whom they were already separated by accidents of origin.

The social effects of the system of slave officials appeared with classical clarity in Turkey. During the heyday of Ottoman power the administrative and military functionaries did not establish a hereditary officialdom,[89] and they prevented the hereditary leaders of the militia cavalry, who were supported by office land (*khasses, ziamets,* and *timars*),[90] from attaining more than secondary and subordinate positions of power.

In this set-up political eunuchs were not altogether absent,[w] but they only bulwarked an autocratic edifice that was essentially a "government by a slave class." [91] The functionaries of this government were so thoroughly disciplined and, even in the civilian sphere, so well integrated that Machiavelli saw no chance of upsetting the Turk-

v. The Turkish word *"kul"* like the Arab word *"mamluk"* means "slave."

w. In the Mamluk empire eunuchs were in charge of the training of the Mamluks (Ayalon, 1951: 14 ff.). The Turkish sultans made the chief White Eunuch the head of the Palace School, where the military and administrative leaders of the state were educated (Miller, 1941: 64, 88). Another high-ranking White Eunuch guarded the treasures in the sultan's private treasury (Miller, 1941: 38). The chief White Eunuch, in addition to being in charge of the Palace School and Harem and acting as the grand master of ceremonies, was also the sultan's confidential agent (Miller, 1941: 88).

ish regime through cooperation with dissenters (today we would say a fifth column) as could be done in feudal France. For "in kingdoms governed like that of France . . . it is easy to enter them by winning over some baron of the kingdom, there being always malcontents, and those desiring innovations. These can, for the reasons stated, open the way to you and facilitate victory." [92] Not so with the Turks. "Because, being all slaves and dependent, it will be more difficult to corrupt them, and even if they were corrupted, little effect could be hoped for, as they would not be able to carry the people with them for the reasons mentioned. Therefore, whoever assaults the Turk must be prepared to meet his united forces, and must rely more on his own strength than on the disorders of others." [93]

Contemplating the struggle between the supreme ruler and his serving men, we are not so much surprised that the Turkish office holders advanced eventually to hereditary or semihereditary tenure,[94] but that, over a considerable period, the sultan was able to successfully block these trends by maintaining a socially rootless class of "slave-officials." [x]

7. "Regular" Officials, Control Groups, and the People

SLAVE officials were among the most effective tools that the ruler of a hydraulic state could muster. Political eunuchs or a nobility of tribal conquerors might supervise, weaken, and restrict the "regular" officialdom, but slave officials could replace it. Despite obvious differences, the three groups resembled each other in one significant way. Each of them constituted a control group, which from the autocrat's standpoint was manifestly more effective than the commoners who might be included in the ranks of the officialdom. The priests, who in ancient America, India, and elsewhere were placed in important government positions, most probably fulfilled a similar function.

---

x. The autocratic master of the new class society in the USSR exerts supreme control over the ranking *apparatchiki* by a variety of methods, among them the periodic purging of established groups of functionaries (the "old guard," the "old cadres") and the introduction of technically and politically suitable commoners. From the standpoint of the supreme autocrat, the functionaries' reliability may be expected to be greater, the less they are rooted in any prestige group that preserves elements of social cohesion. The Great Purge of the thirties liquidated the bulk of the Old Bolsheviks, and subsequent purges many other persons of prominence in the party, government, and army. Vyshinsky, who was a Menshevik until the early days of the regime, was ideally fitted to prosecute the Old Bolsheviks. No bonds of comradeship tempered his assault; and his heterodox past made him particularly vulnerable—and particularly ready to please the supreme Party leadership.

The regular officials were remote from, and above, the people. But the members of the control groups, who were particularly close to the despot, were also particularly removed from the people. A well-intentioned regular official or a member of the bureaucratic gentry might develop quasipatriarchal relations to the local population. This was much less likely to be the case with priest officials, slave officials, alien nobles, or eunuchs.

J. SOCIAL PROMOTION

THE political careers of eunuchs, slaves, ex-slaves, and commoners in hydraulic society have a further significance. They demonstrate that social (vertical) mobility means one thing in open and balanced societies, and another in societies which exist under the shadow of total power. Obviously there is more than a single pattern of social mobility. And any discussion of the phenomenon will be satisfactory only to the degree that the facts are placed in their specific institutional setting.

1. RESERVOIRS AND MAINSPRINGS OF SOCIAL PROMOTION

IN open and property-based societies a commoner may rise above his original station, either through political or economic achievement. Members of the upper class may try to prevent his ascent, but they cannot forbid it. They may discriminate against the power *parvenu* or the *nouveau riche* personally, but usually the newcomer's children or grandchildren achieve social acceptance. This was the general pattern in the democratic city states of ancient Greece. And it is increasingly typical for such modern industrial countries as England, Scandinavia, Australia, and the United States.

This pattern of democratic and spontaneous social mobility differs fundamentally from the patterns of social mobility that characterize hydraulic society. In hydraulic society the lowly ones who entered the ruling class rarely came from the ranks of free and prominent commoners. In China the number of persons who could obtain a higher examination degree was carefully restricted; and even this Chinese pattern was by no means typical for the majority of all Oriental civilizations. In general, a vigorous commoner was not likely to become a member of the ruling class. The eunuchs, freedmen, and slaves who rose to political prominence originally ranked below the free commoners. And this was true also for the slave girls, who in the ruler's harem could become the mothers of future rulers.

Members of these groups rose to positions of distinction, not because they overcame barriers of established wealth and power through their own efforts, but because their ruler was sufficiently strong to select whom he pleased and to place the person of his choice where he pleased. What vertical mobility there was in hydraulic society resulted from manipulation from above.

To be sure, there are active elements in passive behavior, just as there are passive elements in active behavior.[a] But this does not negate the validity of the conclusion that under Oriental despotism social mobility was essentially a passive process.

It may be said, of course, that in certain complex and semicomplex Oriental societies some commoners have risen from poor and humble origins to wealth and distinction within their class, improving their status in a way that is typical for property-based open societies. True enough. However, in many hydraulic societies such patterns are almost entirely lacking, and where they do occur they do not involve ascent into the ruling class.

2. Criteria for Social Promotion (Aptitudes "plus" . . .)

Total power promotes prudently and discriminatingly. And it promotes those who may be expected to satisfy the needs of the apparatus state. In such a process the candidate must possess aptitudes "plus." . . . What is this "plus"?

Some who are selected for promotion may be unusually talented; and this certainly is desirable. But all must excel in the key virtue of totalitarianism: total and ingenious servility. This qualification may be expressed in either an ideologically or a ceremonially subtle way (as was the case in Confucian China and Hindu India) or pragmatically and directly (as was the case in many other hydraulic civilizations). But the substance was everywhere the same; and the supreme manipulators of total power would have considered themselves fools if they had not insisted on a qualification that, from their standpoint, was vital.

3. Social Promotion on a Slave Plantation

Social mobility in hydraulic society is not identical with social mobility on a slave-operated plantation. Nevertheless, some features of the latter are not without interest for the former. A plantation owner may raise the most lowly slaves to be his foremen or personal servants,

a. Cf. Wittfogel, 1932: 474 ff. This study has tried to define the potential influence of an object upon the operations to which it is exposed.

but an awareness of this possibility does not favor an independent spirit among their fellows. On the contrary. The fact that promotion is offered essentially to those who are unquestionably submissive tends to stimulate among the opportunistic majority of all slaves attitudes of spectacular servility.

K. THE TOTAL RULING CLASS—A MONOPOLY BUREAUCRACY

1. THE RULING CLASS OF HYDRAULIC SOCIETY AND THE UPPER CLASSES IN OTHER STRATIFIED SOCIETIES

FROM still another angle, the peculiarity of social mobility in hydraulic society indicates the peculiarity of its ruling class. For all practical purposes this ruling class is a closed class. Only by the will of its recognized representatives can members of lower classes be incorporated into it. In this respect it is like the feudal nobility and unlike the upper classes of a modern property-based industrial society.

The peculiarity of the hydraulic variant of a closed ruling class derives mainly from the manner in which it is organized. The active core of the ruling class of hydraulic society is a rigidly cohesive body; in this respect it differs not only from the modern bourgeoisie but also from the feudal nobility. Even where entrepreneurial monopolies coordinate prominent elements of the *haute bourgeoisie,* we do not find the business class as a whole hierarchically and formally organized, as were the vassals of feudal countries. The organizational unity of the feudal lords reached its peak in their combined (national) military actions; but both the scope of these actions and the disciplinary controls exercised by the supreme leader were very restricted. For the most part the lords were independently concerned with their own military, economic, and social affairs.

The serving men of hydraulic despotism were organized as a permanently operating and highly centralized "apparatus." In contrast to the bourgeois upper class, which has no recognized head, and in contrast also to the feudal lords, whose recognized head was the first among equals in a conspicuously decentralized order, the men of the hydraulic apparatus state held their ruler to be the supreme leader, who always and unconditionally determined their position and tasks.

Prior to the rise of the modern industrial apparatus state, the men of a hydraulic government were the only major example of a ruling class, whose operational core permanently functioned as an organized, centralized, and semimilitary entity.

2. Authoritarian Bodies Do Not Necessarily Exert Totalitarian Power

EVEN a formidable authoritarian body cannot prevail totally as long as significant countervailing forces exert a restraining or controlling influence on it. Both in Periclean Athens and in a modern industrial democracy the army is an authoritarian organization; its commanders expect, and have the means to enforce, unquestioning obedience. But in each case it is subordinated to the decisions of an over-all and democratically established political body.

Manifestly no society is without its authoritarian segments, but in a democratic society such segments can be supervised and controlled. Awareness of this fact is essential for a proper evaluation of the effects (and the limitations) of authoritarian patterns in Big Business, Big Labor, and Big Government that appear in modern property-based civilizations.

The absolutist governments of late and postfeudal Europe had to cope with such forces as an organized nobility, the Church, the guilds, and the rising capitalist middle classes. These governments were authoritarian enough, and they strove hard to exert exclusive ("totalitarian") power. But on the whole they were unable to do so, because they were unable to attain a monopoly of societal leadership.

3. Monopoly versus Competition in Societal Leadership

SOCIETAL leadership may be exerted by several groups or classes that in various ways offset one another. Or it may be exerted monopolistically by a single group or class. Manifestly, a group that exerts monopolistic leadership behaves differently from a group that, despite its superior strength, is unable to crush its rivals.

In postfeudal Europe and Japan state power and active (entrepreneurial) property gave rise to several upper classes; and no class succeeded in establishing exclusive (total) prominence. More recently the owners of land and capital are being confronted with a new type of rival: the owners of a special kind of property, labor. Today labor openly contests the political and social leadership of the old upper classes.

In hydraulic society development took a different course. There the rise of propertied classes—artisans, merchants, and landowners—did not involve the rise of competing upper classes. In semicomplex and complex hydraulic societies the ranking officials accepted as inevitable, and in some measure as desirable, the presence of men of wealth who were detached from government. But even when these men were numerous enough to constitute a class, they did not compete with the bureaucratic upper class for social and political leadership. They did not compete because they had no opportunity to engage in a substantial political struggle. Neither at the start nor later did these holders of independent small or large property succeed in coordinating their forces into a national and politically effective rival organization.

In all probability the men of the apparatus were not clearly aware of the threat that a rival organization might pose. Most hydraulic societies originated prior to, and far away from, the balanced agrarian societies that crystallized in ancient Greece and Rome and in Medieval Europe and Japan. And in most simple hydraulic societies the independent propertied groups were too feeble to make their political will felt either in general political assemblies or in estate-like corporations. Democratic tribal traditions—where they existed —were apparently abandoned either when, or before, they became a serious threat to the masters of the agromanagerial regime. This may have happened in proto-Sumerian society, but even in this case the evidence is weak. As a rule the representatives of the young despotic states seem to have kept the owners of private mobile or immobile property politically atomized, sometimes by resorting to violence, but more often without exerting any untoward physical or political effort.

In late medieval and postmedieval times the Orientally despotic states of the Near East and Russia co-existed with European states that were characterized by multiple political organizations. But except for post-Muscovite Russia and 19th-century Turkey, there is little to show that the Western pattern was consciously imitated in these nearby Eastern lands. The Christian crusaders weakened the absolutist power of Late Byzantium, but its men of property were unable to create independent and effective feudal or burgher corporations. In Turkey and Russia multiple political organizations appeared only when the industrial revolution and the impact of Western power created an altogether new national and international situation.

4. Monopoly of Societal Leadership Appears in Oriental Despotism as Monopoly of Bureaucratic Organization ("Monopoly Bureaucracy")

The freedom to compete involves the freedom to organize; and it involves the freedom, when conditions permit, to use bureaucratic devices for developing and perpetuating organizational bonds. The corporate barons and burghers of the feudal world utilized bureaucratic means only to a modest degree. But the history of the medieval Church shows that during that era a powerful nongovernmental body could erect, if it wanted to, impressive bureaucratic structures.

In the modern countries of central and western Europe, in America, Australia and Japan, many smaller and larger bureaucracies exist outside and independent of government. Aristocratic landlords, where they still survive, may employ bureaucratic devices to protect their interests. Merchants, industrialists, and bankers run large enterprises with bureaucratically organized staffs; and when they combine to achieve comprehensive political goals, they create or support bureaucratically organized lobbies or parties. Farmers, too, are resorting more and more to bureaucratically coordinated action. And trade unions and labor parties are gaining economic and political prominence, because they effectively use bureaucratic methods to realize the organizational potential inherent in the concentration of workers in large plants.

Of all these developments, the expansion of large business enterprises into monopolistic giants has been particularly commented upon by certain analysts, who viewed it as so outstanding a feature of our time that they decided to speak of an entire period of "monopoly capitalism."

The concept "monopoly capitalism" is as provocative as it is misleading, but its very deficiencies aid us in putting into proper relief the peculiarities of the Oriental monopoly bureaucracy. The modern giant enterprises are indeed formidable, both in dimension and influence; and they certainly have crushed or absorbed many medium-sized and small rivals. But only rarely have they been able to prevent the operations of other giants in different branches of economy. And never have they been able to prevent the rise of big societal rivals, such as Big Government and Big Labor. "Monopoly capitalism" is therefore a misnomer for an institutional conformation in which multiple societal forces, however monopolistically inclined, counterbalance each other so as to preclude the exclusive leadership of any one of them.

No such checks weaken the monopolistic claims of a total apparatus state. The masters of hydraulic society permit no conspicuous and bureaucratically organized rivals. They exert exclusive leadership by ruthlessly and continually operating as a genuine monopoly bureaucracy.

CHAPTER 9

*C*he rise and fall of the theory of the
Asiatic mode of production

SUCH is hydraulic society, as it emerges from our inquiry. This society persisted over millennia—indeed until it suffered the impact
of the rising industrial and commercial West. Then chain reactions
were set in motion that gave the old order a new shape and a new
direction. Does our analysis of traditional hydraulic society enable
us to understand these recent developments?

At this point the reader who has followed us so far may want to
ask some questions. The concept of hydraulic society, he may say,
seems to have been eminently productive for the study of the past.
But is it also useful for evaluating the present and the future? Isn't
the "feudal" interpretation of Oriental conditions equally appropriate? Certainly it indicates the vigorous condemnation of an evil
heritage—and already it is widely employed in the East and in the
West.

This may well be so. However, in our context vigor and currency
can scarcely be decisive criteria. The history of social and racial
demagoguery shows that false slogans pervert man's thoughts and
deeds—the more disastrously, the more often and the more in-
sistently they are uttered. By equating the Orient and feudal Europe,
we lose sight of basic differences. And by ignoring the existence of
major non-Western societies, we run the danger of abandoning the
freedom of historical choice, because we are paralyzed by the fiction
of a unilinear and irresistible development.

No such danger resulted from the efforts of the 19th-century unilinealists whose errors are easily recognized. Essentially it is a product
of contemporary Marxism-Leninism, which combines ideological
and political means to liquidate both the theory of Oriental society
and the concept of a multilinear development.

Unidentified, this Marxist-Leninist force may block the analysis
of hydraulic society in transition—not by open argument, but by
creating an enervating atmosphere of ambivalence and distrust. Prop-

erly identified, it will give a new impetus to the study of the facts—
and the potentialities—of a multiform and changing world.

A. OLD AND NEW CONSTRUCTS OF A UNILINEAR DEVELOPMENT DISREGARD HYDRAULIC SOCIETY

1. 19TH-CENTURY UNILINEALISTS

THE unilinealists of the 19th century disregarded hydraulic society,
not because they shunned the reality of bureaucratic despotism but
because they were inspired by the stupendous consequences of the
industrial revolution. Overgeneralizing the experience of a rapidly
changing Western world, they naively postulated a simple, unilinear,
and progressive course of societal growth.

Man seemed to move irresistibly toward freedom (Hegel), toward
universal harmony (Fourier), toward a just and rational society
(Comte), toward general happiness (Spencer). Archaeologists began
to distinguish a scale of "ages" based on the use of stone, bronze, and
iron; and ethnologists arranged selected features of primitive life in
consecutive "stages." By defining the "Paleolithic" and "Neolithic"
as forerunners of the "Metal Age," Lubbock completed in 1865 what
Thomson had initiated in 1836. And in 1877 Morgan formulated his
much cited typological sequence: Old Stone Age (savagery), New
Stone Age (barbarism), and Iron Age (civilization).

2. NEGATIVE CRITICISMS

THE 19th-century evolutionists should certainly be praised for their
efforts to find structure and orderly change in the turbulent currents
of history. But their performance can hardly be deemed satisfactory,
for they were able to depict the higher civilizations as progressing
unilineally only by disregarding the fate of over one-half of the people of the globe. Nor did the criticism that was subsequently leveled
against them close the gap, for it, too, failed to take into account the
stagnation of the hydraulic world.

A wealth of new anthropological and archaeological data enabled
scholars such as Boas to demonstrate that the 19th-century theoreticians "erred in assuming a single unilinear evolution." [1] But the new
insights were accompanied by a stubborn reluctance to draw upon the
facts of Western and Oriental institutional history for a new multilinear pattern of development. Said Boas: "Laws of development,
except in most generalized form, cannot be established and a detailed
course of growth cannot be predicted. All we can do is to watch and
judge day by day what we are doing by what we have learned and

to shape our steps accordingly." [2] True, even this cautious statement suggests a "course of growth" of some kind. But instead of trying to determine its character, Boas contented himself with an impressionistic "day by day" evaluation of man's experience.

3. A THEORETICAL VACUUM

BOAS' arguments carried great weight both inside and outside his discipline. And his adevelopmental attitude gained wide support among social scientists generally during the first decades of the 20th century. A sociologist of knowledge, observing this agnosticism, could have quickly discerned the resulting theoretical vacuum. And he could have predicted that major conflicts and crises would inspire new questions and, ultimately, new answers.

Spengler's concept of compartmentalized civilizations that grow and decay like living organisms was so obviously based on biological rather than historical premises that it failed to satisfy the social scientists. For a different reason Toynbee's attempt failed also. Being a historian by profession, Toynbee approached the fate of mankind historically. But a lack of incisive major concepts handicapped his analysis. Overemphasis on details prevented him from recognizing major patterns of societal change. Overemphasis on the peculiarities of individual "societies" prevented him from recognizing the common institutional denominators that compel their classification in larger units. In the realm of taxonomy the "splitter" is as likely to err as is the lumper.[3] The intriguing trees that dot Toynbee's landscape [a] do not reveal the character of the woods of which they form a part.

4. THE SPREAD OF A "MARXIST-LENINIST" NEO-UNILINEALISM

BUT the demand for new historical vistas arose even before the appearance of Toynbee's *Study of History*. Economic and political earthquakes, starting with the Depression, had made Spengler's romantic speculations appear as unrealistic as the findings of an overmethodologized, overcompartmentalized and overquantified sociology.

Impressed by the brutal directness with which Marxism-Leninism discussed the burning conflicts of the day, numerous writers accepted

---

a. A landscape, let it be added, that was rich and suggestive in many ways. Toynbee's attempt to see structure and process in the life of "societies" will be acknowledged also by those who find the major conclusions of his sociohistorical studies intellectually problematic or morally paralyzing.

significant elements of the Soviet scheme of societal development together with the Marxist-Leninist explanation of capitalism and imperialism. They did not hesitate to call the traditional institutions of China, India and the Near East "feudal." They equated post-Mongol Russia and Western feudalism. And they were convinced that Communist Russia—and recently also mainland China—had attained a higher socialist or protosocialist level of development, because they had prevailed over both "feudalism" and capitalism.

5. THE NEED FOR A REEXAMINATION OF MARX', ENGELS', AND LENIN'S VIEWS ON THE "ASIATIC SYSTEM" AND ORIENTAL DESPOTISM

THIS being so, no responsible student of hydraulic society will deny the importance of reviewing the ideas of Marx, Engels, and Lenin about the "Asiatic system," Oriental despotism, and societal development. Manifestly such an examination is necessary from the standpoint of our subject matter. And it is highly dramatic, because Marx and Engels, and even the pre-October Lenin, accepted the very Asiatic concept that the high priests of Marxist-Leninist ideology are rejecting today.

B. MARX, ENGELS, AND LENIN ACCEPT THE ASIATIC CONCEPT

1. MARX FOLLOWS HIS CLASSICAL PREDECESSORS WITH REGARD TO THE INSTITUTIONAL STRUCTURE AND THE DEVELOPMENTAL POSITION OF THE ORIENT[a]

MARX' concept of Asiatic society was built largely on the views of such classical economists as Richard Jones and John Stuart Mill, who in their turn had developed generalized ideas held by Adam Smith and James Mill. Adam Smith noted similarities of hydraulic enterprise in China and "several other governments of Asia"; and he commented particularly on the acquisitive power of the rulers in China, ancient Egypt, and India.[1] James Mill considered the "Asiatic model of government" a general institutional type; [2] and he rejected forced analogies to European feudalism.[3] Richard Jones outlined

---

a. Marxist writers have seldom troubled to trace the sources of Marx' Asiatic concept (see Kautsky's note to Plechanoff, 1891: 447; Kautsky, 1929, II: 209 ff.; and Plekhanov, FPM: 40, 50). In my earlier writings I pointed to the geographer Ritter and to Hegel as possibly having influenced Marx (Wittfogel, 1929: 492–496; *ibid.,* 1931a: 354); but I did not then realize the fundamental dependence of Marx on the classical economists.

an over-all picture of Asiatic society in 1831,[4] when Marx was thirteen years old. And John Stuart Mill placed this society in a comparative frame in 1848,[5] when the authors of the *Communist Manifesto,* despite an occasional reference to the "East," [6] betrayed no awareness of a specific Asiatic society. It was only after Marx resumed his study of the classical economists in London [b] that he emerged as a vigorous adherent of the "Asiatic" concept.

From 1853 until his death Marx upheld the Asiatic concept together with the Asiatic nomenclature of the earlier economists. In addition to the formula "Oriental despotism," he employed for the whole institutional order the designation "Oriental society," used by John Stuart Mill,[7] and also (and with apparent preference) the designation "Asiatic society," used by Richard Jones.[8] He expressed his specific concern for the economic aspect of Asiatic society by speaking of an "Asiatic system" of landownership,[9] a specific "Asiatic mode of production," [10] and, more concisely, "Asiatic production." [11]

In the 1850's the notion of a specific Asiatic society struck Marx with the force of a discovery. Temporarily abandoning party politics, he applied himself intensely to the study of industrial capitalism as a distinct socio-economic and historical phenomenon. His writings during this period—among others, the first draft of *Das Kapital* which he set down in 1857–58 [c]—show him greatly stimulated by the Asiatic concept. In this first draft as well as in the final version of his *magnum opus,* he systematically compared certain institutional features in the three major types of agrarian society ("Asia," classical antiquity, feudalism) and in modern industrial society.[12]

b. In London, Marx resumed his economic and sociohistorical studies by reading Mill's *Principles of Political Economy* (from September 1850 on), Smith's *Wealth of Nations* (March 1851), Jones' *Introductory Lecture* [on Political Economy] (June 1851), Prescott's *Conquest of Mexico* and *Conquest of Peru* (August 1851), Bernier's *Voyages* (May–June 1853), James Mill's *History of British India* (probably—mentioned on July 7, 1853) (KMCL: 96, 103, 107, 110, 139; cf. also MEGA, III, Pt. 1: 133; Marx, NYDT, July 7, 1853).

c. In its original form this draft appeared in print for the first time in two volumes in 1939 and 1941 respectively. Marx rewrote and published part of it in 1859 under the title, *Zur Kritik der Politischen Ökonomie.* In the preface to this book he made his most systematic statement on social structure and change, a statement which ended with the enumeration of four major socio-economic orders, the Asiatic, the ancient, the feudal, and the capitalist modes of production. From the summer of 1863 on, Marx reorganized and reworked his earlier draft into what he now called *Das Kapital* (see Grossmann, 1929: 310 ff.). The history of pertinent theories, which Marx planned to publish as the fourth volume of *Das Kapital* (*ibid.:* 311), was eventually published as a separate work under the title *Theorien über der Mehrwert* (*Theories on Surplus Value*).

2. Marx' Asiatic Interpretation of India, China, and Post-Mongol Russia

WE need not in the present context examine every aspect of Marx' views on Asiatic society. For our purposes it is enough to underline his Asiatic interpretation of three countries that today are again prominent on the global political scene: India, China, and Russia.

a. India ("Asiatic Society" . . .)

IN two articles published in the *New York Daily Tribune* in 1853 [d] Marx discussed the character of Asiatic society and the possibilities of its progressive dissolution. In these articles he cited India as a representative of "old Asiatic society" and the Hindus as having certain crucial institutions in common with "all Oriental people." He argued that "climate and territorial conditions" made "artificial irrigation by canals and waterworks the basis of Oriental agriculture." And he observed that water control "necessitated in the Orient, where civilization was too low and the territorial extent too vast to call into life voluntary association, the interference of the centralizing power of the government."

Thus it was the need for government-directed water works that according to Marx gave birth to the Asiatic state. And it was the "dispersed" condition of the "Oriental people" and their agglomeration in "self-supporting" villages (combining small agriculture and domestic handicraft) that permitted its age-long perpetuation.[13]

Factually, the second statement requires qualification. Ideologically, it is most consequential. Only when we keep Marx' notion of the role of the "dispersed" Oriental villages in mind can we fully understand Marx' own, as well as Engels' and Lenin's, characterization of Oriental despotism.

b. China (". . . Asiatic Production" and Private Peasant Landholding)

LIVING in England, as he did for the greater part of his adult life, Marx was more alert to conditions in India than in China. But from the 1850's on he viewed China, like India, as characterized by "Asiatic" institutions,[14] and he found "the economic structure of Chinese society depending upon a combination of small agriculture and domestic industry (1859).[15] In Volume 3 of *Das Kapital*, while dis-

---

d. Marx, NYDT, June 25 and August 8, 1853. In his correspondence with Engels, Marx had gone far in clarifying his concept of an "Asiatic" or "Oriental" society (see MEGA, III, Pt. 1: 445 ff., 470 ff., and especially 475 ff., 480 ff., and 486 ff.).

cussing the impact of English trade on India and China, he made this point again. But here he also commented on the absence of a communal system of land tenure in contemporary China. In India and China "the broad foundation of the mode of production is shaped by the unity of small agriculture and domestic industry, to which, in India, is added the pattern of *the village community based on communal property, which, by the way, was also the original form in China.*" And remarking on the slow dissolution of the self-sufficient rural economy in contemporary India (where Britain intervened directly) and the slower dissolution of this economy in China ("where no direct political power aids it"), he concluded that "different from English trade, the Russian trade leaves the economic foundations of *Asiatic production* untouched." [16]

As early as the 1850's Marx was aware of the fact that the Chinese "Crown" permitted most of the peasants to "hold their lands, which are of a very limited extent, in full property." [17] And the just cited passage from *Das Kapital* shows clearly that in his opinion the disappearance of "communal landownership" in China had not, in any significant way, undermined "the economic foundations of Asiatic production."

c. Russia ("Oriental Despotism" . . . Perpetuated)

To the best of my knowledge, Russia was first called a "semi-Asiatic" country in an article signed by Marx, but written by Engels, which appeared in the *New York Daily Tribune* on April 18, 1853.[18] On August 5, 1853, and this time in an article that was genuinely his, Marx contrasted certain "semi-Eastern" developments involving Tsarist Russia with "completely Eastern" events in China. From the start the term "semi-Asiatic," as applied by Marx and Engels to Russia, referred not to that country's geographic location but to its "traditions and institutions, character and conditions." [19]

The articles of 1853 did not discuss Russia's institutional peculiarity in detail. However, in 1881 Marx spoke of Russia's isolated villages and the strongly centralized form of despotism that had arisen everywhere on this foundation.[20] Shortly before, Engels had emphasized this point. Indeed the Marxian interpretation of Russia received its greatest currency through two statements made by Engels in the 1870's. The first, written in 1875, reads as follows: "Such a complete isolation of the individual [village] communities from each other, which in the whole country creates identical, but the exact opposite of common, interests, is the natural foundation of Oriental despotism, and from India to Russia this societal form, wherever it prevailed, has always produced despotism and has always found therein its supplement. Not only the Russian state in general, but even its specific form, the despotism of the Tsar, far from being suspended in mid-air, is the necessary and logical product of the Russian social conditions." [21] The second, contained in his critique of Dühring, expresses the same idea more briefly: "The ancient communes, where they continued to exist, have for thousands of years formed the basis of the most barbarous form of state, Oriental despotism, from India to Russia." [22]

How long did Russian Oriental despotism endure? Marx insisted that Peter the Great, far from eliminating it, "generalized" it.[23] And he expected the emancipation of the serfs to strengthen the absolutist regime, because it would destroy both the power of the nobles over the serfs and the self-government of the rural communities.[24]

Marx did not explain how in Russia modern capitalism could develop under Oriental rule. His failure to do so is one of the most serious deficiencies in his treatment of marginal and transitional patterns of hydraulic society. But in terms of his views on the position of capitalism in the Orient,[25] he was consistent when, in 1881, he considered Russia's modern quasi-Western capitalism a predatory, middleman-like force.[26]

3. Marx Warns against Confusing the State-Controlled Agrarian Order of Asia with Slavery or Serfdom

RETURNING to the over-all problems of the Asiatic mode of production, we may say: no matter what Marx thought about the exact nature of landownership in the Orient, he felt certain it was not feudal. In 1853, when Engels noted "that the Orientals did not advance toward landownership,[e] not even to a feudal one," Marx warned against a too sweeping assumption of the absence of Oriental landownership.[27] But while he then saw some evidence of private landholding in India,[28] and later also in China, he did not call their systems of land tenure "feudal."

Oversimplifying a complicated pattern of proprietary relations, Marx, nevertheless, recognized a basic trend when he noted that under the "Asiatic system" the state was "the real landlord." [29] Later he refined this early notion. In *Das Kapital*, Volume 3, he explained that under the Asiatic system there existed "no private landowner-

---

e. Engels means private landownership, as can be seen from Marx' preceding letter, which, taking up Bernier's view, expressly speaks of *Privatgrundeigentum* (MEGA, III, Pt. 1: 477).

ship, but both private and communal possession and usage of the soil." [30]

This position led Marx to brand the confusion of Asiatic-Egyptian land tenure with systems based on slavery and serfdom as the worst mistake that can be made in the analysis of ground rent.[31] And it immunized him against viewing the Indian *zamindars* as a variant of European feudal landlords. He classified the traditional *zamindars* as "native tax-gatherers." And he ridiculed the attempt to equate the British-made *zamindar*-landlords with England's landed gentry: "A curious sort of English landlord was the zemindar, receiving only one-tenth of the rent, while he had to make over nine-tenths of it to the Government." [f]

4. "General Slavery"

THUS in the "Orient" the state ruled supreme over both the labor and property of its subjects. Marx commented on the despot's position as the actual and apparent coordinator of the population's labor for hydraulic and other communal works; [32] and he considered the individual land-possessing peasant *"au fond* the property, the slave" of the head of the Oriental community.[33] Consistently he spoke of the "general slavery of the Orient." [34] In contrast to the private slavery of classical antiquity, a type whose insignificance in the Orient he understood,[35] and in contrast to the decentralized patterns of feudal control, which he also understood,[36] Marx viewed the relation between Oriental despotism and the most important group in the population as one of *general* (state) slavery.[g]

5. For Many Years Lenin Also Upheld the Asiatic Concept

IT is difficult to harmonize these statements with the "feudal" interpretation of the Orient offered today by persons calling themselves

f. Marx, NYDT, August 5, 1853. For reasons that will be discussed below, the Indian Communist edition of *Karl Marx: Articles on India* (cited as Marx, 1951) which attached "feudal" comments to Marx' Asiatic views contains neither this piece nor the one published on June 7, 1858, also dealing with the Indian land system.

g. In an elliptic remark made in 1887, Engels said that "class oppression" in both Asiatic and classical antiquity had the form of "slavery." Since Engels, like Marx, recognized the irrelevance in the Orient of private slavery (see below), he was obviously referring to the "general slavery" of Oriental despotism. His claim that in both cases slavery involved "not so much the expropriation of the masses from the land as the appropriation of their persons" (Engels, 1887: iii) fits the Orient, but not classical antiquity.

"Marxists." It is even difficult to present such an interpretation in the name of Leninism. Starting as an orthodox Marxist, Lenin upheld the idea of a special "Asiatic system" for the better part of three decades, speaking precisely, from 1894 to 1914.

a. "Asiatic Despotism," a Totality of Traits "with Special Economic, Political, and Sociological Characteristics"

THE young Lenin joined the Social Democratic movement in 1893. After a zealous study of Marx' and Engels' writings, he accepted, in 1894, the "Asiatic mode of production" as one of the four major economic configurations of society.[37] In his first important book, *The Development of Capitalism in Russia*, published in 1899, he began to designate his country's Asiatic conditions as the *Aziatchina*,[38] the "Asiatic system." And he termed Tsarist control over land and peasants a "fiscal land ownership." [39]

In 1900 he referred to the government of traditional China as "Asiatic"; [40] and he rejected as "pharisaic" the equation of European and Asiatic institutions.[41] In 1902 he noted the crushing character of Asiatic oppression.[42] In 1905 he denounced "the cursed heritage of bondage of the *Aziatchina* and the shameful treatment of man," [43] and he contrasted the retarded development of "Asiatic capitalism" and the comprehensive and fast development of European capitalism.[44] In 1906 and 1907 he engaged in a passionate debate with Plekhanov which underlined his awareness of the Asiatic system and its implications for a "semi-Asiatic" Russia.[45] In 1911 he reemphasized the peculiarity of "the Oriental system," the "Asiatic system," and the stagnation of the Orient.[46]

In 1912, on the occasion of the Chinese revolution, he recognized the "Asiatic" quality of traditional China by speaking of "Asiatic China" [47] and of the "Asiatic" president of China.[48] In 1914 in a discussion with Rosa Luxemburg, he defined "Asiatic despotism" as a "totality of traits" with special "economic, political, and sociological characteristics," and he ascribed its great stability to "utterly patriarchal pre-capitalist traits and an insignificant development of commodity production and class differentiation." [49] In the fall of that year he wrote an article on Marx for the *Encyclopaedia Granat*, in which once more he listed Marx' four major socio-economic configurations, "the Asiatic, the ancient, the feudal, and the modern bourgeois modes of production." [50]

Thus from 1894 to 1914 Lenin upheld basic features of Marx' concept of Asiatic society, the Asiatic mode of production, and Oriental despotism.

b. Lenin Elaborates Marx' Semi-Asiatic Interpretation of Tsarist Russia

LENIN, however, approached the Asiatic problem more narrowly and more broadly than Marx. Marx defined the peculiarities of precapitalist societies in order to deepen his understanding of capitalist society; and his comments on the Asiatic mode of production primarily served this end. But he did not employ the Asiatic concept either to analyze or to influence his sociopolitical environment.

Lenin was much less interested in macrohistorical comparisons. Living in a society which Marx had characterized as semi-Asiatic, and fighting a state which Marx had characterized as Orientally despotic, Lenin was vitally interested in applying the Asiatic concept to his immediate environment. Most of his references to "Asiatic" conditions pertain to Russia.

Following Marx and Engels, Lenin called Russian society "semi-Asiatic," [51] and the Tsarist regime "Oriental despotism." Western socialists loathed Bismarck because of his antisocialist measures; and some Russian socialists, such as Ryazanov, equated Russian and Prussian absolutism.[h] But Lenin considered Bismarck's repressive state a "pygmy" compared to Russian absolutism, which, probably remembering Marx' characterization of Tatar despotism,[52] he called a "monster." [53]

c. Lenin Holds the Term "Feudal" Unsuited to Traditional Russia

LENIN expressed his acceptance of the Asiatic concept positively by using such terms as *Aziatchina* and "Asiatic" and negatively by his reluctance to apply the term "feudal" to traditional Russia. The Russian peasants lived under conditions of *krepostnichestvo*, literally "attachment"; [i] and Lenin thus designated the Russian system of land tenure. We translate it "bondage."

Lenin made his position clear in 1902, when he criticized the first

h. A Western interpretation of historical Russia was suggested by the scholarly Ryazanov, who perhaps more than any other Russian socialist familiarized Western Marxists with Marx' Asiatic views on Russia. Ryazanov explained the rise of Muscovite autocracy as a spontaneous response to "the Tatar danger," comparable to Austria's response to "the Turkish danger." The analogy is manifestly faulty, since the Austrians never lived under a Turkish "yoke." But Ryazanov made it the starting point for his equation of Russian and Austrian absolutism, and he bracketed Prussian absolution and Tsarist Russia (Rjasanoff, 1909: 28).

i. Readers unfamiliar with the Russian language are warned against relying on the official Communist translations of Lenin's and Stalin's works. These translations almost always render *krepostnichestvo* as "feudal." Disregarding a distinction that

draft of the program of the Russian Social-Democratic party for having "almost intentionally" confused the issue by ascribing a "feudal-craft period" to Medieval Russia. Noting that the appropriateness of the term "feudalism" to the Russian Middle Ages was being questioned, he found it "least applicable to Russia." [54] In 1905 he again, with reference to Russia, insisted that the word *krepostnichestvo* be employed instead of *feodalisma*.[55] In 1911 he apologized for using the term "feudal" in the Russian context, since this was "a not quite exact general *European* expression." [56]

C. RETREAT FROM TRUTH

DOES all this mean that Marx, Engels, and Lenin upheld the classical concept of Asiatic society fully and without oscillation? It does not. Several times Lenin came close to withdrawing from his original Asiatic position before abandoning it altogether in 1916. But the retrogressive trend began prior to Lenin. Significantly, the first Marxist to accept the concept of an Asiatic society was the first to cripple it: Marx himself. Significantly also, he crippled it by dropping the idea of a bureaucratic ruling class.

1. MARX

a. Marx "Mystifies" the Character of the Ruling Class

IN his effort to determine class rule Marx, like Adam Smith and his successors, asked: Who controls the decisive means of production and the "surplus" created by them? And he found that these advantages were enjoyed in antiquity by the "slaveholders," in feudal society by the "feudal landlords," in modern industrial society by "the capitalists," and in Asiatic society by "the sovereign" or "the state." [1] Thus in the three types of private-property-based society of his schema, Marx established a ruling class as the main beneficiaries of economic privilege, whereas with regard to government-dominated Oriental society he was satisfied to mention a single person, the ruler, or an institutional abstraction, "the state."

This was a strange formulation for a man who ordinarily was eager to define social classes and who denounced as a mystifying "reification" the use of such notions as "commodity" and "the state," when the underlying human (class) relations were left unexplained.[a]

---

for many years Lenin deemed essential, they misrepresent his view of Russian society during these years.

a. When Marx discussed the "fetishistic" character of commodities, he stereotyped ideas already formulated by his classical predecessors. He admitted this none too

But it may be said, perhaps Marx did not know of any persons who, in Asiatic society, shared the surplus with the sovereign? No such plea can be made. Marx had thoroughly studied John Stuart Mill's *Principles*,[2] which, in addition to the ruler's household and favorites, listed as the beneficiaries of the Asiatic state revenue "the various functionaries of the government." [3] And in his historical survey of the theories of surplus value, he had inserted *verbatim* Jones' statement that "The surplus revenue from the soil, the only revenues except those of the peasants of any considerable amount, were (in Asia, and more especially in India) distributed by the state and its officers," [4] as well as Bernier's comment that in India the state revenues supported large numbers of serving men.[5]

Marx' interest in the class issue, the data at his disposal, and his objection to the mystification of social relations point to one conclusion, and one conclusion only. They all suggest that from his own standpoint Marx should have designated the functional bureaucracy as the ruling class of Oriental despotism. But Marx did nothing of the kind. Instead of clarifying the character of the Oriental ruling class he obscured it. Measured by the insights reached by Bernier, Jones, and Mill, Marx' mystification (reification) of the character of the ruling class in Oriental society was a step backward.

b. Further Retrogressions

MARX took this step backward in the 1850's, at the very time he was accepting the classical concept of Asiatic society. In the '60's and '70's he regressed further. A comparison of the first volume of *Das Kapital* and his writings of 1853 and 1857–58 shows him in the early years more precise on the hydraulic aspect of Oriental despotism. The many passages in *Das Kapital* and the *Theorien über der Mehrwert* that contrast Oriental and ancient, feudal, and/or capitalist conditions reveal both the later Marx' determination to view Asiatic society as a specific institutional conformation and his reluctance to discuss the managerial aspect of Oriental despotism.[6]

In the writings of the later period he emphasized the technical side of large-scale water works,[7] where previously he had emphasized their political setting. He now lumped together control of water "in Egypt, Lombardy, Holland, etc.," [8] where previously he had distinguished the centralized and despotic governments of the Orient from the

---

gracefully in Volume I of *Das Kapital* (I: 47 n.). But he was more generous in Volume III, where he commented that the exposure of the false "personification of things and the reification of production relations" was "the greatest merit of classical economy" (Marx, DK, III, Pt. 2: 366).

private-enterprise-based "voluntary associations" of Flanders and
Italy.[9] He now mentioned the agrohydraulic function of a single state,
India,[10] where previously he had spoken of this "economic function"
as devolving upon "all Asiatic governments." [11]

A frequently cited passage in *Das Kapital,* Volume 1, appears to
face the problem of the ruling class in Oriental society. Actually, however, it blurs the issue by introducing what, from the Marxian point
of view, is a most peculiar determinant of economic dominance. Attached to the phrase "The regulation of water in Egypt" is the following note: "The necessity to calculate the periodic movements of the
Nile created Egyptian astronomy and with it the rule of the priest
caste as leader of agriculture." By making astronomy the basis for
economic leadership, Marx dropped his standard criterion: control
over the means of production. And by stressing the hereditary
("caste") status of the "leaders" rather than their class, he further
confused the matter.[b]

Moreover, in Volume 3 of *Das Kapital* he asserted that "in despotic
states, the labor of supreme supervision and the ubiquitous interference of the government" is demanded in "the execution of the
common tasks evolving from the nature of *all* [sic!] commonwealths
as well as the specific functions that stem from the antagonisms between the government and the mass of the people." [12]

In writing thus, Marx obscured the specific managerial functions
of the despotic state of the Orient, which in the '50's had intrigued
him so greatly.

2. ENGELS

a. Asiatic Society—Yes! (Engels' Basic Attitude)

MARX' retrogressions in the treatment of Asiatic society are little
known. Those of Engels have been widely publicized. Indeed the
frequent references to certain passages in his book, *The Origin of the
Family, Private Property, and the State,* have beclouded the fact that
from 1853 until his death in 1895 Engels upheld, in largest part, the
theory of Oriental society.

Engels' early role in clarifying Marx' understanding of the hydraulic aspect of the Orient and the validity of an "Asiatic" interpretation
of India and Russia [c] has already been noted. In his critique of Eugen

b. Marx, DK, I: 478, n. 5. The sentence is followed by a quotation from Cuvier's
Discours sur les revolutions du globe, which relates the need for astronomy to the
annual rise of the Nile and the [seasonal] agricultural activities of the Egyptians.

c. See above. Since neither Marx nor Engels had explained how, under the influence
of foreign capitalism, an Orientally despotic government could encourage modern

Dühring (the *Anti-Dühring*) he went further than Marx by suggesting that the execution of important "socio-administrative functions" [13] might lead to the formation of a "ruling class." And he underscored this point by noting that each of the many "despotic governments which rose and fell in India and Persia . . . knew full well that it was first of all the total entrepreneur [*Gesamtunternehmerin*] of irrigation in the river valleys, without which no agriculture is possible there." [14] In his critique of Dühring as well as in his book on the family Engels contrasted the "domestic slavery" of the Orient and the "work slavery" of antiquity.[15] And in a passage inserted in *Das Kapital,* Volume 3, published in 1894, eleven years after Marx' death, he described the peasants of both India and Russia as being exploited by the mercilessly grinding "tax-screw of their despotic governments." [16]

b. Asiatic Society—Yes and No! (The Anti-Dühring)

THIS long-range trend was interrupted by two major lapses—one manifested in the *Anti-Dühring,* the other in *The Origin of the Family, Private Property, and the State.*

In the *Anti-Dühring* Engels suggested a dual origin for the state and for its ruling class. In the first case, these two forces came into being because of excessive political power, in the second because of the growth of private property and private-property-based production. The first development involved the rise of important socio-administrative functions and the ability of the governing persons to defy control to the extent that the original "servant" of society became its "master." [17]

In this context Engels mentioned "an Oriental despot or satrap, the Greek tribal prince, the chieftain of a Celtic clan and so on." His two Western examples bring to mind Marx' ideas on societal dominance based on political-military function.[18] According to Marx, this

---

capitalist forms of private enterprise, Engels was introducing a new concept when in 1894 he called Russia's new bourgeoisie a dominant force (Marx and Engels, 1952: 240). He did not elaborate this point, nor did he reconcile it with a statement made four years earlier on the incompatibility of Oriental despotism and capitalism: "Turkish, like any other oriental domination, is incompatible with a capitalistic economy; the surplus value extorted is not safe from the hands of greedy satraps and pashas. The first basic condition of bourgeois acquisition is lacking: the security of the person and the property of the trader" (Marx and Engels, 1952: 40). Engels' statement of 1894 also contradicts the insertion in *Das Kapital,* III, in which he described Russia's despotic government as the great exploiter of the peasantry (Marx, DK, III, Pt. 2: 259 ff.). But however different their emphasis, Engels' various utterances on post-Emancipation Russia had one thing in common: they all implied that Tsarist despotism was still a going concern.

type of dominance soon yielded to dominance based on private property and private-property-rooted labor (slave labor and serf labor).[19] Only in the form of Oriental despotism did societal dominance based on public function spread far and last long.

Although Engels, in the *Anti-Dühring*, twice noted the enormous staying power of Oriental despotism ("thousands of years"),[20] in neither instance did he elaborate this point. But he did list the Oriental despot first; and later in speaking of the despotic regimes of Persia and India he did specify their "socio-administrative" function: their "first duty was the general maintenance of irrigation throughout the valleys." [21] Engels even noted that dominance based on socio-administrative function united the "individual ruling persons into a ruling class." [22]

Thus far Engels' presentation, despite its lack of subtlety, was scientifically legitimate and in agreement with Marx' version of the classical concept of Oriental society. Equally legitimate, and again in agreement with relevant ideas of Smith, Mill, and Marx, was his statement on the second origin of classes and the state: [23] the rise of slave-based production and of private property in slaves involved the rise of a private-property-based ruling class; and this development paved the way for an evolution that led via classical Greece and the Roman Empire to "modern Europe." [24] And it also involved the rise of a type of state which, because of irreconcilable contradictions in the new private-property-based economy, was used by the propertied classes to protect their privileged position.[25]

We need not criticize here the primitive ideas on the relation of wealth and government that Marx shared with John Locke, Adam Smith, and others.[26] In the present context we are interested only in the fact that Engels, in the earlier part of the *Anti-Dühring*, indicated two different patterns of societal development ("Side by side with this [the socio-administrative] origin of class there occurred still another") [27] and that in the last part of this same book, he abruptly abandoned this notion of a multilinear development. There he spoke of state and class rule as if they had resulted exclusively from antagonisms based on conditions of private property. And he climaxed his slanted presentation by listing only three class societies based respectively on slavery, serfdom, and wage labor.[28]

c. Asiatic Society—No! (*The Origin of the Family, Private Property, and the State*)

IN Engels' much quoted book on the family, which links the basic ideas of Morgan's *Ancient Society* and certain Marxian views, Asiatic society as a major societal order has altogether disappeared. Here Engels discusses the origin of the state as if he had never heard of the "socio-administrative" state in general and of Oriental despotism in particular.

This omission cannot be ascribed to any lack of interest in societies of the "barbarian" type, for Engels elaborated on the conditions of "barbarism" [d] in ancient Greece, Rome, and the Celtic and Germanic Middle Ages.[29] Nor can it be ascribed to the general exclusion of matters pertaining to the Orient. Although more remiss in this respect than Morgan [30] (Engels refrained for reasons of "space" from dealing with the pertinent history of "Asiatic" peoples),[31] he did speak of Asia, the Asiatics, and Oriental institutions; [32] and as already related, he contrasted the "domestic slavery" of the Orient with the "work slavery" of antiquity.[33] But unconcerned with what he had formerly designated as the "new division of labor"—a division which, subsequent to the natural division of labor within a community,[e] caused the rise of "functional" governments and power-based ruling classes —and also unconcerned with what both he and Marx had written regarding the exploitative quality of Oriental despotism, Engels now asserted categorically that *"the first great social division of labor initiated the first great division of society into two classes: masters and slaves, exploiters and exploited."* [34]

The slavery-based society was governed by a state of slave owners, just as the feudal and capitalist types of society were governed respectively by a state of feudal nobles and a state of capitalists.[35] In all these societies economic dominance led to political dominance.[36] And eco-

d. Marx and Engels adopted the terms "barbarism" and "civilization" not from Adam Smith (see Smith, 1937: 666, 669, esp. 735), but from Fourier, whose typology of development Engels praised in the forties [MEGA, I, Pt. 4: 413 (1846); I, Pt. 6: 398 ff. (1848)], and again with undiminished enthusiasm in the seventies (Engels, 1935: 269). Even in 1884, when he adopted Morgan's schema, Engels still referred to Fourier's "brilliant critique of civilization," and he commented on the fact that Fourier, like Morgan, viewed private landownership as a key feature of this phase (Engels, 1921: 187 n.).

Under the influence of Morgan, Marx and Engels modified these categories. But they did not discard them. It was with these categories in mind that Engels, in 1848, spoke of "semi-barbarous" countries, such as India and China (MEGA, I, Pt. 6: 506), that Marx, in the fifties, spoke of the "barbarism" of China and the "semi-barbarian" emperor of China (Marx, 1951a: 48, 50, 55) and its "patriarchal constitution" (*ibid.*: 56), of "barbaric" Turkey and Persia (*ibid.*: 47), of the "semi-barbarian, semi-civilized communities" of India (Marx, NYDT, June 25, 1853), of Eastern "barbarism" (*ibid.*, April 12, 1853), and "the barbarian" sovereign of Russia (Marx and Engels, 1920, I: 251).

e. Engels, 1935: 165. In the same work Engels referred to the "primeval division of labor in the agricultural family" (*ibid.*: 183). Marx (DK, I: 44 and 316) considered the division of labor according to sex and age its primeval form.

nomic dominance, as Engels stressed, involved *private ownership of the decisive means of production.*[37]

Thus societal leadership and exploitation were essentially rooted in private property. The despotic masters of the functional state, whose ruthless methods of exploitation Engels had once so eloquently described, remained unnoted. "With *slavery,* which in civilization developed most fully, there occurred *the first great split of society into an exploiting and an exploited class.* This cleavage lasted throughout the whole period of civilization. *Slavery is the first form of exploitation,* which is specific for the ancient world; it was succeeded by serfdom in the Middle Ages and wage labor in more recent times. These are the three great forms of servitude, characteristic of the three great epochs of civilization." [38]

The references to "civilization" do not correct the notion of a unilinear pattern of development created by these sentences. But they show Engels aware of what he was doing—or better: of what he was hiding. In Engels' terminology, "civilization" was identical with the predominance of private property. Through his qualifying clause, he backhandedly admitted that his statement did not include the "barbarian" world of Oriental despotism.

d. Retrogressive Trends in a Supposedly Progressive Position

i. MARX DEFENDS SCIENTIFIC OBJECTIVITY AGAINST ALL EXTRANEOUS CONSIDERATIONS

THIS is not a pretty picture. The founding fathers of scientific socialism, who claimed to be basing their political practice on the most advanced theory of societal development, harmed rather than helped the cause of truth when they were confronted with the most important historical manifestation of total power. Why? Did Marx have so little regard for scientific truth that he bent it easily? This certainly was not the case. The care with which he documented his own economic views and the elaborate way in which he presented opposing views demonstrate that he fully recognized the demands of scholarship.

And Marx himself was explicit on this point. Commenting on the scientific behavior of Malthus and Ricardo, he condemned all who abandoned scientific truth and the interest of mankind in general for special interests of any kind. A scholar, he held, should seek the truth in accordance with the immanent needs of science, no matter how this affected the fate of any social class: capitalists, landowners, and workers. Marx praised Ricardo for taking this attitude,[39] which he called "not only scientifically honest, but also scientifically required." [40] For the same reasons, he condemned as "mean" anyone who subordinated scientific objectivity to extraneous purposes: "a man who tries to accommodate science to a standpoint which is not derived from its own interest, however erroneous, but from outside, alien, and extraneous interests, [such a man] I call 'mean' (gemein)." *f*

Marx was entirely consistent when he held the refusal to accommodate science to the interests of any class to be "stoic, objective, scientific." [41] He was entirely consistent also, when he concluded on a note which from the standpoint of Leninist-Stalinist partisanship sounds heretically humanitarian: "As far as this can be done without sin against his science, Ricardo is always a philanthropist, as he indeed was in practice." [42] And he was equally consistent when he branded the reverse behavior a "sin against science." [43]

ii. MARX' AND ENGELS' "SIN AGAINST SCIENCE"

IN view of these strongly worded principles, Marx' retrogressions in analyzing Asiatic society assume special significance. Obviously the concept of Oriental despotism contained elements that paralyzed his search for truth. As a member of a group that intended to establish a total managerial and dictatorial state and was ready to use "despotic measures" [44] to achieve its socialist ends, Marx could scarcely help recognizing some disturbing similarities between Oriental despotism and the state of his program.

The classical economist John Stuart Mill, who, in his *Principles*, wrote about the Oriental state, warned in the same book against an all-interfering state, against the dangers of an intellectually elitist despotism ("the government of sheep by their shepherd, without anything like so strong an interest as the shepherd has in the thriving of his flock"), against "political slavery," [45] and a "dominant bureaucracy." [46] Did these and other academic exhortations induce Marx in the '50's to hide the bureaucratic aspect of Oriental despotism? This we do not know. But we do know that in the '60's and '70's anarchist writers leveled much less academic criticisms at the Marxian principles of state socialism.

When Marx was writing the final version of *Das Kapital*, Volume 1, he was in open conflict with the Proudonists.[47] And from the late '60's on, both he and Engels were manifestly disturbed by the claim of the Bakunists that state socialism would inevitably involve the despotic rule of a privileged minority over the rest of the population, the

f. Marx, TMW, II, Pt. 1: 312 ff. In this context the German word *gemein*, like the related English "mean," has the connotations "vicious," "shabby."

workers included.[48] In 1873 Bakunin continued the attack in his book *Statism and Anarchism,* which insisted that the Marx-envisaged socialist state "begets despotism on the one hand and slavery on the other." [49] The Marxist theory "is a falsehood, behind which lurks the despotism of a governing minority, a falsehood which is all the more dangerous in that it appears as the ostensible expression of the people's will." [50]

The political solutions offered by the anarchists were without doubt Utopian. But their criticism cut deep, as can be inferred from Marx' interpretation of the Paris Commune (which the Anarchists held to be a clownish reversal of his earlier position),[51] and from the secrecy with which, in 1875, Marx and Engels shrouded their ideas on state socialism and the dictatorship of the proletariat.[52] In his personal copy of *Statism and Anarchism* Marx made extensive notes, but he never answered Bakunin's acid arguments in public.

Engels confused the issue of Oriental despotism most seriously in the years following the appearance of Bakunin's book. His insertion in *Das Kapital,* Volume 3, dealing with the exploitative despotic regimes of Russia and India was made in the '90's [53]—when, according to Engels' own statement, he was no longer bothered by the anarchists.[g]

iii. FROM PROGRESSIVE TO REACTIONARY UTOPIANISM

THE authors of the *Communist Manifesto* accused the "Utopian" socialists of giving a "fantastic description of the society of the future." [54] But Marx and Engels did exactly this when they pictured their socialist state. The fathers of "scientific socialism," who realistically, if imperfectly, analyzed the problems of capitalist economy, failed to make any comparable effort to analyze the problems of the dictatorial and functional state, a socialist variant of which they were seeking to establish. Substituting "fanatical superstitions" [55] for scientific inquiry, they made the very mistake for which they had so harshly criticized the early Utopians.

And they suffered the same fate. The Utopian views, which in Marx' and Engels' opinion originally had a progressive ("revolutionary") quality, lost "all practical value and all theoretical justification," when new progressive societal forces emerged. Their significance bore "an inverse relation to historical development." Eventually they became outright "reactionary." [56]

g. For the later Engels' evaluation of the anarchist criticism as a past issue, see his foreword to *The Critique of the Gotha Programme,* published in 1891: "These considerations do not now exist" (Marx, 1935: 41).

Under different circumstances and in a much more devastating way, the Utopian state socialists also closed the circle. Their economic and functional approach to history stimulated the social sciences of the 19th and early 20th centuries. And their social criticism stimulated the struggle against the monstrous conditions that characterized the earlier phases of the modern industrial system.[57] But the original vision lost its progressive quality as realization neared. On the theoretical plane its reactionary potential was manifested early in Marx' and Engels' retrogressive attitude toward the Asiatic variant of managerial and bureaucratic despotism. On the practical plane this reactionary potential was manifested on a colossal scale when, nine months after the fall of the semimanagerial apparatus state of Tsarism, the Bolshevik revolution paved the way for the rise of the total managerial apparatus state of the USSR.

3. LENIN

a. Lenin Further Cripples Marx' Crippled Version of the Asiatic Concept

i. CONSISTENT DISREGARD OF THE MANAGERIAL ASPECT OF ORIENTAL DESPOTISM

THE factors which increasingly distorted Marx' and Engels' views of Oriental despotism increasingly produced retrogressive results in the case of Lenin.

During the first twenty years of his political career Lenin had generally accepted Marx' version of the classical concept of Asiatic society, but from the start his attitude was peculiarly selective. He never mentioned the managerial functions of Oriental despotism, although he certainly knew Engels' pertinent statements in the *Anti-Dühring* (from which he frequently quoted) and although these functions were emphasized in the correspondence between Marx and Engels (with which he was familiar). Nor was his disinclination to explore the functional aspect of Asiatic despotism weakened by the knowledge that this aspect was stressed by Kautsky, whose "orthodox" Marxism he admired, and by Plekhanov, whom he considered the leading authority on Marxist philosophy even after they broke politically.

Lenin thus closed his eyes not only to crucial realities in traditional Asia but also to essential features of the Tsarist regime, whose managerial activities he could observe at close range. In his *Development of Capitalism in Russia* (1899), he accomplished the extraordinary feat of describing the rise of a private-property-based industry in his native land without indicating the dimension of the state-managed enterprises which for almost two hundred years had dominated Russia's large-scale industry and which, with significant modifications, were still extremely important.

By neglecting the managerial role of Tsarist despotism, Lenin seriously falsified the picture of Russia's economic order. By underplaying its exploitative role, he falsified it still more. In 1894 Engels noted the crushing effect of taxation on the Russian peasants. And a few years later, Nicolai-on and Milyukov showed that the government, through direct—and indirect—taxes, was depriving the Russian peasants of about 50 per cent of their income.[58] Although he dealt with Nicolai-on's work at length, Lenin said nothing about the indirect taxes, which were numerous and heavy, and this procedure led him to the problematic conclusion that among the peasant group on which he had detailed data the taxes absorbed only about 15 per cent or "one seventh of the gross expenditure." [59]

ii. A CONFUSED PRESENTATION OF RUSSIA'S RULING CLASS

LENIN's treatment of the ruling class under Oriental despotism was equally unsatisfactory. Marx' retrogressions in this respect, although enormously important for the interpretation of managerial despotism in general, did not seriously affect his analysis of modern Western society, which after all was his major concern. On the other hand, Lenin's discussion of the ruling class of Oriental despotism was anything but academic. It pertained to the very society which he was endeavoring to revolutionize.

If, as Lenin assumed, Tsarism was a variant of Oriental despotism, and if under Oriental despotism landlordism originated from a non-feudal form of state dependency, then he could be expected to hold that Tsarist society was controlled not by feudal or postfeudal landowners but by bureaucrats; and if this was his opinion, he could be expected to say so. If it was not, he could be expected to give substantial reasons for rejecting this view.

Actually he did neither. Instead he described Russia's ruling class now in one way, now in another. At times he spoke of a "dictatorship of the bureaucracy," [60] and he saw its officials towering "over the voiceless people like a dark forest." [61] At times he spoke of the Tsarist government as having "bourgeois" tendencies [62] and being subservient to the "big capitalists and nobles." [63] Most frequently he described it as being dominated by noble landowners.[64]

b. A Power-Strategist's Treatment of Truth

OBSERVING these inconsistencies, we may well wonder how a revolutionary leader whose ideas on the ruling class were so blurred could seize power. But we have only to recall Hitler's perverted interpretation of German conditions and his smashing victories over his internal enemies to realize that enormous political successes can be won on the basis of ideas that are at best semirational.

Lenin's stress on objective and absolute truth [65] did not prevent him from demanding that socialist writers and artists follow the principle of partisanship, *partinost*.[66] Throughout his career he himself did so even when it meant the abrogation of the most elementary rules of scientific propriety.[67]

Certainly Lenin's inconsistency in defining Russia's ruling class had no scientific justification. And his tricky verbal acrobatics in and after the Stockholm debate on Russia's Asiatic Restoration foreshadow his later readiness to blackout the truth completely.[h]

c. The Threat of the Asiatic Restoration (1906–07)

PREPARING for the Stockholm Congress of the Russian Social Democratic party in 1906, Plekhanov, speaking for the Mensheviks, challenged Lenin's plan for the nationalization of the land. Both the debate at the Congress itself and Lenin's subsequent utterances show him seriously upset by Plekhanov's argument, which, recalling Russia's Asiatic heritage, warned of the possibility of an Asiatic restoration.

The reason for Plekhanov's apprehensions can be quickly told. Encouraged by the experiences of 1905, Lenin believed that the Social Democratic party would be able to seize power if it could rally behind it Russia's small working class and the numerically strong peasantry. To win the support of the latter, he suggested that the nationalization of the land be made part of the revolutionary program. Plekhanov branded the idea of a socialist seizure of power as premature and the plan to nationalize the land as potentially reactionary. Such a policy, instead of discontinuing the attachment of the land and its tillers to the state, would leave "untouched this survival of an old semi-Asiatic order" and thus facilitate its restoration.[68]

This was the dreaded historical perspective that Lenin alternately designated as "the restoration of the Asiatic mode of production," [69] "the restoration of our old 'semi-Asiatic' order," [70] the restoration of

---

h. Plekhanov in 1906 compared Lenin to a brilliant lawyer who, in order to bulwark a problematic case, defies logic (*Protokoly*, 115).

Russia's "semi-Asiatic nationalization," [71] "the restoration of the semi-Asiatic order," [72] "the return to the *Aziatchina*," [73] and Russia's " 'Asiatic' restoration." [74]

Plekhanov, in developing his theme, adhered to Marx' and Engels' idea that under Mongol rule Russia became semi-Asiatic and that despite important modifications it remained so even after the Emancipation.[75] He noted that eventually [in 1762] the *pomeshchiki* were made the owners of their former service land without any further obligation to serve the government, while the peasants were still allotted their land [by the state and the *pomeshchiki*]. Resenting the striking injustice of the situation, the peasants wanted the old system of state control over the land restored.

Plekhanov, who recognized the revolutionary aspect of this position, at the same time dreaded what he considered its reactionary implications. Through a restoration of Russia's old economic and governmental order "the wheel of Russian history would be powerfully, very powerfully reversed." [76] Invoking the example of the Chinese statesman Wang An-shih, who allegedly sought to make the state the owner of all land and the state officials the managers of all production,[i] Plekhanov exclaimed: "We expect nothing but damage from the projects of Russian Wang An-shihs, and we bend all our efforts to make such projects economically and politically impossible." [77] "We want no *kitaishchina*"—no Chinese system.[78]

With these experiences in mind, Plekhanov fought Lenin's program to establish a dictatorial government based on a small proletarian minority that could do little to prevent a restoration. Instead he advocated the municipalization of the land, a measure that would place "organs of public self-government . . . in possession of the land" and thus "erect a bulwark against reaction." [79]

Would the "bulwark" of municipalization have been strong enough to counter the infinitely greater power of the new state that Lenin intended to create? It hardly seems so. Would it have been strong enough to hold in bounds a variant of the old-fashioned despotic bureaucracy that Plekhanov apparently saw as the beneficiaries of a possible future restoration? This is not quite as unlikely as Lenin made it appear.

But whatever the effect of municipalization might have been, Plekhanov certainly was on firm ground when he pointed to Russia's Asiatic heritage and when he stressed "the necessity to eliminate that economic foundation through which our people have approached

---

i. Plekhanov took up the argument as it was presented by Reclus (1882: 577 ff.). For a historically more correct evaluation of Wang An-shih's aims, see Williamson, WAS, II: 163 ff.

more and more closely the Asiatic people." [80] This formulation implies what Plekhanov in the same debate and in conformity with Marx' and Engels' views said explicitly—that in Russia, Oriental despotism, although very much weakened, still persisted after the Emancipation. And he was only drawing the logical conclusion from this premise when he warned that the decay of the hoped-for revolution would lead to an Asiatic restoration.

The significance of Plekhanov's arguments explains why Lenin kept reverting to them at the Stockholm Congress, in a subsequent *Letter to the Petersburg Workers,* in a lengthy pamphlet on the Party's agrarian program, published in 1907, and in a digest of this pamphlet for a Polish Socialist paper. Manifestly, his revolutionary perspective was being challenged by the very Asiatic interpretation of Russian society that until then had been for him a Marxist axiom.

But although Lenin was greatly disturbed by this fact, he could not, in the then climate of Russian Marxism, abandon the Asiatic concept. Despite his aggressive rejection of Plekhanov's arguments, he admitted the reality of Russia's Asiatic heritage when he demanded that "the restoration of our old semi-Asiatic order must be distinguished from the restoration that took place in France, on the basis of capitalism." [81] He admitted it when he noted that the "shell" of the old order was "still strong in the Peasant Reform," and that, even after the '80's the bourgeois development of rural Russia advanced "very slowly." [82] And he admitted it when he asserted that land nationalization would "far more radically eliminate the economic foundations of the Aziatchina" than municipalization.[83]

These are important affirmations. And they become even more important when we recall Lenin's conviction that because of Russia's backwardness a protosocialist revolution there was bound to fail if it was not supported by a socialist revolution in one or more of the industrially advanced countries of the West. "The only guarantee against restoration is the socialist revolution in the West." [84] In view of the just-cited statements, the dreaded Russian restoration could only be an Asiatic restoration.

Plekhanov, in harmony with socialist teachings which Lenin also accepted, condemned Lenin's plan to seize power as "Utopian," and he referred to Napoleon's remark that a general who counts on the simultaneous occurrence of all favorable conditions is a bad general.[85] But Lenin was determined to take the Great Gamble. And it was for this reason that during and immediately after the Stockholm Congress, he minimized and obscured Russia's Asiatic heritage.

In his concluding speech at Stockholm and in his digest of the

subsequent pamphlet in the Polish paper he discussed the problem
of the restoration without mentioning the possibility of an Asiatic
restoration. In his *Letter to the Petersburg Workers* he mentioned
the issue, but he belittled its significance by describing the Asiatic
mode of production in Russia as a phenomenon of the past. If the
dreaded restoration should occur, it would not be a restoration of the
Asiatic mode of production or even a restoration of the 19th-century
type. For "in Russia from the second half of the 19th century on,
the capitalist mode of production became stronger, and in the 20th
century, it became absolutely predominant." [86]

Recalling Lenin's remark in 1905—that so far Russia had developed only a restricted "Asiatic" capitalism—this statement seems
fantastic, and in his 1907 pamphlet, he did not repeat it. Indeed, as
noted above, he admitted here that Russian agriculture developed
along the bourgeois path "very slowly." And his assertion that the
"medieval system of landownership" presented obstacles to the
growth of bourgeois farming in Russia explains what he meant when
he said that the foundations of the *Aziatchina* still needed eliminating.

A leader who in one year deals with the facts of a crucial problem
in four different ways (by omission, ambiguity, denial of their importance, and recognition of their importance) is not too sure of his
course. From Stockholm on, Lenin increasingly avoided the "Asiatic"
nomenclature, and this even when he was dealing with Asiatic institutions.[87] He increasingly called the "Asiatic" heritage "medieval,"
"patriarchal," or "precapitalist." And although he still spoke of
Russian "bondage" (*krepostnichestvo*), he increasingly spoke of Russian "feudalism." [j]

d. Further Oscillations (1907–14)

DESPITE these oscillations, Lenin stuck by a concept for which
apparently he knew no substitute. In the fall of 1910 he again drew
closer to Plekhanov,[88] and in January 1911 he demonstrated his
continued adherence to the Asiatic views by characterizing the Russia of Tolstoy's writings as a land in which "the Oriental system,
the Asiatic system" prevailed until 1905, this year being "the be-

j. Lenin employed the term "state feudalism" for the Asiatic land system in his
1907 pamphlet, naming Plekhanov and "subsequently also" Martynov as persons who
had used this formula (Lenin, S, XIII: 301). Martynov did indeed say at Stockholm
"our feudalism is a state feudalism" (*Protokoly,* 90), but I have not found any similar
phrase in Plekhanov's speeches. However, even if Plekhanov had occasionally used this
formula, throughout the year 1906 he kept insisting that Russia's institutional heritage
was not feudal but semi-Asiatic (see esp. *Protokoly,* 116).

ginning of the end of 'Oriental' stagnation." [k] In 1912 he discussed traditional China in "Asiatic" terms; [89] and in 1914, he spoke of the Asiatic despotism of Russia as a living reality.[90]

e. Full Retreat (1916–19)

i. LENIN'S IMPERIALISM (1916)

WORLD WAR I abruptly terminated Lenin's adherence to the Asiatic concept. In October 1914 he expressed the hope that the war would permit the radical socialists to initiate a comprehensive political and social revolution.[91] And in 1915 he was convinced that a gigantic cataclysm was in the making.[92] To prepare his followers for their daring revolutionary role, he wrote two small books that evidence a crucial turn in his sociohistorical views: *Imperialism: the Highest Stage of Capitalism* in 1916 and *State and Revolution* in 1917.

In *Imperialism* Lenin depicted capitalism as a "monopolistic" and imperialistic system which, as its sterile and stationary condition revealed, had reached the end of its historical road. And following Hilferding, he viewed "finance capital" as the master of a modern country's credit system and, on this account, also the master of its economy. The next logical step, or so it seems, would have been the demonstration that these ideas had validity not only for Western Europe and America but also for Russia, the chief target of his theoretical and political concern. In the case of Russia such a demonstration would have been both simple and instructive, for it was generally known that the Tsarist government had supreme control of the Russian credit system. The "Asiatic" interpretation of Russian society suggested that this circumstance gave the Tsarist bureaucracy supreme control over the country's economy.

Lenin recognized the premise, but he dodged the conclusion. He mentioned the financial key position of the Tsarist government; [93] but he did so without emphasis and without explaining its implications for the economy, as he had done for the private-property dominated West. Having failed to stress the managerial functions of the Russian state for the past, he also failed to stress them for the

k. Lenin, S, XVII: 31. This periodization appeared again in an article in 1916 by Zinoviev, then a close collaborator of Lenin, who wrote that the analysis made by Engels in 1890 met with the general approval of the Russian socialists (Zinowjew, 1919: 46). The Revolution of 1905, he added, initiated a new situation. Then, the rise of a politically conscious proletariat and the pro-Tsarist turn of the bourgeoisie (*ibid.:* 46 ff., 49, 60, 70 ff.) "changed the entire social structure of Russia, the relative strength of the various classes" (*ibid.:* 69). Tsarist autocracy now faced a new enemy; but Zinoviev did not deny that in 1916 it had still existed.

present. He thus hid an essential institutional feature that might link the country's "semi-Asiatic" past either with a state-Socialist or with an "Asiatic" future.

ii. STATE AND REVOLUTION (1917)

STATE AND REVOLUTION carried the deception still further. In this treatise Lenin explained the need for replacing the existing state, which was dominated by the ruling class, by a new type of a state which, like the Paris Commune, would be controlled from below. He based this significant decision not on an examination of the facts of history but on Marx' relevant comments.

To make good his claim to restore Marxist orthodoxy, Lenin promised to present "the totality" of Marx' and Engels' views on the state. For this purpose, "all, or at least all the most decisive, passages in the works of Marx and Engels on the subject of the state must necessarily be given as fully as possible." [94]

A reader interested in certain ideas of a certain author will want to be introduced first to that author's major work, if these ideas are discussed there, and then to his other pertinent writings. How did Lenin proceed in *State and Revolution?* As shown by his remark in 1907, the coming Russian revolution still had to eliminate the economic foundations of Oriental despotism. As shown by his remark in 1912, the year 1905 was only "the beginning of the end" of Russia's stationary "Oriental" conditions. And as shown by his remark in 1914, he still considered the contemporary "state system of Russia" as characterized by a "totality of traits which as a whole produces the concept 'Asiatic despotism.'" Thus in 1916–17, when Lenin promised to give all of Marx' and Engels' important observations on the state, we could expect him to give, along with Marx' ideas on the proprietary foundations of the state, his ideas on its functional foundations and on the related Russian state system. We could expect him to cite from *Das Kapital,* Marx' major work, which contains many significant references to the Asiatic state, as well as from those among his other writings which deal with this topic. And of course we could expect him to cite from Engels' writings also, giving special attention to his statement in 1875 on Russia's Oriental despotism.

But Lenin did nothing of the kind. In the book in which he allegedly was going to present all of Marx' decisive comments on the state, *Das Kapital* is not even mentioned. And all other comments of Marx and Engels on the functional state in general and on Russia's Oriental despotism in particular are equally shunned. In fact, Marx' and Engels' idea of a functional despotic state disappeared.

The only kind of state to which Lenin referred was Marx' and Engels' private-property-based variant: the non-Oriental state.

Consistent in his selectivity, Lenin cited only three statements which were concerned with the three private-property-based societal orders of the Marxist schema: antiquity, feudalism, and capitalism. And these statements he found most readily at hand not in Marx but in the later sections of Engels' *Anti-Dühring* and in the weakest link of Engels' sociohistorical writings: *The Origin of the Family, Private Property, and the State.*[95]

iii. LENIN'S LECTURE ON THE STATE (1919)

IN 1916, when Lenin was organizing his notes for *State and Revolution,* Russian absolutism, however weakened, still persisted. In the summer of 1917, when the book was completed, the Tsar had fallen; the Bolsheviks were trying to carry out Lenin's program of 1905–06, including the nationalization of the land which, according to Plekhanov, would greatly increase the chance of an Asiatic restoration.

Thus Lenin misled his readers on the key issues of the revolution he was promoting. And he continued to do so immediately after the October revolution and later when the Bolsheviks were consolidating their monopolistic managerial power. The climax of his ideological turnabout came in a lecture, "On the State," delivered on July 11, 1919.

In *State and Revolution* Lenin had failed to cite *Das Kapital;* but he had at least quoted some of Marx' secondary writings. In his lecture "On the State" he mentioned neither Marx' name nor the word "Marxism." Instead he gave Engels as his only authority in the matter of "contemporary Socialism." And he recommended Engels not for his many insights on the Asiatic state and Russia's Oriental despotism, or even for his *Anti-Dühring,* but only for his 1884 popularization of Morgan. Said Lenin: "I trust that concerning the question of the state you will familarize yourselves with Engels' work, *The Origin of the Family, Private Property, and the State.* This is one of the basic works of contemporary [m] Socialism, every phrase of which can be accepted with confidence." [96]

But even though Lenin recommended every phrase of this book as authoritative, he distorted some of its key ideas. Two instances are of particular interest to our inquiry, both involving the significance of slavery and both tending to strengthen the belief that societal development was a unilinear process.

m. Note that Lenin did not use the formula "scientific" socialism, usually associated with Marxist socialism.

As stated above, Engels indicated in his book on the family that slavery was not an essential element of production either in the "Orient" or in the European Middle Ages (the Orient knew only "domestic slavery"; and the Celtic and Germanic tribes, avoiding the "morass" of slavery, moved directly from a primitive "gens" society to feudal serfdom). Lenin, however, brushed aside these important distinctions and defined the "slave-owning society" as a virtually universal phase of development. "Through this [phase] passed *all* of contemporary civilized Europe—slavery ruled supreme two thousand years ago. Through this passed the great majority of the peoples in other parts of the world." [97] And one allegedly general type of private-property-based order necessarily led to the next: slave-owning society to serf-owning society; serf-owning society to capitalism; and capitalism to socialism.[98]

This unilinear scheme of development left no room for an Asiatic society and an Asiatic restoration. Rather it demonstrated "scientifically" that the Bolshevik revolution, by crushing the evil forces of private property, initiated the inescapable next stage of human progress: socialism.

f. Lenin's Last Period: the Specter of the Aziatchina Reemerges

IF Lenin had discarded his earlier convictions entirely, our account of the Big Myth could stop here. But Lenin was a "subjective socialist." And although the regime he headed from its inception bore little resemblance to the protosocialist government envisaged by Marx or by himself before the October revolution, he continued to reassert his earlier convictions. Thus while for the sake of power he betrayed his socialist principles, there is no doubt that he did so with a bad conscience. And there is no doubt either that he was uneasy when he obscured the Asiatic issue.

In *State and Revolution* Lenin indirectly recognized the existence of Oriental despotism, the decisive "barbarian" system of oppression and exploitation, by attaching the qualifying phrase "in the period of civilization" [99] to his remarks on the private-property-based state. This gesture did little to counteract the misleading effect of his main thesis, but it did show him aware of his "sin against science."

In his lecture "On the State" Lenin used the term "bondage" (*krepostnichestvo*) where Engels had used "feudalism." And he concluded his discussion of the bondage state by saying: "This was the bondage state, which in Russia, for instance, or in completely (*sovershenno*)ⁿ backward Asiatic countries, where bondage prevails until today—it differed in form—was either republican or monarchical." [100] Obviously, Lenin still knew that "Asiatic countries" had a special form of bondage. And he still distinguished between "completely" backward Asiatic countries and other (semibackward, semi-Asiatic?) countries, among which he included Russia. Again he made significant admissions, but again he hid his admissions so carefully that they were barely recognizable. And this also continued to be his method after the October revolution.

From the standpoint of Lenin's premises, the Bolshevik seizure of power in the fall of 1917 had little chance to initiate a proto-socialist and socialist development. For in his own opinion the internal "relative" guarantees provided by a state of the Commune type (no bureaucracy, no police, no standing army) could only prevent the dreaded restoration, if the new regime had the support of a revolution in some industrially advanced Western countries. Hence Lenin was overjoyed when a revolution broke out in Germany in November 1918.

But the assassination of the two German Communist leaders, Karl Liebknecht and Rosa Luxemburg, on January 15, 1919, grimly demonstrated the weakness of the revolutionary forces in the West whose aid he craved. Lenin was profoundly shaken. Five days later, in a strange speech before the Second All-Russian Trade Union Congress, he assessed the achievements of the Bolshevik revolution. The French revolution in its pure form, he noted, had only lasted a year—but it accomplished great things. The Bolshevik revolution in the same time did much more.[101] His rambling sentences, however, scarcely veiled his fear that the Bolshevik revolution, like the French revolution before it, was headed for a restoration.

We do not know exactly what kind of a restoration Lenin was envisaging then, but in a speech on April 20, 1921—immediately after the Kronstadt uprising—he drew attention to the antisocialist and antiproletarian dangers inherent in the new Soviet bureaucracy. This bureaucracy was no bourgeois force but something worse. His comparative scale of societal orders suggests what he had in mind: "Socialism is better than capitalism, but capitalism is better than medievalism, *small production, and a bureaucracy connected with the dispersed character of the small producers.*" [102]

Lenin's statement may puzzle those who are unfamiliar with the

---

n. Lenin's formula recalls the distinction Marx had made between the "completely" Eastern troubles in the China of the fifties and the "semi-Eastern" troubles caused by Tsarist Russia (Marx, NYDT, August 5, 1853).

Marxist definition of Oriental despotism. But the initiated will recall Marx' and Engels' view that self-sufficient, dispersed, and isolated
rural communities form the solid and natural foundation of Oriental
despotism.[103] And they will recall Lenin's statement in 1914 that the
"insignificant development of commodity production" was the economic cause of the great stability of Asiatic despotism.[104]

A few paragraphs later, and as if to dispel all doubt as to what he
was driving at, Lenin went still further in characterizing the new
Soviet bureaucracy. To his own question, "What are the economic
roots of bureaucracy?" he answered, "There are two main roots: on
the one hand, the developed bourgeoisie needs a bureaucratic apparatus, primarily a military apparatus, and then a judicial apparatus.
. . . This we have not got. Our bureaucracy has a different economic
root: *it is the fragmented and dispersed character of the small producer, his poverty, the lack of culture, the absence of roads, illiteracy,
the absence of exchange between agriculture and industry, the absence of connection and interaction between them.*" [105]

True, Lenin did not put a label on the phenomenon he was
describing. But the details he cited all elaborated the dispersion
and isolation of the villages over which the new regime ruled. In
Aesopian language *o* he was obviously expressing his fear that an
Asiatic restoration was taking place and that a new type of Oriental
despotism was in the making.

No wonder then that at the end of his political career Lenin
several times called Russia's institutional heritage "bureaucratic"
and "Asiatic." He noted that Russian society had "not yet emerged"
from its "semi-Asiatic" lack of culture.[106] He juxtaposed the "Asiatic"
way in which the Russian peasant traded to the "European" way.[107]
And he criticized the Soviet regime for being unable to "go along
without the particularly crude types of pre-bourgeois culture, i.e.
bureaucratic or bondage culture." [108] Bondage culture—not feudal
culture. And shortly before he suffered the stroke that altogether removed him from the political arena, he went so far as to call the
Soviet state apparatus "to a large extent the survival of the old one.
. . . It is only slightly repainted on the surface." *p*

---

o. Originally Lenin used an "Aesopian" (slave) language to speak to those oppressed
by the government in such a way that the rulers would not realize what he was saying
(cf. Lenin, S, XXII: 175). Now, as the head of the new ruling stratum, he used the
same device to hide his meaning from those who were being ruled.

p. Lenin, S, XXXIII: 440; cf. Lenin, SW, IX: 382. See also Lenin, S, XXXIII: 404
("We still have the old apparatus") and 434 ("Our apparatus . . . which we took over
in its entirety from the preceding epoch").

4. STALIN

LIKE the first Roman emperor, Augustus, the founding father of the
Soviet Union, Lenin, upheld in words what he destroyed by deeds.
But words, too, have their history, and under a regime that fits its
ideas into a rigid frame, words of the official doctrine makers are
not easily cast out. It is no accident that in the USSR arguments defending the concept of an Asiatic society continued to be made openly
as long as "subjective socialists" (members of the "Old Guard")
openly fought the rise of the new totalitarian bureaucracy. And it
is no accident that Stalin, who inherited and developed Lenin's
incipient apparatus state, also inherited and developed Lenin's readiness to destroy inconvenient truths, even when these truths were
uttered by Marx and Engels—or by Lenin himself.

a. The Old Guard Objects

IN 1925 Ryazanov, who was then director of the Marx-Engels Institute, published an article, "Marx on India and China," which
brought together Marx' ideas on Asiatic society and the Asiatic mode
of production.[109] In the same year the top economist, Varga, declared
that government-controlled productive and protective water works
were the basis of Chinese society and that the scholarly administrators, the *literati,* and not the representatives of private property, such
as the landowners, constituted China's ruling class.[110] In 1928 the
Program of the Communist International, which was drafted under
Bukharin's guidance, found in the economy of colonial and semi-
colonial countries "feudal medieval relationships, or 'Asiatic mode
of production' relationships prevailing"; and Varga, in an article
in *Bolshevik,* the theoretical organ of the Communist Party of the
USSR, again defined traditional China as an Asiatic society and
pointed out that in this society the peasants, both owners and tenants,
occupied a very different position from that of the serfs in feudal
society.[111] In 1930 he publicly criticized the Comintern official Yolk
and those editors of the *Problemy Kitaia* who sided with him for
calling the Asiatic mode of production an Asiatic variant of the feudal
mode of production: If Marx had been of this opinion, "he would
have said so." [112] The change suggested by Yolk involved no less than a
"revision of Marxism." Varga therefore demanded that the underlying problem be made the topic of an organized discussion.

Such a discussion was indeed held in Leningrad in February 1931
—that is, shortly after the enforced collectivization which enormously
strengthened the new Stalin-led *apparatchiki* but before the Purges,

which ruthlessly decimated the Old Guard. The date explains why Ryazanov, Varga, Bukharin, and Madyar (the leading younger proponent of the Asiatic concept) were not invited to participate. And it also explains why those who called the great Asian civilizations "feudal" proceeded with a certain restraint when they attacked the defenders of "the theory of the Asiatic mode of production."

b. A Half-hearted Criticism of the Theory of Oriental Society

i. THE LENINGRAD DISCUSSION (1931)

POLITICALLY speaking, the advocates of the "feudal" interpretation of Oriental society were in a strong position, for since 1926 Stalin had repeatedly designated China's agrarian order as "feudal." [113] But Stalin had been more apodictic than convincing when he spoke of China's feudal conditions. He had not driven home his ideas by reference to the known facts of Chinese economy and society. Nor had he shown how to deal with Marx', Engels', and Lenin's utterances concerning the Asiatic system and the Asiatic mode of production.

This lack of direction is reflected in the Comintern statements on China, India, and other Asiatic countries. And it accounts for the caution with which those who stressed Stalin's "feudal" view proceeded during the Leningrad discussion. It was no easy matter to uphold a party line that was fraught with serious doctrinal difficulties.

However, in the course of the Leningrad conference, a few points did emerge clearly.

1) The critics of the Asiatic concept rejected as un-Marxist the idea that a functional bureaucracy could be the ruling class. [114]

2) They rejected the Asiatic-bureaucratic interpretation of the Chinese "gentry." [q]

3) They claimed that the theory of the Asiatic mode of production imperiled the work of the Communist International in the colonial and semicolonial countries of Asia. [r]

q. DASP: 68, cf. 181. It was in this respect that I was singled out for criticism as having stressed the "Asiatic" quality of the Chinese gentry. This indeed I did when I described the group in question as the nonofficiating wing of the bureaucratic ruling class (Wittfogel, 1931: 730). For the elaboration of my earlier view see above, pp. 312 ff.

r. Godes charged that the idea of the "exceptionality" (the non-Western character) of the Orient implied in the theory of Asiatic society tended to encourage some Asian nationalists to reject the doctrinal authority of the Communists and that the idea of a stationary Asia conceded to European capitalism the possibility of a "Messianic" role (DASP: 34). Such a "Messianic" argument was suggested by Marx' evaluation of British

The spokesmen for the feudal interpretation of the Orient bolstered their position by invoking those utterances of Engels and Lenin that ignored Asiatic society. The defenders of the theory of the Asiatic mode of production, on their part, cited supporting statements from Marx, Engels, and Lenin. But they did not mention Marx' or Engels' Oriental interpretation of Russia; and they shied away from Lenin's concept of the *Aziatchina* and his comments on the possibility of an Asiatic restoration.

In this battle of quotations the defenders of the "Asiatic" theory did not fare too badly. The party-line spokesmen, who before the conference had surely consulted with the Politburo, were obviously not instructed on how to deal with Marx' concept of an Asiatic mode of production, as presented in his *Preface* to the *Critique of Political Economy.* Thus Godes and Yolk, who dared to dissociate themselves from the "Asiatic" clause in the Comintern program,[115] still faithfully quoted Marx' famous pronunciamento.[s]

Their doctrinal insecurity found expression also in their political behavior. At the outset Yolk had asserted: "I want to warn against this theory. What is really important is to unmask it politically, and not to establish the 'pure truth' as to whether the 'Asiatic mode of production' existed or not." But his contempt for even the appearance of scientific objectivity was as premature as it was imprudent. Godes tactfully rephrased Yolk's comment,[116] and the printed minutes give only an emasculated version of the original statement.[t] Moreover, while both Godes and Yolk reprimanded some members of the "antifeudal" camp for "Trotskyite" leanings,[117] Godes warned against labeling all members of the group as Trotskyites.[118]

This restraint was certainly not due to the fact that Trotsky had never invoked the Asiatic concept in his fight against Stalin.[u] No

---

rule in India. Marx' attitude greatly embarrassed the Comintern, as may be seen from the heated debate on the problems of "industrialization" and "decolonization" in colonial and semi-colonial countries (see *Inprecor,* 1928: 1225 ff., 1247 ff., 1276, 1312, 1320 ff., 1350, 1352 ff., 1365, 1395 ff., 1402, 1405 ff., 1409 ff., 1412 ff., 1421 ff., 1424, 1425, 1471 ff.).

s. Yolk minimized its importance (DASP: 71), but Godes criticized him for doing so (*ibid.:* 164 ff.).

t. DASP: 59. In the printed report of the Leningrad conference Yolk stresses only the political importance of the Asiatic theory. Happily, however, the editors slipped up on their job. They reproduced not only Godes' rephrasing of Yolk's statement, which showed that Yolk had raised the issue of truth, but also, in the speech of another conferee, a citation of Yolk's exact words (*ibid.:* 89).

u. In the introductory chapters of his books on the Russian revolutions of 1905 and 1917, Trotsky succinctly explained the managerial and exploitative quality of the Tsarist regime which, in his opinion, approached "Asiatic despotism" (Trotsky, 1923:

such contingency would have stopped a Bolshevik propagandist. But if the "feudalists" had denounced the whole "Asiatic" camp as Trotskyite, they would have given the discussion a finality which, at that time, the ideological master strategists apparently did not want. Even the rude Yolk found it necessary to say that the defenders of the Asiatic concept were not repeating bourgeois theories. He merely found that, objectively, "their erroneous positions reflect alien influences." [119]

Thus the political propriety of the upholders of the theory of the Asiatic mode of production was not questioned. Their heresy was a minor one, and it did not deprive them of their good Communist standing.

ii. THE SIGNIFICANCE OF THE 1931 DISCUSSION

FROM the standpoint of immediate results, the Leningrad conference was inconclusive. From the standpoint of the student of the sociology of knowledge, it was highly rewarding. For this conference was the only one in which, to my knowledge, Soviet ideologists discussed the political implications of the theory of Asiatic society with any degree of frankness. Its singularity is underlined by two facts: unlike the other discussions of controversial matters—economic, literary, or biological—the Leningrad conference was not publicized in the international Communist press, nor were the issues involved comprehensively debated in Communist parties outside the USSR.

To summarize these issues briefly: The theory of Asiatic society endangered Communist leadership in Asia in that it depicted the "capitalist" West as capable not only of oppressive, but also of constructive, action. It endangered Communist leadership in that it enabled the nationalist leaders of Asia to reject Moscow-rooted doctrine as their guide. And it endangered the Communist attempt to one-sidedly stress secondary, if serious, problems of property and thus to hide the primary problem of bureaucratic class rule and general state slavery.

The delicate nature of these issues necessitated cautious procedures. But the top leadership of World Communism knew that whatever

---

18 ff.; *ibid.*, 1931: 18 ff.). But in the twenties and thirties he did not discuss Chinese society in "Asiatic" terms, nor did he use the criteria of Oriental despotism when he criticized Stalin's bureaucratic despotism. In 1938 Trotsky wrote a survey of what he held to be Marx' ideas. In his discussion of the types of social relations he mentioned only three—slavery, feudalism, and capitalism (Trotsky, 1939: 8)—just as Stalin did in the same year and Lenin had done in 1919.

the delays, the concept of a managerial-bureaucratic "Asiatic" state ultimately had to wither away.

c. Ideological Twilight

THE ideological erosion of the theory of the Asiatic mode of production advanced unevenly. The Chinese Communists rejected the concept of an Asiatic mode of production for traditional China before the Leningrad conference. They took this step in 1928 at their Sixth National Congress (held in Moscow) in a resolution on Agrarian Relations and the Struggle for Land in China, whose wording showed them more eager to embrace Stalin's "feudal" views than to do justice to Marx' "Asiatic" comments on China.[v] True, the first draft of this resolution had employed the concept of an Asiatic mode of production.[120] But this pathetic effort—which was probably spearheaded by Ch'ü Ch'iu-pai [121] and which led to nothing—only underlined the lack of a serious Marxist tradition in the Chinese Communist movement.

In other parts of the Marxist-Leninist world the idea of an Asiatic society survived in an ideological twilight that endured until the appearance of Stalin's *Dialectical and Historical Materialism* in 1939 and in some Anglo-Saxon countries even after.

It would be interesting to show how, during the 1930's, Soviet writers tried to find a "feudal" explanation for phenomena which they knew Marx considered expressions of an Asiatic mode of production. Note the efforts of Prigozhin (1934),[w] Grinevitch (1936),[x] and Struve (1938).[y] It would be interesting to show how, even within

v. In his study on Mao Tse-tung, B. Schwartz mentioned two theoretical decisions of the Sixth Congress of the CCP, one rejecting the Trotskyite stress on capitalist relations in the Chinese villages, the other rejecting the interpretation of Chinese society as an Asiatic society (Schwartz, 1951: 122 ff.). It is regrettable that *A Documentary History of Chinese Communism* (1952), which Schwartz edited together with John K. Fairbank and C. Brandt, failed to inform its readers on the latter point. According to the *History*, "the only innovation in the 'theoretical' sphere" was "the new estimate of the revolutionary situation" (Brandt, Schwartz, and Fairbank, 1952: 125). The omission is all the more regrettable since only a few years previously Dr. Fairbank in his book, *The United States and China*, had devoted a whole chapter to the discussion of "China as an Oriental Society" (Fairbank, 1948: 53–8).

w. Prigozhin explained the Asiatic mode of production as a special type of feudalism and he spoke of "the so-called Asiatic mode of production" (Prigozhin, 1934: 80, 86).

x. See the *Great Soviet Encyclopaedia*, 1936, XXXII: "China" (esp. pp. 538, 530), where Grinevitch speaks of the "bureaucratic feudalism" and the "bureaucratic despotism" of imperial China.

y. See Struve's ten points on the Asiatic mode of production in Struve, 1940 (1st ed. 1938): 22.

the Comintern itself, the Asiatic concept could still be employed. Note the article "The Flood Disasters in China," by Madyar in the Comintern organ, *International Press Correspondence*, published on September 3, 1931,[z] and Fox' 1935 praise of Marx' "brilliant grasp on the Indian . . . problem" in the same journal.[a] It would be interesting to show how English Marxism, as set forth in Burns' *A Handbook of Marxism*, spread the hydraulic interpretation of the Orient. Note the stress on the managerial and despotic peculiarities of "Oriental societies" in Gordon Childe's *Man Makes Himself*.[b] And it would be interesting to show how in the United States certain writers who based their thinking on Marx' Asiatic-hydraulic concept influenced non-Marxist students of the Orient. Note the impression made by Chi Ch'ao-ting's *Key Economic Areas in Chinese History, as Revealed in the Development of Public Works for Water-Control,* and by myself on Owen Lattimore.[c]

But a detailed review of this many-sided development is outside the scope of the present book. For our purpose it is sufficient to state that during the 1930's and especially in the Anglo-Saxon world Marxism in its most actively proselytizing form reproduced and spread an Asiatic-hydraulic interpretation of Oriental civilizations.

z. Protected by a thin veil of "feudal" verbiage (China's "feudal dismemberment"), Madyar stressed the "tremendous importance" of hydraulic works and the organizing function that, because of them, devolved upon "the Oriental despotism of the Chinese ruling class" (*Inprecor,* 1931: 865).

a. *Inprecor,* 1935: 1336. Fox, who in 1930 had published a comprehensive collection of Marx' statements on the Asiatic mode of production (*Letopis Marksizma,* 1930, XIII: 3–29), drew attention to Marx' ideas on India in a review of *A Handbook of Marxism.* It is a curious accident—if it is an accident—that this *Handbook,* which brought together fifty-two writings by Marx, Engels, and Stalin and which was distributed in the U.S.A. as well as in Great Britain, reproduced Marx' two main articles on India but not Lenin's lecture "On the State."

b. Childe acknowledged the significance of Marx' "realistic concept of history" in this book. And although his notion of the "urban revolution" is a deterioration of Marx' and Engels' (originally: Adam Smith's) ideas on the separation of town and village, and although his notion of the "arrested growth" of Oriental societies (Childe, 1952: 181, 186) lacks the incisiveness of Jones', Mill's, and Marx' statements on this phenomenon, his emphasis on the crucial significance of hydraulic operations for the rise of Oriental societies in Egypt, Mesopotamia, and early India definitely follows the classical Asiatic concept.

c. In his *Inner Asian Frontiers of China* (completed in 1939), Lattimore related that Chi's book first impressed on him "the importance of irrigation and canal transport in Chinese history" (Lattimore, 1940: xxi). In the same book he stated that over two millennia ago China's early feudalism had been superseded by "a bureaucratically administered empire" (*ibid.:* 369 ff., 375 ff.; cf. 368 ff., 373); and he added that "the prime factors" of this transformation had been "authoritatively classified by Wittfogel" (*ibid.:* 370).

d. Stalin "Edits" Marx

HOWEVER, while this development stimulated a number of social historians, from the standpoint of Russia's new totalitarian bureaucracy it was dynamite. Stalin had probably already sensed the danger in the late 1920's, but he probably also sensed the difficulty of abandoning a key idea of Marx that was still being upheld by respected Old Bolsheviks. Significantly, it was only after the Great Purges (1935-38), which liquidated the bulk of these traditionalists, that Stalin dared to lay hands on Marx' decisive statement on the Asiatic mode of production.

But wasn't Stalin himself an Old Bolshevik? Stalin had indeed been schooled in orthodox Marxism. In 1913 he described the Russia of the 1830's as dominated by "a gross Asiatic social and political regime," and he spoke of contemporary Russia as a "semi-Asiatic country." [122] But Stalin wrote these lines under Lenin's influence.[123] And while, on occasion, he employed the term "Asiatic" to characterize particularly oppressive features in his homeland, Georgia,[124] it is doubtful whether he was ever greatly concerned with Marx' theory of Asiatic society. During the Stockholm Party Congress of 1906 Stalin outdid Lenin in pleading for the "black" transfer of the landowners' land to the peasants; [125] but the possibility of an Asiatic restoration, which so deeply stirred Lenin and Plekhanov, evoked no comment from him. In his first popular presentation of Marxism in 1906-07 he listed among the types of society above the level of primitive communism, matriarchy, and patriarchy—slavery, "bondage," and capitalism.[126]

After the middle 1920's Stalin began to emphasize the "feudal" character of China's agrarian order. In 1926 he spoke of China's "medieval feudal survivals," [127] and in 1927, he elaborated the standard formula "feudal survivals" [128] by referring to China's "medieval-feudal forms of exploitation and oppression" [129] and "feudal-bureaucratic apparatus." [130]

There is little reason to believe that an early and complete acceptance would have kept Stalin from discarding the Asiatic concept. Lenin abandoned cherished ideas when strategy demanded it. But his lack of strong "Asiatic" convictions certainly made it easier for Stalin to promote the "feudal" view, just as his lack of subtlety in general made it easier for him to achieve his ends without any concern for consistency.

As discussed above, Engels had not, in his most problematic non-Asiatic statements, denied the socio-evolutionary importance of the ecological factor which he and Marx had emphasized in their earlier comments on Asiatic society. And neither Engels nor Lenin had tampered with Marx' programmatic statement on the four antagonistic modes of production as set forth in his famous *Preface*.

Stalin did both. He rejected the "geographical environment" as a *"determining* cause of social development, for that which remains almost unchanged in the course of tens of thousands of years cannot be the chief cause of development." [d] And instead of by-passing Marx' programmatic declaration as others had done, he brazenly invoked—and mutilated—it. Having pontifically presented his unilinear scheme of development, which included only three types of class societies (slave-holding, feudal, and capitalist), he fulsomely praised the "brilliant formulation of the essence of historical materialism given by Marx in 1859 in his historic *Preface* to his famous book, *Critique of Political Economy.*" And he quoted the "historic" passage word for word—until just before the sentence which contains Marx' reference to the Asiatic mode of production.[131] Stalin thus demonstrated for all concerned that Marx, too, could be "edited," when necessary, *modo Tatarico*—with a meat cleaver.

e. Delayed Reaction in the Anglo-Saxon World

THE supreme judge of Marxist-Leninist doctrine had spoken—the Asiatic concept need no longer embarrass the faithful. However, the *Short Course* appeared in book form and in many foreign languages in the spring of 1939 [e]—at a time when the world was tense with the fear of an approaching catastrophe. From September 1939 on, the spreading war prevented the political strategists of the Soviet Union from pressing doctrinal issues. In fact, during these years they made substantial ideological concessions to the peoples of the USSR as well as to the Western democracies.

These circumstances go far to explain why, in 1940, the leading

---

d. Stalin, 1939: 118 ff. In rejecting environment and population growth as major determinant factors, Stalin was closely following the argument of Bukharin (Bukharin, 1934: 121, 124), who, shortly before his execution in 1938, had been publicly ridiculed by Vyshinsky as a "theoretician in quotation marks" (see above, p. 160). In Chap. 1 of the present inquiry I noted that the Marxian view of the relation between man and nature underrated the cultural factor, but this limitation notwithstanding, Marx' concept of the historically changing character of nature is far removed from the static view promoted by Bukharin, and following him, Stalin. Obviously, both Lenin and Plekhanov were closer to Marx' than to Bukharin's position (see Wittfogel, 1929: 504–21 and 698–724).

e. In the USSR the work began to appear in installments in the fall of 1938 (see *Inprecor*, 1938: 1067, 1108, 1132, 1157, 1197).

British Marxist-Leninist theoretician, R. P. Dutt, in a book *India To-day*, and in an Introduction to *Karl Marx, Articles on India*, enthusiastically reproduced Marx' ideas on Asiatic society in general and Indian society in particular.[f] They also go far to explain why, in 1942, Childe in another general sociohistorical study, *What Happened in History*, carried his discussion of the peculiarities of "Oriental societies" still further than he had in 1936.[132] In his second study he noted that the Bronze and Iron ages gave birth to four distinct institutional orders: irrigation-based agrarian societies, whose surplus "was concentrated in the hands of a relatively narrow circle of *priests and officials*"; classical Graeco-Roman civilizations, in which the primary producers and artisans were ultimately impoverished or enslaved; European feudalism; and the modern "bourgeois capitalist" world.[133] Semantically these four orders are identical with Marx' four major antagonistic societal conformations.

f. The Rout of the Notorious Theory of the Asiatic Mode of Production

WHEN the war ended, the ideological twilight ended also. Dutt, who a few years previously had vigorously recommended the application of the theory of the Asiatic mode of production to the scientific analysis of India and China, no longer discussed this theory, which he had once found singularly rewarding.[g]

f. Dutt presented Marx' pertinent articles of 1853 as "among the most fertile of his writings, and the starting-point of modern thought on the questions covered" (Dutt, 1940: 93). Marx' ideas on Asia that for half a century were almost unknown now begin "increasingly to influence current thought on Indian questions. To-day modern historical research is increasingly confirming the main outlines of their approach" [*ibid.*: 92. Cf. Dutt, 1951 (written 1940): *passim*]. An approving digest of *India To-day*, including Marx' "Asiatic" argument, by T. A. Bisson, was published in *Amerasia*, IV, No. 9, 1940.

g. In 1942 Dutt still upheld his earlier position, if in a diluted way [Dutt, 1943 (Engl. ed. 1942): 38 ff., 43, 71, 73 ff., 76 ff., 87]. He stopped doing so after the end of the War. While he still on occasion pointed to Marx' writings on India (*Labour Monthly*, XXXII, 1950: 43; XXXV, 1953: 105), the reader can draw no "Asiatic" conclusion from his vaguely phrased remarks. Viewed isolatedly, Dutt's scattered comments on "feudal" conditions in India (*ibid.*, XXVIII, 1946: 321; XXIX, 1947: 211) may not have created a new, non-"Asiatic" image. However, Dutt glorified Stalin, the great Marxist theoretician and author of the *Short Course* (*ibid.*, XXXI, 1949: 357); he dutifully praised S. A. Dange's crudely unilinear historical sketch, *India, from Primitive Communism to Slavery* (*ibid.*, XXXII, 1950: 41 ff.); and he reproduced in his magazine, and at length, the 1952 Soviet discussion on the Eastern countries, which was very specific in its emphasis on the "feudal survivals" and the "feudal" or "semi-feudal" character of rural India (*ibid.*, XXXV, 1953: 40, 41, 44, 84, 86). All this, taken together, definitely encouraged the feudal interpretation of traditional India.

Chi Ch'ao-ting, too, lost interest in the hydraulic-bureaucratic thesis that underlay his study of China's *Key Economic Areas*. Neither as an employee of the Chinese Nationalist government nor as a high-ranking official of the Chinese Communist regime did he elaborate his earlier "Asiatic" arguments.

And Lattimore, who in the 1930's was so impressed by Chi's and my own hydraulic-bureaucratic views and who still in 1944 considered the loosely used terms "semi-feudal" and "feudal survivals" scientifically obscuring, in the later '40's characterized the traditional societies of Asia as "feudal." [h]

The case of Childe is different. Childe, who since the '30's identified himself with Marx' interpretation of history, who in the '40's began to invoke Stalin's sociological authority,[134] and who in 1951 hailed Stalin as "the leading exponent of Marxism today," [135] established a frame of reference that makes his recent changes ideologically quite understandable. Having previously spoken of four major types of class societies, Childe in 1951 mentioned only three: classical, medieval, and modern.[i] And having previously stated that *"priests*

h. In 1936, Lattimore, as the then editor of *Pacific Affairs*, published a bibliography of the Chinese Soviet Movement, prepared by the staff of the American Council of the Institute of Pacific Relations. The authors of the bibliography described the position that "characterizes Chinese economy as 'semi-feudal' " as "the viewpoint adopted by official documents of the Communist International and the Communist Party of China"; but they also indicated that Madyar, who upheld the idea of an "Asiatic Mode of Production," although officially criticized for doing so, nevertheless, had exerted in the USSR "considerable influence . . . in the field" (*Pacific Affairs*, IX, 1936: 421 ff.).

As noted above, Lattimore, in his *Inner Asian Frontiers of China* (1940), upheld the "bureaucratic" against the feudal interpretation of imperial Chinese society. And in March 1944 he still classed Stalin's concept of "feudal survivals" among the "paramount Communist theses" that "a Communist writer has . . . to maintain" when he discusses Chinese society (Lattimore, 1944: 83). Commenting on a number of recent Soviet studies on China, he objected to the "emphasis on 'feudal' thought later than the Christian era" (*ibid.:* 87) for China, and he held that "the social data are somewhat obscured by loosely used terms like 'semi-feudal' and 'feudal survivals' " (*ibid.:* 85, 87). In 1948 members of a research group directed by Lattimore published a survey of Sinkiang which applied to the typically hydraulic conditions of that area a variety of "feudal" terms: "semi-feudal agrarian relations," "the purely feudal system of the past," "the survival of feudal land" (*Far Eastern Survey*, March 10, 1948: 62 ff.). And in 1949 Lattimore himself spoke of Asia's "feudal land tenure" (Lattimore, 1949: 67). Of course, Lattimore is free to hold whatever sociohistorical ideas he wants and to change them in whatever way he deems fit. But in view of his previous statements concerning the politically motivated and scientifically harmful character of the feudal interpretation of China, he may legitimately be asked to explain his recent position in the light of his earlier appraisal.

i. In his 1951 study Childe claimed that Marx had developed his sociohistorical concepts "from historical data furnished by civilized societies—classical, medieval, and

and officials" were the controllers of the surplus in the Orient, Childe in 1953 ascribed this prerogative—the prerogative of the ruling class —to "the divine king and *a very small class of noble landowners."* [136] In the new formulation, the emphasis on private property replaced the emphasis on bureaucratic functions that Childe had clearly recognized in the past

Behind the Iron Curtain the enforced withdrawal from the theory of Asiatic society was part of an intellectual tragedy whose scope and intensity are difficult for the outsider to comprehend. A complaint made in 1942 that "for a long time" the young Soviet Orientalists had been excessively interested in the problem of the socioeconomic character of the Orient—which included the problem of "the so-called Asiatic mode of production [137]—is indicative of a trend that obviously persisted after that year. In 1950 an official report on recent Soviet Oriental studies listed as the outstanding achievement in the field "the rout of the notorious theory of the 'Asiatic mode of production.' " [138]

D. THREE FORMS OF THE BLACKOUT OF THE THEORY OF THE ASIATIC MODE OF PRODUCTION

THE fall of the theory of the Asiatic mode of production was as extraordinary as its rise. In 1748 Montesquieu opened up an area of inquiry that included Oriental despotism as an important issue. In 1848 John Stuart Mill, drawing upon the earlier classical economists, hammered out a new concept of Oriental society. And in the 1850's, Marx, who sought to predict the future of societal development by determining its past, added the idea of a specific Asiatic mode of production.

However, the managerial-bureaucratic implications of the Asiatic concept soon embarrassed its new adherent, Marx. They also increasingly disturbed his friend Engels. And they caused a complete ideological retreat in the movement which, under the banner of Marxism-Leninism, engaged in establishing a totalitarian "socialist" state. What one hundred years previously had seemed a highly illuminating idea and what, for a time, had been an accepted Marxist concept, became the "so-called" and eventually the "notorious" theory of the Asiatic mode of production.

The resulting ideological blackout has three major forms. It is

---

modern" (Childe, 1951: 10). Invoking the term "civilized," as Engels and Lenin had done under similar circumstances, Childe by-passed "barbarian" Oriental society, which certainly influenced Marx' sociohistorical thinking—and which happened also to be a major concern of Childe's own studies.

overt and official in the Communist third of the world. It is covert
and limited in most private-property-based industrial societies. And
it is thinly camouflaged and disturbingly successful in many non-
Communist countries of the Orient.

The third condition will occupy our attention when we discuss the
institutional and ideological aspects of hydraulic society in transition.
The first condition is largely beyond the reach of our influence. It
is part of the general intellectual blackout that results from total
managerial power; and it is not substantially relieved by modifications in detail. Sundry attempts may be made to improve on the
Engels of 1884, the Lenin of 1919, and the Stalin of 1939. Of course
they, too, will bulwark the total managerial regime that initiates
them, and they, too, will remain inconsistent. However, even a torn
rag can smother a helpless victim. For all practical purposes the
official blackout is sufficient to keep the people behind the Iron Curtain ideologically paralyzed.

The second condition is our most immediate concern. In the
property-based industrial societies some elements of the Soviet scheme
of development have been widely circulated, but the scheme in its
entirety is so contrived that recognition usually leads to rejection.
This being the case, critical explanation serves a vital purpose. In
the rational treatment of big ideas, as in the control of big water,
protective and productive action go hand in hand.

CHAPTER 10

Oriental society in transition

RECOGNITION of the peculiarity of hydraulic society is the decisive stumbling block for any unilinear scheme of development. It is crucial in the formulation of a multilinear pattern of societal evolution. And it is the starting point for any institutional analysis of the recent changes in the East.

The many students who, examining Oriental civilizations, found them to be substantially different from feudal societies often did not draw the developmental consequences suggested by their research. Others, using the comparative method, perceived hydraulic society as part of a multilinear pattern of development. John Stuart Mill was one of the first to do this conspicuously.[1] Max Weber's relevant observations, although never integrated, were global in scope and trail blazing in detail. Childe's use of Marx' ideas confused rather than refined the underlying concepts. But even in Childe's version, these concepts proved extremely productive. And the friendly reception they received indicates the need to deepen our understanding of societal structure and function ("type") and change ("development").

This state of affairs gives particular importance to the recent search for developmental regularities undertaken by archaeologists such as J. O. Brew [2] and G. R. Willey [3] and to the recent efforts to establish the principles of a multilinear development undertaken by science-philosophers such as J. S. Huxley [4] and ethnologists such as J. H. Steward.[a]

Having employed, and elaborated, the concept of multilinear development in the course of the present inquiry, I will now briefly emphasize some key aspects which may help in clarifying the position and perspective of hydraulic society in transition.

---

a. Steward, 1949: 2 ff.; *ibid.*, 1953: 318 ff.; *ibid.*, 1955: 1 ff. Willey (1953: 378) mentions as students of "developmental parallelism" on an area level: W. C. Bennet, R. Larco Hoyle, W. D. Strong, J. Bird, P. Armillas, and himself (we might add D. Collier, R. Adams, and A. Palerm). And he singles out Steward for having made "world-wide comparative evaluations."

413

A. BASIC CONCEPTS OF SOCIETAL TYPE AND DEVELOPMENT

1. SOCIETAL TYPES

a. Essential, Specific, and Nonspecific Elements of Society

SOCIETY changes in an orderly and recognizable way. This thesis implies the existence of social entities whose structure and transformation can be discerned. The present inquiry is based on this thesis. It accepts in substance John Stuart Mill's principle of the "Uniformity of Co-existence," [5] which postulates a definable relation between the major aspects of society. But it rejects the assumption concerning the necessity for coexistence.

Among the ideological, technical, organizational, and social features that appear in any given society, some are essential for the society's proper functioning, some are not. Among the essential features some are specific, some are not. A third group is neither essential nor specific.

Agromanagerial despotism is essential to hydraulic society, and as far as we know it is specific to it. The feudal system of limited and conditional service (not unconditional subservience), vassalage (not bureaucracy), and fief (not office land) is essential to the medieval societies of Europe and Japan. It occurs so rarely elsewhere that it may be considered specific to these societies.

Corvée labor is an essential element of hydraulic and feudal societies, and serfdom (the attachment of the peasant to his land or village) is essential to the helotage-based [6] societies of ancient Greece, to feudal society, and to most simple and semicomplex Oriental societies. That is, both institutions are essential to more than one type of society and specific to none.

Large government-managed works of irrigation and flood control are probably essential to all primary hydraulic societies, and they remain essential to the core areas of secondary hydraulic societies. But they are not specific to either. Hydraulic installations were built in ancient Greece and Rome, and hydraulic enterprises of various kinds appear also in postfeudal Western societies. Slavery may have been essential to the agriculture of late republican and early imperial Rome. It was compatible with, but not essential to, many other societies.

Innumerable elements of technology, custom, art, and belief occur widely and without being either essential or specific to the conditions of power, status, and property—that is, to the crucial relations within any society. These elements may fulfill an essential cultural function, human life being organized not only in societal but also in cultural "going concerns"; [7] and their interrelations within a specific societal order may color their appearance. But being compatible with several types of societies, they are more or less free floating. The ease with which certain elements of Chinese culture—such as the script, Confucianism, and architecture—flowed to Japan, and the persistence with which China's bureaucratic patterns of power, property, and class were kept out of Japanese society illustrate this point. A similar flow of societally irrelevant elements characterized the relations between classical Greece and Western Asia, between Kievan Russia and Byzantium, between Christian and Muslim Spain, and between nonhydraulic Egypt and the hydraulic areas in general. A comparison of the German part of Switzerland and Hitler Germany demonstrates strikingly that civilizations may share many technological, artistic, literary, and religious features and yet, from the standpoint of societal structure, be worlds apart. Recognition of these facts should go far in correcting the idea of a "necessary relation between *all* possible aspects of the same social organism." [b]

Evidently, then, the discrete cultural traits of a given civilization do not always clearly and surely reveal its specific societal structure. Nor is this structure necessarily clarified by the recognition of unique and specific essential institutional features. Specific occurrence is more the exception than the rule. Usually an essential element becomes specific through its dimension and/or through the type of configuration in which it occurs. The corvée is not confined to hydraulic societies; forced labor of nonslaves appears also in other societal types. It is specific in that in agrohydraulic civilizations, different from feudalism, corvée labor is imposed on the mass of the population by the state.

But specific or not, essential features are usually not numerous. Nor do they occur in many combinations. It is a basic fact of history that the key institutions of power, property, and social relations have constituted only a limited number of effective going concerns—societies.

Hydraulic society is such a going concern. Its dimension and staying power have made it prominent in the history of man. Yet it is only one among several types of stratified societies that emerged prior to the rise of the modern industrial world. A brief glance at these other types will aid us in defining more clearly the peculiarity of hydraulic society.

b. Comte, approvingly quoted by Mill, 1947: 599, cf. 600 (italics mine). For a one-sidedly economic version of the same thesis see Marx, 1939: 27.

b. Pre-industrial Stratified Societies

i. PASTORAL SOCIETY

STATE-CENTERED hydraulic societies may have preceded all other stratified civilizations; but in all probability the early hydraulic societies were soon confronted by groups which combined nonhydraulic farming with extensive stock raising and which were dominated by tribal aristocracies. The Aryan conquerors of India apparently were semipastoralists of this kind.[8]

However, it was only after the first great cavalry revolution, when man learned to ride the horse and the camel, that he gained easy access to the steppe and established powerful societies based essentially on herding. Interacting with hydraulic and nonhydraulic sedentary neighbors, stratified pastoralists [c] affected the course of history greatly, persisting mainly in Inner Asia and the Near East until modern times.[d]

ii. SEVERAL TYPES OF ANCIENT SOCIETIES

THE higher agrarian civilizations of Greece and Rome, which existed side by side with the self-perpetuating East for almost a millennium,

c. We cannot discuss here the possible subtypes of stratified pastoral societies. Max Weber's stress upon the social peculiarities of "small cattle pastoralism" as practiced by the early Jews (Weber, RS, III: 44 ff.) indicates the possibility of at least one subdivision.

d. Why did Marx omit Mill's stratified pastoral societies from his list of "progressive epochs in the economic system of society"? (see Marx, 1921: lvi). As explained in Chap. 9, above, Marx did not, in this context, view "progress" in terms of an actual historical development; and Plekhanov's efforts to correct Marx on this point therefore sought to remove an obstacle that was not there (Plekhanov, FPM: 50). Reminiscent in a way of Hegel's "worlds," which differed from each other in the degree of freedom they enjoyed and which did not constitute a developmental sequence, Marx set up a series of "antagonistic" societies, which, although different with respect to the increase and importance of private property, also did not constitute a developmental sequence. The despotic states of Asiatic society controlled the villages, and they did not break up their communal landed property (Marx, 1939: 376 ff., 380, 383). The societies of Greece and Rome made the first major attempts to establish private property, but they also preserved a part of the communally held landed property as *ager publicus* (*ibid.*: 378 f., 380, 382). Medieval ("feudal") society went further in reducing communal property (*ibid.*: 380 ff., 399 ff.). And in modern "bourgeois" society private ownership of the means of production prevails completely (*ibid.*: 375, 402 ff.).

Marx' famous scheme did not take into account the fact, of which he later became aware (cf. Marx, DK, III, Pt. 1: 318), that certain Asiatic societies, such as China, abolished the communal system of land tenure. Moreover, it is contrived with regard to "ancient" and feudal land tenure. The inclusion of another stratified and property-based conformation, pastoral society, would have made his typology even more artificial.

were neither hydraulic nor feudal. Nor can they be subsumed under a single major societal type, which was penetrated and, finally, ruined by slave labor.

A well-integrated upper stratum maintained its hegemony in Crete, Sparta, Thessaly, and also, under different conditions, in Rome, while in the Greek city states of the Athenian type loosely associated aristocracies eventually lost their political dominance. In Sparta native serfs tilled the fields for their alien masters, and the free peasants of Rome were ultimately, and largely, replaced by slaves. Conversely, in the city states of the Athenian type, farming remained predominantly in the hands of free peasants, and the increase of slave labor primarily affected urban industry.[9]

Without trying to disentangle all the threads of this institutional tissue, we are probably safe in saying that prior to the spread of Hellenism, the civilizations of Greece and Rome—and for that matter Spain and France—embraced more than a single societal type. Among them the helotage-based Spartan type is noteworthy for both the stability of its over-all pattern and the insignificance of slave labor.[10]

iii. FEUDAL SOCIETY

THE ancient societies of Greece and Rome, whatever their original form, were eventually Orientalized. The agrarian societies of Europe and Japan were not. In fact, these latter developed specific feudal relations which, on the agrarian level, are unmatched both in their multicenteredness and in their capacity for growth. It was this feudal order that led to a limping and multicentered type of absolutism and, eventually, to multicentered and private-property-based industrial society.

The similarities between the feudal civilizations of Europe and Japan are evident. In both cases there existed, alongside and below the sovereign, numerous lords (vassals) who rendered only limited and conditional services and who were not members of a bureaucratic state apparatus. But the two institutional configurations were not identical. Along the western flank of the Eurasian continent agriculture, being based on rainfall, was extensive, and it was conducive to a manorial economy that gave rise to centers of large-scale farming. Along the eastern flank farming, being based on irrigation, was intensive and definitely favored small-scale production. Furthermore, the independent Church and the guild cities of Europe had no parallel in Japan.

Thus we find in Japan and in the early phase of Medieval Europe a simpler form of feudal society in which the ruler shared societal leadership exclusively with his vassals. In Europe this simpler form gave birth to a more complex form in which the ruler had to reckon with a powerful corporated clergy and a variety of burgher associations.

These two variants do not exhaust the subtypes of feudal society. In Medieval Sweden and Kievan Russia the decisive social relations, as expressed in feudal investiture and enfeoffment, never seem to have matured. We may therefore view them as belonging to a third subtype: "marginal" feudal society.

iv. UNWIELDY HYDRAULIC SOCIETY

HYDRAULIC society surpasses all other stratified pre-industrial societies in duration, extent, and the number of persons dominated. This may largely explain why it comprises so many subtypes. Taxonomically speaking, hydraulic society is an unwieldy giant. Should we not then treat certain of its major subtypes as discrete major societal conformations?

Such a decision would be justified if we were faced with basic structural differences in social relations and societal leadership. However, no such differences can be demonstrated, since agromanagerial despotism and a monopoly bureaucracy prevail in all known subtypes of the hydraulic world. In consequence, arbitrary "splitting" would obscure the crucial sociohistorical fact that hydraulic society dwarfed all other agrarian societies in dimension and institutional diversity.

Biological taxonomists, faced with similar problems, have refused "to split up big genera simply because they contain a larger number of species than some other genera and may look 'unbalanced'" or "unwieldy." Knowing that the biological world is characterized by inequality, they feel that scientific "classification should reflect this inequality faithfully." [11]

v. RESIDUAL STRATIFIED PRE-INDUSTRIAL SOCIETIES

THE problem of taxonomical residues, another concern of biotaxonomy, is also suggestive for our inquiry. "It is estimated that less than 2 per cent of the total number of species of birds of the entire world remain still unknown." [12] This optimum is reached only by "a few genera of mammals, butterflies, beetles, mollusks and so forth." [13] Most biologists consider their investigations well advanced when they can establish, in the field of their researches, the major outlines of structure (system) and change (evolution).

Taking the stratified pre-industrial civilizations in their entirety,

how many specific societies can be discerned? Assuming that Greek
and Roman antiquity embraced at least two types, we arrive at a
minimum of five such conformations. And there is good reason to
believe that there are others. The nonhydraulic parts of the "classical"
and preclassical Mediterranean could well be further scrutinized.
So could certain neglected areas of Asia, Africa, the Pacific Islands,
and America.

But while making full allowance for possible new disclosures, we
must warn against overrating their historical significance. The records
of the past and present-day observations indicate that above the level
of primitive tribal life and below the level of modern industrial
society, the great majority of all human beings lived in already identified institutional settings—in stratified pastoral societies, in hydraulic
societies, in helotage-, free peasant-, or slavery-based nonfeudal societies, or in feudal societies.

2. Societal Changes

a. Forms

THE fate of these different types of societies is instructive in several
ways. As stated above, the stratified pastoral societies underwent a
variety of experiences. Some raised crops; some became predominantly agricultural. This may well have been the origin of the early
Greek tribal aristocracies, and it manifestly was the background of
Germanic tribal society. Other herding groups were in contact with
hydraulic civilizations. Some merged with them completely, some,
after a period of conquest or subjugation, withdrew to the steppe.
Some, without an "Oriental" interlude, persisted in their semi-arid
grasslands, remaining in a state of developmental stagnation, until
under the influence of modern neighbor societies they began to lose
their institutional identity.

The higher agrarian societies of ancient Greece and Rome attacked
the Oriental world. But while their conquests brought material advantages to many of their citizens and a great increase in power to
a few, the price paid was the general Orientalization of their society.
This transformation offers a striking example of "diversive" (*externally* conditioned) as juxtaposed to "developmental" (*internally*
conditioned) [14] change.

Feudal society was sufficiently strong to hold its own against hydraulic society. It was sufficiently open to initiate a commercial and
manufacturing way of life. Among higher civilizations it is the outstanding case of societal development.

Hydraulic society is the outstanding case of societal stagnation. Probably originating in several ways [15] and under favorable circumstances developing semicomplex and complex patterns of property and social stratification, hydraulic society did not abandon its basic structures except under the impact of *external* forces.

b. Values

THESE facts show that the morphology of societal change is far from simple. They also show that behind the problems of form lie crucial problems of value which a naive, or politically motivated, developmental optimism is unable or unwilling to see.

Societal change is not identical with development. Development, the transformation effected essentially by internal forces, is only one form of societal change. Equally important is diversive change, the transformation effected essentially by external forces.

Moreover, neither developmental nor diversive change is necessarily progressive: neither necessarily improves the condition of man. Man's control over nature is an enormously significant factor in civilization; but as a criterion of progress it must be examined together with man's relation to his fellow men and to his own convictions (secular and religious). The three relations interlock, and any two are as likely to clash as to harmonize.

The wishful thinker may be frightened by such conflicts. The realist, who accepts tragedy as an inevitable element of life, will accept the possibility of diverse value developments in diverse historical circumstances. He will understand that simultaneous progress in all three relations is less frequent than legend has it and that from the standpoint of human values development may be progressive, ambivalent, or outright retrogressive. To the technologist the emergence of Western absolutism and early industrialism will appear spectacularly progressive. In our opinion this development probably destroyed as many values as it created. To the apologist of Soviet rule the diversive change that laid the groundwork for Muscovite despotism will appear as predominantly progressive.[16] In terms of human values it was definitely retrogressive.

Processes that transform a given society into a society of a different type can be considered *primary* societal changes. For obvious reasons their number is limited. *Secondary* societal changes may produce a new subtype of the same over-all conformation; or they may be circular, leading eventually to the restoration of the original order or suborder. They may—but they need not—be cathartic (regenerative). Certain dynastic changes and many institutional reforms have been of this kind.

Restorative developments occur in all institutional conformations. They are particularly frequent in societies that perpetuate themselves over long periods of time. Above the level of primitive civilizations, hydraulic society therefore offers the richest opportunities for studying societal stagnation and circular change.

B. HYDRAULIC SOCIETY IN TRANSITION

1. FOUR ASPECTS OF THE SELF-PERPETUATION OF HYDRAULIC SOCIETY

a. The Potential for Institutional and Cultural Growth

THE power nuclei of hydraulic society surpassed all other agrarian commonwealths in their capacity for subduing and controlling outlying areas. After a local "formative" period and where opportunity permitted, these nuclei assumed territorial or national dimensions. Under particularly favorable conditions, territorial "florescence" was followed by "imperial" expansion and "fusion." [a] Hydraulic society enduring over millennia had unique opportunities to exhaust the creative potential of each of these situations. The culture history of hydraulic civilization shows how thoroughly these opportunities were realized.

The growth in the magnitude of a sociocultural unit, however, does not necessarily involve a corresponding institutional and cultural growth. Loose interaction between numerous independent units proves more stimulating than island- or oasis-like isolation. It also proves more stimulating than imperial fusion, which tends to give the initiative for experiment and change to a single center. This probably accounts for the fact that the foremost representatives of hydraulic civilization generally achieved the peak of their creativeness when they were part of a cluster of loosely related territorial states.

Virtually all great Chinese ideas on the "Way" (*tao*), on society, government, human relations, warfare, and historiography, crystallized during the classical period of the territorial states and at the beginning of the imperial period. The establishment of the examination system and the psychologically slanted reformulation of Con-

---

a. See Wittfogel, 1955: 47 ff. The terms "formative," "florescence," and "empire" have recently been used to distinguish "periods" in the development of societies ("culture types"). A "formative" period on a local scale may be followed by a "florescent" or "classical" period (growth and maturation on a regional or territorial scale), and this eventually by a period of interarea expansion: "Empire" or "Fusion" (see Steward, 1949: 7 ff.; *ibid.*, 1953: 323).

fucianism followed the reunification of the empire, the transfer
of the economic center to the Yangtze Valley, and the building of an
artificial Nile, the Grand Canal.[1] Other significant changes occurred
during later periods of imperial China in the field of the drama and
the popular novel; but they were partly due to a new influence, the
complete subjugation of China by two "barbarian" conquest dynasties. And none of them shook the Confucian foundation of Chinese
thought.

The climax of creative expression in India is similarly located.
Religion, statecraft, law, and family patterns originated and reached
their "classical" maturity either when India was a network of independent states or during the early phase of imperial unification.

The Arab-dominated conquest societies of the Near East began
on an empire-like level. In this case most of the great ideas concerned with law, statecraft, and man's fate were formulated during
the first and early middle periods of Islamic society.

b. Stagnation, Epigonism, and Retrogression

WITHIN a given framework, creative change does not continue indefinitely. The growth potential of a society varies with its natural
and cultural setting, but when the possibilities for development
and differentiation have in great part been realized, the creative
process tends to slow down. Maturation becomes stagnation. And
given time, stagnation results in stereotyped repetition (epigonism)
or outright retrogression. New conquests and territorial expansions
favor acculturation. But the ensuing changes do not necessarily alter
the existing pattern of society and culture. Eventually they also will
yield to stagnation, epigonism, and retrogression.

The trend toward epigonism and retrogression may merge—and
in the Oriental conquest societies of the Old World it did merge
—with a trend toward reduced hydraulic intensity and increased
personal restriction. In terms of managerial action, personal freedom,
and cultural creativeness, most hydraulic societies of the late "Empire" period probably operated on a level lower than that reached
during the days of regional and early "Empire" florescence.

c. The Staying-Power of Hydraulic Society

BUT whether the institutional and cultural level was lowered or
whether periodically regenerative changes restored earlier "classical"
conditions, hydraulic society, as an institutional configuration, persisted. Dominated by its monopoly bureaucracy, it continued to
muster the technical and intellectual skills necessary to its perpetua-

tion. Its officials frequently possessed learning and subtlety. Its peasants grew their crops with more care than did the serfs of Europe,[b]
and its artisans handled the materials of their crafts with the greatest
refinement. These groups responded to a variety of incentives, but
they did not demand political independence or a popular form of
government.

Nor did the irrational features of hydraulic despotism prevent the
monopoly bureaucracy from perpetuating itself. Measured by the
people's rationality standard, an apparatus state may be overorganized
economically. It may be overdefended militarily. And its masters
may be overprotected police-wise. But as long as the regime maintains
the masters' rationality minimum, it will continue as a going concern. And it will hold its own against open societies with a much
higher rationality coefficient as long as its armed forces are a match
for theirs.

d. Societal Change Dependent on External Influence

ONE important developmental consequence of this fact has already
been discussed. Since the agrarian monopoly bureaucracy prevented
hydraulic society of and by itself from developing a multicentered
type of society, it is clear that when such a transformation occurred,
it occurred only through the direct or indirect influence of external
forces.

Western Rome was crushed by tribal invaders from the north, and
Moorish Spain fell to the feudal warriors of the Iberian Peninsula.
In both cases, internal crisis facilitated the institutional victory of
the aggressors. In Byzantium the European attackers, who were strong
enough to overthrow the decaying absolutist regime, were too weak
to initiate a multicentered order with corporated barons, powerful
guild cities, and an independent Church, such as existed at that time
in their feudal homelands. The external nonhydraulic forces had to
penetrate hydraulic society thoroughly in order to accomplish a full
diversive transformation.

2. RECENT PATTERNS OF EXTERNAL INFLUENCE

DID the impact of the commercial and industrial West produce such
a transformation? John Stuart Mill was convinced that this would be
the case. The "civilized [industrial] nations" [2] would make "all other
countries" follow the course they had taken [3] in technology and
material prosperity, personal security, and voluntary cooperation.[4]

---

b. Japanese farming, based on small-scale irrigation and stimulated by the Chinese
example, was, during the feudal period, as intensive as Chinese farming.

Marx also was convinced that in such colonial countries as India, "England has to fulfill a double mission . . . one destructive, the other regenerating—the annihilation of old Asiatic society and the laying the material foundations of Western society in Asia." [5] And even if he expected the Indians to reap "the fruits of the new elements of society" only after they had attained freedom through labor rule in Great Britain or through their own efforts,[6] he spoke enthusiastically of the newly introduced Western features, mentioning especially political unity, modern communications (telegraph, railways, steamships), a Western-trained army, a free press, private landownership,[c] and a class of modern civil servants.[7]

With regard to Tsarist Russia he was still more optimistic. Although well aware of Russia's Oriental heritage, he nevertheless believed it possible that Russia might cross "the threshold of the capitalist system" and then "submit to the implacable laws of such a system, like the other Western nations." [8]

Mill and Marx were expressing opinions that many of their contemporaries shared. But manifestly they did not know how their predictions would be fulfilled. To the best of my knowledge, Mill did not elaborate on his statement of 1848; and Marx, who in the 50's presented the British-promoted dissolution of India's old rural order as a *fait accompli* and "the only social revolution ever heard of in Asia," [9] noted in Volume 3 of *Das Kapital* that this dissolution was proceeding "only very slowly (*nur sehr allmählich*)." [10] To be sure, in the meantime much has happened in the West as well as in the East, and much has been said about the "changing" (and the "unchanging") Orient. The contrived interpretations of events given by the Communist International do not mean that a truly scientific analysis is not needed. Such an analysis is very much needed, since the issues involved are both complex and momentous.

a. Patterns of Interrelation

To begin with, present-day developments in the hydraulic world follow no single pattern. Different types of interrelation with the West and different conditions within both the influencing and the influenced side inevitably affect the result. Thus on the basis of different intensities of cultural contact and different degrees of military aggression and political control we may distinguish at least four pat-

c. Marx called the *zamindar* and *riotwar* forms of land tenure, which the British had created, "abominable"; but he still welcomed them as "two distinct forms of private property in land—the great desideratum of Asiatic society" (Marx, NYDT, August 8, 1853).

terns of interrelations between the commercial and industrial West and various countries of the Oriental world.

Type I: Aloof independence (representative: Thailand).[d] Thailand suffered only minor military defeats at the hands of the West; and there was no direct, and little indirect, Western interference in the country's internal affairs. Nor was there, until recently, much Western contact of any kind. In consequence, Thailand remained an independent and more or less aloof hydraulic society, which was free to adopt or disregard Western institutions and culture.

Type II: Proximity and independence (foremost representative: Russia). Russia was geographically and culturally close to Western Europe. But in contrast to Ottoman Turkey, its policy was not decisively influenced by foreign "councils"; and in contrast to China, its major cities were not compelled to tolerate foreign settlements. Three disastrous military events—the Crimean War, the war against Japan, and World War I—shook Russia deeply, but they did not force it into a colonial or "semi-colonial" position. A minimum of direct foreign interference was combined with a maximum of peaceful interaction.

Type III: Complete and simple dependency (outstanding representatives: Mexico, Peru, Indonesia, and India). All these countries suffered complete military defeat at the hands of the West, which led to their outright political subjugation (colonization).

Type IV: Limited and multiple dependency (major representatives: Ottoman Turkey and China). Both countries suffered severe military defeats at the hands of the West, and both were subjected to substantial political and economic interference from several foreign powers. But the Turkish and Chinese governments preserved their armies, and although under great pressure from the outside, they still made policy decisions.

b. The Influencing Side

ON the cultural level, diffusion was by no means a one-way process. In the 19th and early 20th centuries Russian literature had a great fascination for the Western world. And long before Turgeniev, Dostoievsky, and Tolstoy, Islamic architecture and poetry and Indian and Chinese philosophy were admired and studied in far-away Western lands. However, in the spheres of technology, government, property, and class, influences moved essentially in one direction, and hydraulic society was definitely on the receiving end.

But these influences were neither identical nor static. In the 16th

d. Prior to 1939 called "Siam."

century, when the Spaniards seized "the Americas," Europe had just
outgrown the feudal way of life, and absolutist governments were
consolidating themselves throughout the continent. In the 17th
century, when the Dutch and English were spreading their domination in South Asia, capitalist elites became socially significant in a
few economically advanced countries. But it was only during the 18th
and 19th centuries that the new bourgeois middle class in its entirety achieved sociopolitical prominence and that representative government came to prevail in the Western world.

This timetable, which by necessity is simplified, throws light on
the colonial history of three major areas of hydraulic society. The
conquest of the Americas was organized, not by private merchant
adventurers, but by an absolutist government, which was enormously
strengthened by its war against the Moors and by its fiscal control of
the Spanish sheep-herding economy. The colonization of Indonesia
and India was accomplished by small groups of privileged businessmen, whose government-supported and quasigovernmental East India
companies came closer to representing a genuine monopoly capitalism than certain recent formations that have been thus designated.

The Dutch East India Company was dissolved in 1798; and Dutch
colonial policy was liberalized after the revolutions of 1848, which
to some extent shifted the center of gravity also in Dutch society.[11]
The British East India Company lost its monopoly in India in 1813
(after the Napoleonic Wars) and its monopoly of the China trade
in 1833 (after the passing of the Reform Bill). Spain's American empire came to an end before the constitutional development of the
19th century made itself felt in the Iberian Peninsula. Yet it is
worth noting that the later phase of Spanish absolutism, especially
the reign of Charles III (1749–88), saw an encouragement of private
enterprise in the form of companies, which until then had played
no role in Spain.[12]

In all these instances Western impact upon a traditionally hydraulic
civilization involved direct colonial domination. In others, several
commercial and manufacturing powers competed for the control of
an economically attractive Oriental territory. Under such circumstances, the relation between the changing conditions in the industrial camp and the form and intensity of the interference are complex.
Nevertheless, certain causal relations can be established. It was only
after the Industrial Revolution that the West was able to force an
open-door policy upon the remote Chinese empire; and it was only
from the second half of the 19th century on, that Western advisors
seriously suggested constitutional and representative governments in
Turkey and China.

c. Institutional Differences in the Target Societies

As demonstrated throughout our inquiry, conditions also varied greatly in the hydraulic countries.

In Mexico hydraulic enterprises were of the "Loose 2" type.[13] In Turkey the metropolis gradually lost control over its hydraulic provinces. Kievan Russia had no agrohydraulic enterprises; and the Tatar Yoke produced no change in this respect. In pre-Spanish Peru and in Siam large-scale private native trade played no role; in Indonesia and Ottoman Turkey it was extremely limited. In Muscovite Russia businessmen other than bureaucratic capitalists were greatly restricted. In Aztec Mexico independent commerce flourished, and in China it assumed large proportions.

In some of these countries there were substantial groups which, given a chance, could have been expected to evolve into a modern middle class. And in some there existed forms of private landowner-ship which, under the impact of private-property-based industrial society, could also have been expected to further the growth of a modern multicentered society. In what manner and to what extent were these possibilities realized?

3. SOCIETAL RESULTS

TRACING the results of the recent Western impact, we need not deal here at length with Thailand.[e] Suffice it to say that despite a number of technical and political innovations, an independent and aloof Thailand has thus far developed neither an indigenous middle class[f] nor a genuinely representative system of government.

a. Russia

LIKE Thailand, Russia remained politically free, but it suffered much more seriously from military attacks. Like the Chinese man-darins, the masters of Russian society were greatly disturbed by the defeats of their armies, but being closer to the West, they were quicker to comprehend the institutional and cultural basis of its military and technical strength. They, therefore, promoted Western forms of strong property, private enterprise, public discussion, and

---

e. For obvious reasons, we must in the present context refrain altogether from discussing the development of Japan. Never having been hydraulic, Japan speedily evolved from a "simple" feudal order into a modern multicentered industrial society.

f. The Chinese business community, which has many features of an incipient middle class, is increasingly excluded from Thailand's economic life. Unless the present trend is reversed, this group will be prevented from playing the developmental role for which it is otherwise well prepared.

local self-government. They introduced these institutions grudgingly
—not because they wanted them to prevail but because they deemed
them necessary and susceptible to continued control.

The deficiences of the emancipation of the serfs have already been
discussed.[14] The *zemstvos*, elected bodies of local self-government,
were, after a brief bloom (1864–66), severely restricted.[15] But even in
their crippled form they wielded much more power than the Beggars'
Democracies of hydraulic despotism. Count Witte was entirely justified in asserting that autocracy and the *zemstvos* could not coexist
for any considerable length of time.[g]

To be sure, the absolutist bureaucracy remained supreme. But its
prestige was weakened by the Turkish war of 1877–78,[16] and it was
deeply shaken by the disasters of the Russo-Japanese War of 1904–05.

State control and oppressive taxation severely handicapped the
growth of a modern economy.[17] But private property now became
secure, and private enterprise, which prior to the middle of the
19th century was already significant in certain light industries,[18]
now advanced vigorously on many fronts.

Between 1893 and 1908, 2,965 million rubles of Russian capital
were invested in industry as compared to 874 million rubles of foreign capital.[19] By 1916–17 government-directed foreign capital prevailed almost completely in mining; but Russian capital was equally
strong, or prevailed, in most other branches of industry. In the
chemical industry it constituted 50 per cent of all capital, in metal
smelting and processing 58 per cent, in wood processing 63 per cent,
and in textiles 72 per cent.[20] The State Bank remained the supreme
master of the credit system; but many private banks came into existence. Private banks increased their own capital plus deposits from
1,289 million rubles in 1909 to 3,375 million rubles in 1913.[21]

This expansion of Russia's modern economy was accomplished not
with forced labor and spectacular police terror but with an increasingly free working class and in an atmosphere of receding despotism.
Take the country's heavy industry: during the two decades before
World War I "the output of coal in the Russian Empire increased
fourfold, and if we exclude Poland, sixfold." [22] From 1893 to 1913
the output of copper "multiplied nearly nine times." [23] Between
1890 and 1913 the output of iron within the empire increased six
times; in the crucial industrial centers of South Russia it increased
"twentyfold." [24] Or take light industry: in 1913 the spindles in the
cotton industry "were two and a half times as numerous, the amount

g. Florinsky, 1953, II: 900; cf. Mavor, 1928: 30. Tsar Nicolas II was therefore right
when he harshly rebuked the representatives of the *zemstvos* for fostering *"senseless
dreams of . . . sharing in the conduct of internal affairs"* (see Birkett, 1918: 488 ff.).

of raw cotton employed three times as great, and the amount of cotton yarn produced two and a half times as great as in 1890." [25]

Russia's first revolution brought about important changes in the political sphere. The Tsar's manifesto of October 1905, although upholding the principle of absolutist power, granted significant constitutional checks and balances. Max Weber, who was deeply aware of the lack of decisive Western phases of development in Russia [26] and who stressed the "Asiatic" or "Mongol" spirit of the Tsarist regime,[h] recognized clearly the enormous advance made by the introduction of even a limited constitution.[i] And indeed, a parliament that could influence the budget and openly criticize the government, political parties that could appeal to the population, a press that enjoyed almost complete freedom of speech,[27] an educational system that was rapidly expanding,[j] commoners who could organize over ten million persons in cooperatives,[28] and workers and other employees who, while prevented from maintaining free trade unions, could share in the administration of health insurance funds [29]—these developments taken together presented a serious challenge to the old single-centered society.

After 1905 Russia's anti-absolutist forces were still not strong enough to establish an open, multicentered society by their own efforts. But when World War I paralyzed the Tsarist army, these forces were sufficiently strong to establish in the spring of 1917 a short-lived but genuinely anti-absolutist and democratic government.

h. Weber spoke of the "cunning Mongol deceit" of the Tsarist bureaucracy (Weber, 1906: 249) and of the regime's "veritable Mongol deceit" (*ibid.:* 394). He criticized the Tsarist police for employing "the most tricky means of the most cunning Asiatic deceit" (*ibid.:* 396).

i. Weber used the not altogether appropriate designation, "pseudoconstitution" (Weber, 1906: 249).

j. Like other countries that had entered the Industrial Age, Russia energetically fostered general education. In 1874, out of one hundred army recruits 21.4 per cent are said to have been literate, in 1894 37.8 per cent, in 1904 55.5 per cent, and in 1914 67.8 per cent. In 1918 among industrial workers aged twenty or below, 77.1 per cent were listed as literate; among those between thirty and thirty-five, 64.8 per cent; and among those over fifty 43.4 per cent (Timasheff, 1946: 35). The high literacy rate of the youngest workers reflects the inauguration by law in 1908 of general secondary education. On the basis of this law almost all children should have been attending school by 1922 (Florinsky, 1953, II: 1237). Florinsky states that progress was slower than anticipated; but he too considers "the modernization and expansion of the school system" impressive (*ibid.:* 1237, 1232). According to the last prerevolutionary estimate, 78 per cent of all Russians were expected to be literate by the late 1930's (Timasheff, 1946: 34, 313). War and revolution retarded performance, but subsequent policy speeded things to some degree. The Soviet census of 1939 asserts that literacy at this time had reached 81.1 per cent (*ibid.:* 314).

b. Colonized Hydraulic Countries

THE Russian experience shows that even in an independent country ruled by a despotic bureaucracy, under favorable international conditions, the germs of a multicentered society may grow fast. This was not the case in the hydraulic areas that, as colonies, fell completely under the sway of Western powers. The Spanish, Dutch, and English colonizers, and also the Portuguese and French, whose ventures we shall not pursue, attempted no thorough modernization of their Oriental possessions. Congruent with their special interests, they introduced Western institutions in a selective and limited way.

The reasons for this are not hard to find. The major areas in hydraulic civilization, being densely populated and for the most part located in tropical and subtropical regions, offered little opportunity for a mass immigration of Europeans. Consequently the conquerors were usually content to establish in their hydraulic colonies a strong administrative apparatus, plus whatever public or private arrangements seemed expedient for economic exploitation.

The Spaniards took this course in the agromanagerial areas of America.[k] The Dutch in Indonesia and the British in India acted similarly. The result was a system of human relations which, despite its differences from traditional hydraulic society, was far from being a replica of Spain, Holland, or England.

Whether the colonizers perpetuated the traditional rural order in a crippled form, as did the Spaniards in Peru and Mexico, whether they left it practically intact, as did the Dutch in Indonesia, or whether they converted communal landholdings into private property, as did the British in India, the administrative masters kept the villages politically impotent. And whether they discarded the native merchants (Mexico and Java), whether they prevented their rise (Peru), or whether they tolerated them (India), the new overlords did little to alter the single-centered society which they had inherited.

Linked to nonhydraulic absolutist or aristocratic regimes, the colonial governments were a curious mixture of Oriental and Occidental absolutism. They were this, despite—or perhaps, to some extent, because of—their continued use of native dignitaries (princes, caciques, curacas), who with certain modifications perpetuated long-established agromanagerial patterns of political, social, and religious control.

k. And also in the nonhydraulic regions. The determination of policy at the center and the excessive strength of the state in the colonial societies in these regions is largely responsible for the continued prominence of the government bureaucracy and for the extraordinary power of its coercive branch, the army.

This roughly was the state of affairs up to the Industrial Revolution, which, in Europe, stimulated the spread of representative governments and which also affected the colonial regimes—where such regimes persisted. The qualification is significant, for India remained a colony until 1949, whereas Spain's American possessions gained their independence shortly after the Napoleonic era.

In postcolonial Mexico and Peru, parliamentary republics were speedily set up. But the innovations benefited primarily the bureaucracy, and still more the army, which in these countries, as in other former Spanish colonies, exerted extraordinary political and economic power.

In Indonesia and India administration was in the hands of a civil service that reflected changing social and political conditions in Holland and England. In both countries popular control over the government increased, and the peculiarities of colonial rule notwithstanding, this fact also influenced the attitudes of the colonial officials toward the native populations. True, the Dutch admitted Indonesians to the regular civil service only in the 20th century,[30] and even then they were reluctant to put them in places of authority. Nevertheless, on the eve of World War II, Indonesians occupied 60.6 per cent of all lower-middle, 38 per cent of all middle, and 6.4 per cent of all higher government positions.[31]

In India a like trend began much earlier and went considerably further. A year after the passage of the Reform Bill, which did so much to strengthen the English middle class, offices in the Indian civil service were opened to all Indians, "irrespective of caste, creed, or race." [32] The Act of 1833 was not much more than a declaration of principle, but subsequent events lent it substance. The British maintained their control over the central government,[33] but they increased Indian authority over the local and provincial administrations until, in 1935, the provinces were given complete self-government.[34]

An ever-larger number of Indians and Indonesians went to Europe to study. Democratic procedures were therefore well known in India and Indonesia before the two countries gained their independence. Indeed the first acts of the new governments showed them eager to promote a parliamentary government, political parties, and free associations of workers, businessmen, peasants, and intellectuals.

What is the developmental meaning of all this? To what extent do the imperfect democracies of Mexico and Peru and the technically advanced democracies of India and Indonesia reveal the rise of new forces that aim at replacing their old single-centered societies with a genuinely multicentered system of human relations?

In Mexico and Peru, Spanish colonial rule did not—except during a short interlude—encourage the growth of private enterprise or the rise of a modern middle class. The independent republics remained governmentally top-heavy. In Mexico the potentials of power and wealth inherent in a bureaucratic or military career further retarded, although they did not block, the spread of independent private enterprise. In Peru the Indians had much less opportunity to engage in middle-class activities than in Mexico. Yet the country's hydraulic and managerial past did not prevent the emergence of large private enterprises in agriculture and industry. Peru's entrepreneurial upper class was (and is) strongly interlinked with foreign capital. And while some of its members profit from close attachment to the government, the group as a whole cannot be viewed as an Andean variant of bureaucratic capitalism.[m]

The Inca empire had no merchant class when the Spaniards came. In Mexico the Spaniards seem to have wiped out the prominent *pochteca* merchants. The Portuguese and their successors, the Dutch, "suppressed Javanese commerce"; and native "merchants and shipbuilders lost their occupation." [35] Thereafter, the Dutch controlled the bulk of big enterprise in Indonesia; and they permitted a group of "Oriental foreigners," the Chinese, to operate on an intermediate level as traders and money lenders. When Indonesia became free, the Dutch were eliminated as administrators and in large part also as businessmen. The Chinese remained distrusted outsiders.[n] And in their own ranks the Indonesians never evolved a sizable industrial, commercial, or banking middle class that could close the gap between the large peasant population and the educated, and mainly bureaucratic, elite.[36] Thus in Indonesia a democratic shell covers a societal structure that is much closer to the single-centered hydraulic patterns of the past than to a modern multicentered industrial society.

The Indian development differs from the Indonesian development in several significant respects. Prior to the arrival of the British, some capitalist enterprise existed in India—probably not so much as is suggested by recent legend [37] but not so little as is claimed by Bernier, who measured Mogul India by Occidental standards. While the British crippled indigenous business activities, they did not forbid them. During the colonial period Indian businessmen organized a number

m. For a comprehensive study of the uneven growth of a modern middle class in the various parts of modern Latin America, see Crevenna, *MECM: passim.*

n. In Indonesia, as in Thailand and other countries of Southeast Asia, there is a substantial Chinese business community. But as in Thailand, the Chinese capitalists of Indonesia are considered aliens; and for this reason they have been unable to fulfill the political functions of a recognized indigenous middle class (see Furnivall, 1944: 414; Kahin, 1952: 28, 475).

of finishing industries, especially cotton, and certain heavy industries, especially steel,[38] and by the time India gained its independence the private sector had increased considerably. However, according to all estimates, this sector—and the modern middle class which reflects its growth—is still small.

Of course, the British also introduced private ownership of land. But contrary to Marx' expectation, this reform did little to aid the growth of Western society in India. Private landownership prevailed in a few hydraulic societies, and was present in lesser degree in many It tended to lead to bureaucratic and absentee landlordism.[39] In general the British recognized the erstwhile holders of office land, the *jagidars,* as landowners. In certain regions they made the previous tax collectors, the *zamindars,* the owners of the lands over which they had exercised fiscal jurisdiction, and in many others they converted the peasant occupiers, the *ryotwari,* into full owners of the land they cultivated. But a land reform that does not protect the peasant owners by appropriate educational, political, and economic measures, especially in the sphere of credit, tends to benefit them only temporarily. The new Indian peasant owners soon fell prey to the money lender. And eventually many were forced to sell their land to an official, *zamindar,* or other person of wealth, who, as an absentee landlord, took half, or more than half, of the crop as rent. In 1950 "about 80 per cent of the land [was] in the hands of absentee landlords, or in other words four-fifths of the land [was] cultivated by people who do not own it." [40] Instead of Westernizing the Indian villages, the British imposed on them one of the worst features of Oriental land tenure: bureaucratic and absentee landlordism.

c. Semidependent ("Semicolonial") Countries

THE recent history of the Near East (roughly the orbit of the former Turkish empire) and of the continental Far East (China) reveals the development of hydraulic countries which, although not colonized, were conspicuously under pressure from the industrial West. In both cases several great powers struggled for control, but none was sufficiently strong to establish its hegemony. In both cases the negative effects of Western interference, which were grave, were to some extent mitigated by the fact that the target areas remained independent and that their governments played an active role in modernizing their countries.

In the Near East a series of military defeats weakened the authority of Constantinople over the Turkish provinces where local masters were seeking to buttress their position, first by abolishing the privileges of such government-attached functionaries as tax collectors and holders of office land, and second by assigning the bulk of the land to those who were tilling it. As in India, many poorly equipped, poorly educated, and poorly organized peasants were soon compelled to sell their newly acquired property to persons of wealth: former tax collectors, civil and military serving men, village sheiks,[41] and rich townsmen with loose or no government ties.

As a result of this process, bureaucratic and absentee landlordism has prevailed until today in Egypt, Syria, Iraq, Lebanon, and other parts of the Near East.[o] And the introduction of certain technical innovations went hand in hand with the perpetuation of quasihydraulic patterns of society that did little to encourage the growth of a modern middle or laboring class or a literate and politically organized peasantry.

The core area of Ottoman power, Anatolia, had a different history. More than the outlying provinces, which gradually broke away, the region was subjected to serious and direct interference from the Great Powers. The Capitulations, which gave privileged foreigners judicial and economic extraterritoriality, were particularly apparent in Constantinople, where most of the beneficiaries lived. Together with the foreign administration of Turkey's debts and the International Council, they did much to lower the country's economy and international prestige.[42]

But the scene of Turkey's greatest humiliation also became the scene of its strongest political and intellectual resurgence. In 1876 a parliamentary constitution was temporarily adopted in Constantinople. Later, the Young Turks began their reform movement in the old metropolitan area. And it was also in this area that Kemal Ataturk and his followers laid the foundations for the new Turkish national state.

Present-day Turkey has almost no middle class in the modern sense.[43] But on the political level a multiparty system has been established, and on the socio-economic level private property and enterprise have been encouraged. An experienced observer, who in 1952 still saw the old vicious circle of bureaucratic power, exploitation, and privilege prevailing in most parts of the former Ottoman empire, found "strong evidence that this circle has at last been broken in one Middle [Near] Eastern country," Turkey.[44]

Has the circle really been broken? Only time will tell. But this

o. See Cooke, 1952: 40. Cooke does not interpret the relation between bureaucratic position and landlordism in these countries as a consequence of traditional bureaucratic rule. But he too recognizes that in the Ottoman empire civil and military office, religious leadership, and landownership overlapped (*ibid.*: 281).

much can be said. The development of modern Turkey, which is both free and closely interlinked with the West, shows significant similarities to later 19th- and early 20th-century Russia, and significant dissimilarities to pre-Communist China.

If the presence of large segments of private property and enterprise were decisive for transforming hydraulic society into a multi-centered Western society, then no country could have been better prepared than China to take this road. In China private property in land was incomparably older than in Turkey or Tsarist Russia, and the tradition of private handicraft and commerce, including big commerce, was equally ancient. But the case of China demonstrates beyond doubt that the emergence of a modern middle class of the Western type depends on more than big private property and enterprise.

From 1840 on, China suffered from outside pressures. Unequal treaties, international concessions, extraterritoriality, and foreign control over the maritime customs weakened the absolutist government to the point where internal enemies were able to overthrow it and set up a republic. But the events which followed the revolution of 1911 revealed both the country's political cohesiveness and its societal inertia. Although temporarily broken up into a number of territorial regimes headed by bureaucratic warlords, China did not evolve a strong modern middle class, and this despite the fact that not a few native business communities in the concessions and abroad supported Dr. Sun Yat-sen's efforts at modernization.

This situation did not change fundamentally when, in 1927–28, the Kuomintang under Chiang Kai-shek accomplished a loose re-unification of China proper. Continued foreign interference, aggravated by Soviet-directed Communist operations, prevented the Nationalist government from gaining full control of the country. And while modern bourgeois forces temporarily exerted some influence over the central government, they remained weak in the provincial administrations, which continued to be largely dominated by a traditional agromanagerial bureaucracy.[45]

But all these obstacles notwithstanding, China did not stand still. Western technology was increasingly welcomed; and Western ideas found expression in education, in the rising position of women, and in a relatively free press. Quit of foreign fetters, the country might have greatly accelerated its cultural and societal transformation.

World War II put an end to the many Western privileges that had crippled China. But relief came too late. It came during a war in which the Japanese, by occupying the treaty ports and the industrial cities, were able to weaken China's modern middle class.[46]

It came during a war in which the Communists were able to thoroughly penetrate the loosely integrated and sorely burdened Chinese society.

In Turkey, when semidependency ended, the road to a modern non-Communist society was clear and open. In China, when this period ended, the opportunities for diversive change, while broadened by the Western powers, were blocked by the Communists.

d. A New Developmental Force Arises: Soviet Communism

IN the 1920's the Soviet Union was too weak to affect decisively even such countries as Turkey, to whom it gave considerable economic aid. In the '30's it began to play a major role in international diplomacy. And after World War II it openly competed with the West for world leadership.

Thus the rise of the USSR presents the heirs of hydraulic society with a new alternative. Where formerly those who strove for institutional change saw only one goal, they now see two, and this because of the Bolshevik revolution. What is the developmental meaning of this revolution?

4. HYDRAULIC SOCIETY AT THE CROSSROADS

a. The Developmental Issue Underlying the Bolshevik Revolution

AMONG the major countries of the Oriental world that were breaking away from their agrodespotic past, the first to turn its back on Western society was Russia. This is of crucial importance because, prior to 1917, Russia had gone far in its Westernization and because, after 1917, it became the most influential source of anti-Western action in Asia and elsewhere.

The extent of Russia's Westernization in the spring of 1917 is indicated by the political prominence of the middle-class party of the "Cadets," the peasant party of the Socialist Revolutionaries, and the Mensheviks, all of whom wanted a parliamentary and democratic government. It was these groups, and not the Bolsheviks, who after the February revolution were supported by the majority of the peasants, workers, and soldiers. The bulk of the peasants followed the Socialist Revolutionaries; [47] the bulk of the workers followed either the Socialist-Revolutionaries or the Mensheviks. (In April 1917 Lenin admitted that "in most of the Soviets of Workers' Deputies" the Bolsheviks constituted "a small minority.") [48] And among the soldiers, who in the main came from the peasantry, the situation was similar.

Even in the elections to the Constitutional Assembly, which were held in the fall of 1917, more soldiers voted for the Socialist Revolutionaries than for the Bolsheviks.[49] In fact, on that occasion the former received 58 per cent of the total vote.[50]

The intelligentsia were even less inclined to follow the Bolsheviks. The pro-Tsarists among them were politically discredited; and the liberals and socialists were "equally alien to Tsarism and to Bolshevism." [51] No wonder then that after the February revolution the democratic parties prevailed not only in the civilian government and army [52] but also in the first soviets,[53] in the new peasant organizations,[54] and in the trade unions.[p]

In their agrarian program the Socialist Revolutionaries had requested the distribution of all "alienated" land to the rural toilers.[55] This was infinitely more attractive to the peasants than Lenin's demand that after the "nationalization of all land" the large estates should be operated as "model farms . . . under the control of the Agricultural Workers' Deputies and for the public account." [q]

As for the war, all the democratic groups, with different arguments, rejected a separate peace with Germany. And while the Bolsheviks introduced a sharp anticapitalist note into the debate, they, too, originally made no such recommendation. In his April Theses Lenin outlined the conditions for a "revolutionary war." While strongly objecting to the prevailing policy of a "revolutionary defence," he urged the utmost patience with the masses who were honestly accepting the war "as a necessity and not as a means of conquest." [56] And as late as June he refused a separate peace, which he held would mean "an agreement with the German robbers, who are plundering just as much as the others." [57]

Lenin's formula of the workers' control over industrial production [58] became increasingly popular in the factory committees.[59] But it did not, prior to the October revolution, make the Bolsheviks the masters of the trade unions.

Manifestly then, there existed in Russia in 1917 a genuinely open historical situation. Had the new leadership defended and developed the new freedoms in a truly revolutionary way, they would have had more than a sporting chance of completing Russia's transformation into a multicentered democratic society. But they lacked both

p. It was the Mensheviks, not the Bolsheviks, who at first controlled the quickly growing labor unions (Florinsky, 1953, II: 1421).

q. Lenin, S, XXIV: 5. In making this demand in his April theses, Lenin repeated a principle of Marxism that had been particularly elaborated by the leading orthodox Marxist, Kautsky. By implication, this policy withholds the land of the large estates from the peasants.

experience and resolve. Afraid of alienating their Western allies, they continued a war they had no strength to fight. And afraid of violating the rules of orderly legal procedure, they postponed the much needed land reform until after the opening of their Constituent Assembly, which was never able to function.

Thus the Bolsheviks got their big chance largely through default. After the July insurrection Lenin, revising his previous position, decided that in the war against the Germans an *"immediate and unequivocal peace must be proposed."* [60] And he soon made an equally daring *volte face* on the internal front. Discarding his orthodox plan to convert the big landed estates into model farms, he took over *in toto* (his opponents said "stole") the Socialist Revolutionary program for distributing land to the peasants, a program which he had recently rejected and which, he openly intimated, he still did not approve of.[61] In addition, he dropped the principle of majority support, which until this time he had considered a basic prerequisite for the seizure of power. Seeing the majority of the population discouraged and confused by the policies of the Provisional Government, which still had their votes, Lenin rallied to his side a minority of urban and rural activists who proved strong enough to place him and his party at the helm of a Soviet dictatorship.

More favorable international conditions—and more understanding and helpful democratic allies—might have tipped the scales in the opposite direction. But the situation being what it was, the political weakness of Russia's Western-oriented forces paralyzed the country's diversive revolution and opened the way for an entirely different type of development.

b. The USSR—Russia's Asiatic Restoration?

WHERE did this lead? Surely not to a socialist order in the sense of Marx and the pre-October Lenin. As shown in Chapter 9, Lenin himself at the close of his life believed that Russia was well on the way to an Asiatic restoration. Lenin's pessimism followed logically from his earlier views and later experiences. It followed from his knowledge of Marx' insistence on primitive democratic control over the protosocialist state, as exemplified in the Paris Commune. It followed from his acceptance of Marx' and Engels' notion that the dispersed rural communities constituted the economic foundation of Oriental despotism generally, and of its Tsarist version particularly.[62] It followed from his own notion that there was only one "absolute" guarantee that would prevent the hoped-for Russian revolution from turning into an Asiatic restoration: the victory of socialism in the highly industrialized West, and only one "relative" guarantee: the strict maintenance of democratic control over the new revolutionary government (no bureaucracy, no army, no police). And it followed from the developments after the October revolution: no socialist revolution occurred in the great industrial countries of the West, and the Soviet regime rapidly set up a new bureaucracy, standing army, and police.

Bukharin, then a top-ranking Bolshevik, had cried out against the new "bureaucratic centralization" and the threatening "enslavement of the working class" as early as the spring of 1918.[63] The Communist party had attacked "the partial revival of the bureaucracy" in its program of 1919. And in 1921 Lenin had depicted the new Soviet bureaucracy in a way that had one meaning and one meaning only: the new bureaucracy was the monster force that was driving Russia toward an Asiatic restoration. In 1922 the "nonproletarian" and "alien" representatives of the new "bureaucratic machine" were so strong that Lenin was no longer certain whether they or the small "Old Guard of the Party" were in the saddle. "Who controls whom?"[64] Only the "undivided prestige" of the Old Guard had so far prevented the complete victory of the new "alien" social forces. And this prestige could be destroyed by "a very slight internal struggle within this structure."[65] It was destroyed shortly after Lenin's death.

This, of course, does not mean that Soviet society originally had a protosocialist quality that was lost by 1922 or shortly thereafter. Lenin's belated warnings indicate the problem, but they show him unwilling to face the reality fully. According to Marx and the pre-October Lenin, socialism is economic planning plus effective popular control over the planners. The Bolsheviks permitted no such control when, after their revolutionary seizure of power, they engaged in economic planning on an ever-growing scale. Measured by Marxist-Leninist standards, there were subjective socialists in Soviet Russia, but there was never socialism.

Nor was there an Asiatic restoration. It is understandable why, in 1921, Lenin had viewed the new Soviet bureaucracy as ruling over fragmented and dispersed small producers. At the end of the civil war, in 1920, large-scale industry was producing not much more than 10 per cent of its prewar output,[66] and most of the industrial workers had returned to their villages. The country relied mainly on a fragmented peasant economy and whatever small-scale industry [r] survived in the villages and shrunken towns.[s] Lenin went so far as to say in 1921, "The proletariat has vanished." [67]

These conditions explain why, between 1921 and 1923, Lenin interpreted the new bureaucracy in terms that Marxists used to designate Oriental despotism. They explain why he spoke of the country's "semi-Asiatic" lack of culture and of the "Asiatic way" in which the peasants traded.[68] Nevertheless, his belief that the men of the new state apparatus were establishing a new version of Russia's old Asiatic system was profoundly wrong.

It was wrong because it underrated the economic mentality of the men of the new apparatus. These men were not satisfied with ruling over a world of peasants and craftsmen. They knew the potential of modern industry. Possessed by a quasireligious socialist vision,[t] they strove to realize it, first within the frame of Russia's previous production maximum and, from the First Five Year Plan on, far beyond it.

Thus while the masters of Soviet Russia perpetuated a key feature of an agrodespotic society, the monopolistic position of its ruling bureaucracy, they did much more than perpetuate that society. Even prior to the collectivization of agriculture, the Soviet *apparatchiki* disposed over a mechanized system of communication and industry that made their semimanagerial position different from and potentially superior to the semimanagerial position of an agrohydraulic bureaucracy. The nationalized industrial apparatus of the new semimanagerial order provided them with new weapons of organization, propaganda, and coercion, which enabled them to liquidate the small peasant producers as an economic category. The completed collectivization transformed the peasants into agricultural workers who toil for a single master: the new apparatus state.[u]

The agrarian despotism of the old society, which, at most, was semimanagerial, combines total political power with limited social and intellectual control. The industrial despotism of the fully developed and totally managerial apparatus society combines total political power with total social and intellectual control.

Remembering Lenin's emphasis on the significance of the "apparatus" as a means for seizing and defending total power, I have

r. In 1920 Russia's small-scale industry still produced around 44 per cent of the output of 1913 (Baykov, 1947: 41).

s. The towns lost from one-third to over one-half of their populations (Baykov, 1947: 41).

t. For the discussion of Marxism-Leninism as a secular religion see Gurian, 1931: 192 ff.

u. For a pioneering analysis of the Soviet Union as a new class society, see Meyer, 1950: *passim*.

designated the genuinely despotic state an "apparatus state." This term covers both the agrarian and industrial forms of total statism. Is there any Marxist label that may be applied specifically to the new industrial apparatus society?

This new apparatus society has been called "neofeudalism" and "state capitalism." Neither formula is appropriate. "Feudalism" certainly does not fit the most highly centralized political order so far known, and "state capitalism" does not fit a conformation that precludes private means of production and an open market for goods and labor.

Marx clearly overrated the oppressiveness of Oriental society, which he held to be a system of "general slavery." [69] Ironically, but suitably, this designation can, however, be used for the new industrial apparatus society. We can truly say that the October revolution, whatever its expressed aims, gave birth to an industry-based system of general (state) slavery.

c. Communist China—the Product of a Genuine "Asiatic Restoration"?

BUT what about Communist China? In contrast to Russia, which in the 20th century made great strides toward industrialization, China was still a predominantly agricultural country when the Communists entered the arena some time after World War I. And there was not much of a modern Chinese middle class when the Communists made their final bid for power after World War II. Is it therefore not a fact that Mao Tse-tung and his followers established an agrarian despotism which, despite superficial modifications, bore a close resemblance to the great despotic regimes of China's past?

Indeed not a few observers have taken Mao's temporary retreat into the countryside as an agrarian deviation from an industry-oriented Marxism-Leninism. But such an interpretation disregards both the strategic aims of the Communist International and the reasons that made the Chinese Communists cling to them during the agrarian phase of their operations.[70]

Man is an ideological animal; he acts in accordance with his innermost conviction; and this is true whether religious or secular issues are at stake. A comprehensive philosophical and political creed, such as Communism, provides its adherents with a map of the world, an arsenal of operational directives (a "guide to action"), a flag, and a powerful political myth. It inspires those who hold it with supreme confidence and paralyzes those among their enemies who are impressed by it.[71]

From the standpoint of the Chinese Communists, the Soviet ideology has proved eminently effective. True, certain features of the developmental scheme have been adjusted; and the new proto-"socialist" or "socialist" order does not fit the Marxian concept of socialism. But these changes involve aspects of the Communist doctrine that probably never were real to the Chinese Communists— or, for that matter, to Communists in "backward" countries generally. We can find tragedy in the career of a Lenin, whose Aesopian warnings against the neo-"Asiatic" trends in Soviet society reveal a pained awareness of having betrayed the principles of his socialist creed. But there is no similar tragedy in a Mao's career, because there is no similar awareness. Mao did not betray the principles of socialism, to which he adhered officially, for the simple reason that for him these principles never had any meaning.

While Lenin's doubts did not bother the Chinese Communists, Moscow's power strategy attracted them immensely. Here was a revolutionary system with popular appeal which, accompanied by proper organization and action, could result in conclusive victory. It had done so in Russia. And properly adapted—the Comintern analysis of global conditions is very detailed—it might prove equally successful in other countries. This system required industrialization in all Communist-dominated areas, not for academic reasons but because ultimately Communist success in the sociopolitical sphere depended directly on Communist success in the industrial sphere.

The relation of these ideas to the long-range perspective of the Chinese Communists is evident. A Mao Tse-tung who viewed entrenchment in the countryside as a permanent principle and not as a temporary strategic device would be no deviant Communist, but merely a fool. He would be like the man who always prefers a stick to a gun, because once in the woods he had only a stick to fight with.

But Mao is no fool. He and his followers never considered themselves leaders of a peasant party,[v] whose actions were motivated, and limited, by the interests of the villages. When the conditions of the civil war forced the Chinese Communists to operate in the countryside, they always expected to return to the cities. And when they seized the cities, they did exactly what the Bolsheviks had done after the October revolution. They restored, consolidated, and developed whatever industries there were; and they were noticeably eager to

v. Lattimore claimed that during the ten years preceding the Sino-Japanese War the Chinese Communists, "cut off from cities and urban workers, had become a peasant party" [Lattimore, 1947 (1st ed. 1945): 108].

control modern industry [w] and mechanized communication. Thus they were as little interested in an Asiatic restoration as were the bureaucratic masters of the Soviet apparatus.

With due consideration for the peculiarities of their country's "backward" and "semicolonial" situation, the Chinese Communists moved quickly to establish a new semimanagerial order, which differs both in structure and developmental intent from the semimanagerial order of agrarian despotism. The rapid integration of the Chinese peasants into primitive collectives, called Producers' Cooperatives, indicates that Communist China is moving quickly from a semimanagerial to a total managerial order. According to an account given by Mao on December 27, 1955, the mass of all Chinese peasants may be members of semisocialist cooperatives (which still recognize a certain tie between the land and the farmer-peasant owner) by the end of 1956; and by 1959 they may be organized in a "completely" socialist way.[x]

C. WHITHER ASIA?

FOR obvious reasons the rise of a Communist regime in China affected the colonial and ex-colonial countries of the Orient much more directly than did the rise of the USSR. The Russia in which Lenin seized power appeared to the Eastern observers as a European country—and one that until recently had exercised imperialist control over vast expanses of Asia. The China in which Mao's party seized power was still an Oriental country and one that had suffered seriously from Western and Japanese imperialism.

Of course, Communist anti-imperialism appealed to the national revolutionists of Asia before the Chinese Communists took over the mainland. The Soviet Union established friendly relations with Ataturk's Turkey as early as 1920 and with Sun Yat-sen and his Canton government in 1923. And Nehru was conspicuous in the Communist-organized First Congress of the League against Imperialism at Brussels in 1927.[1]

But while, in the 1920's, the Asian national revolutionists were

w. Five years after the establishment of the Chinese People's Republic, 71 per cent of the output of all industrial enterprises, in terms of value, came from state-owned "joint state-private" and cooperative enterprises, the first complex supplying 59 per cent of the total, the second 12 per cent, and the third 4 per cent. At that time the value of the output of private industry had shrunk to 25 per cent of the total (*Jen-min Jih-pao*, September 23, 1955, Peking).

x. For Mao's above cited statement see *Izvestia*, January 13, 1956. Cf. Wittfogel, 1955a; Walker, 1955: 149 ff.; Tang (MS).

able to disregard the Soviet conquest of Georgia and Turkestan, they could not remain blind to Moscow's expansion in Eastern Europe after World War II and to Peiping's occupation of Tibet, a large Inner Asian country, whose right to be free Mao Tse-tung had publicly recognized in the 1930's.[2] They responded to these developments by resorting to a semi-anti-imperialism [a] which is as quick to attack the insecure forces of an old and shrinking capitalist imperialism as it is reluctant to criticize the brazen operations of the young and growing Communist imperialism.

Such behavior makes it clear that hostility to Western imperialism is only one reason for the popularity of the Communist regimes in non-Communist Asia. Another enormously compelling reason is the affinity to, and admiration of, the Communist system of managerial statism.

The political scientist who considers only the form of government may argue that today almost all non-Communist countries of the Orient have parliamentary governments and that in several countries, such as India, the leading policy makers take their democratic creed very seriously. Quite so. But the political scientist, who examines the phenomenon of government in depth, knows that in different institutional contexts the same form may have entirely different meanings. The Roman senate in the heyday of the republic had little in common with the body which, under the same name, operated in the empire; and Augustus' sentimental concern for Rome's glorious traditions did not restore the republic, for Augustus was careful to keep the supreme center of power outside and above all effective control.

Whither Asia? When answering this question, we must remember that capitalist colonization during the three hundred years of its dominance failed in the Orient to develop multicentered societies based on a strong middle class, organized labor, and an independent peasantry. We must remember that most constitutions of the new sovereign Asian nations, directly or indirectly, proclaim statism as a basic feature of their government.[b] We must remember that in many cases—we exclude Ataturk [3]—the will to statism was bulwarked

a. An excellent example of this semi-anti-imperialist attitude is Panikkar's *Asia and Western Dominance*. The Indian author is very outspoken in his criticism of Western imperialism in Asia and very gentle with Communist imperialism. Citing Lattimore, Panikkar finds kind words also for Tsarist imperialism, which he obviously considers the forerunner of modern Soviet imperialism (Panikkar, AWD: 249 ff.).

b. The principle of statism is solemnly proclaimed in Article 2 of the Turkish Constitution. Semantically, this principle is also invoked in the constitutions of Nationalist China, India, Burma, and Indonesia.

by democratic-socialist principles and that, in most of these cases
—we exclude Sun Yat-sen—the professed democratic socialists were
also professed admirers of Marx.

The student of Asia naturally wants to know how seriously the
Asian socialists take Marx' Asiatic ideas: his theory of the Asiatic
mode of production, which stresses private property as a key necessity for overcoming state-heavy Asiatic society; his multilinear concept of development, which warns against any simple scheme of unilinear development; his definition of socialism, which includes popular control as an essential element and which makes it impossible
to call Communist Russia and Communist China socialist or protosocialist; and his "Oriental" interpretation of Tsarist Russia, which
made Plekhanov and Lenin consider the dangers of an Asiatic
restoration.

Strange as it may seem, the Asian socialists are as indifferent to
these ideas as are the Asian Communists. And this is true for the
spokesmen of socialist parties as well as for socialists like Nehru
who do not belong to any such organizations. Nehru, who found
"Marx's general analysis of social development . . . remarkably correct," [4] apparently was unimpressed by Marx' analysis of the social
development of India, which he can hardly have missed seeing, since
Marx' writings on this subject circulated in India in several edi-
tions.

To be sure, the official representatives of the various Asian socialist parties sharply attack Russian and Chinese Communism for their
totalitarianism. But disregarding Marx' views on Asiatic society
and socialism, they disregard what, from the standpoint of "scientific
socialism," would be the decisive critical test. And they hide the
grave implications of their own societal past by calling this past
"feudal" and by placing it into a crude scheme of unilinear development.[5]

Such procedures cannot be excused by asserting that the democratic Marxists of Europe also neglected Marx' Asiatic views. For
while the European socialists did not draw the political conclusions
Plekhanov drew, they certainly recognized Marx' concept of the
Asiatic mode of production. In fact, Rosa Luxemburg, who is highly
esteemed by the leading Indian Socialist Mehta,[6] expressly discussed
the hydraulic and stationary character of Oriental societies.[7]

But even if the European socialists had neglected these societies,
which to them constituted a remote issue, this would not excuse
the Asian socialists. Being concerned primarily with Asia, they should
have paid particular attention to what Marx had to say on this

subject. However, instead of doing this, they remain stubbornly aloof from Marx' and Engels' theory of Asiatic society.

This omission does not keep the Asian socialists from opposing the "excessive growth of bureaucracy" in their own part of the world [8] and from rejecting the Russian and Chinese Communist regimes.[9] However, it gives tacit support to a policy which endeavors to abandon as soon as possible what Marx called "the greatest desideratum of Asian society"—private property in land.[10]

And far from precluding, it indirectly encourages a sympathetic appraisal of the managerial statism of the USSR and Communist China. In the 1930's Nehru viewed the Soviet Union as "run by representatives of the workers and peasants" and as being "in some ways . . . the most advanced country in the world." [11] In the 1940's he approvingly cited Tagore's opinion that the USSR "is free from all invidious distinction between one class and another," its regime being based not on exploitation but on cooperation.[12] And in the 1950's he equated the despotic masters of Communist Russia and China and their peoples; and he depicted Mao and his lieutenants as advancing the freedom of those they rule.[13]

Like his Indian counterpart, the prime minister of Burma, U Nu, is not unaware of the dangers of Communist expansion. But in 1954 he noted with pride the internal and external strength of Mao's regime. And he lauded the Chinese Communists for having abolished corruption and for improving the condition of the "downtrodden teeming millions." [14] He said this about a regime which openly and repeatedly had admitted being plagued by corruption. And he said it at a time when Mao's policy of enforced "cooperativization" was breaking the backbone of the Chinese peasantry.[15]

Excepting Japan—which never was a hydraulic civilization—and making full allowance for regional differences, we find most non-Communist nations of the Orient institutionally ambivalent and influenced by a semi- or crypto-Communist ideology which, by enhancing the authority of Marxism-Leninism, as the Leningrad discussion of 1931 explained, tends to weaken their political independence.

Does this mean that one after the other the ideologically penetrated countries will cease resisting the political erosion to which Communist strategy is exposing them? Such a turn is entirely possible. And although its consequences would entail far more than an "Asiatic restoration," in one respect it deserves this title: it would be a spectacular manifestation of a retrogressive societal development.

D. WHITHER WESTERN SOCIETY—WHITHER
MANKIND?

CAN the West prevent this development, which would extend the system of bureaucratic state slavery to two-thirds of mankind? The history of pre-Bolshevik Russia shows that countries of the Oriental type which are independent and in close contact with the West may vigorously move toward a multicentered and democratic society. As described above, a diversive transformation of this kind has begun in many non-Communist countries of the Orient; and given time and opportunity, it may assume momentous dimensions. But will there be time? Will there be opportunity?

Time is already running out. And opportunity, if it is to be seized with any chance of success, presupposes a West whose attitude toward bureaucratic totalitarianism is both informed and bold. Today, the attitude of the West is neither.

Public opinion in the leading Western countries is ambivalent about the form and function of managerial bureaucracy; and it is ambivalent also about the form and function of private property and enterprise. The Second Industrial Revolution, which we are now experiencing, is perpetuating the principle of a multicentered society through large bureaucratized complexes that mutually—and laterally [a]—check each other: most importantly, Big Government, Big Business, Big Agriculture, and Big Labor. But the destruction of one major nongovernmental complex may bring about the downfall of others. Under Fascism and National Socialism, the liquidation of Big Labor so strengthened Big Government that eventually Big Business and Big Agriculture were also threatened. [b] And in Soviet Russia the liquidation of Big Business and Big Agriculture quickly enabled Big Government to subdue labor.

These experiences should alert us to the dangers inherent in unchecked bureaucratic dominance. To what extent can we trust the members of any "Big" group to use supreme and total power, once

a. The decrease of vertical controls from below (by voters, shareholders, and rank-and-file trade union members) goes hand in hand with the increase of lateral controls. These last are not new (cf. the history of factory legislation in England). But while their significance has grown, the recent Communist and Fascist revolutions show that their capacity to prevent a totalitarian accumulation of power is limited.

b. Before the end of World War II some attempts were made to analyze the institutional trends in Italian and German Fascism; but comparison with Communist totalitarianism was superficial or avoided altogether. In recent years there has been little interest in comparative studies of modern totalitarianism that include Fascism. Moscow's role in Hitler's rise to power is a similarly neglected issue.

they gain it, to serve the people's interest and not their own? To what extent can we trust the judgment of officiating or nonofficiating members of our segmented bureaucracies who view the Communist monopoly bureaucracy as a progressive form of totalitarianism? [c]

Western writers, teachers, and practicing politicians who do not understand the meaning of their institutional and cultural heritage are poorly equipped to unleash its creative potential. And they are also poorly equipped to combat Communist totalitarianism. For however necessary military preparedness and a courageous economic policy may be, they are only two among several essentials. Equally important is the judicious implementation of institutional change. And most important, because most fundamental, is a thorough grasp of the multiform course of history and of the opportunities and responsibilities it imposes on free man.

No doubt we are in the midst of an open historical situation, and no doubt there is freedom of effective choice. But our past blunders and present deliberations show that so far we have not used our opportunities competently. We did not give full scope to the antitotalitarian forces in the Western world. And failing to do this, we did little to strengthen the antitotalitarian forces in the hydraulic societies in transition.

But while the realm of freedom is rapidly shrinking, the desire to defend and expand it is growing. Shocked into a vigorous reappraisal of our position, we may still learn how to wrest victory from defeat. A new insight that is fully perceived, convincingly communicated, and daringly applied may change the face of a military and ideopolitical campaign. It may change the face of a historical crisis. Ultimately, the readiness to sacrifice and the willingness to take the calculated risk of alliance against the total enemy depend on the proper evaluation of two simple issues: slavery and freedom.

The good citizens of classical Greece drew strength from the determination of two of their countrymen, Sperthias and Bulis, to resist the lure of total power. On their way to Suza, the Spartan envoys were met by Hydarnes, a high Persian official, who offered to make them mighty in their homeland, if only they would attach themselves to the Great King, his despotic master. To the benefit of Greece—and to the benefit of all free men—Herodotus has preserved their answer. "Hydarnes," they said, "thou art a one-sided counselor. Thou hast experience of half the matter; but the other

c. When John K. Fairbank stressed "the distinction between fascist-conservative and *communist-progressive forms of totalitarianism*" (Fairbank, 1947: 149; italics mine), he expressed in print, and very succinctly, an opinion shared today by many intellectuals and officials.

half is beyond thy knowledge. A slave's life thou understandest; but, never having tasted liberty, thou canst not tell whether it be sweet or no. Ah! hadst thou known what freedom is, thou wouldst have bidden us fight for it, not with the spear only, but with the battle-axe."

NOTES

INTRO.

1. For documentation concerning these statements, see below, Chap. 7, notes to first part.
2. Mill, 1909: 210.
3. *Ibid.*: 211.
4. Bury, 1910: 1.
5. See below, Chaps. 4 and 8.
6. See below, Chap. 4.
7. DASP, 1931: 89.
8. Tolstov, 1950: 3.
9. Marx, TMW, II, Pt. 1: 310 ff.
10. For documentary evidence for the above statements see Chap. 9, *passim.*
11. Wittfogel, 1924: 122, cf. 49.
12. *Ibid.*: 117.
13. *Ibid.*, 1926: 25.
14. *Ibid.*: 16.
15. *Ibid.*: 20–7.
16. *Ibid.*, 1927: 314, 315 ff., 320 ff., 324 ff.
17. *Ibid.*, 1929: 606.
18. *Ibid.*, 1931: *passim.*
19. *Inostrannaya Kniga* (Moscow), No. 1, 1931: 20.
20. Marx, NYDT, June 22, 1853.

1, C

1. Widtsoe, 1926: 64.

1, D

1. Nelson, 1938: 8.
2. Widtsoe, 1926: 5.

2, A

1. Wittfogel, 1956: 157.
2. Wittfogel, 1931: 312, 424, 337–44. *Ibid.*, 1956: 158.
3. Buck, 1937: 61.
4. See Wittfogel, 1931: 253 ff., 261 ff., 267 ff.
5. Buckley, 1893: 10. Cf. Marshall, 1931, I: 6.
6. RRCAI: 359. Cf. Saha, 1930: 12.
7. See Strabo 16.1.10.
8. Wittfogel and Fêng, 1949: 661, n. 52.
9. Willcocks, 1904: 70.
10. See Humboldt, 1811, II: 193 ff.
11. Beech, 1911: 15.
12. Parsons, 1939, I: 111.
13. Gutmann, 1909: 20.
14. Eck and Liefrinck, 1876: 228 ff.
15. Deimel, 1928: 34. *Ibid.*, 1931: 83.
16. Sethe, 1912: 710 ff.
17. *Arthaçāstra*, 1926: 60. *Arthaśāstra*, 1923: 51 ff.

18. Blas Valeras = Garcilaso, 1945, I: 245.
19. Sahagun, 1938, I: 292, 296.
20. Ramirez, 1944: 52, 75. Tezozomoc, 1944: 381, 385.
21. Willcocks, 1889: 274.
22. *Ibid.:* 279.
23. *Ibid.*
24. Gutmann, 1926: 369, 374.
25. Parsons, 1939, I: 124–6. Wittfogel and Goldfrank, 1943: 29.

2, C

1. Cf. Wittfogel, 1931: 456 ff., 680 ff. *Ibid.*, 1938: 98 ff. Wittfogel and Fêng, 1949: 123, 467.
2. Herodotus 2.109.

2, D

1. Reed, 1937: 373. Robins, 1946: 91 ff., 129 ff.
2. For Palenque see Stephens, ITCA, II: 321, 344. For Aztec Mexico see Tezozomoc, 1944: 23, 379 ff.; Chimalpahin Quauhtlehuanitzin: 117, 128.
3. Cf. Pietschmann, 1889: 70.
4. Cf. Cahen, 1940: 132.
5. Jacobsen and Lloyd, 1935: 31. Luckenbill, AR, II: 150. Cf. Olmstead, 1923: 332; Thompson and Hutchinson, 1929: 129 ff.
6. See below, Chap. 6.
7. Heichelheim, 1938: 728. See also below, Chap. 7.
8. Williams, 1910: 168. Cf. Sombart, 1919, I: 396; II: 252.
9. Kulischer, AW, II: 381 ff.
10. Williams, 1910: 168.
11. Sombart, 1919, II: 251.
12. Williams, 1910: 168.
13. Kees, 1933: 129, cf. 109. Breasted, 1927: 147 and *passim*.
14. Thompson, 1941: 515.
15. See *Shih Chi*, 29.3a–b, 4b–5a, 5b–6a, 7b–8a, 126.15b. *Han Shu*, 29.2b–3a, 4a–b, 5a–b, 7a–8a, 89.14b–15a. For translation and comment see MS HCS, Ch'in-Han, II (3) (4) (36) (43) (54) (55) (56) (72).
16. See *Shih Chi*, 29.2a–b, 4a–b. *Han Shu*, 29.1b–2a, 3b–4a, 64A.6b. *Hou Han Shu*, 35.3b. For translation and comment see MS HCS, Ch'in-Han, IV (1) (6) (32) (66).
17. *Sui Shu*, 3.11a, cf. 5a.
18. Kulischer, AW, II: 6.
19. King, 1927: 97 ff.
20. Dundas, 1924: 73; cf. Widenmann, 1899: 63 ff.
21. Dundas, 1924: 73.
22. *Ibid.:* 95 ff.
23. *Ibid.* Cf. Widenmann, 1899: 63 ff.
24. Cortes, 1866: *passim*. Díaz, 1944: *passim*. Cf. Vaillant, 1941: 135.
25. Armillas, 1944: *passim*. Vaillant, 1941: 219.
26. Jerez, 1938: 38. Sancho de la Hos, 1938: 177 ff. Cieza, 1945: 206 ff., 245. Ondegardo, 1872: 75 ff. Garcilaso, 1945, II: 31, 146 ff. Espinosa, 1942: 565 ff. Cobo, HNM, IV: 65 ff., 207 ff. Cf. Rowe, 1946: 224 ff.
27. Cobo, HNM, III: 272. Garcilaso, 1945, II: 147.
28. *Arthaśāstra*, 1923: 54 ff.
29. *Shih Chi*, 88.1b.
30. Meissner, BA, I: 340.

31. *Ibid.:* 340 ff. Olmstead, 1923: 334.
32. Herodotus 5.52 f.; 8.98. Cf. Xenophon 8.6.17.
33. Rostovtzeff, 1941, I: 133, 135, 173 ff., 484, 517.
34. For Diocletian's achievements in this sphere see Bury, 1931, I: 95 ff.; and Ensslin, 1939: 397.
35. Mez, 1922: 461.
36. For the Mamluks see Sauvaget, 1941: 35. For the Ottoman Turks see Taeschner, 1926: 203 ff.
37. *Arthaçāstra,* 1926: 60, and esp. 74. Strabo 15.1.50.
38. Cf. Smith, 1914: 135.
39. Appadorai, 1936, I: 424 ff.
40. Sabahuddin, 1944: 272 ff.
41. Haig, 1937: 57.
42. Smith, 1926: 413 ff.
43. *Kuo Yü,* 2.22 ff.
44. *Han Shu,* 51.2a. For translation and comment see MS HCS, Ch'in-Han, IV (4).
45. Jerez, 1938: 55. Estete, 1938: 83 ff., 97 ff., 244 ff. Sancho de la Hos, 1938: 175. Pizarro, 1938: 259. CPLNC: 310. Cieza, 1945: *passim.* Sarmiento, 1906: 88. Ondegardo, 1872: 12. Cf. Garcilaso, 1945, II: 242 and *passim;* Cobo, HNM, III: 260 ff.
46. Pizarro, 1938: 259.
47. *Chin Shih Ts'ui Pien,* 5.13a–b. For translation see MS HCS, Ch'in-Han, IV (75), n. 305.
48. Widenmann, 1899: 70.
49. Ixtlilxochitl, OH, II: 174.
50. I Kings 5: 14. For ancient Mesopotamia see Schneider, 1920: 92; Mendelsohn, 1949.
51. Marshall, 1928: 587 ff.
52. *Shih Chi,* 6.31a–b. For translation and comment see MS HCS, Ch'in-Han, III (12).
53. *Shih Chi,* 6.13b–14a, 24a–25a. For translation and comment see MS HCS, Ch'in Han, III (10) (11).
54. See above.
55. *Sui Shu,* 3.9b.
56. *Sui Shu,* 24.16a.
57. Barton, 1929: 3 ff. Thureau-Dangin, 1907: 3 and *passim.* For epigraphic references to the temples of Babylonia and Assyria see Meissner, BA, I: 303 ff.; and Luckenbill, AR: *passim.*
58. Breasted, 1927, I: 186, 244, 336; II: 64, 72, 245, 311, 318; III: 96 ff.; IV: 116 ff., 179 ff., and *passim.*
59. Ramirez, 1944: 39.
60. Ixtlilxochitl, OH, II: 184.
61. Chimalpópoca, 1945: 49.
62. *Ibid.:* 52.
63. Cieza, 1943: 150 ff.
64. *Ibid.:* 241. Cf. Garcilaso, 1945, I: 245, 257 ff.

2, E

1. Cf. Bengtson, 1950: 38.

2, F

1. Glotz, 1926: 152, cf. 267.
2. Kulischer, AW, I: 224.
3. Sombart, 1919, II: 792. Cf. Cole, 1939, II: 458 ff.
4. Cf., for Ottoman Turkey, Anhegger, 1943: 5, 8 ff., 22 ff., 123 ff., 126 ff.

5. Boulais, 1924: 728.
6. Pant, 1930: 70.

2, G

1. See below, Chap. 6.

3, A

1. Milukow, 1898: 111.

3, B

1. Garcilaso, 1945, II: 23 ff., 25 ff. Cobo, HNM, III: 295 ff. Rowe, 1946: 264.
2. Torquemada, 1943, II: 546 ff.
3. *Kuo Yü*, 1.8 ff.
4. *Shih Chi*, 6.50a. See MS HCS, Ch'in-Han, I, 3, n. 17.
5. *Kuan Tzŭ*, 3.17–18.
6. *Hou Han Shu*, 10A.4a. For translation and comment see MS HCS, Ch'in-Han, I, 3 (8).
7. *Kuan T'ang Chi Lin*, 11.5b–6a. See MS HCS, Ch'in-Han, I, 3, n. 21.
8. *Han Shu*, 28A, 28B. *Hsü Han Chih*, 19–23. See MS HCS, Ch'in-Han, I, 1, Tables.
9. *Arthaçāstra*, 1926: 86 ff.
10. Smith, 1926: 376.
11. Strabo 15.50 f.
12. Appadorai, 1936, II: 683 ff.
13. Deimel, 1924: *passim. Ibid.*, 1927, 1928.
14. Breasted, 1927, I: 54, 59, and *passim.* Cf. Meyer, GA, I, Pt. 2: 159 ff.
15. Wilcken, 1912: 173 and n. 3.
16. *Ibid.:* 173.
17. *Ibid.:* 178 ff., 206.
18. *Ibid.:* 192 ff.
19. *Ibid.:* 237 ff. For further data on the cadasters under Arab rule see de Sacy, 1923, II: 220 ff.
20. Gaudefroy-Demombynes, 1923: xli. Wiet, 1937: 482. *Ibid.*, 1932: 257. Cf. Björkman, 1928: *passim.*
21. Wright, 1935: 119. Cf. Lybyer, 1913: 167 ff.; and Gibb and Bowen, 1950: 167 ff.
22. *Chou Li*, 16.5a. cf. Biot, 1851, I: 367.
23. Herodotus 3.117.
24. Eck and Liefrinck, 1876: 231.
25. Wirz, 1929: 13.
26. *Ibid.*
27. *Ibid.:* 14.
28. *Ibid.*
29. Eck and Liefrinck, 1876: 230.
30. Wittfogel, 1931: 263.
31. Willcocks, 1889: 339.
32. Sombart, 1919, II: 373 ff.
33. Cf. Grant, 1937: 241.
34. Prescott, 1936: 29.
35. Torquemada, 1943, II: 536.
36. Cieza, 1943: 125. Rowe, 1946: 231.
37. Cieza, 1943: 126.
38. Herodotus 5.52 f.; 7.239; 8.98. Cf. Christensen, 1933: 283 ff.; Olmstead, 1948: 299.
39. Herodotus 7.239.
40. Xenophon 8.6.17.

41. Cf. Seeck, 1901: 1847 ff.
42. Suetonius Augustus, 1886: 61.
43. Riepl, 1913: 459. Hudemann, 1878: 81 ff.
44. Bréhier, 1949: 324.
45. Procopius, *Anecdota* 3.1.30 = Bréhier, 1949: 326.
46. Christensen, 1944: 129.
47. Gaudefroy-Demombynes, 1923: 239, n. 1. Björkman, 1928: 40.
48. Mez, 1922: 461.
49. Ibn Khordâdhbeh, 1889: 114.
50. Mez, 1922: 70.
51. *Ibid.*: 71.
52. Björkman, 1928: 41.
53. Sauvaget, 1941: *passim.* Gaudefroy-Demombynes, 1923: 239 ff. Grant, 1937: 239.
54. Björkman, 1928: 43. See also Sauvaget, 1941: 44 ff.
55. Grant, 1937: 243.
56. Strabo 15.1.48.
57. *Arthaśāstra*, 1923: 256 ff., and *passim;* Manu, 1886: 387 ff. Cf. Vishnu, 1900: 17.
58. Saletore, 1943: 256 ff.
59. Cf. Sabahuddin's instructive account of the postal system in Muslim India (Sabahuddin, 1944: 273 ff., 281). Cf. also Ibn Batoutah, 1914: 95; Bâbur, 1921: 357.
60. Smith, 1926: 382.
61. *Ibid.*: 414.
62. See *Kuo Yü,* 2.22 ff.
63. *Hou Han Shu,* 86.5a, 89.22b, 87.22b–23a. For translation and comment see MS HCS, Ch'in-Han IV (73).
64. *Han Shu,* 63.11a. For translation and comment see MS HCS, Ch'in-Han IV (43).
65. *Hou Han Shu,* 16.34b–35a. For translation and comment see MS HCS, Ch'in-Han IV (77).
66. Wittfogel and Fêng, 1949: 161 ff.
67. *Ibid.*: 162.
68. Marco Polo, 1929, I: 434 ff.
69. *Ibid.*: 435.
70. MS HCS, Ch'ing IV.
71. Delbrück, GK, III: 102 ff., 172. Lot, 1946, I: 303, 305. Stubbs, CHE, I: 432; II: 277. Vinogradoff, 1908: 61 and nn. 2, 3.
72. Lot, 1946, I: 303 ff.
73. Delbrück, GK, III: 103, 172.
74. Tout, 1937: 140 ff.
75. Full list in Lot, 1946, II: 212.
76. Delbrück, GK, III: 260 ff., 263 ff., 304 ff.
77. Herodotus 9. 62.
78. Herodotus 7. 104. Cf. Delbrück, CK, I: 38 ff.
79. Oman, 1924, I: 204.
80. *Ibid.*: 204–5.
81. *Ibid.*: 205.
82. *Ibid.*: 251.
83. *Ibid.*: 252. Cf. Delbrück, GK, III: 305, 307, 333, 338 ff.
84. Atiya, 1934: 71.
85. Rowe, 1946: 274.
86. Herodotus 7. 25.
87. Oman, 1924, I: 190 f.
88. Cf. Fries, 1921: 12 ff.; Horn, 1894: 57 ff.; Løkkegaard, 1950: 99; and Gibb, 1932: 39.

89. See Wittfogel and Fêng, 1949: 523 ff., 526 ff. Cf. MS HCS, Ch'in-Han and Ch'ing, sec. XV.
90. Delbrück, GK, III: 303, 333 ff.
91. *Arthaçāstra*, 1926: 64 ff., 399 ff., 406 ff., 522, 526 ff.
92. Delbrück, GK, III: 207–9. Wittfogel and Fêng, 1949: 536. Huuri, 1941: 71 ff.
93. Koran, 61. 4. For discipline in Muhammad's army see Buhl, 1930: 242, n. 97.
94. Wüstenfeld, 1880: *passim*. Ritter, 1929: 116, 144 ff. Huuri, 1941: 94 ff.
95. *Ca.* 500 b.c. See Wittfogel and Fêng, 1949: 534, n. 438.
96. *Han Shu*, 30. 25b ff.
97. Sun Tzŭ, 1941: 39.
98. *Han Shu*, 30. 25b–28a.
99. Bandelier, 1877: 131, 133 ff.
100. Cobo, HNM, III: 270; Rowe, 1946: 278.
101. Wittfogel and Fêng, 1949: 519.
102. *Ibid.:* 532 ff.
103. Lot, 1946, I: 98, 122 ff.
104. Kremer, CGO, I: 223 ff. Lot, 1946, I: 59 ff.
105. See Kremer, CGO, I: 213, 216, n. 4.
106. *Ibid.:* 244.
107. Lot, 1946, II: 257, n. 1.
108. *Ibid.:* 257.
109. *Ibid.*, I: 56.
110. Herodotus 7. 184.
111. *Ibid.* 7. 83.
112. Delbrück, GK, I: 41.
113. Smith, 1914: 125.
114. *Ibid.*
115. *Ibid.* Cf. Strabo 15. 1. 52.
116. Smith, 1914: 126 and n. 2.
117. Horn, 1894: 40 ff.
118. *Chan-kuo Ts'ê*, 8. 76, 14. 20, 19. 56, 22. 94, 26. 30, 29. 55.
119. Wittfogel and Fêng, 1949: 516, 519.
120. Williamson, WAS, I: 185.
121. *Ch'ing Shih Kao*, 137. 13b, 13b–19a, 19a–20b.
122. *Han Shu*, 24A.11a. Cf. MS HCS, Ch'in-Han, II (18).
123. For this figure see Kahrstedt, 1924: 660.
124. For the data on which these percentages are based see *ibid.:* 660 ff.
125. For the basic data see Inama-Sternegg and Häpke, 1924: 672, 680.

3, c

1. Parsons, 1939, I: 157–8, 495, 534; II: 790, 893, 901, 904, 909, 1131.
2. Gutmann, 1909: 111.
3. Deimel, 1922: 20, 22. Cf. *ibid.*, 1931: 83.
4. Poma, 1936: 1050.
5. Legge, CC, IV: 600 ff.
6. Breasted, 1927, IV: 194, cf. 157, 178, 185. Cf. also Kees, 1933: 45 ff.
7. Wan, KT, 1933: 38. Ma, SF, 1935: 218–19.
8. Glotz, 1926: 154.
9. *Ibid.:* 153 ff.
10. Stubbs, CHE, I: 583. See below, Chap. 6.
11. Meissner, BA, I: 125.
12. Genesis 47:24. Cf. Kees, 1933: 46.

13. *Arthaçāstra,* 1926: 372.
14. Meissner, BA, I: 125.
15. *Arthaśāstra,* 1923: 72 ff.
16. *Ibid.:* 77.
17. See Kees, 1933: 42, 47, 223 ff., 226. For the system of land tenure during this period see below, Chap. 7.
18. Kees, 1933: 42, 226.
19. Wilson, 1950: 212. Cf. Kees, 1933: 47, n. 7, 224.
20. Hummel, ECCP, I: 289.
21. *Arthaśāstra,* 1923: 75 ff.
22. *Ibid.:* 74.
23. *Ibid.:* 75.
24. *Ibid.:* 72.
25. *Ibid.:* 76. *Arthaçāstra,* 1926: 100.
26. *Arthaçāstra,* 1926: 100. *Arthaśāstra,* 1923: 77.
27. *Arthaśāstra,* 1923: 70.
28. *Ibid.:* 76 and n.
29. *Mez,* 1922: 109.
30. *Ibid.:* 110.
31. *Ibid.*
32. *Ibid.:* 127 ff.
33. *Arthaçāstra,* 1926: 373.
34. *Ibid.:* 374.
35. *Ibid.:* 378.
36. *Ibid.:* 380.
37. *Arthaśāstra,* 1923: 296.
38. *Ibid.*
39. *Mez,* 1922: 107.
40. *Ibid.:* 110 ff.

3, D

1. Mitteis, 1912: 231. Kreller, 1919: 182. Taubenschlag, 1944: 158. Kees, 1933: 83.
2. Hammurabi, sec. 165. Cf. Meissner, BA, I: 159.
3. Meek, 1950: 185, 188. Meissner, BA, I: 178.
4. *Arthaçāstra,* 1926: 255 ff., 456 f. Keith, 1914, I: 232, 191. Cf. Hopkins, 1922: 244; Āpastamba, 1898: 134 ff.; Gautama, 1898: 303 ff.; Vasishtha, 1898: 88 ff.; Manu, 1886: 348 and n. 117; Rangaswami, 1935: 30 ff.; Baudhāyana, 1898: 224 ff.; Vishnu, 1900: 40; Nārada, 1889: 201; and Yājnavalkya, 53 ff., 68 ff.
5. Cf. Juynboll, 1925: 253 ff.; Kremer, CGO, I: 527 ff.; and Schacht, 1941: 513 ff.
6. Boulais, 1924: 199.
7. Ondegardo, 1872: 37 ff.
8. Zurita, 1941: 144.
9. Fei and Chang, 1945: 302.
10. Schacht, 1941: 516.
11. Ondegardo, 1872: 38.
12. Glotz, 1926: 247.
13. *Ibid.:* 248.
14. Myers, 1939: 20.
15. Morris, 1937: 554 ff.
16. *Ibid.*
17. Aristotle, *Politics* 2.7.
18. Pöhlmann, 1912, I: 206 ff.

19. Jetterson, 1944: 440.
20. Beard, 1941: 149.
21. Beard, 1927, I: 292.
22. *Ibid.:* 413.
23. Bloch, 1949, II: 244.
24. Tout, 1937: *passim.*
25. McIlwain, 1932: 673.
26. *Ibid.*
27. *Ibid.*
28. Morris, 1937: 554.
29. *Ibid.:* 553 ff.
30. Murdock, 1949: 37 ff.
31. *Shih Chi* 53.4b–5b. For translation and comment see MS HCS, Ch'in-Han, II (14).

                    3, E
1. Weber, WG: 241 ff.
2. Deimel, 1920: 21.
3. *Ibid.:* 31.
4. *Ibid.:* 21. Cf. Meissner, BA, II: 53.
5. Deimel, 1920: 31.
6. *Ibid.*
7. Glotz, 1929: 39.
8. Bury, 1937: 46. Cf. Stengel, 1920: 33 ff.; and Bengtson, 1950: 97.
9. Bengtson, 1950: 62.
10. Busolt, GS, I: 515.
11. *Ibid.:* 498.
12. Lamprecht, DG: 17 ff., 34. Petit-Dutaillis, 1949: 23.
13. Petit-Dutaillis, 1949: 92.
14. *Ibid.:* 333.
15. Cf. Ranke, 1924, I: 32.
16. Garcilaso, 1945, I: 58 ff. Cobo, HNM, III: 122 ff. Means, 1931: 370. Rowe, 1946: 257.
17. Garcilaso, 1945, I: 61. Means, 1931: 370.
18. Means, 1931: 370, 374. Rowe, 1946: 265. Cf. Garcilaso, 1945, I: 84.
19. Garcilaso, 1945, I: 84, 175 ff. Means, 1931: 407, 370. Rowe, 1946: 299.
20. Ondegardo, 1872: 18 ff. Cobo, HNM, III: 246 ff. Rowe, 1946: 265 ff.
21. Cobo, HNM, III: 254 ff. Rowe, 1946: 266 ff.
22. Sethe, PT, II: 139. Breasted, 1927, I: 108, 114, 242, 327; II: 11, 25, and *passim;* III: 17 and *passim;* IV: 15, 27 and *passim.*
23. Breasted, 1927, II: 12 and *passim;* III: 17 and *passim;* IV: 28 and *passim.*
24. Breasted, 1927, I: 70, 114, and *passim.*
25. *Ibid., passim.*
26. *Ibid.,* II: 80 and *passim;* III: 56 and *passim.*
27. Erman and Ranke, 1923: 73.
28. Engnell, 1943: 5 ff.
29. Erman and Ranke, 1923: 73.
30. Breasted, 1927, I: 100 and *passim.* Kees, 1933: 242 ff.
31. Cf. Breasted, 1927, I: 103.
32. Kees 1933: 252.
33. See above, p. 89.
34. Breasted, 1927, IV: 346 and *passim,* 419, 452, 482.
35. Engnell, 1943: 4.
36. *Ibid.:* 16.

37. Barton, 1929: 31 ff., 37, 43, 99. Labat, 1939: 53 ff. Engnell, 1943: 16 and nn.
38. Labat, 1939: 63.
39. Cf. Labat, 1939: *passim;* Engnell, 1943: 16 ff., 33; McEwan, 1934: 7 ff.; and Nilsson, 1950: 129 and n. 2.
40. Barton, 1929: 31, 35, 97, 137 ff., 325.
41. Labat, 1939: 131.
42. Engnell, 1943: 31. Cf. Labat, 1939: 202 ff.
43. Cf. Deimel, 1920: 21 ff.
44. Meissner, BA, I: 68. Labat, 1939: 135.
45. Labat, 1939: 202.
46. *Ibid.:* 168.
47. *Ibid.:* 234.
48. Meissner, BA, II: 59 ff.
49. *Ibid.:* 60.
50. *Ibid.*
51. Cf. Christensen, 1944: 229; and McEwan, 1934: 18 and n. 116.
52. McEwan, 1934: 17.
53. *Ibid.:* 19.
54. Nilsson, 1950: 145 ff., 149 ff., 156 ff.
55. *Ibid.:* 161 ff.
56. Taylor, 1931: 58 ff.
57. *Ibid.:* 185 ff.
58. Bury, 1931, II: 360.
59. Bréhier, 1949: 61 ff.
60. See below, p. 97.
61. De Groot, 1918: 141 ff.
62. *Ibid.:* 180 ff. Cf. Wittfogel, 1940: 123 ff.
63. De Groot, 1918: 182 ff.
64. *Ibid.:* 219 ff.
65. *Ibid.:* 226 ff.
66. *Ibid.:* 247 ff.
67. *Ibid.:* 270 ff.
68. *Ibid.:* 276 ff.
69. Seler, GA, III: 332 ff.
70. *Ibid.:* 107 ff.
71. Seler, 1927: 238, 171. Cf. Sahagun, 1938, I: 211.
72. Seler, 1927: 104. Cf. Sahagun, 1938, I: 139.
73. Seler, 1927: 354.
74. Paul Kirchhoff, personal communication.
75. Priests as warriors: Seler, 1927: 115. *Ibid.,* GA, II: 606, 616. For priests as judges see *ibid.,* GA, III: 109.
76. Christensen, 1933: 257, 291.
77. *Ibid.:* 289.
78. Bréhier, 1949: 61.
79. Ostrogorsky, 1940: 18.
80. Cf. Arnold, 1941: 291 ff.
81. *Ibid.:* 295.
82. Pedersen, 1941: 445.
83. Fick, 1920: 98 ff.
84. Manu, 1886: 14.
85. *Ibid.:* 216 f.
86. Keith, 1922: 127 ff. Cf. *ibid.,* 1914, I: 109, 279; II: 599 ff.

87. Fick, 1920: 166 ff.
88. Manu, 1886: 228.
89. Baudhāyana, 1898: 200.
90. Manu, 1886: 26.
91. *Ibid.:* 509.
92. *Ibid.:* 253 f. Gautama, 1898: 237 ff.
93. Fick, 1920: 174.
94. *Ibid.:* 173 ff.
95. Dubois, 1943: 290.
96. *Ibid.*
97. Fick, 1920: 79 ff.

4, A

1. Cf. Têng and Biggerstaff, 1936: 139 ff.
2. Cf. Hopkins, 1922: 277 ff.
3. Hsieh, 1925: 34.
4. Rangaswami, 1935: 103 ff.
5. Bury, 1910: 26.
6. Arnold, 1924: 53.
7. Schacht, 1941: 676 f. Cf. Laoust, 1939: 54; Horster, 1935: 5 ff.; and Gaudefroy-Demombynes, 1950: 154.
8. Arnold, 1924: 47. Cf. Gaudefroy-Demombynes, 1950: 110.
9. Rangaswami, 1935: 69.
10. Wittfogel and Goldfrank, 1943: 30 and n. 139.
11. Krause and With, 1922: 26 ff.
12. For Hindu India see Manu, 1886: 397 ff.; Fick, 1920: 103; and *Arthaçāstra*, 1926: lxiii ff., 822. For Muslim thoughts see al-Fakhrî, 1910: 56. Cf. Hasan Khan, 1944: 36 ff.
13. For the contrary view see Hsieh, 1925: 11.
14. Wittfogel and Fêng, 1949: 398 ff.
15. Reid, 1936: 25.
16. Mommsen, 1875: 1034.
17. Bury, 1910: 9.
18. Diehl, 1936: 729.
19. Bury, 1910: 8.
20. *Ibid.:* 8 ff.
21. Kornemann, 1933: 143.
22. Boulais, 1924: 464.
23. For Egypt see Kees, 1933: 184. For India see *Arthaśāstra*, 1923: 28 ff.; and Manu, 1886: 224 ff. For China see Hsieh, 1925: 83.
24. For China see Ch'ü, TT, 1947: 206–8.

4, B

1. Cf. Clark, 1937: 145 ff.
2. Garcilaso, 1945, I: 246.
3. De Groot, 1940: *passim.*
4. For intermediate constellations see below, Chap. 7.
5. Marx, 1939: 371, 375, 386, 429.
6. Manu, 1886: 24.
7. Legge, CC, I: *passim.*
8. For Chagga see Gutmann, 1909: 167; and Dundas, 1924: 158 ff. For Hawaii see Alexander, 1899: 66 ff., 72 ff.

9. Ch'ü, TT, 1947: 7 ff.

10. *Ibid.:* 20.

11. Hammurabi, sec. 117.

12. Koran, 17.24 ff. Cf. Daghestani, FM: 134.

13. Daghestani, FM: 136. Cf. Gaudefroy-Demombynes, 1950: 128.

14. Jolly, 1896: 78.

15. Vāsishṭha, 1898: 75.

16. Rowe, 1946: 263 ff. Cobo, HNM, III: 232 ff.

17. Zurita, 1941: 90.

18. Breasted, 1927, II: 278 ff. Kees, 1933: 36 ff.

19. Cf. Wiedemann, 1920: 68.

20. Jouguet, 1911: 59 ff., 62. Wilcken, 1912: 275. San Nicolo, PR, I: 162 ff. Johnson and West, 1949: 98. Tomsin, 1952: 117 ff.

21. Jouguet, 1911: 59.

22. San Nicolo, PR, I: 171.

23. Jouguet, 1911: 213.

24. Harper, 1928: 142 ff.

25. Cf., for the end of the "ancient" period, Rostovtzeff, 1910: 259; and San Nicolo, PR, I: 160, n. 1. Cf. also below, Chap. 7.

26. Rostovtzeff, 1910: 259.

27. *Ibid.:* 258. Broughton, 1938: 629.

28. Johnson, 1951: 133.

29. Steinwenter, 1920: 52 ff.

30. *Ibid.:* 49 ff.

31. *Ibid.:* 54.

32. Gibb and Bowen, 1950: 262.

33. *Ibid.:* 263. Cf. Kremer, 1863, I: 255.

34. Kremer, 1863, I: 255.

35. Fick, 1920: 160 ff. Rhys-Davids, 1950: 35.

36. Rhys-Davids, 1950: 35. Jolly, 1896: 93. Cf. Matthai, 1915: 10.

37. Fick, 1920: 114, n. 1.

38. Jolly, 1896: 93. Fick, 1920: 161.

39. Matthai, 1915: 15.

40. Smith, 1899: 227 ff. Yang, 1945: 173.

41. Smith, 1899: 228.

42. Williams, 1848: 384 ff.

43. Smith, 1899: 233 ff.

44. Smith, 1897: 230.

45. Rostovtzeff, 1941, II: 1062 f. (italics mine).

46. Stöckle, 1911: 82.

47. For the market inspector see Ibn al-Ukhuwwa, 1938: 5. Cf. Gaudefroy-Demombynes, 1938: 450 ff.; and Lévi-Provençal, 1947: 42 ff.

48. Maurer, GSD, III: 30 ff. Inama-Sternegg, 1901: 353–4.

49. Gibb and Bowen, 1950: 278.

50. *Jātakam, passim.* Fick, 1920: 257 ff.

51. Fick, 1920: 285. Cf. Hopkins, 1902: 172.

52. Hopkins, 1902: 171.

53. Fick, 1920: 285.

54. C. A. F. Rhys-Davids, 1922: 210 ff.

55. *Chiu T'ang Shu,* 48.11b.

56. Kato, 1936: 62.

57. *Ibid.*
58. Grunebaum, 1946: 179.
59. *Ibid.:* 185.
60. Scheel, 1943: 8, 16.
61. Grunebaum, 1946: 185.
62. Wittfogel and Fêng, 1949: 292 and n. 19.
63. De Groot, 1940, I: 102 ff.
64. *Ibid.:* 107.
65. *Ibid.:* 109 ff.
66. *Ibid.:* 113.
67. *Ibid.:* 116.
68. For China see Ch'ü, TT, 1947: 18–19. For India see Manu, 1886: 260.
69. Harper, 1928: *passim.*
70. Johnson, 1951: 133.
71. Gibb and Bowen, 1950: 263.
72. Dubois, 1943: 88 ff.
73. *Ibid.:* 89.
74. See Appadorai, 1936, I: 152.
75. *Ibid.*
76. Fick, 1920: 120. Baden-Powell, 1896: 441 ff.
77. Letter of January 15, 1954, of Dr. K. C. Hsiao.
78. Smith, 1899: 229.
79. *Ibid.:* 228.
80. Manu, 1886: 260 and n. 41.
81. For Ottoman Turkey see Gibb and Bowen, 1950: 227. For Byzantium see Stöckle, 1911: *passim.* For China see Ch'üan, HS, 1934: *passim.*
82. Gibb and Bowen, 1950: 277.
83. *Ibid.:* 278.
84. *Ibid.:* 277 (italics mine).
85. De Groot, 1940, I: 116.
86. Macdonald, 1941: 96.
87. Smith, 1899: 229.
88. De Groot, 1940: *passim.*
89. Grunebaum, 1946: 184.
90. Stöckle, 1911: 138.
91. Massignon, 1937: 216.
92. Gibb and Bowen, 1950: 281, n. 5.
93. C. A. F. Rhys-Davids, 1922: 210 ff.
94. Wittfogel, 1931: 572 ff. Cf. Hintze, 1941: 152 ff.
95. Wittfogel, 1931: 580 ff.

4, C
1. *Yüan Shih,* 146.4a. Cf. Wittfogel, 1949: 10.
2. Koran, 2.266 (267). For irrigation in ancient Arabia see Grohmann, 1933: 19 ff. For irrigation near Mecca see Lammens, 1922: 141 ff.
3. Wittfogel, 1949: 10.
4. Garcilaso, 1945, I: 43.
5. Legge, CC, I: 215.
6. *Ibid.,* II: 128 ff.
7. Garcilaso, 1945, II: 21.
8. *Ibid.:* 9.
9. Garcilaso, 1945, II: 81.

10. For Ch'ing see *Ta Ch'ing Lü Li*, 17.26a ff.; Boulais, 1924: 389 ff. Cf. Ch'ü, TT, 1947: Chap. 3.
11. Manu, 1886: 37 ff. Āpastamba, 1898: 9 ff. Gautama, 1898: 176 ff. Baudhāyana, 1898: 150. Vāsishṭha, 1898: 56 ff. Vishnu, 1900: 114 ff.
12. Erman and Ranke, 1923: 238 ff.
13. Meissner, BA, I: 130 ff.
14. Porphyrogénète, 1939: 34 ff. Cf. Stein, 1949: 844; Lopez, 1945: 2.
15. Kremer, CGO, II: 218 ff.; Mez, 1922: 217.
16. Makrizi, 1845: 72.
17. Björkman, 1941: 756.
18. *Han Shu*, 24A.11b–12a. For translation and comment see MS HCS, Ch'in-Han VII, 1 (18).
19. Bernier, 1891: 225.
20. *Ibid.*: 226.
21. Cf. Meissner, BA, I: 147 ff.
22. Locke, 1924: 162–3.
23. *Ibid.*: 162.
24. Acton, 1948: 364.
25. *Arthaśāstra*, 1923: 296.
26. Stalin, S, XII: 368.

5, A

1. Fromm, 1941: *passim*.

5, B

1. Manu, 1886: 219.
2. Legge, CC, I: 267.
3. Manu, 1886: 218.
4. *Ibid.*: 220.
5. *Ibid.*: 219 (italics mine).
6. *Ibid.*
7. *Ibid.*
8. *Ibid.* (italics mine).
9. Barton, 1929: 31 and *passim*.
10. Jacobsen, 1946: 143.
11. *Ibid.*: 144.
12. *Ibid.*
13. Barton, 1929: 31 and *passim*.
14. Hammurabi: Prologue.
15. Erman and Ranke, 1923: 64, 460.
16. al-Fakhrî, 1910: 36.
17. Thucydides 1.6.
18. *Ibid.*
19. Bauer, 1893: 350.
20. Eisenhower, 1948: 467 ff.

5, C

1. Lenin, S, XXVIII: 216.
2. Vyshinsky, 1948: 92 ff.
3. Gutmann, 1909: 26.
4. *Ibid.*
5. Alexander, 1899: 26 ff. Blackman, 1899: 22 ff.
6. Sethe, PT, II: 137 ff., 156 ff.

7. Price, 1927: 17, 60.
8. Kees, 1933: 224.
9. Mallon, 1921: 137 ff.
10. Cromer, 1908, II: 402.
11. Garcilaso, 1945, I: 246.
12. Erman, 1923: 247.
13. Kees, 1933: 23, 220, cf. 224.
14. Mez, 1922: 126 ff. Cf. Goldziher, 1905: 108; Juynboll, 1925: 317, n. 1; Schacht, 1935: 117; Santillana, 1938: 48.
15. Mez, 1922: 126.
16. *Arthaçāstra*, 1926: 228.
17. Boulais, 1924: 215 ff.
18. Kees, 1933: 224.
19. Breasted, 1927, IV: 270. Cf. Spiegelberg, 1892: 85.
20. *Arthaśāstra*, 1923: 269 (italics mine). Cf. *Arthaçāstra*, 1926: 343.
21. *Arthaśāstra*, 1923: 269. Cf. *Arthaçāstra*, 1926: 344.
22. *Arthaśāstra*, 1923: 269.
23. *Ibid.*: 270.
24. *Ta Ch'ing Lü Li* 2.34b. Boulais, 1924: 5 ff.
25. Cf. Doolittle, 1876, I: 335–46.
26. Mez, 1922: 349. The quotation is taken from Masçudi, VIII: 154.
27. Cromer, 1908, II: 403.
28. Busolt, GS, I: 555 ff.
29. *Ibid.*: 280.
30. Glotz, 1926: 281.
31. *Ibid.*
32. Busolt, GS, I: 555 ff.; II: 1180. Cf. Aristotle, *Rhetoric* 1.15; Freudenthal, 1905: 14.
33. Schiller, 1893: 223. Mommsen, 1905: 5. Hitzig, 1905: 43.
34. Hitzig, 1905: 43 ff. Williams, 1911: 73 ff.
35. Helbing, 1926: 46 ff.
36. Brunner, 1905: 58. Cf. Lea, 1892: 275 ff., 117 ff.
37. Lea, 1892: 200 ff., 483.
38. Helbing, 1926: 101 ff.
39. Lea, 1908, I: 217 ff. Helbing, 1926: 112. Williams, 1911: 74.
40. Williams, 1911: 75 ff. Lea, 1892: 483, 527 (Protestant Germany), 566 ff. (Protestant England without formal integration in the law), 572 ff. (Scotland).
41. See below, Chap. 6.
42. Cf. Kennan, 1891, II: 52.
43. Hammurabi: *passim*.

5, D

1. Jaeger, 1939: 104.
2. *Ibid.*: 88 ff.
3. Díaz, 1949: 91 ff.
4. Parsons, 1939, I: 53, 108. Goldfrank, 1945: 527 ff. Wittfogel and Goldfrank, 1943: 30.
5. Gutmann, 1909: 21.
6. Jacobsen, 1946: 202.
7. *Ibid.*: 202 ff.
8. *Ibid.*: 202.
9. *Ibid.*: 203.
10. Grapow, 1924: 150, 153.
11. Wilson, 1950: 414.

12. Manu, 1886: 391.

13. Koran, 4.62.

14. al-Fakhrî, 1910: 44.

15. **Legge, CC, I: 245.**

16. *Ibid.:* 246.

17. *Ibid.:* 178.

18. *Ibid.:* 211.

19. Bühler, 1948: 175 ff.

20. *Ibid.:* 296 ff.

21. *Ibid.:* 298.

22. Jacobsen, 1946: 202.

23. *Ibid.*

24. Wilson, 1950: 414.

25. Manu, 1886: 71.

26. *Lun Yü*, 1.1b.

27. Østrup, 1929: 27 ff.

28. *Ibid.:* 27.

29. Dundas, 1924: 282.

30. Cf. Gutmann, 1926: 531.

31. Cobo, HNM, III: 279–80. Rowe, 1946: 259.

32. Seler, 1927: 328.

33. *Ibid.*

34. Sahagun, 1938, IV: 51. Seler, 1927: 483.

35. Kuo, MJ, 1935: 20b, 30b, 39a, 46a, 55a–b, 57a, 60b, 61a–b, 62b, 65b, 68a ff. Legge,
    CC, III: 424, 432, 437 f., 446, 449, 508, 511.

36. Strabo 15.1.67. Manu, 1886: 43, 54.

37. Saletore, 1943: 179 ff. Beal, *Si-yu-ki*, I: 85. *Ta T'ang Hsi-yü Chi*, Chap. 1.

38. Jahāngīr, 1909: 203.

39. Dubois, 1943: 132.

40. Breasted, 1927, I: 214.

41. Grapow, 1924: 121 ff. Cf. Erman and Ranke, 1923: 82; Kees, 1933: 183; and
    Østrup, 1929: 31.

42. Erman and Ranke, 1923: 82.

43. *Ibid.* Breasted, 1927, IV: 204, 422, 427 f., 430, 437 ff.

44. Barton, 1929: 27. Meissner, BA, I: 70. Østrup, 1929: 32. Cf. Horst, 1932: 55.

45. Herodotus 1.134.

46. Horst, 1932: 103 ff.

47. *Ibid.:* 27, 103.

48. Ṭabarī, 1879: 93, 367.

49. Kornemann, 1933: 142.

50. Bréhier, 1949: 70.

51. Mez, 1922: 135 ff. Sauvaget, 1946: 62. Gaudefroy-Demombynes, 1950: 110. Kremer,
    CGO, II: 247.

52. Schramm, 1924: 220.

53. Kantorowicz, 1931: 76, 91.

    5, E

1. Wilson, 1950: 418.

2. *Arthaśāstra*, 1923: 42, 45.

3. *Ibid.:* 24.

4. *Ibid.:* 42.

5. *Ibid.:* 43.

6. *Ibid.*
7. *Ibid.:* 34.
8. *Ibid.:* 34 ff.
9. *Ibid.:* 302.
10. Kai Kā'ūs ibn Iskandar, 1951: 191.
11. Smith, 1897: 257.
12. *Ibid.:* 242. Cf. Doolittle, 1876, I: 346.
13. *Han Shu*, 62.14a–22a.
14. Howorth, HM, III: 588 ff.
15. *Ibid.:* 561.
16. *Ibid.:* 588.
17. *Ibid.:* 588 ff.
18. *Ibid.*
19. Trotsky, 1928: 322.
20. ASBRT: 627.
21. *Ibid.:* 644.
22. *Ibid.:* 697.

6, A

1. For Marx' and Engels' ideas concerning the Asiatic issue see below, Chap. 9, *passim.*

6, B

1. Westermann, 1921: 169 ff. *Ibid.,* 1922: 22 ff. Schnebel, 1925: 8 ff.
2. Westermann, 1922: 27. Erman and Ranke, 1923: 203 ff. Schnebel, 1925: 11, 274. Kees, 1933: 32, 40, 49.
3. *Han Shu*, 28B.20b. MS HCS, Ch'in-Han, I, 2 (3).
4. *Shih Chi*, 8.16b. Cf. MS HCS, Ch'in-Han, I, 2 (4).
5. See Wittfogel, 1931: 454; *ibid.,* 1938: 110.
6. Mez, 1922: 423–8.
7. *Ibid.:* 423.
8. *Ibid.:* 423–8.
9. Gardiner, 1948, II: 9, 69, 88, 163.
10. Wilcken, 1912: 182 ff., 212 ff.
11. *Ibid.:* 183 ff., 212 ff., 230. Wallace, 1938: 286 ff. Johnson and West, 1949: 299, 321 ff.
12. Wilcken, 1912: 230–1.
13. Mez, 1922: 125. Cf. Becker, IS, I: 237, 239, and *passim.*
14. See above, Chap. 4.
15. Cf. Lybyer, 1913: 147.
16. For occasional and exceptional efforts see Longrigg, 1925: 127.
17. Wittfogel, 1949: 10.
18. Lammens, 1907: 131 ff., 140. *Ibid.,* 1914: 179 ff. Miles, 1948: 236 ff. Wellhausen, 1927: 252 and n. 1, 331 ff. Gabrieli, 1935: 12 ff., 22, 128 ff.
19. See below, pp. 276 and 288.
20. Hardy, 1931: 59 ff., 113. Johnson and West, 1949: 11.

6, C

1. Ramsay, 1890: 74 ff.
2. *Ibid.* Cf. Bréhier, 1949: 328 ff.
3. Cf. Ramsay, 1890: 74. Taeschner, 1926: 202 ff.
4. Ostrogorsky, 1940: 261. Honigmann, 1935: 44 and *passim.* For the character and purpose of these fortifications see Ramsay, 1890: 200.
5. Ostrogorsky, 1940: 261.
6. Ramsay, 1890: 199.

7. Bréhier, 1949: 262.

8. *Ibid.*: 328 ff. Cf. the description of the Byzantine post at the close of the 9th century given by Hārūn b. Yaḥyā (Marquart, 1903: 207 ff.).

9. Bréhier, 1950: 220 ff.

10. See above, Chap. 3.

11. See Karamsin, HER, VI: 439 (Ivan III); Herberstein, NR, I: 95 (Vasili III); and Staden, 1930: 57 (Ivan IV). Cf. Kluchevsky, HR, II: 126 ff., 138; III: 235 ff.; and Milukow, 1898: 129 ff.

12. Karamsin, HER, VI: 448 (Ivan III). Herberstein, NR, I: 108 (Vasili III).

13. Herberstein, NR, I: 111. Staden, 1930: 52 ff. Fletcher, 1856: 57 ff. Cf. Kulisher, 1925: 345 ff.; and Lyashchenko, 1949: 224 ff.

14. Ostrogorsky, 1940: 57, n. 4.

15. Stein, 1920: 50 ff. Cf. Ostrogorsky, 1940: 57, n. 4.

16. Ostrogorsky, 1940: 57 ff., 87.

17. *Ibid.*: 262.

18. *Ibid.*: 232.

19. *Ibid.*: 344.

20. *Ibid.*: 216. *Ibid.*, 1942: 209.

21. Dölger, 1927: 94 n.

22. Ostrogorsky, 1940: 262 ff.

23. See Stepniak, 1888: 155 ff.; and Nicolai-on, 1899: 171. Cf. Milukow, 1898: 142 ff.

24. See Robinson, 1949: 129 ff., 268, 270.

25. Wittfogel, 1950: 452. Cf. Prokopowitsch, 1913: 17 ff., 31, 39 ff.; and Lyashchenko, 1949: 534 ff., 716.

26. Lyashchenko, 1949: 701, 706.

27. Cf. Wittfogel, 1950: 453.

28. See below, Chap. 10.

29. Wittfogel and Fêng, 1949: 123 ff., 136.

30. *Ibid.*: 365, 371, 373 f.

31. *Ibid.*: 371.

32. *Ibid.*: 373.

33. *Ibid.*: 160, 165.

34. *Ibid.*: 370.

35. *Ibid.*: 365, 373, 522.

36. *Ibid.*: 367 ff.

37. *Ibid.*: 366.

38. *Ibid.*: 112 ff., 370 ff., 520, 559.

39. *Ibid.*: 162.

40. *Ibid.*: 533.

41. *Ibid.*: 65 ff.

42. *Ibid.*: 66 ff.

43. *Ibid.*: 45, 65, n. 29.

44. *Ibid.*: 310 ff.

45. *Chin Shih*, 96.4b. Cf. Wittfogel and Fêng, 1949: 296.

46. Wittfogel and Fêng, 1949: 124, 296, 572.

47. Cortes, 1866: 24.

48. Landa, 1938: 225. Cf. Tozzer, 1941: 187 and n. 975.

49. Roys, 1933: 75, 175.

50. RY, I: 116 and *passim*.

51. Landa, 1938: 226.

52. Stephens, 1848, I: 335; II: 144 and *passim*.

53. *Ibid.*, I: 357.

54. *Ibid.* Casares (1907: 221) agrees with this conjecture.

55. Casares, 1907: 217.

56. Stephens, 1848, I: 231.

57. *Ibid.*, ITCA, II: 429.

58. Casares, 1907: 218.

59. Stephens, 1848, I: 250.

60. See Ruppert and Denison, 1943: 3 and *passim.*

61. Stephens, 1848, II: 213.

62. Tozzer, 1941: 86 = Landa, 1938: 104.

63. Stephens, 1848, II: 211 ff.

64. Ruppert and Denison, 1943: *passim.*

65. *Ibid.* Cf. Morley, 1947: 43.

66. Landa, 1938: 104, 209. Tozzer, 1941: 85 ff., 170 ff. Cf. Morley, 1947: 174.

67. Tozzer, 1941: 174, n. 908. Landa, 1938: 212. Morley, 1947: 339 ff. and plate 55. Roys, 1943: 51.

68. Landa, 1938: 104.

69. *Ibid.*

70. Tozzer, 1941: 87 = Landa, 1938: 105.

71. Roys, 1943: 63.

72. *Ibid.*

73. Tozzer, 1941: 28 and n. 154; 64, n. 292.

74. Roys, 1943: 66.

75. *Ibid.*: 67.

76. *Ibid.*

77. *Ibid.*: 61.

78. *Ibid.*

79. *Ibid.*

80. Kljutschewskij, 1945, I: 162.

81. *Ibid.*: 163.

82. *Ibid.*: 164 ff.

83. *Ibid.*, II: 91.

84. Wittfogel and Fêng, 1949: 398 ff.

85. *Ibid.*: 466 ff., 502.

86. *Ibid.*: 213, 259, and *passim.*

87. Tozzer, 1941: 99 = Landa, 1938: 114.

88. Ostrogorsky, 1940: 173.

89. *Ibid.*: 348.

90. Sumner, 1949: 177.

91. *Ibid.*: 178.

92. *Ibid.*: 184.

93. *Ibid.*: 178.

94. *Ibid.*: 184.

95. Wittfogel and Fêng, 1949: 217 ff.

96. Roys, 1943: 60.

97. *Ibid.*: 79.

98. Tozzer, 1941: 27, n. 149.

99. Beaglehole, 1937: 30. Wittfogel and Goldfrank, 1943: 25. Titiev, 1944: 186. Parsons, 1939, I: 111.

100. Das, 1904: 52, 98, 102. Cf. Hedin, 1917: 280, 295, 299, 320.

101. For this term see Das, 1904: 233.

102. *Ibid.*: 234, 244 ff.

103. *Ibid.*: 245 ff.

104. *Ibid.:* 231. Bell, 1927: 158.
105. See Rockhill, 1891: 292 ff. Das, 1904: 241 ff.

6, D

1. Glotz, 1925: 10.
2. *Ibid.:* 115–17.
3. *Ibid.:* 117, 186 ff., 402.
4. *Ibid.:* 151.
5. *Ibid.:* 119, 150 ff.
6. *Ibid.:* 150.
7. Ehrenberg, 1946: 8.
8. *Ibid.*
9. *Ibid.* Cf. Meyer, GA, I, Pt. 2: 776, 779. Glotz, 1925: 202 ff.
10. Ehrenberg, 1946: 8.
11. Bengtson, 1950: 41. Meyer, GA, II, Pt. 1: 244 ff.
12. Bengtson, 1950: 41.
13. *Ibid.*
14. *Ibid.:* 42.
15. Horst, 1932: 23.
16. Herodotus 7.136. Arrian 4.10 ff.
17. Bengtson, 1950: 38.
18. *Ibid.*
19. Cf. Glotz, 1926: 268, 271.
20. Ehrenberg, 1946: 22.
21. Homo, 1927: 110.
22. Voigt, 1893: 274, 358.
23. Homo, 1927: 120.
24. *Ibid.:* 217, 243.
25. Asakawa, 1929: 71.
26. Nihongi, 1896, II: 225 ff.
27. See Sansom, 1938: 93 ff.; and Reischauer, 1937, I: 146 ff.
28. Nihongi, 1896, I: 164, 183, 283. Asakawa, 1929a: 193 and n. 6.
29. Asakawa, 1903: 270. See also Sansom, 1938: 101, contradicting his statement on p. 159.
30. Nihongi, 1896, II: 250 ff., 255. Cf. Florenz, 1903: 163.
31. Nihongi, 1896, II: 208, 241.
32. Asakawa, 1911: 178 ff. Cf. Rathgen, 1891: 142.
33. Takekoshi, 1930, I: 161.
34. Sansom, 1938: 457.
35. Takekoshi, 1930, III: 394, 412.
36. *Ibid.*
37. Sansom, 1938: 455 ff. Takekoshi, 1930, I: 253.
38. Honjo, 1935: 241.
39. Sansom, 1938: 470.
40. Vernadsky, 1943: 327.
41. Struve, 1942: 421.
42. *Ibid.*
43. Nestor, 1931: 101.
44. *Ibid.:* 180.
45. *Ibid.:* 122, 124.
46. Hötzsch, 1912: 545.
47. Nestor, 1931: 11, 16. Cf. Vernadsky, 1943: 276 ff. For a recent Soviet presentation cf. Grekov, 1947: 130.

48. Vernadsky, 1943: 338.

49. *Ibid.:* 168 ff.

50. Borosdin, 1908 (presenting the finds of Pavlov-Silvansky): 577. Hötzsch, 1912: 546. Struve, 1942: 427.

51. Mitteis, 1933: 87 ff., 528.

52. Vernadsky, 1948: 190.

53. Struve, 1942: 422.

54. Vernadsky, 1948: 191.

55. Ostrogorsky, 1940: 130.

56. Nestor, 1931: 11, 56, cf. 43; cf. also 14.

57. *Ibid.:* 43; Miakotine, 1932: 101.

58. Goetz, RR, II: 228.

59. *Ibid.,* I: 247 ff.; IV: 144.

6, E

1. Goldfrank, 1945a: *passim.*

2. Wittfogel and Fêng, 1949: 505 ff.

3. *Ibid.:* 120 ff.

4. Vladimirtsov, 1948: 102.

5. *Ibid.:* 101 ff.

6. Wittfogel, 1949: 5 ff.

7. Wittfogel and Fêng, 1949: 664.

8. Riasanovsky, 1937: 102.

9. *Ibid.:* 95.

10. Rostovtzeff, 1910: 230 ff.

11. *Ibid.:* 230.

12. *Ibid.:* 237.

13. *Ibid.:* 237 and n.

14. Frank, 1928: 795.

15. Gelzer, 1943, II: 49 ff.

16. Stevenson, 1934: 211 ff.

17. Jones, 1934: 180.

18. Stevenson, 1934: 191 ff.

19. *Ibid.:* 216. Cf. Last, 1936: 428 ff.

20. Stevenson, 1934: 185 ff.

21. Charlesworth, 1934: 686 ff.

22. *Ibid.:* 123. Stevenson, 1934: 192 ff.

23. Riepl, 1913: 435 ff., 459.

24. Stevenson, 1934: 189. Charlesworth, 1934: 686 ff.

25. See below, Chap. 8.

26. Frank, 1940: 300.

27. Miller, 1939: 24.

28. Oertel, 1939: 272.

29. *Ibid.*

30. *Ibid.:* 273.

31. *Ibid.:* 256.

32. Cf. (for Spain) Van Nostrand, 1937: 127 ff.; (for Gaul) Grenier, 1937: 493 ff.; (for England) Collingwood, 1937: 14 ff.

33. Stein, 1928: 515–17.

34. *Ibid.:* 343.

35. Reiske, 1830: 271.

36. See Lot, 1951: 405 ff.

37. Bloch, 1937: 209.
38. Maitland, 1921: 1 ff.
39. Haskins, 1918: 5 ff.
40. *Ibid.*: 4.
41. Maitland, 1948: 9.
42. *Ibid.*
43. Haskins, 1911: 435.
44. *Ibid.*: 436.
45. *Ibid.*: 664 ff.
46. Wittfogel and Fêng, 1949: 507 ff.
47. Koebner, 1942: 52.
48. Sánchez-Albornoz, EM, I: 281. Cf. Lévi-Provençal, 1932: 99 ff.
49. Sánchez-Albornoz, EM, I: 213 ff.
50. Cf. Mieli, 1938: 205 ff. *Ibid.*, 1946: 165 ff. Lévi-Provençal, 1932: 173 ff.
51. Mieli, 1938: 184 ff., 197 ff. *Ibid.*, 1946: 132, 141 ff.
52. Dozy, 1932, II: 173.
53. Bücher, 1922, I: 382.
54. Rogers, 1884: 117.
55. al-Makkari, 1840, I: 215, cf. 214.
56. *Primera Crónica General:* 767 (chap. 1124). Cf. Laborde, 1808: 9; and Schirrmacher 1881: 410.
57. Seybald, 1927: 176. Cf. Lafuente Alcantara, 1845: 136.
58. Dozy, 1932, II: 173.
59. *Ibid.*: 200, 222. Sanchez-Albornoz, EM, I: 344.
60. See Sanchez-Albornoz, EM, I: 349, 351.
61. Hintze, 1901: 406.
62. *Ibid.*: 413.
63. *Ibid.*: 411.
64. Altamira, 1930: 61.
65. *Ibid.*: 104 ff.
66. See *ibid.*: 62 ff.
67. *Ibid.*: 160.
68. *Ibid.*: 138.
69. Hintze, 1930: 241.
70. Altamira, 1930: 63.
71. See Klein, 1920: 34 ff.
72. *Ibid.*: 17 ff., see esp. the map following p. 18.
73. *Ibid.*: 75, 77 ff., 157 ff., 170, 173, 175 ff.
74. *Ibid.*: 279.
75. Quoted by *ibid.*: 317.
76. *Ibid.*: 325.
77. Kliuchevskii, *Kurs,* II: 260.
78. Kluchevsky, HR, II: 112.
79. *Ibid.*, II: 112 ff.
80. *Ibid.*, I: 117.
81. *Ibid.*, I: 269.
82. Kliuchevskii, *Kurs,* II: 174.
83. *Ibid.*, II: 22–3.
84. *Ibid.*, II: 23.
85. Kluchevsky, HR, II: 126 ff., 138; III: 235 f., 237 ff., 241.
86. Kliuchevskii, *Kurs,* II: 23.
87. Spuler, 1943: 333, 338. Vernadsky, 1953: 219 ff.

88. Vernadsky, 1953: 357 ff.
89. *Ibid.*: 358 (italics mine).
90. Kluchevsky, HR, III: 227.
91. Kliuchevskii, *Kurs,* II: 436.
92. See Karamsin, HER, VI: 448.
93. Spuler, 1943: 409 ff. Karamsin, HER, IV: 393 ff. Vernadsky, 1953: 221, 357.
94. Kluchevsky, HR, I: 304 ff.
95. *Ibid.,* II: 123.
96. *Ibid.:* 124 ff.
97. *Ibid.,* III: 52.
98. Kliuchevskii, *Kurs,* II: 272–3.
99. *Ibid.:* 277.
100. *Ibid.:* 278.
101. Kovalewsky, 1903: 43.
102. Vernadsky, 1953: 372.
103. *Ibid.:* 367.
104. See Wipper, 1947: 15, 30, 37, 42 ff.

7, E

1. See Murdock, 1949: 38 ff.
2. Lips, 1938: 516.
3. *Ibid.*
4. Beech, 1911: 16.
5. *Ibid.:* 34.
6. *Ibid.*
7. Parsons, 1939, I: 20.
8. Titiev, 1944: 184. Cf. Beaglehole, 1937: 15.
9. Titiev, 1944: 61.
10. *Ibid.:* 64.
11. Beech, 1911: 15.
12. *Ibid.:* 34.
13. Dundas, 1924: 302.
14. Merker, 1904: 217.
15. Widenmann, 1899: 68. Dundas, 1924: 266. Gutmann, 1926: 440 ff
16. Gutmann, 1926: 455.
17. *Ibid.:* 442.
18. *Ibid.*
19. *Ibid.:* 442, 448.
20. *Ibid.:* 446 ff.
21. Dundas, 1924: 298.
22. Gutmann, 1926: 382 ff.
23. Gutmann, 1909: 12.
24. Dundas, 1924: 286.
25. Widenmann, 1899: 87.
26. Merker, 1903: 34.
27. Waitz, 1880, I: 338 ff.

7, F

1. Dundas, 1924: 287.
2. Widenmann, 1899: 87.
3. Gutmann, 1909: 12. Cf. Widenmann, 1899: 87.
4. Widenmann, 1899: 87.

5. Gutmann, 1926: 368.
6. Dundas, 1924: 287.
7. Gutmann, 1926: 370.
8. See *ibid.*: 369 ff.
9. *Ibid.*: 497 ff.
10. So also, with a few exceptions, Gutmann, 1909: 9 and *passim; ibid.*, 1914: *passim*; and *ibid.*, 1926: *passim*.
11. Kepelino, 1932: 122, 124, 134. Cf. Fornander, HAF, V: 72, 478.
12. Kepelino, 1932: 122, 126, 146.
13. Lydgate, 1913: 125.
14. Alexander, 1899: 28. Cf. Fornander, HAF, V: 208 ff., 262; and Perry, 1913: 93 ff.
15. Perry, 1913: 92, 95. Handy, 1940: 36.
16. Malo, 1903: 84. Cf. Fornander, HAF, IV: 356; Kepelino, 1932: 146; and Handy, 1933: 34.
17. Ellis, 1826: 395. Alexander, 1899: 28, 59 ff. Kepelino, 1932: 148, 150. Handy, 1933: 34.
18. Kepelino, 1932: 150.
19. Gutmann, 1926: 302 ff.
20. *Ibid.*: 16.
21. *Ibid.*: 428.
22. Ellis, 1826: 296 ff.
23. Alexander, 1899: 24.
24. *Ibid.*: 88. Blackman, 1899: 55.
25. Lind, 1938: 140.
26. Ellis, 1826: 401. Alexander, 1899: 88.
27. Ellis, 1826: 296 ff.
28. Cf. Alexander, 1899: 156; and Blackman, 1899: 188.
29. Cook, 1944: 337.
30. Fornander, HAF, V: 478, 610 ff., 630. Vancouver, 1798, II: 116. Ellis, 1826: 89.
31. Alexander, 1899: 82.
32. Malo, 1903: 105; Cook, 1944: 436.
33. For lists of such objects see Blackman, 1899: 54 ff.; Alexander, 1899: 80 ff.; and Cook, 1944: 337 ff.
34. Kepelino, 1932: 124.
35. *Ibid.*: 134.
36. Sarmiento, 1906: 90.
37. Cieza, 1945: 180, 116 ff.
38. *Ibid.*: 272. Garcilaso, 1945, II: 82. Cf. Cobo, HNM, III: 43 ff.; and Means, 1931: 314 ff.
39. Cieza, 1945: 243, 278 ff. Cf. Garcilaso, 1945, I: 237, 180.
40. Estete, 1938: 94.
41. Garcilaso, 1945, I: 251.
42. CPLNC: 309. Jerez, 1938: 38. Garcilaso, 1945, I: 187, 189 ff.
43. Cieza, 1945: 144, 165.
44. CPLNC: 309. Cf. Jerez, 1938: 38.
45. Sancho de la Hos, 1938: 181.
46. Garcilaso, 1945, I: 185.
47. Sombart, 1919, II: 769 ff., 837. Kulischer, AW, II: 156 ff.
48. See above, pp. 79 f.
49. Breasted, 1927, IV: 164. Spiegelberg, 1896: 21, 25.
50. Kees, 1933: 103.
51. *Ibid.*: 103–4.
52. *Ibid.*: 104.
53. Newberry, BH, I: 46.

54. Erman and Ranke, 1923: 112. Kees, 1933: 164. Cf. Klebs, 1915: 116; and Erman, 1923: 102 ff.

55. See Kees, 1933: 165.

56. *Ibid.*

57. Breasted, 1927, II: 401 and *passim*.

58. *Ibid.: passim.* Kees, 1933: 166 ff.

59. Kees, 1933: 103.

60. *Ibid.:* 165.

61. *Ibid.:* 164.

62. *Ibid.:* 167.

63. *Ibid.*

64. Ch'ü, TT, 1937: 200–1.

65. Duyvendak, 1928: 49, 177, 179, 183.

66. *Shih Chi,* 6.21b. For translation and commentary see MS HCS, Ch'in-Han, VII, 1 (7).

67. See Legge, CC, III: 381, 439; and Kuo, MJ, 1935: 102b, 114a, 125b.

68. Legge, CC, III: 414, 516; IV: 439, cf. 582. Kuo, MJ, 1935: 118a.

69. Ch'ü, TT, 1947: 200.

70. Falkenstein, 1936: 58 ff.

71. Schneider, 1920: 21, 23.

72. Deimel, 1924b: 25. Schneider, 1920: 108 ff.

73. Schneider, 1920: 92.

74. Deimel, 1927: 58 ff., 61. *Ibid.,* 1928: 116 ff. *Ibid.,* 1929: 82, 85 f. Cf. Schneider, 1920: 80, 85.

75. Deimel, 1927: 60 ff. *Ibid.,* 1931: 108 f., 112.

76. Schneider, 1920: 83.

77. *Ibid.:* 32.

78. Scholtz, 1934: 36, 137.

79. Deimel, 1931: 39. Schneider, 1920: 66 ff. Cf. Scholtz, 1934: 79, 92.

80. Schneider, 1920: 67 ff. Scholtz, 1934: 115. Leemans, 1950: 45 ff.

81. Schneider, 1920: 68.

82. Scholtz, 1934: 171.

83. *Ibid.:* 115.

84. Schneider, 1920: 68.

85. Leemans, 1950: 46.

86. Sethe, 1908: 8. Breasted, 1927, I: 209; II: 208 ff.; III: 20 ff.

87. Sethe, 1908: 8 ff.; Breasted, 1927, IV: 284.

88. TEA, I: 83 ff.

89. *Ibid.:* 279 ff.

90. *Ibid.:* 75, 89, 97, 281, 287, 291.

91. *Ibid.:* 93. Breasted, 1927, II: 114.

92. TEA, I: 93.

93. *Ibid.:* 93, 99, 281, 283, 297. Breasted, 1927, IV: 282 ff.

94. Cf. Wittfogel, 1951: 34.

95. Schneider, 1920: 66 ff.

96. Thureau-Dangin, 1907: 67 ff., 77, 103 ff. Barton, 1929: 181 ff., 217 ff., 143. Price, 1927: 58 ff., 16.

97. Thureau-Dangin, 1907: 31, 103, 105–7. Barton, 1929: 47, 131, 145. Price, 1927: 63, 71 19 ff.

98. Thureau-Dangin, 1907: 71, 107. Barton, 1929: 185, 221. Price, 1927: 63, 20–1.

99. Price, 1927: 20.

100. Leemans, 1950: 113.

101. *Ibid.:* 118.
102. *Ibid.:* 120 ff.
103. *Ibid.:* 122.

7, G

1. Acosta, 1945: 39 ff.
2. Bandelier, 1878: 426 and n. 98. *Ibid.*, 1880: 600. Monzon, 1949: *passim*
3. Zurita, 1941: 146. Oviedo, HGNI, II, Pt. 2: 535 ff. Cf. Bandelier, 1880: 602 and n. 73.
4. For various categories of Aztec craftsmen see Sahagun, 1938, III: 28 ff.; II: 385, 394;
    Díaz, 1944, I: 349; Torquemada, 1943, II: 486; and Motolinia, 1941: 243.
5. Motolinia, 1941: 206. Oviedo, HGNI, II, Pt. 2: 536. Tezozomoc, 1944: 105. Torque-
    mada, 1943, II: 555, 559. Cf. Cortes, 1866: 103.
6. Monzon, 1949: 44. Bandelier, 1878: 426, n. 98.
7. Zurita, 1941: 146 ff. Monzon, 1949: 26.
8. Tezozomoc, 1944: 100, 105, 123, 148.
9. Sahagun, 1938, II: 356 ff. Tezozomoc, 1944: 143, 156.
10. Sahagun, 1938, II: 341, 344 ff., 354 ff., 359.
11. Tezozomoc, 1944: 125.
12. Cf. Sahagun, 1938, II: 102, 196.
13. Ramirez, 1944: 86. Tezozomoc, 1944: 148.
14. Roys, 1943: 46.
15. See above, Chap. 6.
16. See Roys, 1943: 46.
17. *Ibid.:* 51.
18. Landa, 1938: 94 ff.
19. Bréhier, 1950: 183 ff., 201 ff.
20. Stöckle, 1911: 11, 16, and *passim*. Bréhier, 1950: 182 ff., 221.
21. Fletcher, 1856: 57.
22. Herberstein, NR, I: 111. Cf. Staden, 1930: 11 ff.
23. Herberstein, NR, I: 111.
24. Kulischer, 1925: 349 ff.
25. Kilburger, quoted by Kulischer, 1925: 350. Lyashchenko, 1949: 224 ff.
26. Kulischer, 1925: 343 ff. Mavor, 1925, I: 118 ff.
27. Kulischer, 1925: 344 ff.
28. *Ibid.:* 349 ff. Lyashchenko, 1949: 224 ff.
29. Kilburger, quoted by Kulischer, 1925: 350.
30. *Ibid.*
31. Fletcher, 1856: 62 ff.
32. *Ibid.:* 61.
33. *Ibid.:* 62.
34. Gsell, HA, I: 98.
35. Polybius 15. 1. 6 f.
36. Hammurabi, sec. 271. Cf. Meissner, BA, I: 153, 361, 163, 230 ff.
37. Roys, 1943: 34.
38. Grassman, RV, I: 341. Whitney, 1905: 899. Cf. Keith, 1922: 100; and Banerjee, 1925:
    115.
39. Banerjee, 1925: 155. Cf. Whitney, 1905: 111.
40. Hopkins, 1922: 258 ff.
41. *Ibid.:* 267.
42. *Ibid.*
43. Fick, 1920: 277.
44. Banerjee, 1925: 192.

45. Hopkins, 1902: 173.

46. Buddhist Suttas: 3.

47. Rhys-Davids, 1922: 175.

48. *Ibid.*: 178. Law, 1923: *passim.* Ibid., 1941: 163 ff. Buddhist Suttas: 131.

49. Buddhist Suttas: 3.

50. *Jātakam,* I: 155; III: 317; IV: 195; V: 35 and esp. 441 ff.

51. Fick, 1920: 137 ff. Rhys-Davids, 1950: 13, 16. Law, 1923: 116, 138 ff., 172 ff., 180, 196, 202.

52. Rhys-Davids, 1950: 1. *Ibid.*, 1922: 190 ff. Law, 1941: 119–38.

53. See *Jātakam,* I: 65, 79; II: 378 ff.; III: 66, 144, 321 ff.; IV: 1; V: 185, 210, and *passim.*
    Cf. C. A. F. Rhys-Davids, 1922: 207.

54. Fick, 1920: 258 ff. Cf. *Jātakam,* I: 336, 342 ff.; II: 59, 74; III: 134, 322; IV: 74; V: 414 and *passim.*

55. Fick, 1920: 257 ff.

56. See *Jātakam,* I: 178, 203; II: 268, 491; III: 523 ff.; IV: 80 and *passim.*

57. See *Jātakam,* I: 436, 438.

58. C. A. F. Rhys-Davids, 1922: 207.

59. Fick, 1920: 260. Cf. *Jātakam,* V: 412 ff.; VI: 391 ff.; VII: 224.

60. C. A. F. Rhys-Davids, 1922: 207.

61. *Ibid.*

62. *Ibid.*: 211.

63. *Ibid.*: 210 ff.

64. Hopkins, 1902: 175.

65. *Ibid.*: 175, n. 2.

66. GBP, 1882: 406 (italics mine).

67. *Ibid.*: 405.

68. See Burnouf, 1876: 220.

69. Speiser, 1942: 60. Jacobsen, 1943: 165 ff. Kramer, 1950: 45 ff.

70. Boas, 1938: 610. Wittfogel and Goldfrank, 1943: 17.

71. Kramer, 1948: 156 ff.

72. Jacobsen, 1943: 159 ff.

73. *Ibid.*: 160.

74. Kramer, 1948: 162.

75. Götze, 1933: 67.

76. *Ibid.*: 67, 71.

77. Landsberger, 1925: 10, 23.

78. Götze, 1933: 71 and nn. 18–20.

79. Landsberger, 1925: 9.

80. Götze, 1933: 70 and nn. 22–25.

81. Jacobsen, 1943: 161. Cf. Götze, 1933: 70.

82. Landsberger, 1925: 9.

83. Jacobsen, 1943: 162. Cf. Walther, 1917: 12 ff.; and Cuq, 1929: 354 ff.

84. Cf. esp. Walther, 1917: 22 ff.

85. Jacobsen, 1943: 164 ff.

86. Cuq, 1929: 358.

87. *Ibid.*

88. Cf. Krückmann, 1932: 446; and Walther, 1917: 74, 75 ff.

89. Weber, RS, II: 88 ff.

7, H

1. Ostrogorsky, 1940: 192.

2. *Ibid.*

3. Mukerjee, 1939: 219.
4. Edgerton, 1947: 156. Kees, 1933: 45.
5. Wilcken, 1912: 278 ff.
6. Cuq, 1929: 363.
7. See above, Chap. 4.
8. For the main date see Bodde, 1938: 238 ff. For a fuller treatment of the matter see MS HCS, Ch'in-Han, I, 1.
9. Smith, 1926: 365.
10. Gibb and Bowen, 1950: 254 ff.
11. See Kees, 1933: 42.
12. Alexander, 1899: 29.
13. Edgerton, 1947: 159 ff.
14. See Kees, 1933: 23, 42, 44; and Breasted, 1927, I: 76 ff., 93, 166 ff.; II: 6, 9; IV: 405.
15. Zurita, 1941: 148 ff. Oviedo, HGNI, II, Pt. 2: 535. Monzon, 1949: 44.
16. Appadorai, 1936, I: 135 ff.
17. Hardy, 1931: 22, 25. Johnson and West, 1949: 22 ff., 65.
18. Poliak, 1939: 36, 39.
19. Gibb and Bowen, 1950: 253.
20. Ostrogorsky, 1940: 179, 194.
21. Boulais, 1924: 244.
22. Oviedo, HGNI, II, Pt. 2: 535.
23. *Jātakam*, II: 427; VI: 98.
24. *Shih-chi*, 30.11a. For translation and comment see MS HCS, Ch'in-Han II (45)
25. Lang, 1946: 87, 94.
26. See Wittfogel, 1956: 157 ff.
27. Haxthausen, SR, III: 46 ff.
28. *Ibid.*: 47.
29. Segrè, 1943: 107.
30. Appadorai, 1936, I: 115.
31. Kees, 1933: 42.
32. Alexander, 1899: 29.
33. Leemans, 1950: 53.
34. Seidl, 1951: 46.
35. Kees, 1933: 42.
36. Jolly, 1896: 94.
37. Appadorai, 1936, I: 152.
38. Leemans, 1950: 53.
39. Meissner, BA, I: 188.
40. Schawe, 1932: 434.
41. Cuq, 1929: 105.
42. *Ibid.*: 92 ff.
43. *Ibid.*: 103.
44. *Ibid.*: 100.
45. Dubberstein, 1939: 36.
46. Rostovtzeff, 1941, I: 465. Christensen, 1933: 271.
47. Rostovtzeff, 1910: 246 ff.
48. Segrè, 1943: 88, 133.
49. Tarn, 1927: 113 ff. Cf. Bikerman, 1938: 183 ff.; and Rostovtzeff, 1910: 249 ff.
50. Tarn, 1927: 123, 150 ff.
51. *Ibid.*: 131.
52. *Ibid.*: 150. Cf. Bell, 1948: 46; Schubart, 1922: 229 ff.; and Johnson, 1951: 67 ff.
53. Rostovtzeff, 1941, I: 289.

54. *Ibid.:* 290.
55. Berger, 1950: 314.
56. Wilcken, 1912: 285 ff. Cf. Tarn, 1927: 150.
57. Wilcken, 1912: 307. Cf. Bell, 1948: 74.
58. Wellhausen, 1927: 32.
59. Becker, IS, I: 237.
60. Cf. Tritton, 1930: 146 ff.
61. Steinwenter, 1920: 51.
62. Becker, IS, I: 237. Cf. *ibid.*, 1903: 94.
63. Cf. Wellhausen, 1927: 275.
64. Becker, 1903: 94.
65. Becker, IS, I: 238.
66. Johnson, 1951: 86.
67. Becker, IS, I: 237.
68. Becker, 1903: 121 ff. Wellhausen, 1927: 31 ff.
69. Becker, 1903: 121 ff.
70. *Ibid.:* IS, I: 239 ff.
71. Poliak, 1939: 24.
72. *Ibid.:* 36 ff.
73. *Ibid.:* 32 ff.
74. *Ibid.:* 39.
75. Gibb and Bowen, 1950: 238.
76. *Ibid.:* 256.
77. *Ibid.:* 239.
78. *Ibid.:* 261.
79. *Ibid.:* 258.
80. *Ibid.*
81. *Ibid.*
82. Roys, 1943: 36.
83. *Ibid.:* 37.
84. Landa, 1938: 111. Tozzer, 1941: 96 and n. 429. Roys, 1943: 37.
85. Monzon, 1949: 45 ff.
86. Zurita, 1941: 148.
87. *Ibid.:* 143 ff., 148 ff., 152 ff.
88. *Ibid.:* 144.
89. Oviedo, HGNI, II, Pt. 2: 535.
90. Monzon, 1949: 41 ff. Cf. Oviedo, HGNI, II, Pt. 2: 535 ff.
91. Monzon, 1949: 45.
92. Zurita, 1941: 153, cf. 144.
93. *Ibid.:* 153.
94. *Ibid.:* 144.
95. Monzon, 1949: 45.
96. Mommsen, 1921: 573, n. 1. Wilcken, 1912: 287. Bell, 1948: 74.
97. Johnson and West, 1949: 18, 39.
98. Wilcken, 1912: 298, 303.
99. *Ibid.:* 298, 307 ff. Bell, 1948: 74.
100. Wilcken, 1912: 287, 302, 307.
101. *Ibid.:* 303.
102. *Ibid.:* 298, 302. Johnson and West, 1949: 18.
103. Cf. Johnson, 1951: 72 ff.
104. Wilcken, 1912: 312, 319 ff., 322.

105. See *ibid.:* 322.
106. *Ibid.:* 322 ff. Hardy, 1931: 22, 25, 136, 138. Johnson and West, 1949: 22 ff., 65. Johnson, 1951: 97. Cf. Bell, 1948: 122 ff.
107. Cf. Wilcken, 1912: 323; Johnson and West, 1949: 46; and Hardy, 1931: 230.
108. Hardy, 1931: 54 ff. Bell, 1948: 124. Johnson, 1951: 86, 97.
109. Hardy, 1931: 82 ff. Johnson, 1951: 83 ff.
110. Cf. Hardy, 1931: 23; and Johnson and West, 1949: 46.
111. See Hardy, 1931: 59 ff.; Bell, 1948: 124 ff.; and Johnson and West, 1949: 30.
112. Johnson and West, 1949: 240.
113. *Ibid.*
114. Cf. *ibid.;* and Johnson, 1951: 123.
115. Johnson, 1951: 86.
116. *Ibid.*
117. *Han Shu,* 24A.14b.
118. *Ibid.:* 11a–b, 14b–15a.
119. *Shih Chi,* 30.11a, 15a ff. *Han Shu,* 24B.12a, 14a ff. MS HCS, Ch'in-Han, II (45) (50).
120. Wan, KT, 1933: 163 ff. Cf. Balázs, BWT, I: 43 ff.
121. *Agrarian China:* 2.
122. *Ibid.:* 23 ff.

7, I

1. Scheil, 1900: 86, 99. Meissner, BA, I: 367. Cuq, 1929: 130. Cf. Speiser, 1942: 59.
2. See above, Chap. 6.
3. *Jātakam,* II: 37 ff. For the function of the appraiser see also IV: 160 ff.
4. See Kees, 1933: 48; Hammurabi, secs. 273 ff.; Meissner, BA, I: 163, 231; and *Jātakam* III: 316, 443, 488, 490.
5. Cf. *Arthaśāstra,* 1923: 76.
6. Cf. *Jātakam, passim;* and *Arabian Nights: passim.*
7. For China see Lang, 1946: 94.

8, A

1. Smith, 1937: 248.
2. *Ibid.*
3. *Ibid.:* 776.

8, C

1. For the history of the term see Emge, 1950: 1205 ff.
2. Stalin, 1942: 352 ff.
3. These facts have been established by Lienche Tu Fang through an analysis of bureaucratic underlings in the Ch'ing dynasty as part of the Ch'ing work of the Chinese History Project (MS).
4. Weber, RS, I: 331 ff.
5. *Ibid.:* 332.
6. Cf. Meyer, GA, IV, Pt. 1: 45 ff. and n.; and Christensen, 1944: 137, n. 1.
7. Cf. Gray and Cary, 1939: 196; and Meyer, GA, IV, Pt. 1: 49.
8. Meyer, GA, IV, Pt. 1: 48.
9. *Ibid.:* 50.
10. *Ibid.:* 49, 67 ff. Gray and Cary, 1939: 198.
11. Gray and Cary, 1939: 198.
12. Cf. Herodotus 5.96; Gray and Cary, 1939: 197; and Meyer, GA, IV, Pt. 1: 49.
13. Herodotus 5.32, Meyer, GA, IV, Pt. 1: 49.
14. Xenophon 8.6.10. Gray and Cary, 1939: 196. Meyer, GA, IV, Pt. 1: 49.

15. Xenophon 8.6.10 ff.
16. Gray and Cary, 1939: 197.
17. *Ibid.*
18. *Ibid.:* 198.
19. *Ibid.:* 199.
20. Meyer, GA, IV, Pt. 1: 50, cf. 53.
21. *Ibid.:* 59 and n. 1.
22. Gray and Cary, 1939: 196.
23. Meyer, GA, IV, Pt. 1: 51.
24. Rowe, 1946: 273.
25. Moreland, 1929: 9.
26. *Ibid.:* 8.
27. *Ibid.:* 119 ff.
28. Wittfogel, in *Commentary,* October 1950: 337.
29. Rowe, 1946: 267.
30. Wittfogel and Fêng, 1949: 441.
31. Kees, 1953: 4.
32. See above, Chap. 8.
33. Fick, 1920: 253.
34. *Ibid.*
35. *Ibid.*
36. *Jātakam,* IV: 541 ff.; VI: 317.
37. Jolly, 1896: 148 ff. Cf. Vishnu, 1900: 190 ff.
38. See C. A. F. Rhys-Davids, 1922: 205.
39. See above, Chap. 7.
40. For the social position of landholders see *Jātakam,* I: 130, 167, 185, 232 ff., 376; II: 73, 98, 234 ff., 300, 384, 388, 425; III: 59, 105, 171, 222 ff., 224, 554; IV: 449; V: 168, 475, 506 ff.; VI: 317.
41. See Stein, 1951: 131. Cf. Hardy, 1931: 25 ff.
42. Ondegardo, 1872: 37 ff.
43. See above, Chap. 7.
44. Ch'ü, TT, 1937: 172.
45. See above, sec. C, n. 3.
46. See esp. Hammurabi, secs. 28 ff.
47. Wilcken, 1912: 184.
48. Johnson and West, 1949: 290.
49. Cf. Poliak, 1939: 49.
50. Gibb and Bowen, 1950: 261.
51. Cf. Otto, PT, II: 243 ff.
52. See above, Chap. 4.
53. Legge, CC, I: *passim.*

8, D

1. See above, Chap. 7.
2. Cf. above, Chap. 2.
3. Wittfogel, 1931: 393 ff. *Ibid.,* 1938: 96 ff.
4. Meissner, BA, I: 180, 377. Mendelsohn, 1949: 66 ff.
5. Kees, 1933: 48, 130. Cf. Erman and Ranke, 1923: 144.
6. Westermann, 1937: 75.
7. Meyer, 1924, I: 190.
8. Mendelsohn, 1949: 121.
9. Wittfogel, 1931: 408 ff.

8, E

1. For this term see Wittfogel, 1949: 15.
2. Lowie, 1927: 42. Cf. MacLeod, 1924: 12, 39.
3. Lowie, 1927: 38.
4. See MacLeod, 1924: *passim*. Cf. Lowie, 1927: 33 ff.
5. Wittfogel and Fêng, 1949: 505 ff.
6. Wittfogel, 1949: 10 ff.

8, F

1. MEGA, I, Pt. 6: 534.
2. *Ch'ing Shih Kao,* 11.2a.
3. *Ibid.,* 11.4b.
4. *Yen T'ieh Lun,* I: 14a. Cf. Gale, 1931: 35.
5. *Peking Gazette,* 1898: 92.

8, G

1. Mavor, 1925, I: 306 ff.
2. Lyashchenko, 1949: 279.
3. *Ibid.:* 280. Cf. Mavor, 1925, I: 306, 310.
4. Wittfogel, 1924: 93. Cf. Lamprecht, DG, IV: 200 ff.

8, H

1. See above, Chap. 5. Cf. Gutmann, 1909: 111.
2. Cf. Erman and Ranke, 1923: 138; and Erman, 1923: 247.
3. Kees, 1933: 46.
4. For China see Wittfogel, 1931: 578 ff. For Mamluk Egypt see Poliak, 1934: 268.
5. For China see Wittfogel, 1931: 579, nn. 355 f.
6. Boulais, 1924: 184.
7. *Peking Gazette,* 1898: 43.
8. Nöldeke, 1892: 158, 162.
9. *Ibid.:* 155, 158.

8, I

1. See above, sec. C, n. 3.
2. *Huang-ch'ao Ching-shih Wên Hsü-p'ien.*
3. See above, sec. C, n. 3. Reference to *Ch'ing Shih Lu* (Chia-ch'ing), 55.18a–19a.
4. *Ibid.*
5. Boulais, 1924: 654 ff.
6. See Kulischer, AW, I: 280 ff.
7. "The Han Officials, a Statistical Study," MS prepared by the Chinese History Project. The basic data were collected by Mrs. Ch'ü Tseng-ch'iu and analyzed by Esther S. Goldfrank.
8. Helck, 1939: 14 ff.
9. *Ibid.:* 71 ff.
10. Wiet, 1937: 399.
11. See Kornemann, 1949: 257 ff.
12. Ostrogorsky, 1940: 225.
13. *Ibid.* Cf. Stein, 1951: 129.
14. Ostrogorsky, 1940: 241 (italics mine).
15. For the concept of powerful families see Wittfogel and Fêng, 1949: 285.
16. *Peking Gazette,* 1896: 60.
17. *Ibid.,* 1872: 4.
18. *Ibid.,* 1890: 55.

19. Mavor, 1925, I: 398.
20. *Ibid.:* 415.
21. *Ibid.*
22. *Ibid.:* 410 ff.
23. See Berle and Means, 1944: 94, 117, 121; and Gordon, 1945: 28, 49, 52, 108 ff., 272 ff., 301 ff.
24. Wittfogel and Fêng, 1949: 441.
25. *Ibid.:* 199 ff.
26. *Ibid.:* 416, n. 51.
27. *Han Shu*, 97A.21b–23a. *San Kuo Chih, Wei* 5.1a.
28. Lybyer, 1913: 58 and n. 2.
29. See above, Chap. 4.
30. *Tso Chuan Chu Shu*, 42.6a–b. *Shih Chi*, 68.9b.
31. Jones, 1831: 113.
32. See above, Chap. 3.
33. Cf. *Jātakam*, III: 369; and Fick, 1920: 173.
34. Dubois, 1943: 290. See above, Chap. 3.
35. Manu, 1886: 141.
36. *Ibid.:* 24.
37. Roys, 1943: 34.
38. Wittfogel, 1947: 24.
39. See Aristotle, *Politics* 4.15.1300b.
40. See MS "The Han Officials."
41. For this phrase see Wittfogel, 1949: 15 ff.
42. Wittfogel and Fêng, 1949: 454.
43. Wittfogel, 1947: 25 and nn. 57–61. Cf. Kracke, 1953: 70 and n. 61.
44. Wittfogel, 1947: 26.
45. *Ibid.:* 30 ff.
46. *Ibid.:* 32–8.
47. Wittfogel and Fêng, 1949: 463.
48. *Ibid.*
49. For a discussion of this edict see MS Chang, CG.
50. Kracke, 1947: 120.
51. See Olmstead, 1948: 90, 227, 267, 312, 314, and *passim*.
52. Herodotus 8.105. Xenophon 7.5.64.
53. Cf. Mez, 1922: 336.
54. *Hou Han Shu*, 78.6b–7a. For translation and comment see MS HCS, Ch'in-Han III (76).
55. See Wittfogel, 1935: 55, n. 2.
56. *Shih Chi*, 87.22b ff. Cf. Bodde, 1938: 52 ff.
57. *Hou Han Shu*, 78.2b.
58. *Han Shu*, 93.1a.
59. *Hou Han Shu*, 78.2b.
60. *Han Shu*, 93.4b.
61. *Hou Han Shu*, 78.3b.
62. *Ibid.*, 68.4a ff.
63. For this term see Wittfogel, 1949: 24.
64. *Ming Shih*, 304.21b–28a.
65. Hug, 1918: 451 f.
66. *Ibid.:* 452.
67. *Ibid.*
68. Ostrogorsky, 1940: 175.

69. Runciman, 1933: 204.
70. *Ibid.*
71. *Ibid.:* 203. Schubart, 1943: 27, 220.
72. Schubart, 1943: 206, 102. Mez, 1922: 335.
73. Runciman, 1933: 203 ff.
74. *Ibid.*
75. Amari, 1935: 301, 312. Mez, 1922: 335.
76. Runciman, 1933: 203.
77. Ostrogorsky, 1940: 175.
78. Runciman, 1933: 203.
79. Mez, 1922: 335.
80. For this term see Fischer, 1948: 634.
81. Mez, 1922: 332.
82. Wittfogel and Fêng, 1949: 529, 560 ff.
83. *Ibid.:* 569.
84. *Ibid.:* 464.
85. *Peking Gazette,* 1899: 82, 84 ff., 86, 87 f.
86. Stevenson, 1934: 188 ff. Charlesworth, 1934: 686. Momigliano, 1934: 727. Last, 1936: 426 ff., 432. Duff, 1936: 757 ff.
87. Miller, 1941: 14.
88. Ayalon, 1951: 16 ff., 27 ff., 29 ff., 31 ff., 34 ff.
89. Lybyer, 1913: 39, 117 ff. Miller, 1941: 70, 73.
90. Lybyer, 1913: 100 ff.
91. Miller, 1941: 71.
92. Machiavelli, 1940: 16 ff.
93. *Ibid.:* 16.
94. Lybyer, 1913: 69, 92, cf. 49.

9, A

1. Boas, 1937: 102.
2. *Ibid.,* 1928: 236.
3. See Arkell and Moy-Thomas, 1941: 397, 408. Mayr, 1942: 280 ff., 286, 289.

9, B

1. Smith, 1937: 645 ff., 687 ff., 789.
2. See Mill, 1820, I: 175 ff.
3. *Ibid.,* II: 175 ff.; cf. I: 182 ff., and II: 186. For other references to the nonfeudal conditions of India see II: 25 ff., 166 ff., 176, 189 ff., 202.
4. Jones, 1831: 7 ff., 109 ff.
5. Mill, 1909: 12 ff.
6. MEGA, I, Pt. 6: 630.
7. Mill, 1909: 20.
8. Jones, 1859: 447. Cf. *ibid.,* 1831: 111 ff.
9. Marx, NYDT, August 5, 1853.
10. Marx, 1921: lvi. *Ibid.,* DK, I: 45; III, Pt. 1: 318.
11. Marx, DK, III, Pt. 1: 318.
12. See Marx, DK, I: 42 ff.; III, Pt. 1: 310, 315, 317, n. 50; III, Pt. 2: 136, 174, 324. *Ibid.,* 1921, II: 482 ff.
13. For the above cited passages see Marx, NYDT, June 25, 1853.
14. Marx and Engels, 1920, I: 197.
15. Marx, NYDT, December 3, 1859.
16. Marx, DK, III, Pt. 1: 318 (italics mine).
17. Marx, NYDT, December 3, 1859.

18. MEGA, III, Pt. 1: 455, 459. See Marx and Engels, 1920, I: 475.
19. Marx and Engels, 1920, I: 160.
20. Marx, 1927: 333.
21. Engels, 1894: 56.
22. Engels, 1935: 165.
23. Marx, 1857: 227.
24. Marx, 1927: 144.
25. Marx, DK, III, Pt. 1: 315; III, Pt. 2: 136.
26. Marx and Engels, 1952: 225.
27. MEGA, III, Pt. 2: 487.
28. *Ibid.*
29. Marx, NYDT, August 5, 1853.
30. Marx, DK, III, Pt. 2: 324.
31. *Ibid.:* 174.
32. Marx, 1939: 376 ff.
33. *Ibid.:* 393.
34. *Ibid.:* 395.
35. *Ibid.:* 392 ff.
36. *Ibid.*, DK, I: 683 ff.
37. Lenin, S, I: 121.
38. *Ibid.*, III: 56.
39. *Ibid.:* 58.
40. *Ibid.*, IV: 351.
41. *Ibid.:* 390.
42. *Ibid.*, VI: 13.
43. *Ibid.*, IX: 43.
44. *Ibid.:* 33, 32.
45. *Ibid.*, XIII: 300 ff.
46. *Ibid.*, XVII: 31.
47. *Ibid.*, XVIII: 144.
48. *Ibid.:* 145.
49. *Ibid.*, XX: 375.
50. *Ibid.*, XXI: 40.
51. *Ibid.*, II: 312; XIII: 300 ff.
52. Marx, 1857: 218.
53. Lenin, S, V: 345.
54. *Ibid.*, VI: 28.
55. *Ibid.*, IX: 114.
56. *Ibid.*, XVII: 118 (italics mine).

9, c

1. Marx, DK, I: 104; III, Pt. 1: 316; III, Pt. 2: 237. *Ibid.*, TMW, I: 371; III: 452 ff.,
479 ff.
2. MEGA, III, Pt. 1: 133.
3. Mill, 1909: 12 ff.
4. Marx, TMW, III: 501. For the original version see Jones, 1859: 448 ff.
5. MEGA, I: 476 ff. See Bernier, 1891: 220, 381, cf. 204 ff., 205 ff., 213 ff.
6. See Marx, DK, I: 45 ff.; III, Pt. 1: 316 f.; III, Pt. 2: 136, 157, 174, 323 ff., 337, 367.
Ibid., TMW, I: 397; II, Pt. 1: 205; III: 451, 452 ff., 473 ff., 479 ff., 482 ff., 495 ff.,
497, 498 ff.
7. Marx, DK, I: 478.
8. *Ibid.*

9. Marx, NYDT, June 25, 1853.
10. *Ibid.*
11. *Ibid.* Cf. Marx, 1939: 337.
12. Marx, DK, III, Pt. 1: 370 (italics mine).
13. Engels, 1935: 183.
14. *Ibid.*
15. Engels, 1935: 183. *Ibid.*, 1921: 185.
16. Marx, DK, III, Pt. 2: 259 ff.
17. Engels, 1935: 183.
18. Marx, 1939: 378.
19. *Ibid.:* 391.
20. Engels, 1935: 164, 185.
21. *Ibid.:* 183.
22. *Ibid.*
23. *Ibid.*
24. *Ibid.:* 184.
25. *Ibid.:* 291.
26. See above, Chap. 8, sec. A, n. *a.*
27. Engels, 1935: 183.
28. *Ibid.:* 291.
29. Engels, 1921: *passim.*
30. Morgan, 1877: 372 ff.
31. Engels, 1921: 132.
32. *Ibid.:* 165 f., 44 ff.
33. *Ibid.:* 185. Cf. Engels, 1935: 184 ff., 395.
34. Engels, 1921: 167 (italics mine).
35. *Ibid.:* 180.
36. *Ibid.*
37. *Ibid.:* 181.
38. *Ibid.:* 331 (italics mine).
39. Marx, TMW, II, Pt. 1: 310.
40. *Ibid.*
41. *Ibid.*, II, Pt. 1: 313.
42. *Ibid.*
43. *Ibid.*
44. MEGA, I, Pt. 6: 545.
45. Mill, 1909: 949.
46. *Ibid.:* 961.
47. MEGA, III, Pt. 3: 217, 224, 302, 341.
48. Guillaume, IDS, I: 78 ff. Bakunin, 1953: *passim.*
49. Bakunin, 1953: 288.
50. *Ibid.:* 287.
51. Guillaume, IDS, II: 192.
52. Cf. Wittfogel, 1953: 358, n. 34.
53. See Engels and Kautsky, 1935: 306, 310, 313 ff.
54. MEGA, I, Pt. 6: 554.
55. *Ibid.*
56. *Ibid.:* 555.
57. Cf. Mill, 1909: 208.
58. See above, p. 180.
59. Lenin, S, III: 126.
60. *Ibid.*, V: 271, 275 f.

61. *Ibid.,* VI: 334.
62. *Ibid.,* I: 272, n. 2.
63. *Ibid.,* IV: 350.
64. *Ibid.,* II: 103–4; VI: 333, 343.
65. *Ibid.,* XIV: *passim.*
66. *Ibid.,* X: 27 ff.
67. See below, p. 396.
68. *Protokoly:* 116.
69. Lenin, S, X: 303.
70. *Ibid.,* XIII: 300.
71. *Ibid.*
72. *Ibid.,* XIII: 301.
73. *Ibid.:* 302.
74. *Ibid.:* 303.
75. Plekhanov, 1906: 12 ff. *Protokoly:* 44.
76. Plekhanov, 1906: 16.
77. *Ibid.:* 14.
78. *Ibid.:* 17 (italics mine).
79. *Protokoly:* 45.
80. *Ibid.:* 116.
81. Lenin, S, XIII: 300.
82. *Ibid.,* XIII: 302.
83. *Ibid.:* 301.
84. *Protokoly:* 103 ff. See also Lenin, S, XIII: 299.
85. *Protokoly:* 45.
86. Lenin, S, X: 303.
87. *Ibid.,* XIII: 301, 387.
88. Lenin, 1937: 288.
89. See above, sec. B, nn. 47, 48.
90. See above, sec. B, n. 49.
91. Lenin, S, XXI: 17.
92. *Ibid.:* 17 ff., 78 ff., 257, 336.
93. *Ibid.,* XXII: 226.
94. *Ibid.,* XXV: 357 ff.
95. *Ibid.:* 358 ff.
96. *Ibid.,* XXIX: 436. Cf. *ibid.,* SW, XI: 642.
97. Lenin, S, XXIX: 438 (italics mine).
98. *Ibid.:* 438 ff.
99. *Ibid.,* XXV: 362.
100. *Ibid.,* XXIX: 445.
101. *Ibid.,* XXVIII: 401.
102. *Ibid.,* XXXII: 329 (italics mine).
103. See MEGA, III, Pt. 1: 487; Marx, DK, I: 323; and Marx and Engels, 1952: 211 ff.
104. See above, sec. B, n. 49.
105. Lenin, S, XXXII: 330 (italics mine).
106. *Ibid.,* XXXIII: 423.
107. *Ibid.:* 430.
108. *Ibid.:* 445.
109. Rjasanoff, 1925: 374 ff.
110. *Inprecor,* 1925: 1280 ff.
111. Varga, 1928: 19 ff.
112. *Problemy Kitaia* (Moscow), Nos. 4–5, 1930: 223.

113. See below, p. 407.
114. DASP: 2 ff., 14 ff., 66 ff.
115. *Ibid.*: 72, 181.
116. *Ibid.*: 182.
117. *Ibid.*: 5, 62.
118. *Ibid.*: 20, 24.
119. *Ibid.*: 74.
120. *Ibid.*: 3.
121. See *Inprecor*, 1928: 1249, 1254.
122. Stalin, S, II: 337 f.
123. See Wolfe, 1948: 582 ff.
124. Stalin, S, II: 118, 124 f., 128.
125. *Ibid.*, I: 237 ff.
126. *Ibid.*: 311.
127. *Ibid.*, VIII: 359.
128. *Ibid.*, IX: 240 ff., 285 ff., 290, 336 ff.
129. *Ibid.*: 240.
130. *Ibid.*: 241.
131. Stalin, 1939: 131.
132. Childe, 1946 [originally 1942]: 76, 161, 203, 223, 272, and *passim*.
133. *Ibid.*: 18 ff. (italics mine).
134. Childe, 1944: 23.
135. Childe, 1951: 35.
136. Childe, 1953: 72 (italics mine).
137. Guber, 1942: 275, 279.
138. Tolstov, 1950: 3.

10, A

1. Mill, 1909: 10–20.
2. Brew, 1946: 44 ff.
3. Willey, 1953a: 378 ff.
4. Huxley, 1955: 9 ff., 15, 21.
5. Mill, 1947: 959.
6. For this term see Westermann, 1937: 76, 13.
7. For this term see Veblen, 1947: 133.
8. Piggott, 1950: 263 ff.
9. Westermann, 1937: 75 ff.
10. *Ibid.*: 76.
11. Arkell and Moy-Thomas, 1941: 408.
12. Mayr, 1942: 5.
13. *Ibid.*
14. See Kroeber, 1948: 261.
15. See above, Chap. 1.
16. See Wipper, 1947: 39, 81.

10, B

1. See Wittfogel, 1935: 52.
2. Mill, 1909: 696 ff., 701. Cf. Smith, 1937: 736.
3. Mill, 1909: 697, 701.
4. *Ibid.*: xlvii, 699–701.
5. Marx, NYDT, August 8, 1853.
6. *Ibid.*
7. *Ibid.*

8. Marx and Engels, 1952: 217.
9. Marx, NYDT, June 25, 1853.
10. *Ibid.*, DK, III, Pt. 1: 318.
11. Furnivall, 1944: 148. Vandenbosch, 1949: 81.
12. Altamira, 1930: 168 ff.
13. See above, p. 166.
14. See above, Chap. 6.
15. Florinsky, 1953, II: 900.
16. *Ibid.:* 1067, 1081 ff.
17. Prokopowitsch, 1913: 52 ff.
18. Tugan-Baranowsky, 1900: 70 ff., 76 ff., 85 ff.
19. Prokopowitsch, 1913: 58. Cf. Lyashchenko, 1949: 716.
20. *Ibid.*
21. *Ibid.:* 703.
22. Zagorsky, 1928: 7.
23. *Ibid.:* 8.
24. *Ibid.*
25. *Ibid.:* 6.
26. Weber, 1906: 324, cf. 398.
27. Florinsky, 1953, II: 1238. Wolfe, 1948: 564.
28. Kayden, 1929: 14.
29. Florinsky, 1953, II: 1228.
30. Furnivall, 1944: 252.
31. Kahin, 1952: 35.
32. *Imperial Gazetteer of India,* II: 514.
33. Appleby, 1953: 51.
34. Schuster and Wint, 1941: 72.
35. Furnivall, 1944: 43.
36. Kahin, 1952: 471, cf. 29 ff.
37. Nehru, 1946: 283 ff.
38. *Ibid.:* 332 ff., 415 ff., cf. 420 ff.
39. See above, Chap. 7.
40. *Agriculture in India:* 35.
41. Warriner, 1948: 15, 85 ff. Bonné, 1948: 188.
42. Jäckh, 1944: 78 ff.
43. See *ibid.:* 187, 191; Thornburg, Spry, and Soule, 1949: 180, 199: and Bismarck-Osten, 1951: 9.
44. Cooke, 1952: 283.
45. See Taylor, 1936: 13.
46. *Ibid.,* 1942: 132.
47. Chamberlin, 1935, I: 248 ff.
48. Lenin, S, XXIV: 4.
49. *Ibid.,* XXX: 237.
50. *Ibid.:* 230 ff.
51. Chamberlin, 1935, I: 281.
52. See *ibid.:* 229.
53. *Ibid.:* 159.
54. *Ibid.:* 249 ff.
55. See Lenin, S, XXVI: 227 ff.
56. *Ibid.,* XXIV: 4.
57. *Ibid.,* XXV: 20.
58. *Ibid.,* XXIV: 5.

59. Chamberlin, 1935, I: 266 ff.
60. Lenin, S, XXV: 267.
61. *Ibid.*, XXVI: 228.
62. See *ibid.*, XX: 375. For Marx' and Engels' basic statements see above; Chap. 9, see B, nn. 20 ff.
63. Lenin, SWG, XXII: 646 ff.
64. *Ibid.*, S, XXXIII: 258.
65. *Ibid.*, XXIII: 229.
66. Baykov, 1947: 8.
67. Lenin, S, XXXIII: 43.
68. *Ibid.*: 423, 430.
69. Marx, 1939: 395.
70. See Mao, 1954: 64, 122, 172, 188, 267, 269–71, 278, cf. 105 ff., 189, 196. *Ibid.*, 1945: 35. *Ibid.*, 1945a: 58.
71. See Wittfogel, 1950: 335.

10, C

1. See *Inprecor*, 1927: 292, 328, 330 ff.; 1942: 123 ff. Cf. Nehru, 1942a: 123 ff.
2. See Wittfogel, 1951: 33.
3. See Jäckh, 1944: 191.
4. Nehru, 1946: 19.
5. See *Socialist Asia*, II, No. 10: 2; III, No. 2: 10; III, No. 3: 5; III, No. 8: 17; Rangoon Tracts, I: 5, 7 ff., 11, 13, 16, 20 ff. See also Mehta, 1954: 40, 59, 149, 152 ff., 165. For statements made by Nehru about India's "feudal" heritage see Nehru, 1946: 284, 307, 319, 320 ff., 324 ff., 334, 352 ff.
6. See Mehta, 1954: 43 ff.
7. Luxemburg, 1951: 604 ff.
8. Rangoon Tracts, I: 5.
9. *Ibid.*, I: 4.
10. See *ibid.*, I: 8, 9.
11. Nehru, 1942: 597.
12. *Ibid.*, 1946: 376.
13. *Hindu Weekly Review* (Madras), November 1, 1954.
14. *Socialist Asia*, III, No. 4: 3, 4.
15. See Wittfogel, 1955a: *passim*.

BIBLIOGRAPHY

THE TITLES LISTED BELOW refer to books and articles cited in this study. In our notes these works are cited by the author's name and date of publication. However, those of more than one volume whose publication was spread over several years (e.g. Meissner, BA) and articles published serially over several years (e.g. Bandelier, DH) are designated by author and title initials. Abbreviations appearing in the notes without an author's name (e.g. RDS) should be found in proper alphabetical position in the list. Titles of collections or periodicals which appear more than twice in the list are cited by the following symbols:

AA   *American Anthropologist.*

ANET   *Ancient Near Eastern Texts, Relating to the Old Testament,* ed. James B. Pritchard. Princeton, 1950.

ASS   *Archiv für Sozialwissenschaft und Sozialpolitik.*

BCPP   *Biblioteca de Cultura Peruana-Premera,* Ser. 2, *Los Cronistas de la Conquista,* ed. Horacio H. Urtega. Paris, 1938.

CAH   *The Cambridge Ancient History,* ed. S. A. Cook, F. E. Adcock, and M. P. Charlesworth. 12 vols. Cambridge, 1923–39.

CEHE   *The Cambridge Economic History of Europe from the Decline of the Roman Empire,* ed. J. H. Clapham and Eileen Power. 2 vols. Cambridge, 1942–52.

CHI   *The Cambridge History of India,* ed. E. J. Rapson. Vols. 1, 3, 4. New York and Cambridge, 1922–37.

CIW   Carnegie Institution of Washington Publications.

CMH   *The Cambridge Medieval History,* planned by J. B. Bury, ed. by H. M. Gwatkin and J. P. Whitney. 8 vols. Cambridge, 1913–36.

ESAR   *An Economic Survey of Ancient Rome,* ed. Tenney Frank in collaboration with T. R. S. Broughton, R. G. Collingwood, A. Grenier, and others. 5 vols. Baltimore, 1933–40.

ESS   *Encyclopaedia of the Social Sciences,* ed. Edwin R. A. Seligman and Alvin Johnson. 15 vols. New York, 1937.

HWI   *Handwörterbuch des Islam,* ed. A. J. Wensinck and J. H. Kramers. Leiden, 1941.

HZ   *Historische Zeitschrift.*

IC   *Islamic Culture.*

JNES   *Journal of Near Eastern Studies.*

NZ   *Die Neue Zeit.*

OCRAA   *Orientalia commentarii de rebus Assyro-Babylonicis, Arabicis, Aegyptiacis,* etc.

PMAAE   Peabody Museum of American Archaeology and Ethnology, Harvard University.

PM   Dr. A. Petermanns Mitteilungen aus Justus Perthes Geographischer Anstalt.

RA   Reallexikon der Assyriologie, ed. Erich Ebeling and Bruno Meissner. 2 vols. Berlin and Leipzig, 1932–38.

SBE   Sacred Books of the East, ed. F. Max Müller. 50 vols. Oxford and New York, 1879–1910.

SIBAE   Smithsonian Institution, Bureau of American Ethnology Publications.

UBM   Unter dem Banner des Marxismus.

Acosta, Fray Joseph de. 1894. Historia natural y moral de las Indias, published in Seville, 1590. 2 vols. Madrid.

Acosta Saignes, Miguel. 1945. Los Pochteca. Acta Anthropologica, I, No. 1. Mexico City.

Acton, John Emerich Edward Dalberg-. 1948. Essays on Freedom and Power. Boston.

Agrarian China. Selected Source Materials from Chinese Authors, comp. and trans. by the Institute of Pacific Relations, with an introduction by R. H. Tawney. Chicago (preface dated 1938).

Agriculture in India. The Publications Division, Ministry of Information and Broadcasting, Government of India, Delhi. April 1950.

Aitken, Barbara. 1930. "Temperament in Native American Religions," Journal of the Royal Anthropological Institute of Great Britain and Ireland, LX: 363–400.

Alexander, W. D. 1899. Brief History of the Hawaiian People. New York, Cincinnati, and Chicago.

Altamira, Rafael. 1930. A History of Spanish Civilization, trans. P. Volkov. London.

Amari, Michele. 1935. Storia dei Musulmani di Sicilia, II. 2nd ed. Catania.

Amerasia. A review of America and Asia. 1938–47.

Ammianus Marcellinus. Ammiani Marcellini rerum gestarum libri qui supersunt, ed. V. Gardthausen. 2 vols. Leipzig, 1874–75.

Anhegger, Robert. 1943. Beitraege zur Geschichte des Bergbaus im osmanischen Reich, I. Istanbul.

Âpastamba. 1898. In Sacred Laws of the Âryas, trans. Georg Bühler. SBE, II. New York.

Appadorai, A. 1936. Economic Conditions in Southern India (1000–1500 A.D.). 2 vols. Madras University Historical Series, 12 and 12-bis. Madras.

Appleby, Paul H. 1953. "Report of a Survey," Public Administration in India. Cabinet Secretariat. New Delhi.

Aristotle. "Politics," in *Basic Works of Aristotle,* ed. Richard McKeon: 1114–1316. New York, 1941.

—— "Rhetoric," in *Basic Works of Aristotle:* 1317–1451.

Arkell, W. J. and Moy-Thomas, J. A. 1941. "Palaeontology and the Taxonomic Problem," in *The New Systematics,* ed. Julian Huxley: 395–410. London.

Armillas, Pedro. 1944. "Revista Mexicana de estudios anthropologicos," in *Sociedad Mexicana de Anthropologia,* VI, No. 3, September 1942–December 1944. Mexico City.

—— 1948. "A Sequence of Cultural Development in Meso-America," in *A Reappraisal of Peruvian Archaeology,* assembled by Wendell C. Bennett. Society of American Archaeology, *Memoirs,* IV: 105–11. April 1948.

—— 1951. "Tecnología, formaciones socio-económicas y religión en Mesoamérica," *Selected Papers of the XXIXth International Congress of Americanists:* 19–30. Chicago.

Arnold, Thomas W. 1924. *The Caliphate.* Oxford.

—— 1941. "*Khalīfa*," HWI: 291–296. Leiden.

Arrian. *The Anabasis of Alexander* in *The Greek Historians,* trans. Edward J. Chinnock, II: 402–620. New York, 1942.

Arthaçāstra. 1926. *Das altindische Buch vom Welt- und Staatsleben des Arthaçāstra des Kauṭilya,* trans. Johann Jakob Meyer. Leipzig.

Arthaśāstra. 1923. *Kauṭilya's Arthaśāstra,* trans. R. Shamasastry. 2d ed. Mysore.

Asakawa, Kanichi. 1903. *The Early Institutional Life of Japan. A Study in the Reform of 645 A.D.* Tokyo.

—— 1911. "Notes on Village Government in Japan after 1600, II," *Journal of the American Oriental Society,* XXI: 151–216.

—— 1929. *The Documents of Iriki,* Yale Historical Publications, X. New Haven.

—— 1929a. "The Early *Sho* and the Early Manor: a Comparative Study," *Journal of Economic Business History,* I, No. 2: 177–207.

ASBRT. *Report of Court Proceedings in the Case of the Anti-Soviet "Bloc of Rights and Trotskyites,"* heard before the Military Collegium of the Supreme Court of the USSR, Moscow, March 2–13, 1938, *in re* N. I. Bukharin etc. Moscow, 1938.

Atiya, Aziz Suryal. 1934. *The Crusade of Nicopolis.* London.

Atkinson, Charles Francis. 1910. "Army," *Encyclopaedia Britannica,* II: 592–625. 11th ed. New York.

Ayalon, David. 1951. *L'Esclavage du Mamelouk.* Israel Oriental Society Publications, No. 1. Jerusalem.

Bābur. 1921. *Memoirs of Zehīr-ed-Dīn Muhammed Bābur,* II, trans. John Leyden and William Erskine, annotated and revised by Sir Lucas King. London, etc.

Baden-Powell, B. H. 1892. *The Land-Systems of British India.* 3 vols. London and New York.

—— 1896. *The Indian Village Community.* London, New York, and Bombay.

Bakunin. 1953. *The Political Philosophy of Bakunin: Scientific Anarchism,* comp. and ed. G. P. Maximoff. Glencoe, Ill.

Balázs, Stefan. BWT. "Beiträge zur Wirtschaftsgeschichte der T'ang-Zeit (618–906)," *Mitteilungen des Seminars für orientalische Sprachen,* XXXIV: 1–92; XXXV: 1–73; XXXVI: 1–62. 1931–33.

Bandelier, Adolph E. DH. "Documentary History of the Rio Grande Pueblos, New Mexico," *New Mexico Historical Review,* IV: 303–34; V: 38–66, 154–85. 1929, 1930.

—— FR. *Final Report of Investigations among the Indians of the Southwestern United States, Carried on Mainly in the Years from 1880 to 1885,* Archaeological Institute of America, American Series, *Papers,* III, 1890; IV, 1892. Cambridge, Mass.

—— 1877. "On the Art of War and Mode of Warfare of the Ancient Mexicans," PMAAE, *Reports,* II: 95–161. Cambridge, Mass.

—— 1878. "On the Distribution and Tenure of Lands, and the Customs with Respect to Inheritance, among the Ancient Mexicans," PMAAE, *Reports,* II, No. 2: 385–448. Cambridge, Mass.

—— 1880. "On the Social Organization and Mode of Government of the Ancient Mexicans," PMAAE, *Reports,* II: 557–699. Cambridge, Mass.

Banerjee (Narayan Chandra Bandyopadhyaya). 1925. *Hindu Period.* Vol. I of *Economic Life and Progress in Ancient India.* Calcutta.

Barton, George A. 1929. *The Royal Inscriptions of Sumer and Akkad.* New Haven and London.

Baudhāyana. 1898. In *Sacred Laws of the Āryas,* trans. Georg Bühler. SBE, II: 143–336. New York.

Bauer, Adolf. 1893. "Die griechischen Kriegsaltertümer," in *Die griechischen Privat- und Kriegsaltertümer* by Iwan von Müller and Adolf Bauer: 270–469. Munich.

Baykov, Alexander. 1947. *The Development of the Soviet Economic System.* Cambridge and New York.

Beaglehole, Ernest. 1937. *Notes on Hopi Economic Life.* Yale University Publications in Anthropology, XV.

Beal, Samuel. *Si-yu-ki. Buddhist Records of the Western World.* 2 vols. in one, London, no date.

Beard, Charles A. 1941. *An Economic Interpretation of the Constitution of the United States.* New York.

Beard, Charles A. and Mary R. 1927. *The Rise of American Civilization.* 2 vols. New York.

Beck, F. and Godin, W. 1951. *Russian Purge and the Extraction of Confession.* New York.

Becker, Carl H. IS. *Islamstudien.* 2 vols. Leipzig, 1924–32.

———— 1903. *Beiträge zur Geschichte Ägyptens unter dem Islam,* II. Strassburg.

Beech, Merwyn W. H. 1911. *The Suk, Their Language and Folklore.* Oxford.

Bell, Sir Charles. 1927. *Tibet Past and Present.* London.

Bell, H. Idris. 1948. *Egypt from Alexander the Great to the Arab Conquest.* Oxford.

Bengtson, Hermann. 1950. *Griechische Geschichte.* Munich.

Berger, Adolph. 1950. "Emphyteusis," *Oxford Classical Dictionary:* 314. Oxford.

Berle, Adolf A., Jr., and Means, Gardiner C. 1944. *The Modern Corporation and Private Property.* New York.

Bernier, François. 1891. *Travels in the Mogul Empire* A.D. *1656–1668.* Rev. ed. based upon Irving Brock's trans., by Archibald Constable: *Constable's Oriental Miscellany, I: Bernier's Travels.* Westminster.

Bhagavadgītā. 1900. Trans. Kāshināth Trimbak Telang. SBE, VIII. New York.

Bikerman, E. 1938. *Institutions des Seleucides.* Paris.

Biot, Edouard. 1851. *Le Tcheou-Li ou Rites des Tcheou.* 2 vols. Paris.

Birkett, G. A. 1918. "From 1801 to 1917," in *Russia from the Varangians to the Bolsheviks,* by Raymond Beazley, Nevill Forbes, and (introduction by) Ernest Barker: 347–557. Oxford.

Bismarck-Osten, Ferdinand von. 1951. *Strukturwandlungen und Nachkriegsprobleme der türkischen Volkswirtschaft.* Kieler Studien, XVI. Kiel.

Björkman, Walther. 1928. *Beiträge zur Geschichte der Staatskanzlei im islamischen Ägypten.* Abhandlungen aus dem Gebiet der Auslandskunde, 28. Hamburg University.

———— 1941. "Turban," *HWI:* 754–8. Leiden.

Blackman, William Fremont. 1899. *The Making of Hawaii.* New York and London.

Bloch, Marc. 1937. "Feudalism: European," *ESS,* V: 203–10. New York.

———— 1949. *La Société féodale.* Paris.

Blom, F. and LaFarge, O. TT. *Tribes and Temples.* 2 vols. New Orleans, 1926–27.

Boas, Franz. 1928. *Anthropology and Modern Life.* New York.

———— 1937. "Anthropology," *ESS,* II: 73–110. New York.

———— 1938. "Mythology and Folklore," in *General Anthropology,* ed. Boas: 609–26. Boston and New York.

Bodde, Derk. 1938. *China's First Unifier*. Leiden.

Bonné, Alfred. 1948. *State and Economics in the Middle East*. London.

Borosdin, J. 1908. "Eine neue Arbeit über den Feudalismus in Russland," review of N. Pawlow-Silwansky, *Der Feudalismus im alten Russland*, in *Vierteljahrschrift für Social- und Wirtschaftsgeschichte*, VI: 572–8.

Boulais, Guy. 1924. *Manuel du Code Chinois*. Shanghai.

Brandt (Conrad), Schwartz (Benjamin), and Fairbank (John K.). 1952. *A Documentary History of Chinese Communism*. Cambridge, Mass.

Breasted, James Henry. 1927. *Ancient Records of Egypt*. 5 vols. Chicago.

Bréhier, Louis. 1949. *Les Institutions de l'Empire Byzantin. L'Evolution de l'humanité*. Paris.

—— 1950. *La Civilisation Byzantine. L'Evolution de l'humanité*. Paris.

Brew, John Otis. 1946. *Archaeology of Alkali Ridge, Southeastern Utah*. PMAAE, *Reports*, XXI. Cambridge, Mass.

Broughton, T. R. S. 1938. "Roman Asia," in *ESAR*, IV: 499–916. Baltimore.

Brown, Delmer M. 1948. "The Impact of Firearms on Japanese Warfare, 1543–98," *Far Eastern Quarterly*, VII, No. 3: 236–53.

Brückner, A. 1896. *Geschichte Russlands bis zum Ende des 18. Jahrhunderts*. Gotha.

Brunner, H. 1905. "Antworten: Germanisch," in Mommsen, 1905: 53–62. Leipzig.

Bücher, Karl. 1922. *Die Entstehung der Volkswirtschaft*. 2 vols. Tübingen.

Büchner, V. F. 1941. *"Madjūs," HWI*: 378–82. Leiden.

Buck, John Lossing. 1937. *Land Utilization in China*. Chicago.

Buckley, Robert Burton. 1893. *Irrigation Works in India and Egypt*. London and New York.

Buddhist Suttas. Trans. T. W. Rhys-Davids, SBE, VII, Pt. 2. New York, 1900.

Buhl, Frants. 1930. *Das Leben Muhammeds*, trans. Hans Heinrich Schaeder. Leipzig.

Bühler, Johannes. 1948. *Die Kultur des Mittelalters*. Stuttgart.

Bukharin, Nikolai. 1934. *Historical Materialism*. New York.

Burnouf, E. 1876. *Introduction à l'histoire du Buddhisme Indien*. 2d ed. Paris.

Bury, J. B. 1910. *The Constitution of the Later Roman Empire*. Cambridge.

—— 1931. *History of the Later Roman Empire*. 2 vols. London.

—— 1937. *A History of Greece to the Death of Alexander the Great*. Modern Library. New York.

Busolt, George. GS. *Griechische Staatskunde: Handbuch der klassischen Altertums-Wissenschaft*, ed. Iwan von Müller (Vol. I) and Walter Müller (Vol. II). Munich, 1920, 1926.

Cahen, Claude. 1940. *La Syrie du Nord à l'époque des croisades,* Institut Français de Damas Bibliothèque Orientale, I. Paris.

Casares, David. 1907. "A Notice of Yucatan with some Remarks on its Water Supply," *Proceedings of the American Antiquarian Society,* new ser., XVII: 207–30.

Castañeda. 1896. "Translation of Narrative of Castañeda" in George Parker Winship, "Coronado Expedition 1540–1542," SIBAE, *Fourteenth Annual Report,* Pt. 1: 470–546. Washington.

Chamberlin, William Henry. 1935. *The Russian Revolution 1917–1921.* 2 vols. New York.

Chan-kuo Ts'ê. Commercial Press, Shanghai, 1934.

Chang Chung-li. GI. "Gentry Income." MS.

——— CG. *The Chinese Gentry. Studies on Their Role in Nineteenth-Century Chinese Society.* Introduction by Franz Michael. University of Washington Press, Seattle. 1955. (This book was cited from the manuscript.)

Charlesworth, M. P. 1934. "The Triumph of Octavian, Parts II and III" and "Gaius and Claudius," CAH, X: 116–26 and 653–701. Cambridge.

Chavannes, Edouard. MH. *Les Mémoires historiques de Se-ma Ts'ien.* 5 vols. Paris, 1895–1905.

Chi Ch'ao-ting. 1936. *Key Economic Areas in Chinese History.* London.

Childe, V. Gordon. 1944. "Archaeological Ages as Technological Stages," *Journal of the Royal Anthropological Institute of Great Britain and Ireland,* LXXIV: 7–24.

——— 1946. *What Happened in History.* Penguin Books, New York (Published originally in 1942).

——— 1951. *Social Evolution.* London.

——— 1952. *Man Makes Himself.* Mentor Book, New York (published originally in 1936).

——— 1953. *What Is History?* Schuman's College Paperbacks, New York.

Chimalpahin Quauhtlehuanitzin. *Annales de Domingo Francisco de San Anton Muñon Chimalpahin Quauhtlehuanitzin,* trans. Remi Simeon, Bibliothèque Linguistique Américaine, XII. Paris, 1889.

Chimalpópoca, Códice. Anales de Cuauhtitlan y leyenda de los soles, trans. Primo Feliciano Velazquez. Publicaciones del Instituto de Historia, Ser. 1, No. 1. Mexico, 1945.

Chin Shih. Po-na ed. Commercial Press.

Chin Shih Ts'ui Pien, by Wang Ch'ang. *Ching-hsün t'ang* edition, 1805.

Ch'ing Shih Kao. Published by Ch'ing Shih Kuan.

Chiu T'ang Shu. Po-na ed. Commercial Press.

Chou Li Chu Shu. Ssŭ-pu Pei-yao. Shanghai, 1936.

Christensen, Arthur. 1933. "Die Iranier," in *Kulturgeschichte des alten Orients,* by A. Alt, A. Christensen, A. Götze, A. Grohmann, H. Kees, and B. Landsberger. Vol. III, Pt. 1: 203–310. Munich.

———— 1944. *L'Iran sous les Sassanides.* 2d ed. Copenhagen.

Ch'ü T'ung-tsu. 1937. *Chung-kuo Fêng-chien Shih-hui.* Commercial Press, Shanghai.

———— 1947. *Chung-kuo Fa-lü Yü Chung-kuo Shih-hui.* Commercial Press, Shanghai.

Ch'üan Han-shêng. 1934. *Chung-kuo Hang-hui Chih-tu Shih.* Hsin-shêng-ming, Shanghai.

Cieza de León, Pedro. 1943. *Del Señorío de los Incas,* prologue and notes by Alberto Mario Salas. Buenos Aires.

———— 1945. *La Crónica del Perú.* Buenos Aires and Mexico.

Clark, John Maurice. 1937. "Diminishing Returns," *ESS,* V: 144–6. New York.

CM. *Climate and Man.* Yearbook of Agriculture, Washington, D.C. 1941.

Cobo, Bernabé. *HNM. Historia del Nuevo Mundo . . .* ed. Marcos Jiménez de la Espada. Sociedad de Bibliófilos Andaluces. 4 vols. Seville, 1890–95.

Cole, Charles Woolsey. 1939. *Colbert and a Century of French Mercantilism.* 2 vols. New York.

Collingwood, R. G. 1937. "Roman Britain," in *ESAR,* III: 1–118. Baltimore.

Contenau, Georges. 1950. *La Vie quotidienne à Babylone et en Assyrie.* Paris.

Cook, James. 1944. *Captain Cook's Voyages of Discovery,* ed. John Barrow. Everyman's Library, London and New York.

Cooke, C. Wythe. 1931. "Why the Mayan Cities of the Péten district, Guatemala, Were Abandoned," *Journal of Washington Academy of Science,* XXI: 283–7.

Cooke, Hedley V. 1952. *Challenge and Response in the Middle East.* New York.

Cortes, Don Pascual de Gayangos. 1866. *Cartas y relaciónes de Hernán Cortés al Emperador Carlos V.* Paris.

CPLNC. "La Conquista del Perú llanda la nueva Castilla," in *BCPP:* 307–28. Paris, 1938.

Creel, H. G. 1949. *Confucius, the Man and the Myth.* New York.

Crevenna, Theodore T. *MECM. Materiales para el estudio de la clase media en la America Latina.* 6 vols. Washington, D.C., 1950–51.

Cromer, Earl of. 1908. *Modern Egypt.* 2 vols. London.

Crum, W. E. 1925. "Koptische Zünfte und das Pfeffermonopol," *Zeit-*

schrift für ägyptische Sprache und Altertumskunde, LXX: 103–11.

Cuq, Edouard. 1929. *Etudes sur le droit Babylonien. Les Lois Assyriennes et les lois Hittites.* Paris.

Daghestani, Kazem. FM. *La Famille Musulmane contemporaine en Syrie.* Paris, no date.

Das, Sarat Chandra. 1904. *Journey to Lhasa and Central Tibet.* New York.

DASP. 1931. *Diskussia ob Aziatskom Sposobe Proizvodstva* (Discussion of the Asiatic Mode of Production). Moscow and Leningrad.

DCF. *Die chinesische Frage. Auf dem 8. Plenum der Exekutive der Kommunistischen Internationale Mai 1927.* Hamburg and Berlin, 1928.

De Groot, J. J. M. 1918. *Universimus.* Berlin.

—— 1940. *Sectarianism and Religious Persecution in China.* 2 vols. Reprint.

Deimel, Anton. 1920. "Die Reformtexte Urukaginas," *OCRAA,* No. 2: 3–31.

—— 1922. "Die Bewirtschaftung des Tempellandes zur Zeit Urukaginas," *OCRAA,* No. 5: 1–25.

—— 1924. *Wirtschaftstexte aus Fara.* Leipzig.

—— 1924a. "Die Vermessung der Felder bei den Šumerern um 3000 v. Chr . . . " *OCRAA,* No. 4:1–55.

—— 1924b. "Die Verarbeitung des Getreides," *OCRAA,* No. 14: 1–26.

—— 1927. "Listen über das Betriebspersonal des *é^d Ba-ú* (Konscriptionslisten)," *OCRAA,* No. 26: 29–62.

—— 1928. "Die Lohnlisten aus der Zeit Urukaginas und seines Vorgängers: I sě-ba-Texte d. h. Gerste-Lohn-Listen . . ." *OCRAA,* No. 5, 34–35: 1–129.

—— 1929. "Die Lohnlisten aus der Zeit Urukaginas und seines Vorgängers (Fortsetzung)," *OCRAA,* Nos. 43–44.

—— 1931. "Šumerische Tempelwirtschaft zur Zeit Urukaginas und seiner Vorgänger," Analecta Orientalia, No. 2.

—— 1932. "Beamter," *RA,* I: 441–4. Berlin and Leipzig.

Delbrück, Hans. GK. *Geschichte der Kriegskunst im Rahmen der politischen Geschichte.* 5 vols. Berlin, 1900–27.

Díaz del Castillo, Bernal. 1944. *Historia verdadera de la conquista de la Nueva España,* with introduction and notes by Joaquin Ramirez Cahanas. 3 vols. Mexico.

Díaz de Gámez. 1949. "The Chivalric Ideal," in *The Portable Medieval Reader,* ed. James Bruce Ross and Mary Martin McLaughlin. New York.

Diehl, Charles. 1936. "The Government and Administration of the Byzantine Empire," *CMH,* IV: 726–44. Cambridge.

Diodorus. *Diodorus of Sicily,* with an English trans. by C. H. Oldfather. 10 vols. London and New York, 1933.

Dölger, Franz. 1927. "Beiträge zur Geschichte der byzantinischen Finanzverwaltung besonders des 10. und 11. Jahrhunderts," *Byzantinisches Archiv,* IX.

Doolittle, Justus. 1876. *Social Life of the Chinese.* 2 vols. New York.

Dozy, R. 1932. *Histoire des Musulmans d'Espagne,* new ed. revised by E. Lévi-Provençal. 3 vols. Leiden.

Dubberstein, Waldo H. 1939. "Comparative Prices in Later Babylonia," *American Journal of Semitic Languages and Literature,* LVI: 20–43.

Dubois, J. A. 1943. *Hindu Manners, Customs and Ceremonies,* trans. Henry K. Beauchamp. Oxford.

Duff, J. Wight. 1936. "Social Life in Rome and Italy," *CAH,* XI: 743–74. Cambridge.

Dundas, Charles. 1924. *Kilimanjaro and Its People.* London.

Dutt, R. Palme. 1940. *India To-day.* London.

—— 1943. *The Problem of India.* New York.

—— 1951. Introduction to *Karl Marx: Articles on India.* Bombay. See also below, *Labour Monthly.*

Duyvendak, J. J. L. 1928. *The Book of Lord Shang.* London.

Ebeling, E. 1932. "Beamte der neubabylonischen Zeit," *RA,* I: 451–7. Berlin and Leipzig.

Eberhard, Wolfram. 1952. *Conquerors and Rulers. Social Forces in Medieval China.* Leiden.

Eck, R. van, and Liefrinck, F. A. 1876. "Kertå-Simå op Gemeente- en Waterschaps-Wetten op Bali," *Tijdschrift voor Indische Taal-, Land- en Volkenkunde,* XXIII: 161–215.

Edgerton, William F. 1947. "The Government and the Governed in the Egyptian Empire," *JNES,* VI: 152–60.

Ehrenberg, Victor. 1946. *Aspects of the Ancient World.* New York.

Eisenhower, Dwight D. 1948. *Crusade in Europe.* Garden City.

Elliot, Sir H. M. and Dowson, John. 1877. *The History of India,* VII. London.

Ellis, William. 1826. *Narrative of a Tour through Hawaii, or Owhyee.* London.

Emge, Carl August. 1950. "Bürokratisierung unter philosophischer und soziologischer Sicht," *Akademie der Wissenschaften und der Literatur. Abhandlungen der Geistes- und Sozialwissenschaftlichen Klasse,* XVIII: 1205–23. Mainz.

Engels, Friedrich. 1887. *The Condition of the Working Class in England in 1844,* Appendix written in 1886, preface in 1887, trans. Florence Kelley Wischnewetzky. New York.

Engels, Friedrich. 1894. "Soziales aus Russland (Volksstaat, 1875)" in *Internationales aus dem Volksstaat (1871–75)*: 47–60. Berlin.

—— 1921. *Der Ursprung der Familie, des Privateigenthums, und des Staats*. 20th ed. Stuttgart.

—— 1935. *Herrn Eugen Dührings Umwälzung der Wissenschaft. Dialektik der Natur. 1873–1882*. Moscow.

Engels, Friedrich and Kautsky, Karl. 1935. *Aus der Frühzeit des Marxismus. Engels Briefwechsel mit Kautsky*. Prague.

Engnell, Ivan. 1943. *Studies in Divine Kingship in the Ancient Near East*. Uppsala.

Ensslin, W. 1939. "The Senate and the Army," *CAH*, XII: 57–95. Cambridge.

Erman, Adolf. 1923. *Die Literatur der Aegypter*. Leipzig.

Erman, Adolf, and Ranke, Hermann. 1923. *Aegypten und aegyptisches Leben im Altertum*, revised by Ranke. Tübingen.

Espejo, Antonio. 1916. "Account of the Journey to the Provinces and Settlements of New Mexico. 1583," in *Spanish Explorations in the Southwest 1542–1706*, ed. Herbert Eugene Bolton: 163–92. New York.

Espinosa, Antonio Vázquez de. 1942. *Compendium and Description of the West Indies*, trans. Charles Upson Clark. The Smithsonian Institution, Washington, D.C., Miscellaneous Collections, CII.

Estete, Miguel de. 1938. "La Relación del viaje que hizo el Señor Capitán Hernando Pizarro por mandado del Señor Gobernador, su hermano, desde el Pueblo de Caxamalca a Pachacama y de allí a Jauja" and "Noticia del Perú," in *BCPP*: 77–98, 195–251. Paris.

Fairbank, John King. 1947. "China's Prospects and U. S. Policy," *Far Eastern Survey*, XVI, No. 13: 145–9.

—— 1948. *The United States and China*. Cambridge, Mass.

al-Fakhrî. 1910. Ibn aṭ-Tiqṭaqâ. al-Fakhrî. *Histoires des dynasties musulmanes*, trans. Emile Amar. Archives Marocaines, XVI. Paris.

Falkenstein, Adam. 1936. *Archaische Texte aus Uruk bearbeitet und herausgegeben von . . . Ausgrabungen der deutschen Forschungsgemeinschaft in Uruk-Warka*, II. Berlin.

Fei Hsiao-tung. 1946. "Peasantry and Gentry: an Interpretation of Chinese Social Structure and its Changes," *American Journal of Sociology*, LII: 1–17.

—— 1953. *China's Gentry*. Essays in Rural-Urban Relations, revised and ed. Margaret Park Redfield, with an introduction by Robert Redfield. Chicago.

Fei Hsiao-tung and Chang Chih-i. 1945. *Earthbound China*. Revised Engl. ed. prepared in collaboration with Paul Cooper and Margaret Park Redfield. Chicago.

Fick, Richard. 1920. *The Social Organisation in North-East India in*

Buddha's Time, trans. Shishirkumar Maitra. University of Calcutta.

Fischel, Walter J. 1937. *Jews in the Economic and Political Life of Mediaeval Islam.* London.

Fischer, Ruth. 1948. *Stalin and German Communism.* Cambridge.

Fletcher, Giles. 1856. "Of the Russe Common Wealth: or Maner of Government by the Russe Emperour etc.," in *Russia at the Close of the Sixteenth Century,* Hakluyt Society, XX. London.

Florenz, Karl. 1903. *Japanische Annalen,* A.D. *592–697 Nihongi,* supplement of *Mitteilungen der deutschen Gesellschaft für Natur- und Völkerkunde Ostasiens.* Tokyo.

Florinsky, Michael T. 1953. *Russia. A History and an Interpretation.* 2 vols. New York.

Fornander, Abraham. HAF. *Fornander Collection of Hawaiian Antiquities and Folk-lore,* Memoirs of Bernice P. Bishop Museum, IV–VI. Honolulu, 1916–20.

———— PR. *An Account of the Polynesian Race, Its Origin and Migrations and the Ancient History of the Hawaiian People to the times of Kamehameha I.* 3 vols. London, 1878–85.

Frank, Tenney. 1928. "Rome after the Conquest of Sicily," *CAH,* VII: 793–821. Cambridge.

———— 1940. *Rome and Italy of the Empire. ESAR,* V. Baltimore.

Freudenthal, Berthold. 1905. "Antworten, Griechisch," in Mommsen, 1905: 9–19. Leipzig.

Fries, Nicolaus. 1921. *Das Heereswesen der Araber zur Zeit der Omaijaden nach Ṭabarî.* Tübingen.

Fromm, Erich. 1941. *Escape from Freedom.* New York.

Furnivall, J. S. 1944. *Netherlands India,* intro. by A. C. D. De Graeff. Cambridge and New York.

Gabrieli, Francesco. 1935. *Il Califfato di Hishâm.* Memoires de Société Royale d'Archéologie d'Alexandrie, VII, No. 2. Alexandria.

Gale, Esson M. 1931. *Discourses on Salt and Iron.* Leiden.

Gallegos. 1927. "The Gallegos Relation of the *Rodriguez Expedition to New Mexico,*" trans. George P. Hammond and Agapito Rey, Historical Society of New Mexico, Publications in History, II: 239–68, 334–62.

Garcilaso de la Vega, Inca. 1945. *Commentarios Reales de los Incas,* ed. Ángel Rosenblat. 2d ed. 2 vols. Buenos Aires.

Gardiner, Alan H. 1948. *The Wilbour Papyrus.* 3 vols. Published for the Brooklyn Museum at the Oxford University Press.

Gaudefroy-Demombynes, Maurice. 1923. *La Syrie à l'époque des Mamelouks d'après les auteurs Arabes.* Paris.

———— 1931. "Le Monde Musulman," in *Le Monde Musulman et Byzantin jusqu'aux Croisades,* by Gaudefroy-Demombynes and Platonov: 29–451. Paris.

Gaudefroy-Demombynes, Maurice. 1938. "Sur quelques ouvrages de ḥisba," *Journal Asiatique,* CCXXX: 449–57.

—— 1950. *Muslim Institutions,* trans. John P. MacGregor. London.

Gautama. 1898. In *Sacred Laws of the Âryas,* trans. Georg Bühler. SBE, II. New York.

GBP. 1882. *Gazetteer of the Bombay Presidency,* XIII, Pt 2: "Thána." Bombay.

Gelzer, Matthias. 1943. *Vom roemischen Staat.* 2 vols. Leipzig.

Gibb, H. A. R. 1932. *The Damascus Chronicle of the Crusades.* London.

Gibb, H. A. R. and Bowen, Harold. 1950. *Islamic Society and the West.* Vol. I: *Islamic Society in the Eighteenth Century.* London, New York, and Toronto.

Glotz, Gustave. 1925. *The Aegean Civilization.* London and New York.

—— 1926. *Ancient Greece at Work.* New York.

—— 1929. *The Greek City and Its Institutions.* London and New York.

Goetz, Leopold Karl. RR. *Das russische Recht.* 4 vols. Stuttgart, 1910–13.

Goldfrank, Esther S. 1945. "Socialization, Personality, and the Structure of Pueblo Society," *AA,* XLVII, No. 4: 516–39.

—— 1945a. "Irrigation Agriculture and Navaho Community Leadership: Case Material on Environment and Culture," *AA,* XLVII, No. 2: 262–77.

Goldziher, Ignaz. 1889. *Muhammedanische Studien,* I. Halle.

—— 1905. "Antworten: Islam," in Mommsen, 1905: 101–12. Leipzig.

Gordon, Robert Aaron. 1945. *Business Leadership in the Large Corporation.* Washington, D.C.

Götze, Albrecht. 1933. "Kleinasien," in *Kulturgeschichte des alten Orients,* by A. Alt, A. Christensen, A. Götze, A. Grohmann, H. Kees, and B. Landsberger. III, Pt. 1: 3–199. Munich.

Grant, Christina Phelps. 1937. *The Syrian Desert.* London.

Grapow, Hermann. 1924. *Die bildlichen Ausdrücke des Aegyptischen; vom Denken und Dichten einer altorientalischen Sprache.* Leipzig.

Grassman, Hermann. RV. *Rig-Veda.* 2 vols. Leipzig, 1876–77.

Gray, G. B. and Cary, M. 1939. "The Reign of Darius," *CAH,* IV: 173–228. Cambridge.

Grekov, B. D. 1939. "La Horde d'Or et la Russie," Pt. 2 of B. Grekov and A. Iakoubovski: *La Horde d'Or,* trans. François Thuret: 163–251. Paris.

—— 1947. *The Culture of Kiev Rūs,* trans. Pauline Rose. Moscow.

Grenier, Albert. 1937. "La Gaule Romaine," *ESAR,* III: 379–644. Baltimore.

Grohmann, Adolf. PAP. "Probleme der arabischen Papyrusforschung, II," *Archiv Orientální,* V: 273–83; VI: 377–98. Prague, 1933–34.

—— 1933. *Südarabien als Wirtschaftsgebiet,* Pt. 2. Schriften der Philosophischen Fakultät der Deutschen Universitat in Prag, XIII. Brünn, Prague, Leipzig, and Vienna.

Grossmann, Henry. 1929. "Die Änderung des ursprünglichen Aufbauplans des Marxschen 'Kapital' und ihre Ursachen," *Archiv für die Geschichte des Sozialismus und der Arbeiterbewegung*, XIV: 305–38.

Grunebaum, Gustave E. von. 1946. *Medieval Islam*. Chicago.

Gsell, Stephane. HA. *Histoire ancienne de l'Afrique du Nord*. 8 vols. Paris, 1914–28.

Guber, A. A. 1942. "Izuchenie Istorii Stran Vostoka v SSSR za 25 let," in *Dvadtsat pyat let istoricheskoi nauki v SSSR*: 272–84. Academy of Sciences of the USSR. Moscow and Leningrad.

Guillaume, James. IDS. *L'Internationale. Documents et souvenirs (1864–1878)*, I and II. Paris, 1905–07.

Guiraud, Jean. 1929. *The Mediaeval Inquisition*, trans. E. C. Messenger. London.

Gumplowicz, Ludwig. 1905. *Grundriss der Soziologie*. Vienna.

Gurian, Waldemar. 1931. *Der Bolschewismus*. Freiburg im Breisgau.

Gutmann, Bruno. 1909. *Dichten und Denker der Dschagganeger*. Leipzig.

–––––– 1914. *Volksbuch der Wadschagga*. Leipzig.

–––––– 1926. *Das Recht der Dschagga*. Munich.

Hackett, Charles Wilson. 1923. *Historical Documents Relating to New Mexico, Nueva Vizcaya, and Approaches Thereto, to 1773*, collected by A. F. A. and F. R. Bandelier. 2 vols. CIW, CCCXXX. Washington, D.C.

Hackman, George Gottlob. 1937. *Temple Documents of the Third Dynasty of Ur from Umna. Babylonian Inscriptions in the Collection of James B. Nies, Yale University*, V. New Haven and London.

Haig, Wolseley. 1937. "Sher Shāh and the Sūr Dynasty. The Return of Humāyūn," *CHI*, IV: 45–69. Cambridge.

Hall, W. H. 1886. *Irrigation Development Report*, Pt. 1. Sacramento.

Hammurabi. "Collections of Laws from Mesopotamia and Asia Minor," trans. Theophile J. Meek, *ANET*: 163–80. Princeton, 1950.

"The Han Officials." A statistical study prepared by the Chinese History Project (MS).

Han Shu. Po-na ed. Commercial Press.

Handbook of Marxism. 1935, ed. Emile Burns. New York.

Handy, E. S. Craighill. 1933. "Government and Society," in *Ancient Hawaiian Civilizations*: 31–42. Honolulu.

–––––– 1940. *The Hawaiian Planter, I: His Plants, Methods and Areas of Cultivation*. Bernice P. Bishop Museum Bulletin, CLXI.

Hardy, Edward Rochie. 1931. *The Large Estates of Byzantine Egypt*. New York.

Harper, George McLean, Jr. 1928. "Village Administration in the Roman Provinces of Syria," *Yale Classical Studies,* I: 105–68. New Haven and London.

Hasan Khan, M. 1944. "Medieval Muslim Political Theories of Rebellion against the State," *IC,* 18: 36–44.

Haskins, Charles Homer. 1911. "England and Sicily in the Twelfth Century," *English Historical Review,* XXVI: 433, 447, 641–65.

———— 1918. *Norman Institutions.* Harvard Historical Studies, XXIV. Cambridge, Mass.

Haxthausen, August Freiherr von. SR. *Studien über die innern Zustände, das Volksleben und insbesondere die ländlichen Einrichtungen Russlands.* 3 vols. Hanover and Berlin, 1847–52.

HCS, Ch'in-Han. "History of Chinese Society, Ch'in-Han" (in preparation by the Chinese History Project).

HCS, Ch'ing. "History of Chinese Society, Ch'ing" (in preparation by the Chinese History Project).

Hedin, Sven. 1917. *Southern Tibet, II: Lake Manasarovar and the Sources of the Great Indian Rivers.* Stockholm.

Heichelheim, Fritz M. 1938. *Wirtschaftsgeschichte des Altertums.* 2 vols. Leiden.

Helbing, Franz. 1926. *Die Tortur,* revised by Max Bauer, with postface by Max Alsberg. 2 parts. Berlin.

Helck, Hans-Wolfgang. 1939. *Der Einfluss der Militärführer in der 18. Ägyptischen Dynastie,* Untersuchungen zur Geschichte und Altertumskunde Aegyptens, XIV. Leipzig.

Herberstein, Sigismund von. NR. *Notes upon Russia; Being a Translation of the Earliest Account of That Country Entitled Rerum Moscoviticarum Commentarii,* trans. and ed. R. H. Major. 2 vols. Hakluyt Society, X, XII. London, 1851–52.

Herodotus. 1942. "The Persian Wars," trans. George Rawlinson in *The Greek Historians,* I: 1–563. New York.

Hewitt, James Francis. 1887. "Village Communities in India, Especially Those in the Bengal Presidency, the Central Provinces, and Bombay," *Journal of the Society of Arts,* XXXV: 613–25.

Hintze, Otto. 1901. "Der österreichische und der preussische Beamtenstaat im 17. und 18. Jahrhundert," *HZ,* LXXXVI, new ser., L: 401–44.

———— 1930. "Typologie der ständischen Verfassungen des Abendlandes," *HZ,* CXLI: 229–48.

———— 1941. *Staat und Verfassung.* Leipzig.

Hirth, Paul. 1928. *Die künstliche Bewässerung.* Kolonial-Wirtschaftliches Komitee, XXI, No. 3. Berlin.

Hitzig, H. F. 1905. "Antworten: Römisch," in Mommsen, 1905: 31–51. Leipzig.

Homo, Léon. 1927. *Primitive Italy and the Beginnings of Roman Imperialism*. New York.

Honigmann, Ernst. 1935. *Die Ostgrenze des byzantinischen Reiches von 363 bis 1071*. . . . Brussels.

Honjo, Eijiro. 1935. *The Social and Economic History of Japan*. Kyoto.

Hopkins, Edward Washburn. 1888. *The Social and Military Position of the Ruling Caste in Ancient India as Represented by the Sanskrit Epic*, reprinted from the *Journal of American Oriental Society*, XIII.

────── 1902. *India Old and New*. New York and London.

────── 1922. "Family Life and Social Customs as They Appear in the Sūtras," "The Princes and Peoples of the Epic Poems," and "The Growth of Law and Legal Institutions," *CHI*, I: 227–95. New York.

Horn, Paul. 1894. *Das Heer- und Kriegswesen der Grossmoghuls*. Leiden.

Horst, D. Johannes. 1932. *Proskynein*. Gütersloh.

Horster, Paul. 1935. *Zur Anwendung des islamischen Rechts im 16. Jahrhundert*. Stuttgart.

Hötzsch, Otto. 1912. "Adel und Lehnswesen in Russland und Polen und ihr Verhältnis zur deutschen Entwicklung," *HZ*, CVIII: 541–92.

Hou Han Shu. Po-na ed. Commercial Press.

Howorth, H. H. HM. *History of the Mongols*. 4 vols. London, 1876–1927.

Hsiao, K. C. "Rural China, Imperial Control in the Nineteenth Century" (MS).

Hsieh, Pao Chao. 1925. *The Government of China (1644–1911)*. Baltimore.

Hsü Han Chih. Po-na ed. Commercial Press.

Huang-ch'ao Ching-shih Wên Hsü-p'ien. Edition of 1888.

Hudemann, E. E. 1878. *Geschichte des römischen Postwesens während der Kaiserzeit*. Berlin.

Hug. 1918. "Eunuchen," *Pauly-Wissowa-Kroll*, Suppl. 3: 450–5. Stuttgart.

Humboldt, Al. de. 1811. *Essai politique sur le royaume de la Nouvelle-Espagne*. 5 vols. Paris.

Hummel, Arthur W. ECCP. *Eminent Chinese of the Ch'ing Period*. 2 vols. Washington, D.C., 1943–44.

Huuri, Kalervo. 1941. *Zur Geschichte des mittelalterlichen Geschützwesens aus orientalischen Quellen*. Helsinki.

Huxley, Julian S. 1955. "Evolution, Cultural and Biological," in the *Yearbook of Anthropology*, Wenner-Gren Foundation for Anthropological Research: 3–25. New York.

Ibn Batoutah. 1914. *Voyages d'Ibn Batoutah*, III, trans. C. Defrémery and B. R. Sanguinetti. Paris.

Ibn Khordādhbeh. 1889. *Kitāb a-Masālik wa'l-Mamālik (Liber viarum et regnorum)* by Ibn Khordādhbeh (Arabic and French translation), ed.

and trans. M. J. de Goeje in *Bibliotheca geographorum arabicorum*, VI: vii–xxiii and 1–144, Arabic text 1–183. Leiden and Batavia.

Ibn al-Ukhuwwa. 1938. *The Ma'ālim al-Qurba*, trans. and ed. Reuben Levy. E. J. W. Gibb Memorial New Series, XII. London.

Imperial Gazetteer of India. The Indian Empire. new ed. 4 vols. Oxford, 1907–09.

Inama-Sternegg, Karl Theodor von. 1901. *Deutsche Wirtschaftsgeschichte*, III. 2. Leipzig.

Inama-Sternegg and Häpke. 1924. "Die Bevölkerung des Mittelalters und der neueren Zeit bis Ende des 18. Jahrhunderts in Europa," *Handwörterbuch der Staatswissenschaften*, II: 670–87. 4th ed. Jena.

Inostrannaya Kniga, No. 1, 1931. Moscow.

Inprecor. International Press Correspondence. English ed. Vienna and London, 1921–38.

Ixtlilxochitl, Don Fernando de Alba. OH. *Obras Historicas*, ed. Alfredo Chavero. 2 vols. Mexico, 1891–92.

Jäckh, Ernest. 1944. *The Rising Crescent, Turkey Yesterday, Today, and Tomorrow*. New York and Toronto.

Jacobsen, Thorkild. 1943. "Primitive Democracy in Ancient Mesopotamia," *JNES*, II, No. 3: 159–72.

———— 1946. "Mesopotamia: the Cosmos as a State" in *The Intellectual Adventure of Ancient Man* by Frankfort, Wilson, Jacobsen, and Irwin: 125–219. Chicago.

Jacobsen, Thorkild, and Lloyd, Seton. 1935. *Sennacherib's Aqueduct at Jerwan*. Chicago.

Jaeger, Werner. 1939. *Paideia: the Ideals of Greek Culture*, trans. Gilbert Highet. New York.

Jahāngīr. 1909. *The Tūzuk-i-Jahāngīrī*, or *Memoirs of Jahāngīr*, trans. Alexander Rogers and ed. Henry Beveridge. Oriental Translation Fund, new ser. XIX. London.

Jātakam. Trans. from the Pali by Julius Dutoit. 7 vols. Leipzig and Munich, 1908–21.

Jefferson, Thomas. 1944. *Basic Writings of Thomas Jefferson*, ed. Philip S. Foner. New York.

Jen-min Jih-pao. Peking.

Jerez, Francisco de. 1938. ". . . la Conquista del Perú . . . " in *BCCP*: 15–115. Paris.

Johnson, Allan Chester. 1951. *Egypt and the Roman Empire*. Ann Arbor.

Johnson, Allan Chester, and West, Louis C. 1949. *Byzantine Egypt: Economic Studies*. Princeton.

Jolly, Julius. 1896. "Recht und Sitte" in *Grundriss der Indo-Arischen*

Philologie und Altertumskunde, II, Fasc. 8, ed. G. Bühler. Strassburg.

Jones, Sir Henry Stuart. 1934. "Senatus Populusque Romanus," *CAH,* X: 159–81. Cambridge.

Jones, Richard. 1831. *An Essay on the Distribution of Wealth, and on the Sources of Taxation.* London.

——— 1859. *Literary Remains, Consisting of Lectures and Tracts on Political Economy,* with a prefatory notice by William Whewell. London.

Josephus, Flavius. JW. *The Works of Flavius Josephus, Containing Twenty Books of the Jewish Antiquities, Seven Books of the Jewish War,* I, trans. William Whiston, revised by Samuel Burder. New York, no date.

Jouguet, Pierre. 1911. *La Vie municipale dans l'Egypte Romaine.* Bibliothèque des Ecoles Française et de Rome, Fasc. 104. Paris.

Juan, George, and Ulloa, Antonio de. 1806. *A Voyage to South America,* trans. John Adams. 2 vols. London.

Juynboll, Th. W. 1925. *Handleiding tot de Kennis van De Mohammedaansche Wet volgens de Leer der Sjāfi'itische School.* 3d ed. Leiden.

Kahin, George McTurnan. 1952. *Nationalism and Revolution in Indonesia.* Ithaca, New York.

Kahrstedt, Ulrich. 1924. "Die Bevölkerung des Altertums," *Handwörterbuch der Staatswissenschaften,* II: 655–70. 4th ed. Jena.

Kai Kā'ūs ibn Iskandar. 1951. *A Mirror for Princes. The Qābus Nāma by Kai Kā'ūs Ibn Iskandar,* trans. Reuben Levy. New York.

Kantorowicz, Ernst. 1931. *Kaiser Friedrich der Zweite.* Berlin.

Karamsin, M. HER. *Histoire de l'empire de Russie,* trans. St.-Thomas and Jauffret. 11 vols. Paris, 1819–26.

Kato, Shigeshi. 1936. "On the Hang or the Associations of Merchants in China," *Memoirs of the Research Department of the Toyo Bunko,* VIII: 45–83.

Kautsky, Karl. 1929. *Die Materialistische Geschichtsauffassung.* 2 vols. Berlin.

Kayden, Eugene M. 1929. "Consumers' Cooperation," in *The Cooperative Movement in Russia during the War,* Vol. VI of *Economic and Social History of the World War,* Russian Series: 3–231. New Haven.

Kees, Herman. 1933. *Ägypten.* Munich.

——— 1938. "Herihor und die Aufrichtung des thebanischen Gottesstaates," *Nachrichten von der Gesellschaft der Wissenschaften in Göttingen,* Philologisch-Historische Klasse, new ser., Section I: *Nachrichten aus der Altertumswissenschaft,* II: 1–20.

——— 1953. *Das Priestertum im ägyptischen Staat.* Vol. I of *Probleme der Ägyptologie.* Leiden and Cologne.

Keith, Arthur Berriedale. 1914. *The Veda of the Black Yajus School En-*

titled Taittiriya Sanhita. Harvard Oriental Series, XVIII, XIX. 2 vols. Cambridge.

—— 1922. "The Age of the Rigveda," *CHI,* I: 77–113. New York.

Kennan, George. 1891. *Siberia and the Exile System.* 2 vols. New York.

Kepelino. 1932. *Kepelino's Traditions of Hawaii,* ed. Martha Warren Beckwith. Bernice P. Bishop Museum Bulletin, XCV. Honolulu.

King, F. H. 1927. *Farmers of Forty Centuries.* London.

Klebs, Luise. 1915. *Die Reliefs des alten Reiches (2980–2475 v. Chr.),* *Material zur ägyptischen Kulturgeschichte,* Abhandlungen der Heidelberger Akademie der Wissenschaften, Philologisch-Historische Klasse, III.

Klein, Julius. 1920. *The Mesta. A Study in Spanish Economic History 1273–1836.* Cambridge.

Kliuchevskii, V. O. *Kurs russkoi istorii.* 5 vols. Moscow, 1908–37.

Kljutschewskij, W. O. 1945. *Russische Geschichte von Peter dem Grossen bis Nikolaus I,* trans. Waldemar Jollos. 2 vols. Zurich.

Kluchevsky, V. O. HR. *A History of Russia,* trans. C. J. Hogarth. 5 vols. London, 1911–31.

KMCL. *Karl Marx Chronik Seines Lebens in Einzeldaten.* Moscow, 1934.

Koebner, Richard. 1942. "The Settlement and Colonisation of Europe," *CEH,* I: 1–88. Cambridge.

Koran, the (Qur'an), trans. E. H. Palmer. London, New York, and Toronto, 1942.

Kornemann, Ernest. 1933. "Die Römische Kaiserzeit," in *Römische Geschichte* by J. Vogt and E. Kornemann: 57–186. Leipzig and Berlin.

—— 1949. *Von Augustus bis zum Sieg der Araber.* Vol. II of *Weltgeschichte des Mittelmeer-Raumes.* Munich.

Kovalewsky, Maxime. 1903. *Institutions politiques de la Russie,* trans. from the English by Mme. Derocquigny. Paris.

Kracke, E. A., Jr. 1947. "Family vs. Merit in Chinese Civil Service Examinations under the Empire," *Harvard Journal of Asiatic Studies,* X: 103–23.

—— 1953. *Civil Service in Early Sung China, 960–1067.* Cambridge.

Kramer, Samuel Noah. 1948. "New Light on the Early History of the Ancient Near East," *American Journal of Archaeology,* LII, No. 1: 156–64.

—— 1950. "Sumerian Myths and Epic Tales," in *ANET:* 37–59. Princeton.

Krause, Gregor, and With, Karl. 1922. *Bali.* Hagen i. W.

Kreller, Hans. 1919. *Erbrechtliche Untersuchungen Aufgrund der graeco-aegyptischen Papyrusurkunden.* Leipzig and Berlin.

Kremer, Alfred von. CGO. *Culturgeschichte des Orients unter den Chalifen.* 2 vols. Vienna, 1875–77.

—— 1863. *Aegypten.* 2 parts, Leipzig.

Kroeber, A. L. 1948. *Anthropology*. Rev. ed. New York.

Krückmann, O. 1932. "Die Beamten zur Zeit der ersten Dynastie von Babylon," *RA*, I: 444–51. Berlin and Leipzig.

Kuan T'ang Chi Lin by Wang Kuo-wei. 1927. In *Wang Chung Ch'üeh Kung I Shu, Ch'u-chi*.

Kuan Tzŭ. Commercial Press, Shanghai, 1934.

Kulischer, Josef. AW. *Allgemeine Wirtschaftsgeschichte des Mittelalters und der Neuzeit*. 2 vols. Munich and Berlin, 1928–29.

―――― 1925. *Russische Wirtschaftsgeschichte*, I. Jena.

Kuo Mo-jo. 1935. *Liang Chou Chin Wên Tz'ŭ Ta Hsi K'ao Shih*. Tokyo.

Kuo Yü. Commercial Press, Shanghai, 1935.

Labat, René, 1939. *Le Caractère religieux de la royauté Assyro-Babylonienne*. Paris.

Laborde, Alexandre de. 1808. *Itinéraire descriptif de l'Espagne* etc., IV. Paris.

Labour Monthly. Ed. R. Palme Dutt. London.

Lafuente Alcantara, D. Miguel. 1845. *Historia de Granada* etc., III. Granada.

Lambton, Ann K. S. 1938. "The Regulation of the Waters of the Zāyande Rūd," *Bulletin of the School of Oriental Studies* (University of London), IX: 663–73.

―――― 1948. "An Account of the Tārīkhi Qumm," *Bulletin of the School of Oriental Studies*, XII: 586–96.

Lammens, Henri. 1907. "Etudes sur le règne du calife Omaiyade Mo'awia Ier," *Mélanges de la Faculté Orientale* (Université Saint-Joseph, Beyrouth), II: 1–172.

―――― 1914. *Le Climat—les Bédouins*. Vol. I of *Le Berceau de l'Islam*. Rome.

―――― 1922. "La Cité Arabe de Ṭāif a la veille de l'Hégire," *Mélanges de l'Université Saint-Joseph Beyrouth (Syrie)*, VIII: 115–327.

Lamprecht, Karl. DG. *Deutsche Geschichte*. Vol. II, 1909; Vol. IV, 1911. Berlin.

Landa, Diego de. 1938. *Relación de las cosas de Yucatan*, with introduction and notes by Hector Perez Martinez. 7th ed. Mexico.

Landsberger, Benno. 1925. "Assyrische Handelskolonien in Kleinasien aus dem dritten Jahrtausend," *Der Alte Orient*, XXIV, Fasc. 4.

Lane, Edward William. 1898. *An Account of the Manners and Customs of the Modern Egyptians*. London.

Lang, Olga. 1946. *Chinese Family and Society*. New Haven.

Laoust, Henri. 1939. *Essai sur les doctrines sociales et politiques de Taḳi-d-Din Aḥmad b. Taimīya*. Recherches d'Archéologie, de Philologie et d'Histoire, X. Cairo.

Last, Hugh. 1936. "The Principate and the Administration," *CAH*, XI: 393–434. Cambridge.

Lattimore, Owen. 1940. *Inner Asian Frontiers of China*. New York.

—— 1944. "A Soviet Analysis of Chinese Civilization," *Pacific Affairs*, XVII: 81–9.

—— 1947. *Solution in Asia*. Boston (first published February 1945).

—— 1949. *The Situation in Asia*. Boston.

Lauts. 1848. *Het eiland Balie en de Balienezen*. Amsterdam.

Law, Bimala Charan. 1923. *Some Kṣatriya Tribes of Ancient India*, with a foreword by A. Berriedale Keith. Calcutta and Simla.

—— 1941. *India as Described in Early Texts of Buddhism and Jainism*. London.

Lea, Henry Charles. 1892. *Superstition and Force*. Philadelphia.

—— 1908. *A History of the Inquisition of the Middle Ages*, I. New York and London.

Leemans, W. F. 1950. *The Old-Babylonian Merchant, His Business and His Social Position*. Leiden.

Legge, James. CC. *The Chinese Classics*. 7 vols. Oxford 1893–95.

Lenin, Vladimir Ilych. S. *Sochinenia*, 4th ed. 35 vols. Moscow, 1941–50.

—— SW. *Selected Works*. 12 vols. New York, 1943.

—— SWG. *Sämtliche Werke*. Vienna and Berlin, later Moscow and Leningrad.

—— 1937. *The Letters of Lenin*, trans. Elizabeth Hill and Doris Mudie. New York.

Letopis Marksizma. Moscow.

Lévi-Provençal, E. 1932. *L'Espagne Musulmane au Xème siècle*. Paris.

—— 1947. *Séville Musulmane au debut du XIIe siècle. Le Traite d'ibn 'Abdun sur la vie urbaine et les corps de métiers*. Paris.

Lind, Andrew W. 1938. *An Island Community. Ecological Succession in Hawaii*. Chicago.

Lips, Julius E. 1938. "Government," in *General Anthropology*, ed. F. Boas: 487–534.

Locke, John. 1924. *Of Civil Government*. Everyman's Library. London and New York.

Løkkegaard, Frede. 1950. *Islamic Taxation in the Classic Period*. Copenhagen.

Longrigg, Stephen Hemsley. 1925. *Four Centuries of Modern Iraq*. Oxford.

Lopez, R. S. 1945. "Silk Industry in the Byzantine Empire," *Speculum*, XX, No. 1: 1–42.

Lot, Ferdinand. 1946. *L'Art militaire et les armées au moyen âge en Europe et dans le Proche Orient*. 2 vols. Paris.

Lot, Ferdinand. 1951. *La Fin du monde antique et le debut du moyen âge.* L'Evolution de l'humanité, XXXI. Paris.

Lowie, Robert H. 1927. *The Origin of the State.* New York.

———— 1938. "Subsistence," in *General Anthropology,* ed. F. Boas: 282–326.

Luckenbill, Daniel David. AR. *Ancient Records of Assyria and Babylonia.* 2 vols. Chicago, 1926–27.

Lun Yü Chu Shu in *Ssŭ Pu Pei Yao.* Shanghai, 1936.

Lundell, C. L. 1937. *The Vegetation of Petén.* CIW, 478. Washington, D.C.

Luxemburg, Rosa. 1951. *Ausgewählte Reden und Schriften,* with a foreword by Wilhelm Pieck. 2 vols. Berlin.

Lyashchenko, Peter I. 1949. *History of the National Economy of Russia,* trans. L. M. Herman. New York.

Lybyer, Albert Howe. 1913. *The Government of the Ottoman Empire in the Time of Suleiman the Magnificent.* Cambridge and London.

Lydgate, John M. 1913. "The Affairs of the Wainiha Hui," *Hawaiian Almanac and Annual for 1913:* 125–37.

Ma Shêng-fêng. 1935. *Chung-kuo Ching-chi Shih* I. Nanking.

Macdonald, D. B. 1941. "*Dhimma,*" HWI: 96. Leiden.

Machiavelli, Niccolò. 1940. *The Prince and the Discourses.* Modern Library. New York.

MacLeod, William Christie. 1924. *The Origin of the State Reconsidered in the Light of the Data of Aboriginal North America.* Philadelphia.

Maitland, Frederic William. 1921. *Domesday Book and Beyond.* Cambridge.

———— 1948. *The Constitutional History of England.* Cambridge.

al-Makkarí, Ahmed Ibn Mohammed. 1840. *The History of the Mohammedan Dynasties in Spain,* extracted from the *Nafhu-t-tíb min Ghosni-l-Andalusi-r-rattíb wa Tárikh Lisánu-d-din Ibni-l-khattíb,* trans. Pascual de Gayanges y Arce, I. Oriental Translation Fund. London.

Makrizi, Taki-eddin-Ahmed- . 1845. *Histoire des sultans Mamlouks, de l'Egypte,* II, Pt. 4, trans. M. Quatremere. Oriental Translation Fund. Paris.

Mallon, Alexis. 1921. "Les Hebreux en Egypte," *OCRAA,* No. 3.

Malo, David. 1903. *Hawaiian Antiquities.* Honolulu.

Manu. 1886. *The Laws of Manu,* trans., with extracts from seven commentaries, by G. Bühler. SBE, XXV. Oxford.

Mao Tse-tung. 1945. *China's New Democracy.* New York.

———— 1945a. *The Fight for a New China.* New York.

———— 1954. *Selected Works of Mao Tse-tung,* I. London.

Marco Polo. 1929. *The Book of Ser Marco Polo,* trans. Colonel Sir Henry Yule, 3d ed. Revised by Henri Cordier. 2 vols. New York.

Markham, Clements R. 1892. *A History of Peru.* Chicago.

Marquart, J. 1903. *Osteuropäische und ostasiastische Streifzüge.* Leipzig.

Marshall, Alfred. 1946. *Principles of Economics.* London.

Marshall, John. 1928. "The Monuments of Muslim India," *CHI,* III: 568–640. New York and Cambridge.

―――― 1931. *Mohenjo-daro and the Indus Civilization.* 3 vols. London.

Marx, Karl. DK. *Das Kapital.* 4th, 2d, and 1st ed. 3 vols. Hamburg, 1890–94.

―――― NYDT. Articles in the *New York Daily Tribune.*

―――― TMW. *Theorien über den Mehrwert.* From the posthumous manuscript "Zur Kritik der politischen Ökonomie," published by Kaul Kautsky. 3 vols. Stuttgart, 1921.

―――― 1857. "Revelations of the Diplomatic History of the Eighteenth Century," *The Free Press,* IV: 203–4, 218, 226–8, 265–7. Feb. 4, 18, 25; April 1.

―――― 1921. *Zur Kritik der Politischen Ökonomie.* 8th ed. Stuttgart.

―――― 1927. *Herr Vogt,* trans. J. Molitor. 3 vols. Paris.

―――― 1935. *Critique of the Gotha Programme.* New York.

―――― 1939. *Grundrisse der Kritik der Politischen Oekonomie* (Rohentwurf), 1857–58. Moscow.

―――― 1951. *Articles on India,* with an introduction by R. P. Dutt. Bombay.

―――― 1951a. *Marx on China 1853–1860.* Articles from the *New York Daily Tribune,* with an introduction and notes by Dona Torr. London. See also KMCL.

Marx, Karl, and Engels, Friedrich. 1920. *Gesammelte Schriften 1852 bis 1862,* ed. N. Rjasanoff. 2 vols. Stuttgart.

―――― 1952. *The Russian Menace to Europe,* a collection of articles ed. Paul W. Blackstock and Bert F. Hoselitz. Glencoe, Ill. See also below, *MEGA.*

Massignon, Louis. 1937. "Guilds," *ESS,* VII: 214–16. New York.

Matthai, John. 1915. *Village Government in British India.* London.

Maurer, Georg Ludwig von. GSD. *Geschichte der Städteverfassung in Deutschland.* 4 vols. Erlangen, 1869–71.

Mavor, James. 1925. *An Economic History of Russia.* 2d ed. 2 vols. London, Toronto, and New York.

―――― 1928. *The Russian Revolution.* London.

Mayr, Ernst. 1942. *Systematics and the Origin of Species.* New York.

McEwan, Calvin W. 1934. *The Oriental Origin of Hellenistic Kingship,* The Oriental Institute of the University of Chicago, Studies in Ancient Oriental Civilization, XIII. Chicago.

McIlwain, C. H. 1932. "Medieval Estates," *CMH,* VII: 665–715. New York and Cambridge.

Means, Philip Ainsworth. 1931. *Ancient Civilizations of the Andes*. New York and London.

Meek, Theophile J. 1950. "The Middle Assyrian Laws," in *ANET:* 180–8. Princeton.

MEGA. Karl Marx and Friedrich Engels. *Historisch-kritische Gesamtausgabe*. Marx-Engels Institute, Moscow, 1927–

Mehta, Asoka. 1954. *Democratic Socialism*. 2d ed. Hyderabad.

Meissner, Bruno. BA. *Babylonien und Assyrien*. 2 vols. Heidelberg, 1920–25.

Mendelsohn, Isaac. 1949. *Slavery in the Ancient Near East*. New York.

Mendoza, Juan González de. 1854. *The History of the Great and Mighty Kingdom of China*, II. Hakluyt Society, XV. London.

Mercer, Samuel A. B. 1952. *The Pyramid Texts*. 4 vols. New York, London, and Toronto.

Merker, M. 1903. "Rechtsverhältnisse und Sitten der Wadschagga," *PM*, XXX, No. 138.

——— 1904. *Die Masai*. Berlin.

Meyer, Eduard. GA. *Geschichte des Altertums*. 4 vols. Stuttgart and Berlin, 1926–39.

——— 1924. *Kleine Schriften*. 2d ed. 2 vols. Halle.

Meyer, Peter. 1950. "The Soviet Union: a New Class Society" in *Verdict of Three Decades*, ed. Julien Steinberg: 475–509. New York.

Mez, Adam. 1922. *Die Renaissance des Islams*. Heidelberg.

Miakotine, V. 1932. "Les Pays russes, des origines à la fin des invasions tatares," *Histoire de Russie*, by Paul Milioukov, Ch. Signobos, and L. Eisenmann, I: 81–124. Paris.

Mieli, Aldo. 1938. *La Science Arabe et son role dans l'évolution scientifique mondiale*. Leiden.

——— 1946. *Panorama general de historia de la ciencia*. Madrid.

Miles, George C. 1948. "Early Islamic Inscriptions Near Ṭa'if in the Hijāz," *JNES*, VII: 236–42.

Mill, James. 1820. *The History of British India*. 2d ed. 12 vols. London.

Mill, John Stuart. 1909. *Principles of Political Economy*. London, New York, Bombay, and Calcutta.

——— 1947. *A System of Logic Ratiocinative and Inductive*. London, etc.

Miller, Barnette. 1941. *The Palace School of Muhammad the Conqueror*. Cambridge.

Miller, S. N. 1939. "The Army and the Imperial House," *CAH*, XII: 1–56. Cambridge.

Milukow, Paul. 1898. *Skizzen Russischer Kulturgeschichte*, I. Leipzig.

Ming Shih. Po-na ed. Commercial Press.

Minorsky, V. 1943. *Tadhkirat al-Mulūk.* E. J. W. Gibb Memorial Series, new ser., XVI. London.

Mitteis, Heinrich. 1933. *Lehnsrecht und Staatsgewalt. Untersuchungen zur mittelalterlichen Verfassungsgeschichte.* Weimar.

Mitteis, L. 1912. *Juristischer Teil, erste Hälfte: Grundzüge.* Vol. II of *Grundzüge und Chrestomathie der Papyruskunde,* by L. Mitteis and U. Wilcken. Leipzig and Berlin.

Momigliano, A. 1934. "Nero," *CAH,* X: 702–42. Cambridge.

Mommsen, Theodor. 1875. *Römisches Staatsrecht,* II, Pt. 2. Leipzig.

——— 1905. *Zum ältesten Strafrecht der Kulturvölker. Fragen zur Rechtsvergleichung gestellt von . . .* Leipzig.

——— 1921. *Römische Geschichte,* V. 9th ed. Berlin.

Monzon, Arturo. 1949. *El Calpulli en la organización social de los Tenochca.* Mexico City.

Moreland, W. H. 1929. *The Agrarian System of Moslem India.* Cambridge.

Morgan, Lewis H. 1877. *Ancient Society or Researches . . . through Barbarism to Civilization.* Chicago.

Morley, S. C. 1938. *The Inscriptions of Petén,* CIW, 437. Washington, D.C.

——— 1947. *The Ancient Maya.* 2d ed. Stanford University.

Morris, Richard B. 1937. "Entail," *ESS,* V: 553–6. New York.

Motolinia, Fr. Toribio de Benavente o. 1941. *Historia de los Indios de la Nueva España* (1541). Mexico City.

Mukerjee, Radhakamal. 1939. "Land Tenures and Legislation," in *Economic Problems of Modern India,* I: 218–45. London.

Munier, Henri. 1932. "L'Egypt Byzantine de Dioclétien à la conquête Arabe," *Précis de l'Histoire d'Egypte,* II: 3–106. Cairo.

Munro, J. A. R. 1939. "Xerxes' Invasion of Greece," *CAH,* IV: 268–316. Cambridge.

Murdock, George Peter. 1949. *Social Structure.* New York.

Myers, Gustavus. 1939. *The Ending of Hereditary American Fortunes.* New York.

Nârada. 1889. In the *Minor Law-Books,* trans. Julius Jolly, Pt. 1: 1–267. SBE, XXXIII. Oxford.

Nehru, Jawaharlal. 1942. *Glimpses of World History.* New York.

——— 1942a. *Toward Freedom.* New York.

——— 1946. *The Discovery of India.* New York.

Nelson, N. C. 1938. "Geological Premises" and "Prehistoric Archaeology," in *General Anthropology,* ed. F. Boas: 7–16, 146–237.

Nestor. 1931. *Die Altrussische Nestorchronik Povest' Vremennych Let,*

trans. Reinhold Trautmann, Slavisch-Baltische Quellen und Forschungen, VI. Leipzig.

Newberry, Percy Edward. BH. *Beni Hasan. Archaeological Survey of
Egypt,* Pts. 1–4. London, 1893–94.

Nicolai-on. 1899. *Die Volkswirtschaft in Russland,* trans. Georg Polonsky.
Munich.

Nihongi. 1896. *Nihongi, Chronicles of Japan from the Earliest Times to
A.D. 697.* Transactions and Proceedings of the Japan Society, London,
Suppl. 1. 2 vols. London.

Nilsson, Martin P. 1950. *Geschichte der Griechischen Religion.* Vol. II
of *Die Hellenistische und Römische Zeit.* Munich.

Nöldeke, Theodor. 1892. *Orientalische Skizzen.* Berlin.

Obregon. 1928. *Obregon's History of the 16th Century Explorations in
Western America,* trans. G. P. Hammond and A. Rey. Los Angeles.

Oertel, F. 1939. "The Economic Life of the Empire," *CAH,* XII: 232–
81. Cambridge.

Oldenberg, Hermann. 1915. *Die Lehre der Upanishaden und die Anfänge
des Buddhismus.* Göttingen.

Olmstead, A. T. 1923. *History of Assyria.* New York and London.

———— 1948. *History of the Persian Empire.* Chicago.

Oman, Charles. 1924. *A History of the Art of War in the Middle Ages.*
2d ed. 2 vols. London.

Ondegardo, Polo de. 1872. "Relación de los fundamentos acerca del
notable Daño que resulta de no guardar á los Indios sus fueros," in
Coleccion de Documentos Inéditos . . . de América y Oceanía, XVII:
5–177. Madrid.

Oppenheimer, Franz. 1919. *Der Staat.* Frankfurt am Main.

Ostrogorsky, Georg. 1940. *Geschichte des byzantinischen Staates.* Munich.

———— 1942. "Agrarian Conditions in the Byzantine Empire in the Middle Ages," *CEHE,* I: 194–223. Cambridge.

Østrup, J. 1929. *Orientalische Höflichkeit,* trans. K. Wulff. Leipzig.

Otto, Walter. PT. *Priester und Tempel im hellenistischen Ägypten.* 2
vols. Leipzig and Berlin, 1905–08.

Oviedo y Valdes, Gonzalo Fernandes de. HGNI. *Historia general y
natural de las Indias,* ed. Jose Amador de los Rios. 3 pts. in 4 vols.
Madrid, 1851–55.

Pacific Affairs. Published by the Institute of Pacific Relations.

Palerm, Ángel. 1952. "La Civilización urbana," *Historia Mexicana,* II:
184–209.

———— 1954. "La Distribución del regadío en el área central de Mesoamérica," *Ciencias Sociales,* V: 2–15, 64–74.

———— 1955. "La Base agricola de la civilización urbana en Mesoamérica," in *Las Civilizaciónes antiguas del Viejo Mundo y de América.* Estudios Monograficos, 1. Union Panamericana, Washington, D.C.

Panikkar, K. M. AWD. *Asia and Western Dominance.* A survey of the Vasco Da Gama epoch of Asian history 1498–1945. New York, no date.

Pant, D. 1930. *The Commercial Policy of the Moguls.* Bombay.

Parsons, Elsie Clew. 1932. "Isleta, New Mexico," SIBAE, *Forty-seventh Annual Report:* 201–1087.

—— 1939. *Pueblo Indian Religion.* 2 vols. Chicago.

Pedersen, J. 1941. "*Masdjid,*" *HWI:* 423–48. Leiden.

Peking Gazette. English translation. Shanghai, 1872–99.

Perry, Antonio. 1913. "Hawaiian Water Rights," *The Hawaiian Almanac and Annual for 1913:* 90–9. Honolulu.

Petit-Dutaillis, Ch. 1949. *The Feudal Monarchy in France and England,* trans. E. D. Hunt.

Pietschmann, Richard. 1889. *Geschichte der Phönizier.* Berlin.

Piggott, Stuart. 1950. *Prehistoric India.* Pelican Books. Harmondsworth.

Pizarro, Hernando. 1938. "A Los Magnificos señores, los señores oidores de la audiencia real de Su Majestad, que residen en la cuidad de Santo Domingo," *BCPP:* 253–64. Paris.

Plato. *The Trial and Death of Socrates.* Vol. III of *The Dialogues of Plato,* trans. J. Jowett. New York, no date.

Platonov, S. F. 1925. *History of Russia,* trans. E. Aronsberg. New York.

Plekhanov, G. V. FPM. *Fundamental Problems of Marxism.* Marxist Library, I. ed. D. Riazanov. New York, no date.

—— 1891. (Plechanoff). "Die Zivilisation und die grossen historischen Fluesse," *NZ,* IX, No. 1: 437–48.

—— 1906. "On the Agrarian Question in Russia," *Dnevnik Sotsial-Demokrata,* No. 5, March.

Pod Znamenem marxizma. Nos. 2–3, 6, 7–8, 1929.

Pöhlmann, Robert von. 1912. *Geschichte der sozialen Frage und des Sozialismus in der antiken Welt.* 2 vols. Munich.

Poliak, A. N. 1934. "Les Révoltes populaires en Egypte à l'époque des Mamelouks et leurs causes économiques," *Revue des Etudes Islamiques,* VIII: 251–73.

—— 1939. *Feudalism in Egypt, Syria, Palestine, and the Lebanon, 1250–1900.* London.

Polybius. *The Histories,* with an English trans. by W. R. Paton. 6 vols. New York, 1925.

Poma de Ayala, Felipe Guaman. 1936. *Nueva corónica y buen gobierno.* Travaux et mémoires de l'Institut d'Ethnologie, XXIII. Paris.

Porphyrogénète, Constantin VII. 1939. *Le Livre des cérémonies,* II, Bk. 1, chaps. 47–92, trans. Albert Vogt. Paris.

Prescott, William H. 1838. *History of the Reign of Ferdinand and Isabella, the Catholic.* 3 vols. Boston.
—— 1936. *History of the Conquest of Mexico and History of the Conquest of Peru.* Modern Library. New York.
Price, Ira Maurice. 1927. *The Great Cylinder Inscriptions A and B of Gudea,* Pt. 2. Leipzig and New Haven.
Prigozhin, A. G. 1934. "Karl Marks i problemy istorii Dokapitalisticheshikh formatsiy," in *Sbornik k pyatidesyatiletiyu so dnya smerti Karla Marxa,* ed. N. Ya Marr. Moscow and Leningrad.
Primera crónica general ó sea estoria de España que mandó componer Alfonso el Sabio y se continuaba bajo Sancho IV en 1289, I, ed. Ramón Menéndez Pidal. Madrid, 1906.
Problemy Kitaia, Nos. 4, 5, 1930. Moscow.
Prokopowitsch, Sergej. 1913. "Uber die Bedingungen der industriellen Entwicklung Russlands," *ASS,* Suppl. X.
Protokoly Obyedinitelnovo Syezda Rossyskoi Sotsialdemokraticheskoi Rabochei Partii (Protocols of the Unification Congress of the RSDRP), held in Stockholm, 1906. Moscow, 1907.
Ramirez, Codice. 1944. *Codice Ramirez. Manuscrito del Siglo XVI intitulado: Relación del origen de los Indios que habitan esta Nueva España, segun sus historias,* ed. Manuel Orozco y Berra. Mexico City.
Ramsay, W. M. 1890. *The Historical Geography of Asia Minor.* Supplementary Papers of the Royal Geographical Society, IV. London.
Rangaswami Aiyangar, K. V. 1935. *Considerations on Some Aspects of Ancient Indian Polity.* 2d ed. University of Madras.
Rangoon Tracts, 1. *Resolutions of the First Asian Socialist Conference, Rangoon, 1953.* Asian Socialist Conference, Rangoon.
Ranke, Leopold. 1924. *Deutsche Geschichte im Zeitalter der Reformation.* 3 vols. Munich and Leipzig.
Rapson, E. J. 1922. "Peoples and Languages and Sources of History," *CHI,* I: 37–64. New York and Cambridge.
Rathgen, Karl. 1891. "Japan's Volkswirtschaft und Staatshaushalt," *Staats- und socialwissenschaftliche Forschungen,* ed. Gustav Schmoller, X, No. 4. Leipzig.
RDS. 1896. "Translation of the *Relacion del Suceso,* account of what happened on the journey which Francisco Vazquez made to discover Cibola," in George Parker Winship, "Coronada Expedition 1540–1542," SIBAE, *Fourteenth Annual Report,* 1892–93, Pt. 1: 572–9.
Reclus, Elisée. 1882. *L'Asie Orientale.* Vol. VII of *Nouvelle geographie universelle.* Paris.
Reed, Thomas H. 1937. "Water Supply," *ESS,* XV: 372–7. New York.
Reid, J. S. 1936. "The Reorganisation of the Empire," *CMH,* I: 24–54. Cambridge.

Reischauer, Robert Karl. 1937. *Early Japanese History*. 2 vols. Princeton.

Reiske, J. J. 1830. *Constantinus Porphyrogenitus. Constantini Porphyrogeniti Imperatoris de Cerimoniis Aulae Byzantinae*, II. Bonn.

Renou, Louis. 1950. *La Civilisation de l'Inde ancienne*. Paris.

C. A. F. Rhys-Davids (Mrs.). 1922. "Economic Conditions according to Early Buddhist Literature," *CHI*, I: 198–219. New York.

Rhys-Davids, T. W. 1922. "The Early History of the Buddhists," *CHI*, I: 171–97. New York.

―――― 1950. *Buddhist India*. 1st Indian ed. Susil Gupta.

Riasanovsky, V. A. 1937. *Fundamental Principles of Mongol Law*. Tientsin.

Ricketson, Oliver G. 1937. "The Excavations," Pt. 1 of *Uaxactun, Guatemala Group E, 1926–31*, CIW, 477: 1–175.

Riepl, Wolfgang. 1913. *Das Nachrichtenwesen des Altertums mit besonderer Rücksicht auf die Römer*. Leipzig and Berlin.

Ritter, Carl. 1858. *Klein-Asien*. Vol. IX, Pt. 1, of *Die Erdkunde von Asien*, Berlin.

Ritter, H. 1929. "La Parure des Cavaliers und die Literatur über die ritterlichen Künste," *Der Islam*, XVIII: 116–54.

Rjasanoff, N. (Ryazanov). 1909. "Karl Marx über den Ursprung der Vorherrschaft Russlands in Europa," Suppl. to *NZ*, XXVII, Pt. 1, No. 5.

―――― 1925. "Introduction to *Marx über China und Indien*," *UBM*, I, No. 2: 370–8.

Robins, F. W. 1946. *The Story of Water Supply*. London, New York, and Toronto.

Robinson, Geroid Tanguary. 1949. *Rural Russia under the Old Régime*. New York.

Rockhill, William Woodville. 1891. *The Land of the Lamas*. New York.

Rogers, James E. Thorold. 1884. *Six Centuries of Work and Wages*. New York.

Rostovtzeff, M. (Rostowzew). 1910. *Studien zur Geschichte des Römischen Kolonates*. Leipzig and Berlin.

―――― 1941. *The Social and Economic History of the Hellenistic World*. 3 vols. Oxford.

Rowe, John Howland. 1946. "Inca Culture at the time of the Spanish Conquest," *Handbook of South American Indians*, II: 183–330. SIBAE, CXLIII.

Roys, Ralph L. 1933. *The Book of Chilam Balam of Chumayel*. CIW, 438.

―――― 1943. *The Indian Background of Colonial Yucatan*. CIW, 548.

RRCAI. *Report of the Royal Commission on Agriculture in India, Presented to Parliament by Command of His Majesty*, June 1928. Abridged.

Runciman, Steven. 1933. *Byzantine Civilisation*. New York and London.

Ruppert, Karl and Denison, John H., Jr. 1943. *Archaeological Reconnaissance in Campeche, Quitana Roo, and Peten*. CIW, 543.

Rüstow, Alexander. OG. *Ortsbestimmung der Gegenwart*. 2 vols. Erlenbach-Zurich, 1950–52.

RY. "Relaciones de Yucatán," in *Colección de documentos inéditos relativos al descubrimiento conquista y organización de las antiguas posesiones Españolas de Ultramar*, ser. 2, Vols. XI, XIII. Madrid, 1898 and 1900.

Sabahuddin, S. 1944. "The Postal System during the Muslim Rule in India," *IC*, XVIII, No. 3: 269–82.

Sacy, Silvestre de. 1923. *Bibliothèque des Arabisants Français contenant les mémoires des Orientalistes Français relatifs aux études Arabes*, published under the direction of George Foucart, Ser. 1, Vol. II. Cairo.

Saha, K. B. 1930. *Economics of Rural Bengal*, with a foreword by Sir Jehangir Coyajee. Calcutta.

Sahagun, Bernardino de. 1938. *Historia general de las cosas de Nueva España*. 5 vols. Mexico City.

Saletore, Rajaram Narayan. 1943. *Life in the Gupta Age*. Bombay.

San Kuo Chih, Wei. Po-na ed. Commercial Press.

Sánchez-Albornoz, Claudio. EM. *La España Musulmana*, I. Buenos Aires, no date.

Sancho de la Hos, Pedro. 1938. "Relación para S. M. de lo Sucedido en la conquista y pacificación de estas provincias de la Nueva Castille y de la Calidad de la Tierra," *BCPP*: 117–93. Paris.

San Nicolò, Mariano. PR. *Ägyptisches Vereinswesen zur Zeit der Ptolemäer und Römer*. 2 vols. Munich, 1913–15.

Sansom, George B. 1938. *Japan, a Short Cultural History*. New York and London.

Santillana, David. 1938. *Teoria Generale delle obbligazione*. Vol. II of *Istituzioni di diritto Musulmano Malichita*. Rome.

Sarmiento de Gamboa, Pedro. 1906. "Geschichte des Inkareiches," ed. Richard Pietschmann, in *Abhandlungen der Königlichen Gesellschaft der Wissenschaften zu Göttingen, Philologisch-Historische Klasse*, VI, Fasc. 4.

Sauvaget, J. 1941. *La Poste aux chevaux dans l'empire des Mamelouks*. Paris.

—— 1946. *Historiens Arabes*. Paris.

Schacht, Joseph. 1935. *G. Bergsträsser's Grundzüge des islamischen Rechts*. Berlin and Leipzig.

—— 1941. "*Mīrāth*" and "*Sharī'a*," *HWI*: 511–17, 673–8. Leiden.

Schawe, J. 1932. "*Bauer*," *RA*, I: 434. Berlin and Leipzig.

Scheel, Helmuth. 1943. "Die staatsrechtliche Stellung der ökumenischen Kirchenfürsten in der alten Türkei," *Abhandlungen der Preussischen Akademie der Wissenschaften, Philologisch-Historische Klasse,* Fasc. 9.

Scheil, V. 1900. *Textes Elamites-Sémitiques,* Ser. 1. Delegation en Perse, *Mémoires,* II. Paris.

Schiller, Herman. 1893. "Staats- und Rechtsaltertümer," *Die römischen Staats-, Kriegs- und Privataltertümer,* by Schiller and Moritz Voigt: 1–268. Munich.

Schirrmacher, Friedrich Wilhelm. 1881. *Geschichte von Spanien,* Vol. IV of *Geschichte der europäischen Staaten,* ed. A. H. L. Heeren, F. A. Ufert, and W. von Giesebrecht. Gotha.

Schnebel, Michael. 1925. *Der Betrieb der Landwirtschaft,* Vol. I of *Die Landwirtschaft im hellenistischen Ägypten.* Munich.

Schneider, Anna. 1920. *Die Anfänge der Kulturwirtschaft: die sumerische Tempelstadt.* Essen.

Scholtz, Rudolf. 1934. *Die Struktur der sumerischen Engeren Verbalpräfixe (Konjugationspräfixe). Speziell dargelegt an der I. and II. Form (E- und Mu-Konjugation).* Mitteilungen der Vorderasiatisch-Aegyptischen Gesellschaft, XXXIX, No. 2. Leipzig.

Schramm, Percy Ernst. 1924. "Das Herrscherbild in der Kunst des Frühen Mittelalters," *Bibliothek Warburg, Vorträge 1922–23,* I: 145–224. Leipzig.

Schubart, Wilhelm. 1922. *Ägypten von Alexander dem Grossen bis auf Mohammed.* Berlin.

———— 1943. *Justinian und Theodora.* Munich.

Schuster, Sir George, and Wint, Guy. 1941. *India & Democracy.* London.

Schwartz, Benjamin I. 1951. *Chinese Communism and the Rise of Mao.* Cambridge, Mass.

Scott, George Ryley. 1943. *The History of Torture throughout the Ages.* London.

Sears, Paul B. 1951. "Pollen Profiles and Culture Horizons in the Basin of Mexico," *Selected Papers of the XXIXth International Congress of Americanists:* 57–61. Chicago.

Seeck, Otto. 1901. "Cursus Publicus," *Pauly-Wissowa,* IV: 1846–63. Stuttgart.

Segrè, Angelo. 1943. *An Essay on the Nature of Real Property in the Classical World.* New York.

Seidl, Erwin. 1951. *Einführung in die ägyptische Rechtsgeschichte bis zum Ende des neuen Reiches.* Glückstadt, Hamburg and New York.

Seler, Eduard. GA. *Gesammelte Abhandlungen zur Amerikanischen Sprach- und Alterthumskunde.* 5 vols. Berlin, 1902–23.

Seler, Eduard. 1927. *Fray Bernardino de Sahagun*. Stuttgart.

Seligman, Edwin R. A. 1914. *Principles of Economics*. New York and London.

Sethe, Kurt. PT. *Übersetzung und Kommentar zu den altägyptischen Pyramidentexten*. 4 vols. Glückstadt, Hamburg and New York, 1935–39.

—— 1908. "Zur ältesten Geschichte des ägyptischen Seeverkehrs mit Byblos und dem Libanongebiet," *Zeitschrift für ägyptische Sprache und Altertumskunde*, XLV: 7–14.

—— 1912. "R. Weill, Les Décrets royaux de l'ancien empire égyptien," *Göttingische gelehrte Anzeigen*, CLXXIV: 705–26.

Seybald, C. F. 1927. "Granada," *Encyclopaedia of Islam*, II: 175–7. Leiden and London.

Shattuck (George Cheever), Redfield (Robert), and MacKay (Katheryn). 1933. "Part I: General and Miscellaneous Information about Yucatan," chaps. 1–5 of *The Peninsula of Yucatan*, CIW, 431.

Shih Chi. Po-na ed. Commercial Press.

SLRUN. *Slave Labor in Russia. The Case Presented by the American Federation of Labor to the United Nations*. A. F. of L., 1949.

SM. *Soils and Men. Yearbook of Agriculture, 1938*. Washington, D.C.

Smith, Adam. 1937. *An Inquiry into the Nature and Causes of The Wealth of Nations*. Modern Library, New York.

Smith, Arthur H. 1897. *Chinese Characteristics*. Edinburgh and London.

—— 1899. *Village Life in China*. New York.

Smith, Vincent A. 1914. *The Early History of India*. 3d ed. Oxford.

—— 1926. *Akbar, the Great Mogul, 1542–1605*. 2d ed. Oxford.

—— 1928. *The Oxford History of India*. 2d ed. Oxford.

Smith, Wilfred Cantwell. 1946. "Lower-class Uprisings in the Mughal Empire," *IC*, XX, No. 1: 21–40.

—— 1946a. *Modern Islam in India*. London.

Socialist Asia. Published monthly by the Asian Socialist Conference, Rangoon.

Sombart, Werner. 1919. *Der moderne Kapitalismus*. 2 vols. Munich and Leipzig.

Speiser, E. A. 1942. "Some Sources of Intellectual and Social Progress in the Ancient Near East," in *Studies in the History of Science*: 51–62. Philadelphia, 1941. Revised reprint.

Spiegelberg, Wilhelm. 1892. *Studien und Matèrialen zum Rechtswesen des Pharaonenreiches*. Hanover.

—— 1896. *Rechnungen aus der Zeit Setis, I*. Text. Strassburg.

Spuler, Bertold. 1943. *Die Goldene Horde. Die Mongolen in Russland 1223–1502*. Leipzig.

—— 1952. *Iran in Früh-Islamischer Zeit*. Wiesbaden.

Staden, Heinrich von. 1930. *Aufzeichungen über den Moskauer Staat*, ed. Fritz Epstein. Hamburg University, Abhandlungen aus dem Gebiet der Auslandskunde, XXXIV. Hamburg.

Stalin, Joseph. S. *Sochinenia*. 13 vols. Moscow, 1946–51.

———— 1939. "Dialectical and Historical Materialism," in *History of the Communist Party of the Soviet Union* (Bolsheviks), *Short Course*, ed. by a Commission of the Central Committee of the CPSU (B.), and authorized by the Central Committee of the CPSU (B.). New York.

———— 1942. *Selected Writings*. New York.

Stamp, L. Dudley. 1938. *Asia, a Regional and Economic Geography*. 4th ed. New York.

Stein, Ernst. 1920. "Ein Kapitel vom persischen und vom byzantinischen Staate," *Byzantinisch-Neugriechische Jahrbücher*, I: 50–89.

———— 1928. *Vom römischen zum byzantinischen Staate. Geschichte des spätrömischen Reiches*, I. Vienna.

———— 1949. *De la Disparition de l'empire d'Occident à la mort de Justinien* (476–565). Vol. II of *Histoire du Bas-Empire*. Paris, Brussels and Amsterdam.

———— 1951. "Introduction à l'histoire et aux institutions byzantines," *Traditio*, VII: 95–168.

Steinwenter, Artur. 1920. *Studien zu den koptischen Rechtsurkunden aus Oberägypten*. Leipzig.

Stengel, Paul. 1920. *Die griechischen Kultusaltertümer*. Munich.

Stephens, John L. ITCA. *Incidents of Travel in Central America, Chiapas, and Yucatan*. 12th ed. 2 vols. New York, 1863–77.

———— 1848. *Incidents of Travel in Yucatan*. 2 vols. New York.

Stepniak. 1888. *The Russian Peasantry*. New York.

Stevenson, G. H. 1934. "The Imperial Administration," *CAH*, X: 182–217. Cambridge.

Steward, Julian H. 1949. "Cultural Causality and Law: a Trial Formulation of the Development of Early Civilizations," *AA*, LI: 1–27.

———— 1953. "Evolution and Process," in *Anthropology Today*, ed. Kroeber: 313–26. Chicago.

———— 1955. "Introduction: the Irrigation Civilizations, a Symposium on Method and Result in Cross-Cultural Regularities," in *Irrigation Civilizations: a Comparative Study*: 1–5. Social Science Monographs, 1. Pan-American Union, Washington, D.C.

Stöckle, Albert. 1911. *Spätrömische und byzantinische Zünfte. Klio. Beiträge zur alten Geschichte*. Leipzig.

Strabo. *The Geography of Strabo*, with an English trans. by Horace Leonard Jones. 8 vols. New York, 1917–32.

Strong (William Duncan), Kidder (A.), and Paul (A. J. D., Jr.). 1938. *Harvard University Archaeological Expedition to Northwestern Honduras*,

1936. Smithsonian Miscellaneous Collections, XCVII, No. 1. Washington, D.C.

Struve, Peter. 1942. "Russia," in *CEHE*, I: 418–37. Cambridge.

Struve, V. V. 1940. "Marksovo opredelenie ranneklassovogo obshchestva," *Sovetskaya Etnografia, Sbornik Statei*, Fasc. 3: 1–22.

Stubbs, William. CHE. *The Constitutional History of England*. 2 vols. Oxford, 1875–78.

Suetonius Augustus. *C. Suetoni Tranquilli quae supersunt omnia,* ed. Karl Ludwig Roth. Leipzig, 1886.

Sui Shu. Po-na ed. Commercial Press.

Sumner, B. H. 1949. *A Short History of Russia*. Revised ed. New York.

Sun Tzu. 1941. "On the Art of War," in *Roots of Strategy,* ed. Thomas R. Phillips: 21–63, trans. Lionel Giles. Harrisburg, Pa.

Ta Ch'ing lü-li hui chi pien lan. Hupeh, 1872.

Ta T'ang Hsi-yü Chi in *Ssŭ-pu Ts'ung K'an*.

Tabari. 1879. *Geschichte der Perser und Araber zur Zeit der Sasaniden aus der arabischen Chronik des Tabari,* trans. T. Nöldeke. Leiden.

Taeschner, Franz. 1926. "Die Verkehrslage und das Wegenetz Anatoliens im Wandel der Zeiten," *PM*, LXXII: 202–6.

Takekoshi, Yosoburo. 1930. *The Economic Aspects of the History of the Civilization of Japan*. 3 vols. London.

Tang, Peter. MS. "Communist China Today: Domestic and Foreign Policy." In press.

Tarn, W. W. 1927. *Hellenistic Civilisation*. London.

Taubenschlag, Raphael. 1944. *The Law of Greco-Roman Egypt in the Light of the Papyri*. New York.

Taylor, George E. 1936. *The Reconstruction Movement in China*. Royal Institute of International Affairs, London.

—— 1942. *America in the New Pacific*. New York.

Taylor, Lily Ross. 1931. *The Divinity of the Roman Emperor*. Middletown, Conn.

TEA. 1915. *Tell-el-Amarna Tablets. Die El-Amarna-tafeln* . . . ed. J. A. Knudtzon, revised by Otto Weber and Erich Ebeling. 2 vols. Leipzig.

Têng Ssŭ-yü and Biggerstaff, Knight. 1936. *An Annotated Bibliography of Selected Chinese Reference Works*. Harvard-Yenching Institute, Peiping.

Tezozomoc, Hernando Alvarado. 1944. *Crónica Mexicana escrita hacia el ano de 1598,* notes by Manuel Orozco y Berra. Mexico City.

Thompson, R. Campbell, and Hutchinson, R. W. 1929. *A Century of Exploration at Nineveh*. London.

Thompson, Virginia. 1941. *Thailand: the New Siam*. New York.

Thornburg (Max Weston), Spry (Graham), and Soule (George). 1949. *Turkey: an Economic Appraisal*. New York.

Thucydides. 1942. "The Peloponnesian War," *The Greek Historians*, trans. Benjamin Jowett, ed. Francis R. B. Godolphin: 567–1001. New York.

Thureau-Dangin, F. 1907. *Die sumerischen und akkadischen Königsinschriften*, Vorderasiatische Bibliothek, I, Pt. 1. Leipzig.

Timasheff, Nicholas S. 1946. *The Great Retreat. The Growth and Decline of Communism in Russia*. New York.

Titiev, Mischa. 1944. *Old Oraibi—a Study of the Hopi Indians of the Third Mesa*. PMAAE, *Reports*, XXII, No. 1. Cambridge, Mass.

Tolstov, S. 1950. "For Advanced Soviet Oriental Studies," *Kultura i zhizn*, Aug. 11, trans. in *Current Digest of the Soviet Press*, XI, No. 33: 3–4.

Tomsin, A. 1952. "Etude sur les πρεσβύτεροι des villages de la χώρα égyptienne," *Bulletin de la Classe des Lettres et des Sciences Morales et Politiques, Académie Royale de Belgique*, Ser. 5, XXXVIII: 95–130.

Torquemada, Fray Juan de. 1943. *Monarquia Indiana*. 3d ed. 3 vols. Mexico City.

Tout, T. F. 1937. *Chapters in the Administrative History of Mediaeval England*, II. Manchester University Press.

Tozzer, Alfred M. 1941. *Landa's relación de las cosas de Yucatan*, trans. with notes, PMAAE, *Reports*, XVIII, Cambridge, Mass.

Tritton, A. S. 1930. *The Caliphs and Their Non-Muslim Subjects*. London and Madras.

Trotsky, Leon. (Trotzki). 1923. *Die russische Revolution 1905*. Berlin.

———— 1928. *The Real Situation in Russia*, trans. Max Eastman. New York.

———— (Trotzki). 1931. *Geschichte der russischen Revolution. Februarrevolution*. Berlin.

———— 1939. *The Living Thoughts of Karl Marx Based on Capital: a Critique of Political Economy*. Philadelphia.

Tso Chuan Chu Shu. Ssǔ-pu Pei-yao.

Tugan-Baranowsky, M. 1900. *Geschichte der russischen Fabrik*, ed. B. Minzes. Suppl. to *Zeitschrift für Sozial- und Wirtschaftsgeschichte*, V–VI.

Vaillant, George C. 1941. *Aztecs of Mexico*. Garden City, New York.

Vancouver, Captain George. 1798. *A Voyage of Discovery to the North Pacific Ocean and Round the World*. 3 vols. London.

Vandenbosch, Amry. 1949. "Indonesia," in Mills and Associates, *The New World of Southeast Asia*: 79–125. New York.

Van Nostrand, J. J. 1937. "Roman Spain," in *ESAR*, III: 119–224. Baltimore.

Varga, E. 1928. "Osnovniye problemy kitaiskoi revolyutsii" (Fundamental Problems of the Chinese Revolution), *Bolshevik*, VIII: 17–40. Moscow.

Vâsishtha. 1898. In *Sacred Laws of the Âryas*, trans. Georg Bühler, SBE, II: 1–140. New York.

Veblen, Thorstein. 1945. *What Veblen Taught*, selected writings, ed. Wesley C. Mitchell. New York.

—— 1947. *The Engineers and the Price System*. New York.

Vernadsky, George. 1943: *Ancient Russia*. 1948: *Kievan Russia*. 1953: *The Mongols and Russia*. Vols. I–III of *History of Russia*, by G. Vernadsky and M. Karpovich. New Haven.

Vinogradoff, Paul. 1908. *English Society in the Eleventh Century*. Oxford.

Vishnu. 1900. "The Institutes of Vishnu," trans. Julius Jolly, SBE, VIII. New York.

Vladimirtsov, B. 1948. *Le Régime social des Mongols. Le Féodalisme nomade*, trans. Michel Carsow. Paris.

Voigt, Moritz. 1893. "Privataltertümer und Kulturgeschichte," *Die römischen Staats-, Kriegs- und Privataltertümer*, by Herman Schiller and Voigt: 271–465. Munich.

Vyshinsky, Andrei Y. 1948. *The Laws of the Soviet State*, trans. Hugh W. Babb, with an intro. by John N. Hazard. New York.

Waitz, Georg. 1880. *Deutsche Verfassungsgeschichte*, I. 3d ed. Berlin.

Walker, Richard L. 1955. *China under Communism. The First Five Years*. New Haven.

Wallace, Sherman Le Roy. 1938. *Taxation in Egypt*. Princeton.

Walther, Arnold. 1917. "Das altbabylonische Gerichtswesen," *Leipziger Semitistische Studien*, VI: Fasc. 4–6.

Wan Kuo-ting. 1933. *Chung-kuo T'ien Chih Shih*. Nanking.

Warriner, Doreen. 1948. *Land and Poverty in the Middle East*. Royal Institute of International Affairs. London and New York.

Wb. *Wörterbuch der ägyptischen Sprache*, IV–VI, ed. Adolf Erman and Hermann Grapow. Berlin and Leipzig, 1930–31, 1950.

Weber, Max. RS. *Gesammelte Aufsätze zur Religionssoziologie*. 3 vols. Tübingen, 1922–23.

—— WG. *Wirtschaft und Gesellschaft. Grundriss der Sozialökonomik*, Pt. 3. Tübingen, 1921–23.

—— 1906. "Russlands Übergang zum Scheinkonstitutionalismus," *ASS*, V: 165–401.

Weissberg, Alexander. 1951. *The Accused*. New York.

Wellhausen, J. 1927. *The Arab Kingdom and its Fall*, trans. Margaret Graham Weir. University of Calcutta.

Wên-hsien T'ung-k'ao. Commercial Press, Shanghai.

Werner, E. T. C. 1910. *Descriptive Sociology: or, Groups of Sociological*

Facts, Classified and Arranged by Herbert Spencer. Chinese. Compiled by E. T. C. Werner, ed. Henry R. Tedder. London.

Westermann, William Linn. 1921. "The 'Uninundated Lands' in Ptolemaic and Roman Egypt," Pt. 2, *Classical Philology,* XVI: 169–88.

―――― 1922. "The 'Dry Land' in Ptolemaic and Roman Egypt," *Classical Philology,* XVII: 21–36.

―――― 1937. "Greek Culture and Thought," and "Slavery, Ancient," *ESS,* I: 8–41; XIV: 74–7.

White, Leslie A. 1932. "The Acoma Indians," SIBAE, *Forty-seventh Annual Report:* 17–192.

―――― 1942. *The Pueblo of Santa Ana, New Mexico.* Memoir Series, American Anthropological Association, LX.

Whitney, William Dwight. 1905. *Artharva-Veda Saṁhitā,* revised by Charles Rockwell Lanman. Harvard Oriental Series, VII. Cambridge.

Widenmann, A. 1899. "Die Kilimandscharo-Bevölkerung Anthropologisches und Ethnographisches aus dem Dschaggalande," *PM,* Suppl. XXVII, No. 129.

Widtsoe, John A. 1926. *The Principles of Irrigation Practice.* New York and London.

―――― 1928. *Success on Irrigation Projects.* New York and London.

Wiedemann, A. 1920. *Das alte Ägypten.* Heidelberg.

Wiet, Gaston. 1932. "L'Egypte Musulmane de la conquête Arabe à la conquête Ottomane," *Précis de l'Histoire d'Égypte,* II: 107–294.

―――― 1937. *L'Egypte Arabe de la conquête Arabe à la conquête Ottomane,* Vol. IV of *Histoire de la Nation Egyptienne.* Paris.

Wilbur, C. Martin. 1943. *Slavery in China during the Former Han Dynasty.* Chicago.

Wilcken, Ulrich. 1899. *Griechische Ostraka aus Aegypten und Nubien.* 2 vols. Leipzig and Berlin.

―――― 1912. *Historischer Teil: Grundzüge,* Vol. I, Pt. 1, of *Grundzüge und Chrestomathie der Papyruskunde,* by L. Mitteis and U. Wilcken. Leipzig and Berlin.

Willcocks, W. 1889. *Egyptian Irrigation.* London and New York.

―――― 1904. *The Nile in 1904.* London and New York.

Willey, Gordon E. 1953. *Prehistoric Settlement Patterns in the Virú Valley, Perú.* SIBAE, CLV.

―――― 1953a. "Archeological Theories and Interpretation: New World," *Anthropology Today,* ed. A. L. Kroeber: 361–85. Chicago.

Williams, Sir Edward Leader. 1910. "Canal," *Encyclopaedia Britannica,* V: 168–71. 11th ed.

Williams, James. 1911. "Torture," *Encyclopaedia Britannica,* XXVII: 72–9. 11th ed.

Williams, S. Wells. 1848. *The Middle Kingdom*. 2 vols. New York and London.

Williamson, H. B. WAS. *Wang-An-Shih, a Chinese Statesman and Educationalist of the Sung Dynasty*. 2 vols. London, 1935–37.

Wilson, John A. 1950. "Egyptian Myths, Tales, and Mortuary Texts," "Documents from the Practice of Law: Egyptian Documents," and "Proverbs and Precepts: Egyptian Instructions," in *ANET*: 3–36, 212–17, 412–25. Princeton.

———— 1951. *The Burden of Egypt*. Chicago.

Wipper, R. 1947. *Ivan Grozny*, trans. J. Fineberg. Moscow.

Wirz, Paul. 1929. *Der Reisbau und die Reisbaukulte auf Bali und Lombok*. Leiden.

Wittfogel, Karl August. 1924. *Geschichte der bürgerlichen Gesellschaft*. Vienna.

———— 1926. *Das erwachende China*. Vienna.

———— 1927. "Probleme der chinesischen Wirtschaftsgeschichte," *ASS*, LVIII, No. 2: 289–335.

———— 1929. "Geopolitik, geographischer Materialismus und Marxismus," *UBM*, III: 17–51, 485–522, 698–735.

———— 1929a. "Voraussetzungen und Grundelemente der chinesischen Landwirtschaft," *ASS*, LXI: 566–607.

———— 1931. *Wirtschaft und Gesellschaft Chinas, Erster Teil, Produktivkräfte, Produktions- und Zirkulationsprozess*. Leipzig.

———— 1931a. "Hegel über China," *UBM*, V: 346–62.

———— 1932. "Die natürlichen Ursachen der Wirtschaftsgeschichte," *ASS*, LXVII: 466–92, 579–609, 711–31.

———— 1935. "The Foundations and Stages of Chinese Economic History," *Zeitschrift für Sozialforschung*, IV: 26–60.

———— 1936. "Wirtschaftsgeschichtliche Grundlagen der Entwicklung der Familienautorität," *Studien über Autorität und Familie, Schriften des Instituts für Sozialforschung*, V. Paris.

———— 1938. "Die Theorie der orientalischen Gesellschaft," *Zeitschrift für Sozialforschung*, VII: 90–122.

———— 1938a. *New Light on Chinese Society*. International Secretariat, Institute of Pacific Relations.

———— 1940. "Meteorological Records from the Divination Inscriptions of Shang," *Geographical Review*, XXX: 110–33.

———— 1947. "Public Office in the Liao Dynasty and the Chinese Examination System," *Harvard Journal of Asiatic Studies*, X: 13–40.

———— 1949. "General Introduction," *History of Chinese Society, Liao*: 1–35. Philadelphia.

———— 1950. "Russia and Asia," *World Politics*, II, No. 4: 445–62.

———— 1951. "The Influence of Leninism-Stalinism on China," *Annals of the American Academy of Political Science,* CCLXXVII: 22–34.

——— 1953. "The Ruling Bureaucracy of Oriental Despotism: a Phenomenon That Paralyzed Marx," *Review of Politics,* XV, No. 3: 350–9.

——— 1955. "Developmental Aspects of Hydraulic Societies," in *Irrigation Civilizations: a Comparative Study:* 43–52. Social Science Monographs, 1. Pan-American Union, Washington, D.C.

——— 1955a. *Mao Tse-tung. Liberator or Destroyer of the Chinese Peasants?* Published by the Free Trade Union Committee, A. F. of L., New York.

——— 1956. "Hydraulic Civilizations," *Man's Role in Changing the Face of the Earth,"* ed. William L. Thomas, Jr., Wenner-Gren Foundation. Chicago.

Wittfogel, Karl A., and Fêng Chia-shêng. 1949. *History of Chinese Society, Liao,* American Philosophical Society, *Transactions,* XXXVI. Philadelphia.

Wittfogel, Karl A., and Goldfrank, Esther S. 1943. "Some Aspects of Pueblo Mythology and Society," *Journal of American Folklore,* January–March 1943: 17–30.

Wolfe, Bertram D. 1948. *Three Who Made a Revolution.* New York.

Wright, Walter Livingston, Jr. 1935. *Ottoman Statecraft.* Princeton.

Wüstenfeld, F. 1880. "Das Heerwesen der Muhammedaner nach dem Arabischen," *Abhandlungen der Historisch-Philologischen Classe der Königlichen Gesellschaft der Wissenschaften zu Göttingen,* XXIV, No. 1.

Xenophon. 1914. *The Education of Cyrus.* Everymans Library. London and New York.

Yājnavalkya Smṛiti. With Mitâkṣarâ. *The Law of Inheritance,* trans. Pandit Mohan Lal, in Sacred Books of the Hindus, II, No. 2. Allahabad City, no date.

Yang, Martin C. 1945. *A Chinese Village.* New York.

Yen T'ieh Lun by Huan K'uan. Shanghai, 1934.

Yüan Shih. Po-na ed. Commercial Press.

Yüeh Hai Kuan Chih. Tao-Kuang edition.

Zagorsky, S. O. 1928. *State Control of Industry in Russia during the War,* Vol. II of *Economic and Social History of the World War,* Russian Series. New Haven.

Zinowjew, G. 1919. "Der russische Sozialismus und Liberalismus über auswärtige Politik der Zarismus," *Archiv für die Geschichte des Sozialismus und der Arbeiterbewegung,* VIII: 40–75.

Zurita. 1941. "Breve relación de los señores de la Nueva España," *Nueva colección de documentos para la historia de Mexico,* XVI: 65–205.

GENERAL INDEX

Abbreviations: HS—hydraulic society; OD—Oriental despotism; OS—Oriental society

Absolutism
  insufficiently studied, 2
  genuine in OD, 103
  limited Western, 45 ff., 78
    multicentered society, 45 and *passim;*
    strong property, 82 ff., 189, 300, 360
  limited Japanese, 200, 366
  and autocracy, 106
  See also Autocracy, Europe, Japan, Mercantilism, OD, Total power
Absorption of conquerors, legend and
  reality, 326. *See also* Conquest societies
Acton, Lord, 133
Administrative returns
  law of changing, 109 ff.
    in hydraulic economy, 109 ff.; in
    sphere of social control, 111 ff.
  law of diminishing, 109 f., 113
Aesopian language
  originally used by slaves, 400
  used by masters of USSR, 400, 442
Agriculture
  essential natural conditions for, 13 ff.
  rainfall, 18 ff.
  hydroagriculture, 3, 18
    primary and secondary origin, 17
  hydraulic, 3
    origins, 18 ff.; multiple, 19 ff.; intensive, 23, 322
  See also Division of labor, Hydraulic economy
Agrobureaucratic regime, synonymous
  with OD, 3, 8, and *passim*
Agrodespotic regime. *See* Oriental despotism
Agromanagerial society, synonymous with
  HS, 3, 8
Akbar, 48, 274, 309
Alexander the Great, 44, 157, 160, 207 f.
Akida (Chagga official), 240 f.
Alienation
  patterns of, 156 ff.
  partial, 157
  total, 157, 160
  See also Loneliness
Altiplano. See Andean zone, Inca society
America, ancient (pre-Conquest)
  hydraulic civilizations, 3
  masters of, great builders, 42 f.
  priests, 362

no evidence of eunuchism, 354 f.
institutional effect on Latin America,
  8, 430
See also Andean zone, Inca society,
  Maya society, Mexico, Pueblo Indians
Anarchists, criticize Marxist state socialism
  for involving despotism and slavery,
  388
Andean zone
  hydraulic landscape, 19, 24, 247
  hypothetical origin of HS, 19
  coastal area, 163, 166
  aqueducts, 31
  trade, 257
  pre-Inca conditions, surmised, 163, 257
  See also Inca society
Apparatus state
  term, 440 f.
  ruling class a monopoly bureaucracy,
  368
Apparatchiki, 335 and *passim*
Arab civilizations
  origins, 127, 154, 359
  Umayyad Caliphate
    a conquest dynasty, 359; upheld by
    tribal supporters, 359 f.; eunuchs insignificant, 359; army, 64, 215, 327; hydraulic concern of, 127, 171; taxation,
    168; prostration, 154; collapse, 205,
    327
  Abbassid Caliphate
    hydraulic core areas, 167; hydraulic
    management, 53; tribal support discarded, 205; army, 215; bureaucratic
    density, 167; eunuchs, 358; terror, 139,
    142 ff., 156; taxation, 168; confiscation,
    76 f;. slaves as bodyguards, 360; slave
    girls, mothers of caliphs, 344
  See also Islamic civilizations, Near East
Architecture, hydraulic
  monumental pubiic structures, 43 ff.
  introvert private edifices, 86
  compared with that of Medieval Europe,
  44 ff.
Aristotle, 160, 208, 219, 263
Army. *See* Military organization
Artisans
  part time, 233
  professional, 246
  government-attached, 246, 248 ff., 250

INDEX OF AUTHORS AND WORKS

For full reference to each see the Bibliography